Honda Jazz
Owners Workshop Manual
R M Jex

Models covered

(4735 - 304)

Jazz Hatchback with 1.2 litre (1246 cc) & 1.4 litre (1339 cc) petrol engines, including special/limited editions

Does NOT cover 'new' Jazz range introduced 2008

© Haynes Publishing 2008

ABCDE
FGHIJ
KLMNO
PQRST

A book in the **Haynes Owners Workshop Manual Series**

ISBN **978 1 84425 735 5**

British Library Cataloguing in Publication Data
A catalogue record for this book is available from the British Library.

Printed in the USA

Haynes Publishing
Sparkford, Yeovil, Somerset BA22 7JJ, England

Haynes North America, Inc
861 Lawrence Drive, Newbury Park, California 91320, USA

Haynes Publishing Nordiska AB
Box 1504, 751 45 UPPSALA, Sverige

Contents

LIVING WITH YOUR HONDA JAZZ

MAINTENANCE

Routine maintenance and servicing

Contents

REPAIRS AND OVERHAUL

REFERENCE

Advanced driving

Many people see the words 'advanced driving' and believe that it won't interest them or that it is a style of driving beyond their own abilities. Nothing could be further from the truth. Advanced driving is straightforward safe, sensible driving - the sort of driving we should all do every time we get behind the wheel.

An average of 10 people are killed every day on UK roads and 870 more are injured, some seriously. Lives are ruined daily, usually because somebody did something stupid. Something like 95% of all accidents are due to human error, mostly driver failure. Sometimes we make genuine mistakes - everyone does. Sometimes we have lapses of concentration. Sometimes we deliberately take risks.

For many people, the process of 'learning to drive' doesn't go much further than learning how to pass the driving test because of a common belief that good drivers are made by 'experience'.

Learning to drive by 'experience' teaches three driving skills:

☐ Quick reactions. (Whoops, that was close!)
☐ Good handling skills. (Horn, swerve, brake, horn).
☐ Reliance on vehicle technology. (Great stuff this ABS, stop in no distance even in the wet...)

Drivers whose skills are 'experience based' generally have a lot of near misses and the odd accident. The results can be seen every day in our courts and our hospital casualty departments.

Advanced drivers have learnt to control the risks by controlling the position and speed of their vehicle. They avoid accidents and near misses, even if the drivers around them make mistakes.

The key skills of advanced driving are **concentration,** effective all-round **observation, anticipation** and **planning.** When **good vehicle handling** is added to these skills, all driving situations can be approached and negotiated in a safe, methodical way, leaving nothing to chance.

Concentration means applying your mind to safe driving, completely excluding anything that's not relevant. Driving is usually the most dangerous activity that most of us undertake in our daily routines. It deserves our full attention.

Observation means not just looking, but seeing and seeking out the information found in the driving environment.

Anticipation means asking yourself what is happening, what you can reasonably expect to happen and what could happen unexpectedly. (One of the commonest words used in compiling accident reports is 'suddenly'.)

Planning is the link between seeing something and taking the appropriate action. For many drivers, planning is the missing link.

If you want to become a safer and more skilful driver and you want to enjoy your driving more, contact the Institute of Advanced Motorists at www.iam.org.uk, phone 0208 996 9600, or write to IAM House, 510 Chiswick High Road, London W4 5RG for an information pack.

Working on your car can be dangerous. This page shows just some of the potential risks and hazards, with the aim of creating a safety-conscious attitude.

General hazards

Scalding

• Don't remove the radiator or expansion tank cap while the engine is hot.
• Engine oil, automatic transmission fluid or power steering fluid may also be dangerously hot if the engine has recently been running.

Burning

• Beware of burns from the exhaust system and from any part of the engine. Brake discs and drums can also be extremely hot immediately after use.

Crushing

• When working under or near a raised vehicle, always supplement the jack with axle stands, or use drive-on ramps. *Never venture under a car which is only supported by a jack.*
• Take care if loosening or tightening high-torque nuts when the vehicle is on stands. Initial loosening and final tightening should be done with the wheels on the ground.

Fire

• Fuel is highly flammable; fuel vapour is explosive.
• Don't let fuel spill onto a hot engine.
• Do not smoke or allow naked lights (including pilot lights) anywhere near a vehicle being worked on. Also beware of creating sparks
(electrically or by use of tools).
• Fuel vapour is heavier than air, so don't work on the fuel system with the vehicle over an inspection pit.
• Another cause of fire is an electrical overload or short-circuit. Take care when repairing or modifying the vehicle wiring.
• Keep a fire extinguisher handy, of a type suitable for use on fuel and electrical fires.

Electric shock

• Ignition HT voltage can be dangerous, especially to people with heart problems or a pacemaker. Don't work on or near the ignition system with the engine running or the ignition switched on.

• Mains voltage is also dangerous. Make sure that any mains-operated equipment is correctly earthed. Mains power points should be protected by a residual current device (RCD) circuit breaker.

Fume or gas intoxication

• Exhaust fumes are poisonous; they often contain carbon monoxide, which is rapidly fatal if inhaled. Never run the engine in a confined space such as a garage with the doors shut.
• Fuel vapour is also poisonous, as are the vapours from some cleaning solvents and paint thinners.

Poisonous or irritant substances

• Avoid skin contact with battery acid and with any fuel, fluid or lubricant, especially antifreeze, brake hydraulic fluid and Diesel fuel. Don't syphon them by mouth. If such a substance is swallowed or gets into the eyes, seek medical advice.
• Prolonged contact with used engine oil can cause skin cancer. Wear gloves or use a barrier cream if necessary. Change out of oil-soaked clothes and do not keep oily rags in your pocket.
• Air conditioning refrigerant forms a poisonous gas if exposed to a naked flame (including a cigarette). It can also cause skin burns on contact.

Asbestos

• Asbestos dust can cause cancer if inhaled or swallowed. Asbestos may be found in gaskets and in brake and clutch linings. When dealing with such components it is safest to assume that they contain asbestos.

Special hazards

Hydrofluoric acid

• This extremely corrosive acid is formed when certain types of synthetic rubber, found in some O-rings, oil seals, fuel hoses etc, are exposed to temperatures above 400°C. The rubber changes into a charred or sticky substance containing the acid. *Once formed, the acid remains dangerous for years. If it gets onto the skin, it may be necessary to amputate the limb concerned.*
• When dealing with a vehicle which has suffered a fire, or with components salvaged from such a vehicle, wear protective gloves and discard them after use.

The battery

• Batteries contain sulphuric acid, which attacks clothing, eyes and skin. Take care when topping-up or carrying the battery.
• The hydrogen gas given off by the battery is highly explosive. Never cause a spark or allow a naked light nearby. Be careful when connecting and disconnecting battery chargers or jump leads.

Air bags

• Air bags can cause injury if they go off accidentally. Take care when removing the steering wheel and/or facia. Special storage instructions may apply.

Diesel injection equipment

• Diesel injection pumps supply fuel at very high pressure. Take care when working on the fuel injectors and fuel pipes.

⚠️ *Warning: Never expose the hands, face or any other part of the body to injector spray; the fuel can penetrate the skin with potentially fatal results.*

Remember...

DO

• Do use eye protection when using power tools, and when working under the vehicle.

• Do wear gloves or use barrier cream to protect your hands when necessary.

• Do get someone to check periodically that all is well when working alone on the vehicle.

• Do keep loose clothing and long hair well out of the way of moving mechanical parts.

• Do remove rings, wristwatch etc, before working on the vehicle – especially the electrical system.

• Do ensure that any lifting or jacking equipment has a safe working load rating adequate for the job.

DON'T

• Don't attempt to lift a heavy component which may be beyond your capability – get assistance.

• Don't rush to finish a job, or take unverified short cuts.

• Don't use ill-fitting tools which may slip and cause injury.

• Don't leave tools or parts lying around where someone can trip over them. Mop up oil and fuel spills at once.

• Don't allow children or pets to play in or near a vehicle being worked on.

Taking the world by surprise at its launch in November 2001, the all-new Honda Jazz has gone on to be a huge sales success in its home market, as well as here in the UK. Its 'one-box' design is similar to that seen in the current generation of mini-MPVs, but the Jazz excels in its clever use of interior space and flexible seating. The fuel tank is mounted under the front seats, and this, combined with compact rear suspension, allows a low floor, maximising the available space.

The engine is also all-new, and designated i-DSI (intelligent Dual Sequential Ignition). The engine is 'only' an 8-valve design (most modern 4-cylinder engines being 16-valve), with a chain-driven single camshaft, but unusually features two spark plugs per cylinder. This configuration gives a high torque output at lower engine speeds, very clean emissions, and compact dimensions. At its launch, the only engine option was a 1.4 litre petrol, but in September 2004 a 1.2 litre petrol version was added.

As expected of a modern design, the Jazz offers high levels of passenger safety, scoring four stars in the Euro NCAP safety tests. To an impact-absorbing bodyshell with side impact beams are added front airbags and seat belt tensioners, with side airbags also fitted on some later models. Many models also feature ABS with EBD and Brake Assist.

The model range is limited to just the 5-door Hatchback, but a wide variety of standard equipment (and colours) have been available during the car's lifespan. Even the base model is well-equipped – besides the valuable safety equipment already mentioned, all have electric power steering, rolling code engine immobiliser, central locking, electric mirrors and electric front windows. Air conditioning (or climate control), an electric sunroof, and a CD player feature higher up the range, while Sport models have their own bodykit and alloy wheels.

The range received a minor facelift in October 2004, with revised light units and bumpers.

All models have front-wheel-drive, with a five-speed manual transmission as standard. One of the most popular options has been the CVT-7 automatic transmission, which offers manual shifting using steering wheel-mounted buttons or paddles.

The front suspension is of conventional MacPherson strut type, incorporating lower arms and an anti-roll bar; at the rear, a compact H-section axle is used.

Your Honda Jazz manual

The aim of this manual is to help you get the best value from your car. It can do so in several ways. It can help you decide what work must be done (even should you choose to get it done by a garage). It will also provide information on routine maintenance and servicing, and give a logical course of action and diagnosis when random faults occur. However, it is hoped that you will use the manual by tackling the work yourself. On simpler jobs it may even be quicker than booking the car into a garage and going there twice, to leave and collect it. Perhaps most important, a lot of money can be saved by avoiding the costs a garage must charge to cover its labour and overheads.

The manual has drawings and descriptions to show the function of the various components so that their layout can be understood. Tasks are described and photographed in a clear step-by-step sequence. References to the 'left' and 'right' of the car are in the sense of a person in the driver's seat, facing forwards.

Acknowledgements

Thanks are due to Draper tools Limited, who provided some of the workshop tools, and to all those people at Sparkford who helped in the production of this manual.

We take great pride in the accuracy of information given in this manual, but car manufacturers make alterations and design changes during the production run of a particular car of which they do not inform us. No liability can be accepted by the authors or publishers for loss, damage or injury caused by any errors in, or omissions from, the information given.

The following pages are intended to help in dealing with common roadside emergencies and breakdowns. You will find more detailed fault finding information at the back of the manual, and repair information in the main chapters.

If your car won't start and the starter motor doesn't turn

☐ If it's a model with automatic transmission, make sure the selector is in P or N.

☐ Open the bonnet and make sure that the battery terminals are clean and tight.

☐ Switch on the headlights and try to start the engine. If the headlights go very dim when you're trying to start, the battery is probably flat. Get out of trouble by jump starting (see next page) using a friend's car.

If your car won't start even though the starter motor turns as normal

☐ Is there fuel in the tank?

☐ Has the engine immobiliser been deactivated? This should happen automatically when the key is inserted and turned to the first position.

☐ Is there moisture on electrical components under the bonnet? With the ignition off, wipe off any obvious dampness with a dry cloth. Spray a water-repellent aerosol product (WD-40 or equivalent) on ignition and fuel system electrical connectors like those shown in the photos. Pay special attention to the ignition coil wiring connectors.

☐ Is the engine management warning light (also known as the malfunction indicator light) on? This is an orange 'engine' symbol, on the left-hand side of the instrument panel. If the light stays on when trying to start the engine, it indicates a fault with the fuel or ignition systems, which will have to be diagnosed using dedicated test equipment (see Chapter 4A).

A Check the condition and security of the battery connections.

B Check that the ignition coils are securely connected.

C With the ignition off, check the fuses and relays in the engine compartment fusebox. Fuse No 3 in particular controls the ignition system.

Check that electrical connections are secure (with the ignition switched off) and spray them with a water-dispersant spray like WD-40 if you suspect a problem due to damp

Jump starting

When jump-starting a car using a booster battery, observe the following precautions:

✔ Before connecting the booster battery, make sure that the ignition is switched off.

✔ Ensure that all electrical equipment (lights, heater, wipers, etc) is switched off.

✔ Take note of any special precautions printed on the battery case.

✔ Make sure that the booster battery is the same voltage as the discharged one in the vehicle.

✔ If the battery is being jump-started from the battery in another vehicle, the two vehicles MUST NOT TOUCH each other.

✔ Make sure that the transmission is in neutral (or PARK, in the case of automatic transmission).

 HAYNES HiNT *Jump starting will get you out of trouble, but you must correct whatever made the battery go flat in the first place. There are three possibilities:*

1 *The battery has been drained by repeated attempts to start, or by leaving the lights on.*

2 *The charging system is not working properly (alternator drivebelt slack or broken, alternator wiring fault or alternator itself faulty).*

3 *The battery itself is at fault (electrolyte low, or battery worn out).*

1 Connect one end of the red jump lead to the positive (+) terminal of the flat battery

2 Connect the other end of the red lead to the positive (+) terminal of the booster battery.

3 Connect one end of the black jump lead to the negative (-) terminal of the booster battery

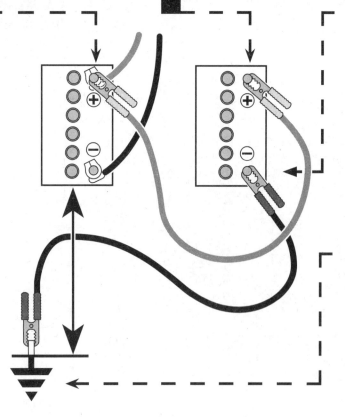

4 Connect the other end of the black jump lead to a bolt or bracket on the engine block, well away from the battery, on the vehicle to be started.

5 Make sure that the jump leads will not come into contact with the fan, drive-belts or other moving parts of the engine.

6 Start the engine using the booster battery and run it at idle speed. Switch on the lights, rear window demister and heater blower motor, then disconnect the jump leads in the reverse order of connection. Turn off the lights etc.

Wheel changing

Warning: Do not change a wheel in a situation where you risk being hit by other traffic. On busy roads, try to stop in a lay-by or a gateway. Be wary of passing traffic while changing the wheel – it is easy to become distracted by the job in hand.

Preparation

☐ When a puncture occurs, stop as soon as it is safe to do so.

☐ Park on firm level ground, if possible, and well out of the way of other traffic.

☐ Use hazard warning lights if necessary.

☐ If you have one, use a warning triangle to alert other drivers of your presence.

☐ Apply the handbrake and engage first or reverse gear (or P on models with automatic transmission).

☐ Chock the wheel diagonally opposite the one being removed – a couple of large stones will do for this.

☐ If the ground is soft, use a flat piece of wood to spread the load under the jack.

Changing the wheel

1 The spare wheel and tools are under the boot floor panel. Lift up the panel's rear edge, take out the tool kit, then unscrew the spare wheel retainer, and lift out the spare wheel. The jack is tucked in at the rear – unscrew ('lower') it slightly to remove.

2 Where applicable, prise off the wheel trim to access the nuts. Use the wheelbrace to loosen each wheel nut by half a turn.

3 Locate the jack head into the jacking point nearest the wheel to be changed. The jacking points are elongated tabs on the base of the door sills at the front and rear – the slotted jack head should locate on the tab. Turn the jack handle clockwise until the wheel is raised clear of the ground.

4 Remove the nuts, and lift the punctured wheel clear. Fit the spare wheel, which is a narrow 'space-saver' type (the wheel trim will not fit a space-saver wheel, so it should be stored in the boot). Refit the wheel nuts, and tighten moderately with the wheelbrace.

5 Lower the car to the ground, then finally tighten the wheel nuts in a diagonal sequence. Ideally, the wheel nuts should be slackened and retightened to the specified torque at the earliest opportunity.

Finally . . .

☐ Remove the wheel chocks.

☐ Stow the jack and tools in the correct locations in the car. On models with alloy wheels, the plastic centre cap must be pushed out before the retainer bolt can be used to hold the punctured wheel in place.

☐ Check the tyre pressure on the wheel just fitted. If it is low, or if you don't have a pressure gauge with you, drive slowly to the nearest garage and inflate the tyre to the right pressure.

☐ The space-saver spare wheel is for temporary use only. Drive with extra care, especially when cornering – limit yourself to a maximum of 50 mph, and to the shortest possible journeys, while it is fitted.

☐ Have the damaged tyre or wheel repaired as soon as possible.

Identifying leaks

Puddles on the garage floor or drive, or obvious wetness under the bonnet or underneath the car, suggest a leak that needs investigating. It can sometimes be difficult to decide where the leak is coming from, especially if the engine bay is very dirty already. Leaking oil or fluid can also be blown rearwards by the passage of air under the car, giving a false impression of where the problem lies.

 Warning: Most automotive oils and fluids are poisonous. Wash them off skin, and change out of contaminated clothing, without delay.

 The smell of a fluid leaking from the car may provide a clue to what's leaking. Some fluids are distinctively coloured. It may help to clean the car carefully and to park it over some clean paper overnight as an aid to locating the source of the leak. Remember that some leaks may only occur while the engine is running.

Sump oil

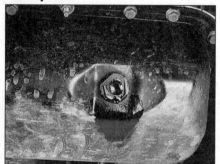

Engine oil may leak from the drain plug...

Oil from filter

...or from the base of the oil filter.

Gearbox oil

Gearbox oil can leak from the seals at the inboard ends of the driveshafts.

Antifreeze

Leaking antifreeze often leaves a crystalline deposit like this.

Brake fluid

A leak occurring at a wheel is almost certainly brake fluid.

Towing

When all else fails, you may find yourself having to get a tow home – or of course you may be helping somebody else. Long-distance recovery should only be done by a garage or breakdown service. For shorter distances, DIY towing using another car is easy enough, but observe the following points:

☐ Use a proper tow-rope – they are not expensive. The vehicle being towed must display an ON TOW sign in its rear window.
☐ Always turn the ignition key to the 'On' position when the vehicle is being towed, so that the steering lock is released, and the direction indicator and brake lights work.
☐ A towing eye is provided in the car's toolkit. To use it, unclip the access panel in the front bumper (below the left-hand headlight), then screw the towing eye in tightly.
☐ On models with automatic transmission, the car **must** be towed with its front wheels raised clear of the ground, or transmission damage may occur. Even on manual transmission models, if the front wheels cannot be suspended, the towing distance must not exceed 50 miles, at a maximum speed of 35 mph.
☐ Before being towed, release the handbrake and select neutral on the transmission.
☐ Note that greater-than-usual pedal pressure will be required to operate the brakes, since the vacuum servo unit is only operational with the engine running.

☐ If the ignition is not switched on, or the battery is flat, the electric power steering may not work, resulting in very heavy steering.
☐ The driver of the car being towed must keep the tow-rope taut at all times to avoid snatching – this can be achieved by applying the brakes very gently, where this is appropriate.
☐ Make sure that both drivers know the route before setting off.
☐ Only drive at moderate speeds and keep the distance towed to a minimum. Drive smoothly and allow plenty of time for slowing down at junctions.

Introduction

There are some very simple checks which need only take a few minutes to carry out, but which could save you a lot of inconvenience and expense.

These *Weekly checks* require no great skill or special tools, and the small amount of time they take to perform could prove to be very well spent, for example:

☐ Keeping an eye on tyre condition and pressures, will not only help to stop them wearing out prematurely, but could also save your life.

☐ Many breakdowns are caused by electrical problems. Battery-related faults are particularly common, and a quick check on a regular basis will often prevent the majority of these.

☐ If your car develops a brake fluid leak, the first time you might know about it is when your brakes don't work properly. Checking the level regularly will give advance warning of this kind of problem.

☐ If the oil or coolant levels run low, the cost of repairing any engine damage will be far greater than fixing the leak, for example.

Underbonnet check points

◄ **1.4 litre petrol engine (1.2 litre similar)**

A *Engine oil level dipstick*

B *Engine oil filler cap*

C *Radiator cap*

D *Expansion tank filler cap*

E *Brake fluid reservoir*

F *Clutch fluid reservoir*

G *Washer fluid filler neck*

H *Battery*

Note: *All models have electric power steering. As this is not a hydraulically-operated system, no power steering fluid reservoir is present.*

Engine oil level

The correct oil
Modern engines place great demands on their oil. It is very important that the correct oil for your car is used (see *Lubricants and fluids*).

Before you start
✔ Make sure that the car is on level ground.
✔ Check the oil level before the car is driven, or at least 5 minutes after the engine has been switched off.

 If the oil is checked immediately after driving the vehicle, some of the oil will remain in the upper engine components, resulting in an inaccurate reading on the dipstick.

Car care
● If you have to add oil frequently, you should

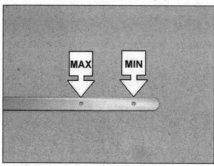

check whether you have any oil leaks. Place some clean paper under the car overnight, and check for stains in the morning. If there are no leaks, then the engine may be burning oil (see *Fault finding*).
● Always maintain the level between the upper and lower dipstick marks (see photo 2). If the level is too low, severe engine damage may occur. Oil seal failure may result if the engine is overfilled by adding too much oil.

1 The dipstick is at the front of the engine, and has an orange handle (see *Underbonnet check points*). Pull out the dipstick.

2 Using a clean rag or paper towel, wipe all the oil from the dipstick. Insert the clean dipstick into the tube as far as it will go, then withdraw it again. Note the oil level on the end of the dipstick, which should be between the lower (or MIN) and upper (or MAX) marks. Adding approximately 1.0 litre of oil will raise the level from the lower to the upper mark.

3 Oil is added through the filler cap on top of the engine. Unscrew the filler cap, then top-up the level – use a funnel to reduce spillage. Add the oil in small amounts, checking the level on the dipstick often – allow a minute or so for the oil added to reach the sump. Take care not to overfill.

Coolant level

 Warning: Do not attempt to remove the radiator cap nor the expansion tank cap when the engine is hot, as there is a very great risk of scalding. Do not leave open containers of coolant about, as it is poisonous.

Car Care
● With a sealed-type cooling system, adding coolant should not be necessary on a regular basis. If frequent topping-up is required, it is likely there is a leak. Check the radiator, all hoses and joint faces for signs of staining or wetness, and rectify as necessary.

● It is important that antifreeze is used in the cooling system all year round, not just during the winter months. Don't top up with water alone, as the antifreeze will become diluted. Genuine Honda antifreeze comes pre-mixed, ready to use.

1 First, the expansion tank level should be checked. The tank is at the front, next to the radiator. When the engine is cold, the level should be between the MIN and MAX marks. When the engine is hot, the level may rise slightly above the MAX mark.

2 If topping-up is necessary, wait until the engine is cold, then remove the cap on the expansion tank. Using a funnel, add a mixture of water and antifreeze to the expansion tank, until the coolant is up to the MAX mark. Use antifreeze of the same type (and colour) as that which is already in the system. Refit the cap securely.

3 If the expansion tank was very low, the level in the radiator should also be checked. For this, the engine must be cold. Turn the radiator cap anti-clockwise to the first stop, then press down and continue turning to remove it. The level should be up to the filler neck. Refit the cap securely on completion.

Brake and clutch fluid levels

Before you start

✔ Make sure that the car is on level ground.
✔ Cleanliness is of great importance when dealing with the hydraulic system, so take care to clean around the reservoir cap before topping-up. Use only clean brake fluid.

Safety first!

● If the reservoir requires repeated topping-up, this is an indication of a fluid leak somewhere in the system, which should be investigated immediately.
● The fluid level in the brake fluid reservoir will drop slightly as the brake pads wear down, but the fluid level must never be allowed to drop below the MIN mark.
● If a leak is suspected, the car should not be driven until the braking system has been checked. Never take any risks where brakes are concerned.

 Warning: Brake fluid can harm your eyes and damage painted surfaces, so use extreme caution when handling and pouring it. Do not use fluid which has been standing open for some time, as it absorbs moisture from the air, which can cause a dangerous loss of braking effectiveness.

1 The two reservoirs are located next to each other, at the rear of the engine bay on the driver's side. The larger of the two is the brake reservoir. Both reservoirs have MAX and MIN level marks – the fluid level must be kept between these two marks.

3 Unscrew the brake reservoir cap. If the fluid in the reservoir is dark or dirty, it should be changed. Carefully add fluid, avoiding spilling it on surrounding paintwork. Use only the specified hydraulic fluid. After filling to the correct level, refit the cap securely, and wipe off any spilt fluid.

2 If topping-up is necessary, peel off the rubber seal at the back of the engine compartment, and unclip the reservoir access panel.

4 Unscrew the clutch reservoir cap, then take out plastic inner cap and the black rubber seal (rest them on a clean piece of paper towel). Topping-up the fluid level is the same as the brake reservoir – on completion, refit the rubber seal, then the inner cap, then tighten the outer cap securely.

Washer fluid level

● Screenwash additives not only keep the windscreen clean during bad weather, they also prevent the washer system freezing in cold weather – which is when you are likely to need it most. Don't top-up using plain water, as the screenwash will become diluted, and will freeze in cold weather.

Caution: On no account use engine coolant antifreeze in the screen washer system – this may damage the paintwork.

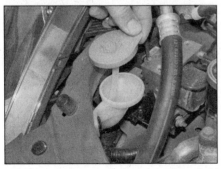

1 The windscreen/tailgate washer fluid reservoir filler neck has a blue cap, and is located at the front of the engine compartment, behind the right-hand headlight. Unclip and remove the cap.

2 A dipstick is attached to the cap – use the markings on the dipstick as a guide, but note that the bottle can safely be filled to the very top.

3 When topping-up the reservoir, a screenwash additive should be added in the quantities recommended on the bottle.

Tyre condition and pressure

It is very important that tyres are in good condition, and at the correct pressure - having a tyre failure at any speed is highly dangerous. Tyre wear is influenced by driving style - harsh braking and acceleration, or fast cornering, will all produce more rapid tyre wear. As a general rule, the front tyres wear out faster than the rears. Interchanging the tyres from front to rear ("rotating" the tyres) may result in more even wear. However, if this is completely effective, you may have the expense of replacing all four tyres at once!

Remove any nails or stones embedded in the tread before they penetrate the tyre to cause deflation. If removal of a nail does reveal that

the tyre has been punctured, refit the nail so that its point of penetration is marked. Then immediately change the wheel, and have the tyre repaired by a tyre dealer.

Regularly check the tyres for damage in the form of cuts or bulges, especially in the sidewalls. Periodically remove the wheels, and clean any dirt or mud from the inside and outside surfaces. Examine the wheel rims for signs of rusting, corrosion or other damage. Light alloy wheels are easily damaged by "kerbing" whilst parking; steel wheels may also become dented or buckled. A new wheel is very often the only way to overcome severe damage.

New tyres should be balanced when they are fitted, but it may become necessary to re-balance them as they wear, or if the balance weights fitted to the wheel rim should fall off. Unbalanced tyres will wear more quickly, as will the steering and suspension components. Wheel imbalance is normally signified by vibration, particularly at a certain speed (typically around 50 mph). If this vibration is felt only through the steering, then it is likely that just the front wheels need balancing. If, however, the vibration is felt through the whole car, the rear wheels could be out of balance. Wheel balancing should be carried out by a tyre dealer or garage.

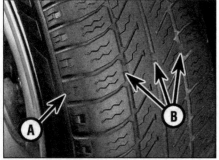

1 *Tread Depth - visual check*
The original tyres have tread wear safety bands (B), which will appear when the tread depth reaches approximately 1.6 mm. The band positions are indicated by a triangular mark on the tyre sidewall (A).

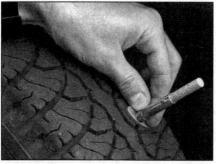

2 *Tread Depth - manual check*
Alternatively, tread wear can be monitored with a simple, inexpensive device known as a tread depth indicator gauge.

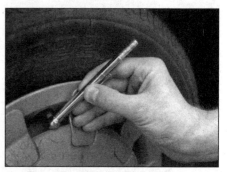

3 *Tyre Pressure Check*
Check the tyre pressures regularly with the tyres cold. Do not adjust the tyre pressures immediately after the vehicle has been used, or an inaccurate setting will result.

Tyre tread wear patterns

Shoulder Wear

Underinflation (wear on both sides)
Under-inflation will cause overheating of the tyre, because the tyre will flex too much, and the tread will not sit correctly on the road surface. This will cause a loss of grip and excessive wear, not to mention the danger of sudden tyre failure due to heat build-up.
Check and adjust pressures
Incorrect wheel camber (wear on one side)
Repair or renew suspension parts
Hard cornering
Reduce speed!

Centre Wear

Overinflation
Over-inflation will cause rapid wear of the centre part of the tyre tread, coupled with reduced grip, harsher ride, and the danger of shock damage occurring in the tyre casing.
Check and adjust pressures

If you sometimes have to inflate your car's tyres to the higher pressures specified for maximum load or sustained high speed, don't forget to reduce the pressures to normal afterwards.

Uneven Wear

Front tyres may wear unevenly as a result of wheel misalignment. Most tyre dealers and garages can check and adjust the wheel alignment (or "tracking") for a modest charge.
Incorrect camber or castor
Repair or renew suspension parts
Malfunctioning suspension
Repair or renew suspension parts
Unbalanced wheel
Balance tyres
Incorrect toe setting
Adjust front wheel alignment
Note: *The feathered edge of the tread which typifies toe wear is best checked by feel.*

Wiper blades

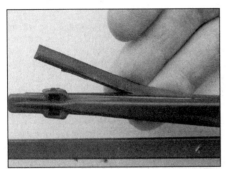

1 Check the condition of the wiper blades; if they are cracked or show any signs of deterioration, or if the glass swept area is smeared, renew them. For maximum clarity of vision, wiper blades should be renewed annually, as a matter of course. The wiper rubbers can be renewed separately if wished, but most people renew the blades complete.

2 To remove a windscreen wiper blade, pull the arm fully away from the screen until it locks. Swivel the blade through 90°, then depress the locking clip at the base of the mounting block, and slide the blade out of the hooked end of the arm.

3 Don't forget to check the tailgate wiper blade as well, which unclips directly from the arm.

Battery

Caution: Before carrying out any work on the vehicle battery, read the precautions given in 'Safety first!' at the start of this manual.

✔ Make sure that the battery tray is in good condition, and that the clamp is tight. Corrosion on the tray, retaining clamp and the battery itself can be removed with a solution of water and baking soda. Thoroughly rinse all cleaned areas with water. Any metal parts damaged by corrosion should be covered with a zinc-based primer, then painted.

✔ Periodically (approximately every three months), check the charge condition of the battery as described in Chapter 5A.

✔ If the battery is flat, and you need to jump start your vehicle, see *Roadside Repairs*.

✔ The original-equipment battery is described as 'maintenance-free', but some have removable cell covers, and the electrolyte level can be seen through the battery casing. If the level in any cell is obviously low, there is no harm in topping-up with a little distilled water.

Battery corrosion can be kept to a minimum by applying a layer of petroleum jelly to the clamps and terminals after they are reconnected.

1 The battery is located at the rear of the engine compartment, on the passenger's side. The battery should be inspected periodically for damage such as a cracked case. Honda batteries have a condition indicator window, which should show either blue or green if all is well.

2 Check the tightness of the battery cable clamps to ensure good electrical connections. You should not be able to move them. Also check each cable for cracks and frayed conductors.

3 If corrosion (white, fluffy deposits) is evident, remove the cables from the battery terminals, clean them with a small wire brush, then refit them. Automotive stores sell a tool for cleaning the battery post . . .

4 . . . as well as the battery cable clamps.

Electrical systems

✔ Check all external lights and the horn. Refer to the appropriate Sections of Chapter 12 for details if any of the circuits are found to be inoperative.

✔ Visually check all accessible wiring connectors, harnesses and retaining clips for security, and for signs of chafing or damage.

 If you need to check your brake lights and indicators unaided, back up to a wall or garage door and operate the lights. The reflected light should show if they are working properly.

1 If a single indicator light, brake light or headlight has failed, it is likely that a bulb has blown and will need to be renewed. Refer to Chapter 12 for details. If both brake lights have failed, it is possible that the brake pedal position switch, operated by the brake pedal, is to blame. Refer to Chapter 9 for details.

2 If more than one indicator light or headlight has failed, it is likely that either a fuse has blown, or that there is a fault in the circuit (see Chapter 12). The interior fuses are mounted underneath the steering column – pull out the fusebox lid using the handle provided. The fuse list is shown inside the lid.

3 To renew a blown fuse, first ensure the ignition is switched off (take out the key). Remove the fuse using the plastic tweezer tool provided (where applicable). Fit a new fuse of the same rating, available from car accessory shops. It is important that you find the reason that the fuse blew (see *Electrical fault finding* in Chapter 12).

Lubricants and fluids

Engine	Engine oil, SAE 5W-30, 5W-40, 10W-30 or 10W-40, to specification API SJ or SL
Cooling system	Ethylene glycol-based antifreeze suitable for use in mixed-metal engines – Honda All Season Type 2
Manual transmission	Honda Manual Transmission Fluid (MTF) – fully synthetic gear oil
Automatic transmission	Honda ATF-Z1
Brake and clutch systems	Hydraulic fluid to DOT 3 or DOT 4

Tyre pressures

Note 1: *Pressures given here are a guide only, and apply to original-equipment tyres – the recommended pressures may vary if any other make or type of tyre is fitted. Check with the car's handbook for latest recommendations, and for usage other than that quoted below.*
Note 2: *The tyre pressures are printed on a sticker attached to the driver's door pillar.*

Normal use	**Front**	**Rear**
Typical	32 psi (2.2 bar)	30 psi (2.1 bar)
Emergency spare tyre		
All usage, front or rear	61 psi (4.2 bar)	

The tyre pressures are given on a sticker on the driver's door pillar

Chapter 1
Routine maintenance and servicing

Contents

Degrees of difficulty

Easy, suitable for novice with little experience	**Fairly easy,** suitable for beginner with some experience	**Fairly difficult,** suitable for competent DIY mechanic 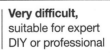	**Difficult,** suitable for experienced DIY mechanic	**Very difficult,** suitable for expert DIY or professional

Lubricants and fluids

Refer to *Weekly checks* on page 0•17

Capacities*

Engine oil (including oil filter)	3.6 litres
Cooling system:	
Change	4.0 litres
Total	5.6 litres
Manual transmission	1.5 litres
Automatic transmission:	
Change	3.2 litres
Total	5.4 litres
Fuel tank	42 litres (9.2 gallons)

* All capacities are approximate.

Lubricants and fluids

Refer to *Weekly checks* on page 0•17

Engine

Engine codes	See Chapter 2A
Valve clearances (engine cold):	
Inlet	0.15 to 0.19 mm (0.006 to 0.007 in)
Exhaust	0.26 to 0.30 mm (0.010 to 0.012 in)
Idle speed (air conditioning off):	
1.2 litre engine (all)	700 ± 50 rpm
1.4 litre engine:	
Manual transmission	650 ± 50 rpm
Automatic transmission	750 ± 50 rpm
Idle CO	0.1% max
Auxiliary drivebelt deflection (midway between pulleys)*:	
New belt	4.5 to 6.0 mm
Used belt	7.5 to 10.5 mm

* **Note:** Adjust a new belt to the 'new' tension, run the engine for 5 minutes, the re-adjust to the 'used' tension.

Ignition system

Spark plugs:	
Type	NGK BKR6E-11 or Denso K20PR-U11
Electrode gap	1.0 to 1.1 mm (0.037 to 0.043 in)

Brakes

Friction material minimum thickness:	
Front brake pads	1.6 mm
Rear brake pads	1.6 mm
Rear brake shoes	1.0 mm
Disc minimum thickness:	
Front disc	19.0 mm
Rear disc	8.0 mm
Drum maximum inside diameter	181 mm
Handbrake adjustment	6 to 10 clicks

Torque wrench settings

	Nm	lbf ft
Alternator adjuster lockbolt	24	18
Alternator lower mounting bolt	44	32
Automatic transmission drain plug	49	36
Engine block coolant drain plug	78	58
Ignition coil mounting bolts	10	7
Manual transmission drain plug	39	29
Manual transmission filler/level plug	44	32
Roadwheel nuts	108	80
Spark plugs	18	13
Sump drain plug	39	29
Valve adjuster locknut	14	10

The maintenance intervals in this manual are provided with the assumption that you, not the dealer, will be carrying out the work. These are the minimum maintenance intervals recommended by us for cars driven daily. If you wish to keep your car in peak condition at all times you may wish to perform some of these procedures more often. We encourage frequent maintenance because it enhances the efficiency, performance and resale value of your car.

If the car is driven in dusty areas, used to tow a trailer, or driven frequently at slow speeds (idling in traffic) or on short journeys, more frequent maintenance intervals are recommended.

When the car is new, it should be serviced by a dealer service department (or other workshop recognised by the car manufacturer as providing the same standard of service) in order to preserve the warranty. The car manufacturer may reject warranty claims if you are unable to prove that servicing has been carried out as and when specified, using only original-equipment parts, or parts certified to be of equivalent quality.

Every 6000 miles or 6 months, whichever comes first

☐ Renew the engine oil and filter (Section 3)

Note: *Frequent oil and filter changes are good for the engine, so we recommend halving Honda's current interval, which is 12 000 miles or 12 months.*

Every 12 000 miles or 12 months, whichever comes first

In addition to the items listed above, carry out the following:

☐ Check the braking system (Section 4)
☐ Check the steering and suspension components for condition and security (Section 5)
☐ Check the condition of the driveshaft gaiters (Section 6)
☐ Engine management and exhaust emission test (Section 7)
☐ Check the engine idle speed (Section 8)
☐ Check the operation of all electrical systems (Section 9)
☐ Check the exhaust system (Section 10)
☐ Check all components, pipes and hoses for fluid leaks (Section 11)
☐ Renew the pollen filter – models with air conditioning (Section 12)
☐ Check the automatic transmission fluid level (Section 13)
☐ Check the manual transmission fluid level (Section 14)
☐ Lubricate all door locks and hinges, door stops, bonnet lock and release, and tailgate lock and hinges (Section 15)
☐ Carry out a road test (Section 16)

Every 24 000 miles or 2 years, whichever comes first

In addition to the items listed above, carry out the following:

☐ Check and if necessary adjust the valve clearances (Section 17)
☐ Renew the air filter element (Section 18)
☐ Check the auxiliary drivebelt, and adjust or renew if necessary (Section 19)
☐ Renew the spark plugs (Section 20)

Every 48 000 miles or 4 years, whichever comes first

☐ Renew the automatic transmission fluid (Section 21)*

* Note: *On a car used mainly for short journeys, the automatic transmission fluid change interval should be halved to 24 000 miles or 2 years. As with engine oil changes, changing the fluid will help to prolong the transmission's life.*

Every 72 000 miles or 6 years, whichever comes first

In addition to the items listed above, carry out the following:

☐ Renew the fuel filter (Section 22)
☐ Renew the manual transmission fluid (Section 23)*

* Note: *On a car used mainly for short journeys, the manual transmission fluid change interval should be halved to 36 000 miles or 3 years. As with engine oil changes, changing the fluid will help to prolong the transmission's life.*

Every 3 years, regardless of mileage

☐ Renew the brake fluid (Section 24)

Every 5 years, regardless of mileage

☐ Renew the coolant (Section 25)

Note: *Some models may have been filled with Honda coolant which is claimed to have a 10-year life (check with your Honda dealer if in doubt). If this is confirmed, and only this coolant is used in the system, the 10-year renewal interval can be observed. The DIY owner may prefer to use the suggested shorter interval, especially if the coolant in the system is of unknown type.*

Underbonnet view

1   Front suspension strut
     upper mounting
2   Brake fluid reservoir
3   Clutch fluid reservoir
4   Inlet manifold
5   Engine oil filler cap
6   Throttle body
7   Battery negative lead
8   Air cleaner
9   Radiator filler cap
10 Engine oil dipstick
11 Alternator
12 Ignition coils (front bank)
13 EGR valve
14 Engine compartment
     fusebox
15 Air conditioning
     refrigerant pipe
16 ABS unit
17 Washer filler cap

Front underbody view

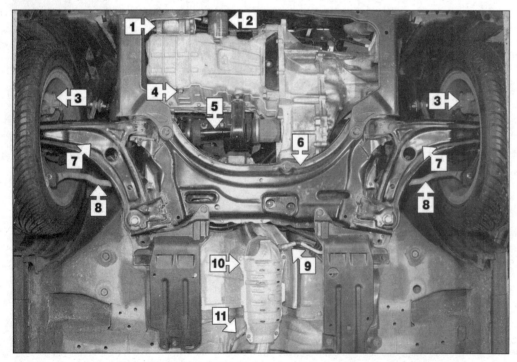

1   Air conditioning
     compressor
2   Oil filter
3   Front brake caliper
4   Engine oil drain plug
5   Right-hand driveshaft
6   Front subframe
7   Front lower suspension
     arm
8   Track rod end
9   Primary oxygen sensor
10 Catalytic converter
11 Secondary oxygen sensor

Rear underbody view

1 Exhaust rear silencer
2 Rear brake caliper
3 Rear coil spring
4 Rear brake hose
5 Rear axle
6 Handbrake cable
7 Fuel filler pipe
8 Fuel breather pipe
9 Exhaust mounting
10 Brake pipes

Maintenance procedures

1 General information

1 This Chapter is designed to help the home mechanic maintain his/her car for safety, economy, long life and peak performance.

2 The Chapter contains a master maintenance schedule, followed by Sections dealing specifically with each task in the schedule. Visual checks, adjustments, component renewal and other helpful items are included. Refer to the accompanying illustrations of the engine compartment and the underside of the car for the locations of the various components.

3 Servicing your car in accordance with the mileage/time maintenance schedule and the following Sections will provide a planned maintenance programme, which should result in a long and reliable service life. This is a comprehensive plan, so maintaining some items but not others at the specified service intervals, will not produce the same results.

4 As you service your car, you will discover that many of the procedures can – and should – be grouped together, because of the particular procedure being performed, or because of the proximity of two otherwise-unrelated components to one another. For example, if the car is raised for any reason, the exhaust can be inspected at the same time as the suspension and steering components.

5 The first step in this maintenance pro-gramme is to prepare yourself before the actual work begins. Read through all the Sections relevant to the work to be carried out, then make a list and gather all the parts and tools required. If a problem is encountered, seek advice from a parts specialist, or a dealer service department.

2 Regular maintenance

1 If, from the time the car is new, the routine maintenance schedule is followed closely, and frequent checks are made of fluid levels and high-wear items, as suggested throughout this manual, the engine will be kept in relatively good running condition, and the need for additional work will be minimised.

2 It is possible that there will be times when the engine is running poorly due to the lack of regular maintenance. This is even more likely if a used car, which has not received regular and frequent maintenance checks, is purchased. In such cases, additional work may need to be carried out, outside of the regular maintenance intervals.

3 If engine wear is suspected, a compression test (refer to Chapter 2A) will provide valuable information regarding the overall performance of the main internal components. Such a test can be used as a basis to decide on the extent of the work to be carried out. If, for example, a compression test indicates serious internal engine wear, conventional maintenance as described in this Chapter will not greatly improve the performance of the engine, and may prove a waste of time and money, unless extensive overhaul work is carried out first.

4 The following series of operations are those most often required to improve the perfor-mance of a generally poor-running engine:

Primary operations

a) Clean, inspect and test the battery (refer to Weekly checks).
b) Check all the engine-related fluids (refer to Weekly checks).
c) Check the condition and tension of the auxiliary drivebelt (Section 19).
d) Renew the spark plugs (Section 20).
e) Check the condition of the air filter, and renew if necessary (Section 18).
f) Check the condition of all hoses, and check for fluid leaks (Section 11).
g) Check the valve clearances (Section 17).

5 If the above operations do not prove fully effective, carry out the following secondary operations:

Secondary operations

All items listed under Primary operations, plus the following:

a) Check the charging system (refer to Chapter 5A).
b) Check the ignition system (refer to Chapter 5B).
c) Check the fuel system (refer to Chap-ter 4A).

3.3 Removing the engine oil filler cap will help the oil to drain faster

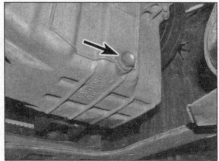

3.5a Remove the engine oil drain plug . . .

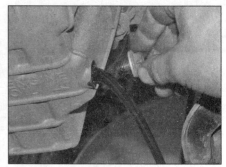

3.5b . . . and allow the oil to drain

Every 6000 miles or 6 months

3 Engine oil and filter renewal

1 Frequent oil and filter changes are the most important preventative maintenance procedures which can be undertaken by the DIY owner. As engine oil ages, it becomes diluted and contaminated, which leads to premature engine wear.

2 Before starting this procedure, gather together all the necessary tools and materials. Also make sure that you have plenty of clean rags and newspapers handy, to mop-up any spills. Ideally, the engine oil should be warm, as it will drain more easily, and more built-up sludge will be removed with it. Take care not to touch the exhaust or any other hot parts of the engine when working under the car. To avoid any possibility of scalding, and to protect yourself from possible skin irritants and other harmful contaminants in used engine oils, it is advisable to wear gloves when carrying out this work.

3 Remove the oil filler cap and pull out the dipstick (see illustration).

4 Firmly apply the handbrake, then jack up the front of the car and support it on axle stands (see Jacking and vehicle support).

5 The drain plug is at the back of the sump.

Using a spanner, or preferably a suitable socket and bar, slacken the drain plug about half a turn. Position the draining container under the drain plug, then remove the plug completely (see illustrations).

6 Allow some time for the oil to drain, noting that it may be necessary to reposition the container as the oil flow slows to a trickle.

7 After all the oil has drained, wipe the drain plug and the sealing washer with a clean rag. Fit a new sealing washer, then clean the area around the drain plug opening. Refit the plug and washer, and tighten it to the specified torque.

8 Move the container into position under the oil filter, which is located on the front face of the sump (see illustration). Remove the engine undertray (see Chapter 11, Section 23), for access.

9 Use an oil filter removal tool to slacken the filter initially, then unscrew it by hand the rest of the way (see illustration). Empty the oil from the old filter into the oil drain container. Check the filter to make sure the filter sealing ring has come off with it – if not, it may still be stuck to the sump, and should be removed.

10 Use a clean rag to remove all oil, dirt and sludge from the filter sealing area on the engine.

11 Apply a light coating of clean engine oil to the sealing ring on the new filter, then screw the filter into position. Tighten the filter firmly

by hand only – do not use any tools. Refit the front undertray.

12 Remove the old oil and all tools from under the car, then lower the car to the ground.

13 Fill the engine through the filler hole, using the correct grade and type of oil (refer to Weekly checks for details of topping-up). Pour in half the specified quantity of oil first, then wait a few minutes for the oil to run into the sump. Continue to add oil, a small quantity at a time, until the level is up to the lower mark on the dipstick (see illustration).

14 Start the engine and run it for a few minutes, while checking for leaks around the oil filter seal and the sump drain plug. Note that there may be a delay of a few seconds before the low oil pressure warning light goes out when the engine is first started, as the oil circulates through the new oil filter and the engine oil galleries before the pressure builds-up.

15 Stop the engine, and wait a few minutes for the oil to settle in the sump once more. With the new oil circulated and the filter now completely full, recheck the level on the dipstick, and add more oil as necessary.

16 Dispose of the used engine oil safely with reference to General repair procedures. It should be noted that used oil filters should not be included with domestic waste. Most local authority used oil 'banks' also have used filter disposal points alongside.

3.8 The oil filter is on the front of the sump

3.9 Unscrew the oil filter, anticipating some oil spillage

3.13 Fill the engine slowly, checking the dipstick often

4.6a On the front caliper, only the inner pad can be seen

4.6b On models with rear disc brakes, both pads are visible

Every 12 000 miles or 12 months

4 Braking system check

⚠️ *Warning: The dust created by the brake system is harmful to your health. Never blow it out with compressed air and don't inhale any of it. An approved filtering mask should be worn when working on the brakes. Do not, under any circumstances, use petroleum-based solvents to clean brake parts. Use brake system cleaner only. Try to use non-asbestos parts whenever possible.*

1 In addition to the specified intervals, the brakes should be inspected every time the wheels are removed or whenever a defect is suspected.

2 Any of the following symptoms could indicate a potential brake system defect:

a) *The car pulls to one side when the brake pedal is depressed.*
b) *The brakes make squealing or dragging noises when applied.*
c) *Brake pedal travel is excessive.*
d) *The brake pedal pulsates when applied (if this happens during emergency braking only, this could be due to ABS operation, which can be felt through the pedal, and is not a cause for concern).*
e) *Brake fluid leaks, usually onto the inside of the tyre or wheel.*

3 Loosen the wheel nuts.

4 Raise the car and place it securely on axle stands (see *Jacking and vehicle support*).

5 Remove the wheels.

Disc brakes

6 There are two pads (an outer and an inner) in each caliper. The inner pad is visible through the inspection hole in the front of each caliper, while the outer pad can be viewed from above and behind **(see illustrations)**.

7 If the lining material is less than the thickness listed in this Chapter's Specifications, renew the pads. **Note:** *Keep in mind that the lining material is bonded to a metal backing plate – the metal plate is not included in this measurement.*

8 If it is difficult to determine the exact thickness of the remaining pad material by the above method, or if you are at all concerned about the condition of the pads, remove the caliper(s), then remove the pads from the calipers for further inspection (refer to Chapter 9).

9 Once the pads are removed from the calipers, clean them with brake cleaner and re-measure them with a ruler or a vernier caliper.

10 Measure the disc thickness with a micrometer to make sure that it still has service life remaining. If a micrometer is not available, assessing the thickness is harder – measuring the disc edge with a ruler, for instance, will not give an accurate result. If the disc has a pronounced lip on its edge, and shows deep grooving, this indicates a disc which is badly worn.

11 If any disc is thinner than the specified minimum thickness, renew it (refer to Chapter 9). Even if the disc has service life remaining, check its condition. Look for scoring, gouging and burned spots. If these conditions exist, new discs should be fitted (see Chapter 9) – ideally, new pads should be fitted with the new discs.

12 Before installing the wheels, check all brake pipes and hoses for damage, wear, deformation, cracks, corrosion, leakage, bends and twists, particularly in the vicinity of the rubber hoses at the calipers. Check the clamps for tightness and the connections for leakage. Make sure that all hoses and pipes are clear of sharp edges, moving parts and the exhaust system. If any of the above conditions are noted, repair, reroute or renew the pipes and/or fittings as necessary (see Chapter 9).

Drum brakes

13 The only satisfactory way to check the rear drum brake linings (and to check the drum for scoring) is to remove the drums as described in Chapter 9. This will also allow an inspection to be made of the rear wheel cylinder, which should be checked for signs of fluid leakage.

Brake servo check

14 Sit in the driver's seat and perform the following sequence of tests.

15 With the brake fully depressed, start the engine – the pedal should move down a little when the engine starts.

16 With the engine running, depress the brake pedal several times – the travel distance should not change.

17 Depress the brake, stop the engine and hold the pedal in for about 30 seconds – the pedal should neither sink nor rise.

18 Restart the engine, run it for about a minute and turn it off. Then firmly depress the brake several times – the pedal travel should decrease with each application.

19 If the brakes do not operate as described, the brake servo or its vacuum hose may have failed. Refer to Chapter 9.

Handbrake

20 Slowly pull up on the handbrake and count the number of clicks you hear until the handle is up as far as it will go. The adjustment is correct if you hear approximately 8 clicks, using normal effort. If you hear more clicks, the handbrake needs adjusting (see Chapter 9); fewer clicks, and the cables may have seized, or the brakes are dragging (not releasing).

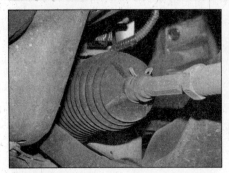

5.4 Steering rack gaiters may get twisted, and split, after the tracking is adjusted

5 Suspension and steering check

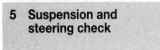

Wheel nut tightness check

1 Work around each wheel in turn, and check the tightness of the wheel nuts using a torque wrench. Where applicable, remove the wheel trim to access the nuts.

2 If you suspect that the nuts have been overtightened (as sometimes happens in certain garages), loosen and then tighten each nut (one at a time) to the specified torque.

Front suspension and steering

3 Raise the front of the car, and securely support it on axle stands (see *Jacking and vehicle support*).

4 Visually inspect the balljoint dust covers and the steering rack-and-pinion gaiters for splits, chafing or deterioration. Any wear of these components will cause loss of lubricant, together with dirt and water entry, resulting in rapid deterioration of the balljoints or steering gear **(see illustration)**.

5 Check the suspension strut for signs of fluid leakage from the shock absorber – if evident, this indicates that the shock absorber has failed (the car would fail an MoT in this condition). **Note:** *Shock absorbers should always be renewed in pairs on the same axle.*

6 Grasp the roadwheel at the 12 o'clock and 6 o'clock positions, and try to rock it **(see illustration)**. Very slight free play may be felt, but if the movement is appreciable, further

6.1 Check the condition of the outer CV gaiters

5.6 Checking for wheel bearing wear

investigation is necessary to determine the source. Continue rocking the wheel while an assistant depresses the footbrake. If the movement is now eliminated or significantly reduced, it is likely that the hub bearings are at fault. If the free play is still evident with the footbrake depressed, then there is wear in the suspension joints or mountings.

7 Now grasp the wheel at the 9 o'clock and 3 o'clock positions, and try to rock it as before. Any movement felt now may again be caused by wear in the hub bearings or the steering track rod balljoints. If the outer balljoint is worn, the visual movement will be obvious. If the inner joint is suspect, it can be felt by placing a hand over the rack-and-pinion rubber gaiter and gripping the track rod. If the wheel is now rocked, movement will be felt at the inner joint if wear has taken place.

8 Using a large screwdriver or flat bar, check for wear in the suspension mounting bushes by levering between the relevant suspension component and its attachment point. Some movement is to be expected, as the mountings are made of rubber, but excessive wear should be obvious. Also check the condition of any visible rubber bushes, looking for splits, cracks or contamination of the rubber.

9 With the car standing on its wheels, have an assistant turn the steering wheel back-and-forth, about an eighth of a turn each way. There should be very little, if any, lost movement between the steering wheel and roadwheels. If this is not the case, closely observe the joints and mountings previously described. In addition, check the steering column universal

6.4 The inner gaiters should also be checked

joints for wear, and also check the rack-and-pinion steering gear itself.

10 The Jazz has an electric power steering system, so there are no fluid hoses to check. However, the system has an EPS warning light on the instrument panel, which should come on with the ignition, then go out as the engine starts. If this warning light operates correctly (and the other checks described previously are carried out) it can be assumed that the steering system is fault-free.

11 The efficiency of the shock absorbers may be checked by bouncing the car at each corner. Generally speaking, the body will return to its normal position and stop after being depressed. If it rises and returns on a rebound, the shock absorber is probably suspect.

Rear suspension

12 Chock the front wheels, then jack up the rear of the car and support securely on axle stands (see *Jacking and vehicle support*).

13 Working as described previously for the front suspension, check the rear hub bearings, the suspension bushes and the struts/shock absorbers for wear.

6 Driveshaft (CV) gaiter check

1 With the car raised and securely supported on stands, turn the steering onto full lock, then slowly rotate the roadwheel. Inspect the condition of the outer constant velocity (CV) joint rubber gaiters while squeezing the gaiters to open out the folds **(see illustration)**.

2 Check for signs of cracking, splits or deterioration of the rubber, which may allow the grease to escape and lead to water and grit entry into the joint.

3 Check the security and condition of the retaining clips.

4 Repeat these checks on the inner CV joints **(see illustration)**.

5 If any damage or deterioration is found, the gaiters should be renewed as described in Chapter 8.

7 Engine management and exhaust emission check

1 This check involves checking the engine management system operation by plugging an electronic tester into the system diagnostic socket to check the electronic control module (ECM) memory for faults (see Chapter 4A).

2 In addition, the exhaust emissions should be checked using suitable equipment. In the UK, the exhaust emissions are checked anyway at the annual MoT test for cars over 3 years old.

3 In reality, if the car is running correctly and the engine management warning light in

10.2a Check all the exhaust joints for black stains, which indicate a leak

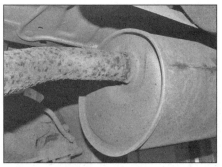

10.2b Leaks often occur where the pipe enters an exhaust box

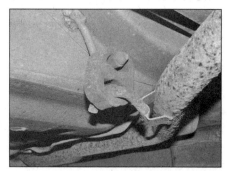

10.2c Check the mounting rubbers for cracks

the instrument panel is functioning normally (coming on with the ignition lights, then going out), then this check need not be carried out. However, if any unusual running problems have been noted, it may be worth having a Honda dealer (or other competent garage with the necessary diagnostic equipment) carry out the check – it may be that a fault has occurred, and the car is running in its 'limp-home' back-up mode.

8 Idle speed check

1 Engine idle speed is the speed at which the engine runs when no throttle is applied, when the car is completely stopped. Note that it is normal for the idle speed to be held up for a second or two, before dropping to base idle – most cars will also run above idle while rolling to a stop, when coasting downhill, or when the air conditioning is switched on. The speed is critical to the performance of the engine itself, as well as many sub-systems.
2 The idle speed is under the control of the engine management module (ECM) and is not adjustable manually. If the idle speed is significantly different from that specified (which is also for an engine at full operating temperature), in the first instance, check the accelerator cable and throttle body.
3 Poor idle quality could be due to poor maintenance – change the engine oil, and carry out the primary operations listed in Section 2.
4 As a rough guide, an idle speed which is too high may be due to an 'air leak' – the engine is sucking in excess air somewhere (perhaps from a loose or split air or vacuum hose), and the ECM is compensating for the extra air by adding fuel.
5 An engine prone to stalling could be suffering a problem with one of the engine-driven ancillaries, such as the alternator, or the problem could be low fuel pressure. Also check the brake pedal position switch and vehicle speed sensor (see Chapter 4A, Section 11).
6 Ultimately, a persistent idle speed problem will have to be referred to a Honda dealer for diagnosis.

9 Electrical systems check

1 Check the operation of all electrical equipment, ie, lights, direction indicators, horn, wash/wipe system, etc. Refer to the appropriate Sections of Chapter 12 for details if any of the circuits are found to be inoperative.
2 Visually check all accessible wiring connectors, harnesses and retaining clips for security, and for signs of chafing or damage. Rectify any faults found.

10 Exhaust system inspection

1 With the engine cold (at least three hours after the car has been driven), check the complete exhaust system from the engine to the end of the tailpipe. Ideally, the inspection should be done with the car on a hoist to permit unrestricted access. If a hoist isn't available, raise the car and support it securely on axle stands (see *Jacking and vehicle support*).
2 Check the exhaust pipes and connections for evidence of leaks, severe corrosion and damage. Make sure that all brackets, hangers and rubbers are in good condition **(see illustrations)**.
3 At the same time, inspect the underside of

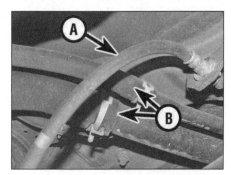

11.2 Check the brake hoses (A) and fuel lines (B)

the body for holes, corrosion, open seams, etc, which may allow exhaust gases to enter the passenger compartment. Seal all body openings with silicone or body filler.
4 Rattles and other noises can often be traced to the exhaust system, especially the mounts and hangers. Try to move the pipes, silencer and catalytic converter. If the components can come into contact with the body or suspension parts, secure the exhaust system with new mounts.

11 Hose and fluid leak check

1 Visually inspect the engine joint faces, gaskets and seals for any signs of water or oil leaks. Pay particular attention to the areas around the cylinder head cover, cylinder head, oil filter and sump joint faces. Bear in mind that, over a period of time, some very slight seepage from these areas is to be expected – what you are really looking for is any indication of a serious leak. Should a leak be found, renew the offending gasket or oil seal by referring to the appropriate Chapters in this manual.
2 Also check the security and condition of all the engine-related pipes and hoses, all braking system pipes and hoses, and the fuel lines **(see illustration)**. Ensure that all cable-ties or securing clips are in place, and in good condition. Clips which are broken or missing can lead to chafing of the hoses, pipes or wiring, which could cause more serious problems in the future.
3 Carefully check the radiator hoses and heater hoses along their entire length. Renew any hose which is cracked, swollen or deteriorated. Cracks will show up better if the hose is squeezed. Pay close attention to the hose clips that secure the hoses to the cooling system components. Hose clips can pinch and puncture hoses, resulting in cooling system leaks. If spring-type hose clips are used, it may be a good idea to substitute Jubilee clips **(see illustrations)**.
4 Inspect all the cooling system components (hoses, joint faces, etc) for leaks.
5 Where any problems are found on cooling

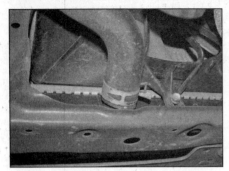

11.3a Check the large radiator hoses . . .

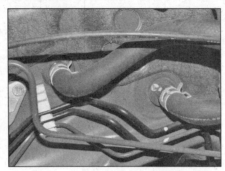

11.3b . . . and the smaller heater hoses

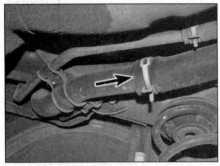

11.6 Check the fuel filler-to-tank
connection for leaks

11.8 Check the condition of the engine-
related vacuum and breather hoses

system components, renew the component or gasket with reference to Chapter 3.

6 With the car raised, inspect the fuel tank and filler neck for punctures, cracks and other damage. The connection between the filler neck and tank is especially critical **(see illustration)**. Sometimes a rubber filler neck or connecting hose will leak due to loose retaining clamps or deteriorated rubber.

7 Carefully check all rubber hoses and metal fuel lines leading away from the fuel tank. Check for loose connections, deteriorated hoses, crimped lines, and other damage. Pay particular attention to the vent pipes and hoses, which often loop up around the filler neck and can become blocked or crimped. Follow the lines to the front of the car, carefully inspecting them all the way. Renew damaged sections as necessary. Similarly, whilst the car is raised, take the opportunity to inspect all underbody brake fluid pipes and hoses.

8 From within the engine compartment, check the security of all fuel, vacuum and brake hose attachments and pipe unions, and inspect all hoses for kinks, chafing and deterioration **(see illustration)**.

9 Where applicable, check the condition of the automatic transmission fluid pipes and hoses.

12 Pollen filter renewal

1 All models with air conditioning are equipped with a filter under the facia that cleans the air entering the car through the ventilation system. This filter is fine enough, apparently, to remove airborne pollen, so it doesn't take long for it to get blocked – when it does, the air output will be greatly reduced.

2 Open the glovebox. If the glovebox is full, it may be advisable to empty it now. Gently pull the glovebox 'liner' towards you, and withdraw it from the glovebox – note that it has a protruding tab on the back, which locates in a slot in the crossmember behind the facia **(see illustration)**.

3 Release the side catches and pull out the pollen filter tray now visible, together with the filter element **(see illustrations)**.

4 Lift the filter element from its tray, noting how it fits.

5 Observing the direction-of-fitting markings on the side of the element (the airflow arrows should point downwards), fit the new element into the tray **(see illustration)**.

6 As far as possible, wipe the inside of the housing clean.

7 Insert the filter tray back into the slot, and push it home.

8 Slide the glovebox liner back into place, making sure the tab locates into the metal crossmember behind. Close the glovebox to complete.

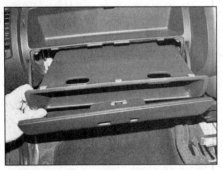

12.2 Open the glovebox, and pull out the
'liner'

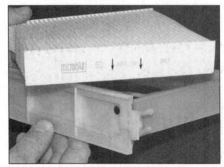

12.3a Release the side catches . . .

12.3b . . . and pull out the filter tray

13 Automatic transmission fluid level check

1 The level of the automatic transmission fluid should be carefully maintained. Low fluid level can lead to slipping or loss of drive, while overfilling can cause foaming, loss of fluid and transmission damage.

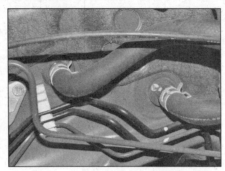

12.5 Fit the new filter to the tray, with the
airflow arrows pointing downwards

2 The transmission fluid level should only be checked with the car parked on level ground.

3 Start the engine, warm it up to operating temperature (wait until the radiator fan comes on, and cuts out), then switch it off. The fluid level should be checked within 60 to 90 seconds of switching off the engine – take care not to burn yourself on hot engine components.

4 Remove the dipstick – it's accessed behind the coolant filler cap, and has a yellow loop on top. Note that the dipstick may have to be twisted slightly to remove it – it has a sealing cap built into the stick **(see illustration)**.

5 Wipe the fluid from the dipstick with a clean rag, and re-insert it.

6 Pull the dipstick out again and note the fluid level, which should be between the upper and lower marks on the dipstick, either side of the word HOT. If the level is low, add the specified automatic transmission fluid through the dipstick opening, using a funnel.

7 Add just enough of the specified fluid to fill the transmission to the proper level. Add the fluid a little at a time, and keep checking the level until it is correct.

8 If the transmission fluid level is ever checked when the engine is cold, use the marks either side of the word COLD on the dipstick.

9 The condition of the fluid should also be checked along with the level. If the fluid at the end of the dipstick is black or a dark reddish brown colour, or if it emits a burned smell, the fluid should be changed (see Section 21). If you are in doubt about the condition of the fluid, purchase some new fluid and compare the two for colour and smell.

14 Manual transmission fluid level check

1 The manual transmission does not have a dipstick. To check the fluid level, raise the car and support it securely on axle stands (see *Jacking and vehicle support*). The filler/level plug is just behind the left-hand driveshaft (the drain plug is directly below the driveshaft, at the base of the housing). Remove the plug, and recover the sealing washer – a new washer should be used when refitting **(see illustrations)**. If the lubricant level is correct, it should be up to the lower edge of the hole.

2 If the transmission needs more lubricant (if the level is not up to the hole), add more through the filler/level hole. If there is sufficient access, a funnel can be used, but most transmission fluid bottles have a flexible tube attached, which is better suited – by squeezing the bottle, fluid can be added from almost any angle **(see illustration)**. Stop filling the transmission when the lubricant begins to run out of the hole.

3 Refit the plug with a new washer, and tighten it securely. Drive the car a short distance, then check for leaks.

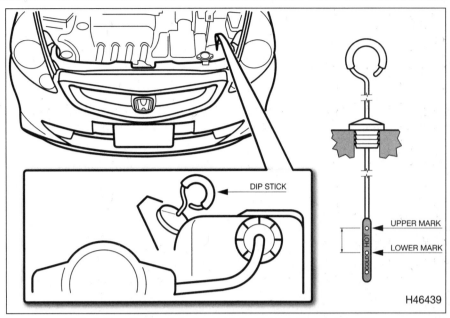

13.4 Automatic transmission fluid dipstick location and markings

15 Hinge and lock lubrication

1 Work around the car and lubricate the hinges of the bonnet, doors and tailgate with a light machine oil **(see illustration)**.

2 Lightly lubricate the bonnet release mechanism and exposed section of inner cable with a smear of grease.

3 Check the security and operation of all hinges, latches and locks, adjusting them where required. Check the operation of the central locking system.

4 Check the condition and operation of the tailgate struts, renewing them both (as described in Chapter 11) if either is leaking or no longer able to support the tailgate securely when raised.

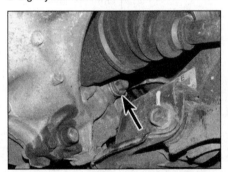

14.1a The manual transmission filler/level plug is behind the left-hand driveshaft

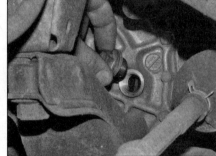

14.1b Unscrew the plug, noting its sealing washer

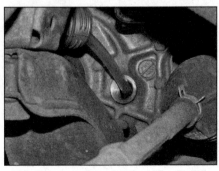

14.2 Top-up using a bottle with a flexible tube

15.1 Oil the door hinges and check straps

16 Road test

Instruments and electrical equipment

1 Check the operation of all instruments and electrical equipment.
2 Make sure that all instruments read correctly, and switch on all electrical equipment in turn, to check that it functions properly.

Steering and suspension

3 Check for any abnormalities in the steering, suspension, handling or road 'feel'.
4 Drive the car, and check that there are no unusual vibrations or noises.
5 Check that the steering feels positive, with no excessive 'sloppiness', or roughness, and check for any suspension noises when cornering and driving over bumps.

Drivetrain

6 Check the performance of the engine, clutch, transmission and driveshafts.
7 Listen for any unusual noises from the engine, clutch and transmission.
8 Make sure that the engine runs smoothly when idling, and that there is no hesitation when accelerating.
9 Check that, where applicable, the clutch action is smooth and progressive, that the drive is taken up smoothly, and that the pedal travel is not excessive. Also listen for any noises when the clutch pedal is depressed.
10 Check that all gears can be engaged smoothly without noise, and that the gear lever action is smooth and not abnormally vague or 'notchy'.
11 On automatic transmission models, make sure that all gearchanges occur smoothly, without snatching, and without an increase in engine speed between changes. Check that all of the gear positions can be selected with the car at rest. If any problems are found, they should be referred to a Honda dealer or specialist.
12 Listen for a metallic clicking sound from the front of the car, as the car is driven slowly in a circle with the steering on full-lock. Carry out this check in both directions. If a clicking noise is heard, this indicates wear in a driveshaft joint (see Chapter 8).

Braking system

13 Make sure that the car does not pull to one side when braking, and that the wheels do not lock when braking hard.
14 Check that there is no vibration through the steering when braking.
15 Check that the handbrake operates correctly, without excessive movement of the lever, and that it holds the car stationary on a slope.

Every 24 000 miles or 2 years

17 Valve clearance check and adjustment

1 The valve clearances must be checked and adjusted with the engine cold.
2 Remove the cylinder head cover as described in Chapter 2A.
3 Set No 1 piston to TDC by turning the engine using a socket or spanner (19 mm) on the crankshaft pulley bolt. Initially be guided by the red and white ignition timing marks on the crankshaft sprocket which align with a notch on the timing cover. The engine is at TDC when the white mark is aligned – however, this could mean either No 1 or No 4 is at TDC, so the camshaft sprocket marks must also be used.
4 The camshaft sprocket has an UP mark on one of its spokes, and two line markings opposite each other, just below the chain (use an electric torch, as the marks are hard to spot). At No 1 TDC, the UP mark should be uppermost (at the twelve o'clock position), and the two line marks aligned horizontally with the cylinder head top surface **(see illustration)**.
5 With the engine in this position, the two valves for No 1 cylinder can be checked and adjusted. Note that the cylinders are numbered from the timing chain end, and that the inlet valves are at the front, with the exhaust valves at the rear.
6 Start with the intake valve clearance. Insert a feeler gauge of the correct thickness (see this Chapter's Specifications) between the valve stem and the rocker arm. Withdraw it, and you should feel a slight drag. If there's no drag or a heavy drag, loosen the locknut and undo the adjuster screw. Carefully tighten the adjuster screw until you can feel a slight drag on the feeler gauge as you withdraw it.
7 Hold the adjuster screw with a screwdriver (to stop it turning) and tighten the locknut (some mechanics leave the feeler blade inserted while this is done). Recheck the clearance to make sure it hasn't changed. Repeat the check-and-adjust procedure on the No 1 cylinder exhaust valve **(see illustration)**.
8 Rotate the crankshaft pulley 180° clockwise (the camshaft sprocket will turn 90°) until No 3 piston is at TDC. With No 3 at TDC, instead of the UP mark, a number 3 will be visible on the camshaft sprocket, and a single horizontal line marking to the right, which should line up with the top of the cylinder head. Check and adjust the two valves for No 3 cylinder.
9 Rotate the crankshaft pulley 180° clockwise until No 4 piston is at TDC, indicated by a number 4 appearing on the camshaft

17.4 The camshaft sprocket UP mark and line markings at No 1 TDC

17.7 Adjusting the No 1 exhaust valve clearance

18.2a Release the spring clips (or remove the screws) . . .

18.2b . . . and take off the air cleaner cover

18.3 Lift out the air cleaner element

sprocket, and another horizontal cylinder head alignment mark. The white crankshaft sprocket timing mark used previously will also be aligned. Check and adjust the two No 4 cylinder valves.

10 Rotate the crankshaft pulley 180° clockwise to bring No 2 piston to TDC. Now the camshaft sprocket should show a 2 marking at twelve o'clock, as well as the horizontal line to the right, in line with the surface of the cylinder head. Check and adjust No 2 cylinder valves.

11 Though there should be no real need, the engine can be turned again to bring No 1 (and the UP mark) back to TDC, and the No 1 clearances can be rechecked. If the engine is then turned further in sequence, the clearances for the remaining three cylinders can be rechecked.

12 On completion, refit the cylinder head cover as described in Chapter 2A.

18 Air filter element renewal

1 One of two different designs of air cleaner may be fitted, depending on model. These different air cleaners also have filter elements of a different shape, so be sure to obtain the correct new filter. One air cleaner has a cover secured by four spring clips, and has a square element – the other cover is secured using six screws, and contains an elongated rectangular element.

2 Either remove the screws or release the clips securing the air cleaner cover, and lift it off for access to the element – the clip-type cover pulls out of the rubber boot at the rear **(see illustrations)**.

3 Lift the air filter element out of the housing, and wipe out the inside of the air cleaner housing with a clean rag **(see illustration)**.

4 While the air cleaner cover is off and the element is removed, be careful not to drop anything down into the air cleaner assembly.

5 Fit the new element into the air cleaner housing, making sure it seats properly.

6 Install the air cleaner cover, and secure with the clips or screws (the clips can be snapped into place by pressing on the curved part of the clip).

19 Auxiliary drivebelt check, adjustment and renewal

Checking

1 Due to their function and material makeup, a drivebelt is prone to failure after a long period of time, and should therefore be inspected regularly.

2 Though it may be possible to view the belt from above, the best access is gained from below. Loosen the right-hand front wheel nuts, then jack up the front of the car, and support it on axle stands (see *Jacking and vehicle support*). Remove the right-hand front wheel. Also unbolt and remove the engine undertray (see Chapter 11, Section 23).

3 With the engine stopped, inspect the full length of the drivebelt for cracks and separation of the belt plies. It will be necessary to turn the engine (using a spanner or socket and bar on the crankshaft pulley bolt) in order to move the belt from the pulleys so that the belt can be inspected thoroughly. Twist the

belt between the pulleys so that both sides can be viewed. Also check for fraying, and glazing which gives the belt a shiny appearance. Check the pulleys for nicks, cracks, distortion and corrosion.

4 The belt tension is checked by pushing the belt at a distance halfway between the pulleys. Push firmly with your thumb and see how much the belt moves (deflects) **(see illustrations)**.

5 Renew the belt if it shows any sign of wear or damage.

Adjustment

6 In all cases, the drivebelt is adjusted by moving the alternator – an adjuster bolt is fitted above the unit. The water pump and, where applicable, the air conditioning compressor, are rigidly mounted.

7 Loosen the left-hand front wheel nuts, then jack up the front of the car, and support it on axle stands (see *Jacking and vehicle support*). Remove the left-hand front wheel.

8 Loosen the alternator lower mounting bolt (on the 'back' of the unit), and the lockbolt which secures the adjuster bolt on the 'front'

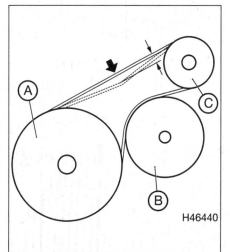

19.4a Auxiliary drivebelt tension checking point – models without air conditioning

A *Crankshaft pulley*
B *Water pump pulley*
C *Alternator*

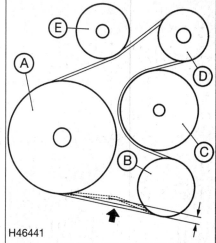

19.4b Auxiliary drivebelt tension checking point – models with air conditioning

A *Crankshaft pulley*
B *Air conditioning compressor*
C *Water pump pulley*
D *Alternator*
E *Idler pulley*

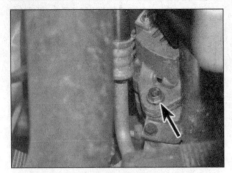

19.8a Loosen the alternator lower mounting bolt . . .

19.8b . . . and the lockbolt on the adjuster bolt

19.9 Auxiliary drivebelt adjuster bolt

19.13 Removing the auxiliary drivebelt

10 When the belt tension is satisfactory, tighten the lower mounting bolt and lockbolt to their specified torques. Recheck the belt tension when all the bolts have been tightened, as tightening them can affect the tension.

11 If a new belt has been fitted, refit the wheel and lower the car to the ground. Run the engine for about 5 minutes, and recheck the belt tension. Honda recommend that, after this 5-minute period, the tension is reset to the deflection specified for a used belt.

12 On completion, refit the wheel once more, then lower the car to the ground and tighten the wheel nuts to the specified torque.

Renewal

13 To renew a belt, follow the above procedure for drivebelt adjustment, but loosen the adjuster bolt enough to slip the belt off the pulleys and remove it **(see illustration)**.

14 Take the old belt with you when purchasing a new one, in order to make a direct comparison for length, width and design.

15 Fit the new belt around the pulleys, making sure the belt ribs sit properly in the pulley grooves – turn the engine using the crankshaft pulley bolt to ensure the belt has seated before adjusting it as described previously in this Section.

(see illustrations). The lower mounting bolt is hard to see – access may be best from below.
9 Turn the adjuster bolt to adjust the belt tension **(see illustration)**. Use the belt deflection figures specified as a guide – to some extent, setting belt tension is a matter

of experience and 'feel'. Clearly the belt must not be too loose (though multi-ribbed belts are less likely to slip than the older vee-belt type), but don't overadjust, as this will lead to expensive wear in the alternator and compressor bearings.

20 Spark plug renewal

Note: *The Jazz is unusual in having EIGHT spark plugs, not the more usual four.*

1 The correct functioning of the spark plugs is vital for the correct running and efficiency of the engine. It is essential that the plugs fitted are appropriate for the engine; suitable types are specified at the beginning of this Chapter, or in the car's handbook. If the correct type is used and the engine is in good condition, the spark plugs should not need attention between scheduled renewal intervals. Spark plug cleaning is rarely necessary, and should not be attempted unless specialised equipment is available, as damage can easily be caused to the firing ends.

2 Ensure that the ignition is switched off (take out the key).

3 Remove the plastic cover from the inlet manifold – this is secured by two domed bolts **(see illustration)**.

4 Unclip the rear wiring harness from the two brackets at either end of the engine. At the air cleaner end, release a tab and the harness slides off rearwards, then the other end slides sideways towards the air cleaner. Releasing two more clips at the driver's end gives the harness more movement, if wished, as does disconnecting the MAP sensor on top of the engine. Move the harness clear – there is no need to disconnect it **(see illustrations)**.

5 Wipe around the coils and the engine as far as possible – it is essential that dirt does not enter the engine when the spark plugs are removed.

20.3 Remove the inlet manifold's plastic cover

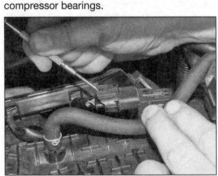

20.4a By disconnecting the MAP sensor wiring plug on top . . .

20.4b . . . and releasing the harness from this bracket . . .

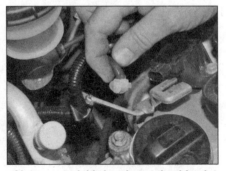

20.4c . . . and this bracket at the driver's side . . .

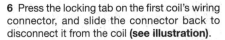

20.4d ... the harness can be moved well back from the rear bank of coils

20.6 Press the locking tab and pull back to disconnect the coil plug

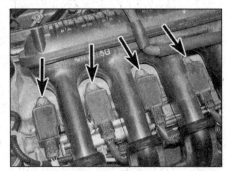

20.7 Ignition coil mounting bolts (front bank)

6 Press the locking tab on the first coil's wiring connector, and slide the connector back to disconnect it from the coil **(see illustration)**.

7 Unscrew the bolt securing each ignition coil to the top of the engine – there are four along the front, and four more at the rear **(see illustration)**.

8 Lift the coil out of the engine **(see illustrations)**. The four front coils and the four rear coils appear to be identical, but they cannot be interchanged front to rear. It may be wise to complete work on one coil/spark plug at a time, before moving on to the next one.

9 Using a slim spark plug socket, unscrew and remove the first spark plug. The spark plugs on these models are recessed, so an extension bar will also be necessary. On the rear plugs, access is reduced – we found the socket and extension had to be inserted first, and only then could the socket handle be fitted to it **(see illustrations)**.

10 Examination of the spark plugs will give a good indication of the condition of the engine. As each plug is removed, examine it as follows.

11 If the insulator nose of the spark plug is clean and white, with no deposits, this is indicative of a weak mixture or too hot a plug (a hot plug transfers heat away from the electrode slowly, a cold plug transfers heat away quickly).

12 If the tip and insulator nose are covered with hard black-looking deposits, then this is indicative that the mixture is too rich. Should the plug be black and oily, then it is likely that the engine is fairly worn, as well as the mixture being too rich. If the insulator nose is covered with light tan to greyish-brown deposits, then the mixture is correct and it is likely that the engine is in good condition.

13 Where multi-electrode plugs are fitted, the electrode gaps are all preset, and **no** attempt

should be made to bend the electrodes – fit the plugs straight out of the packet.

14 If standard single-electrode plugs are fitted, the spark plug electrode gap is of considerable importance. If the gap is too large or too small, the size of the spark and its efficiency will be seriously impaired and it will not perform correctly under all engine speed and load conditions. The gap quoted at the start of this Chapter is suitable for the plugs also specified, but may not be if other makes of plug are used.

15 To set the gap, measure it with a feeler blade or spark plug gap gauge, then carefully bend the outer plug electrode until the correct gap is achieved. The centre electrode should never be bent, as this may crack the insulator and cause plug failure, if nothing worse. If using feeler blades, the gap is correct when the appropriate-size blade is a firm sliding fit **(see illustrations)**.

20.8a Lift the ignition coil off the spark plug (front bank) ...

20.8b ... at the rear, access is reduced, but the coil will still come out

20.9a The spark plugs are deeply recessed ...

20.9b ... but the front ones can be removed easily

20.9c There is room to use a socket handle and extension on the rear plugs ...

20.9d ... but to remove/fit the plug, the handle had to be removed first

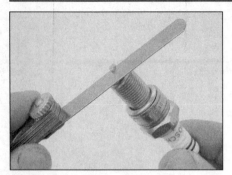

20.15a Measuring the spark plug gap with a feeler blade

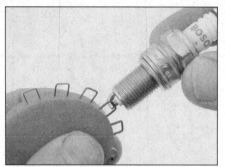

20.15b Measuring the spark plug gap with a wire gauge

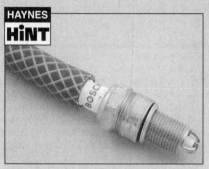

HAYNES HiNT

It's often difficult to insert spark plugs into their holes without cross-threading them. To avoid this possibility, fit a short length of rubber or plastic hose over the end of the spark plug. The flexible hose acts as a universal joint, to help align the plug with the plug hole. Should the plug begin to cross thread, the hose will slip on the spark plug, preventing thread damage to the aluminium cylinder head.

16 Special spark plug electrode gap adjusting tools are available from most motor accessory shops, or from some spark plug manufacturers.

17 Before fitting the spark plugs, check that the threaded connector sleeves on top are tight, and that the plug exterior surfaces and threads are clean. Though not essential, a little copper grease applied to the plug threads may make the plugs easier to remove next time.

18 Fit the new plug into the spark plug socket, then offer it into the engine with the long extension. A proper spark plug socket has a rubber insert fitted, which is very useful for gripping the plug during this stage of fitting – use an ordinary deep socket, and the plug will fall out.

19 Tighten the plug initially by hand – this way, it is possible to feel whether the plug is going in correctly (there should be little or no effort needed), or whether it is misaligned and is cross-threading **(see Haynes Hint)**. After several turns, the plug will be felt to 'seat' (contact the cylinder head).

20 Using a torque wrench, tighten the plug to the specified torque (remember that, during tightening, a new plug's sealing washer is crushed). Alternatively, tighten the plug no more than about half a turn after it seats. Do not overtighten the plugs, or the alloy threads in the cylinder head will be damaged.

21 Offer the ignition coil into the engine so that the hole in the coil mounting plate aligns with the mounting bolt hole on the engine, and fit it over the plug. Press the coil firmly down onto the plug, then reconnect the coil wiring plug, ensuring that a good connection is made. Fit the coil mounting bolt, and tighten it securely.

22 Repeat the procedure for the remaining coils and spark plugs. As previously stated, the four front coils and the four rear coils appear to be identical, but they cannot be interchanged front to rear. It may be wise to complete work on one coil/spark plug at a time, before moving on to the next one.

23 On completion, clip the rear wiring harness back into place, then refit the plastic cover over the inlet manifold, and secure with the two domed bolts.

Every 48 000 miles or 4 years

21 Automatic transmission fluid renewal

1 The fluid should be drained when hot, preferably immediately after the car has been driven.

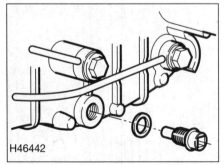

21.4 Automatic transmission fluid drain plug

⚠️ *Warning: Fluid temperature can exceed 120°C in a hot transmission. Wear protective gloves.*

2 Raise the front of the car and place it on axle stands for access to the transmission drain plug (see *Jacking and vehicle support*).

3 Move the tools and drain pan under the car, being careful not to touch any of the hot exhaust components.

4 The transmission drain plug is located on the right-hand side of the transmission at the bottom, adjacent to the two fluid pipe unions. A square key will be needed to undo it (it may be possible to use the square fitting on a socket handle or extension bar) **(see illustration)**. Be sure the drain pan is in position, as fluid will come out with some force.

5 Unscrew the drain plug, which will be quite tight (try not to drop it), and recover the sealing washer. Once the fluid is drained, clean the drain plug and refit it with a new sealing washer, then tighten it to the specified torque. Lower the car to the ground.

6 Pull out the dipstick, then add new fluid to the transmission through the dipstick tube. Use a funnel to prevent spills. It is best to add a little fluid at a time, continually checking the level with the dipstick (see Section 13). Use the two dipstick markings either side of the word COLD – ignore the upper mark above HOT at this stage.

7 When the fluid level reaches the mark just above COLD on the dipstick, refit the dipstick.

8 With one foot on the brake, start the engine and slowly shift the selector into all positions, then shift into P and apply the handbrake. Let the engine warm-up to operating temperature (wait until the radiator fan has come on, and gone off).

9 Turn off the engine and check the fluid level as described in Section 13. With the transmission at operating temperature, the dipstick marks either side of the word HOT should be used.

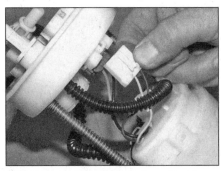

22.3 Disconnect the sender unit wiring plug

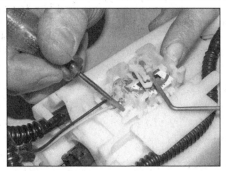

22.4a Use a screwdriver to depress the clip, and push upwards . . .

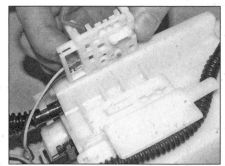

22.4b . . . to release the sender unit from the assembly

Every 72 000 miles or 6 years

22 Fuel filter renewal

Note: *The fuel filter is not a conventional externally-mounted canister-type filter element – rather, it constitutes more than half of the in-tank fuel pump/sender unit. Though it is part of Honda's maintenance schedule to renew the filter at this interval, Honda also state that the filter should be renewed when the fuel pressure drops below the value quoted in Chapter 4A Specifications. If the fuel pressure is checked, and found to be acceptable, it may be arguable that fuel filter renewal could be postponed, though this is* up to the individual. A Honda dealer should be consulted if in doubt.

1 Remove the fuel pump/sender unit as described in Chapter 4A.
2 With the assembly drained of fuel and removed to a clean working area, dismantling can begin.
3 Disconnect the upper wiring plug (on our car, this had yellow and black wires) which supplies the level sender unit **(see illustration)**.
4 Using a small screwdriver, depress the locating tab and remove the sender unit upwards from the side of the assembly **(see illustrations)**.
5 Release the fuel hose connection from the base of the sediment bowl **(see illustration)**.

6 Release the three securing tabs, and slide off the sediment bowl **(see illustrations)**.
7 Disconnect the pump wiring plug (on our car, this had blue and black wires) **(see illustration)**.
8 Carefully release the plastic tube clipped to the side of the assembly – this makes room to unclip the pump lower cover **(see illustration)**.
9 Release the three securing tabs, and take out the pump lower cover. Recover the rubber seat which fits between the pump and its cover, noting how it fits **(see illustrations)**.
10 Pull the pump down and out of the assembly – there will be some resistance from the pump's upper O-ring. Recover the O-ring from the assembly if it was not removed with

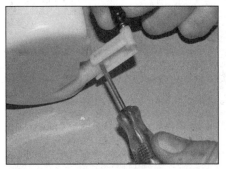

22.5 Unclip the hose connection on the base of the bowl

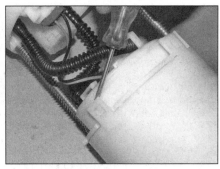

22.6a Release the securing tabs with a small screwdriver . . .

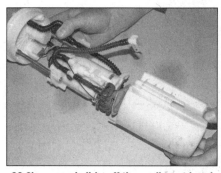

22.6b . . . and slide off the sediment bowl

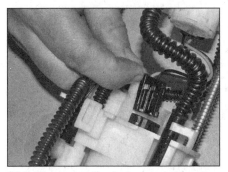

22.7 Disconnect the fuel pump wiring plug

22.8 Unclip the plastic tube from the side, and just move it clear

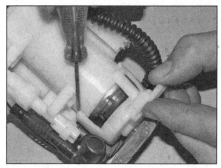

22.9a Release the securing tabs, and take out the pump lower cover

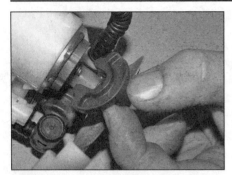

22.9b Recover the rubber seat from the base of the pump

22.10a Pull out the fuel pump . . .

22.10b . . . and if necessary, recover the old O-ring

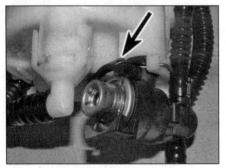

22.11 Pull up the metal clip securing the fuel pressure regulator

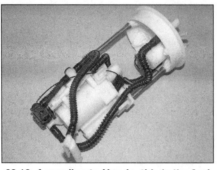

22.12 According to Honda, this is the fuel filter

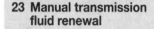

23 Manual transmission fluid renewal

the pump – however, a new O-ring should really be used when reassembling **(see illustrations)**.

11 Pull up the metal securing clip, then pull the fuel pressure regulator out of the assembly **(see illustration)**. Recover the two O-rings from the regulator – new ones should be used when refitting.

12 The assembly which is left should be, effectively, the fuel filter **(see illustration)**. Transfer any parts to the new filter if necessary.

13 Fit two new O-rings to the pressure regulator, then press it home and secure with the metal clip (squeeze the clip legs together, and fit it from the top).

14 Fit a new upper O-ring to the pump, then offer it in position and press it into the new filter assembly.

15 Refit the rubber seat to the pump lower cover, then clip the cover onto the base of the pump, ensuring that the tabs engage properly. Once this is done, the plastic tube on the side of the assembly can also be clipped back in place.

16 Reconnect the pump wiring plug.

17 Refit the sediment bowl, again making sure the tabs engage properly. Clip the hose connection back onto the bowl.

18 Clip the sender unit back onto the side of the assembly, and reconnect its wiring plug.

19 Refit the fuel pump/sender unit as described in Chapter 4A.

1 The fluid should be drained when hot, preferably immediately after the car has been driven. Park the car on level ground to begin with.

2 Raise the front of the car and place it on axle stands for access to the transmission drain plug (see *Jacking and vehicle support*).

3 Move the tools and drain pan under the car, being careful not to touch any of the hot exhaust components.

4 Place the drain pan under the transmission and remove the drain plug – it's located on the left-hand side of the transmission, directly below the left-hand driveshaft at the bottom, and a square key will be needed (we found that the 3/8-inch square fitting on a socket handle or extension bar will fit). Be sure the drain pan is in position, as fluid will come out with some force **(see illustrations)**.

5 Once the fluid is drained, clean and refit the drain plug, using a new sealing washer and tightening it to the specified torque. Lower the car to the ground, and make sure that it is level.

6 Remove the filler/level plug, which is located higher up the transmission casing, behind the left-hand driveshaft. Add new fluid until it begins to run out of the filler hole (see Section 14). On completion, refit the filler/level plug – use a new sealing washer and tighten it to the specified torque.

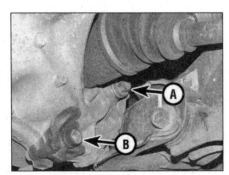

23.4a Manual transmission fluid plugs – filler/level (A) and drain (B)

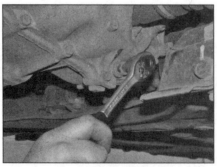

23.4b The drain plug's a 3/8-inch square fitting

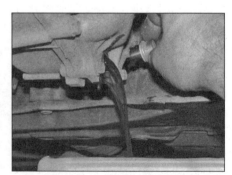

23.4c Remove the drain plug (and washer), and let the fluid drain

Every 3 years (regardless of mileage)

24 Brake fluid renewal

⚠️ *Warning: Brake hydraulic fluid can harm your eyes and damage painted surfaces, so use extreme caution when handling and pouring it. Do not use fluid that has been standing open for some time, as it absorbs moisture from the air. Excess moisture can cause a dangerous loss of braking effectiveness.*

1 The procedure is similar to that for the bleeding of the hydraulic system as described in Chapter 9.

2 Working as described in Chapter 9, open the first bleed screw in the sequence, and pump the brake pedal gently until nearly all the old fluid has been emptied from the master cylinder reservoir. Top-up to the MAX level with new fluid, and continue pumping until only the new fluid remains in the reservoir, and new fluid can be seen emerging from the bleed screw. Tighten the screw, and top the reservoir level up to the MAX level line.

3 Work through all the remaining bleed screws in the sequence until new fluid can be seen at all of them. Be careful to keep the master cylinder reservoir topped-up to above the MIN level at all times, or air may enter the system and greatly increase the length of the task.

HAYNES HiNT *Old hydraulic fluid is invariably much darker in colour than the new, making it easy to distinguish the two.*

4 When the operation is complete, check that all bleed screws are securely tightened, and that their dust caps are refitted. Wash off all traces of spilt fluid, and recheck the master cylinder reservoir fluid level.

5 Check the operation of the brakes before taking the car on the road.

Every 5 years (regardless of mileage)

25 Coolant renewal

⚠️ *Warning: Refer to Chapter 3 and observe the warnings given. In particular, never remove the radiator cap or expansion tank filler cap when the engine is running, or has just been switched off, as the cooling system will be pressurised and hot, and the consequent escaping steam and scalding coolant could cause serious injury. If the engine is hot, the electric cooling fan may start rotating even if the engine is not running, so be careful to keep hands, hair and loose clothing well clear when working in the engine compartment.*

Note: *Some models may have been filled with Honda coolant which is claimed to have a 10-year life (check with your Honda dealer if in doubt). If this is confirmed, and only this coolant is used in the system, the 10-year renewal interval can be observed. The DIY owner may prefer to use the suggested shorter interval, especially if the coolant in the system is of unknown type.*

⚠️ *Warning: Wait until the engine is cold before starting this procedure.*

Cooling system draining

1 To drain the system, first remove the radiator cap. Place a thick cloth over the radiator cap, then turn the cap anti-clockwise as far as the first stop and wait for any pressure to be released, then depress it and turn it further anti-clockwise to remove it. Similarly, remove the expansion tank cap **(see illustrations)**.

2 If additional working clearance is required, apply the handbrake, then jack up the front of the car and support it on axle stands (see *Jacking and vehicle support*).

3 Remove the engine undertray (see Chapter 11, Section 23), then place a large drain tray underneath, and loosen the radiator drain tap. Allow the coolant to drain into the tray **(see illustrations)**. On completion, refit the drain tap with a new O-ring, and tighten it securely. **Note:** *The radiator drain tap is accessible through a hole in the undertray, but if the undertray is not removed, draining will be messy. Also, the engine block drain plug will not be accessible.*

4 Move the drain tray underneath the oil filter.

25.1a Remove the radiator cap . . .

25.1b . . . and the expansion tank cap when draining the system

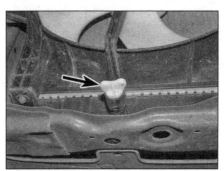

25.3a Unscrew the radiator drain tap . . .

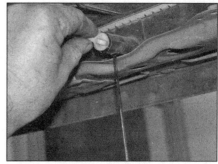

25.3b . . . and allow the coolant to drain

25.4a Engine block coolant drain plug – seen from above, with inlet manifold removed

25.4b Unscrew the plug . . .

25.4c . . . and allow the coolant to drain

Directly above the oil filter is the engine block coolant drain plug – we found that the oil filter had to be removed to gain access to the plug (if so, anticipate oil spillage from the filter as it is unscrewed). Unscrew the coolant drain plug and allow the rest of the system contents to drain into the tray **(see illustrations). Note:** *There is a slight risk of coolant splashing the alternator as the engine block drains – it may be advisable to temporarily wrap the alternator in a plastic bag.*

5 When the block has been drained of coolant, refit the drain plug using a new washer. Tighten the block drain plug to the specified torque, then refit the undertray. Where necessary, lower the car to the ground.
6 Honda also stipulate that the contents of the expansion tank should be drained when renewing the coolant. Realistically, unless suitable syphoning equipment is available (and remember, antifreeze is poisonous), this will mean removing the tank to pour out the contents. To remove the tank, unscrew the mounting bolt at the top, and lift the tank off its lower mounting.

Cooling system flushing

7 If coolant renewal has been neglected, or if the antifreeze mixture has become diluted, then in time, the cooling system may gradually lose efficiency, as the coolant passages become restricted due to rust, scale deposits, and other sediment. The cooling system efficiency can be restored by flushing the system clean.
8 The radiator should be flushed independently of the engine, to avoid unnecessary contamination.

Radiator flushing

9 Disconnect the top and bottom hoses and any other relevant hoses from the radiator, with reference to Chapter 3.
10 Insert a garden hose into the radiator top inlet. Direct a flow of clean water through the radiator, and continue flushing until clean water emerges from the radiator bottom outlet.
11 If after a reasonable period the water still does not run clear, the radiator can be flushed with a good proprietary cleaning agent. It is important that the manufacturer's instructions

are followed carefully. If the contamination is particularly bad, remove the radiator, insert the hose in the radiator bottom outlet, and reverse-flush the radiator.

Engine flushing

12 Remove the thermostat as described in Chapter 3 then, if the radiator top hose has been disconnected from the engine, temporarily reconnect the hose.
13 With the top and bottom hoses disconnected from the radiator, insert a garden hose into the radiator top hose. Direct a clean flow of water through the engine, and continue flushing until clean water emerges from the radiator bottom hose.
14 Alternatively, a degree of engine flushing can be achieved by simply filling the system with clean water only, running the engine for a few minutes, then draining the system as described previously in this Section.
15 On completion of flushing, refit the thermostat and reconnect the hoses with reference to Chapter 3.

Antifreeze mixture

 HAYNES HiNT *It is rare to ever drain the cooling system completely – a small quantity will remain. If the system has been extensively flushed with clean water, this remaining quantity will in fact be plain water. For this reason, some people will first fill the system with the required quantity of neat antifreeze (half the total system capacity, for a 50% mixture), and then complete the filling process with plain water. This ensures that the resulting coolant (once it has mixed inside the engine) is not 'diluted' by old coolant or water remaining in the system.*

16 Honda state that, if the only antifreeze used is the type with which the system was first filled at the factory (see *Lubricants and fluids*) it will last 10 years. This is subject to it being used in the recommended concentration, unmixed with any other type of antifreeze or additive, and topped-up when

necessary using only that antifreeze. No other type of antifreeze should be mixed with it – if this happens; to restore the 10-year life, the system must be drained and thoroughly reverse-flushed before fresh coolant is poured in.
17 If the car's history (and therefore the quality of the antifreeze in it) is unknown, owners who wish to follow Honda's recommendations are advised to drain and thoroughly reverse-flush the system, before refilling with fresh coolant.
18 If any antifreeze other than Honda's is to be used, the coolant must be renewed at regular intervals to provide an equivalent degree of protection; the conventional recommendation is to renew the coolant every five years.
19 Honda's own antifreeze is usually supplied pre-mixed at 50/50 strength, and is therefore ready to use. If you are using any other type of antifreeze, to give the recommended mixture ratio, 50% (by volume) of neat antifreeze must be mixed with 50% of clean, soft water; however, always note the antifreeze manufacturer's instructions **(also see the Haynes Hint).**
20 Before adding antifreeze, the cooling system should be completely drained, preferably flushed, and all hoses checked for condition and security. Fresh antifreeze will rapidly find any weaknesses in the system.
21 After filling with antifreeze, a label should be attached to the expansion tank, stating the type and concentration of antifreeze used, and the date installed. Any subsequent topping-up should be made with the same type and concentration of antifreeze.

Cooling system filling

22 Before attempting to fill the cooling system, make sure that all hoses and clips are in good condition, and that the clips are tight. If removed, refit the expansion tank.
23 Fill the expansion tank until the level reaches the MAX mark, then refit the expansion tank cap.
24 Slowly fill the system through the radiator filler cap until the coolant level reaches the base of the radiator filler neck **(see illustration).** Wait a few minutes for the level in the radiator to stabilise, then **loosely** refit the radiator cap. The cap is fitted loosely at

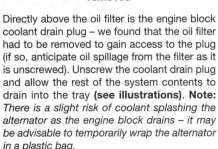

this stage to prevent a build-up of pressure in the system, and to allow the release of any trapped air.

25 Start the engine and let it run at idle until the engine reaches normal operating temperature, as indicated by the temperature gauge, or by the radiator cooling fan cutting in and out at least twice. Also check for hot air output from the heater – if this is not evident, an airlock may be the cause (often, an airlock like this will clear after a short drive).

26 Switch off the engine, then check the level in the radiator and expansion tank, and top-up if necessary.

27 Refit the radiator cap tightly, then run the engine again briefly, and check for leaks.

28 Switch off the engine, and allow it to cool for at least an hour or, preferably, leave overnight.

29 With the engine completely cold, check and top-up the coolant level in the radiator and expansion tank as necessary.

Airlocks

30 If, after draining and refilling the system, symptoms of overheating are found which did not occur previously, then the fault is almost certainly due to trapped air at some point in the system, causing an airlock and restricting the flow of coolant; usually, the air is trapped because the system was refilled too quickly.

31 If an airlock is suspected, first try gently squeezing all visible coolant hoses. A coolant hose which is full of air feels quite different to one full of coolant, when squeezed. After refilling the system, most airlocks will clear once the system has cooled, and been topped-up.

32 While the engine is running at operating temperature, switch on the heater and heater fan, and check for heat output. Provided there is sufficient coolant in the system, any lack of heat output could be due to an airlock in the system.

33 Airlocks can have more serious effects than simply reducing heater output – a severe airlock could reduce coolant flow around the engine. Check that the radiator top hose is hot when the engine is at operating temperature – a top hose which stays cold could be the result of an airlock (or a non-opening thermostat).

34 If the problem persists, stop the engine and allow it to cool down **completely** before unscrewing the radiator and expansion tank caps or loosening the hose clips and squeezing the hoses to bleed out the trapped air. In the worst case, the system will have to be at least partially drained (this time, the

25.24 Fill the radiator to the base of the filler neck

coolant can be saved for re-use) and flushed to clear the problem.

Radiator cap check

35 Clean the radiator cap, and inspect the seal inside the cap for damage or deterioration. If there is any sign of damage or deterioration to the seal, fit a new pressure cap. If the cap is old, it is worth considering fitting a new one for peace of mind – they are not expensive. If the pressure cap fails, excess pressure will be allowed into the system, which may result in the failure of hoses, the radiator, or the heater matrix.

Notes

Chapter 2 Part A:
Engine in-car repair procedures

Contents

Degrees of difficulty

Easy, suitable for novice with little experience	Fairly easy, suitable for beginner with some experience	Fairly difficult, suitable for competent DIY mechanic	Difficult, suitable for experienced DIY mechanic	Very difficult, suitable for expert DIY or professional

Specifications

General

Engine type	Four-cylinder, in-line, single overhead cam (SOHC)
Designation	i-DSI (intelligent Dual Sequential Ignition)
Engine code:	
1.2 litre engine	L12A
1.4 litre engine	L13A
Capacity:	
1.2 litre engine	1246 cc
1.4 litre engine	1339 cc
Bore	73.0 mm
Stroke:	
1.2 litre engine	74.4 mm
1.4 litre engine	80.0 mm
Compression ratio	10.8 : 1
Firing order	1-3-4-2 (No 1 cylinder at timing chain end)
Direction of crankshaft rotation	Clockwise (seen from right-hand side of car)

Compression pressures

Minimum	142 psi
Maximum difference between cylinders	28 psi

Valves

Valve clearances (engine cold):	
Inlet	0.15 to 0.19 mm (0.006 to 0.007 in)
Exhaust	0.26 to 0.30 mm (0.010 to 0.012 in)
Valve stem diameter	5.42 to 5.49 mm
Valve stem-to-guide clearance:	
Inlet	0.020 to 0.050 mm
Exhaust	0.050 to 0.080 mm
Valve spring free length:	
Inlet	50.52 mm
Exhaust	57.37 mm

Cylinder head

Maximum permissible gasket surface distortion	0.08 mm
Cylinder head height	119.9 to 120.1 mm
Resurface limit	0.2 mm

Camshaft

Running clearance	0.045 to 0.084 mm, 0.1 mm max
Endfloat	0.05 to 0.25 mm, 0.5 mm max

Cylinder block

Gasket face distortion	0.10 mm max
Cylinder bore diameter.	73.00 to 73.02 mm, 73.07 mm max
Cylinder bore taper.	0.05 mm max
Cylinder reboring limit	0.25 mm

Pistons and piston rings

Piston diameter	72.97 to 72.99 mm
Piston ring end gap – installed:	
Top compression ring.	0.15 to 0.30 mm, 0.60 mm max
Second compression ring.	0.35 to 0.50 mm, 0.65 mm max
Oil control ring	0.20 to 0.70 mm, 0.80 mm max
Piston ring-to-groove clearance:	
Top compression ring.	0.065 mm to 0.090 mm, 0.15 mm max
Second compression ring.	0.030 mm to 0.055 mm, 0.13 mm max

Gudgeon pin

Diameter.	17.997 to 18.000 mm
Pin-to-piston clearance	0.010 to 0.017 mm

Crankshaft and bearings

Main bearings.	5
Main bearing journal diameter	49.976 to 50.000 mm
Big-end bearing journal diameter.	39.976 to 40.000 mm
Crankshaft endfloat	0.10 to 0.35 mm, 0.45 mm max
Runout	0.04 mm max

Connecting rods

Big-end bore diameter.	43.0 mm
Small-end bore diameter	17.964 to 17.977 mm
Running clearance	0.020 to 0.036 mm
Endfloat	0.15 to 0.30 mm

Lubrication

Oil pressure relief valve operating range (min. values).	10 psi @ idle, 50 psi @ 3000 rpm
Oil pump clearances:	
Inner rotor to outer rotor.	0.02 to 0.14 mm, 0.20 mm max
Housing to outer rotor	0.10 to 0.18 mm, 0.20 mm max
Housing to rotor endfloat	0.02 to 0.07 mm, 0.15 mm max

Torque wrench settings

	Nm	lbf ft
Air cleaner mounting bracket bolts	24	18
Air conditioning compressor mounting bolts	22	16
Auxiliary drivebelt idler pulley bolt	24	18
Big-end bearing cap bolts*:		
Stage 1	10	7
Stage 2	Angle-tighten through a further 90°	
Camshaft position (TDC) sensor mounting bolt.	12	9
Camshaft sprocket bolt	56	41
Camshaft thrust cover bolts.	10	7
Crankshaft pulley bolt:		
Stage 1 (new bolt or new crankshaft ONLY).	177	131
Stage 2 (new bolt or new crankshaft ONLY).	Loosen fully	
Stage 3 (all).	54	40
Stage 4 (all).	Angle-tighten through a further 90°	
Cylinder head bolts:		
Stage 1	29	21
Stage 2	Angle-tighten through a further 130°	
Cylinder head cover bolts	12	9

Torque wrench settings (continued)

	Nm	lbf ft
Driveplate mounting bolts	74	55
Driveplate-to-flywheel bolts	12	9
Engine mountings:		
Front mounting:		
Bracket-to-transmission bolts	44	32
Bracket-to-body bolts	39	29
Through-bolt nut	59	44
Left-hand mounting**:		
Mounting bracket nuts/bolt	49	36
Through-bolt	44	32
Rear mounting:		
Subframe and rear bracket bolts	44	32
Through-bolt	59	44
Right-hand mounting:		
Adjustment nut	74	55
Mounting-to-wing bolts	49	36
Mounting bracket nuts	39	29
Flywheel mounting bolts	118	87
Main bearing bridge bolts*:		
Stage 1	25	18
Stage 2	Angle-tighten through a further 40°	
Oil pressure switch	18	13
Oil pump mounting bolts	10	7
Oil pump pick-up/strainer nuts/bolt	10	7
Oil pump pressure relief valve bolt	39	29
Rocker shaft mounting bolts	29	21
Sump drain plug	39	29
Sump mounting bolts:		
Front bolt, transmission end	24	18
Transmission-to-sump bolts	64	47
All other bolts	12	9
Timing chain cover bolts:		
6 mm bolts	12	9
8 mm bolts	31	23
Timing chain front guide bolts	12	9
Timing chain tensioner arm lower pivot bolt	22	16
Timing chain tensioner bolts	12	9
Transmission-to-engine bolts	64	47
Water pump pulley bolts	14	10

* Use new bolts
** Left and right are as seen from the driver's seat

1 General information

How to use this Chapter

This Part of Chapter 2 is devoted to in-car repair procedures. All procedures concerning engine removal and refitting, and engine block/cylinder head overhaul, can be found in Chapter 2B.

Refer to *Vehicle identification numbers* in the Reference Section at the end of this manual for details of engine code locations.

Most of the operations included in this Chapter are based on the assumption that the engine is still installed in the car. Therefore, if this information is being used during a complete engine overhaul, with the engine already removed, many of the steps included here will not apply.

Engine description

The engine is a single overhead cam, water-cooled, four cylinder in-line design, designated i-DSI by Honda (intelligent Dual Sequential Ignition). An all-new design, the 'dual sequential ignition' tag refers to the fact that this engine, unusually, has two spark plugs per cylinder – this, and the two valve-per-cylinder design, helps to boost low-speed torque, as well as cleaning-up the exhaust emissions. The more compact engine dimensions allowed by a single overhead camshaft design are also clearly important in a space-efficient package like the Jazz. The engine is mounted transversely at the front of the car together with the transmission to form a combined power unit.

The crankshaft is supported in five shell-type main bearings, combined into a one-piece bearing cap bridge. The connecting rod big-end bearings are also split shell-type, and the small ends are attached to the pistons by interference-fit gudgeon pins. Each piston is fitted with two compression rings and one oil control ring.

Drive for the overhead camshaft is provided by a spring-tensioned timing chain. The eight valves are operated by a rocker shaft assembly, with screw-and-locknut adjustment on the rocker arms for the valve clearances; the valves are each closed by a single valve spring, and operate in guides integral in the aluminium alloy cylinder head.

The oil pump is mounted externally on the crankcase, and is driven directly by the 'nose' of the crankshaft.

Operations with engine in car

The following work can be carried out with the engine in the car:

a) Rocker shaft and camshaft – removal, inspection and refitting.
b) Cylinder head – removal and refitting.
c) Crankshaft oil seals – renewal.
d) Timing chain, sprockets and tensioner – removal, inspection and refitting.
e) Oil pump – removal and refitting.
f) Sump – removal and refitting.
g) Connecting rods and pistons – removal and refitting*.
h) Flywheel/driveplate – removal, inspection and refitting.
i) Engine/transmission mountings – inspection and renewal.

* Although the operation marked with an asterisk can be carried out with the engine in the car after removal of the sump, it is better for the engine to be removed in the interests of cleanliness and improved access. For this reason, the procedure is described in Part B of this Chapter.

2 Compression test – description and interpretation

1 When engine performance is down, or if misfiring occurs which cannot be attributed to the ignition or fuel systems, a compression test can provide diagnostic clues as to the engine's condition. If the test is performed regularly, it can give warning of trouble before any other symptoms become apparent.

2 The engine must be fully warmed-up to operating temperature, the oil level must be correct and the battery must be fully-charged. The help of an assistant will also be required.

3 To completely disable the ignition system for the test, remove fuses 2 and 24 from the interior fusebox. Remove the front row of spark plugs (four out of eight), referring to Chapter 1 if necessary.

4 The fuel pump must also be disabled, by removing the fuel pump relay from the interior fusebox (this is relay A at the right-hand end of the row above the fuses). Alternatively, remove the fuel pump fuse (No 11) – although this fuse is shared with the airbag system, and removing it may cause an airbag fault. **Note:** *Removing the fuel pump relay and the ignition coil fuses may cause a temporary fault code to be stored in the ECM, so the engine management warning light may be lit on completion. After a number of successful starts, the codes should clear themselves – if not, refer to Chapter 4A, Section 10.*

5 Fit a compression tester to one of the No 1 cylinder spark plug holes – the type of tester which screws into the spark plug thread is preferable.

6 Arrange for an assistant to hold the accelerator pedal fully depressed to the floor, while at the same time cranking the engine over for several seconds on the starter motor.

Observe the compression gauge reading. The compression will build-up fairly quickly in a healthy engine. Low compression on the first stroke, followed by gradually-increasing pressure on successive strokes, indicates worn piston rings. A low compression on the first stroke which does not rise on successive strokes, indicates leaking valves or a blown head gasket (a cracked cylinder head could also be the cause). Deposits on the underside of the valve heads can also cause low compression. Record the highest gauge reading obtained, then repeat the procedure for the remaining cylinders.

7 Due to the variety of testers available, and the fluctuation in starter motor speed when cranking the engine, different readings are often obtained when carrying out the compression test. For this reason, the specified compression pressure figures may have to be treated as a guide. However, the most important factor is that the compression pressures are uniform in all cylinders, and that is what this test is mainly concerned with. Repeat the test if any suspect readings are produced to confirm your findings.

8 Add some engine oil (about three squirts from a plunger type oil can) to each cylinder through the spark plug holes, and then repeat the test.

9 If the compression increases after the oil is added, the piston rings are probably worn. If the compression does not increase significantly, the leakage is occurring at the valves or the head gasket. Leakage past the valves may be caused by burned valve seats and/or faces, or warped, cracked or bent valves.

10 If two adjacent cylinders have equally low compressions, it is most likely that the head gasket has blown between them. The appearance of coolant in the combustion chambers or on the engine oil dipstick would verify this condition.

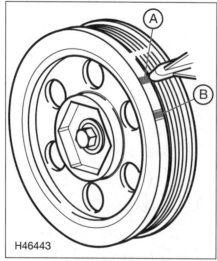

3.3 Crankshaft pulley's white TDC mark (A) and red ignition timing mark (B)

11 If one cylinder is about 20 percent lower than the other, and the engine has a slightly rough idle, a worn lobe on the camshaft could be the cause.

12 On completion of the checks, refit the spark plugs and ignition coils. Refit the fuel pump relay and the ignition coil fuses to the fusebox.

3 Top Dead Centre (TDC) for No 1 piston – locating

1 Top dead centre (TDC) is the highest point of the cylinder that each piston reaches as the crankshaft turns. Each piston reaches its TDC position at the end of its compression stroke, and then again at the end of its exhaust stroke. For the purpose of engine timing, TDC at the end of the compression stroke for No 1 piston is used. No 1 cylinder is at the crankshaft pulley/timing chain end of the engine (nearest the driver's-side inner wing). Proceed as follows.

2 Ensure that the ignition is switched off. Turning the engine will be easier if the front-row spark plugs are removed as described in Chapter 1, but this is not essential.

3 Turn the engine over by hand (using a 19 mm socket or spanner on the crankshaft pulley bolt) until the TDC notch in the crankshaft pulley (which may be painted white) is aligned with the pointer above the pulley. Note that the crankshaft pulley will also have an ignition timing mark before top dead centre (BTDC), which may be painted red – as the pulley is turned clockwise, the TDC notch will be the second of the two marks to come into alignment **(see illustration)**.

4 In this position, No 1 and No 4 pistons will be at TDC, but one will be on the compression stroke, and the other on exhaust. Without removing the cylinder head cover as described in Section 4, the only way to check this is as follows. Remove one of the spark plugs from No 1 cylinder as described in Chapter 1, then turn the engine back from TDC by approximately 90°. Have an assistant cover the open spark plug hole with their hand, then turn the engine forwards to TDC – as this is done, it should be possible to feel compressed air coming from the open plug hole. If not, turn the engine round a full turn until the TDC mark is again aligned, and repeat the check.

5 Further confirmation of TDC on No1 cylinder can only be achieved by removing the cylinder head cover as described in Section 4 – as this involves removing the inlet manifold, the importance of this will depend on what other work is being carried out. With the cylinder head cover removed, check that the UP marking on the camshaft sprocket is visible, and the two horizontal marks are aligned with the cylinder head top surface **(see illustration)**.

6 Once No 1 cylinder has been positioned at

3.5 Camshaft sprocket UP marking and horizontal lines at TDC

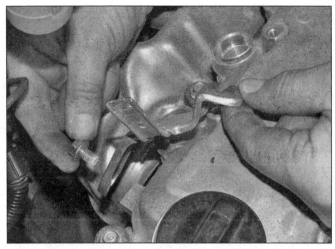

4.3 Unbolt the wiring harness support bracket from the back of the cover

TDC on the compression stroke, TDC for any of the other cylinders can then be located by rotating the crankshaft clockwise (in its normal direction of rotation), 180° at a time, and following the firing order (see *Specifications*).

7 Where removed, refit the spark plug(s) and cylinder head cover, referring to Chapter 1 and Section 4 as necessary.

4 Cylinder head cover – removal and refitting

Removal

1 Remove the inlet manifold as described in Chapter 4A.

2 Remove all eight ignition coils, as described in Chapter 5B.

3 Remove the bolt securing the wiring harness bracket behind the oil filler cap, and take off the bracket, noting which way round it fits **(see illustration)**.

4 Disconnect the wiring plug from the EGR valve at the front corner of the cylinder head cover – this improves access to the cover bolt at the front corner **(see illustration)**.

5 If not already done, pull off the breather hose at the transmission end of the cylinder head cover.

6 Remove the eight bolts securing the cylinder head cover, then lift it off the top of the engine **(see illustration)**. Recover the rubber gasket – this may be re-used if it is in good condition.

Refitting

7 Thoroughly clean the cylinder head cover, and the mating surface of the cylinder head. Besides removing any oil, in particular, clean off any sealant at the cylinder head-to-timing chain cover joint.

8 Check the condition of the old gasket. Providing it's not crushed, perished or distorted, it can be refitted into the cover groove **(see illustration)**. Similarly, check the

condition of the cover bolt washers, and fit new ones if necessary.

9 Apply two 3.0 mm blobs of RTV sealant (Honda Liquid Gasket 1216E, part number 08C70-K0334M, or equivalent) to the joint between the cylinder head and the timing chain cover **(see illustration)**. Once the sealant has been applied, the cover should be fitted within 5 minutes.

10 Refit the cylinder head cover, making sure the gasket stays in place. Once the cover is down, slide it back-and-forth very slightly, to ensure that the gasket is properly seated.

11 Fit the cover bolts and washers. Working from the centre bolts outwards, tighten them in stages, in a diagonal sequence, to the specified torque.

12 Further refitting is a reversal of removal, noting the following points:

a) *Refit the ignition coils as described in Chapter 5B.*

b) *Refit the inlet manifold as described in Chapter 4A.*

c) *Wait at least 30 minutes before starting the engine, to give the sealant time to cure.*

4.4 Disconnect the EGR valve wiring plug to access the front corner bolt

4.6 Removing the cylinder head cover

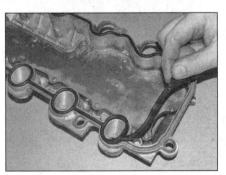

4.8 Fit the cover gasket into its groove

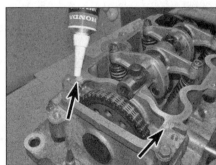

4.9 Apply sealant to the cylinder head/ timing cover joint

5.3 Unbolt and remove the drivebelt idler pulley (air conditioning models only)

5.4 Take off the water pump pulley

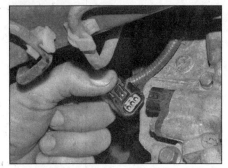

5.9 Disconnect the crankshaft position sensor wiring plug

5.12 Unbolt the air conditioning refrigerant pipe bracket above the mounting

5 Timing chain and related components – removal, inspection and refitting

Removal

Timing chain

1 Loosen (but do not yet remove) the three water pump pulley bolts – this is more easily done before the auxiliary drivebelt is removed.

2 Remove the auxiliary drivebelt as described in Chapter 1. In addition, unbolt and remove the alternator adjuster bolt bracket from the engine, and ensure that the alternator lower mounting bolt is loose enough that the alternator can pivot forwards, clear of the timing chain cover.

3 On models with air conditioning, unbolt and remove the drivebelt idler pulley, noting carefully the fitted sequence of washers and spacers (see illustration).

4 Remove the three water pump pulley bolts, and take off the pulley (see illustration).

5 Remove the cylinder head cover as described in Section 4.

6 Set the engine to TDC on No 1 cylinder, as described in Section 3. As the cylinder head cover has been removed, check that the camshaft sprocket UP mark and horizontal lines are correctly aligned.

7 Remove the crankshaft pulley as described in Section 6.

8 Remove the sump as described in Section 10.

9 At the back of the timing chain cover, disconnect the wiring plug from the crankshaft position sensor (see illustration). Trace the wiring up the back of the timing chain cover, release the two harness clips and move the wiring clear.

10 The weight of the engine must now be supported, as the right-hand mounting must be removed. As the sump has been removed, supporting from below is made more difficult – take care not to involve the crankshaft, nor to damage the oil pump pick-up. Use a jack, with a block of wood on the edge of the block, and just take the weight of the engine.

11 Where applicable, unbolt the earth strap in front of the right-hand mounting, and move it clear.

12 On models with air conditioning, one of the refrigerant hoses passes close to the right-hand mounting, and is secured to the inner wing by a support bracket. It may be useful to remove the hose support bracket bolt, to give some movement in the hose (see illustration).

13 With the engine supported from below, loosen the bolts securing the right-hand mounting to the inner wing. The mounting upper bracket is secured to the engine by two nuts – one on top, and the other removed from below. Remove the two nuts, then unscrew the mounting-to-wing bolts, and lift out the mounting assembly, manoeuvring it past the refrigerant hose where applicable (see illustrations).

14 The timing chain cover is secured by a total of twelve bolts, of 6 mm and 8 mm diameter. Remove the bolts, and store them carefully – we pushed the bolts through a piece of card, in their fitted pattern (see

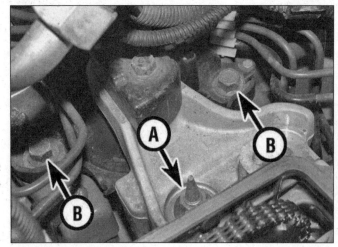

5.13a Engine right-hand mounting upper nut (A) and two of the wing bolts (B)

5.13b Removing the engine right-hand mounting

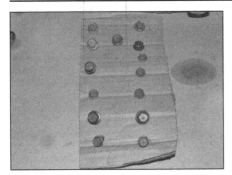

5.14 Store the timing cover bolts in a piece of card

5.15 Removing the timing chain cover

5.16 Removing the crankshaft position sensor pulse generator plate

illustration). If not already done, pivot the alternator forwards, clear of the cover (or, if preferred, remove it completely, referring to Chapter 5A).

15 The cover is fitted using a bead of sealant, so will probably be stuck. Start by pulling it at the top, and work downwards until it is free, and can be removed – prising between the joint faces may cause damage and an oil leak on reassembly. Slide the cover off the nose of the crankshaft, and remove it (see illustration). **Note:** *While the timing chain cover is removed, consider fitting a new crankshaft oil seal which is fitted to it – this job is far easier to do with the cover off. Refer to Section 14.*

16 Slide off the crankshaft position sensor's pulse generator plate (this looks like a slim sprocket), noting how it is fitted (see illustration).

17 Apply a little oil as necessary to the timing chain tensioner's slider. Use a screwdriver in the hole provided at the back of the tensioner to release the chain tension. As this is done, loosen the tensioner's lower bolt, and remove the upper bolt (see illustrations).

18 Withdraw the screwdriver, then take out the lower bolt and remove the tensioner from the engine (see illustration).

19 Remove the lower pivot bolt, and take off the curved tensioner arm from the back of the chain (see illustration).

20 Remove the two bolts securing the guide in front of the chain, and take off the guide (see illustration).

21 Before removing the chain, note the fitted positions of the blue-steel links – there should be one at the base of the crankshaft sprocket, and two more at the top of the camshaft sprocket. If the chain is to be re-used, if necessary, clean the marked links and apply fresh paint.

22 With all tension removed from the chain, it can be checked for wear (the chain should be renewed as a matter of course if the engine is being overhauled). Try to lift the chain upwards off the camshaft sprocket, at the top. If the chain is worn, it may be possible to lift it clear so that the sprocket teeth are visible – a chain this worn should always be renewed.

23 Using an open-ended spanner (the

5.17a The chain tensioner has two bolts, and a slot behind for a screwdriver

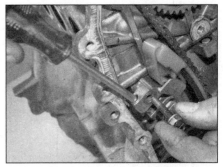

5.17b Hold the tensioner with a screwdriver, and remove the upper bolt

correct size appears to be 29 mm, but we found that a 30 mm spanner would do) on the camshaft flats provided, hold the camshaft while the sprocket bolt is loosened. Unscrew the sprocket bolt, then slide the sprocket and

chain from the camshaft (note the position of the locating keyway – at the top), and withdraw it (see illustration). Remove camshaft sprocket from the chain.

24 Slide the crankshaft sprocket and the

5.18a Take out the lower bolt . . .

5.18b . . . and remove the timing chain tensioner

5.19 Remove the lower bolt, and take off the curved rear arm

5.20 Unbolt and remove the chain front guide

5.23 Remove the camshaft sprocket bolt, and slide off the sprocket with the chain

5.24 Slide off the crankshaft sprocket and chain

5.38 The chain's two blue-steel links sit either side of a vertical mark near the UP

chain off the nose of the crankshaft (see illustration). Remove the sprocket from the chain. Note that the sprocket's Woodruff key (which is fitted with its curved surfaces pointing downwards) will be loose – remove it for safekeeping.

25 Note that, while it is removed, Honda advise keeping the chain away from magnetic fields (presumably, this also applies to a new chain).

Camshaft sprocket

26 In theory, the camshaft sprocket can be removed without removing the chain completely – this would also save removing the timing chain cover. For details, refer to the camshaft removal procedure in Section 8.

27 In practice, removing the camshaft sprocket from the chain, and then refitting it, is nearly impossible while the timing cover is still in place – there is just too little working room. If the sprocket must be removed, refer to the timing chain removal procedure described previously in this Section.

Crankshaft sprocket

28 The crankshaft sprocket can only be removed or refitted with the timing chain, as described previously in this Section.

Timing chain tensioner

29 The chain tensioner can be removed as described previously in this Section (paragraphs 1 to 18). If the tensioner is being renewed, attention should also be paid to the tensioner arm (paragraph 19) and the chain front guide (paragraph 20).

Inspection

30 Check the chain for wear, which will be evident in the form of excess play between the links. If the chain can be lifted at either 'end' of its run so that the sprocket teeth are visible, it has stretched excessively. If there is any doubt as to the chain's condition, a new one should be fitted – timing chain failure is a lot rarer than timing belt failure, but would still be catastrophic to the engine.

31 If the chain is worn, examine the sprocket teeth closely – if their teeth have taken on a 'hooked' appearance, new ones should be fitted. It is generally considered a false economy to fit a new timing chain on worn sprockets.

32 Assessing wear in the chain tensioner is not easy. Particularly if the tensioner is known to have covered a very high mileage, and/or if a new chain is being fitted, it is recommended that an old tensioner is not re-used.

33 Examine the tensioner arm and front guide for scoring or wear ridges, and renew if necessary. If a new timing chain is being fitted, it would make sense to renew the arm and guide also.

Refitting

34 Check that the crankshaft is set to TDC – in this position, a punched mark on one of the crankshaft sprocket teeth will be aligned with an arrowhead marking on the oil pump. Temporarily refit the crankshaft sprocket (the right way round) to check.

35 The camshaft should also be set to TDC – in this position, the word UP should

be uppermost, and the two horizontal lines should align with the top of the cylinder head. Temporarily refit the camshaft sprocket to check. If the marks are not aligned, turn the camshaft sprocket only very slightly, as turning it by more than a few degrees could bend the valves. If the camshaft must be turned significantly, turn the crankshaft approximately 90° first, so the pistons are down the bores – reset the camshaft, then bring the crankshaft back to TDC.

36 Remove the camshaft and crankshaft sprockets, if they were temporarily refitted.

37 Find a clean working area, to lay out the timing chain and the two sprockets.

38 Fit the chain around the camshaft sprocket. The two blue-steel links should sit either side of a near-vertical line, just to the right of the word UP on the sprocket (see illustration).

39 Now fit the timing chain around the crankshaft sprocket, so that the single blue-steel link sits exactly over the sprocket tooth with the punched mark on it (see illustration).

40 If removed, refit the crankshaft's Woodruff key, with its curved surface pointing downwards (see illustrations).

41 Offer in the chain and two sprockets as an assembly (see illustration). Slide the crankshaft sprocket onto the crankshaft, and over the Woodruff key, then fit the camshaft sprocket onto the camshaft's locating keyway. Refit the camshaft sprocket bolt.

42 With the chain in place, again check that the two sprockets are correctly aligned.

5.39 The single blue-steel link sits over the crankshaft sprocket's punch mark

5.40a Refit the Woodruff key, curved face downwards . . .

5.40b . . . so that it sits in the groove as shown

5.41 Fit the chain and sprockets as an assembly

5.42 The crankshaft sprocket's single link aligns with the oil pump arrowhead mark

Note that the single blue-steel link around the crankshaft sprocket should align with the arrowhead on the oil pump (see illustration).

43 Fit the chain front guide, and tighten the two bolts to the specified torque (see illustration).

44 Fit the curved tensioner arm in position on the rear run of the chain, then oil the pivot bolt, and tighten it to the specified torque (see illustration).

45 Offer up the chain tensioner, and fit the lower bolt, hand-tight only at this stage (see illustration).

46 Apply a little engine oil to the tensioner's sliding surface (where it contacts the curved tensioner arm). Using a screwdriver in the hole provided, turn the tensioner clockwise (towards the chain), and refit the upper bolt (see illustrations). Tighten the upper and lower bolts to the specified torque.

47 Using an open-ended spanner (the correct size appears to be 29 mm, but we found that a 30 mm spanner would do) on the camshaft flats provided, hold the camshaft. Tighten the camshaft sprocket bolt to the specified torque (see illustration).

48 Slide on the crankshaft position sensor's pulse generator plate ('sprocket'), as noted on removal. Note that this plate has an arrowhead marking, which, at TDC, should align with the identical marking on the oil pump (see illustrations).

49 Temporarily refit the crankshaft pulley bolt, and use a spanner or socket to slowly turn the engine through two complete revolutions. Check that the TDC marks described in paragraphs 34 and 35 come back into alignment. If the crankshaft binds or seems to hit something, do not force it, as the valves

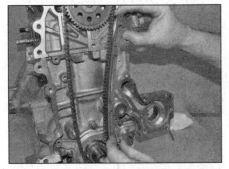

5.43 Fit the chain front guide, and secure with the two bolts

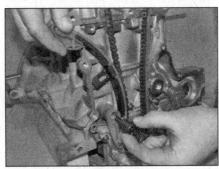

5.44 Fit the curved rear arm and the lower pivot bolt

5.45 Fit the chain tensioner with the lower bolt hand-tight

5.46a Apply a little engine oil to the tensioner's curved surface . . .

5.46b . . . then use a screwdriver to turn the tensioner, and fit the upper bolt

5.47 Use a spanner to hold the camshaft, and tighten the sprocket bolt

5.48a Slide on the crankshaft position sensor pulse plate . . .

5.48b . . . noting that, at TDC, its arrowhead mark aligns with that on the oil pump

54 Offer the cover over the end of the crankshaft, taking care not to damage the oil seal in the cover. Seat the cover onto the engine, and guide it into place by fitting two or more of the bolts (the bolts are two different sizes, and should be fitted to their original locations) **(see illustrations)**.

55 The cover will 'float' on the sealant, even with all the bolts in place (there are no locating dowels). Although the cover alignment doesn't appear to be critical, use a straight-edge across the top surfaces of the cover and cylinder head, to ensure they are level.

56 Fit all the remaining cover bolts. Starting in the middle of the cover, tighten the bolts evenly, and finally to their respective torques.

57 Clip the crankshaft position sensor wiring harness to the rear of the timing cover, and reconnect the wiring plug.

58 Refit the engine right-hand mounting with reference to Section 17. Also refit the earth strap in front of the mounting, and (where removed) the refrigerant hose mounting bracket bolt.

59 The remainder of refitting is a reversal of removal, noting the following points:

a) *Refit the sump as described in Section 10.*

b) *Refit the crankshaft pulley as described in Section 6.*

c) *Refit the cylinder head cover as described in Section 4.*

d) *If the alternator was removed, refit it as described in Chapter 5A.*

e) *Refit the water pump pulley, with the bolts hand-tight to begin with (it will be easier to tighten them to the specified torque once the auxiliary drivebelt has been refitted and tensioned, as described in Chapter 1).*

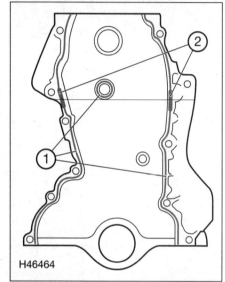

H46464

5.53a Sealant application details (to head and block) when refitting timing chain cover

1 *Bead of sealant, 1.5 mm diameter*
2 *Bead of sealant, 3.0 mm diameter*

may be hitting the pistons. If this happens, the chain is incorrectly fitted. If necessary, reset the engine to TDC, then remove the chain and repeat the refitting procedure.

50 Remove the crankshaft pulley bolt.

51 Before refitting the timing cover, check the condition of the crankshaft oil seal which is fitted to it. This seal is much easier to renew

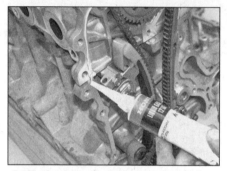

5.53b Applying the sealant to the engine, prior to fitting the timing cover

when the cover is removed – see Section 14 for details.

52 Clean off all traces of old sealant from the cover, engine faces, cover bolts and bolt holes. Take care not to mark the mating faces. Wash the cover and engine mating faces with suitable solvent, and dry them before continuing.

53 Apply a bead of RTV sealant (Honda Liquid Gasket 1216E, part number 08C70-K0334M, or equivalent) to the timing cover mating faces on the engine block and cylinder head, as shown. The bead should be 1.5 mm diameter all round, except in the area where the block and head join – here the bead should be doubled up to 3.0 mm **(see illustration)**. Run the sealant inside the bolt holes – try not to get any down the holes themselves, as this may affect the bolt tightening. Once the sealant has been applied, the cover should be fitted within 5 minutes.

6 Crankshaft pulley – removal and refitting

1 Remove the auxiliary drivebelt as described in Chapter 1.

2 The crankshaft pulley has a white TDC marking on its outer rim (there is also a red mark, indicating the BTDC ignition timing point). The engine does not have to be set to TDC if just the pulley is being removed, but if other work is to be carried out requiring the engine to be at TDC, the engine should be set in this position as described in Section 3 before the pulley is removed.

3 The crankshaft pulley must now be held stationary while the bolt is loosened. Since the bolt is extremely tight, the method (for manual transmission models only) of having an assistant engage a gear and apply the footbrake, is unlikely to work.

4 Jack up the front of the car, and support it on axle stands (see *Jacking and vehicle support*). Remove the metal cover plate on the base of the transmission bellhousing, which is secured by three bolts – this gives access to the flywheel ring gear **(see illustrations)**. By jamming a suitable tool into the ring gear, the

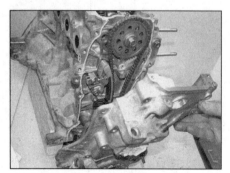

5.54a Offer up the timing cover . . .

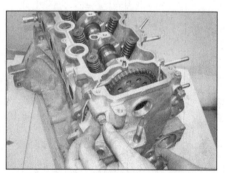

5.54b . . . and use the bolts to guide it into position

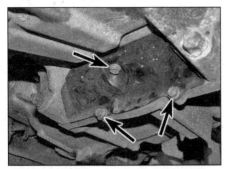

6.4a At the base of the transmission bellhousing, undo the three bolts . . .

if something slips, it may result in injury. For extra leverage, use a long-handled breaker (or 'cracker') bar, or slip a piece of substantial tubing over the socket handle, to make it longer. Don't use a ratchet handle if possible – the ratchet may fail under load. If an extension bar is used on the socket, rest the outer end of the extension bar (the end nearest the handle) on another axle stand, to keep it horizontal – this improves leverage, and reduces the chance of the socket slipping off under load.

6.4b . . . and take off the metal cover plate

engine will be locked, and the pulley bolt can be loosened.

5 Because the pulley bolt is so tight, we felt that jamming a screwdriver blade in the ring gear would not be sufficient (or safe). We made our own angled tool from some thick steel strip – this could have been bent over at the end, but we welded on a piece of angled steel bar instead. This tool slots into the base of the bellhousing, and into the ring gear (see illustrations). It worked very well, and can also be turned around to hold the flywheel for tightening the pulley bolt.

6 Before loosening the pulley bolt, ensure that the car is securely supported. Only use good-quality, close-fitting tools for this job –

 If the bolt proves difficult to undo, use plenty of penetrating spray, and let it soak in. Also, give the bolt a few sharp taps with a hammer, taking care not to burr the bolt head in the process.

7 Unscrew and remove the bolt (which has an integral washer), and slip off the pulley (see illustration). Note which way up the pulley fits – it engages on a keyway. Where applicable, the Woodruff key which sits in the crankshaft may be loose – it's best to recover it, and store it with the pulley.

8 If the engine had to be set to TDC before the pulley was removed (see paragraph 2), loosely refit the pulley and bolt, and reset the engine to TDC, as it is likely that the pulley may have

turned during removal. Once the setting is conformed, remove the bolt and pulley again.

Refitting

9 Wipe clean the pulley and the mating surfaces of the crankshaft and its sprocket. Also clean the pulley bolt and washer. Though not specifically required by Honda, consider using a new bolt when refitting – this should be done in any case if the bolt appears damaged.

10 Offer in the pulley, the same way up as was noted on removal, and fit it over the crankshaft key. Lightly oil the bolt threads and the underside of the bolt head, then tighten the bolt by hand, and check that the pulley is properly seated (see illustrations).

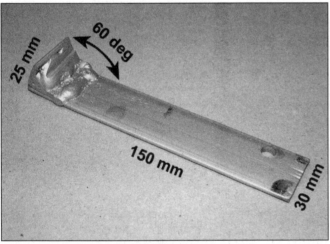

6.5a The angled flywheel locking tool . . .

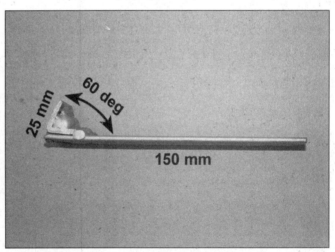

6.5b . . . which we made from thick steel strip . . .

6.5c . . . sits in the base of the bellhousing, and engages the ring gear

6.7 Removing the crankshaft pulley

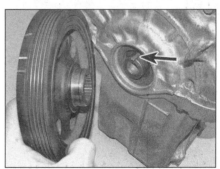

6.10a Fit the pulley over the crankshaft key

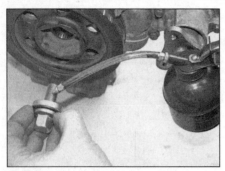

6.10b Lightly oil the bolt threads and head . . .

6.10c . . . then fit the bolt and tighten it by hand

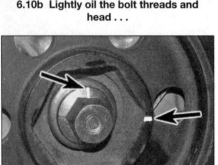

6.12a Before the final tightening, paint a mark on the bolt and pulley . . .

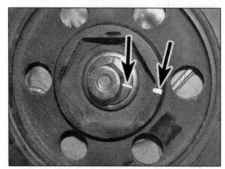

6.12b . . . the marks will align after a quarter-turn

11 Using the same method as for removal, prevent the crankshaft pulley from turning as the bolt is tightened.
12 If a new bolt is being used (or if a new crankshaft has been fitted), there are two initial stages to tightening to be observed first. Otherwise, just tighten the bolt to the specified

Stage 3 torque, then through the Stage 4 angle (which is equivalent to a quarter-turn). A quarter-turn can be made easier to judge by painting a mark on the bolt and the pulley, as we did (see illustrations).
13 Refit and tension the auxiliary drivebelt as described in Chapter 1.

7.5 Removing the rocker shaft assembly

7.9 Refit the shaft locating dowel

7.10 Apply clean engine oil to the cam lobes and valve tops

7.11 Tie the rockers together in pairs, to make fitting easier

7 Rocker shaft assembly – removal, inspection and refitting

Removal

1 Remove the cylinder head cover (see Section 4).
2 Completely loosen (but do not remove) all the valve adjuster screws, to remove all valve spring pressure from the rocker shaft components.
3 Set the engine to No 1 on TDC as described in Section 3.
4 Loosen the five rocker shaft mounting bolts a half-turn at a time, working in the **reverse** of the tightening sequence shown later in this Section.
5 When all the bolts are loose, remove them. Lift off the rocker shaft assembly, noting that it locates on a dowel at the timing chain end (see illustration).

Inspection

6 If you wish to dismantle and inspect the rocker arm assembly, the locating dowel at the timing chain end of the shaft should be removed first. Slip the rocker arms, washers and springs off the timing chain end of the shaft, keeping them in fitted order – they must be reassembled in the same positions they were removed from.
7 Thoroughly clean the components and inspect them for wear and damage. Check the rocker arm faces that contact the camshaft – if any wear is found, the corresponding camshaft lobes should also be checked – and the rocker arm tips. Check the surfaces of the rocker shaft that the rocker arms ride on, as well as the bearing surfaces inside the rocker arms, for scoring and excessive wear. Renew any parts that are damaged or excessively worn. Also, make sure the oil holes in the shaft are not blocked.

Refitting

8 Lubricate all components with clean engine oil, and reassemble the rocker arms, washers and springs onto the timing chain end of the shaft, in their correct fitted order.
9 Refit the shaft locating dowel to the head, at the timing chain end (see illustration).
10 Coat the camshaft lobes, valve tops, and the bolt threads and heads, with clean engine oil (see illustration).
11 Before offering the assembled shaft into place, each pair of rockers should be 'tied' together with a cable-tie, to compress the springs (see illustration). We found this was necessary, otherwise the rockers and washers catch on the camshaft bearing housings as the shaft is tightened down, which carries a risk of component damage.
12 Refit the five rocker shaft bolts. Starting with the centre bolt and working outwards, tighten the bolts half a turn at a time until they are all seated fully. Working in the same

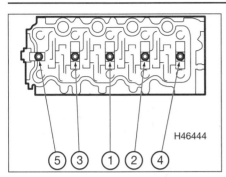

7.12a Rocker shaft bolt tightening sequence

7.12b Tighten the bolts until the shaft is seated, then to the specified torque

7.13 On completion, cut the cable-ties and remove them

sequence, tighten the bolts to the specified torque **(see illustrations)**.

13 When the shaft is fully tightened, cut the cable-ties and remove them **(see illustration)**.

14 Adjust the valve clearances as described in Chapter 1, then refit the cylinder head cover as described in Section 4.

15 Run the engine and check for oil leaks and proper operation.

8 Camshaft – removal, inspection and refitting

Removal

1 Remove the rocker shaft assembly as described in Section 7.

2 The following procedure assumes that the timing chain will not be removed completely. If the chain is to be removed, refer to Section 5.

3 There are no camshaft bearing caps to remove – therefore, the camshaft can only be withdrawn by sliding it out of the head, at the transmission end. This means that the camshaft sprocket has to be unbolted, and removed from the camshaft with the timing chain still attached.

4 Support the engine from below, as the right-hand mounting must be removed. Use a large piece of wood between the jack head and the sump, to spread the load, and just take the weight of the engine.

5 Where applicable, unbolt the earth strap in front of the right-hand mounting, and move it clear.

6 On models with air conditioning, one of the refrigerant hoses passes close to the right-hand mounting, and is secured to the inner wing by a support bracket. It may be useful to remove the hose support bracket bolt, to give some movement in the hose.

7 With the engine supported from below, loosen the bolts securing the right-hand mounting to the inner wing. The mounting upper bracket is secured to the engine by two nuts – one on top, and the other removed from below. Remove the two nuts, then unscrew the mounting-to-wing bolts, and lift out the mounting assembly, manoeuvring it past the refrigerant hose where applicable.

8 Using the spout of an oil can through the cylinder head's oil return hole behind the camshaft sprocket, lightly lubricate the sliding surfaces of the chain tensioner.

9 Unscrew and remove the access bolt and washer, located halfway down the timing cover, at the rear (the access bolt is brass-coloured, unlike the silver cover bolts) **(see illustrations)**. Have ready a 6 mm diameter bolt, approximately 60 mm in length, to insert into this hole.

10 Prise out the large plastic plug from the end of the head, which covers the camshaft sprocket bolt **(see illustration)**. Recover the plug's O-ring seal – note that a new plug and O-ring must be obtained for refitting.

11 The crankshaft must now be prevented from turning for the next step. This could be achieved by holding the pulley bolt itself (though this is the direction for unscrewing the pulley bolt, the bolt is so tight, there should be

no danger of it loosening). Alternatively, refer to Section 6 and use the ring gear locking method described.

12 With the crankshaft locked, have an assistant use a spanner on the camshaft sprocket bolt to apply firm pressure on the sprocket clockwise (the sprocket should hardly turn) – this will force the tensioner and its arm rearwards. Attached to the tensioner arm is a slotted bracket – when the arm is forced back by the chain, the slot uncovers a 6 mm threaded hole in the end of the block **(see illustration)**.

13 Holding the camshaft sprocket clockwise, insert a 6 mm bolt, at least 60 mm long, into the threaded hole, and screw it in as far as possible (the bolt will be under some strain, and screwing in by a few threads will not be enough) **(see illustration)**. Have the assistant release the sprocket. The tensioner arm is now locked in the retracted position, releasing the

8.9a The chain tensioner access bolt can be seen from below . . .

8.9b . . . and is brass-coloured – note its sealing washer

8.10 Prise out the plastic plug which covers the camshaft sprocket bolt

8.12 Turning the sprocket bolt moves the slotted bracket to reveal a hole . . .

8.13 . . . into which a locking bolt can be screwed (timing cover removed for clarity)

8.14 Tie the camshaft sprocket and chain together

8.15 Hold the camshaft with a large spanner while the sprocket bolt is loosened

We found that two short pieces of stiff wire could be passed through the sprocket's upper holes, and folded over the head and timing cover, to support the sprocket and chain. This method of support will only work if the timing cover is not being removed.

chain tension – this can be confirmed by the play that will now be present in the camshaft sprocket.

14 The chain and camshaft sprocket are removed together. Pass a cable-tie through one of the camshaft sprocket holes, and wrap it tight around the chain – this keeps the chain and sprocket together, in the correct fitted position **(see illustration)**.

15 Using an open-ended spanner (actual size 29 mm, but a 30 mm spanner will do) on the camshaft flats provided, hold the camshaft while the sprocket bolt is loosened **(see illustration)**. Only loosen the bolt by half a turn at this stage – do not remove it.

16 There is a slight risk that, if upward tension is not maintained on the chain, the chain will drop off the crankshaft sprocket, making it near-impossible to put back on without removing the sump. We found that the guide below the crankshaft sprocket

always kept the chain engaged with it, however.

17 With the timing cover still fitted, the danger is that the camshaft sprocket and chain might drop down inside the cover, and that they would be impossible to retrieve, so it is advisable to keep the chain and sprocket supported while removed. This can be done by passing some stiff wire or cable-ties through the camshaft sprocket holes **(see Haynes Hint)**.

18 With the camshaft sprocket supported, remove the bolt and release the sprocket from the keyway at the top of the camshaft, by moving it to the side. Once the sprocket is released, support the chain and sprocket before continuing.

19 Remove the battery as described in Chapter 5A.

20 Remove the lower bolt securing the wiring harness to the end of the head, and also unbolt the earth strap from the camshaft thrust cover. Release the wiring harness from the support bracket at the rear **(see illustrations)**.

21 To improve access, remove the two bolts securing the wiring harness support bracket, and remove it from the head **(see illustrations)**.

22 At the rear of the head, disconnect the wiring plug from the camshaft position (TDC) sensor, then remove the single mounting bolt and withdraw the sensor, recovering its O-ring seal – a new seal should be used when refitting **(see illustrations)**. The camshaft position sensor is the higher of the two sensors fitted in this area, the other being the coolant temperature sensor.

8.20b . . . and unbolt the earth strap from the camshaft thrust cover

8.20a Remove the bolt securing the wiring harness to the end of the head . . .

8.20c Slide the wiring harness rearwards off the support bracket

8.21a To remove the wiring harness support bracket, take out one bolt from behind . . .

8.21b . . . and one from the end of the head

8.22a Disconnect the camshaft position sensor wiring plug . . .

8.22b . . . then unbolt and remove the sensor

8.23a Remove the two thrust cover mounting bolts . . .

8.23b . . . then withdraw the cover, noting its large O-ring seal

8.25 Keep the camshaft as horizontal as possible while removing it

8.29 Oil the camshaft bearings in the cylinder head

23 Remove the two camshaft thrust cover bolts, and withdraw the cover. It's likely that the cover will prove difficult to remove, as there is a large O-ring seal inside – take care not to damage the mating faces if the cover has to be prised off **(see illustrations)**. Recover the O-ring seal – a new one should be used when refitting.

24 Before removing the camshaft, note that the camshaft sprocket locating keyway is positioned at 12 o'clock, at TDC.

25 Carefully slide out the camshaft, keeping it as horizontal as possible **(see illustration)**. If the shaft catches as it is withdrawn, slide it back in and try to free it by turning it slightly – there is a danger of damaging the cam lobes if the shaft is roughly handled. Once it is completely removed, rest the shaft on clean newspaper or rags, to protect the lobes.

Inspection

26 Examine the camshaft lobes for score marks, pitting, galling (wear due to rubbing) and evidence of overheating (blue, discoloured areas). Look for flaking away of the hardened surface layer of each lobe. Renew the camshaft if any of these conditions are apparent.

27 If any of the lobes is damaged, check the corresponding rocker finger's surfaces for similar signs – it probably wouldn't be wise to fit a new camshaft and re-use the old rocker shaft assembly, as both would have suffered wear. Seek the advice of an engine rebuilding specialist if in doubt.

28 As far as possible, examine the condition of the camshaft bearing surfaces in the cylinder head. If the head bearing surfaces are worn excessively, the cylinder head will need to be renewed.

Refitting

29 Liberally oil the camshaft lobes and the camshaft bearings in the cylinder head **(see illustration)**.

30 Slide the camshaft into the head, keeping it horizontal to avoid catching the lobes, which might cause damage **(see illustration)**. Turn the camshaft so that the sprocket locating keyway is in the TDC position (12 o'clock), as noted before removal.

31 Fit a new (lightly oiled) O-ring seal to the thrust cover, then press the cover into position and secure with the two bolts, tightened to the specified torque **(see illustrations)**.

32 Similarly, refit the camshaft position (TDC) sensor to the back of the engine, with a new, lightly-oiled O-ring. Tighten the sensor mounting bolt to the specified torque.

33 Refit the wiring harness support bracket.

8.30 Slide in the camshaft, keeping it horizontal

8.31a Fit a new O-ring to the thrust cover . . .

8.31b . . . then press the cover into place, and secure with the two bolts

8.40 Fit a new plug into the sprocket bolt access hole, and tap it home

Fit the harness itself back onto the bracket, then refit the earth strap and lower bolt.

34 Align the sprocket onto the keyway, and refit the bolt. Once the bolt is at least hand-tight, the wire and/or cable-ties can be removed from the sprocket.

35 Check that the sprocket is aligned in the TDC position (UP mark uppermost, horizontal marks in line with the head), turning the camshaft if necessary to achieve this. The alignment mark made prior to removal between the chain and sprocket should also correspond.

36 Hold the camshaft using a spanner on the flats provided, and tighten the sprocket bolt to the specified torque.

37 Use the method employed during removal to stop the crankshaft turning during the next step.

38 Have an assistant apply firm pressure clockwise on the camshaft sprocket bolt, so

9.3 Disconnect the coolant hoses from the throttle body

9.7 Unbolt and remove the drivebelt idler pulley (air conditioning models only)

that the 6 mm bolt fitted to the timing cover earlier is released. Unscrew the 6 mm bolt, then release the pressure on the sprocket, so that the chain tensioner arm takes up the chain tension once more. Refit the access bolt and washer, and tighten it securely.

39 Use a spanner or socket on the crankshaft pulley bolt to slowly turn the engine through two complete revolutions. Check that the TDC marks described in Section 3 come back into alignment. If the crankshaft binds or seems to hit something, do not force it, as the valves may be hitting the pistons. If this happens, the chain is incorrectly fitted. If necessary, reset the engine to TDC, then remove the chain from the camshaft sprocket and repeat the refitting procedure.

40 Fit a new cylinder head plug (and O-ring) into the camshaft sprocket bolt access hole, and tap it home **(see illustration)**.

41 Refit the engine right-hand mounting with reference to Section 17. Also (where removed) refit the earth strap in front of the mounting, and the refrigerant hose mounting bracket bolt.

42 Refit the rocker shaft assembly as described in Section 7.

43 Refit the battery as described in Chapter 5A.

9 Cylinder head –
removal and refitting

Note: *To avoid the possibility of warping the cylinder head, Honda state that the cylinder*

9.4 Disconnect the radiator and other coolant hoses from the thermostat housing

9.8 Take off the water pump pulley

head bolts should only be loosened when the engine has cooled down completely. In reality, this will always be the case.

Removal

1 Refer to Chapter 1 and drain the cooling system.

2 Remove the air cleaner as described in Chapter 4A.

3 Disconnect the two coolant hoses from the throttle body **(see illustration)**.

4 Release the spring clips, and disconnect the radiator top and bottom hoses from the thermostat housing **(see illustration)**. Similarly, disconnect the two smaller hoses at the rear of the housing, and the remaining heater hose from the back of the head – mark the hoses for position using tape.

5 Loosen (but do not yet remove) the three water pump pulley bolts – this is more easily done before the auxiliary drivebelt is removed.

6 Remove the auxiliary drivebelt as described in Chapter 1. In addition, unbolt and remove the alternator adjuster bolt bracket from the engine, and ensure that the alternator lower mounting bolt is loose enough that the alternator can pivot forwards, clear of the timing chain cover.

7 On models with air conditioning, unbolt and remove the drivebelt idler pulley, noting carefully the fitted sequence of washers and spacers **(see illustration)**.

8 Remove the three water pump pulley bolts, and take off the pulley **(see illustration)**.

9 Remove the inlet manifold and fuel rail as described in Chapter 4A.

10 Either remove the exhaust manifold, or disconnect the catalytic converter from it, as described in Chapter 4A. Removing the manifold will make it easier to lift the head off, and out of the engine compartment.

11 Disconnect the following wiring plugs from the following components around the engine:

a) *Camshaft position (TDC) sensor, from the rear of the head, at the transmission end* **(see illustration)**.

b) *Coolant temperature sensor, below the TDC sensor* **(see illustration)**.

c) *Radiator fan switch, from the side of the thermostat housing* **(see illustration)**.

12 At the transmission end of the head, remove the two bolts from above, and take

9.11a Disconnect the wiring plugs from the TDC sensor . . .

9.11b ... coolant temperature sensor ...

9.11c ... and from the radiator fan switch

9.12a Remove the bolt securing the wiring harness to the end of the head ...

off the air cleaner mounting bracket (where applicable). Remove the lower bolt securing the wiring harness to the end of the head, and also unbolt the earth strap from the camshaft thrust cover. Release the wiring harness from the support bracket at the rear (see illustrations).

13 The rigid coolant pipe at the front of the head must now be removed. Release the clips, and slide the rubber hose section down the pipe. Unscrew the single bolt securing the coolant pipe to the front of the thermostat housing, and pull the pipe off, noting that it has an O-ring seal which must be renewed when reconnecting (see illustrations).

14 Release the spring clip and disconnect the coolant hose from the base of the EGR valve (at the front corner of the head) (see illustrations).

15 Remove the cylinder head cover as described in Section 4.

9.12b ... and unbolt the earth strap from the camshaft thrust cover

16 Set the engine to TDC on No 1 cylinder, as described in Section 3. As the cylinder head cover has been removed, check that the camshaft sprocket UP mark and horizontal lines are correctly aligned.

9.12c Slide the wiring harness off the bracket at the rear

17 Remove the crankshaft pulley as described in Section 6.

18 At the back of the timing chain cover, disconnect the wiring plug from the crankshaft position sensor (see illustration). Trace the

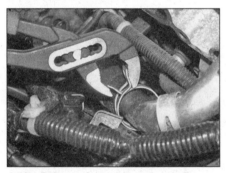

9.13a Release the two large hose clips ...

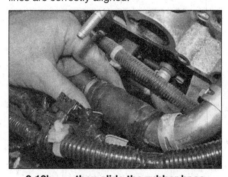

9.13b ... then slide the rubber hose section down the rigid pipe sections

9.13c Unbolt the rigid pipe section from the head ...

9.13d ... then prise it free and remove it, noting the O-ring seal

9.14a Release the spring clip ...

9.14b ... and disconnect the coolant hose from the EGR valve

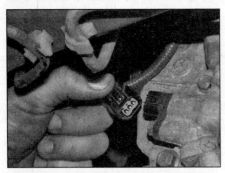

9.18 Disconnect the crankshaft position sensor wiring plug

9.20 Unbolt the earth strap from the front of the head

9.21 Unbolt the air conditioning refrigerant pipe bracket above the mounting

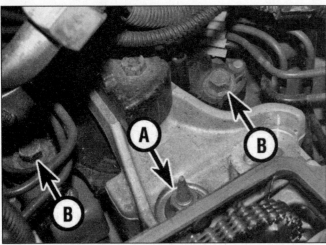

9.22a Engine right-hand mounting upper nut (A) and two of the wing bolts (B)

9.22b Removing the engine right-hand mounting

wiring up the back of the timing chain cover, release the two harness clips and move the wiring clear.

19 The weight of the engine must now be supported from below, as the right-hand mounting must be removed. Use a large piece of wood between the jack head and the sump, to spread the load, and just take the weight of the engine.

20 Where applicable, unbolt the earth strap in front of the right-hand mounting, and move it clear **(see illustration)**.

21 On models with air conditioning, one of the refrigerant hoses passes close to the right-hand mounting, and is secured to the

inner wing by a support bracket. It may be useful to remove the hose support bracket bolt, to give some movement in the hose **(see illustration)**.

22 With the engine supported from below, loosen the bolts securing the right-hand mounting to the inner wing. The mounting upper bracket is secured to the engine by two nuts – one on top, and the other removed from below. Remove the two nuts, then unscrew the mounting-to-wing bolts, and lift out the mounting assembly, manoeuvring it past the refrigerant hose where applicable **(see illustrations)**.

23 The timing chain cover is secured by a

total of fourteen bolts (including two straight up at the base of the cover, from the sump), of 6 mm and 8 mm diameter. Remove the bolts, and store them carefully – we pushed the bolts through a piece of card as they were removed, to store them in their fitted pattern **(see illustration)**. If not already done, pivot the alternator forwards, clear of the cover.

24 The cover is fitted using a bead of sealant, so will probably be stuck. Start by pulling it at the top, and work downwards until it is free, and can be removed – prising between the joint faces is not recommended, as this may give rise to an oil leak on reassembly. Slide the cover off the nose of the crankshaft, and remove it **(see illustration)**. **Note:** *While the timing chain cover is removed, consider fitting a new crankshaft oil seal which is fitted to it – this job is far easier to do with the cover off. Refer to Section 14.*

25 Using the spout of an oil can through the cylinder head's oil return hole behind the camshaft sprocket, lightly lubricate the sliding surfaces of the chain tensioner.

26 Chock the front wheels, and apply the handbrake firmly. Engage a gear (or P), and have an assistant apply the footbrake firmly, to stop the crankshaft turning during the next step. Alternatively, lock the engine using the tool described in Section 6.

27 Use a socket on the camshaft sprocket

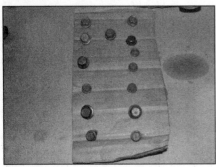

9.23 Store the timing cover bolts in a piece of card

9.24 Removing the timing chain cover

9.27 Turning the sprocket bolt moves the slotted bracket to reveal a hole . . .

9.28 . . . into which a locking bolt can be screwed

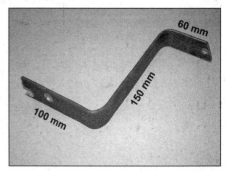

9.32 Home-made bracket to support the camshaft sprocket (dimensions not critical)

bolt to apply firm pressure on the sprocket clockwise (the sprocket should hardly turn) – this will force the tensioner and its arm rearwards. Attached to the tensioner arm is a slotted bracket – when the arm is forced back by the chain, the slot uncovers a 6 mm threaded hole in the end of the block **(see illustration)**.

28 Holding the camshaft sprocket clockwise, insert a 6 mm bolt, at least 60 mm long, into the threaded hole, and screw it in as far as possible (the bolt will be under some strain, and screwing in by a few threads will not be enough) **(see illustration)**. Have the assistant release the sprocket. The tensioner arm is now locked in the retracted position, releasing the chain tension – this can be confirmed by the play that will now be present in the camshaft sprocket.

29 Using an open-ended spanner (actual size 29 mm, but a 30 mm spanner will do) on the camshaft flats provided, hold the camshaft while the sprocket bolt is loosened. Only loosen the bolt by half a turn at this stage – do not remove it.

30 The chain and camshaft sprocket are removed together. Pass a cable-tie through one of the camshaft sprocket holes, and wrap it tight around the chain – this keeps the chain and sprocket together, in the correct fitted position.

31 There is a slight risk that, if upward tension is not maintained on the chain, the chain will drop off the crankshaft sprocket, making it near-impossible to put back on without removing the sump. We found that the guide

below the crankshaft sprocket always kept the chain engaged with it, however.

32 To be on the safe side, it may be advisable to keep the chain and sprocket supported while removed. This could be done using wire or cable-ties, but we made up an S-shaped metal bracket which we were able to bolt to the right-hand inner wing **(see illustration)**.

33 With an assistant supporting the camshaft sprocket, remove the bolt and release the sprocket from the keyway at the top of the camshaft, by moving it to the side. Support the camshaft sprocket and chain while removed **(see illustrations)**.

34 Remove the top bolt from the chain front guide, so that the guide is released from the head **(see illustration)**.

35 Working in the **reverse** of the tightening sequence shown later in this Section, loosen each head bolt by a quarter-turn each time,

repeating the sequence until all bolts are completely loose, and can be removed **(see illustration)**. If new bolts are not being fitted (this is not something we would recommend), lay the old bolts out in their fitted order, so they can be refitted in the same place.

36 Carefully lift off the head, and place it on a clean surface – do not allow the lower face to be damaged, or even a new gasket will not seal properly **(see illustration)**. If the head is stuck, try rocking it backwards to free it, using a blunt lever (such as a wooden hammer handle) in the inlet ports on the front – space permitting, try the same approach on the exhaust ports at the rear. Once the gasket seal has been broken, the head should come off. Hitting the head is not advisable, as the alloy is easily damaged. Also note that the head is located on two dowels.

37 Recover the old head gasket **(see**

9.33a Slide the camshaft sprocket off its keyway with the chain attached . . .

9.33b . . . and support the assembly while it is removed

9.34 Remove the top bolt from the timing chain front guide

9.35 Loosen the head bolts a quarter-turn each, in sequence

9.36 Lifting off the cylinder head

9.37 Take off the old head gasket, and keep it for comparison

9.47a Refit the dowels to their original locations . . .

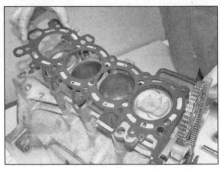

9.47b . . . and lay the new head gasket in position

illustration). Though it should not be re-used, it may be useful to hold onto it for now, to compare with the new one as verification.

38 If the head is to be dismantled for overhaul, remove the rocker shaft and camshaft as described in Sections 7 and 8, then refer to Part B of this Chapter.

Preparation for refitting

39 The mating faces of the cylinder head and cylinder block/crankcase must be perfectly clean before refitting the head. Remove the two dowels (note their positions) and use a hard plastic or wood scraper to remove all traces of gasket and carbon; also clean the piston crowns.

40 Take particular care during the cleaning operations, as aluminium alloy is easily damaged. Also, make sure that the carbon is not allowed to enter the oil and water passages – this is particularly important for the lubrication system, as carbon could block the oil supply to the engine's components. Using adhesive tape and paper, seal the water, oil and bolt holes in the cylinder block/crankcase.

41 Take care that as little debris as possible gets onto the timing chain (and that the supported chain is not disturbed during cleaning) – anything more than a little dirt will risk getting caught up in the crankshaft sprocket, and may cause damage to the timing chain.

> **HAYNES HINT** To prevent carbon entering the gap between the pistons and bores, smear a little grease in the gap. After cleaning each piston, use a small brush to remove all traces of grease and carbon from the gap, then wipe away the remainder with a clean rag.

42 Check the mating surfaces of the cylinder block/crankcase and the cylinder head for nicks, deep scratches and other damage. If slight, they may be removed carefully with a file, but if excessive, machining may be the only alternative to renewal.

43 If warpage of the cylinder head gasket surface is suspected, use a straight-edge to check it for distortion. Refer to Part B of this Chapter if necessary.

44 As stated previously, we recommend that the old head bolts should not be re-used. Do not be tempted, either for convenience or saving money, to ignore this advice – if the bolts or their threads 'let go' when they're tightened, the bottom half of the engine could be reduced to scrap very quickly.

45 Although not essential, if a suitable tap-and-die set is available, it's worth running the correct-size tap down the bolt threads in the cylinder block. This will clean the threads of any debris, and go some way to restoring any

damaged threads. Make absolutely sure the tap is the right size and thread pitch, and lightly oil the tap before starting. Failing this, choose one of the old head bolts, clean its threads with a wire brush, then lightly oil it, and run it fully into each bolt hole, cleaning it between each one.

46 If possible, clean out the bolt holes in the block using compressed air, to ensure no oil or water is present. Screwing a bolt into an oil- or water-filled hole can (in extreme cases) cause the block to fracture, due to the hydraulic pressure created.

Refitting

47 Ensure the two locating dowels are refitted to their original positions on the block top surface – the dowels correspond to bolts 3 and 10 in the tightening sequence. Check that the new cylinder head gasket is the same type as the original, and that any TOP or UP marking is facing upwards, then locate it onto the top face of the cylinder block and over the dowels. Ensure that it is correctly aligned with the coolant passages and oilways **(see illustrations)**.

48 Lower the head onto the block, taking care not to disturb the supported timing chain, and making sure the gasket does not move. Locate the head on the two dowels **(see illustration)**.

49 Lightly oil the threads and heads of the new head bolts before fitting them.

50 Following the tightening sequence, first tighten the bolts to the specified Stage 1 torque **(see illustration)**. Note: *If any bolt*

9.48 Place the cylinder head on the block, aligning it on the dowels

9.50 Cylinder head bolt tightening sequence

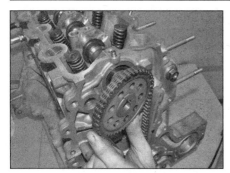

9.52a Fit the camshaft sprocket (and chain) . . .

9.52b . . . then fit the sprocket bolt, and tighten it by hand

9.53 Refit the timing chain front guide's top bolt

starts creaking during tightening, Honda suggest loosening it completely, and start tightening again. If the bolts are lubricated as stated in the previous paragraph, no creaking should be evident.

51 Now the head bolts should be tightened further, to their specified Stage 2 angle. It is strongly recommended that an angle gauge is used for this task – these are not expensive, and are available from any good car accessory shop or motor factors. Again, follow the tightening sequence.

52 Align the camshaft sprocket (and chain) onto the keyway, and refit the sprocket bolt (by hand at this stage) **(see illustrations)**.

53 Refit the chain front guide's top bolt, and tighten it to the specified torque **(see illustration)**.

54 Check that the sprocket is aligned in the TDC position (UP mark uppermost, horizontal marks in line with the head). The alignment mark made prior to removal between the chain and sprocket should also correspond.

55 Hold the camshaft using a spanner on the flats provided, and tighten the sprocket bolt to the specified torque.

56 Chock the front wheels, and apply the handbrake firmly. Engage a gear (or P), and have an assistant apply the footbrake firmly, to stop the crankshaft turning during the next step. Alternatively, lock the engine using the tool described in Section 6.

57 Using a socket on the camshaft sprocket bolt, apply pressure clockwise on the sprocket, so that the 6 mm bolt fitted earlier is released. Unscrew the 6 mm bolt, then release the pressure on the sprocket, so that the chain tensioner arm takes up the chain tension once more.

58 Before refitting the timing cover, check the condition of the crankshaft oil seal which is fitted to it. This seal is much easier to renew when the cover is removed – see Section 14 for details.

59 Clean off all traces of old sealant from the cover, engine and sump faces, cover bolts and bolt holes. Take care not to mark the mating faces. Wash the cover and engine/sump mating faces with suitable solvent, and dry them before continuing.

60 Apply a bead of RTV sealant (Honda Liquid Gasket 1216E, part number

08C70-K0334M, or equivalent) to the timing cover mating faces on the engine block and cylinder head, as shown. The bead should be 1.5 mm diameter all round, except in the area where the block and head join – here the bead should be doubled up to 3.0 mm **(refer to illustration 5.53a)**.

61 Similarly, the bead should be 1.5 mm on the sump mating face at the 'ends', but 5 mm diameter on the central, curved section **(see illustration)**. Run the sealant inside the bolt holes – try not to get any down the holes themselves, as this may affect the bolt tightening. Once the sealant has been applied, the cover should be fitted within 5 minutes.

62 Offer the cover over the end of the crankshaft, taking care not to damage the oil seal in the cover. Seat the cover onto the engine, and guide it into place by fitting two or more of the bolts (the bolts are two different sizes, and should be fitted to their original locations).

63 The cover will 'float' on the sealant, even with all the bolts in place (there are no locating dowels). Although the cover alignment doesn't appear to be critical, use a straight-edge across the top surfaces of the cover and cylinder head to ensure they are level.

64 Fit all the remaining cover bolts. Starting in the middle of the cover, tighten the bolts evenly, and finally to their respective torques.

65 Clip the crankshaft position sensor wiring harness to the rear of the timing cover, and reconnect the wiring plug.

66 Refit the engine right-hand mounting with reference to Section 17. Also (where removed) refit the earth strap in front of the mounting, and the refrigerant hose mounting bracket bolt.

67 The remainder of refitting is a reversal of removal, noting the following points:

a) Use a new O-ring when reconnecting the rigid coolant pipe to the front of the thermostat housing.

b) Refit the crankshaft pulley as described in Section 6.

c) Before refitting the cylinder head cover (Section 4), check and adjust the valve clearances as described in Chapter 1.

d) Refit the water pump pulley, with the bolts hand-tight to begin with (it will be easier to tighten them to the specified torque

once the auxiliary drivebelt has been refitted and tensioned, as described in Chapter 1).

e) Refit the fuel rail and inlet manifold as described in Chapter 4A. On completion, switch the ignition on and off a few times, to run the fuel pump, then check for signs of fuel leakage.

f) When all the coolant pipes and hoses have been reconnected, refill the cooling system as described in Chapter 1.

10 Sump – removal and refitting

Removal

1 Jack up the front of the car, and support it on axle stands (see Jacking and vehicle support).

2 Drain the engine oil as described in Chapter 1, then refit the drain plug. Remove the oil filter – unusually, this is mounted on the sump's front face. It makes sense to fit a new oil filter on completion, but this is not essential.

3 On models with air conditioning, the compressor is bolted to the sump's front face. Disconnect the compressor wiring plug. Remove the four bolts, then move the compressor forwards, clear of the sump. Support the compressor using wire or cable-ties, so that the refrigerant hoses (which must not be disturbed) are not strained **(see illustrations)**.

4 At the rear of the sump, remove the three

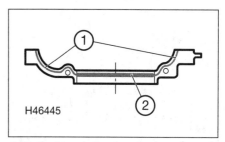

9.61 Sealant application details (to sump) when refitting timing chain cover

1 Bead of sealant, 1.5 mm diameter
2 Bead of sealant, 5.0 mm diameter

10.3a Disconnect the air conditioning compressor wiring plug

10.3b Remove the four mounting bolts . . .

10.3c . . . then move the compressor forwards and tie it up

mounting bolts (two above, one below) securing the curved heat shield around the right-hand driveshaft CV joint, and take off the shield (see illustration).

5 Withdraw the dipstick, and place it to one side. Remove the single bolt securing the dipstick tube to the front of the engine, then pull the tube upwards to release its lower O-ring, and remove it (see illustration). A new O-ring should be used when refitting.

6 At the sump-to-transmission joint, remove three bolts and take off the small cover plate from below the flywheel/driveplate. Also remove the two large sump-to-transmission bolts (see illustrations).

7 Remove the remaining bolts securing the sump to the base of the engine – note that the front bolt at the transmission end is larger than the others, and that the two bolts next to the flywheel are longer. The sump is fitted

using sealant, so will likely remain stuck. Note that the sump is located on two dowels.

8 Honda suggest prising the sump down at the four corners, but this carries the risk of damaging the mating faces, making it hard to seal. Try removing the drain plug once more, and use a tool such as a screwdriver inserted in the drain hole as a lever to prise the sump free (take care not to damage the drain hole threads). Keep the sump level as it is lowered, to prevent spillage of any remaining oil in it. Also be prepared for oil drips from the crankcase when the sump is removed.

9 Recover the U-shaped gasket from the transmission end of the sump – a new one must be used when refitting.

10 Similarly, recover the O-ring fitted to the oil filter supply passage, and the locating dowel behind it, if it is loose. A new O-ring must be used when refitting.

11 A further small dowel is fitted at the transmission end of the sump – recover this dowel if it is loose.

12 Clean any sealant from the sump and engine mating faces – care must be taken not to damage the soft aluminium of the sump. Wipe the mating faces with a suitable solvent, and allow to dry. While the sump is off, check that the oil pick-up/strainer on the base of the engine is clear, cleaning it if necessary.

Refitting

13 Fit a new U-shaped gasket to the transmission end of the sump, ensuring that it locates fully in the groove (see illustration).

14 Fit a new O-ring to the oil filter supply passage at the front of the sump. Ensure that the two sump locating dowels are still in place (see illustrations).

15 Apply a bead of RTV sealant (Honda Liquid

10.4 Unbolt the curved heat shield from the back of the sump

10.5 Pull out the dipstick tube

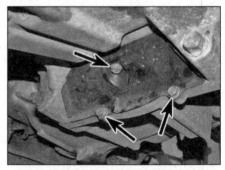

10.6a At the base of the transmission bellhousing, undo the three bolts . . .

10.6b . . . and take off the metal cover plate (sump-to-transmission bolts arrowed)

10.13 Fit a new U-shaped gasket to the sump groove

10.14a Fit a new O-ring to the oil filter supply passage (note locating dowel)

10.14b Make sure the other locating dowel is in place at the transmission end

Gasket 1216E, part number 08C70-K0334M, or equivalent) to the sump's mating face. The bead should be 1.5 mm diameter all round, except in the curved area where the sump meets the timing chain cover – here the bead should be 5.0 mm. Run the sealant inside the bolt holes **(see illustrations)**. Once the sealant has been applied, the sump should be fitted within 5 minutes.

16 Lining up the sump is tricky. It is helpful to have an assistant available to guide the sump over the timing cover end – the large bead of sealant has a tendency to apply itself to the teeth of crankshaft position sensor pulse plate otherwise. We temporarily fitted a longer bolt at the timing cover end, to get the alignment right.

17 Offer up the sump, and locate it on the two dowels **(see illustration)**. Fit the bolts to retain it, tightened by hand only initially. Note that the two longer bolts are fitted at the flywheel end, and the larger-diameter bolt is number 1 in the tightening sequence.

18 Working in sequence, and in two or three stages, tighten the nuts and bolts to the specified torque **(see illustration)**. Note that the larger bolt on the front at the transmission end (number 1 in the tightening sequence) has a higher tightening torque than the others.

19 Refit the two sump-to-transmission bolts, and tighten them to the specified torque.

20 Similarly, refit the small cover plate from below the flywheel/driveplate, and secure with the three bolts.

21 Refit the dipstick tube, using a new O-ring, and tighten the tube mounting bolt securely.

22 At the rear of the sump, refit the curved heat shield around the right-hand driveshaft CV joint, and tighten the three bolts securely – tighten the top two bolts before the lower one.

23 On models with air conditioning, refit the compressor, and tighten the four bolts to the specified torque. Reconnect the compressor wiring plug.

24 Fit the oil filter, tightening it by hand only – do not use any tools.

25 Allow at least 30 minutes (and preferably, several hours) for the sealant used on the sump to cure, then refill the engine with oil as described in Chapter 1.

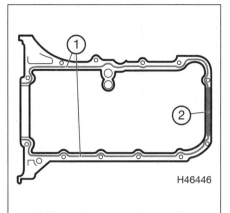

H46446

10.15a Sealant application details when refitting the sump

1 *Bead of sealant, 1.5 mm diameter*
2 *Bead of sealant, 5.0 mm diameter*

10.17 Offer the sump into position

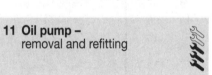

11 Oil pump – removal and refitting

Removal

1 Remove the timing chain and crankshaft sprocket as described in Section 5.

2 Remove the two nuts and bolt securing the oil pick-up/strainer to the bottom of the engine. Recover the gasket from the oil pump flange – a new one must be used when refitting.

11.3 Unscrew the oil pump mounting bolts

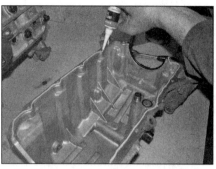

10.15b Run the sealant inside the bolt holes

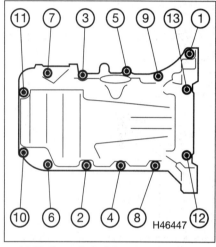

H46447

10.18 Sump bolt tightening sequence

3 Unscrew and remove the seven bolts securing the oil pump to the block (note that three of the bolts are shorter than the rest) **(see illustration)**. Withdraw the oil pump from the front of the crankshaft – recover the two locating dowels, and the O-ring from the oil supply passage.

Inspection

4 Remove the pressure relief valve bolt, and extract the spring and pressure relief valve plunger from the pump housing **(see illustration)**. Check the spring for distortion and the relief valve plunger for scoring. Renew parts as necessary.

11.4 Oil pump pressure relief valve bolt, spring and plunger

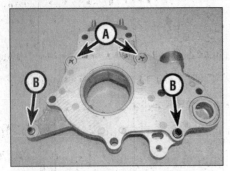

11.5a Remove the two screws (A) – note the locating dowels (B) . . .

11.5b . . . and take off the inner cover

11.6a Check the pump inner-to-outer rotor clearance . . .

11.6b . . . the housing-to-outer rotor clearance . . .

11.6c . . . and the housing-to-rotor endfloat

11.7 Lightly oil the pump rotors when refitting

5 Undo the screws and dismantle the oil pump. You may need to use an impact screwdriver to loosen the two pump inner cover screws without stripping the heads (see illustrations).

6 Check the oil pump inner-to-outer rotor

clearance, housing-to-outer rotor clearance, and the housing-to-rotor endfloat (see illustrations). Compare your measurements to the figures listed in the Specifications. Renew the pump if any of the measurements exceed the specified limits. It is generally considered

good practice to fit a new oil pump if the engine is being overhauled.

7 If removed, lightly oil and refit the pump rotors (see illustration).

8 Apply thread-locking compound to the pump inner cover screws, refit the cover and tighten the screws securely. Refit the oil pressure relief valve and spring assembly, then refit the bolt, and tighten to the specified torque.

Refitting

9 Refit the two locating dowels on the back of the pump, and fit a new O-ring to the oil supply passage (see illustration).

10 Offer the pump onto the engine, aligning the pump's inner rotor with the drive slot on the crankshaft, and refit the seven bolts (see illustrations).

11 Tighten the oil pump mounting bolts to the specified torque.

11.9 Fit a new O-ring to the back of the oil pump

11.10a Offer the oil pump into position . . .

11.10b . . . and refit the bolts – we've left the four longer bolts loose here

11.12a Fit a new pipe flange gasket . . .

11.12b . . . then refit the oil pick-up/ strainer . . .

12 Refit the oil pick-up/strainer using a new gasket on the pipe flange, and tighten the nuts/bolt to the specified torque **(see illustrations)**.
13 Remove the crankshaft sprocket and timing chain as described in Section 5.

12 Oil pressure switch – removal and refitting

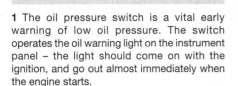

1 The oil pressure switch is a vital early warning of low oil pressure. The switch operates the oil warning light on the instrument panel – the light should come on with the ignition, and go out almost immediately when the engine starts.
2 If the light does not come on, there could be a fault on the instrument panel, the switch wiring, or the switch itself. If the light does not go out, low oil level, worn oil pump (or sump pick-up blocked), blocked oil filter, or worn main bearings could be to blame – or again, the switch may be faulty.
3 If the light comes on while driving, the best advice is to turn the engine off immediately, and not to drive the car until the problem has been investigated – ignoring the light could mean expensive engine damage.

Removal

4 The oil pressure switch is located on the front face of the engine, directly above the oil filter.
5 Access to the switch is easiest from below – raise the front of the car, and support it on axle stands (see *Jacking and vehicle support*). Though not essential, access to the switch is improved by unscrewing the oil filter – anticipate oil spillage when this is done.
6 Disconnect the wiring plug from the switch.
7 Unscrew the switch from the block and remove it – a deep socket or large spanner will be required **(see illustration)**. There should only be a very slight loss of oil when this is done.

Inspection

8 Examine the switch for signs of cracking or splits. If the top part of the switch is loose, this is an early indication of impending failure.
9 Check that the wiring terminals at the switch are not loose, then trace the wire from the switch connector until it enters the main loom – any wiring defects will give rise to apparent oil pressure problems.

Refitting

10 Refitting is the reverse of the removal procedure, noting the following points:
a) If the same switch is being refitted, clean any old sealant from the switch threads.
b) Apply a little RTV sealant to the switch threads, then tighten the switch to the specified torque **(see illustrations)**.
c) Reconnect the switch connector, making sure it clicks home properly. Ensure that

11.12c . . . and secure with the flange nuts and mounting bolt

the wiring is routed away from any hot or moving parts.
d) If removed, refit the oil filter, tightening it securely by hand only (do not use any tools).
e) Check the engine oil level and top-up if necessary (see Weekly checks).
f) Check for signs of oil leaks once the engine has been restarted and warmed-up to normal operating temperature.

13 Camshaft oil seals – renewal

1 There are no conventional camshaft oil seals on this engine, but O-ring seals are fitted to covers at either end of the camshaft.

Timing chain end

2 If an oil leak has been noted from the timing

12.7 Unscrew and remove the oil pressure switch

12.10b . . . before refitting and tightening it

chain end of the engine, it may be coming from the cylinder head cover (Section 4) or the timing chain cover (Section 5).
3 However, there is a small plastic plug fitted to the timing chain cover, in line with the camshaft. If oil is weeping from this plug, the seal can be renewed as follows.
4 Support the engine from below, as the right-hand mounting must be removed. Use a large piece of wood between the jack head and the sump, to spread the load, and just take the weight of the engine.
5 Where applicable, unbolt the earth strap in front of the right-hand mounting, and move it clear.
6 On models with air conditioning, one of the refrigerant hoses passes close to the right-hand mounting, and is secured to the inner wing by a support bracket. It may be useful to remove the hose support bracket bolt, to give some movement in the hose.
7 With the engine supported from below, loosen the bolts securing the right-hand mounting to the inner wing. The mounting upper bracket is secured to the engine by two nuts – one on top, and the other removed from below. Remove the two nuts, then unscrew the mounting-to-wing bolts, and lift out the mounting assembly, manoeuvring it past the refrigerant hose where applicable.
8 Prise out the large plastic plug from the end of the head, which covers the camshaft sprocket bolt. Recover the plug's O-ring seal.
9 Clean the location in the timing chain cover, then fit a new plug and O-ring, pressing the plug home firmly **(see illustration)**.

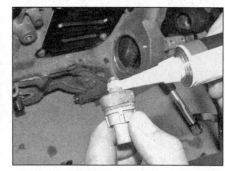

12.10a Apply a little sealant to the switch threads . . .

13.9 Fit the new timing cover plug and O-ring (seen with cylinder head cover removed)

13.14a Remove the bolt securing the wiring harness to the end of the head . . .

13.14b . . . and unbolt the earth strap from the camshaft thrust cover

13.14c Slide the wiring harness rearwards off the support bracket

13.15a Remove the two thrust cover mounting bolts . . .

13.15b . . . then withdraw the cover, noting its large O-ring seal

13.16a Fit a new O-ring to the thrust cover . . .

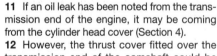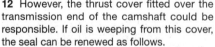

13.16b . . . then press the cover into place, and secure with the two bolts

14.6 Tap the oil seal into the timing cover using a tube or socket

there is a large O-ring seal inside – take care not to damage the mating faces if the cover has to be prised off **(see illustrations)**.

16 Fit a new (lightly oiled) O-ring seal to the thrust cover, then press the cover into position and secure with the two bolts, tightened to the specified torque **(see illustrations)**.

17 Refit the wiring harness to the mounting bracket, then refit the earth strap and lower bolt. Refit the air cleaner mounting bracket, and tighten the two bolts to the specified torque.

18 Refit the air cleaner as described in Chapter 4A.

14 Crankshaft oil seals – renewal

Timing chain end

1 Remove the crankshaft pulley as described in Section 6.

2 Before removing the old seal, note its fitted depth in the timing cover carefully, especially if the seal is being renewed with the timing cover still fitted.

3 Using a suitable claw tool, extract the oil seal, but take care not to damage the seal housing. As it is removed, note the fitted orientation of the seal in the cover.

HAYNES HiNT *Sometimes, a seal can be loosened by pushing it in on one side – this tilts the seal outwards on the opposite side, and it can then be gripped with pliers and removed.*

4 Clean the seal location in the timing cover as far as possible. Also, check for any sharp edges which may damage the new seal, either during fitting or in service.

5 Honda do not state whether the new seal should be oiled before fitting, so we fitted our (genuine Honda) seal without oiling it first. If possible, seek clarification on this from your parts supplier.

6 Offer the new seal into position. If the timing cover has been removed, the seal can be tapped home to the fitted depth noted previously, using a tube or socket of roughly the same outside diameter as the seal **(see illustration)**. If the

10 Refit the engine right-hand mounting with reference to Section 17. Also refit the earth strap in front of the mounting, and (where removed) the refrigerant hose mounting bracket bolt.

Transmission end

11 If an oil leak has been noted from the transmission end of the engine, it may be coming from the cylinder head cover (Section 4).

12 However, the thrust cover fitted over the transmission end of the camshaft could be responsible. If oil is weeping from this cover, the seal can be renewed as follows.

13 Remove the air cleaner as described in Chapter 4A.

14 Remove the two bolts from above, and take off the air cleaner mounting bracket at the transmission end of the cylinder head. Remove the lower bolt securing the wiring harness to the end of the head, and also unbolt the earth strap from the camshaft thrust cover. Release the wiring harness from the support bracket at the rear **(see illustrations)**.

15 Remove the two camshaft thrust cover bolts, and withdraw the cover. It's likely that the cover will prove difficult to remove, as

timing cover is still fitted, there is limited working room to tap the seal home, and it may have to be pressed in with a suitable blunt instrument – make sure the seal isn't damaged, and is fitted to the same depth as the old one.

7 Refit the crankshaft pulley as described in Section 6.

Transmission end

8 Remove the flywheel or driveplate as described in Section 15.

9 Using a suitable claw tool, extract the oil seal, but take care not to damage the seal housing. Alternatively, carefully drill a small hole in the seal, then fit a self-tapping screw and pull out the seal **(see illustrations)**. As it is removed, note the fitted orientation of the seal, and its fitted depth.

10 Clean the seal location as far as possible. Also, check for any sharp edges which may damage the new seal, either during fitting or in service.

11 Honda do not state whether the new seal should be oiled before fitting, so we fitted our (genuine Honda) seal without oiling it first. If possible, seek clarification on this from your parts supplier.

12 Offer the new seal into position, and tap it home to the fitted depth noted previously (this is effectively flush with the crankcase/block). If possible, use a tube or socket of roughly the same outside diameter as the seal – failing this, work around the seal, tapping it progressively home with a blunt instrument to make sure the seal isn't damaged **(see illustrations)**.

13 Refit the flywheel or driveplate as described in Section 15.

15 Flywheel/driveplate –
removal, inspection and refitting

Removal

Manual transmission models

1 Remove the transmission as described in Chapter 7A, then remove the clutch as described in Chapter 6.

2 Jam a suitable tool into the ring gear teeth to prevent the flywheel/crankshaft from rotating as the bolts are removed **(see illustration)**.

15.2 We bolted a home-made tool to lock the flywheel ring gear

14.9a Drill a small hole in the seal . . .

14.12a Offer the seal into position . . .

3 Unscrew the six retaining bolts, and remove the flywheel from the rear flange of the crankshaft – take care not to drop the flywheel, as it is heavy **(see illustrations)**.

Automatic transmission models

4 Remove the transmission as described in Chapter 7B. Unusually, the flywheel and driveplate are separate – the flywheel is removed with the transmission.

5 The driveplate must now be prevented from turning while its bolts are loosened – this should be possible by passing a suitable tool through one of the flywheel mounting bolt holes, and jamming it against a suitable point on the engine.

6 Unscrew the six retaining bolts, take off the support plate, then remove the driveplate from the rear flange of the crankshaft.

Inspection

7 If on removal, the flywheel bolts are found

15.3a Unscrew the six flywheel bolts . . .

14.9b . . . then fit a screw and use it to pull out the seal

14.12b . . . and tap it home using a block of wood

to be in poor condition (stretched threads, etc) they must be renewed.

8 Inspect the starter ring gear on the flywheel for any broken or excessively-worn teeth. If evident, the ring gear must be renewed; this is a task best entrusted to a Honda dealer or a competent garage. Alternatively, obtain a complete new flywheel.

9 On manual transmission models, the clutch friction surface on the flywheel must be carefully inspected for grooving or hairline cracks (caused by overheating). If these conditions are evident, it may be possible to have the flywheel surface-ground, however this work must be carried out by an engine overhaul specialist. If surface-grinding is not possible, the flywheel must be renewed.

Refitting

10 Check that the mating faces of the flywheel/driveplate and crankshaft are clean

15.3b . . . and take off the flywheel

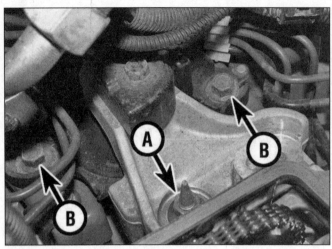
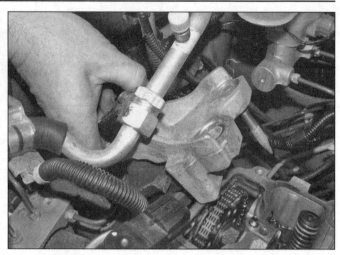

17.11a Engine right-hand mounting upper nut (A) and two of the wing bolts (B)

17.11b Removing the engine right-hand mounting

before refitting. Lubricate the threads of the retaining bolts with engine oil before they are screwed into position.

Manual transmission models

11 Locate the flywheel onto the crankshaft, then insert and hand-tighten the bolts.
12 Prevent the flywheel turning as for removal. Tighten the bolts progressively to the specified torque.
13 If removed, refit the starter motor as described in Chapter 5A. Refit the clutch as described in Chapter 6, then refit the transmission as described in Chapter 7A.

Automatic transmission models

14 Locate the driveplate onto the crankshaft, with the support plate, then insert and hand-tighten the bolts.
15 Prevent the driveplate turning as for removal. Tighten the bolts progressively to the specified torque.
16 Refit the transmission as described in Chapter 7B.

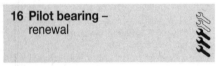

16 Pilot bearing – renewal

Note: *A pilot bearing is only fitted to manual transmission models.*

1 The pilot bearing is located in the end of the crankshaft, and supports the end of the transmission input shaft. Whenever the transmission is removed (such as when the clutch is being renewed), the pilot bearing should be checked for wear.
2 Remove the transmission as described in Chapter 7A.
3 The pilot bearing can be accessed through the centre of the flywheel. Turn the bearing by hand, and check it for roughness, excess play, or any other sign of wear.
4 The bearing is press-fitted into the end of the crankshaft, and the only way to remove it is by using a suitable slide hammer.

5 The new bearing should be lightly oiled, then tapped home to the shoulder inside the crankshaft, using a socket or tube which bears on the new bearing's outer race.
6 Refit the transmission as described in Chapter 7A.

17 Engine/transmission mountings – inspection and renewal

Inspection

1 The engine/transmission mountings seldom require attention, but broken or deteriorated mountings should be renewed immediately, or the added strain placed on the driveline components may cause damage or wear.
2 During the check, the engine/transmission must be raised slightly, to remove its weight from the mountings.
3 Apply the handbrake, then jack up the front of the car and support it on axle stands (see *Jacking and vehicle support*). Position a jack under the sump, with a large block of wood between the jack head and the sump, then carefully raise the engine just enough to take the weight off the mountings.
4 Check the mountings to see if the rubber is cracked, hardened or separated from the metal components. Sometimes, the rubber will split right down the centre.
5 Check for relative movement between each mounting's brackets and the engine or body (use a large screwdriver or lever to attempt to move the mountings). If movement is noted, lower the engine and check the mounting nuts and bolts for tightness.

Renewal

Note: *References to 'left' and 'right' are as seen from the driver's seat.*

Right-hand mounting

6 Support the weight of the engine from below. Use a large piece of wood between the

jack head and the sump, to spread the load, and just take the weight of the engine.
7 Where applicable, unbolt the earth strap in front of the mounting, and move it clear.
8 On models with air conditioning, one of the refrigerant hoses passes close to the right-hand mounting, and is secured to the inner wing by a support bracket. It may be useful to remove the hose support bracket bolt, to give some movement in the hose.
9 To improve access to the engine mounting bolts, lift the engine compartment fusebox off its mounting – this creates a small amount of movement in the fusebox.
10 Loosen the bolts securing the right-hand mounting to the inner wing – three bolts on manual transmission models, two bolts on those with automatic transmission.
11 The mounting upper bracket is secured to the engine by two nuts – one on top, and the other removed from below. Remove the two nuts, then unscrew the mounting-to-wing bolts, and lift out the mounting assembly, manoeuvring it past the refrigerant hose where applicable **(see illustrations)**.
12 Refit the mounting loosely, then check that there is a clearance of at least 6 mm between the upper bracket and the wing mounting – providing the adjustment nut (fitted over the stud with the square end fitting) has not been disturbed, it is unlikely to have changed. If necessary, loosen the adjustment nut slightly, and push the engine as required until the clearance is correct. Tighten the adjustment nut to the specified torque on completion.
13 The remainder of refitting is a reversal of removal. Tighten the mounting bolts, then the nuts, to the specified torque. Also refit the earth strap in front of the mounting, and (where removed) the refrigerant hose mounting bracket bolt.

Left-hand mounting

14 Support the weight of the transmission from below. Use a large piece of wood between the jack head and the transmission, to spread the load, and just take the weight

17.17 Unbolt the radiator hose support bracket from the transmission bracket

17.18 Unbolt the earth strap in front of the left-hand mounting

17.19 Unscrew the mounting through-bolt

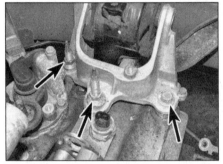

17.20a To remove the mounting bracket, undo the two nuts and single bolt . . .

17.20b . . . then lift the mounting off

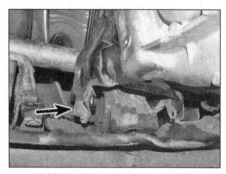

17.25 Unscrew the rear mounting through-bolt

of the engine. **Note:** *If the front or rear mountings are also to be removed, support the transmission so as not to impede access to the other mountings.*

15 Remove the air cleaner as described in Chapter 4A.

16 Remove the battery and battery tray as described in Chapter 5A.

17 Lift out the radiator top hose from the support bracket which is bolted to the transmission bracket. Unbolt the hose bracket and withdraw it **(see illustration)**.

18 Unbolt the earth strap in front of the mounting, and move it clear **(see illustration)**.

19 Unscrew and remove the mounting through-bolt **(see illustration)**. On automatic transmission models, lower the transmission slightly on the jack, to separate the mounting (on manual transmission models, the front mounting will prevent the unit from moving far).

20 To remove the transmission bracket, unscrew the two mounting nuts and single bolt on top of the transmission **(see illustrations)**. If required, the other part of the mounting can be unbolted from the inner wing/chassis leg.

21 Refitting is a reversal of removal. Tighten the bracket nuts/bolt, then the through-bolt, to their specified torques. Also refit the earth strap in front of the mounting.

Rear mounting

22 To remove the engine rear mounting, apply the handbrake, then jack up the front of the car and support it on axle stands (see *Jacking and vehicle support*).

23 Removing the rear mounting will only allow the engine to move on its remaining mountings, so providing they are in sound condition, removing the rear mounting will not leave the engine dangerously unsupported.

24 Where necessary to improve access, remove the clip and take off the rear undershield.

25 To separate the mounting, unscrew and remove the through-bolt **(see illustration)**.

26 The subframe bracket has two bolts from above and one from below. Three further bolts secure the rear bracket to the transmission **(see illustrations)**.

27 Refitting is a reversal of removal. Tighten the bolts to the specified torque.

Front mounting (manual transmission models only)

28 To remove the transmission front mounting, apply the handbrake, then jack up the front of the car and support it on axle stands (see *Jacking and vehicle support*).

29 Removing the front mounting will only allow the engine to move on its remaining mountings, so providing they are in sound

17.26a The mounting's subframe bracket has two bolts from above . . .

17.26b . . . and one from below

17.26c The mounting's rear bracket has three bolts to the transmission

17.31 Unscrew the front mounting through-bolt . . .

17.32a . . . then unscrew the two body bolts from below . . .

17.32b . . . and remove the mounting

17.33a If required, the front mounting inner bracket's three bolts can be unscrewed . . .

17.33b . . . and the bracket removed

condition, removing the front mounting will not leave the engine dangerously unsupported.

30 Unbolt and remove the engine undertray.

31 Separate the mounting by unscrewing the through-bolt at the front **(see illustration)**.

32 Unbolt the outer bracket by removing the two bolts from below, securing it to the inner wing **(see illustrations)**.

33 Now the inner bracket can be unbolted from the transmission (three bolts) and removed if required **(see illustrations)**.

34 Refitting is a reversal of removal. Tighten the bracket bolts to the specified torque, and tighten the through-bolt securely.

Chapter 2 Part B:
Engine removal and overhaul procedures

Contents

Degrees of difficulty

Easy, suitable for novice with little experience ⚒	Fairly easy, suitable for beginner with some experience ⚒	Fairly difficult, suitable for competent DIY mechanic ⚒	Difficult, suitable for experienced DIY mechanic ⚒	Very difficult, suitable for expert DIY or professional ⚒

Specifications

Engine overhaul data and torque wrench settings

Refer to Specifications in Chapter 2A.

1 General information

Included in this part of Chapter 2 are the general overhaul procedures for the cylinder head, cylinder block/crankcase and internal engine components.

The information ranges from advice concerning preparation for an overhaul and the purchase of parts, to detailed step-by-step procedures covering removal, inspection, renovation and refitting of internal engine parts.

The following Sections have been compiled based on the assumption that the engine has been removed from the car. For information concerning in-car engine repair, as well as the removal and refitting of the external components necessary for the overhaul, refer to Part A, and to Section 5 of this Part.

2 Engine overhaul – general information

It is not always easy to determine when, or if, an engine should be completely overhauled, as a number of factors must be considered.

High mileage is not necessarily an indication that an overhaul is needed, while low mileage does not preclude the need for an overhaul.

Frequency of servicing is probably the most important consideration. An engine which has had regular and frequent oil and filter changes, as well as other required maintenance, will most likely give many thousands of miles of reliable service. Conversely, a neglected engine may require an overhaul very early in its life.

Excessive oil consumption is an indication that piston rings, valve stem oil seals and/or valves and valve guides are in need of attention. Make sure that oil leaks are not responsible before deciding that the rings and/or guides are to blame. Perform a cylinder compression check to determine the extent of the work required.

Check the oil pressure with a gauge fitted in place of the oil pressure switch, and compare it with the value given in the Specifications. If it is extremely low, the main and big-end bearings and/or the oil pump are probably worn out.

Loss of power, rough running, knocking or metallic engine noises, excessive valve gear noise and high fuel consumption may also point to the need for an overhaul, especially if they are all present at the same time. If a complete tune-up does not remedy the situation, major mechanical work is the only solution.

An engine overhaul involves restoring the internal parts to the specifications of a new engine. During an overhaul, the pistons and rings are renewed, and the cylinder bores are reconditioned. New main bearings and connecting rod (big-end) bearings are generally fitted, and if necessary, the crankshaft may be reground to restore the journals. The valves are also serviced as well, since they are usually in less-than-perfect condition at this point. While the engine is being overhauled, other components, such as the starter and alternator, can be overhauled as well. The end result should be a like-new engine that will give many trouble-free miles. **Note:** *Critical cooling system components such as the hoses, auxiliary drivebelt, thermostat and water pump MUST be renewed when an engine is overhauled. The radiator should be checked carefully, to ensure that it is not clogged or leaking. Also, it is a good idea to renew the oil pump whenever the engine is overhauled.*

Before beginning the engine overhaul, read through the entire procedure to familiarise yourself with the scope and requirements of the job. Overhauling an engine is not difficult if you follow all of the instructions carefully, have the necessary tools and equipment, and pay close attention to all specifications; however, it can be time-consuming. Plan on the car being tied up for a minimum of two weeks, especially if parts must be taken to an engineering works for repair or reconditioning. Check on the availability of parts, and make sure that any necessary special tools and equipment are obtained in advance. Most work can be done with typical hand tools, although a number of precision measuring tools are required for inspecting parts to determine if they must be renewed. Often the engineering works will handle the inspection of parts, and offer advice concerning reconditioning and renewal. **Note:** *Always wait until the engine has been completely dismantled, and all components, especially the engine block, have been inspected before deciding what service and repair operations must be performed by an engineering works. Since the condition of the block will be the major factor to consider when determining whether to overhaul the original engine or buy a reconditioned unit, do not purchase parts or have overhaul work done on other components until the block has been thoroughly inspected.* As a general rule, time is the primary cost of an overhaul, so it does not pay to fit worn or sub-standard parts.

As a final note, to ensure maximum life and minimum trouble from a reconditioned engine, everything must be assembled with care, and in a spotlessly-clean environment.

Engine overhaul

The home mechanic is faced with a number of options when performing an engine overhaul. The decision to renew the engine block, piston/connecting rod assemblies and crankshaft depends on a number of factors, with the number one consideration being the condition of the block. Other considerations are cost, access to engineering workshop facilities, parts availability, time required to complete the project and the extent of prior mechanical experience.

Give careful thought to which alternative is best for you and discuss the situation with local automotive engineering workshops, automotive parts dealers and experienced reconditioners before ordering or purchasing renewal parts.

Some of the rebuilding alternatives include:

Individual parts

If the inspection procedures reveal the engine block and most engine components are in re-usable condition, purchasing individual parts may be the most economical alternative. The block, crankshaft and piston/connecting rod assemblies should all be inspected carefully. Even if the block shows little wear, the cylinder bores should be surface-honed.

4.6 Disconnect the EVAP hose from the rigid pipe behind the throttle body

Short block

A short block consists of an engine block with a crankshaft and piston/connecting rod assemblies already refitted. All new bearings are incorporated, and all clearances will be correct. The existing camshaft, valvetrain components, cylinder head and external parts can be bolted to the short block with little or no engineering work necessary.

Long block

A long block consists of a short block plus an oil pump, sump, cylinder head, cylinder head cover, camshaft and valvetrain components, timing sprockets and chain. All components are installed, with new bearings, seals and gaskets incorporated throughout. The refitting of manifolds and external parts is all that's necessary.

3 Engine removal – methods and precautions

If you have decided that an engine must be removed for overhaul or major repair work, several preliminary steps should be taken.

Locating a suitable place to work is extremely important. Adequate work space, along with storage space for the car, will be needed. If a garage is not available, at the very least a flat, level, clean work surface is required.

Cleaning the engine compartment and engine before beginning the removal procedure will help keep tools clean and organised.

The engine is normally removed as a unit with the transmission – the transmission can be removed on its own first, but this hardly offers any benefits if the engine must also be removed. The car's body should be raised and supported securely, sufficiently high that the subframe can be removed, then the engine/transmission is unbolted as a single unit and lowered to the ground; the engine/transmission can then be withdrawn from under the car and separated. An engine hoist, crane or A-frame is ideal for supporting the engine and lowering it out, but the job can also be accomplished using an engine support bar, mounted across the engine bay on the inner wing channels. Supporting the engine/transmission from below should be considered a last resort. Make sure the equipment is rated in excess of the combined weight of the engine and transmission. Safety is of primary importance, considering the potential hazards involved in removing the engine/transmission from the car.

If the engine is being removed by a novice, an assistant should be available. Advice and aid from someone more experienced would also be helpful. There are many instances when one person cannot simultaneously perform all of the operations required when removing the engine from the car.

Plan the operation ahead of time. Arrange for, or obtain, all of the tools and equipment you will need, prior to beginning the job.

Some of the equipment necessary to perform engine removal and installation safely and with relative ease are (in addition to an engine hoist) a heavy-duty trolley jack, complete sets of spanners and sockets as described at the end of this manual, wooden blocks, and plenty of rags and cleaning solvent for mopping-up spilled oil, coolant and fuel. If the hoist must be hired, make sure that you arrange for it in advance, and perform all of the operations possible without it beforehand. This will save you money and time.

Plan for the car to be out of use for quite a while. An engineering works will be required to perform some of the work which the do-it-yourselfer cannot accomplish without special equipment. These places often have a busy schedule, so it would be a good idea to consult them before removing the engine, in order to accurately estimate the amount of time required to rebuild or repair components that may need work.

Always be extremely careful when removing and refitting the engine. Serious injury can result from careless actions. Plan ahead, take your time, and you will find that a job of this nature, although major, can be accomplished successfully.

4 Engine – removal, separation and refitting

1 Open the bonnet, and support it in the fully-open position by using the lower support hole.
2 Depressurise the fuel system with reference to Chapter 4A.
3 Remove the air cleaner as described in Chapter 4A.
4 Remove the battery and its tray as described in Chapter 5A.
5 Disconnect the accelerator cable, referring to Chapter 4A if necessary.
6 Release the hose clip, and disconnect the EVAP hose from the rigid pipe at the rear of the throttle body **(see illustration)**.
7 Similarly, disconnect the brake servo hose from the rear of the inlet manifold, nearest the timing chain end of the engine **(see illustration)**.

4.7 Disconnect the brake servo vacuum hose from the inlet manifold

4.8a Pull out each gearchange cable's split pin . . .

4.8b . . . take off the washers . . .

4.8c . . . and lift off the cable end fitting

4.8d Unscrew the three cable support bracket bolts . . .

4.8e . . . noting that one of them has a wiring harness bracket attached . . .

4.8f . . . and remove the bracket with cables

8 On manual transmission models, disconnect the shift and selector cables from their levers on the transmission – each is secured by a split pin, and there are two washers. Unhook the cables, then unscrew the three bolts securing the cable support bracket to the transmission (note that one bolt has a wiring harness attached), and lift it clear, taking care not to bend the cables (**see illustrations**).

9 Also on manual transmission models, trace the fluid pipe back from the slave cylinder to the fluid hose union. Remove the single bolt from the pipe/union support bracket, then release the pipe from the clip at the front of the transmission. Remove the two slave cylinder bolts, and move the slave cylinder and pipe clear (**see illustrations**).

Caution: Be careful not to bend or kink the clutch hydraulic pipe, and don't depress the clutch pedal while the slave cylinder is removed.

10 On automatic transmission models, the selector cable is also secured by a split pin, and there are two washers. Unhook the cable, then unscrew the two bolts securing the cable support bracket to the transmission. Lift the bracket clear, disconnecting the wiring harness from it, and taking care not to bend the cables.

11 Loosen the front wheel nuts, then jack up the front of the car, and support it on axle stands (see *Jacking and vehicle support*). Remove the front wheels.

12 On models with air conditioning, remove the auxiliary drivebelt as described in

Chapter 1. Disconnect the compressor wiring plug. Remove the four bolts securing the compressor to the front of the sump – move the compressor clear, and tie it up using

4.9a Remove the pipe/union support bracket bolt . . .

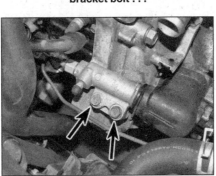

4.9c Remove the slave cylinder mounting bolts . . .

wire or cable-ties, without disconnecting the refrigerant hoses (**see illustrations**).

13 Drain the cooling system as described in Chapter 1.

4.9b . . . then release the clutch pipe from the clip

4.9d . . . and move the slave cylinder clear

4.12a Disconnect the air conditioning compressor wiring plug

4.12b Remove the four mounting bolts . . .

4.12c . . . then move the compressor forwards and tie it up

4.20a Disconnect the reversing light switch

4.20b Unclip the wiring harness from the transmission

4.21 Disconnect the two radiator hoses from the thermostat housing

14 Drain the transmission fluid as described in Chapter 1 – if this is not done, be prepared for fluid spillage when the driveshafts are removed.

15 If the engine is being dismantled, drain the engine oil with reference to Chapter 1.

16 Remove the catalytic converter as described in Chapter 4A.

17 Disconnect the drop links from the anti-roll bar, referring to Chapter 10 if necessary.

18 Remove both driveshafts as described in Chapter 8.

19 On automatic transmission models, release the hose clips and disconnect the fluid cooler hoses from the transmission. Plug or tape over the open connections, to prevent dirt entry.

20 Work around the transmission, disconnecting the various wiring plugs, unclipping the wiring harness and unbolting the wiring support brackets, as necessary (see illustrations). There will be considerably more plugs/wiring on the automatic transmission.

21 Release the hose clips and disconnect the radiator hoses from the thermostat housing. Similarly, disconnect the two smaller hoses at the rear of the housing, and the remaining heater hose from the back of the head – label the hoses if necessary, to ensure correct refitting (see illustration).

22 Just behind the front subframe, remove the clip each side securing the plastic undershields (see illustrations).

23 Referring to Chapter 10 if necessary, unbolt and remove the three mounting brackets securing the steering gear to the subframe (each small bracket has two bolts) (see illustration). Use wire or cable-ties to

4.22a Prise out the clip at the front . . .

4.22b . . . and remove the two small undershields behind the subframe

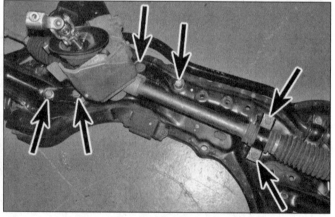

4.23 Steering gear-to-subframe bracket bolts (subframe removed)

4.26a Remove the front . . .

4.26b . . . and rear subframe bolts

support the steering gear from a convenient point on the bulkhead, for when the subframe is lowered out.

24 On automatic transmission models, if the transmission is to be separated from the engine, it is easier if the driveplate-to-flywheel bolts are removed now. Under the car, at the transmission-to-engine joint, remove the three bolts and take off the small cover plate. There are six driveplate-to-flywheel bolts to remove – one should be visible, but the engine will have to be turned (use the crankshaft pulley bolt) to access all six.

25 Referring to Chapter 2A if necessary, unbolt the front (manual transmission models only) and rear engine mountings. Provided the left- and right-hand mountings have not been disturbed, this will only result in increased movement of the engine.

26 With the aid of an assistant (or a pair of carefully-positioned trolley jacks), support the front subframe from below, then progressively remove the four subframe bolts **(see illustrations)**. Lower out the subframe, and withdraw it from under the car. Note that four new subframe bolts will be needed for refitting.

27 Make a final check round the engine and transmission, to make sure nothing (apart from the left- and right-hand mountings) remains attached or in the way which will prevent it from being lowered out. Also make sure there is enough room under the front of the car for the engine/transmission to be lowered out and withdrawn.

> **HAYNES HiNT**
> *Lowering the engine/transmission onto a large board, some strong card, or even an old piece of carpet, will not only protect it from damage, but will make it easier to drag out from under the car.*

28 Securely attach the engine/transmission unit to a suitable engine crane or hoist, and

raise it so that the weight is just taken off the two remaining engine mountings. It is helpful at this stage to have an assistant available, either to work the crane or to guide the engine out.

29 With the engine securely supported, where applicable, unbolt the earth strap in front of the left-hand (transmission) mounting, and move it clear. Unscrew and remove the mounting through-bolt, then lower the engine/transmission slightly, to separate the mounting. Unscrew the two mounting nuts and single bolt on top of the transmission, and take off the mounting bracket.

30 Unbolt the earth strap in front of the right-hand mounting, and move it clear **(see illustration)**. On models with air conditioning, one of the refrigerant hoses passes close to the right-hand mounting, and is secured to the inner wing by a support bracket. It may be useful to remove the hose support bracket bolt, to give some movement in the hose.

31 Loosen the bolts securing the right-hand mounting to the inner wing – three bolts on manual transmission models, two bolts on those with automatic transmission.

32 The mounting upper bracket is secured to the engine by two nuts – one on top, and the other removed from below. Remove the two nuts, then unscrew the mounting-to-wing bolts, and lift out the mounting assembly,

manoeuvring it past the refrigerant hose where applicable.

33 With the help of an assistant, carefully lower the assembly from the engine compartment, making sure it clears the surrounding components and bodywork **(see illustration)**. Be prepared to steady the engine when it touches down, to stop it toppling over. Withdraw the assembly from under the car, and remove it to wherever it will be worked on.

Separation

34 Remove the starter motor as described in Chapter 5A.

Manual transmission models

35 Progressively unscrew and remove the transmission-to-engine bolts.

36 With the help of an assistant, withdraw the transmission directly from the engine, making sure that its weight is not allowed to bear on the clutch friction disc.

Automatic transmission models

37 Progressively unscrew and remove the transmission-to-engine bolts.

38 The driveplate-to-flywheel bolts should have been removed at this stage – if not, refer to paragraph 23. Note that, as the bolts are accessed through a small hole at the base of the transmission, and the engine must be

4.30 Unbolt the earth strap at the front of the head

4.33 Lowering out the engine/transmission

4.40a Prise out the large grommet at the left rear corner of the engine bay . . .

4.40b . . . and start to feed through the wiring harness

4.40c With the wiring plugs inside the car disconnected, the harness comes right through

turned to bring the bolts into view, this will not be easy with the engine and transmission on the floor.

39 With the help of an assistant, withdraw the transmission directly from the engine. Make an alignment mark between the driveplate and flywheel, to make refitting easier, then slide off the flywheel, noting which way round it fits, and store it carefully.

Refitting

40 Removing the engine as described previously will leave behind the engine wiring loom, which at some point has to be routed around the engine, and reconnected. Owing to the lack of access around the Jazz engine once in-car, this is a daunting task in itself. However, we found that the engine wiring harness can be traced to a number of plugs inside the car, then disconnected and fed back into the engine bay through a bulkhead grommet for removal **(see illustrations)**. The wiring harness can then be refitted to the engine prior to the engine itself being refitted, making the job much easier.

41 Refitting the engine is a reversal of removal, noting the following additional points:

a) *Make sure that all mating faces are clean, and use new gaskets where necessary.*

b) *Tighten all nuts and bolts to the specified torque setting, where given.*

c) *Apply a smear of high melting-point grease to the splines of the transmission input shaft. Do not apply too much, otherwise (on manual transmission models) there is the possibility of the grease contaminating the clutch friction disc.*

d) *Fit the transmission bracket to the engine right-hand mounting, rather than to the transmission, before lifting the engine into place. This is preferable, as it avoids lining up the bracket and the central part of the mounting as the engine is being raised.*

e) *Refer to Chapter 10 when refitting the subframe – new subframe bolts must be used. Also, ensure that the appropriate new nuts and locking/split pins are used when reconnecting the steering/ suspension components.*

f) *Refer to Chapter 2A when refitting the engine right-hand mounting.*

g) *On manual transmission models, check the operation of the clutch, and bleed the system if necessary, as described in Chapter 6. Honda state that new split pins should be used when refitting the gearchange cables.*

h) *Refit the driveshafts as described in Chapter 8.*

i) *Replenish the transmission fluid, and check the level with reference to Chapter 1.*

j) *Refill the cooling system and engine oil as described in Chapter 1.*

k) *Where the accelerator cable was disconnected, reconnect and adjust it as described in Chapter 4A.*

5 Engine overhaul – dismantling sequence

1 It is much easier to dismantle and work on the engine if it is mounted on a portable engine stand. These stands can often be hired from a tool hire shop. Before the engine is mounted on a stand, the flywheel/driveplate should be removed from the engine, so that the engine stand bolts can be tightened into the end of the cylinder block.

2 If a stand is not available, it is possible to dismantle the engine with it blocked up on a sturdy workbench or on the floor. Be extra careful not to tip or drop the engine when working without a stand.

3 If you're going to obtain a reconditioned ('recon') engine, all external components must be removed first, to be transferred to the new engine (just as they will if you are doing a complete engine overhaul yourself). **Note:** *When removing the external components from the engine, pay close attention to details that may be helpful or important during refitting. Note the fitted position of gaskets, seals, spacers, pins, washers, bolts and other small items. These external components include the following:*

a) *Alternator, water pump, air conditioning compressor, etc ('ancillaries').*

b) *Ignition coils and spark plugs.*

c) *Thermostat housing.*

d) *Fuel injection equipment.*

e) *Inlet and exhaust manifolds.*

f) *Oil filter.*

g) *Engine mountings and lifting brackets.*

h) *Coolant pipes and hoses.*

i) *Flywheel/driveplate.*

4 If you are obtaining a 'short' motor (which, when available, consists of the engine cylinder block, crankshaft, pistons and connecting rods all assembled), then the cylinder head, sump, and oil pump will have to be removed also.

5 If you are planning a complete overhaul, the engine can be disassembled and the internal components removed in the following order:

a) *Engine external components (including inlet and exhaust manifolds).*

b) *Timing sprockets and chain.*

c) *Cylinder head.*

d) *Flywheel/driveplate.*

e) *Sump.*

f) *Oil pump.*

g) *Main bearing cap bridge.*

h) *Crankshaft.*

i) *Pistons/connecting rods.*

6 Before beginning the disassembly and overhaul procedures, make sure that you have all of the correct tools necessary. Refer to the reference section at the end of this manual for further information.

6 Cylinder head – dismantling

Note: *New and reconditioned cylinder heads are available from the manufacturers and from engine overhaul specialists. Due to the fact that some specialist tools are required for the dismantling and inspection procedures, and new components may not be readily available, it may be more practical and economical for the home mechanic to purchase a reconditioned head rather than dismantle, inspect and recondition the original head.*

1 Remove the cylinder head as described in Part A of this Chapter.

2 If not already done, remove all external brackets and housings.

3 Again, if not already done, remove the rocker shaft and camshaft as described in Part A of this Chapter.

6.4 Compress the valve spring and remove the two collets

6.7 Pull off the valve stem oil seals with pliers

6.9 A labelled plastic bag can be used to store the valve components

4 Using a valve spring compressor, compress each valve spring in turn until the split collets can be removed; compressors are now widely available from most good motor accessory shops **(see illustration)**. Release the compressor, and lift off the spring upper seat and spring.

5 If, when the valve spring compressor is screwed down, the spring upper seat refuses to free and expose the split collets, gently tap the top of the tool, directly over the upper seat, with a light hammer. This will free the seat.

6 Withdraw the valve through the combustion chamber. If it binds in the guide (won't pull through), push it back in, and de-burr the area around the collet groove with a fine file; take care not to mark the tappet bores.

7 Pull the valve stem seals from the valve guides using a pair of pliers **(see illustration)**. As the seals are removed, note whether they are of different colours for the inlet and exhaust valves – compare with the new parts, and note this for refitting.

8 Remove the valve spring lower seats, and store them with their respective springs.

9 It is essential that the valves are kept together with their collets, spring seats and springs, and in their correct sequence (unless they are so badly worn that they are to be renewed). If they are going to be kept and used again, place them in a labelled polythene bag or similar small container **(see illustration)**. Note that No 1 valve is nearest to the timing chain end of the engine.

7 Cylinder head and valves – cleaning, inspection and renovation

1 Thorough cleaning of the cylinder head and valve components, followed by a detailed inspection, will enable you to decide how much valve service work must be carried out during the engine overhaul.

Cleaning

2 Scrape away all traces of old gasket material and sealing compound from the cylinder head. Take care not to damage the cylinder head surfaces.

3 Scrape away the carbon from the combustion chambers and ports, then wash the cylinder head thoroughly with paraffin or a suitable solvent.

4 Scrape off any heavy carbon deposits that may have formed on the valves, then use a power-operated wire brush to remove deposits from the valve heads and stems.

5 If the head is extremely dirty, it should be steam cleaned. On completion, make sure that all oil holes and oil galleries are cleaned.

Inspection and renovation

Note: *Be sure to perform all the following inspection procedures before concluding that the services of an engine overhaul specialist are required. Make a list of all items that require attention.*

Cylinder head

6 Inspect the head very carefully for cracks, evidence of coolant leakage and other damage. If cracks are found, a new cylinder head should be obtained.

7 Use a straight-edge and feeler blade to check that the cylinder head surface is not distorted **(see illustration)**. If the specified distortion limit is exceeded, machining of the gasket face is permitted up to the specified resurface limit, providing the cylinder head height is not reduced below the minimum amount.

8 Examine the valve seats in each of the combustion chambers. If they are severely pitted, cracked or burned, then they will need to be renewed or recut by an engine overhaul specialist. If they are only slightly pitted, this can be removed by grinding the valve heads and seats together with coarse, then fine, grinding paste as described below.

9 If the valve guides are worn, indicated by a side-to-side motion of the valve in the guide, new guides must be fitted. If necessary, insert a new valve in the guides to determine if the wear is on the guide or valve. If new guides are to be fitted, the valves must be renewed as a matter of course. Valve guides may be renewed using a press and a suitable mandrel, however, the work is best carried out by an engine overhaul specialist, since if it is not done skilfully, there is a risk of damaging the cylinder head.

10 Check the camshaft bores in the cylinder head for wear. If excessive wear is evident, the cylinder head must be renewed.

11 Examine the camshaft bearing surfaces in the cylinder head as described in Chapter 2A.

Valves

12 Examine the head of each valve for pitting, burning, cracks and general wear, and check the valve stem for scoring and wear ridges. Rotate the valve, and check for any obvious indication that it is bent. Look for pits and excessive wear on the end of each valve stem.

13 If the valve appears satisfactory at this stage, measure the valve stem diameter at several points using a micrometer. Any significant difference in the readings obtained indicates wear of the valve stem. Should any of these conditions be apparent, the valve(s) must be renewed.

14 If the valves are in satisfactory condition, or if new valves are being fitted, they should be ground (lapped) into their respective seats to ensure a smooth gas-tight seal.

15 Valve grinding is carried out as follows. Place the cylinder head upside-down on a bench, with a block of wood at each end to give clearance for the valve stems. Take care to protect the camshaft bearing surfaces.

16 Smear a trace of coarse carborundum paste on the seat face, and press a suction grinding tool onto the valve head. With a semi-rotary action, grind the valve head to its seat, lifting the valve occasionally

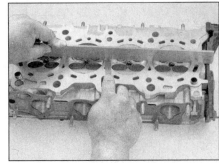

7.7 Check the head for warpage by trying to slip a feeler blade under the straight-edge

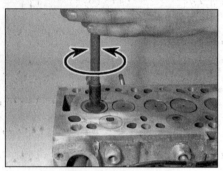

7.16 Grind-in the valve with a reciprocating rotary motion

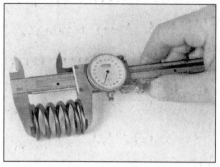

7.19 Measure the free length of each valve spring

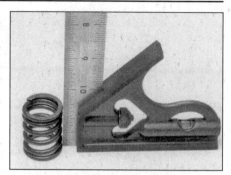

7.20 Check each valve spring for squareness

to redistribute the grinding paste **(see illustration)**.

17 When a dull-matt even surface is produced on both the valve seat and the valve, wipe off the paste and repeat the process with fine carborundum paste. A light spring placed under the valve head will greatly ease this operation.

18 When a smooth unbroken ring of light grey matt finish is produced on both the valve and seat, the grinding operation is complete. Be sure to remove all traces of grinding paste, using paraffin or a suitable solvent, before reassembly of the cylinder head.

Valve components

19 Examine the valve springs for signs of damage and discoloration, and also measure their free length using vernier calipers or a steel rule, or by comparing the existing spring with a new component **(see illustration)**.

20 Stand each spring on a flat surface, and check it for squareness **(see illustration)**. If any of the springs are damaged, distorted or have lost their tension, obtain a complete new set of springs. It is normal to renew the springs as a matter of course during a major overhaul.

Valve stem oil seals

21 The valve stem oil seals should be renewed as a matter of course – new seals should be available with the cylinder head gasket, manifold gaskets, etc, as part of a cylinder head 'set' from parts suppliers.

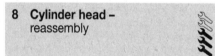

8 Cylinder head – reassembly

1 Fit the valve spring lower seats into their original positions **(see illustration)**.

2 Genuine Honda valve stem oil seals have a colour-coded band – black for the exhaust valves, and white for the inlets. Lubricate the oil seals with clean engine oil, then fit them by pushing into position in the cylinder head using a suitable socket **(see illustrations)**. Ensure that the seals are fully engaged with the valve guide.

3 Lubricate the valve stems, then insert the valves into their original locations **(see illustrations)**. If new valves are being fitted, insert them into the locations to which they have been ground. Take care not to damage the valve stem oil seal as each valve is fitted.

4 Fit the valve springs and upper seats in their original locations, where applicable **(see illustrations)**.

5 Compress the valve spring and locate the split collets in the recess in the valve stem

8.1 Fitting the valve spring lower seat

8.2a The valve stem oil seals have a colour-coded band

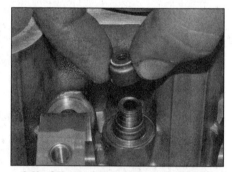

8.2b Offer the valve stem oil seals into position . . .

8.2c . . . and press them home using a suitable deep socket

8.3a Lubricate the valves and the stem seals . . .

8.3b . . . then insert the valve into the head

(see illustrations). Release the compressor, then repeat the procedure on the remaining valves.

 HAYNES HiNT *Applying a little grease to the collets will help to 'stick' them in place until the compressor is released.*

6 With all the valves installed, place the cylinder head flat on the bench and, using a hammer and interposed block of wood, tap the end of each valve stem to settle the components.

7 The previously-removed components can now be refitted with reference to Section 6.

9 Timing chain components – removal and refitting

Refer to Part A, Section 5.

10 Piston/connecting rod assemblies – removal

1 Remove the cylinder head, sump, and oil pump, with reference to Chapter 2A. Place the block on its side on a clean surface (or preferably on an engine stand) so that it can be worked on.

2 Working in the **reverse** order of the tightening sequence shown in Section 18, loosen the ten main bearing cap bridge bolts a quarter of a turn at a time, until all are loose and can be removed.

3 Lift off the main bearing cap bridge and recover the lower bearing shells – store the shells in fitted order, or tape them to their respective locations on the bearing cap bridge.

4 Rotate the crankshaft so that No 1 big-end cap (timing end of the engine) is at the lowest point of its travel. The big-end cap and rod should be numbered with a stamp across the cap and rod, indicating their fitted position (No 1 is at the timing chain end). If no marks are visible, use a marker pen on the cap and rod to identify the cylinder they operate in. **Note:** *On our project car's engine, all the big-end caps/rods were (confusingly) marked with a 3.*

5 Unscrew and remove the big-end bearing cap bolts, and withdraw the cap complete with shell bearing from the connecting rod. Make sure that the shell remains in the cap, and if necessary identify it for position. Also recover the two dowels from each rod/cap if they are loose. Discard the bolts – we recommend that they should not be re-used.

6 If only the bearing shells are being attended to, push the connecting rod up and off the crankpin, and remove the upper bearing shell. Keep the bearing shells and cap together in their correct sequence if they are to be refitted.

8.4a Fit the valve spring . . .

8.4b . . . and spring upper seat

8.5a Compress the valve spring . . .

8.5b . . . and refit the collets using a small screwdriver

7 If the piston is being removed, push the connecting rod up and remove the piston and rod from the top of the bore. Note that if there is a pronounced wear ridge at the top of the bore, there is a risk of damaging the piston as the rings foul the ridge. However, it is reasonable to assume that a rebore and new pistons will be required in any case if the ridge is so pronounced.

8 Repeat the procedure for the remaining piston/connecting rod assemblies. Ensure that the caps and rods are marked before removal, as described previously, and keep all components in order.

11 Crankshaft – removal

1 Carry out the operations described in Section 10, paragraphs 1 to 6. In addition, if not already done, remove the flywheel/driveplate, referring to Chapter 2A if necessary.

2 The pistons/connecting rods must be free of the crankshaft journals, however it is not essential to remove them completely from the cylinder block.

3 Before the crankshaft is removed, check the endfloat. Mount a dial gauge with the probe in line with the crankshaft and just touching the crankshaft.

4 Push the crankshaft fully away from the gauge, and zero it. Next, lever the crankshaft towards the gauge as far as possible, and check the reading obtained.

The distance that the crankshaft moved is its endfloat; if it is greater than specified, new thrustwashers will be required (see Chapter 2A Specifications).

5 If no dial gauge is available, feeler blades can be used. Gently lever or push the crank- shaft in one direction, then insert feeler blades between the crankshaft web and the No 4 upper main bearing (with the thrustwashers) to determine the clearance **(see illustration)**.

6 Lift the crankshaft out from the crankcase, then extract the upper bearing shells, and the side thrustwashers from No 4 bearing. Keep them with their respective caps for correct repositioning if they are to be used again. Remove the crankshaft oil seal, and discard it – a new one should be used when refitting.

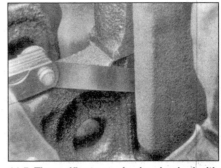
11.5 The endfloat can also be checked with a feeler blade at the thrustwasher journal

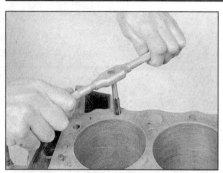

12.6 All bolt holes in the block should be cleaned and restored with a tap

12 Cylinder block/ crankcase and bores – cleaning and inspection

Cleaning

Caution: If cleaning the cylinder block with the crankshaft fitted, it is recommended that only the external surfaces are cleaned, as otherwise the internal oilways and channels may become contaminated, leading to premature wear of the crankshaft and main bearings.

1 For complete cleaning, remove all external components, such as the oil pressure switch, knock sensor and coolant drain bolt, noting their locations.

2 Scrape all traces of gasket or sealant from the cylinder block, taking care not to damage the head and sump mating faces.

3 If the block is extremely dirty, it should be steam-cleaned.

4 After the block has been steam-cleaned, clean all oil holes and oil galleries one more time. Flush all internal passages with warm water until the water runs clear, dry the block thoroughly and wipe all machined surfaces with a light rust-preventative oil. If you have access to compressed air, use it to speed up the drying process and to blow out all the oil holes and galleries.

 Warning: Wear eye protection when using compressed air.

5 If the block is not very dirty, you can do an adequate cleaning job with hot soapy water

and a stiff brush. Take plenty of time, and do a thorough job. Regardless of the cleaning method used, be sure to clean all oil holes and galleries very thoroughly, dry the block completely and coat all machined surfaces with light oil.

6 The threaded holes in the block must be clean to ensure accurate torque wrench readings during reassembly. Run the proper-size tap into each of the holes to remove rust, corrosion, thread sealant or sludge, and to restore damaged threads **(see illustration)**. If possible, use compressed air to clear the holes of debris produced by this operation. Now is a good time to clean the threads on the head bolts and the main bearing cap bolts as well.

7 If the engine is not going to be reassembled right away, cover it with a large plastic bag to keep it clean and prevent it rusting.

Inspection

8 Visually check the block for cracks, rust and corrosion. Look for stripped threads in the threaded holes. If there has been any history of internal water leakage, it may be worthwhile having an engine overhaul specialist check the block with special equipment. If defects are found, have the block repaired, if possible, or renewed.

9 Check the cylinder bores for scuffing and scoring. Normally, bore wear will be evident in the form of a wear ridge at the top of the bore. This ridge marks the limit of piston travel.

10 Measure the diameter of each cylinder at the top (just under the ridge area), centre and base of the cylinder bore, parallel to the crankshaft axis.

11 Next measure each cylinder's diameter at the same three locations across the crankshaft axis. If the difference between any of the measurements is greater than 0.20 mm, indicating that the cylinder is excessively out-of-round or tapered, then remedial action must be considered.

12 Repeat this procedure for the remaining cylinders, then measure the diameter of each piston at right-angles to the gudgeon pin axis, and compare the result with the information given in Chapter 2A Specifications. By comparing the piston diameters with the bore diameters, an idea can be obtained of the clearances.

13 If the cylinder walls are badly scuffed or scored, or if they are excessively out-of-round or tapered, have the cylinder block rebored (where possible) by an engine overhaul specialist. New pistons (oversize in the case of a rebore) will also be required.

14 If the cylinders are in reasonably good condition, then it may only be necessary to renew the piston rings.

15 If this is the case, the bores should be honed in order to allow the new rings to bed-in correctly and provide the best possible seal. The conventional type of hone has spring-loaded stones, and is used with a power drill. You will also need some paraffin or honing oil and rags. The hone should be moved up-and-down the cylinder to produce a crosshatch pattern, and plenty of honing oil should be used.

16 Ideally, the crosshatch lines should intersect at approximately a 60° angle. Do not take off more material than is necessary to produce the required finish. If new pistons are being fitted, the piston manufacturers may specify a finish with a different angle, so their instructions should be followed. Do not withdraw the hone from the cylinder while it is still being turned, but stop it first (keep the hone moving up-and-down the bore while it slows down).

17 After honing a cylinder, wipe out all traces of the honing oil. If equipment of this type is not available, or if you are not sure whether you are competent to undertake the task yourself, an engine overhaul specialist will carry out the work at a moderate cost.

18 Refit all external components and senders in their correct locations, as noted before removal.

13 Piston/connecting rod assemblies – inspection and reassembly

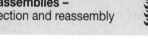

Inspection

1 Before the inspection process can begin, the piston/connecting rod assemblies must be cleaned, and the original piston rings removed from the pistons.

2 Carefully expand the old rings over the top of the pistons. The use of two or three old feeler blades will be helpful in preventing the rings dropping into empty grooves **(see illustration)**. Note that the oil control scraper ring is in three sections.

3 Scrape away all traces of carbon from the top of the piston. A hand-held wire brush or a piece of fine emery cloth can be used once the majority of the deposits have been scraped away.

4 Remove the carbon from the ring grooves in the piston by cleaning them using an old ring **(see illustrations)**. Break the ring in half to do this. Be very careful to remove only the carbon deposits; do not remove any metal, or scratch the sides of the ring grooves. Protect your fingers – piston rings are sharp.

13.2 Use a feeler blade when removing and refitting the piston rings

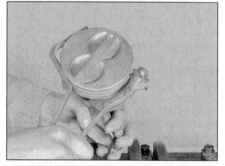

13.4a The piston ring grooves can be cleaned with a special tool, as shown here . . .

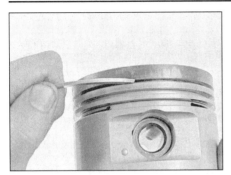

13.4b ... or a section of a broken ring

5 Once the deposits have been removed, clean the piston/connecting rod assembly with paraffin or a suitable solvent, and dry thoroughly. Make sure the oil return holes in the ring grooves are clear.

6 If the pistons and cylinder bores are not damaged or worn excessively, and if the cylinder block does not need to be rebored, the original pistons can be re-used. Normal piston wear appears as even vertical wear on the piston thrust surfaces, and slight looseness of the top ring in its groove. New piston rings, however, should always be used when the engine is reassembled.

7 Carefully inspect each piston for cracks around the skirt, at the gudgeon pin bosses, and at the piston ring lands (between the piston ring grooves).

8 Look for scoring and scuffing on the sides of the skirt, holes in the piston crown, and burned areas at the edge of the crown. If the skirt is scored or scuffed, the engine may have been suffering from overheating and/or abnormal combustion, which caused excessively-high operating temperatures. The cooling and lubricating systems should be checked thoroughly.

9 Scorch marks on the sides of the pistons show that blow-by has occurred and the rings are not sealing correctly. A hole in the piston crown is an indication that abnormal combustion (pre-ignition, knocking or detonation) has been occurring. If any of the above problems exist, the causes must be corrected, or the damage will occur again. Typically, the causes may include inlet air leaks, incorrect fuel/air mixture or incorrect ignition timing.

10 Corrosion of the piston, in the form of small pits, indicates that coolant is leaking into the combustion chamber and/or the crankcase. Again, the cause must be corrected, or the problem may persist in the rebuilt engine.

11 If new rings are being fitted to old pistons, measure the piston ring-to-groove clearance by placing a new piston ring in each ring groove and measuring the clearance with a feeler blade. Check the clearance at three or four places around each groove. If the new ring is excessively tight, the most likely cause is dirt remaining in the groove.

12 The gudgeon pin is an interference fit in the piston – a hydraulic press will be required if they are to be removed.

13 Before refitting the rings to the pistons, check their end gaps by inserting each of them in their cylinder bores. Use the piston to make sure that they are square. Using feeler blades, check that the gaps are within the tolerances given in the Specifications. Genuine rings are supplied pre-gapped; no attempt should be made to adjust the gaps by filing.

Reassembly

14 Install the new rings by fitting them over the top of the piston, starting with the oil control scraper ring sections. Use feeler blades in the same way as when removing the old rings. New rings generally have their

top surfaces identified, and must be fitted the correct way round. Note that the first and second compression rings have different sections – the first ring should be marked R1, and the second just R **(see illustration)**. Be careful when handling the compression rings; they will break if they are handled roughly or expanded too far.

15 With all the rings in position, space the ring gaps as shown **(see illustration)**.

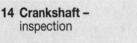

14 Crankshaft –
inspection

1 Clean the crankshaft and dry it with compressed air if available. Be sure to clean the oil holes with a cotton bud or similar probe.

⚠️ *Warning: Wear eye protection when using compressed air.*

2 Check the main and big-end bearing journals for uneven wear, scoring, pitting and cracking.

3 If the crankshaft has been reground, check for burrs around the crankshaft oil holes (the holes are usually chamfered, so burrs should not be a problem unless regrinding has been carried out carelessly). Remove any burrs with a fine file or scraper, and thoroughly clean the oil holes as described previously.

4 Using a micrometer, measure the diameter of the main bearing and connecting rod journals, and compare the results with the Specifications (Chapter 2A). By measuring the diameter at a number of points around each journal's circumference, you will be able to determine whether or not the journal is out-of-round. Take the measurement at each end of the journal, near the webs, to

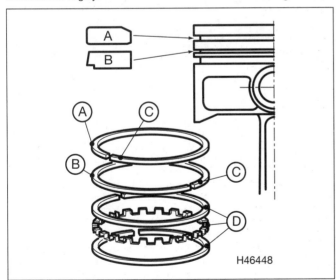

13.14 Piston ring fitting details

A First compression ring
B Second compression ring
C Maker's markings (R1 and R)
D Oil control rings and expander

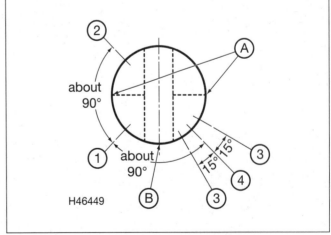

13.15 Piston ring end gap positioning

A Piston thrust surfaces (front/rear) – do not position ring gaps here
B Gudgeon pin axis – do not position ring gaps here

1 Top ring gap position
2 Second ring gap position
3 Oil ring gap positions
4 Oil ring spacer gap position

determine if the journal is tapered. If any of the measurements vary significantly, the crankshaft will have to be reground, and undersize bearings fitted – consult an engine rebuilding specialist for advice.

5 Check the oil seal contact surfaces at each end of the crankshaft for wear and damage. If an excessive groove is evident in the surface of the crankshaft, consult an engine specialist who will be able to advise whether a repair is possible or if a new crankshaft is necessary.

15 Main and big-end bearings – inspection

1 Even though the main and big-end bearings should be renewed during the engine overhaul, the old bearings should be retained for close examination, as they may reveal valuable information about the condition of the engine **(see illustration)**. The size of the bearing shells is stamped on the back metal, and this information should be given to the supplier of the new shells.

2 Bearing failure occurs because of lack of lubrication, the presence of dirt or other foreign particles, overloading the engine, and corrosion. Regardless of the cause of bearing failure, it must be corrected before the engine is reassembled, to prevent it from happening again.

3 When examining the bearings, remove them from the engine block, the main bearing cap bridge, the connecting rods and the rod caps, and lay them out on a clean surface in the same general position as their location in the engine. This will enable you to match any bearing problems with the corresponding crankshaft journal.

4 Dirt and other foreign particles get into the engine in a variety of ways. Dirt may be left in the engine during assembly, or it may pass through filters or the crankcase ventilation system. It may get into the oil, and from there into the bearings. Metal chips from machining operations and normal engine wear are often present. Abrasives are sometimes left in engine components after reconditioning, especially when parts are not thoroughly cleaned using the proper cleaning methods.

5 Whatever the source, these foreign objects often end up embedded in the soft bearing material, and are easily recognised. Large particles will not embed in the bearing, and will score or gouge the bearing and journal. The best prevention for this cause of bearing failure is to clean all parts thoroughly, and keep everything spotlessly-clean during engine assembly. Frequent and regular engine oil and filter changes are also recommended.

6 Lack of lubrication (or lubrication breakdown) has a number of interrelated causes. Excessive heat (which thins the oil), overloading (which squeezes the oil from the bearing face) and oil leakage (from excessive bearing clearances, worn oil pump or high

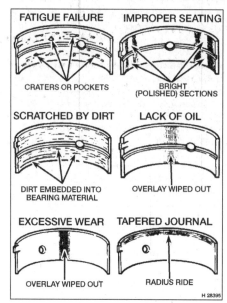

15.1 Typical bearing failures

engine speeds) all contribute to lubrication breakdown. Blocked oil passages, which usually are the result of misaligned oil holes in a bearing shell, will also oil-starve a bearing and destroy it. When lack of lubrication is the cause of bearing failure, the bearing material is wiped or extruded from the steel backing of the bearing. Temperatures may increase to the point where the steel backing turns blue from overheating.

7 Driving habits can have a definite effect on bearing life. Full-throttle, low-speed operation (labouring the engine) puts very high loads on bearings, which tends to squeeze out the oil film. These loads cause the bearings to flex, which produces fine cracks in the bearing face (fatigue failure). Eventually, the bearing material will loosen in pieces and tear away from the steel backing. Short-trip driving leads to corrosion of bearings, because insufficient engine heat is produced to drive off the condensed water and corrcsive gases. These products collect in the engine oil, forming acid and sludge. As the oil is carried to the engine bearings, the acid attacks and corrodes the bearing material.

8 Incorrect bearing installation during engine

17.3a The arrow on the piston crown should face the timing chain end

assembly will lead to bearing failure as well. Tight-fitting bearings leave insufficient bearing oil clearance, and will result in oil starvation. Dirt or foreign particles trapped behind a bearing shell result in high spots on the bearing which lead to failure.

9 *Do not* touch any shell's bearing surface with your fingers during reassembly; there is a risk of scratching the delicate surface, or of depositing particles of dirt on it.

10 As mentioned at the beginning of this Section, the bearing shells should be renewed as a matter of course during engine overhaul; to do otherwise is false economy.

16 Engine overhaul – reassembly sequence

1 Before reassembly begins, ensure that all new parts have been obtained and that all necessary tools are available. Read through the entire procedure to familiarise yourself with the work involved, and to ensure that all items necessary for reassembly of the engine are at hand. In addition to all normal tools and materials, flange sealant and thread-locking compound will be needed during engine reassembly. Do not use any kind of silicone-based sealant on any part of the fuel system or inlet manifold, and never use exhaust sealants upstream (on the engine side) of the catalytic converter.

2 In order to save time and avoid problems, engine reassembly can be carried out in the following order:

   a) Connecting rods/pistons.
   b) Crankshaft.
   c) Main bearing cap bridge.
   d) Cylinder head.
   e) Oil pump.
   f) Timing sprockets and chain.
   g) Sump.
   h) Flywheel/driveplate.
   i) Engine external components (including inlet and exhaust manifolds).

3 Ensure that everything is clean prior to reassembly. As mentioned previously, dirt and metal particles can quickly destroy bearings and result in major engine damage. Use clean engine oil to lubricate during reassembly.

17 Pistons/connecting rods – refitting

1 Clean the backs of the big-end bearing shells, and the recesses in the connecting rods and big-end caps. If new shells are being fitted, ensure that all traces of the protective grease are cleaned off using paraffin. Wipe the shells and connecting rods dry with a lint-free cloth.

2 Lubricate No 1 piston and piston rings, and check that the ring gaps are spaced as described in Section 13.

17.3b Fit a ring compressor, and insert the assembly

18.3 Fit the connecting rod bearing shells

18.4 Fit the upper main bearing shells

3 Fit a ring compressor to No 1 piston, then insert the piston and connecting rod into No 1 cylinder. Make sure that the arrow on the piston crown is facing the timing end of the engine. With No 1 crankpin at its lowest point, drive the piston carefully into the cylinder with the wooden handle of a hammer **(see illustrations)**.

4 Repeat the process and refit the remaining three piston/connecting rod assemblies.

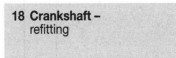

18 Crankshaft – refitting

Selection of new bearing shells

1 Have the crankshaft inspected and measured by a Honda dealer or engine reconditioning specialist. They will be able to carry out any regrinding/repairs, and supply suitable main and big-end bearing shells.

Refitting

2 It is assumed at this point that the cylinder block/crankcase and crankshaft have been cleaned and repaired or reconditioned as necessary. Position the engine on its side.

3 Fit the connecting rod bearing shells in place, making sure the shell's locating tab engages correctly **(see illustration)**.

4 Wipe clean the main bearing shell seats in the crankcase, and clean the backs of the bearing shells. Insert the respective upper shells (dry) into position in the crankcase. Note that the upper shells have grooves and oil holes in them (the lower shells are plain). The shell oil holes must align with the oil supply holes in the crankcase. Where the old main bearings are being refitted, ensure that they are located in their original positions. Make sure that the tab on each bearing shell fits into the notch in the block **(see illustration)**.

5 Place the crankshaft thrustwashers into

position in the crankcase, either side of No 4 bearing, so that their oil grooves are facing outwards (away from the web). Hold them in position with a little grease **(see illustrations)**.

6 Lubricate the main and big-end bearings with clean engine oil **(see illustrations)**.

7 Adjust the position of the connecting rods to allow the crankshaft to be fitted – for instance, by moving all the pistons close to the top of the bores.

8 Make sure the crankshaft journals are clean, then lay the crankshaft back in place in the block **(see illustration)**.

9 Guide each connecting rod onto the crankshaft. Fit the shells to the big-end caps, then lubricate them and fit them **(see illustrations)**. Note that each cap has two dowels to ensure correct positioning – refit the dowels if they were removed earlier.

10 Lightly oil the threads and heads of the

18.5a Apply grease to the back of the thrustwashers to help them 'stick' . . .

18.5b . . . then lay them in place either side of No 4 bearing

18.6a Lubricate the main . . .

18.6b . . . and big-end bearings with engine oil

18.8 Carefully lay the crankshaft into position

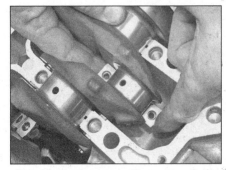

18.9a Guide the connecting rods onto the crankshaft

18.9b Fit the big-end shells to the caps . . .

18.9c . . . then apply engine oil . . .

18.9d . . . and fit them using the locating dowels

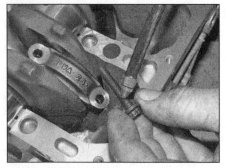

18.10a Lightly oil the new bolt threads . . .

18.10b . . . then fit and tighten them to the Stage 1 torque

18.11a Tighten the bolts through the Stage 2 angle, either using an angle gauge . . .

18.11b . . . or by paint-marking the bolt and cap

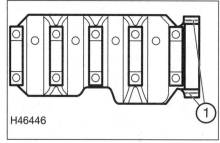

H46446

18.13a Apply sealant to the main bearing cap bridge before fitting

1 Bead of sealant, 1.5 mm diameter

18.13b Applying sealant to the oil seal end of the bridge

new bearing cap bolts, then tighten them to the specified Stage 1 torque **(see illustration)**.
11 Now tighten the bolts to the specified Stage 2 angle (90° is equivalent to a quarter-turn) **(see illustration)**.

12 Refit the remaining connecting rods and big-end caps, turning the crankshaft as little as possible.
13 Clean all traces of sealant from the main bearing cap bridge. Apply fresh RTV sealant

(Honda part number 08C70-K0234M, or equivalent) to the oil seal end of the bridge, as shown **(see illustrations)**. Once the sealant has been applied, the bridge should be fitted within 5 minutes.
14 Clean the bearing surfaces of the shells in the bearing cap bridge, then lubricate them with oil **(see illustration)**.
15 Fit the bearing cap bridge into position. Fit the new bolts, with their threads and heads lightly oiled. Working in sequence, tighten the bridge bolts to the Stage 1 setting **(see illustration)**.
16 With all the main bearing bolts tightened to the Stage 1 setting, go round again in the same sequence and tighten them further to the Stage 2 angle – it is recommended that an angle gauge is used here (these are not expensive, and are available from good car accessory shops or motor factors) **(see illustration)**. Once this is done, clean off any excess sealant.

18.14 Oil the bearing shells in the main bearing bridge

18.15a Fit the main bearing bridge into position . . .

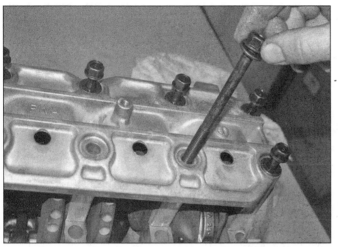

18.15b ... then oil and fit the new bolts

18.15c Main bearing cap bridge bolts tightening sequence

17 Referring to Chapter 2A if necessary, fit a new crankshaft oil seal.

18 Rotate the crankshaft a number of times by hand, to check for any obvious binding.

19 Engine –
initial start-up after overhaul

1 With the engine refitted in the car, double-check the engine oil and coolant levels (see *Weekly checks*). Make a final check that everything has been reconnected, and that there are no tools or rags left in the engine compartment.

2 Disable the ignition system by removing fuses 2 and 24 from the interior fusebox.

3 Similarly, disable the fuel injection system by removing the fuel pump relay (see Chapter 4A, Section 2).

4 Crank the engine on the starter motor until the oil pressure light goes out.

5 Refit the removed fuses and the relay.

6 Start the engine, noting that this may take a little longer than usual.

7 While the engine is idling, check for fuel,

18.15d Tighten the main bearing bolts to the Stage 1 torque

water and oil leaks. Do not be alarmed if there are some odd smells and smoke from parts getting hot and burning off oil deposits.

8 Keep the engine idling until hot water is felt circulating through the top hose, then switch it off.

9 After a few minutes, recheck the oil and coolant levels, and top-up as necessary (see *Weekly checks*).

10 If the engine management light has come

18.16 Tighten the bolts to the Stage 2 angle using an angle gauge

on (possibly during the procedures in paragraphs 2 and 3), refer to Chapter 4A, Section 10 for advice.

11 If new pistons, rings or crankshaft bearings have been fitted, the engine must be run-in for the first 500 miles. Do not operate the engine at full-throttle, nor allow it to labour in any gear during this period. It is recommended that the oil and filter be changed at the end of this period.

Notes

Chapter 3
Cooling, heating and air conditioning systems

Contents

Degrees of difficulty

Easy, suitable for novice with little experience	**Fairly easy,** suitable for beginner with some experience	**Fairly difficult,** suitable for competent DIY mechanic	**Difficult,** suitable for experienced DIY mechanic	**Very difficult,** suitable for expert DIY or professional

Specifications

General
Thermostat opening temperature.	80 to 84°C
Radiator cap relief valve opening pressure	14 to 18 psi

Torque wrench settings
	Nm	lbf ft
Air conditioning compressor mounting bolts....................	22	16
Coolant temperature sensor.................................	12	9
Engine block coolant drain bolt	78	58
Radiator fan switch.......................................	24	18
Radiator top bracket bolt	12	9
Thermostat housing bolts...................................	10	7
Water pump mounting bolts.................................	12	9
Water pump pulley bolts	14	10

1 General information and precautions

General information

The cooling system is of pressurised type, comprising a pump driven by the auxiliary drivebelt, an aluminium crossflow radiator, electric cooling fan, and a thermostat. The system functions as follows: cold coolant from the radiator passes through the hose to the water pump, where it is pumped around the cylinder block and head passages. After cooling the cylinder bores, combustion surfaces and valve seats, the coolant reaches the underside of the thermostat, which is initially closed. The coolant passes through the heater, and is returned via the cylinder block to the water pump.

When the coolant reaches a predetermined temperature, the thermostat opens and the coolant passes through to the radiator. As the coolant circulates through the radiator, it is cooled by the inrush of air when the car is in forward motion. Airflow is supplemented by the action of the electric cooling fan when necessary. Once the coolant has passed through the radiator, and has cooled, the cycle is repeated.

The electric cooling fan, mounted on the rear of the radiator, is controlled by a thermostatic switch in the thermostat housing. At a predetermined coolant temperature, the switch actuates the fan, via the engine management ECM. On models with air conditioning, a second fan is fitted on the rear of the condenser – this too is under ECM control.

The coolant temperature is signalled to the engine ECM, and to the temperature display on the instrument panel, by another sensor fitted on the back of the cylinder head.

An expansion tank is fitted to allow for the expansion of the coolant when hot. The expansion tank is connected to the top of the radiator.

Refer to Section 10 for information on the air conditioning system.

Precautions

 Warning: Do not attempt to remove the radiator filler cap, expansion tank cap, nor disturb any part of the cooling system, while the engine is hot; there is a high risk of scalding. If the filler cap(s) must be removed before the engine and radiator have fully cooled (even though this is not recommended) the pressure in the cooling system must first be relieved. Cover the cap with a thick layer of cloth, to avoid scalding, and slowly unscrew the filler cap until a hissing sound can be heard. When the hissing has stopped, indicating that the pressure has reduced, slowly unscrew the filler cap until it can be removed; if more hissing sounds are heard, wait until they have stopped before unscrewing the cap completely. At all times, keep well away from the filler cap opening.

 Warning: Do not allow antifreeze to come into contact with skin, or with the painted surfaces of the car. Rinse off spills immediately, with plenty of water. Never leave antifreeze lying

2.3a The coolant hoses on the Jazz are secured with spring-type clips . . .

2.3b . . . which are released using pliers

2.3c With the clip released and slid back, pull off the hose

---

around in an open container, or in a puddle on the driveway or garage floor. Children and pets are attracted by its sweet smell, but antifreeze can be fatal if ingested.

 Warning: If the engine is hot, the electric cooling fan may start rotating even if the engine is not running; be careful to keep hands, hair and loose clothing well clear when working in the engine compartment.

Warning: Refer to Section 10 for precautions to be observed when working on models equipped with air conditioning.

2 Cooling system hoses – disconnection and renewal

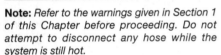

Note: Refer to the warnings given in Section 1 of this Chapter before proceeding. Do not attempt to disconnect any hose while the system is still hot.

1 If the checks described in the relevant part of Chapter 1 reveal a faulty hose, it must be renewed as follows.

2 First drain the cooling system (see Chapter 1). If the coolant is not due for renewal, it may be re-used if it is collected in a clean container.

3 Before disconnecting a hose, first note its routing in the engine compartment, and whether it is secured by any clips or ties. Use a pair of pliers to release the spring clips (or a screwdriver to slacken Jubilee clips) then move them along the hose, clear of the

relevant inlet/outlet union. Carefully work the hose free **(see illustrations)**.

4 Note that the coolant unions are fragile (some are made of plastic); do not use excessive force when attempting to remove the hoses. If a hose proves to be difficult to remove, try to release it by rotating the hose ends before attempting to free it – if this fails, try gently prising up the end of the hose with a small screwdriver to 'break' the seal.

> **HAYNES HINT** *If all else fails, cut the coolant hose with a sharp knife, then slit it so that it can be peeled off in two pieces. Although this may prove expensive if the hose is otherwise undamaged, it is preferable to buying a new radiator.*

5 When fitting a hose, first slide the clips onto the hose, then work the hose into position. If spring-type clips were originally fitted, it is a good idea to update them with Jubilee clips when refitting the hose (if only to make removal easier, next time). If the hose is stiff, use a little soapy water (washing-up liquid is ideal) as a lubricant, or soften the hose by soaking it in hot water.

6 Work the hose into position, checking that it is correctly routed and secured. Slide each clip along the hose until it passes over the flared end of the relevant inlet/outlet union, before tightening the clips securely.

7 Refill the cooling system with reference to Chapter 1.

8 Check thoroughly for leaks as soon as possible after disturbing any part of the cooling system.

3 Radiator – removal, inspection and refitting

Note: If leakage is the reason for removing the radiator, bear in mind that minor leaks can often be cured using a radiator sealant with the radiator in situ.

Removal

1 On models with air conditioning, the condenser must be removed first, as described in Section 11. This means, of course, that the air conditioning system must be discharged (drained) first by a Honda dealer or air conditioning specialist.

2 Drain the cooling system as described in Chapter 1.

3 Remove the front bumper and bumper crossmember as described in Chapter 11.

4 Remove the air cleaner as described in Chapter 4A.

5 Release the spring clip and disconnect the top hose from the radiator. As for the bottom hose, we found it was easier to disconnect this from the thermostat housing, noting that the hose is also clipped to the front of the engine **(see illustrations)**.

6 On automatic transmission models, disconnect the two smaller fluid cooler hoses from the base of the radiator – once disconnected, turn the hose ends upwards to reduce loss of fluid (ideally plug the hoses, to stop dirt entry).

7 Disconnect the radiator (and where

3.5a Release the spring clip and pull off the top hose from the radiator

3.5b It is easier to disconnect the bottom hose from the thermostat housing . . .

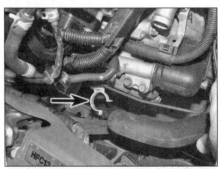

3.5c . . . and then unclip the hose from the front of the engine

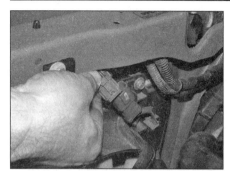

3.7a Disconnect the radiator fan plug from behind the front panel

3.7b On models with air conditioning, there will be two fan plugs to disconnect

3.8a Remove the bolt securing each radiator bracket to the front panel . . .

3.8b . . . then lift them off the peg on top of the radiator

3.9a Release the lower hose clip, then undo the bolt . . .

3.9b . . . and take off the radiator filler neck

applicable, the condenser) cooling fan wiring plugs from the back of the front panel ('slam panel') **(see illustrations)**.

8 Remove the two radiator top brackets, which are secured by a single bolt at the rear

of the front panel. Remove each bolt, and lift the brackets off the locating peg on top of the radiator **(see illustrations)**.

9 Release the lower clip on the radiator filler neck hose. Remove the bolt securing the filler

neck to the front panel, and take out the filler neck **(see illustrations)**. There is no need to disconnect the small hose to the expansion tank, as the tank is removed next.

10 Undo the top bolt, and lift out the expansion tank from the side of the radiator **(see illustrations)**.

11 On models with air conditioning, disconnect the compressor wiring plug from below, on the driver's side. Note that the top half of the plug is clipped to the side of the radiator – slide the plug upwards to release it **(see illustrations)**.

12 Carefully lift out the radiator assembly. The radiator sits in two lower mountings – recover the rubber bush from each one, as they are best refitted attached to the radiator **(see illustrations)**. Remove the assembly from the car.

3.10a Remove the bolt . . .

3.10b . . . and lift out the expansion tank

3.11a Disconnect the air conditioning compressor wiring plug . . .

3.11b . . . and slide up the top half of the plug to release it from the radiator

3.12a Lift out the radiator and fan assembly

3.12b Recover the two rubber bushes from the front of the car

Inspection

13 If the radiator has been removed due to suspected blockage, reverse-flush it as described in Chapter 1. Clean dirt and debris from the radiator fins, using an airline (in which case, wear eye protection) or a soft brush. Be careful, as the fins are easily damaged, and are sharp.

14 If necessary, a radiator specialist can perform a 'flow test' on the radiator, to establish whether an internal blockage exists.

15 A leaking radiator must be referred to a specialist for permanent repair. Do not attempt to weld or solder a leaking radiator, as damage may result.

Refitting

16 If a new radiator is being fitted, the fan(s) should be unbolted and transferred to the new radiator.

4.13a Remove the bolt securing the wiring harness to the end of the head . . .

4.13c Slide the wiring harness rearwards off the support bracket

17 Refitting is a reversal of removal, bearing in mind the following points:
 a) *Check the condition of the two lower mounting bushes, and fit new ones if necessary.*
 b) *Ensure that all hoses are correctly reconnected, and their retaining clips securely refitted (or tightened).*
 c) *Reconnect the radiator fan wiring, and ensure the harness is routed clear of the fan blades or hot components.*
 d) *On completion, refill the cooling system as described in Chapter 1.*
 e) *On models with automatic transmission, check and top-up the fluid level if necessary, as described in Chapter 1.*

4 Thermostat – removal, testing and refitting

1 As the thermostat ages, it will become slower to react to changes in water temperature ('lazy'). Ultimately, the unit may stick in the open or closed position, and this causes problems. A thermostat which is stuck open will result in a very slow warm-up; a thermostat which is stuck shut will lead to rapid overheating.

2 Before assuming the thermostat is to blame for a cooling system problem, check the coolant level. If the system is draining due to a leak, or has not been properly filled, there may be an airlock in the system (refer to the coolant renewal procedure in Chapter 1).

3 If the engine seems to be taking a long

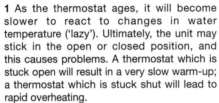

4.13b . . . and unbolt the earth strap from the camshaft thrust cover

4.14 Disconnect the radiator fan switch wiring plug

time to warm up (based on heater output), the thermostat could be stuck open. Don't necessarily believe the temperature gauge reading – some gauges never seem to register very high in normal driving.

4 A lengthy warm-up period might suggest that the thermostat is missing – it may have been removed or inadvertently omitted by a previous owner or mechanic. Don't drive the car without a thermostat – the engine management system's ECU will then stay in warm-up mode for longer than necessary, causing emissions and fuel economy to suffer.

5 If the engine runs hot, use your hand to check the temperature of the radiator top hose. If the hose isn't hot, but the engine clearly is, the thermostat is probably stuck closed, preventing the coolant inside the engine from escaping to the radiator – renew the thermostat. Again, this problem may also be due to an airlock (refer to the coolant renewal procedure in Chapter 1).

6 If the radiator top hose is hot, it means that the coolant is flowing (at least as far as the radiator) and the thermostat is open. Consult the *Fault diagnosis* section at the end of this manual to assist in tracing possible cooling system faults, but a lack of heater output would now definitely suggest an airlock or a blockage. Also consider the possibility of water pump failure – if the pump fails, the coolant won't circulate, causing overheating with reduced heater output.

7 To gain a rough idea of whether the thermostat is working properly when the engine is warming up, without dismantling the system, proceed as follows.

8 With the engine completely cold, start the engine and let it idle, while checking the temperature of the radiator top hose. Periodically check the temperature indicated on the instrument panel – if overheating is indicated, switch the engine off immediately.

9 The top hose should feel cold for some time as the engine warms up, and should then get warm quite quickly as the thermostat opens.

10 The above is not a precise or definitive test of thermostat operation, but if the system does not perform as described, remove and test the thermostat as described below.

Removal

11 Allow the engine to cool completely, then drain the coolant as described in Chapter 1.

12 Remove the air cleaner as described in Chapter 4A.

13 Remove the lower bolt securing the wiring harness to the end of the head, and also unbolt the earth strap from the camshaft thrust cover. Release the wiring harness from the support bracket at the rear **(see illustrations)**.

14 Disconnect the radiator fan switch wiring plug from the side of the thermostat housing **(see illustration)**.

15 Release the spring clips and disconnect the two large radiator hoses from the front and side of the housing **(see illustration)**.

4.15 Disconnect the radiator hoses from the front and side of the housing

4.17 Remove the four thermostat housing bolts

4.18a Pull out the thermostat – note the bleed valve hole at the top

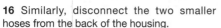
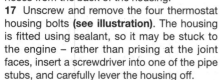
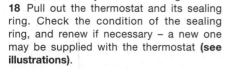

4.18b If necessary, fit a new thermostat sealing ring

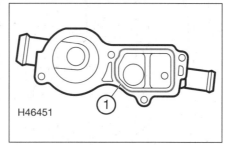

4.26a Sealant application details to the thermostat housing

1 Bead of sealant, 1.5 mm diameter

4.26b Applying sealant to the thermostat housing

16 Similarly, disconnect the two smaller hoses from the back of the housing.

17 Unscrew and remove the four thermostat housing bolts **(see illustration)**. The housing is fitted using sealant, so it may be stuck to the engine – rather than prising at the joint faces, insert a screwdriver into one of the pipe stubs, and carefully lever the housing off.

18 Pull out the thermostat and its sealing ring. Check the condition of the sealing ring, and renew if necessary – a new one may be supplied with the thermostat **(see illustrations)**.

Testing

Note: *Frankly, if there is any question about the operation of the thermostat, it's best to renew it – they are not expensive items. Testing involves heating in, or over, an open pan of boiling water, which carries with it the risk of scalding. A thermostat which has seen more than five years' service may well be past its best already.*

19 If the thermostat remains in the open position at room temperature, it is faulty, and must be renewed as a matter of course.

20 Check to see if there's a open temperature marking stamped on the thermostat.

21 Using a thermometer and container of water, heat the water until the temperature corresponds with the temperature marking stamped on the thermostat. If no marking is found, start the test with the water hot, and heat slowly until it boils.

22 Suspend the (closed) thermostat on a length of string in the water, and check that

maximum opening occurs within two minutes, or before the water boils.

23 Remove the thermostat and allow it to cool down; check that it closes fully.

24 If the thermostat does not open and close as described, or if it sticks in either position, it must be renewed.

Refitting

25 Clean all traces of old sealant from the housing and its mating face on the engine, taking care not to damage the alloy head or housing. Wipe the faces with a suitable solvent, and allow to dry.

26 Apply a bead of RTV sealant (Honda Liquid Gasket 1216E, part number 08C70-K0334M, or equivalent) to the housing mating face as shown **(see illustrations)**. The bead should be 1.5 mm diameter all round. Once the sealant has been applied, the housing should be fitted within 5 minutes.

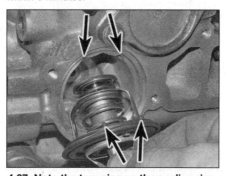

4.27 Note the two pips on the sealing ring, and the recesses in the housing

27 Fit the sealing ring to the thermostat, then fit the thermostat into the housing, with its bleed valve hole ('jiggle pin') at the top. There are also two pips on the back of the sealing ring, which fit into recesses in the housing **(see illustration)**.

28 Offer the housing into position, and secure with the four bolts – tighten them progressively to the specified torque **(see illustration)**.

29 Reconnect the hoses to their original positions, and reconnect the fan switch wiring plug.

30 Refit the wiring harness onto the support bracket, then refit the earth strap and the harness mounting bolt to the end of the head.

31 Refit the air cleaner as described in Chapter 4A.

32 On completion, give the sealant time to cure (at least 30 minutes) before refilling the cooling system as described in Chapter 1.

4.28 Fitting the thermostat housing

5.8a The fans are either bolted top and bottom . . .

5.8b . . . or bolted at the top . . .

5.8c . . . and pegged at the bottom

5 Radiator and condenser fans – testing, removal and refitting

> ⚠ **Warning: To avoid possible injury or damage, DO NOT operate the engine with a damaged fan. Do not attempt to repair fan blades – renew a damaged fan.**

Testing

Note: Models equipped with air conditioning have two complete fan circuits – one for the condenser and one for the radiator. The following procedures apply to both. Both fans

6.4a Disconnect the radiator fan switch . . .

are ultimately controlled through the engine management ECM.

1 To test a fan motor, disconnect the two-pin electrical connector at the motor, and use bridging wires to connect the fan directly to the battery. If the fan still doesn't work, renew the motor.

2 If the motor tests OK, check the fuse and relay (see Chapter 12), the fan switch, the condenser fan relay (also mounted in the engine compartment fusebox) if equipped, or the wiring which connects the components.

3 The radiator fan switch is screwed into the side of the thermostat housing.

4 To test a radiator fan switch, remove the switch wiring plug and, using an ohmmeter, check for continuity across the terminals of the switch with the engine cold. The switch should not have continuity while the coolant is below the specified switch-on temperature. Start the engine and allow the engine to reach normal operating temperature. Stop the engine and check for continuity again. The radiator fan switch should show continuity when the coolant temperature reaches or exceeds the switch-on temperature. If the switch fails to show continuity above this temperature, renew it.

5 If the condenser fan fails to operate with the air conditioning on after all other checks have been completed, this may be due to a low refrigerant charge – have the system checked by a dealership service department or air conditioning specialist.

Removal

6 Disconnect the battery negative lead, and position the lead away from the battery (also see *Disconnecting the battery*).

7 Both fans are bolted to the back of the radiator, and clearance to withdraw them is limited. It appears that the radiator should first be removed as described in Section 3, then both fans can be unbolted from it.

8 With the radiator assembly removed, unbolt the fan(s) **(see illustrations)** – note that the radiator fan is the one nearest the passenger side of the car. While the whole of the radiator is

accessible, take the opportunity to thoroughly clean the fins, using a stiff paintbrush.

Refitting

9 Refitting is a reversal of removal, noting the following points:
a) *Tighten the fan mounting bolts securely.*
b) *Refit the radiator as described in Section 3.*
c) *On completion, check the fan operation, either as described at the start of this Section, or (for the radiator fan only) by starting the engine and allowing it to reach operating temperature – if this method is chosen, do not allow the engine to overheat.*

6 Cooling system switches and sensors – removal and refitting

> ⚠ **Warning: Do not attempt to remove any switch or sensor while the cooling system is hot and/or pressurised, as there is a great risk of scalding.**

1 Allow the engine to cool, then slowly remove the radiator cap to depressurise the cooling system. To avoid any chance of coolant spillage, the system can be drained as described in Chapter 1, but this is not essential if a new sensor is being fitted and can quickly be substituted for the old one. Otherwise, if the system is not drained and the sensor will be left out for some time, a plug of some kind should be inserted to reduce coolant loss.

Radiator fan switch

2 The switch is screwed into the side of the thermostat housing, at the transmission end of the engine.

3 Remove the air cleaner as described in Chapter 4A.

4 Disconnect the switch wiring plug, then unscrew the switch and remove it. Recover the O-ring seal – a new one should be used when refitting **(see illustrations)**.

5 Refitting is a reversal of removal. Use a new

O-ring seal, and tighten the switch to the specified torque (a deep socket will be required).
6 Either refill or top-up the cooling system as described in Chapter 1 or *Weekly checks*.

Coolant temperature sensor

7 The switch is screwed into the rear of the cylinder head, at the transmission end of the engine. Do not confuse the sensor with the camshaft position sensor mounted above it, which has a single mounting bolt.
8 Access to the sensor is not easy, but may be improved by removing the air cleaner as described in Chapter 4A.
9 Disconnect the sensor wiring plug, then unscrew the sensor and remove it. Recover the O-ring seal – a new one should be used when refitting **(see illustrations)**.
10 Refitting is a reversal of removal. Use a new O-ring seal, and tighten the switch to the specified torque (a deep socket will be required) **(see illustration)**.
11 Either refill or top-up the cooling system as described in Chapter 1 or *Weekly checks*.

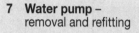

7 Water pump – removal and refitting

Removal

1 Loosen the right-hand front wheel nuts, then jack up the front of the car, and support it on axle stands (see *Jacking and vehicle support*). Remove the right-hand front wheel. Also unbolt and remove the engine undertray and right-hand front wheel arch liner (see Chapter 11, Section 23).
2 Drain the cooling system as described in Chapter 1.
3 Loosen (but do not yet remove) the three water pump pulley bolts – this is more easily done before the auxiliary drivebelt is removed.
4 Remove the auxiliary drivebelt as described in Chapter 1.
5 Unscrew the three bolts, and remove the water pump pulley. If the bolts were not previously loosened, it may be possible to hold the pulley using a tool through the pulley holes **(see illustrations)**.
6 On models with air conditioning, remove the auxiliary drivebelt's idler pulley, which is

7.6 Remove the drivebelt idler pulley to access the pump's top bolt

6.4b . . . then unscrew the switch and recover its O-ring

6.9b . . . then unscrew and remove the sensor

secured by a single bolt **(see illustration)**. Access to the bolt is not easy, but we found it to be possible from below. Removing the pulley greatly improves access to the water pump's top mounting bolt.
7 Unscrew and remove the five mounting

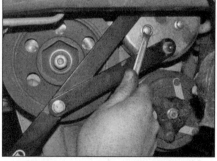

7.5a Using a sprocket-holding tool to loosen the water pump pulley bolts

7.7a Remove the five mounting bolts (one hidden) . . .

6.9a Disconnect the coolant temperature sensor wiring plug . . .

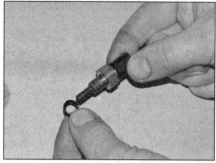

6.10 Use a new O-ring when refitting the sensor

bolts, and withdraw the water pump from the engine **(see illustrations)**. Recover the pump's rubber seal – a new one should be used when refitting. Also note that the pump has two locating dowels fitted – make sure these aren't left behind on the engine.

7.5b Removing the water pump pulley

7.7b . . . then remove the water pump

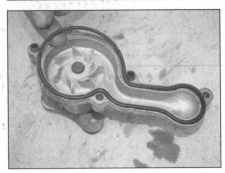

7.12a Fit a new rubber seal (also note the locating dowel positions) . . .

7.12b . . . then offer up the pump . . .

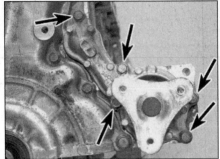

7.12c . . . and refit the five bolts, tightened to the specified torque

Inspection

8 If the pump has been removed for reasons other than to fit a new one (unlikely), inspect it as follows.

9 Check around the drain hole on the pump body for signs of coolant leakage (typically, white or coolant-coloured deposits). Even a slight leak is a sign of impending failure, and the pump should be renewed.

10 Spin the pump impeller, and listen for a noisy bearing. A rough scraping sound indicates that the pump is not worth refitting, and a new one should be obtained.

Refitting

11 Commence refitting by thoroughly cleaning the mating faces of the water pump and the cylinder block.

12 Refit the water pump, using a new rubber seal. Fit the two locating dowels, and

9.3a Remove the single central screw . . .

9.3b . . . then release the end clips with a small screwdriver . . .

tighten the bolts to the specified torque **(see illustrations)**.

13 Further refitting is a reversal of removal, bearing in mind the following points:

a) *Delay fully tightening the water pump pulley bolts until the drivebelt has been fitted.*

b) *Refit the auxiliary drivebelt as described in Chapter 1.*

c) *On completion, refill the cooling system as described in Chapter 1.*

8 Heating and ventilation system – general information

The heater/ventilation system consists of a four-speed blower motor (housed behind the facia), face-level vents in the centre and at each end of the facia, and air ducts to the front footwells.

The control unit is located in the facia, and the controls operate flap valves to deflect and mix the air flowing through the various parts of the heater/ventilation system. The flap valves are contained in the air distribution housing, which acts as a central distribution unit, passing air to the various ducts and vents.

Cold air enters the system through the grille at the rear of the engine compartment and, on air conditioned models, is filtered by a fine-mesh filter mounted behind the glovebox to remove particles like dust and pollen before they enter the cabin.

The air (boosted by the four-speed blower fan if required) then flows through the various

. . . and drop down the curved trim

9.3c

ducts, according to the settings of the controls. Stale air is expelled through ducts at the rear of the car. If warm air is required, the cold air is passed through the heater matrix, which is heated by the engine coolant.

A recirculation control enables the outside air supply to be closed off, while the air inside the car is recirculated. This can be useful to prevent unpleasant odours entering from outside the car, but should only be used briefly, as the recirculated air inside the car will soon deteriorate.

9 Heater/ventilation system components – removal and refitting

Note: *On models with climate control ('automatic' air conditioning), various other heating and ventilation control components are fitted in addition to the items listed in this Section – these are covered in Section 11.*

Heater control panel

Note: *This procedure applies to models without air conditioning, or with the 'manual' air conditioning system. These models can be identified by having three rotary heater control knobs. Details on removing the climate control panel appear later in this Section.*

1 Set the heater controls to the positions listed below – this is not essential, but will make resetting the cables easier on refitting:

a) *Temperature control to full cold (blue control cable).*

b) *Distribution/direction control to vents – fully left (yellow control cable).*

c) *Recirculation control slider to recirculate (grey control cable).*

d) *The blower switch can be anywhere, as it has no cable.*

2 Remove the glovebox, and the facia closing panel on the driver's and passenger's side, as described in Chapter 11, Section 27.

3 Remove the single central screw underneath the blower control, then release the end clips and drop down the curved trim piece fitted below the controls, noting that it also has locating lugs which hook in at the rear edge **(see illustrations)**.

4 Disconnect the two wiring plugs at the base

of the panel, and release the wiring harness from the clip **(see illustration)**.

5 Working through the glovebox aperture, release each cable outer from the spring clip, then unhook the recirculation (grey) and direction control (yellow) cable end fittings from the control levers **(see illustration)**. Do not bend the cables, and try not to turn the levers.

6 Similarly, working underneath the facia, reach up under the glovebox and unclip the cable outer, then unhook the temperature control cable (blue) end fitting **(see illustration)**.

7 Working from below the panel, remove the small cross-head mounting bolt at either end of the panel **(see illustration)**.

8 Reach up through the glovebox aperture and prise forwards the metal frame at the back of the centre panel, using a screwdriver or similar tool – this should release the left-hand top corner clip **(see illustration)**. The clips are particularly strong, and we found that simply pulling the centre panel would not release them.

9 Remove the instrument panel as described in Chapter 12. Working through the aperture behind the instrument panel, prise forwards the metal frame on the back of the centre panel until the right-hand top corner clip releases. Once both top corners are free, the rest of the clips should let go more easily. In all, there are three centre panel clips along the top, and two more on each side **(see illustrations)**.

10 When the panel is free, reach in behind and disconnect the various wiring plugs, which may include the blower and heated rear

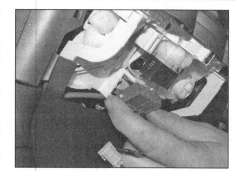

9.4 **Disconnect the two wiring plugs underneath the panel**

9.5 **Working through the glovebox, disconnect the grey and the yellow heater cables**

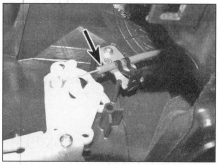

9.6 **From below the glovebox, disconnect the blue heater control cable**

9.7 **Remove the small cross-head bolt at either end of the panel**

window switches, radio unit and aerial lead, among others. Release the wiring harness from any clips as necessary to remove the centre panel **(see illustrations)**.

11 Withdraw the panel from the facia, feeding

out the heater control cables with it – note how the cables are routed, for refitting **(see illustration)**.

12 Carefully pull off the three control knobs from the front of the panel **(see illustration)**.

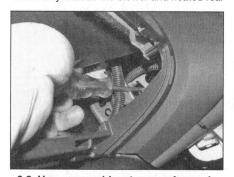

9.8 **Use a screwdriver to press forwards on the metal frame behind the panel**

9.9a **Similarly, press forwards on the other side . . .**

9.9b **. . . until the clips release, and the panel is free**

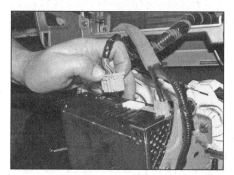

9.10a **Disconnect the wiring plugs from the panel . . .**

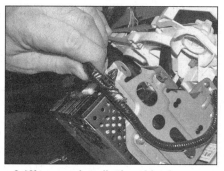

9.10b **. . . and unclip the wiring harness**

9.11 **Withdraw the panel, noting how the cables are routed**

9.12 Pull off the control knobs

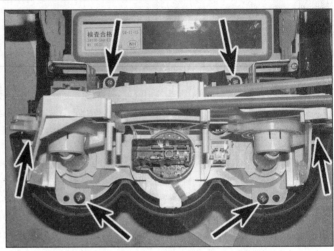

9.13a Remove six screws from behind . . .

13 At the rear of the panel, remove a total of eight screws (six from behind, and one on each side). Pull the frame sides apart to free the locating pegs, and detach the control panel from the centre panel **(see illustrations)**.

14 If one or more cables is being renewed, only remove one at a time, to avoid confusion. First, unhook the cable end from the control lever. To release the cable outer, use a pair of circlip or thin needle-nose pliers to open the plastic 'jaws' securing the cable, and remove it **(see illustration)**. To fit the new cable, feed the end through the jaws, then push the outer into the 'jaws' until it clicks in. On completion,

check that the new cable operates smoothly, through its full range of travel.

15 Refitting is a reversal of removal. When reconnecting the cables, proceed as follows:

a) Set the heater controls to the positions described in paragraph 1.

b) When connecting the temperature control cable, working from underneath, check that the control lever is set fully clockwise (if the lever has not been disturbed, it should be in the right place), then hook the end fitting on, and clip the cable outer back into the spring clip.

c) The direction and recirculation cables are refitted the same way. Note, however, that

the direction control cable lever should be fully anti-clockwise when reconnecting the cable.

Climate control panel

16 Remove the glovebox, and the facia closing panel on the driver's and passenger's side, as described in Chapter 11, Section 27.

17 Remove the single central screw underneath the control panel, then release the end clips and drop down the trim piece fitted below the controls, noting that it also has locating lugs which hook in at the rear edge.

18 Disconnect the wiring plug at the base of the panel, and release the wiring harness from the clip.

19 Working from below the panel, remove the small cross-head mounting bolt at either end of the panel.

20 Reach up through the glovebox aperture and prise forwards the metal frame at the back of the centre panel, using a screwdriver or similar tool – this should release the left-hand top corner clip. The clips are particularly strong, and we found that simply pulling the centre panel would not release them.

21 Remove the instrument panel as described in Chapter 12. Working through the aperture behind the instrument panel, prise forwards the metal frame on the back of the centre panel until the right-hand top corner clip releases. Once both top corners are free, the rest of the clips should let go more easily. In all, there are three centre panel clips along the top, and two more on each side.

22 When the panel is free, reach in behind and disconnect the various wiring plugs, which may include the heated rear window switch, radio unit and aerial lead, among others. Release the wiring harness from any clips as necessary to remove the centre panel. Withdraw the panel from the facia.

23 At the rear of the panel, remove a total of four screws, then pull the frame sides apart to free the locating pegs, and detach the control panel from the centre panel.

24 Refitting is a reversal of removal.

9.13b . . . and one more from each side . . .

9.13c . . . then pull the metal frame sides apart . . .

9.13d . . . and lift out the control panel

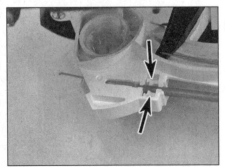

9.14 Prise apart the plastic 'jaws' securing the end of the cable

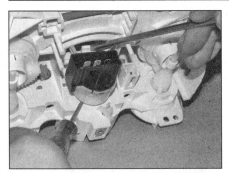

9.25a Use a screwdriver above to release the upper tab, and one to prise it . . .

9.25b . . . and remove the blower switch from the panel

9.30a Blower motor seen from below – mounting screws arrowed

9.30b Disconnect the wiring plug, then remove the screws . . .

9.31 . . . and lower out the motor into the footwell

9.36 Disconnect the blower motor resistor wiring plug . . .

Heater blower motor switch

25 The blower switch is only a separate component on models which have the three rotary controls (models without climate control). On these models, remove the heater control panel as described at the start of this Section – the blower switch is clipped to the back of the panel, and can be removed if required **(see illustrations)**.

26 On models with climate control, the blower switch is part of the control panel, and is not available separately. The climate control panel itself can be removed as described previously in this Section.

Heater/ventilation control cables

27 The temperature, distribution/direction and recirculation control cables can only be renewed by first removing the heater control panel as described at the start of this Section. Cable renewal is also covered in the control panel procedure.

28 Models with climate control have motors for the various control functions (cables are not used) – refer to Section 11 for the motor renewal procedures.

Heater blower motor

29 Remove the facia closing panel on the passenger's side, as described in Chapter 11, Section 27.

30 Disconnect the blower motor wiring plug **(see illustrations)**.

31 Remove the three motor mounting screws from below, then lower the motor out into the passenger footwell **(see illustration)**.

32 Refitting is a reversal of removal.

Heater blower motor resistor

33 If the blower fan will only operate on its fastest speed, or not at all, the resistor pack may be faulty.

34 Remove the facia closing panel on the passenger's side, as described in Chapter 11, Section 27.

35 The resistor pack is a round unit, mounted on the back of the main heater assembly. Access is not easy, but is possible without removing the heater unit itself.

36 Reach in behind the heater assembly, and disconnect the resistor pack wiring plug (a square, four-pin plug, release catches either side) **(see illustration)**.

37 Remove the cross-head screw above and below the resistor pack, and withdraw it from the back of the heater assembly **(see illustrations)**.

38 Refitting is a reversal of removal.

9.37a . . . then undo the two cross-head screws . . .

Heater matrix

⚠ *Warning: On models with air conditioning, the system must be discharged before starting this procedure. The heater assembly must be moved back inside the car to allow the matrix's rigid pipes to clear the bulkhead, and this means detaching the air conditioning pipes where they pass through the bulkhead as well. Discharging the air conditioning system must be carried out by a specialist, or by a Honda dealer.*

39 Drain the cooling system as described in Chapter 1.

40 At the rear of the engine compartment, release the spring-type hose clips and disconnect the two coolant hoses which pass through the bulkhead to the heater **(see illustration)**.

41 Have the air conditioning system

9.37b . . . and withdraw it from the heater assembly

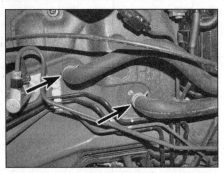

9.40 Disconnect the two heater hoses at the bulkhead

9.42a ONLY with the system discharged, prise out the black part of the clip . . .

9.42b . . . then slide back the green part . . .

9.42c . . . and pull out the refrigerant pipe – note the O-ring (arrowed)

9.44a Using a flat-bladed tool, prise out . . .

9.44b . . . and remove the clip securing the heater air duct

professionally discharged, on models so equipped.

42 On models with air conditioning, there will be two refrigerant pipes passing through the bulkhead – **do not** disturb them unless the system has been discharged first (see Section 10). For maximum personal safety, have the pipes disconnected by the engineer who discharges the system for you, and ensure the system is kept switched off afterwards. For reference, the pipe clips are in two parts – the black plastic clip slides off sideways, and the green part then slides back up the pipe (the green part of the clip is not re-usable, and new clips should be used when refitting). Pull out the pipes, and recover the O-rings – these too should be renewed (see illustrations).

43 Remove the facia panel as described in Chapter 11.

44 Prise out the clip securing the heater assembly to the air intake duct at the top (see illustrations).

45 Underneath the heater blower motor (on the passenger side), take out three bolts and remove the small support bracket (see illustrations).

46 The heater assembly is now secured by a total of three nuts and one bolt. Remove the nuts/bolt, then pull the assembly rearwards into the car. On models with air conditioning, note the small drain tube at the front, at floor level – the drain pipe on the front of the heater assembly must fit into this tube when refitting (see illustrations).

9.45a Remove the three bolts . . .

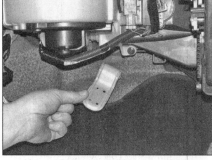

9.45b . . . and take off the heater lower support bracket

9.46a Remove the bolt and nut either side of the blower . . .

9.46b . . . one nut at floor level . . .

9.46c . . . and another to the right, higher up

9.46d Lift and pull the whole assembly back into the car . . .

9.46e . . . and disconnect the drain pipe at the front

9.47a Remove the two screws . . .

9.47b . . . take off the pipe cover . . .

9.47c . . . and remove the pipe clamp screw

9.48 Slide out the heater matrix, taking care not to bend the pipes

47 Remove the two screws and take off the pipe cover on the side of the heater housing, then remove the pipe clamp screw and take off the clamp **(see illustrations)**.

48 Carefully withdraw the heater matrix from the heater housing, without bending the pipework **(see illustration)**.

49 Refitting is a reversal of removal, noting the following points:

a) Check the condition of the rubber grommet(s) where the pipes pass through the bulkhead – if necessary, renew them when refitting.

b) Refit the facia panel as described in Chapter 11.

c) On completion, refill the cooling system as described in Chapter 1.

d) On models with air conditioning, have the refrigerant pipes reconnected (using new O-ring seals) and the system recharged by a specialist or a Honda dealer.

Heater assembly

50 Removal and refitting of the heater assembly are as previously described in this Section for the heater matrix.

Facia vents

Centre vents

51 Taking care not to mark the surrounding trim, use a flat-bladed screwdriver to prise out the vent at its outer pivot, then unhook the inner pivot and remove it **(see illustrations)**. Take care that the pivot bushes do not come off and fall down into the vent duct.

52 Refitting is a reversal of removal. Clip the

vent into its outer pivot first, then clip into the inner pivot.

Facia end vents

53 The end vents can only be accessed after the facia panel has been removed, as described in Chapter 11.

54 Each vent is secured by two screws – remove the screws, and withdraw the vent.

55 Refitting is a reversal of removal. Refit the facia panel as described in Chapter 11.

10 Air conditioning system – general information and precautions

General information

Air conditioning is available on certain models. It enables the temperature of incoming air to be lowered, and also dehumidifies the

9.51a Taking care to protect the trim, prise the outer side of the vent out first . . .

air, which makes for rapid demisting and increased comfort.

The cooling side of the system works in the same way as a domestic refrigerator. Refrigerant gas is drawn into a belt-driven compressor, and passes into a condenser mounted in front of the radiator, where it loses heat and becomes liquid. The liquid passes through an expansion valve to an evaporator, where it changes from liquid under high pressure to gas under low pressure. This change is accompanied by a drop in temperature, which cools the evaporator. The refrigerant returns to the compressor, and the cycle begins again.

Air blown through the evaporator passes to the heater assembly, where it is mixed with hot air blown through the heater matrix, to achieve the desired temperature in the passenger compartment.

The heating side of the system works

9.51b . . . then unhook the inner side, and remove it

TOOL TiP

Many car accessory shops sell one-shot air conditioning recharge aerosols. These generally contain refrigerant, compressor oil, leak sealer and system conditioner. Some also have a dye to help pinpoint leaks.

⚠ *Warning: These products must only be used as directed by the manufacturer, and do not remove the need for regular maintenance.*

in the same way as on models without air conditioning (see Section 8).

The operation of the system is controlled electronically. A thermistor mounted below the passenger airbag monitors the cabin temperature, which allows the system to maintain the value set on the control – for removal and refitting, see Section 11. Any problems with the system should be referred to a Honda dealer or an air conditioning specialist in the first instance **(see Tool tip)**.

Precautions

⚠ *Warning: The air conditioning system is under high pressure. Do not loosen any fittings or remove any components until after the system has been discharged. Air conditioning refrigerant should be properly discharged at a dealer service department or an*

automotive air conditioning repair facility capable of handling R134a refrigerant. Always wear eye protection when disconnecting air conditioning system fittings.

When an air conditioning system is fitted, it is necessary to observe the following special precautions whenever dealing with any part of the system, its associated components, and any items which necessitate disconnection of the system:

a) *While the refrigerant used – R134a – is less damaging to the environment than the previously-used R12, it is still a very dangerous substance. It must not be allowed into contact with the skin or eyes, or there is a risk of frostbite. It must also not be discharged in an enclosed space – while it is not toxic, there is a risk of suffocation. The refrigerant is heavier than air, and so must never be discharged over a pit.*

b) *The refrigerant must not be allowed to come in contact with a naked flame, otherwise a poisonous gas will be created – under certain circumstances, this can form an explosive mixture with air. For similar reasons, smoking in the presence of refrigerant is highly dangerous, particularly if the vapour Is Inhaled through a lighted cigarette.*

c) *Never discharge the system to the atmosphere – R134a is not an ozone-depleting ChloroFluoroCarbon (CFC) like R12, but is instead a hydrofluorocarbon, which causes environmental damage by contributing to the 'greenhouse effect' if released into the atmosphere.*

d) *R134a refrigerant must not be mixed with R12; the system uses different seals (now green-coloured, previously black) and has different fittings requiring different tools, so that there is no chance of the two types of refrigerant becoming mixed accidentally.*

e) *If for any reason the system must be*

disconnected, entrust this task to your Honda dealer or a refrigeration engineer.

f) *It is essential that the system be professionally discharged prior to using any form of heat – welding, soldering, brazing, etc – in the vicinity of the system, before having the car oven-dried at a temperature exceeding 70°C after repainting, and before disconnecting any part of the system.*

11 Air conditioning system components – removal and refitting

⚠ *Warning: Read the precautions given in Section 10, and where necessary, have the system discharged by a Honda dealer or an air conditioning specialist. Apart from work involving the various climate control motors and sensors, the system should always be discharged before starting.*

Compressor

Note: *If the compressor is being removed as part of another procedure, it may not be necessary to have the system discharged. Usually, the compressor can be unbolted and tied to one side without the need to disturb the refrigerant lines.*

1 Remove the auxiliary drivebelt as described in Chapter 1.

2 Disconnect the compressor wiring plug, and release the wiring from the securing clip **(see illustration)**.

3 With the system discharged, unscrew each flange bolt, and disconnect the refrigerant lines from the compressor **(see illustration)**. Discard the O-ring seals – new ones must be used when refitting. Either plug or tape over the open connections, to avoid the entry of moisture and dirt.

4 Support the compressor, then remove the four mounting bolts, and lower the compressor out of the engine bay **(see illustration)**.

11.2 Disconnect the compressor wiring plug

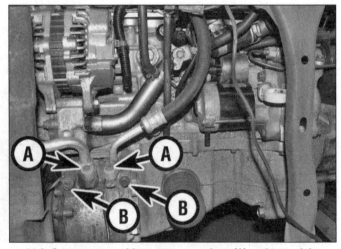

11.3 Compressor refrigerant connections (A) and two of the mounting bolts (B)

11.4 Support the compressor, then remove the mounting bolts

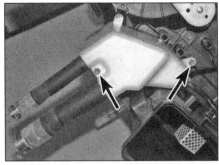

11.7a Remove the two screws . . .

11.7b . . . and take off the evaporator pipe cover

11.8a Remove the two Allen bolts . . .

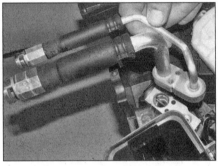

11.8b . . . and lift off the pipes . . .

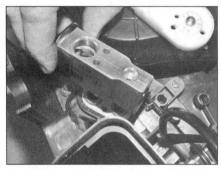

11.8c . . . and the expansion valve

5 Refitting is a reversal of removal, noting the following points:
  a) *Use new O-rings, coated with refrigerant oil, when reconnecting the refrigerant lines.*
  b) *Tighten the compressor mounting bolts to the specified torque.*
  c) *Have the system professionally recharged and tested on completion.*

Evaporator

6 The evaporator is fitted inside its own housing on the side of the heater assembly. Removal and refitting of the heater assembly is described in Section 9. To remove the evaporator, the blower motor housing does not have to be removed.
7 Working on the driver's side of the heater assembly, remove the two screws and take off the pipe cover **(see illustration)**.
8 Remove two further Allen bolts, and take off the pipes and the expansion valve – recover the

two O-rings from each, noting that new ones will be needed when refitting **(see illustrations)**.
9 Disconnect the evaporator temperature sensor wiring plug, and unclip the plug bracket by sliding it downwards **(see illustrations)**.
10 Remove the five screws and take off the

11.9a Disconnect the evaporator temperature sensor wiring plug . . .

evaporator duct from the side of the heater assembly **(see illustrations)**.
11 Slide out the evaporator, and recover the lower support plate **(see illustration)**.
12 Refitting is a reversal of removal. Refit the heater assembly as described in Section 9.

11.9b . . . and slide the plug bracket downwards to unclip it

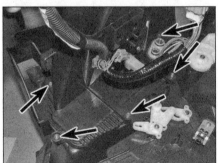

11.10a Remove the five screws . . .

11.10b . . . and take off the evaporator duct

11.11 Removing the evaporator

11.15a Disconnect the upper . . .

11.15b . . . and lower refrigerant lines from the condenser

11.16a Prise up the clip, then unscrew the bolt (arrowed) . . .

11.16b . . . and lift off the mounting bracket either side

11.17 Lift out the condenser

Condenser

13 Remove the front bumper and cross-member as described in Chapter 11.

14 Apply the handbrake, then jack up the front of the car and support securely on axle stands (see *Jacking and vehicle support*).

15 With the system discharged, remove the nut (upper) and bolt (lower) and disconnect the two refrigerant lines from the condenser **(see illustrations)**. Discard the O-rings – new ones must be used when refitting. Either plug or tape over the open connections, to avoid the entry of moisture and dirt.

16 The condenser has an upper mounting

bracket on either side. First, prise up the plastic clip securing the side trim panel to each bracket. Remove each mounting bracket's bolt, and lift off the brackets **(see illustrations)**.

17 Lift the condenser to remove it, taking care not to damage the fins on the surrounding components **(see illustration)**.

18 Refitting is a reversal of removal, noting the following points:

a) *Use new O-rings, coated with refrigerant oil, when reconnecting the refrigerant lines.*

b) *Have the system professionally recharged and tested on completion.*

Climate control components

Main control panel

19 Refer to Section 9.

Cabin temperature sensor

20 The sensor is mounted to the left of the steering wheel, behind a small grille.

21 To access the sensor, remove the instrument panel as described in Chapter 12.

22 Disconnect the sensor air hose on top, and the wiring plug below.

23 Remove the two screws, then withdraw the sensor from its location **(see illustration)**.

24 Refitting is a reversal of removal.

Outside temperature sensor

25 Apply the handbrake, then jack up the front of the car and support securely on axle stands (see *Jacking and vehicle support*).

26 The sensor is mounted on the back of the front bumper crossmember.

27 Lift the locktab on top of the sensor to release it from its location **(see illustration)**.

28 Disconnect the wiring plug from the sensor, and remove it.

29 Refitting is a reversal of removal.

Sun sensor

30 The sun sensor allows the system to compensate for the additional cabin

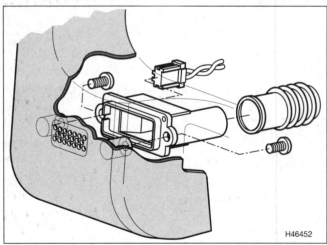

11.23 Cabin temperature sensor removal details

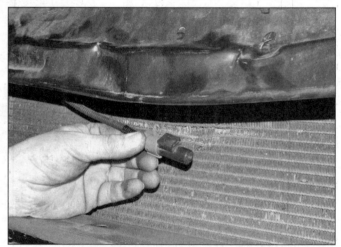

11.27 Removing the outside temperature sensor

temperature generated in sunny conditions. The sensor is located in the centre of the facia panel, just behind the windscreen.

31 Taking care not to scratch the facia, and noting its fitted orientation, prise the sensor out using a small flat-bladed screwdriver.

32 Disconnect the wiring plug from the sensor, and remove it completely **(see illustration)**. Make sure the plug doesn't fall back inside the facia.

33 Refitting is a reversal of removal. Ensure the sensor is fitted the right way round (with its wiring plug at the front).

Temperature control motor

34 Remove the facia closing panel on the passenger's side, as described in Chapter 11, Section 27.

35 Reach up on the left-hand side of the heater assembly, and disconnect the wiring plug from the base of the motor.

36 Remove the two mounting screws, and withdraw the motor – try not to turn it as this is done. Note how the motor operating lever pin engages with the heater linkage.

37 Refitting is a reversal of removal. Engage the motor lever pin into its locating hole, then align the mounting holes.

Distribution control motor

38 Open the glovebox. If the glovebox is full, it may be advisable to empty it now. Gently pull the glovebox 'liner' towards you, and withdraw it from the glovebox – note that it has a protruding tab on the back, which locates in a slot in the crossmember behind the facia.

39 The distribution control motor is on the right-hand side. Working through the glovebox aperture, disconnect the wiring plug from the base of the motor. Do not confuse this motor with the recirculation control motor on the left, which has its wiring plug on the front.

40 Remove the three mounting screws, and withdraw the motor – try not to turn it as this is done.

41 Refitting is a reversal of removal. Engage the motor lever with the linkage, then align the mounting holes.

Recirculation control motor

42 Open the glovebox. If the glovebox is full, it may be advisable to empty it now. Gently pull the glovebox 'liner' towards you, and withdraw it from the glovebox – note that it has a protruding tab on the back, which locates in a slot in the crossmember behind the facia.

43 The recirculation control motor is on the

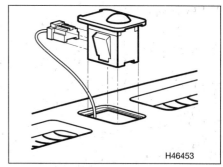

11.32 Sun sensor removal details

left-hand side. Working through the glovebox aperture, disconnect the wiring plug from the front of the motor. Do not confuse this motor with the distribution control motor on the right, which has its wiring plug on the base.

44 Remove the two mounting screws, and withdraw the motor – try not to turn it as this is done. Note how the motor operating lever pin engages with the heater linkage.

45 Refitting is a reversal of removal. Engage the motor lever pin into its locating hole, then align the mounting holes.

Chapter 4 Part A:
Fuel and exhaust systems

Contents

Degrees of difficulty

Easy, suitable for novice with little experience	Fairly easy, suitable for beginner with some experience	Fairly difficult, suitable for competent DIY mechanic	Difficult, suitable for experienced DIY mechanic	Very difficult, suitable for expert DIY or professional

Specifications

General
Manufacturer's engine codes*:
- 1.2 litre engine ... L12A
- 1.4 litre engine ... L13A

* See Vehicle identification in the Reference section for code location

System type
All models ... Honda PGM-FI (Programmed Fuel Injection) multi-point sequential injection system. Electronic throttle control system (ETCS) on some models

Fuel system data
Fuel pump type ... Electric, immersed in tank
Fuel pressure ... 47 to 54 psi
Idle speed (air conditioning off):
- 1.2 litre engine (all) ... 700 ± 50 rpm
- 1.4 litre engine:
  - Manual transmission ... 650 ± 50 rpm
  - Automatic transmission ... 750 ± 50 rpm
Idle CO ... 0.1% max
Injector resistance ... 10 to 13 ohms
Accelerator cable free play (deflection) ... 10 to 12 mm

Recommended fuel
Minimum octane rating ... 95 RON unleaded (UK unleaded premium). Leaded fuel must **not** be used

Torque wrench settings

	Nm	lbf ft
Camshaft position (TDC) sensor mounting bolt	12	9
Coolant temperature sensor	12	9
Crankshaft position sensor mounting bolt	12	9
Exhaust front pipe-to-centre section nuts*	33	24
Exhaust front pipe-to-manifold bolts	22	16
Exhaust manifold nuts/bolts*	44	32
Exhaust rear silencer bolts*	22	16
Floor crossmember bolts	22	16
Fuel rail mounting nuts	12	9
Fuel tank support frame bolts	38	28
Handbrake lever mounting bolts	22	16
Inlet manifold mounting bolts/nuts	22	16
Throttle body mounting bolts	12	9

* Use new nuts/bolts

1 General information and precautions

The fuel system consists of a fuel tank, an electric fuel pump (located in the fuel tank), a fuel pump relay, the fuel rail and fuel injectors, an air cleaner assembly and a throttle body. All models are equipped with a multi-point sequential electronic fuel injection system, which essentially means it has four injectors (one per cylinder) which operate in firing order. Various sensors are used to supply information to the Engine Control Module (ECM), and from this information, the module is able to determine the optimum settings for both fuelling and ignition timing. This Chapter deals with the fuel side of the system – refer to Chapter 5B for ignition-specific details. However, many of the sensors (described in Section 11) have a dual role, with their information being relevant to the correct operation of the fuel and ignition systems.

Fuel injection system

An electric fuel pump, pressure regulator and fuel level sender unit are located inside the fuel tank. Fuel is pumped from the fuel tank to the fuel rail, which is equipped with a pressure damper to smooth out the flow of fuel. The system is 'returnless' – there is no return feed to the tank. Fuel vapours from the tank are stored in a canister at the rear of the tank, and supplied to the throttle body through a separate pipe.

Sequential injection uses timed impulses to inject the fuel directly into the inlet port of each cylinder according to its firing order. The injectors are controlled by the ECM, which monitors various engine parameters and delivers the exact amount of fuel required into the inlet ports. The throttle body serves only to control the amount of air passing into the system. Because each cylinder is equipped with its own injector, much better control of the fuel/air mixture ratio is possible.

The amount of fuel supplied by the injectors is precisely controlled by the ECM. The ECM uses the signals from the crankshaft position sensor and the camshaft position sensor, to trigger each injector separately in cylinder firing order (sequential injection), with benefits in terms of better fuel economy and leaner exhaust emissions.

The ECM is the heart of the entire engine management system, controlling the fuel injection, ignition and emissions control systems. The ECM receives information from various sensors, which is then processed and compared with preset values stored in its memory to determine the required period of injection.

Information on crankshaft position and engine speed is generated by a crankshaft position sensor. The inductive head of the sensor is mounted just behind the crankshaft sprocket, and scans the teeth on a special sensor plate fitted next to the sprocket. As the crankshaft rotates, the sensor transmits a pulse to the ECM every time a tooth passes it. The teeth are 10° apart, and there are two missing teeth together on the sensor plate – the ECM recognises the absence of a pulse from the crankshaft position sensor at this point to establish a reference mark for crankshaft position. Similarly, the time interval between absent pulses is used to determine engine speed. This information is then fed to the ECM for further processing.

The camshaft position sensor is located at the transmission end of the cylinder head, and functions similarly to the crankshaft position sensor, with a reference lug on the camshaft. The sensor signal is used by the ECM to identify the TDC position of No 1 piston, which is key to the sequential fuel injection.

Engine temperature information is supplied by the coolant temperature sensor (see Chapter 3). The sensor is an NTC (Negative Temperature Coefficient) thermistor – that is, a semi-conductor whose electrical resistance decreases as its temperature increases. The sensor provides the ECM with a constantly-varying (analogue) voltage signal, corresponding to the temperature of the engine coolant. This is used to refine the calculations made by the ECM, when determining the correct amount of fuel required to achieve the ideal air/fuel mixture ratio.

Inlet air temperature information is provided by an inlet air temperature sensor. Where this is a separate component, the sensor is fitted into the back of the air cleaner. On models with the electronic throttle control system (ETCS), the air temperature sensor is integral with the MAP sensor.

The manifold absolute pressure (MAP) sensor provides the ECM with information on the vacuum level in the inlet manifold. The ECM uses this to calculate the engine load, and the appropriate fuelling – for example, if the vacuum measured is low, this suggests that the throttle is wide-open, and more fuel will be supplied.

The throttle valve inside the throttle body governs the amount of air entering the engine. A throttle valve sensor tells the ECM how far open the valve is – as more air is admitted, the ECM opens each injector for a longer duration, to increase the amount of fuel delivered to the inlet ports.

Idle speed is under ECM control, and can be raised from the base value if the ECM detects that certain equipment has been switched on (such as the air conditioning), or when the electrical load on the engine is increased (high power steering or alternator loads). When the engine is cold, the idle control system is used by the ECM to provide a faster idle speed. To reduce emissions, the engine also enters 'idle mode' when the brake pedal is pressed. On models with the electronic throttle control system (ETCS), the idle speed is controlled using the throttle actuator to open the throttle valve as necessary. All other models have an ECM-controlled idle air control valve fitted to the throttle body, which allows extra air into the engine to raise the idle speed (as air is added, more fuel is supplied, increasing the idle speed).

On manual transmission models, roadspeed is monitored by the vehicle speed sensor. This component is a Hall-effect generator, mounted on top of the transmission, in place of the old speedometer drive. It supplies the ECM with a series of pulses corresponding to the car's roadspeed, enabling the ECM to control features such as the fuel shut-off on overrun. Automatic transmission models have a similar arrangement, with a CVT speed sensor, and other internal sensors, to determine roadspeed.

An oxygen sensor in the exhaust system provides the ECM with constant feedback – 'closed-loop' control – which enables it to adjust the mixture to provide the best possible operating conditions for the catalytic converter. A further sensor is fitted, downstream of the converter, to monitor the converter's operation, and this provides an even finer degree of emission control.

On models with automatic transmission, the fuel system components and sensors are essentially the same as those with manual transmission. However, because of its additional transmission control parameters, the engine control module for automatic transmission models is instead known by Honda as the Powertrain Control Module, or PCM. For simplicity, we shall refer to the control module in all cases as the ECM.

Electronic throttle control system

Some models feature an electronic throttle control system (ETCS), where a throttle actuator (control motor) is used to open and close the throttle valve inside the throttle body. However, unlike some modern 'fly by wire' systems, an accelerator cable is still fitted, connected to an accelerator pedal position sensor. The position sensor tells the ECM the pedal position and rate of opening/closing, and the ECM then sets the throttle valve position remotely, using the actuator on the throttle body – this offers a greater degree of throttle valve control than is possible with a cable alone.

Exhaust system

The exhaust system includes an exhaust manifold, primary and secondary oxygen sensors, a three-way catalytic converter, a centre section with silencer, and a rear silencer.

The catalytic converter is an emissions control device added to the exhaust system to reduce pollutants. Refer to Chapter 4B for more information regarding the catalytic converter and other emission control components.

Precautions

Extreme caution should be exercised

when dealing with either the fuel or exhaust systems. Fuel is a potentially-explosive liquid, and extreme care should be taken when dealing with the fuel system. The exhaust system is an area for exercising caution, as it will remain hot for some time after the engine is switched off. Serious burns can result from even momentary contact with any part of the exhaust system, and the fire risk is ever-present. The catalytic converter in particular runs at very high temperatures.

When removing the engine control module (ECM), do not touch the terminals, as there is a chance that static electricity may damage the internal electronic components.

⚠️ **Warning: Many of the procedures in this Chapter require the removal of fuel lines and connections, which may result in some fuel spillage. Before carrying out any operation on the fuel system, refer to the precautions given in Safety first! at the beginning of this manual, and follow them implicitly. Petrol is a highly-dangerous and volatile liquid, and the precautions necessary when handling it cannot be overstressed.**

2 Fuel system – depressurisation

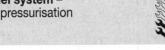

Note: *Refer to the warning in Section 1 before proceeding.*

⚠️ **Warning: The following procedures will merely relieve the pressure in the fuel system – remember that fuel will still be present in the system components, and take precautions accordingly before disconnecting any of them.**

1 The fuel system referred to in this Chapter is defined as the fuel tank and tank-mounted fuel pump/fuel gauge sender unit, the fuel rail, the fuel injectors, and the metal pipes and flexible hoses of the fuel lines between these components. All these contain fuel, which will be under pressure while the engine is running and/or while the ignition is switched on.

2 The pressure will remain for some time after the ignition has been switched off, and must be relieved before any of these components is disturbed for servicing work.

3 Whichever depressurisation method is used, bear in mind the following points:
  a) Plug the disconnected pipe ends, to minimise fuel loss and prevent the entry of dirt into the fuel system.
  b) Note that, once the fuel system has been depressurised and drained (even partially), it will take significantly longer to restart the engine – perhaps several seconds of cranking – before the system is refilled and pressure restored.

Method 1

Note: *Using this method should only be*

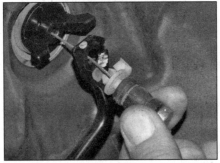
3.2 Unhooking the accelerator cable from the pedal

necessary if the engine has been running within the last few hours. If the engine has been switched off for several hours (such as overnight), the pressure remaining in the system will be greatly reduced – in this case, method 2 described below could safely be used.

4 The simplest depressurisation method is to disconnect the fuel pump electrical supply.

5 Gain access to the relays in the interior fusebox. On early models, remove the driver's side facia closing panel as described in Chapter 11, Section 27, then release the relay holder from the main fusebox. On later models, just remove the fusebox cover.

6 With the ignition switched off, pull out the fuel pump relay from the interior fusebox – this is the No 2 relay, which should be coloured blue. Alternatively, remove the fuel pump fuse (No 11) – although note that this fuse is shared with the airbag system, and removing it may cause an airbag fault.

7 Try to start the engine – if it starts, allow the engine to idle until it stops through lack of fuel. Turn the engine over once or twice on the starter to ensure that all pressure is released, then switch off the ignition. **Note:** *Removing the fuel pump relay (or the fuse) may cause a temporary fault code to be stored in the ECM, so the engine management warning light may be lit on completion. After a number of successful starts, the codes should clear themselves – if not, refer to Section 10.*

8 Refit the relay securely on completion, then ensure that the ignition is not switched on again until work is complete – ideally, if the fuel system is being worked on, the battery should be disconnected, to avoid the risk of sparks.

Method 2

9 Place a suitable container beneath the connection or union to be disconnected, and have a large rag ready to soak up any escaping fuel not being caught by the container. Slowly open the connection or loosen the union nut to avoid a sudden release of pressure, and position the rag around the connection, to catch any fuel spray which may be expelled.

3.3 Accelerator pedal mounting nuts

3 Accelerator pedal – removal and refitting

1 From inside the car, remove the driver's side facia closing panel to gain access to the accelerator pedal (see Chapter 11, Section 27).
2 Working in the driver's footwell, operate the accelerator pedal by hand, and unhook the cable end fitting from the top of the pedal, sliding it out to the right **(see illustration)**.
3 Unscrew the two retaining nuts and remove the pedal assembly from the bulkhead **(see illustration)**.
4 If the pedal is defective, the complete assembly will have to be renewed.
5 Refit the pedal assembly and tighten its retaining nuts securely.
6 Refit the trim panel to the facia on completion.
7 Check the pedal operation before taking the car out on the road – if necessary, adjust the accelerator cable as described in Section 4.

4 Accelerator cable – removal, refitting and adjustment

Note: *The procedure differs according to whether the electronic throttle control system (ETCS) is fitted. Models without this system have a cable which connects directly to the throttle body, and the cable is mounted high at the rear of the engine. On models with ETCS, the cable is mounted lower, and it disappears under the plastic cover fitted over the accelerator pedal position sensor.*

Removal

Models without ETCS

1 Open the throttle body quadrant, and unhook the accelerator cable end fitting from it.
2 Trace the cable back to the mounting bracket. Loosen the adjuster nut and locknut, and lift the cable out of the mounting bracket.

Models with ETCS

3 Trace the accelerator cable from the bulkhead to the pedal position sensor, which

4.3a Prise out the clip . . .

4.3b . . . then lift off the plastic cover

4.4 Loosen the nuts and lift out the cable

4.5 Unhook the end fitting from the quadrant, and remove it

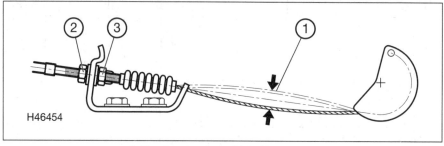

4.12a Accelerator cable adjustment – models without ETCS

1 Cable free play   2 Cable locknut   3 Cable adjuster nut

is mounted behind and below the throttle body, under a plastic cover. Unclip the wiring plug from the cover, then prise out the single clip, and lift the cover off **(see illustrations)**.
4 Loosen the adjuster nut and locknut, and lift the cable out of the mounting bracket **(see illustration)**.
5 Open the position sensor quadrant, and unhook the accelerator cable end fitting from it **(see illustration)**.

All models

6 Trace the cable back round the engine compartment, freeing it from any clips, and noting how it is routed.
7 Remove the driver's side facia closing panel to gain access to the accelerator pedal (see Chapter 11, Section 27).
8 Working in the driver's footwell, operate the accelerator pedal by hand, and unhook the

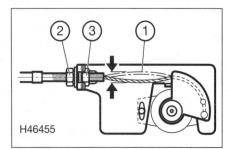

4.12b Accelerator cable adjustment – models with ETCS

1 Cable free play   3 Cable adjuster
2 Cable locknut   nut

cable end fitting from the top of the pedal, sliding it out to the right. Feed the cable back into the engine compartment, releasing the bulkhead grommet.
9 Withdraw the cable from the engine side, and remove it.

Refitting

10 Refitting is a reversal of removal. On completion, adjust the cable as described later in this Section.

Adjustment

11 Once the cable has been refitted, check the free play in the cable between the quadrant and the mounting bracket. The total deflection (up-and-down movement) should be in the range specified. If not, adjustment is required.
12 Loosen the cable adjuster nut and locknut on the mounting bracket, then turn the adjuster

5.3 Some of the fuel line connections have a plastic cover

nut (the one nearest the quadrant) until the free play is as specified **(see illustrations)**. On completion, tighten the locknut up to the mounting bracket, without disturbing the cable or the adjuster nut.
13 Without starting the engine, have an assistant depress the accelerator pedal fully, and check that the throttle quadrant opens fully. Similarly check that the quadrant returns to the idle position when the pedal is released.

5 Fuel lines and fittings – general information

Note: Refer to the warning in Section 1 before proceeding.

1 Quick-release couplings are employed at several unions in the fuel feed and return lines.
2 Before disconnecting any fuel system component, relieve the pressure in the system as described in Section 2, and equalise tank pressure by removing the fuel filler cap. Also note the routing of all hoses and pipes, and the orientation of all clamps and clips to ensure correct refitting.
3 Some of the quick-release connections have a plastic cover over them, which must be unclipped first for access **(see illustration)**.
4 Release the protruding locking lugs on each fuel line union, by squeezing them together (or depressing the lugs with a screwdriver) and carefully pulling the coupling apart **(see illustration)**. Use rag to soak up any spilt fuel.

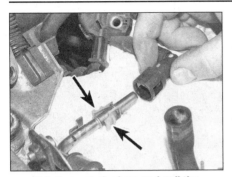

5.4 Depress the lugs and pull the connector apart

6.2 Pull off the air cleaner breather hose

6.3 Loosen the air cleaner-to-throttle body clip

Where the unions are colour-coded, the pipes cannot be confused. Where both unions are the same colour, note carefully which pipe is connected to which, and ensure that they are correctly reconnected on refitting.

5 To reconnect one of these couplings, press them together until they are locked. Switch the ignition on to pressurise the system, and check for any sign of fuel leakage around the disturbed coupling before attempting to start the engine.

6 Checking procedures for the fuel lines are included in Chapter 1.

7 Always use genuine fuel lines and hoses when renewing sections of the fuel system. Do not fit substitutes constructed from inferior or inappropriate material, or you could cause a fuel leak or a fire.

6 Air cleaner – removal and refitting

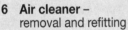

Removal

1 Where applicable, disconnect the inlet air temperature sensor wiring plug at the rear of the air cleaner.

2 Also where applicable, disconnect the air cleaner breather hose **(see illustration)**.

6.4a Unscrew the air cleaner mounting bolt at the front . . .

3 Release the clip securing the air cleaner to the throttle body, and pull the air cleaner sideways (towards the battery) to free it at the rear **(see illustration)**.

4 Unscrew the two air cleaner mounting bolts **(see illustrations)**.

5 At the front, pull the air cleaner sideways (towards the engine) off the duct on the inner wing, and lift it out of the engine compartment **(see illustrations)**.

Refitting

6 Refitting is a reversal of removal, noting the following points:

 a) Ensure that the air cleaner is located properly in the inlet duct and onto the

6.4b . . . and the one at the rear

 throttle body, and that the clip securing it to the throttle body is secure.
 b) Tighten the air cleaner mounting bolts securely.
 c) Where applicable, reconnect the inlet air temperature sensor wiring plug securely.

7 Fuel pump/gauge sender unit – removal and refitting

Removal

1 Unscrew the fuel filler cap – this is done to equalise the pressure in the tank.

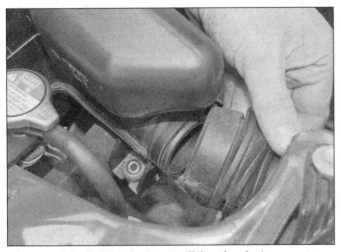

6.5a Pull the air cleaner off the wing duct . . .

6.5b . . . and remove the assembly from the engine bay

7.4a Disconnect the handbrake warning light switch . . .

7.4b . . . then unbolt the handbrake lever, and move it aside

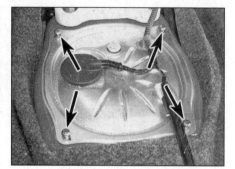

7.5a Remove the four screws . . .

7.5b . . . and lift up the access panel

7.6 Disconnect the wiring plug under the panel

2 Depressurise the fuel system as described in Section 2.

3 Remove the centre console as described in Chapter 11. Also, removing one front seat (and preferably, both) greatly improves access – again refer to Chapter 11 (on some models,

note that the battery must be disconnected before unplugging the seat wiring, as it includes the side airbags).

4 Disconnect the handbrake warning light switch wiring plug, then remove the two handbrake lever mounting bolts and move the

lever to one side, without disconnecting the cable(s) (see illustrations).

5 Unscrew the four screws securing the tank access panel to the car floor, and carefully lift it up – there's wiring attached to it (see illustrations).

6 Disconnect the pump/sender unit wiring plug inside, and move the access panel clear (see illustration).

7 Release the fitting on the fuel supply hose on top of the sender unit, and disconnect it, anticipating a small amount of fuel spillage (see illustrations). Either plug or tape over the hose ends. The quick-release fittings are typically released by squeezing the upper and lower tabs on the plastic collar while sliding the hose off.

8 Noting their fitted positions (attach labels if necessary), disconnect the two vapour hoses on top of the unit (see illustration).

9 The sender unit is secured using a threaded plastic collar, which will be tight. As access to it is limited by the hole in the car floor, Honda mechanics use a special three-legged gripping tool which engages the ribs on the collar's sides. An equivalent to this tool is available from several tool manufacturers. With care, it may be possible to unscrew the collar using large slip-joint water pump pliers, an oil filter strap wrench, or even by tapping the collar round with a screwdriver, but care must be taken not to damage either the collar or the tank. Unscrew and remove the collar (see illustrations).

10 Carefully lift the pump and sender unit out of the tank. Lift the unit straight up, then turn it to keep the fuel level float from catching on

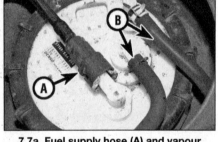

7.7a Fuel supply hose (A) and vapour hoses (B)

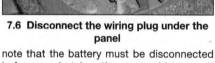

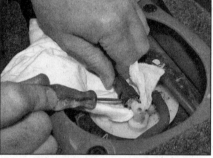

7.7b Depress the tabs, release the supply hose . . .

7.7c . . . and rest it on some clean rag to soak up any spillage

7.8 Release the spring clip and pull off each vapour hose

7.9a Home-made adjustable tool engages in collar ribs, turned using a bar

the tank opening **(see illustrations)**. Recover the sealing ring – if this is in poor condition, a new one should be used when refitting.

11 The unit may be dismantled if required – refer to Chapter 1, Section 22. It appears that spare parts are available, but check this before proceeding.

Refitting

12 If necessary, fit a new sealing ring to the sender unit, prior to fitting.

13 Refit the unit to the tank, taking care not to catch the sender unit's float. Align the rib mark on top of the unit between the two marks at the front of the tank **(see illustration)**.

14 Refit the collar to the fuel tank and tighten it securely.

15 Reconnect the fuel supply hose and vapour hoses to their original positions on the cover, and reconnect the wiring plug. Refit the access cover.

16 Refit the handbrake lever, tightening the mounting bolts to the specified torque. Reconnect the warning light wiring plug.

17 Refit the centre console as described in Chapter 11. If removed, also refit the front seat(s) with reference to Chapter 11 – where applicable, ensure that the battery is off before reconnecting the seat/side airbag wiring.

8 Fuel tank – removal and refitting

Removal

1 Before removing the fuel tank, all fuel must be drained from the tank. Since a fuel tank drain plug is not provided, it is therefore preferable to carry out the removal operation when the tank is nearly empty. The remaining fuel can then be syphoned or hand-pumped from the tank.

2 Unscrew the fuel filler cap – this is done to equalise the pressure in the tank. Depressurise the fuel system as described in Section 2.

3 Remove the centre console as described in Chapter 11. Also, removing one front seat (and preferably, both) greatly improves access – again refer to Chapter 11 (on some models, note that the battery must be disconnected before unplugging the seat wiring, as it includes the side airbags).

7.9b Removing the sender unit collar

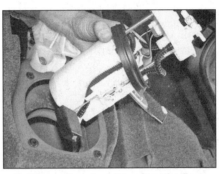

7.10b . . . then turn it to clear the float

4 Disconnect the handbrake warning light switch wiring plug, then remove the two handbrake lever mounting bolts and move the lever to one side, without disconnecting the cable(s).

5 Unscrew the four screws securing the tank access panel to the car floor, and carefully lift it up (see Section 7).

6 Disconnect the pump/sender unit wiring plug inside, and move the access panel clear.

7 Release the fitting on the fuel supply hose on top of the sender unit, and disconnect it, anticipating a small amount of fuel spillage. Either plug or tape over the hose ends. The quick-release fittings are typically released by squeezing the upper and lower tabs on the plastic collar while sliding the hose off.

8 Noting their fitted positions (attach labels if necessary), disconnect the two vapour hoses on top of the unit.

9 Jack up either the front or rear of the car,

7.10a Lift the unit straight up initially . . .

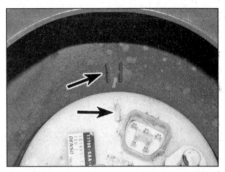

7.13 Align the sender unit rib between the two lines at the front

and support it on axle stands (see *Jacking and vehicle support*). Unusually, the fuel tank is mounted in the centre of the car.

10 Release the clips, then disconnect the filler and breather hoses from the rear of the tank – once the clips are released, twist the hoses off to avoid damage **(see illustration)**.

11 Unbolt and remove the heat shield from in front of the tank.

12 Remove the floor crossmember below the tank – this is secured by four bolts from below, and four more from the rear **(see illustration)**.

13 Position a jack (and a large flat piece of wood, to spread the load) under the tank, and just take its weight. Place the jack and wood centrally, so that the tank's support frame can be lowered.

14 Taking care that the tank does not move, loosen and remove the four support frame mounting bolts, and lower the frame **(see illustration)**.

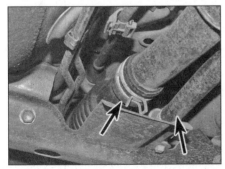

8.10 Disconnect the large filler hose, and the smaller breather hose, from the tank

8.12 Remove the floor crossmember

8.14 One of the four fuel tank support frame mounting bolts

9.1 Remove the screw at the rear of the flap surround

9.2 Unclip and remove the flap and surround as one

9.3 When refitting, tuck the rubber surround over the filler neck

15 With the aid of an assistant to steady the tank on the jack, lower the jack and remove the tank out from under the car. Note that the tank may 'stick' on the underseal. Try and keep the tank as level as possible, especially if it still contains fuel – if the tank tips, the fuel will run to one end, and the tank may slide off the jack.

16 As the tank is lowered, check for any hoses which may still be attached, and disconnect them as they become accessible.

17 If the tank is contaminated with sediment or water, remove the fuel gauge sender unit (Section 7), and swill the tank out with clean fuel. The tank is injection-moulded from a synthetic material – if seriously damaged, it should be renewed. However, in certain cases, it may be possible to have small leaks or minor damage repaired. Seek the advice of a specialist before attempting to repair the fuel tank.

Refitting

18 Refitting is the reverse of the removal procedure, noting the following points:
  a) When lifting the tank back into position, take care to ensure that none of the hoses become trapped between the tank and body. Refit the support frame and tighten the bolts to the specified torque.
  b) Ensure all pipes and hoses are correctly routed, and all hose connections securely remade.
  c) On completion, refill the tank with a small amount of fuel, and check for signs of leakage prior to taking the car out on the road.

9 Fuel filler flap – removal and refitting

1 Open the filler door, then remove the single screw at the rear of the filler surround **(see illustration)**.

2 Take off the filler cap, then unclip and remove the surround and the flap together from the car **(see illustration)**.

3 Refitting is a reversal of removal. Fold the rubber surround over the filler neck as the flap is fitted **(see illustration)**.

10 Fuel injection system – checking and fault code clearing

Note: *Refer to the warning note in Section 1 before proceeding.*

1 If a fault appears in the engine management system, first ensure that all the system wiring connectors are securely connected and free of corrosion. Then ensure that the fault is not due to poor maintenance; ie, check that the air cleaner filter element is clean, the valve clearances are correct, the cylinder compression pressures are correct, and the engine breather hoses are clear and undamaged, referring to Chapter 1 or Chapter 2A.

2 If these checks fail to reveal the cause of the problem, the car should be taken to a suitably-equipped Honda dealer for testing. A diagnostic connector is incorporated in the engine management system wiring harness, into which dedicated electronic test equipment can be plugged – the connector is located under the steering column, on the left, and is accessed after removing the driver's facia closing panel as described in Chapter 11, Section 27 **(see illustration)**. The test equipment is capable of 'interrogating' the engine control module (ECM) electronically and accessing its internal fault log (reading fault codes).

3 Fault codes can only be extracted from the ECM using a dedicated fault code reader. A Honda dealer will obviously have such a reader, but they are also available from other

10.2 Engine management system diagnostic connector

suppliers. It is unlikely to be cost-effective for the private owner to purchase a fault code reader, but a well-equipped local garage or auto-electrical specialist will have one.

4 Using this equipment, faults can be pinpointed quickly and simply, even if their occurrence is intermittent. Testing all the system components individually in an attempt to locate the fault by elimination is a time-consuming operation that is unlikely to be fruitful (particularly if the fault occurs dynamically), and carries a high risk of damage to the ECM's internal components.

5 Experienced home mechanics equipped with a suitable tachometer or other diagnostic equipment may be able to check the engine idle speed; if found to be out of specification, the car must be taken to a suitably-equipped Honda dealer for assessment. The engine idle speed is not manually adjustable; incorrect test results indicate the need for maintenance (check for leaking air/vacuum hoses, or use a proprietary injector cleaning treatment) or a fault within the injection system.

Clearing fault codes

6 Most of the components and sensors which make up the engine management system will log a fault code in the ECM memory in the event of a fault. When this happens, the engine management warning light on the instrument panel will come on. In some cases, the ECM will substitute its own default value instead of the correct sensor reading, and although it can still be driven safely, the car will suffer driveability problems, often especially noticeable when cold.

7 Once the faulty component has been identified and the problem corrected (usually by fitting a new component), the fault code must be cleared. In some cases, this will happen automatically once the ignition has been switched on and off enough times – if the fault does not recur, it may clear itself.

8 To clear fault codes manually requires the use of a fault code reader tool as described at the start of this Section. However, codes may also be cleared by the DIY mechanic, as follows.

9 It appears that it may be sufficient to simply disconnect the battery negative lead for a few minutes to clear any stored codes.

11.2a Disconnect the valve wiring plug . . .

11.2b . . . and disconnect the canister purge valve front and rear (arrowed) hoses . . .

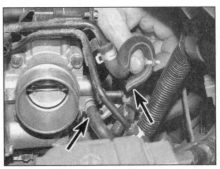

11.6 Disconnect the throttle body coolant hose from the rear, and from the side

Alternatively, with the ignition off, remove fuse No 14 from the interior fusebox for at least 10 seconds, then refit it. Switch the ignition on, and the fault should have cleared.

10 If the engine management light remains on (or comes back on later), either the same fault still exists, or there is another faulty component triggering a different fault code. Check that any new components have been correctly fitted, and especially, that their wiring plugs are clean and secure.

11 Fuel injection system electronic components – removal and refitting

Throttle body

1 Remove the air cleaner as described in Section 6.
2 Disconnect the canister purge solenoid

valve's wiring plug at the rear, then disconnect the front and rear hoses **(see illustrations)**.

Models without ETCS

3 Turn the throttle body quadrant by hand, and unhook the accelerator cable end fitting from it. Trace the cable back to the mounting bracket, then loosen the cable locknut, lift the cable from the bracket and move it to one side.
4 The throttle body has two coolant hoses attached, so either clamp the hoses or be prepared for a small amount of coolant loss (draining the cooling system is the only other option). The hoses are next to each other, at the rear – it may be advisable to mark or label them for position before removal. Release the clips and disconnect the two hoses – turn the hose ends upwards to minimise coolant loss.
5 Disconnect the wiring plugs from the throttle position sensor and the idle air control valve, both on the front of the throttle body.

Models with ETCS

6 The throttle body has two coolant hoses attached, so either clamp them or be prepared for a small amount of coolant loss (draining the cooling system is the only other option). One hose is at the rear, with the other on the side – mark or label them for position before removal. Release the clips and disconnect the two hoses – turn the hose ends upwards to minimise coolant loss **(see illustration)**.
7 Remove the small bolt underneath the throttle body which secures the wiring harness bracket. Release the end catches, and disconnect the main throttle actuator wiring plug at the front. Move the wiring harness clear **(see illustrations)**.

All models

8 Unscrew and remove the four mounting bolts (from the side) and withdraw the throttle body from the inlet manifold **(see illustrations)**.

11.7a Unscrew the wiring harness bolt . . .

11.7b . . . then disconnect the throttle actuator wiring plug . . .

11.7c . . . and move the harness clear

11.8a Unscrew the four mounting bolts . . .

11.8b . . . then remove the throttle body from the manifold . . .

11.8c . . . and recover the rubber seal

11.13 Disconnect the EGR valve wiring plug, and unclip the harness

11.14 Unclip the coil/injector harness from the fuel rail

11.15 Disconnect the four injector wiring plugs

11.16a At the end of the head, unclip the plastic cover . . .

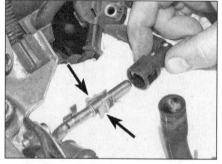

11.16b . . . then release the lugs and disconnect the fuel supply hose

11.17 Unscrew the fuel rail mounting nuts

Recover the rubber seal, noting its locating tab at the top, and discard it. It is essential that a new seal is used whenever the throttle body is disturbed – failure to do so will give rise to air leaks, which will upset the smooth running of the engine.

11.18 Unscrew the fuel rail support bracket bolt

11.19 Lift out the fuel rail

11.20a Slide back the metal locking clip . . .

9 Refitting is a reversal of removal, noting the following points:
a) Use a new rubber seal, and tighten the throttle body bolts to the specified torque.
b) Ensure that the wiring plugs and hoses are correctly refitted. If any of the hoses show signs of perishing or split ends, new hoses should be obtained.
c) Where applicable, refit and adjust the accelerator cable as described in Section 4.
d) Check the coolant level, and top-up if necessary (Weekly checks).

Fuel injectors

10 Depressurise the fuel system as described in Section 2.
11 Remove the air cleaner as described in Section 6.
12 Remove the inlet manifold as described in Section 12.
13 Disconnect the wiring plug from the EGR valve at the front corner of the engine, and unclip the wiring harness (see illustration). The EGR valve harness is part of the same harness which supplies the injectors.
14 Similarly, release the two clips which secure the front ignition coil and injector wiring harness to the fuel rail (see illustration).
15 Disconnect the wiring plugs from all four fuel injectors (it is essential that the injector wiring plugs are not mixed up, though this is unlikely in practice) (see illustration). Move the harness clear of the fuel rail.
16 Unclip the plastic cover, then depress the (green) lugs on the quick-release connection with a small screwdriver, and pull the fuel supply hose from the fuel rail. Have some clean rag ready, to soak up the fuel spillage (see illustrations).
17 Unscrew the two fuel rail mounting nuts (see illustration).
18 At the fuel hose end of the fuel rail, remove the bolt and separate the support bracket from the end of the head (see illustration).
19 Ease the fuel rail out by pulling upwards equally on both ends of the rail – there will be some resistance from the injector lower O-ring seals (see illustration). Recover the injector lower O-ring seals, and the small spacer collar from each mounting stud. Remove the rail to a clean working area.
20 Slide out the metal locking clip which secures each injector to the rail, then pull the injector free, noting which way round they are fitted – again, there will be resistance from the upper O-ring. Remove and discard the upper O-ring – a new set should be obtained for refitting (see illustrations).

21 Refitting is a reversal of removal, noting the following points:

a) Use new O-ring seals, lightly oiled, and ensure the injectors are located in the rail the same way round as noted on removal – the wiring plug sockets should face the front of the car when the rail is installed **(see illustration)**.

b) Fit the two spacer collars over the rail mounting studs **(see illustration)**. Seat the rail and injectors fully home, and tighten the mounting nuts.

c) Refit all hoses and wiring plugs securely.

d) Refit the inlet manifold as described in Section 12, and the air cleaner as described in Section 6.

e) On completion, switch on the ignition to pressurise the system, and check for leaks.

Fuel pressure damper

22 The fuel pressure damper is located in the fuel rail, and its function is to smooth out any fuel pressure peaks from the fuel pump and regulator in the fuel tank. To access the damper, remove the fuel rail and injectors as described previously in this Section. Remove the damper's plastic cover. The damper is secured in its fuel rail housing by a large circlip – remove the circlip and withdraw the damper, noting its O-ring seal.

23 Refitting is a reversal of removal. Use a new O-ring, and ensure the damper is fully seated and secured with the circlip. Refit the plastic cover over the damper. Refit the fuel rail and injectors using the information in this Section.

Fuel pressure regulator

24 The pressure regulator is mounted inside the fuel tank, and forms part of the fuel pump/sender unit.

25 Remove the fuel pump assembly as described in Section 7, then refer to Chapter 1, Section 22.

Fuel filter unit

26 The filter unit is mounted inside the fuel tank, and forms part of the fuel pump/sender unit.

27 Remove the fuel pump assembly as described in Section 7, then refer to Chapter 1, Section 22.

Throttle position sensor

28 The throttle position sensor is fitted to the front of the throttle body, and signals the position of the throttle butterfly to the ECM. The sensor is mated to the throttle body in production, and is not intended to be removed. In the event that a throttle position sensor problem is suspected, consult a Honda dealer or Honda parts specialist for advice, as it appears (at the time of writing) that the only solution is a new throttle body.

Throttle actuator

29 On models with the electronic throttle

11.20b . . . and pull out the injectors from the fuel rail

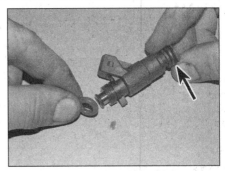

11.20c Take off the injector O-rings – new ones must be used

11.21a Oil the new O-rings before fitting the injectors to the rail

11.21b Fit the fuel rail spacer collars over the studs

control system (ETCS), the actuator is used by the ECM to control the throttle directly. The actuator is combined with the throttle position sensor into one unit, mounted on the front of the throttle body. The actuator is mated to the throttle body in production, and is not intended to be removed. In the event that a throttle actuator problem is suspected, consult a Honda dealer or Honda parts specialist for advice, as it appears (at the time of writing) that the only solution is a new throttle body.

Accelerator pedal position sensor

30 This sensor is only fitted to models with the electronic throttle control system (ETCS), and converts the driver's input from the accelerator cable into a signal which is used by the ECM to operate the throttle valve.

31 Trace the accelerator cable from the bulkhead to the sensor, which is mounted behind and below the throttle body, under a plastic cover. Unclip the wiring plug from the cover, then prise out the single clip, and lift the cover off.

32 Open the position sensor quadrant, and unhook the accelerator cable end fitting from it.

33 Loosen the adjuster nut and locknut, and lift the cable out of the mounting bracket.

34 Disconnect the sensor wiring plug.

35 Unscrew and remove the two mounting bolts, then lift the sensor off its support bracket, and remove it. The sensor is itself attached to a mounting plate, by two further bolts underneath **(see illustrations)**.

36 Refitting is a reversal of removal. Adjust the accelerator cable if necessary, as described in Section 4.

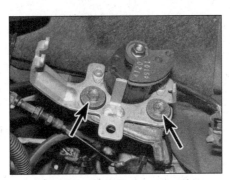

11.35a Unscrew the two mounting bolts . . .

11.35b . . . and lift out the accelerator pedal position sensor

11.35c Undo two further bolts to separate the sensor from its plate

11.38a Disconnect the wiring plug . . .

11.38b . . . then remove the mounting screw . . .

Manifold absolute pressure (MAP) sensor

37 The sensor is mounted on the back of the inlet manifold, at the transmission end.
38 Disconnect the sensor wiring plug, then

11.51 Disconnect the crankshaft position sensor wiring plug

11.52b . . . and withdraw the sensor

11.38c . . . and withdraw the MAP sensor – note the O-ring seal

unscrew the mounting screw and withdraw the sensor from the manifold – note that the sensor has an O-ring seal (see illustrations).
39 Refitting is a reversal of removal. Use a new O-ring if necessary, and tighten the mounting bolt securely.

11.52a Unscrew the mounting bolt . . .

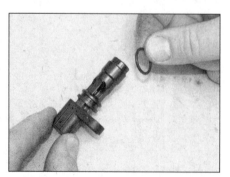

11.53 Use a new O-ring seal when refitting the sensor

Inlet air temperature sensor

40 On models with the electronic throttle control system (ETCS), the air temperature sensor is integral with the MAP sensor, which is removed as described previously in this Section.
41 On all other models, the inlet air temperature sensor is mounted in the back of the air cleaner. Disconnect the wiring plug, then pull the sensor out of the air cleaner, noting its sealing grommet.
42 Refitting is a reversal of removal. Use a new grommet if necessary, and ensure that the sensor is fully seated.

Idle air control valve

43 On models without the electronic throttle control system (ETCS), the idle air control valve is mounted on the front of the throttle body.
44 Remove the air cleaner as described in Section 6.
45 Disconnect the wiring plug from the front of the valve.
46 Remove the two mounting screws and withdraw the valve from the throttle body.
47 Recover the valve's seal – it is strongly recommended that a new one is used when refitting – air leaking past a worn seal will upset the running of the engine.
48 Refitting is a reversal of removal. Use a new seal, and tighten the mounting screws securely.

Coolant temperature sensor

49 Refer to Chapter 3, Section 6.

Crankshaft position sensor

50 The sensor is mounted at the base of the timing chain cover, at the rear. Access not easy, but is best from below. Loosen the right-hand front wheel nuts, then jack up the front of the car, and support it on axle stands (see *Jacking and vehicle support*). Remove the front wheel.
51 Reach up behind the timing chain cover, and disconnect the sensor wiring plug (see illustration).
52 Unscrew the single mounting bolt, then withdraw the sensor. Recover the O-ring seal – a new one should be used when refitting (see illustrations).
53 Refitting is a reversal of removal. Use a new seal, and tighten the sensor mounting bolt to the specified torque (see illustration).

Camshaft position (TDC) sensor

54 The sensor is screwed into the rear of the cylinder head, at the transmission end of the engine. Do not confuse the TDC sensor with the coolant temperature sensor mounted below it. Disconnect the sensor wiring plug (see illustration).
55 Unscrew the single mounting bolt, then withdraw the sensor. Recover the O-ring seal – a new one should be used when refitting (see illustrations).

11.54 Disconnect the camshaft position (TDC) sensor wiring plug

11.55a Unscrew the mounting bolt . . .

11.55b . . . and withdraw the sensor

11.56 Use a new O-ring seal when refitting the sensor

11.63a Unscrew the mounting bolt . . .

11.63b . . . and pull out the vehicle speed sensor

56 Refitting is a reversal of removal. Use a new seal, and tighten the sensor mounting bolt to the specified torque **(see illustration)**.

Oxygen sensors

57 Refer to Chapter 4B.

Canister purge solenoid valve

58 Refer to Chapter 4B.

Exhaust gas recirculation (EGR) valve

59 Refer to Chapter 4B.

Knock sensor

60 Refer to Chapter 5B.

Vehicle speed sensor

61 The vehicle speed sensor is mounted on top of the manual transmission, at the rear, in line with the right-hand driveshaft. Access to the sensor is easiest from below – jack up the front of the car, and support it on axle stands (see *Jacking and vehicle support*).
62 Reach up from behind the transmission, and disconnect the wiring plug from the speed sensor.
63 Unscrew the sensor mounting bolt, then withdraw the sensor from the transmission – there may be some resistance, both from the O-ring seal and from the sensor drivegear **(see illustrations)**.
64 Refitting is a reversal of removal, noting the following points:
a) Clean the mating faces of the sensor and transmission, and use a new O-ring if necessary **(see illustration)**. Expect

the sensor to twist as it meshes with the transmission gear, then turn it to align the mounting bolt hole.
b) Tighten the sensor mounting bolt securely, and ensure that the wiring plug is securely reconnected.

CVT speed sensor

65 Automatic transmission models have a CVT speed sensor mounted on top of the transmission, which is removed and refitted as described previously in this Section for the vehicle speed sensor. However, it is unclear at the time of writing whether the ECM uses only the CVT speed sensor signal to determine vehicle speed, as internal sensors (which monitor the transmission drive and driven pulley speeds) are also fitted – these sensors are not DIY-serviceable. If the CVT speed sensor is thought to be faulty, a Honda dealer or transmission specialist

11.64 Use a new O-ring when refitting

should be consulted before a new sensor is purchased.

Engine control module (ECM)

Note: *The ECM contains the immobiliser coding which was programmed into it when the car was new. If a new ECM is fitted, the immobiliser coding will have to be programmed into it by a Honda dealer before the car will start.*

66 Disconnect the battery negative lead, and position the lead away from the battery (also see *Disconnecting the battery*). This is **essential** when working on the ECM – if the module's wiring connector is unplugged when the battery is still connected, this will almost certainly damage the module.
67 The module is located inside the car, to the left of the glovebox. Access to the module is not easy, but there is a small curved panel below the glovebox which can be unclipped to improve matters **(see illustration)**.

11.67 Unclip this curved panel to gain better access to the ECM

11.71a Lower the ECM and its bracket into the passenger footwell

11.71b The ECM can be separated from its bracket if required

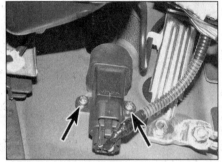

11.78 Disconnect the inertia switch wiring plug, then remove the mounting bolts

11.83 Removing the brake pedal position switch

Brake pedal position switch

80 The brake pedal position switch is fitted above and behind the top of the brake pedal itself – access is from the driver's footwell.
81 Remove the driver's side facia closing panel, as described in Chapter 11, Section 27.
82 Reach up under the facia to the switch mounting bracket, and disconnect the wiring plug from the top of the switch.
83 Turn the switch body anti-clockwise to remove it from the bracket **(see illustration)**.
84 To refit and set the switch, offer the switch into its bracket, so that the switch plunger touches the pedal. Without moving the switch in or out, turn it clockwise to lock it.
85 Reconnect the switch wiring plug to complete, then check the operation of the brake lights.

Electric power steering (signal)

86 The Jazz is equipped with electric power steering (refer to Chapter 10 for more details). The steering system's torque sensor signals the engine management ECM when the steering load is high, as the resultant electrical load on the engine could cause the idle speed to drop.

---

12 Inlet manifold – removal and refitting

Removal

1 Remove the air cleaner as described in Section 6.
2 Remove the plastic cover from the inlet manifold – this is secured by two domed bolts **(see illustrations)**.
3 Release the clip and disconnect the PCV hose from the centre of the manifold, and the brake servo vacuum hose just behind it **(see illustrations)**.
4 Similarly, disconnect the EVAP hose from the throttle body end of the manifold **(see illustration)**.
5 On models without ETCS, using the information in Section 4, disconnect the accelerator cable from the throttle body, and remove it from the mounting bracket on the manifold.

68 Remove the glovebox, passenger side facia closing panel, and the passenger kick panel as described in Chapter 11, Section 27.
69 Unbolt the wiring bracket in front of the ECM, and lower it past the module for access.
70 Disconnect the row of ECM wiring plugs along the base of the module.
71 Remove the two ECM mounting bracket bolts, and remove the module from the car. The module can be separated from the mounting bracket by removing the nut and bolt either side **(see illustrations)**.
72 Refitting is a reversal of removal. Make sure the battery is still disconnected before reconnecting the ECM wiring plugs.

Fuel shut-off (inertia) switch

73 The fuel shut-off switch is a safety device which automatically cuts off the fuel supply in the event of a sudden impact or collision.

The switch may occasionally be triggered in normal driving, for example when driving over badly-maintained roads.
74 The inertia switch is located inside the car, behind the passenger kick panel.
75 Open the glovebox. If the glovebox is full, it may be advisable to empty it now. Gently pull the glovebox 'liner' towards you, and withdraw it from the glovebox – note that it has a protruding tab on the back, which locates in a slot in the crossmember behind the facia.
76 Remove the passenger side facia closing panel, and the passenger kick panel as described in Chapter 11, Section 27.
77 To reset the switch after an impact or shock, depress the button on the top of the switch.
78 To remove the switch, disconnect the wiring plug on the base, then remove the mounting bolts and withdraw the switch **(see illustration)**.
79 Refitting is a reversal of removal.

12.2a Unscrew the two domed bolts . . .

12.2b . . . and take off the plastic cover

12.3a Disconnect the PCV hose in the centre . . .

12.3b . . . and the brake servo hose just behind it

12.4 Also disconnect the EVAP hose nearer the throttle body

12.6a For simplicity, remove the four throttle body bolts . . .

6 We found it best to unbolt the throttle body from the manifold (four bolts), and move it to one side – a new manifold-to-throttle body seal will be needed when refitting **(see illustrations)**. Alternatively, the throttle body can be removed with the inlet manifold, but all the wiring plugs and hoses listed in the Section 11 removal procedure must be disconnected from it first.

7 At the rear of the throttle body, remove the two small bolts from the manifold support bracket **(see illustration)**.

8 Remove the two bolts along the front of the manifold, then move the wiring harness clear, and unclip the coolant bypass hose **(see illustrations)**.

9 Disconnect the wiring plug from the MAP sensor, located on top of the manifold at the transmission end **(see illustration)**.

10 The manifold is secured at the front by three bolts and two nuts. Unscrew the nuts/

12.6b . . . and carefully move it clear without disconnecting

bolts – access to them is not easy, and care must be taken not to hit the radiator **(see illustration)**.

11 Support the manifold at the rear, then withdraw it forwards off its two studs. When

12.7 Remove the two bolts from behind the throttle body

it is clear of the studs, remove it from the engine compartment **(see illustration)**. Treat the manifold with care – do not drop it, as it is made of plastic.

12 Recover the four rubber port seals from the

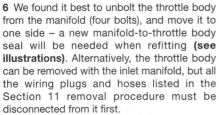

12.8a Remove the two bolts from the front of the manifold . . .

12.8b . . . noting that one of them also secures a pipe support bracket . . .

12.8c . . . and unclip the coolant bypass hose

12.9 Disconnect the MAP sensor wiring plug

12.10 The manifold nuts and bolts are hard to reach – this is one of the nuts

12.11 Removing the inlet manifold

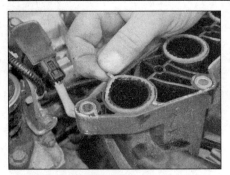

12.12 Recover the four port seals from the manifold – these must be renewed

12.13a Take off the EGR plate . . .

12.13b . . . and the metal gasket behind it

12.16a Fit the new EGR plate gasket . . .

12.16b . . . then slide on the EGR plate itself

12.17 Fit four new port seals to the manifold

manifold, and discard them – new ones **must** be used when refitting **(see illustration)**.

13 The EGR plate should also be removed from the manifold studs, so that a new plate-to-head gasket can be fitted (this should always be renewed when the manifold has been disturbed) **(see illustrations)**.

14 Clean all mating faces prior to refitting, and wipe them dry.

15 Check the manifold for any signs of splitting or cracking – this may be most evident around the mounting holes. If the manifold is damaged, a new one will be needed, although small isolated cracks may be repairable, either with sealant or with the help of a plastics repair specialist.

Refitting

16 Fit a new EGR plate-to-head gasket over the studs, then slide on the EGR plate **(see illustrations)**.

17 Fit four new port seals to the inlet manifold, then slide it onto the studs and up to the injector plate **(see illustration)**.

18 Refit the manifold nuts and bolts, and tighten them fully by hand. Once they are hand-tight, tighten the manifold nuts and bolts by a quarter-turn each at a time to the specified torque, working in a diagonal pattern from the centre outwards.

19 Further refitting is a reversal of removal. On completion, where applicable, refit and adjust the accelerator cable as described in Section 4.

13 Exhaust manifold – removal and refitting

⚠️ *Warning: Inspection and repair of exhaust system components should be done only after the*

system has cooled completely. Apart from the catalytic converter, the manifold is potentially the hottest part of the exhaust.

Removal

1 The exhaust manifold is at the rear of the cylinder head, and access is not easy – part of the job must be done from above, and the rest from below.

2 Remove the three bolts securing the heat shield fitted over the manifold, and lift it off **(see illustrations)**. These bolts often suffer from corrosion, and may be difficult to remove. Use a wire brush and plenty of penetrating oil first if they appear to be rusty. If the bolts are in less-than-perfect condition, new ones should be obtained for reassembly.

3 The manifold is secured with two nuts on top, and three bolts along the bottom edge **(see illustration)**. Loosen (do not yet remove)

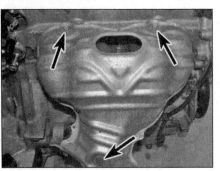

13.2a Remove the three bolts . . .

13.2b . . . and take off the exhaust manifold heat shield

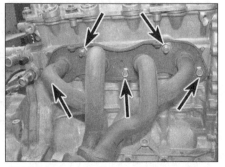

13.3 Exhaust manifold two nuts and three bolts (one hidden)

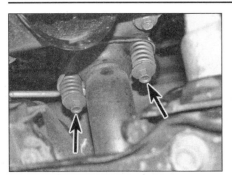

13.7 Manifold-to-downpipe bolts

13.9 Removing the exhaust manifold

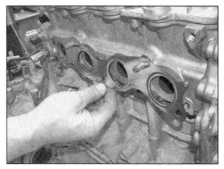

13.10 Always use a new manifold gasket

the nuts and bolts which are accessible from above.

> **HAYNES HiNT**
> *If a nut appears to be sticking, do not try to force it; tighten the nut back half a turn, apply some more penetrating oil to the stud threads, wait several seconds for it to soak in, then gradually unscrew the nut by one turn. Repeat this process until the nut is free. It doesn't matter if the studs are removed with the nuts.*

4 Jack up the front of the car, and support it on axle stands (see *Jacking and vehicle support*).

5 Have a support (such as an axle stand or a small jack) ready to rest the front pipe on.

6 At the manifold-to-downpipe joint, a support bracket is fitted which secures the manifold to the engine – unscrew the bracket-to-engine bolt, so that the bracket is removed with the manifold.

7 Undo the two bolts securing the front pipe to the manifold **(see illustration)**. Recover the springs and the 'olive' gasket – it is recommended that new bolts, springs and a new gasket are used when refitting (these should be available as part of a fitting kit from dealers and parts suppliers).

8 Do not let the front pipe hang down unsupported, as this will strain the oxygen sensor wiring (as well as the pipe itself). Place an axle stand or another jack under the pipe.

9 Unscrew any remaining manifold nuts or bolts which were not accessible from above, then remove those which were previously only loosened. Withdraw the manifold off the studs, and remove it from the engine compartment **(see illustration)**. Recover the manifold gasket from the engine – a new one should always be used when refitting.

Refitting

10 Refitting is a reversal of removal, noting the following points:
a) Clean the manifold and cylinder head mating faces, and fit a new gasket **(see illustration)**.
b) It is recommended that new nuts/bolts are used as a matter of course – even if

the old ones came off without difficulty, they may not stand being retightened. New components will be much easier to remove in future, should this be necessary.
c) If the manifold studs were removed, it's best to obtain a set of new studs and nuts, rather than try to separate the old ones. The new studs can be fitted by tightening two nuts against each other on the stud, then using them to screw the stud into place – once this is done, the nuts can be unscrewed from each other, and removed.
d) If the old studs and bolts are re-used, clean the threads thoroughly to remove all traces of rust.
e) Apply anti-seize compound (copper grease will do) to the manifold studs before fitting the nuts, and to the bolt threads.
f) Tighten the manifold nuts/bolts to the specified torque.
g) Reconnect the front pipe, using a new olive gasket, springs and bolts. Do not apply exhaust jointing compound to the new gasket. Tighten the bolts fully by hand, then by a quarter-turn each at a time to the specified torque.
h) Reconnect the primary oxygen sensor wiring plug, and clip the plug back in place. Ensure that the wiring is routed clear of any hot components.

14 Exhaust system – general information, removal and refitting

> ⚠ **Warning: Inspection and repair of exhaust system components should be done only after the system has cooled completely. This applies particularly to the catalytic converter, which runs at very high temperatures.**

General information

1 The exhaust system consists of three sections: the front pipe and catalytic converter, the centre pipe and silencer, and the rear silencer. The system is unusual because the front-mounted fuel tank means the exhaust is routed around it.

2 The system is suspended throughout its entire length by rubber mountings **(see illustration)**.

3 If any section of the exhaust is damaged or deteriorated, excessive noise and vibration will occur.

4 Carry out regular inspections of the exhaust system, to check security and condition. Look for any damaged or bent parts, open seams, holes, loose connections, excessive corrosion, or other defects which could allow exhaust fumes to enter the car. Deteriorated sections of the exhaust system should be renewed.

5 If the exhaust system components are extremely corroded or rusted together, it may not be possible to separate them. This often happens with the rear silencer, which rusts to the centre section – try twisting the pipes to separate them. Cut off the old components carefully with a hacksaw, and see if any corroded pipe can be removed (perhaps with a chisel) without damaging the remaining exhaust section. Wear safety glasses to protect your eyes, and wear gloves to protect your hands.

6 Here are some simple guidelines to follow when repairing the exhaust system:
a) Work from the back to the front when removing exhaust system components.
b) Apply penetrating fluid to the flange nuts before unscrewing them. If possible, wire-brush any exposed threads to remove corrosion and dirt before trying to loosen the nuts.
c) Use new gaskets and rubber mountings when installing exhaust system components.
d) Apply anti-seize compound (copper grease will do) to the threads of all

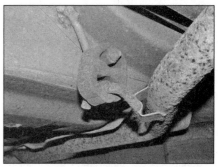

14.2 Check the condition of the exhaust rubber mountings regularly

14.9 The secondary oxygen sensor wiring plug is located in front of the gear lever

    exhaust system studs/bolts during reassembly.

  e) *The downpipe is secured to the manifold, and the rear silencer to the centre section, by two coil springs and bolts. When the bolts are tightened to the specified torque, the pressure of the springs will then be sufficient to make a leak-proof connection. Do not overtighten the bolts to cure a leak, or they may shear. Renew the 'olive' gasket and the springs if a leak is found.*

  f) *Be sure to allow sufficient clearance between newly-installed parts and all points on the underbody, to avoid overheating the floorpan, and possibly damaging the interior carpet and insulation. Pay particularly close attention to the catalytic converter and its heat shield.*

Removal

7 Each exhaust section can be removed individually, or the complete system can be removed as a unit. Even if only one part of the system needs attention, in some cases it will be easier to remove the whole system and separate the sections on the bench.

8 To remove the system or part of the system, first jack up the front or rear of the car, and support it on axle stands. Alternatively, position the car over an inspection pit, or on car ramps.

Front pipe and catalytic converter

9 Trace the wiring from both oxygen sensors to their in-line wiring plugs, and disconnect them (the secondary sensor plug is inside the car – remove the centre console as described in Chapter 11 for access) **(see illustration)**.

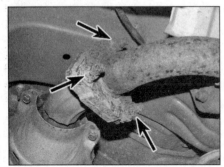

14.12 Catalytic converter rear flange nuts

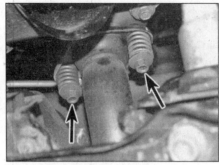

14.11 Exhaust manifold-to-front pipe bolts

Release the wiring from any clips or ties, so that it is free to be removed with the exhaust system.

10 Have a support (such as an axle stand or a small jack) ready to rest the front pipe on as required during removal.

11 Undo the two bolts securing the front pipe to the manifold **(see illustration)**. Recover the springs and the 'olive' gasket – it is recommended that new bolts, springs and a new gasket are used when refitting (these should be available as part of a fitting kit from dealers and parts suppliers).

12 Unscrew the three flange nuts from the joint behind the catalytic converter, and separate the converter flange from the centre section **(see illustration)**. Recover the gasket and discard it – this and the flange nuts should be renewed, and they may also be part of an exhaust fitting kit.

13 Remove the pipe and catalytic converter from underneath the car. Take care that the converter is not dropped or roughly handled.

Centre pipe and silencer

14 Slacken and remove the three flange nuts securing the centre pipe to the catalytic converter, and separate the joint. Recover and discard the 'olive' gasket – a new one must be used when refitting.

15 Undo the two bolts securing the rear silencer to the centre section. Recover the springs and the 'olive' gasket – it is recommended that new bolts, springs and a new gasket are used when refitting (these should be available as part of a fitting kit from dealers and parts suppliers).

14.17 Rear silencer-to-centre section bolts

16 Release the centre section from its three mounting rubbers by pulling it forwards, then remove it from underneath the car.

Rear silencer

17 Undo the two bolts securing the rear silencer to the centre section **(see illustration)**. Recover the springs and the 'olive' gasket – it is recommended that new bolts, springs and a new gasket are used when refitting (these should be available as part of a fitting kit from dealers and parts suppliers).

18 Unhook the rear silencer from its mounting rubbers, and free it from the centre pipe.

Complete system

19 Trace the wiring from both oxygen sensors to their in-line wiring plugs, and disconnect them. Release the wiring from any clips or ties, so that it is free to be removed with the exhaust system.

20 Have a support (such as an axle stand or a small jack) ready to rest the front pipe on as required during removal.

21 Undo the two bolts securing the front pipe to the manifold. Recover the springs and the 'olive' gasket – it is recommended that new bolts, springs and a new gasket are used when refitting (these should be available as part of a fitting kit from dealers and parts suppliers).

22 Free the system from its mounting rubbers, then remove it from underneath the car.

Heat shields

23 The heat shields are secured to the underside of the body by various nuts, bolts and rivets (which will have to be drilled out). Each shield can be removed once the relevant exhaust section has been removed. If a shield is being removed to gain access to a component located behind it, it may prove sufficient in some cases to remove the retaining nuts and/or bolts, and simply lower the shield, without disturbing the exhaust system.

24 The catalytic converter has a two-part clam-shell shield around it, with a further shield above attached to the floor.

Refitting

25 Each section is refitted by reversing the removal sequence, noting the following points:

  a) *Ensure that all traces of corrosion have been removed from the flanges, and renew all necessary gaskets, bolts and springs as applicable.*

  b) *The exhaust system flange nuts are all of self-locking type, and new ones should be used when refitting.*

  c) *Inspect the rubber mountings for signs of damage or deterioration, and renew as necessary.*

  d) *Prior to tightening the exhaust system fasteners, ensure that all rubber mountings are correctly located, and that there is adequate clearance between the exhaust system and underbody.*

  e) *Tighten all flange bolts and nuts fully by hand, then by a quarter-turn each at a time to the specified torque.*

Chapter 4 Part B:
Emission control systems

Contents

Degrees of difficulty

Easy, suitable for novice with little experience		**Fairly easy,** suitable for beginner with some experience		**Fairly difficult,** suitable for competent DIY mechanic		**Difficult,** suitable for experienced DIY mechanic		**Very difficult,** suitable for expert DIY or professional	

Specifications

Torque wrench settings	Nm	lbf ft
EGR valve:		
Housing-to-cylinder head nuts.	24	18
Mounting bolts	21	15
Oxygen sensors	44	32

1 General information

1 All engines are designed to use unleaded petrol, and are controlled by the engine management system to give the best compromise between driveability, fuel consumption and exhaust emission production. In addition, a number of systems are fitted that help to minimise other harmful emissions.

2 A positive crankcase ventilation (PCV) control system is fitted, which reduces the release of pollutants from the engine's lubrication system, and a catalytic converter is fitted which reduces exhaust gas pollutants.

3 An exhaust gas recirculation (EGR) system is fitted, to further reduce emissions.

4 Finally, an evaporative emission control system (known as EVAP) is fitted, which reduces the release of gaseous hydrocarbons from the fuel tank.

Crankcase emissions control

5 The positive crankcase ventilation (PCV or 'breather') system reduces hydrocarbon emissions by scavenging crankcase vapours. It does this by circulating fresh air from the air cleaner through the crankcase, where it mixes with blow-by gases and is then rerouted through a PCV valve to the inlet manifold.

6 The main components of the PCV system are the PCV valve in the front of the block, and the hoses (one from the valve to the inlet manifold, the other from the cylinder head cover to the air cleaner).

7 To maintain idle quality, the PCV valve restricts the flow when the inlet manifold vacuum is high. If abnormal operating conditions (such as piston ring problems) arise, the system is designed to allow excessive amounts of blow-by gases to flow back through the crankcase vent tube into the air cleaner to be consumed by normal combustion.

8 The PCV valve is fitted into the front of the engine, with oil separator passages behind it. The valve can be prised out of its location, noting the grommet it sits in – if this is in poor condition, it should be renewed **(see illustrations)**.

9 The most common reason for problems with the PCV system is blocked or damaged hoses, or a blocked valve. Disconnect the hose at one end, and see whether it can be blown through. If the pipe is blocked with oil sludge, it must be removed and cleaned, or for preference, renewed. Hoses which have perished, been crushed, or which have split ends, should also be renewed.

1.8a The PCV valve can be prised out of its cover

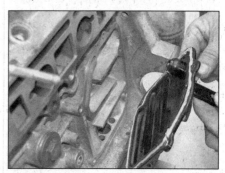

1.8b Refitting the PCV valve cover – note the bead of sealant around the edge

2.1 Disconnect the EGR valve wiring plug

2.2a Unscrew the two bolts, lift off the EGR valve . . .

2.2b . . . and recover the gasket

10 With the engine idling at normal operating temperature, pull off the PCV hose.

11 Place your finger over the hose. If there is no vacuum, check for a blocked hose, manifold port, or the valve itself. Renew any blocked or deteriorated hoses.

Exhaust emissions control

12 To minimise the amount of pollutants which escape into the atmosphere, all models are fitted with a catalytic converter in the exhaust system. The system is of the closed-loop type, in which two oxygen sensors in the exhaust system provide the ECM with constant feedback, enabling the ECM to adjust the mixture to provide the best possible conditions for the converter to operate. One oxygen sensor is located ahead of the catalytic converter, with the second downstream of it, to monitor the converter's efficiency.

13 The oxygen (lambda) sensor has a heating element built-in that is controlled by the ECM through the sensor relay to bring the sensor's tip to an efficient operating temperature quickly. The sensor's tip is sensitive to oxygen and sends the ECM a varying voltage depending on the amount of oxygen in the exhaust gases; if the inlet air/fuel mixture is too rich, the exhaust gases are low in oxygen, so the sensor sends a low voltage signal, the voltage rising as the mixture weakens and the amount of oxygen rises in the exhaust gases.

14 Peak conversion efficiency of all major pollutants occurs if the inlet air/fuel mixture is maintained at the chemically correct ratio for the complete combustion of petrol of

14.7 parts (by weight) of air to 1 part of fuel (the 'stoichiometric' ratio). The sensor output voltage alters in a large step at this point, the ECM using the signal change as a reference point and correcting the inlet air/fuel mixture accordingly by altering the fuel injector pulse width.

Evaporative emissions control

15 The fuel evaporative emissions control system absorbs fuel vapours and, during engine operation, releases them into the inlet manifold where they mix with the incoming air/fuel mixture.

16 The fuel filler cap is fitted with a two-way valve as a safety device. The valve vents fuel vapours to the atmosphere if the evaporative control system fails.

17 The vapours are passed to a charcoal canister mounted at the back of the engine compartment. A two-way valve mounted on top of the canister regulates fuel vapour flow, and ensures that no liquid fuel is passed into the EVAP system.

18 After passing through the two-way valve, fuel vapour passes to the charcoal canister itself. The activated charcoal in the canister absorbs and stores these vapours.

19 When the engine is running and warmed to a preset temperature, a solenoid valve (known as the canister purge solenoid valve) on the throttle body closes, allowing a diaphragm valve in the charcoal canister to be opened by inlet manifold vacuum. Fuel vapours from the canister are then drawn through by inlet manifold vacuum, and burned in the engine.

20 Always check the hoses first. A

disconnected, damaged or missing hose is the most likely cause of a malfunctioning EVAP system. Repair any damaged hoses or renew any missing hoses as necessary.

Exhaust gas recirculation

21 To reduce oxides of nitrogen (NOx) emissions, some of the exhaust gases are recirculated through the EGR valve to the inlet manifold. This has the effect of lowering combustion temperatures.

22 The EGR system consists of the EGR valve, the EGR control solenoid valve, and the Electronic Control Module (ECM). The ECM regulates the amount of exhaust gas which is recycled into the engine, via the solenoid valve. Unusually, the exhaust gas is fed from the exhaust side of the head to the inlet side via an internal passage, meaning there is no external pipework.

2 Exhaust gas recirculation (EGR) system – component renewal

EGR valve

1 The EGR valve is fitted to the cylinder head, directly in front of the oil filler cap. Disconnect the wiring plug from the top of the valve (see illustration).

2 Remove the two mounting bolts, and lift off the EGR valve. Recover the gasket – a new one should be used when refitting (see illustrations).

3 Clean the mating surfaces on the EGR valve and engine.

4 Fit the EGR valve, using a new gasket. Tighten the bolts to the specified torque.

5 Reconnect the wiring plug to complete.

EGR valve housing

6 Remove the EGR valve as described previously in this Section.

7 The housing is supplied with coolant. Either drain the cooling system as described in Chapter 1 first, or be prepared for coolant loss as the housing is removed.

8 Disconnect the coolant pipe from the front of the housing (see illustrations).

9 Remove the two mounting nuts, and withdraw the housing off its studs (see

2.8a Release the spring clip . . .

2.8b . . . and disconnect the coolant hose from the EGR housing

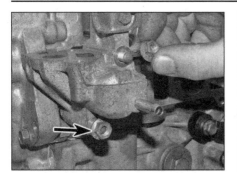

2.9a Unscrew the two mounting nuts . . .

2.9b . . . and slide off the EGR housing

2.11 Use a new gasket when refitting the housing

illustrations). Recover the housing gasket – a new one should be used when refitting.

10 Clean the mating surfaces on the valve housing and engine.

11 Fit the housing, using a new gasket **(see illustration)**. Tighten the nuts to the specified torque.

12 Refit the EGR valve as described previously in this Section.

EGR control solenoid

13 The EGR control solenoid is integral with the valve, and cannot be renewed separately.

3 Evaporative emissions (EVAP) system – component renewal

Canister purge solenoid valve

1 The canister purge solenoid is mounted on top of the throttle body.

2 Disconnect the wiring plug from the back of the solenoid, then release the hose clips and disconnect the two hoses from the front and rear of the valve **(see illustrations)**. Label the hoses to avoid confusion when refitting.

3 Unscrew the two mounting screws and remove the solenoid from the throttle body **(see illustration)**.

4 Refitting is a reversal of removal, noting the following points:
   a) Ensure that the wiring plug and hoses are correctly and securely refitted.
   b) If the hoses show signs of perishing, or split ends, new ones should be fitted.

Charcoal canister

5 The charcoal canister and two-way valve are mounted as an assembly at the rear of the engine compartment, with the two-way valve mounted on top.

6 Disconnect the two hoses from the side of the canister, then lift it out, noting that it fits into a tapered bracket on the bulkhead.

7 Refitting is a reversal of removal, noting the following points:
   a) Ensure that the hoses are correctly and securely refitted.
   b) If the hoses show signs of perishing, or split ends, new ones should be fitted.

4 Catalytic converter – general information and precautions

General information

1 The catalytic converter reduces harmful exhaust emissions by chemically converting the more poisonous gases to ones which (in theory at least) are less harmful. The chemical reaction is known as an 'oxidising' reaction, or one where oxygen is 'added'.

2 Inside the converter is a honeycomb structure, made of ceramic material and coated with the precious metals palladium, platinum and rhodium (the 'catalyst' which promotes the chemical reaction). The chemical reaction generates heat, which itself promotes the reaction – therefore, once the car has been driven several miles, the body of the converter will be very hot.

3.2a Disconnect the solenoid valve wiring plug . . .

3.2c . . . and rear hoses

3 The ceramic structure contained within the converter is understandably fragile, and will not withstand rough treatment. Since the converter runs at a high temperature, driving through deep standing water (in flood conditions, for example) is to be avoided, since the thermal stresses imposed when plunging the hot converter into cold water may well cause the ceramic internals to fracture, resulting in a 'blocked' converter – a common cause of failure. A converter which has been damaged in this way can be checked by shaking it (do not strike it) – if a rattling noise is heard, this indicates probable failure.

Precautions

4 The catalytic converter is a reliable and simple device which needs no maintenance in itself, but there are some facts of which an owner should be aware if the converter is to function properly for its full service life.

3.2b . . . then release the clips and take off the front . . .

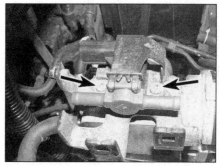

3.3 Remove the mounting screws and take off the valve

6.3 The secondary oxygen sensor wiring plug is located in front of the gear lever

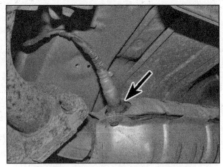

6.4 The heat shield limits access for unscrewing the secondary sensor

6.5 Access to the primary sensor is better

a) *DO NOT use leaded petrol (or lead-replacement petrol, LRP) in a car equipped with a catalytic converter – the lead (or other additives) will coat the precious metals, reducing their converting efficiency and will eventually destroy the converter.*

b) *Always keep the ignition and fuel systems well-maintained in accordance with the manufacturer's schedule (see Chapter 1).*

c) *If the engine develops a misfire, do not drive the car at all (or at least as little as possible) until the fault is cured.*

d) *DO NOT push or tow start the car – this will soak the catalytic converter in unburned fuel, causing it to overheat when the engine does start.*

e) *DO NOT switch off the ignition at high engine speeds – ie, do not 'blip' the throttle immediately before switching off the engine.*

f) *DO NOT use fuel or engine oil additives – these may contain substances harmful to the catalytic converter.*

g) *DO NOT continue to use the car if the engine burns oil to the extent of leaving a visible trail of blue smoke.*

h) *Remember that the catalytic converter operates at very high temperatures. DO NOT, therefore, park the car on dry undergrowth, over long grass or piles of dead leaves after a long run.*

i) *As mentioned above, driving through deep water should be avoided if possible. The sudden cooling effect may fracture the ceramic honeycomb, damaging it beyond repair.*

j) *Remember that the catalytic converter is FRAGILE – do not strike it with tools during servicing work, and take care handling it when removing it from the car for any reason.*

k) *In some cases, a sulphurous smell (like that of rotten eggs) may be noticed from the exhaust. This is common to many catalytic converter-equipped cars, and has more to do with the sulphur content of the brand of fuel being used than the converter itself.*

l) *If a substantial loss of power is experienced, remember that this could be due to the converter being blocked.*

This can occur simply as a result of contamination after a high mileage, but may be due to the ceramic element having fractured and collapsed internally (see paragraph 3). A new converter is the only cure in this instance.

m) *The catalytic converter, used on a well-maintained and well-driven car, should last at least 100 000 miles – if the converter is no longer effective, it must be renewed.*

5 Catalytic converter – removal and refitting

Refer to Chapter 4A. The converter is part of the exhaust system front pipe.

6 Oxygen sensors – testing and renewal

Testing

1 Testing the oxygen sensor is only possible by connecting special diagnostic equipment to the sensor wiring, and checking that the voltage varies from low to high values when the engine is running. **Do not** attempt to 'test' any part of the system with anything other than the correct test equipment. This is beyond the scope of the DIY mechanic, and should be left to a Honda dealer. **Note:** *All models are fitted with two sensors – one before and one after the catalytic converter. This enables more efficient monitoring of the exhaust gas, allowing a faster response time. The overall efficiency of the converter itself can also be checked. The sensors before and after the converter are known as the 'primary' and 'secondary' sensors respectively.*

Renewal

Note: *The sensor is delicate, and will not work if it is dropped or knocked, or if unsuitable cleaning materials are used on it.*

2 Jack up the front of the car, and support it on axle stands (see *Jacking and vehicle support*).

3 Trace the wiring from the sensor body back to its wiring plug, and disconnect it (the secondary sensor plug is inside the car – remove the centre console as described in Chapter 11 for access) **(see illustration)**. The wiring attached to the sensor must be released form any securing clips or ties. Note how the wiring is routed, as it must not come into contact with hot exhaust components.

4 If working on the secondary sensor, note that it is accessible without removing the heat shield fitted around the converter, but take care, as the shield edges may be sharp **(see illustration)**.

5 Unscrew the sensor from the exhaust system – it will be very tight, so be sure to use a good-quality, close-fitting spanner to remove it **(see illustration)**. The secondary sensor is harder to unscrew, as the heat shields limit access, and the sensor wiring prevents the use of a conventional deep socket. Special slotted sockets are available for this task from tool companies and suppliers.

6 It may be beneficial to wipe the sensor clean before refitting it, especially if the sensor tip appears to be contaminated. However, great care must be exercised, as the tip will be damaged by any abrasives, and by certain solvents. Seek the advice of a Honda dealer before cleaning the sensor with any products.

7 Refitting is a reversal of removal, noting the following points:

a) *Apply a little anti-seize compound to the sensor threads, taking care not to allow any on the sensor tip, and tighten the sensor to the specified torque.*

b) *If the special slotted socket is not available, the sensor will have to be tightened securely with just a spanner – use the specified torque as a guide to tightening.*

c) *Reconnect the wiring, ensuring that it is routed clear of any hot exhaust components, and securely clipped in place as required.*

d) *If required, proof that the sensor is working can be gained by having the exhaust emissions checked by a Honda dealer or MoT test station. Remember that a faulty sensor may have generated a fault code – if so, refer to Chapter 4A, Section 10.*

Chapter 5 Part A:
Starting and charging systems

Contents

Degrees of difficulty

Easy, suitable for novice with little experience	Fairly easy, suitable for beginner with some experience	Fairly difficult, suitable for competent DIY mechanic	Difficult, suitable for experienced DIY mechanic	Very difficult, suitable for expert DIY or professional

Specifications

General
System type . . . . 12 volt, negative-earth

Starter motor
Output:
   Manual transmission models . . . . 0.6 kW or 1.0 kW
   Automatic transmission models . . . . 0.7 kW
Minimum brush length . . . . 6.0 mm

Battery
Rating . . . . 28 Ah (typical)

Alternator
Output 75A
Minimum brush length . . . . 5 mm

Torque wrench settings	Nm	lbf ft
Alternator mounting bolts:		
Lower bolt	44	32
Upper bolt	24	18
Starter motor mounting bolts:		
Lower bolt	64	47
Upper bolt	44	32

1 General information and precautions

General information

The engine electrical system consists mainly of the charging and starting systems. Because of their engine-related functions, these are covered separately from the body electrical devices such as the lights, instruments, etc, which are covered in Chapter 12. Refer to Part B of this Chapter for information on the ignition system.

The electrical system is of the 12 volt negative-earth type.

The battery may be of the low maintenance or maintenance-free (sealed for life) type and is charged by the alternator, which is belt-driven from the crankshaft pulley.

Charging system

The charging system includes the alternator, an internal voltage regulator, a charge indicator light, the battery, a fusible link and the wiring between all the components. The charging system supplies electrical power for the ignition system, the lights, the radio, etc. The alternator is driven by the auxiliary drivebelt at the timing chain end of the engine.

The alternator control system within the ECM controls the voltage generated at the alternator in accordance with driving conditions.

Depending upon electric load, vehicle speed, engine coolant temperature, accessories (air conditioning system, radio, power steering, etc) and the inlet air temperature, the system will adjust the amount of voltage generated, creating less load on the engine.

The purpose of the voltage regulator is to limit the alternator's voltage to a preset value. This prevents power surges, circuit overloads, etc, during peak voltage output.

The charging system doesn't ordinarily require periodic maintenance. However, the auxiliary drivebelt, battery, wiring and connections should be inspected at the intervals outlined in Chapter 1.

The instrument panel warning light should come on when the ignition key is turned to the second position, but it should go off immediately after the engine is started. If it is slow to go out, or remains on, there is a malfunction in the charging system (see Section 4).

Starting system

The starting system consists of the battery, the starter motor, the starter solenoid and the wires connecting them. The solenoid is mounted directly on the starter motor.

The solenoid/starter motor assembly is installed at the front of the engine, next to the transmission bellhousing.

When the ignition key is turned to the Start position, the starter solenoid is actuated through the starter control circuit. The starter solenoid then connects the battery to the starter. The battery supplies the electrical energy to the starter motor, which does the actual work of cranking the engine.

The starter on models equipped with automatic transmissions can only be operated when the selector lever is in P or N.

Further details of the various systems are given in the relevant Sections of this Chapter. While some repair procedures are given, the usual course of action is to renew the component concerned.

Precautions

Always observe the following precautions when working on the electrical system:

a) *Be extremely careful when servicing engine electrical components. They are easily damaged if handled improperly, if the wiring connections are reversed, or if testing is carried out carelessly (this is particularly true of alternator testing).*

b) *Never leave the ignition switched on for long periods of time when the engine is not running.*

c) *Don't disconnect the battery leads while the engine is running.*

d) *Maintain correct polarity when connecting a battery lead from another vehicle during jump starting – see the Jump starting Section at the front of this manual.*

e) *Always disconnect the negative lead first, and reconnect it last, or the battery may be shorted by the tool being used to loosen the lead clamps.*

It's also a good idea to review the safety-related information regarding the engine electrical

3.3 Disconnect the battery negative lead

systems shown in the *Safety first!* section at the front of this manual, before beginning any operation included in this Chapter.

Battery disconnection

Refer to *Disconnecting the battery* at the end of this manual.

2 Battery – testing and charging

Testing

1 The simplest way to test a battery is with a voltmeter (or multimeter set to voltage testing) – connect the voltmeter across the battery terminals, observing the correct polarity. The test is only accurate if the battery has not been subjected to any kind of charge for the previous six hours. If this is not the case, switch on the headlights for 30 seconds, then wait four to five minutes before testing the battery after switching off the headlights. All other electrical circuits must be switched off, so check that the doors and tailgate are fully shut when making the test.

2 If the voltage reading is less than 12.0 volts, then the battery is less than healthy. Under 11.5 volts, and the battery needs charging. However, as little as 11.0 volts will still usually be enough to start the engine, though a battery in this condition could not be relied on. A reading of around 10.0 volts suggests that one of the six battery cells has died – a common way for modern batteries to fail.

3 If the battery is to be charged, remove it from the car (Section 3) and charge it as described later in this Section.

Low-maintenance battery

4 If the car covers a small annual mileage, it is worthwhile checking the specific gravity of the electrolyte every three months to determine the state of charge of the battery. Use a hydrometer to make the check, and compare the results with the tool maker's instructions (typically, there will be a colour-coded scale on hydrometers sold for battery testing).

5 If the battery condition is suspect, first check the specific gravity of electrolyte in each cell. A significant variation between any cells indicates loss of electrolyte, or deterioration of the internal plates.

6 If the cell variation is satisfactory but the battery is discharged, it should be charged as described later in this Section.

Maintenance-free battery

7 In cases where a 'sealed for life' maintenance-free battery is fitted, topping-up and testing of the electrolyte in each cell is not possible. The condition of the battery can therefore only be established using the battery condition indicator or a voltmeter.

Charging

Note: *The following is intended as a guide only. Always refer to the manufacturer's*

recommendations (often printed on a label attached to the battery), and always disconnect both terminal leads before charging a battery.

Low-maintenance battery

8 It is advisable to remove the cell caps or covers if possible during charging, but note that the battery will be giving off potentially-explosive hydrogen gas while it is being charged. Small amounts of acidic electrolyte may also escape as the battery nears full charge – keep your face and hands clear. Removing the cell caps will allow you to check whether all six cells are receiving charge – after a while, the electrolyte should start to bubble. If any cell does not bubble, this may indicate that it has failed, and the battery is no longer fit for use.

9 Charge the battery at a rate of 3.5 to 4 amps, and continue to charge the battery at this rate until no further rise in specific gravity is noted over a four-hour period.

10 Alternatively, a trickle charger charging at the rate of 1.5 amps can safely be used overnight.

11 Specially rapid 'boost' charges which are claimed to restore the power of the battery in 1 to 2 hours are not recommended, as they can cause serious damage to the battery plates through overheating.

12 While charging the battery, note that the temperature of the electrolyte should never exceed 38°C.

Maintenance-free battery

13 This battery type takes considerably longer to fully recharge than the standard type, the time taken being dependent on the extent of discharge, but it can take anything up to three days.

14 A constant-voltage type charger is required, to be set, when connected, to 13.9 to 14.9 volts with a charger current below 25 amps. Using this method, the battery should be usable within three hours, giving a voltage reading of 12.5 volts, but this is for a partially-discharged battery and, as mentioned, full charging can take considerably longer.

15 If the battery is to be charged from a fully-discharged state (condition reading less than 12.2 volts), have it recharged by your local automotive electrician, as the charge rate is higher and constant supervision during charging is necessary.

3 Battery – removal and refitting

Removal

1 Before removing the battery, refer to *Disconnecting the battery* in the reference section of this manual.

2 The battery is located at the left-hand side of the engine compartment.

3 Loosen the clamp nut and disconnect the battery negative (–) lead from the terminal **(see illustration)**.

4 Unscrew the nuts at the front and rear of the hold-down clamp, sufficient to unhook the clamp bolts from the battery tray. Lift off the hold-down clamp and bolts **(see illustrations)**.

5 Lift the plastic flap, then loosen the clamp nut and disconnect the battery positive (+) lead from the terminal **(see illustration)**.

6 Slide off the plastic battery box, where fitted **(see illustration)**.

7 Lift out the battery and withdraw it from the engine compartment. Also lift out the plastic tray, noting how it fits **(see illustrations)**.

8 If required, the battery tray can be removed as follows. Unclip the wiring harness at the rear, and move it clear of the tray. The tray itself is secured by three bolts – remove the bolts and lift out the tray **(see illustrations)**.

Refitting

9 Refitting is a reversal of removal, noting the following points:
  a) *Clean the battery tray if necessary.*
  b) *Tighten the battery hold-down clamp securely.*
  c) *Reconnect the battery leads, positive first, negative last.*
  d) *Re-activate the radio, reprogram the electric windows, etc, as described in Disconnecting the battery. If the electric power steering (EPS) does not work properly after the battery is reconnected, refer to Chapter 10, Section 19.*

---

4 Alternator/charging system – testing

Note: *Refer to Section 1 of this Chapter before starting work.*

1 If the charge warning light fails to illuminate when the ignition is switched on, first check the alternator wiring connections for security. If the light still fails to illuminate, check the continuity of the warning light feed wire from the alternator to the instrument panel. Check the condition of the auxiliary drivebelt. Check the condition of the regulator within the alternator as described in Section 6 of this Chapter. If all is satisfactory, the alternator is at fault and should be renewed or taken to an auto-electrician for testing and repair.

2 Similarly, if the charge warning light comes on with the ignition, but is then slow to go out when the engine is started, this may indicate an impending alternator problem. Check all the items listed in the preceding paragraph, and refer to an auto-electrical specialist if no obvious faults are found.

3 If the charge warning light illuminates when the engine is running, stop the engine and check that the drivebelt is correctly tensioned (see Chapter 1) and that the alternator connections are secure. If all is so far satisfactory, check the alternator brushes and slip-rings as described in Section 6. If the fault persists, the alternator should be renewed,

3.4a Loosen the nuts on the hold-down clamp . . .

3.4b . . . until it can be unhooked from the tray and removed

3.5 Disconnect the positive lead, and move it clear

3.6 Slide the plastic box off the battery

or taken to an auto-electrician for testing and repair.

4 If the alternator output is suspect even though the warning light functions correctly, the regulated voltage may be checked as follows.

5 Connect a voltmeter across the battery terminals, and start the engine.

6 Increase the engine speed until the voltmeter reading remains steady; the reading should be approximately 12 to 13 volts, and no more than 14 volts.

3.7a Lift out the battery . . .

3.7b . . . and its plastic tray

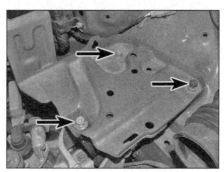

3.8a Unscrew the three bolts . . .

3.8b . . . and lift out the battery tray

5.4a Unscrew the nut and disconnect the supply lead . . .

5.4b . . . then disconnect the main wiring plug

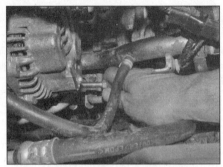

5.5 Removing the alternator lower mounting bolt

7 Switch on as many electrical accessories (such as the headlights, heated rear window and heater blower) as possible, and check that the alternator maintains the regulated voltage at around 13 to 14 volts.

8 If the regulated voltage is not as stated, this may be due to worn brushes, weak brush springs, a faulty voltage regulator, a faulty diode, a severed phase winding or worn or damaged slip-rings. The brushes and slip-rings may be checked (see Section 6), but if the fault persists, the alternator should be renewed or taken to an auto-electrician.

5 Alternator – removal and refitting

Removal

1 Disconnect the battery negative and positive

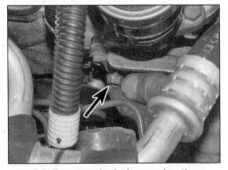

5.6 Remove the bolt securing the alternator adjuster bracket to the engine

leads, and position the leads away from the battery (also see *Disconnecting the battery*). This is **essential** before disconnecting the alternator wiring.

2 Remove the auxiliary drivebelt as described in Chapter 1.

3 The alternator is mounted at the timing chain end of the engine, at the front. Access is not easy, and there is little room to withdraw the unit, once it has been unbolted – especially on models with air conditioning, as the compressor prevents lowering the alternator out. For this reason, on models with air conditioning, the inlet manifold must be removed, as described in Chapter 4A.

4 Unclip the wiring harness, then unscrew the nut and disconnect the battery supply lead. Disconnect the main alternator wiring plug **(see illustrations)**.

5 Unscrew the alternator's upper mounting bolt (on the 'front'), and lower mounting

5.7 Disconnect the front coils, and unclip the harness

bolt (on the 'back') **(see illustration)**. The alternator will remain in place, sitting on its lower bracket.

6 Remove the single bolt securing the alternator adjuster bracket to the engine, and take off the bracket **(see illustration)**. Access to the bolt is not easy, but can be slightly improved by unbolting the air conditioning hose support bracket that's in the way, giving a small amount of movement in the hose.

7 Disconnect the four front ignition coil wiring plugs, then release the clips securing the front ignition coil wiring harness, and move it clear **(see illustration)**.

8 At the front of the engine, take out the engine oil dipstick, then remove the bolt securing the dipstick tube. Pull the tube upwards to withdraw it from the sump – note that there is an O-ring seal at the base of the tube **(see illustrations)**.

9 Lift the alternator off its lower bracket – it may be necessary to 'wiggle' the unit as you pull upwards, as it will typically be a tight fit. We found that by turning the unit so the pulley faces upwards, we were able (just) to withdraw it up and out **(see illustration)**.

Refitting

10 Refitting is a reversal of removal, noting the following points:

a) Where applicable, refit the inlet manifold as described in Chapter 4A.

b) Refit and adjust the auxiliary drivebelt as described in Chapter 1.

c) Check the charging voltage to verify proper operation of the alternator (see Section 4).

5.8a Unscrew the bolt at the top of the dipstick tube

5.8b Removing the engine oil dipstick tube

5.9 Removing the alternator, pulley uppermost

8.6a Unscrew the (shorter) upper mounting bolt . . .

8.6b . . . and the (longer) lower bolt . . .

8.6c . . . and withdraw the starter motor from the engine

6 Alternator – overhaul

Renewing the brushes and regulator on these alternators requires major dismantling, and should be done by a suitable auto-electrical repair specialist. It will probably be most practical to either have it rebuilt or exchange it for a reconditioned unit.

7 Starting system – testing

Note: *Refer to Section 1 of this Chapter before starting work.*

1 If the starter motor fails to operate when the ignition key is turned to the appropriate position, the following possible causes may be to blame:
   a) *The battery is faulty.*
   b) *The electrical connections between the switch, solenoid, battery and starter motor are somewhere failing to pass the necessary current from the battery through the starter to earth.*
   c) *The solenoid is faulty.*
   d) *The starter motor is mechanically or electrically defective.*

2 To check the battery, switch on the headlights. If they dim after a few seconds, this indicates that the battery is discharged – recharge (see Section 2) or renew the battery. If the headlights glow brightly, operate the ignition switch and observe the lights. If they dim, then this indicates that current is reaching the starter motor, therefore the fault must lie in the starter motor. If the lights continue to glow brightly (and no clicking sound can be heard from the starter motor solenoid), this indicates that there is a fault in the circuit or solenoid – see following paragraphs. If the starter motor turns slowly when operated, but the battery is in good condition, then this indicates that either the starter motor is faulty, or there is considerable resistance somewhere in the circuit.

3 If a fault in the circuit is suspected,

disconnect the battery leads (including the earth connection to the body), the starter/solenoid wiring and the engine/transmission earth strap. Thoroughly clean the connections, and reconnect the leads and wiring, then use a voltmeter or test light to check that full battery voltage is available at the battery positive lead connection to the solenoid, and that the earth is sound. Smear petroleum jelly around the battery terminals to prevent corrosion – corroded connections are amongst the most frequent causes of electrical system faults.

4 If the battery and all connections are in good condition, check the circuit by disconnecting the wire from the solenoid blade terminal. Connect a voltmeter or test light between the wire end and a good earth (such as the battery negative terminal), and check that the wire is live when the ignition switch is turned to the start position. If it is, then the circuit is sound – if not the circuit wiring can be checked as described in Chapter 12.

5 The solenoid contacts can be checked by connecting a voltmeter or test light between the battery positive feed connection on the starter side of the solenoid, and earth. When the ignition switch is turned to the start position, there should be a reading or lighted bulb, as applicable. If there is no reading or lighted bulb, the solenoid is faulty and should be renewed.

6 If the circuit and solenoid are proved sound, the fault must lie in the starter motor. Begin checking the starter motor by removing it (see Section 8), and having the brushes checked. If the fault does not lie in the brushes, the motor windings must be faulty. In this event, it may be possible to have the starter motor overhauled by a specialist, but check on the availability and cost of spares before proceeding, as it may prove more economical to obtain a new or exchange motor.

8 Starter motor – removal and refitting

Removal

1 Disconnect the battery negative and positive

leads, and position the leads away from the battery (also see *Disconnecting the battery*). This is **essential** before disconnecting the starter wiring.

2 The solenoid/starter motor assembly is installed at the front of the engine, next to the transmission bellhousing. Access is from below.

3 Jack up the front of the car, and support it on axle stands (see *Jacking and vehicle support*). Unbolt and remove the engine undertray (see Chapter 11, Section 23).

4 Peel back the rubber cover, then unscrew the nut and take off the main starter wire. Disconnect the (spade type) wiring plug from the solenoid.

5 Unbolt the radiator hose support clip from the starter motor (or just unclip the hose).

6 Unscrew and remove the two mounting bolts, withdraw the starter motor from the transmission, and remove it from the engine compartment. Note that the upper mounting bolt is smaller than the lower one (which is one of the transmission-to-engine bolts) **(see illustrations)**.

Refitting

7 Refitting is a reversal of removal, noting the following points:
   a) *Tighten the starter mounting bolts to the specified torque.*
   b) *Ensure that the wiring connections are correctly and securely remade.*

9 Starter motor – overhaul

If the starter motor is thought to be defective, it should be removed from the car and taken to an auto-electrician for assessment. In the majority of cases, new starter motor brushes can be fitted at a reasonable cost. However, check the cost of repairs first, as it may prove more economical to purchase a new or exchange motor.

Chapter 5 Part B:
Ignition system

Contents

Degrees of difficulty

Easy, suitable for novice with little experience	Fairly easy, suitable for beginner with some experience	Fairly difficult, suitable for competent DIY mechanic	Difficult, suitable for experienced DIY mechanic	Very difficult, suitable for expert DIY or professional

Specifications

System type
All models. . . . . Fully-electronic under ECM control, two individual direct-ignition coils and spark plugs per cylinder (i-DSI – intelligent Dual Sequential Ignition)

Firing order. . . . . 1-3-4-2 (No 1 cylinder at timing chain end)

Ignition timing
All models. . . . . 8° BTDC ± 2° at idle (red pulley mark)

Torque wrench settings

	Nm	lbf ft
Ignition coil mounting bolts	10	7
Knock sensor:		
With mounting bolt	22	16
Without mounting bolt	31	23

1 General information

The ignition system fitted to the Jazz is highly unusual, in that it features two direct-ignition coils and two spark plugs per cylinder, making a total of eight. The coils are arranged in two rows of four, along the front and rear of the cylinder head. The engine control module (ECM) takes advantage of this arrangement, and is able to advance or retard the timing on the front or rear bank of coils to boost engine torque at low engine speeds, and also to clean up exhaust emissions.

At idle speed and at high engine speeds, both banks of coils fire simultaneously. However, at low engine speeds with light loads, the ECM advances the timing on the front bank (where the cylinder combustion temperature is lower) to improve fuel consumption. At low engine speeds and higher loads, the front bank timing stays advanced, but now the rear bank timing is retarded, which boosts torque and limits 'pinking' (detonation or knock). The coils operate in firing order, and there is no 'wasted

spark', as seen on earlier systems without a distributor.

Ignition timing is also altered in response to engine speed, coolant temperature, throttle position and vacuum pressure in the intake manifold. These parameters are relayed to the ECM by the crankshaft position and camshaft/TDC sensors, throttle position sensor, coolant temperature sensor and the MAP sensor. Ignition timing is altered during warm-up, idling and warm running conditions by the ECM. This electronic ignition system also consists of the ignition switch, battery, eight direct-ignition coils, and the eight spark plugs.

The knock sensor is mounted on the cylinder block to inform the ECM when the engine is 'pinking'. Its sensitivity to a particular frequency of vibration allows it to detect the impulses which are caused by the shock waves set up when the engine starts to pink (pre-ignite). The knock sensor sends an electrical signal to the ECM which retards the ignition advance setting until the pinking ceases – the ignition timing is then gradually returned to the 'normal' setting. This maintains the ignition timing as close to

the knock threshold as possible – the most efficient setting for the engine under normal running conditions.

Precautions

The following precautions must be observed, to prevent damage to the ignition system components and to reduce risk of personal injury.

a) Ensure the ignition is switched off before disconnecting any of the ignition wiring.
b) Ensure that the ignition is switched off before connecting or disconnecting any ignition test equipment, such as a timing light.
c) Do not earth the coil primary or secondary circuits.

⚠ **Warning: Voltages produced by an electronic ignition system are considerably higher than those produced by conventional ignition systems. Extreme care must be taken when working on the system with the ignition switched on. Persons with surgically-implanted cardiac pacemaker devices should keep well clear of the ignition circuits, components and test equipment**

2.5 Engine management system diagnostic connector

5.3 Disconnect the wiring plug from the sensor . . .

5.4 . . . then unscrew its mounting bolt and remove it from the engine

2 Ignition system – testing

1 The components of ignition systems are normally very reliable; most faults are far more likely to be due to loose or dirty connections, or to 'tracking' of HT voltage due to dirt, dampness or damaged insulation than to the failure of any of the system's components. Always check all wiring thoroughly before condemning an electrical component and work methodically to eliminate all other possibilities before deciding that a particular component is faulty.

Engine will not start

2 If the engine either will not turn over at all, or only turns very slowly, first check the battery and starter motor as described in Chapter 5A.
3 The anti-theft immobiliser system disables the fuel system when in operation, meaning that the engine will turn over as normal, but will not start. The immobiliser should be deactivated when a properly-coded ignition key is inserted into the ignition switch. If possible, substitute a spare key and recheck.
4 Ordinarily, it would be possible to check the ignition coil resistances, but Honda do not publish resistance specifications.
5 Ultimately, the car should be referred to a Honda dealer or diagnostic specialist for testing. A diagnostic connector is incorporated in the engine management system wiring harness, into which dedicated electronic test equipment can be plugged – the connector is located under the steering column, on the left, and is accessed after removing the driver's facia closing panel as described in Chapter 11, Section 27 **(see illustration)**. The tester will locate the fault quickly and simply, alleviating the need to test all the system components individually, which is a time-consuming operation that carries a high risk of damaging the ECM. If necessary, the system wiring and wiring connectors can be checked as described in Chapter 12, ensuring that the

ECM wiring connector is only unplugged with the battery disconnected.

Engine misfires

6 An irregular misfire suggests either a loose connection or intermittent fault in the primary circuit, or an HT fault between the coils and spark plugs.
7 With the ignition switched off, check carefully through the system, ensuring that all connections are clean and securely fastened.
8 Check that the HT coils and their associated wiring connections are clean and dry.
9 Regular misfiring of one spark plug may be due to a faulty spark plug, faulty injector, a faulty coil, or loss of compression in the relevant cylinder. Regular misfiring of all the cylinders suggests a fuel supply fault, such as a clogged fuel filter or faulty fuel pump, especially if it occurs in conditions where fuel demand is high.

3 Ignition coils – removal and refitting

1 Refer to Chapter 1, Section 20. Note that the four front coils and the four rear coils appear to be identical, but they cannot be interchanged front to rear.

4 Ignition timing – checking and adjustment

It is possible to check the ignition timing, but only using Honda diagnostic equipment. Even if this is available, the ignition timing cannot be adjusted, and if a check reveals it to be out of specification, a new engine control module (ECM) will be needed.

If the timing is thought to be incorrect because the engine can be heard pinking, the knock sensor may be faulty (see Section 5).

If performance in general is down, carry out the primary operations listed in Chapter 1, Section 2, before having the engine manage-

ment system checked by a Honda dealer or diagnostic specialist. The principal engine management sensors (described in Chapter 4A) having the most direct bearing on ignition timing are the crankshaft position sensor, camshaft/TDC sensor and MAP sensor.

If the timing chain has recently been disturbed, note that engine performance will suffer if the chain is incorrectly fitted (one or more teeth 'out').

5 Knock sensor – removal and refitting

Removal

1 The knock sensor is mounted on the front of the engine, just below the inlet manifold. Realistically, access is only possible with the inlet manifold removed as described in Chapter 4A, though it may just be possible from below.
2 The knock sensor is next to the engine block coolant drain plug – do not confuse it with the oil pressure switch, which is directly above the oil filter. One of two types of knock sensor may be fitted.

Type 1

3 Disconnect the wiring plug from the sensor **(see illustration)**.
4 Unscrew the mounting bolt in the centre of the sensor, then withdraw the sensor from the engine **(see illustration)**.

Type 2

5 Disconnect the wiring plug from the sensor.
6 Unscrew the sensor (a spanner or deep socket will be needed), then withdraw the sensor from the engine.

Refitting

7 Clean the sensor and engine block mating faces before fitting.
8 Refitting is a reversal of removal. It is critical for the correct operation of the sensor that it, or its mounting bolt, is tightened to the specified torque.

Chapter 6
Clutch

Contents

Degrees of difficulty

Easy, suitable for novice with little experience	**Fairly easy,** suitable for beginner with some experience	**Fairly difficult,** suitable for competent DIY mechanic	**Difficult,** suitable for experienced DIY mechanic	**Very difficult,** suitable for expert DIY or professional

Specifications

General

Type	Single dry plate, diaphragm spring with spring-loaded hub
Operation	Hydraulic
Clutch pedal:	
Minimum disengagement height from floor	61 mm
Pedal free play	6 to 20 mm
Pedal stroke	130 to 140 mm
Standard height	150 mm
Friction disc thickness:	
Nominal	7.3 to 8.0 mm
Wear limit	5.0 mm
Rivet head depth limit	0.2 mm

Torque wrench settings

	Nm	lbf ft
Clutch slave cylinder mounting bolts.	22	16
Master cylinder mounting nuts.	13	10
Pressure plate-to-flywheel bolts.	25	18

1 General information and precautions

All manual transmission models use a single dry plate, diaphragm-spring type clutch. The clutch friction disc has a splined hub which allows it to slide along the splines of the transmission input shaft. The friction disc is held in contact with the flywheel by spring pressure exerted by the diaphragm in the pressure plate.

The clutch release system is operated by hydraulic pressure. The hydraulic release system consists of the clutch pedal, a master cylinder and fluid reservoir, the hydraulic pipe, a slave (release) cylinder which actuates the clutch release lever and the clutch release bearing.

When pressure is applied to the clutch pedal to release the clutch, hydraulic pressure is exerted against the outer end of the clutch release lever. As the lever pivots the shaft, fingers push against the release bearing. The bearing pushes against the fingers of the diaphragm spring of the pressure plate assembly, which in turn releases the clutch friction disc.

When the pedal is released, the diaphragm spring forces the pressure plate back into contact with the linings on the clutch friction disc. The disc is now firmly held between the pressure plate and the flywheel, thus transmitting engine power to the transmission.

The hydraulic system requires no adjustment, since the quantity of hydraulic fluid in the circuit automatically compensates for wear every time the clutch pedal is operated.

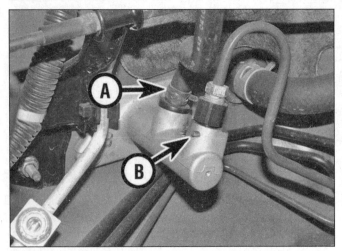

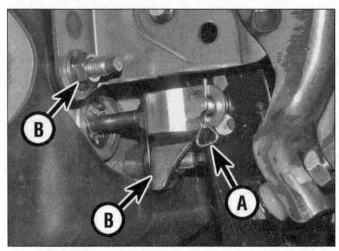

2.1 Master cylinder fluid supply hose (A) and rigid pipe clip (B)

2.4 Master cylinder pushrod pin's spring clip (A) and mounting nuts (B)

Other than to renew components with obvious damage, some preliminary checks should be performed to diagnose clutch problems. These checks assume that the transmission is in good working condition.

a) *The first check should be the fluid level in the clutch master cylinder (see Weekly checks). If the fluid level is low, add fluid as necessary and inspect the hydraulic system for leaks. If the master cylinder reservoir has run dry, bleed the system as described in Section 4 and retest the clutch operation.*

b) *To check 'clutch spin-down time', run the engine at normal idle speed with the transmission in neutral (clutch pedal up – engaged). Disengage the clutch (pedal down), wait several seconds and select reverse. No grinding noise should be heard. A grinding noise would most likely indicate a problem in the pressure plate or the clutch friction disc.*

c) *Visually inspect the pivot bushing at the top of the clutch pedal to make sure there is no binding or excessive play.*

d) *Check that the clutch release lever is solidly mounted on the ball-stud.*

⚠ **Warning: The fluid used in the system is brake hydraulic fluid, which is poisonous. Take care to keep it off bare skin, and in particular not to get splashes in your eyes. The fluid also attacks paintwork, and may discolour carpets, etc – keep spillages to a minimum, and wash any off immediately with cold water. Finally, hydraulic fluid is highly flammable, and should be handled with the same care as petrol.**

⚠ **Warning: Dust produced by clutch wear and deposited on clutch components may be hazardous to your health. DO NOT blow it out with compressed air and DO NOT inhale it. DO NOT use petrol or petroleum-based solvents to remove the dust. Brake system cleaner should be used to flush the dust into a drain pan.**

2 Master cylinder – removal, overhaul and refitting

Note: *Refer to the hydraulic fluid warning in Section 1 before proceeding.*

Removal

1 Clamp the fluid supply hose from the reservoir, then release the spring clip, and pull the hose off the master cylinder's rear port – quickly turn the hose end upwards, to reduce fluid spillage **(see illustration)**. Take care not to drip hydraulic fluid onto the paintwork or hot engine components.

2 To disconnect the rigid line from the front port, pull the clip out to the side, then pull up the pipe to detach it. Wrap the end of the pipe with clean tissue or cloth, to reduce leakage and stop dirt entry. Note that a new pipe clip should be used when refitting.

3 Remove the driver's side facia closing panel as described in Chapter 11, Section 27.

4 Working under the facia, remove the spring clip from the master cylinder pushrod clevis pin **(see illustration)**. Pull out the clevis pin to the left, to disconnect the pushrod from the pedal.

5 Unscrew the two master cylinder mounting nuts in front of the pedal, then return to the engine compartment and withdraw the master cylinder from the bulkhead. Recover the gasket fitted behind the cylinder, and the O-ring fitted inside the fluid pipe connection – new ones should be used when refitting.

Overhaul

Note: *Check availability of overhaul kits prior to dismantling the cylinder.*

6 Remove the nut from the end of the cylinder, hold the pushrod into the cylinder body, and prise out the circlip.

7 Remove the stopper, then ease out the pushrod, and pull out the piston assembly. If necessary, use compressed air to force the piston from the cylinder body.

8 Carefully examine the bore of the cylinder for rust, scratches, gouges and general wear. If the bore is damaged, the complete cylinder must be renewed. If the bore is in good condition, thoroughly clean the assembly, and renew the seals as described below.

9 Take note of the seal orientation on the piston, and using a small screwdriver, lever the seals from the grooves on the piston.

10 Fit the new seals to the piston, ensuring the seal lips point towards the spring end of the piston. Smear the seals with the assembly grease supplied in the overhaul kit.

11 Insert the piston assembly into the cylinder, spring end first. Ensure the seal lips enter the cylinder bore without catching or folding back.

12 Compress the piston with the pushrod, fit the stopper, then secure with the circlip. Refit and tighten the nut to complete.

Refitting

13 Refitting is a reversal of removal, noting the following points:

a) *Use a new bulkhead gasket and pipe connection O-ring.*

b) *Tighten the mounting nuts to the specified torque.*

c) *When the rigid pipe is reconnected, secure using a new clip, and splay the clip ends open to retain the pipe securely.*

d) *Use a new spring clip to secure the pedal clevis pin.*

e) *Top-up the reservoir, then bleed the system as described in Section 4.*

3 Slave cylinder – removal, overhaul and refitting

Note: *Refer to the hydraulic fluid warning in Section 1 before proceeding.*

Removal

1 Remove the air cleaner as described in Chapter 4A.

2 Remove the battery and its tray as described in Chapter 5A.

3 Pull out the two roll-pins from the front of the cylinder, at the bleed screw end.

4 Anticipating some fluid spillage, disconnect the fluid pipe union and recover the O-ring – a new one must be used when refitting. Either plug or tape over the open connections.

5 Unscrew and remove the two mounting bolts, then withdraw the cylinder from the transmission **(see illustration)**.

Overhaul

Note: *Check availability of overhaul kits prior to dismantling the cylinder.*

6 Unclip the dust boot from the cylinder body, and pull the pushrod out. Extract the piston and spring. If necessary, use compressed air to force the piston from the bore. Recover the piston spring.

7 Carefully examine the bore of the cylinder for rust, scratches, gouges and general wear. If the bore is damaged, the complete cylinder must be renewed. If the bore is in good condition, thoroughly clean the assembly, and renew the seals as described below.

8 Note their fitted locations, then using a small screwdriver, prise the seals from the piston.

9 Fit the new seals to the piston, ensuring they are fitted as noted on removal. Coat the seals with assembly grease (supplied in the overhaul kit).

10 Insert the spring, large diameter end towards the cylinder bleed nipple, followed by the piston. Ensure the seals lips enter the cylinder bore without catching or folding back.

11 Squeeze some brake grease into the dust boot, then refit the boot and pushrod.

Refitting

12 Refitting is a reversal of removal, noting the following points:

 a) *If not already done, pull back the dust boot, and apply a little brake grease to the end of the slave cylinder pushrod.*

 b) *Tighten the slave cylinder mounting bolts to the specified torque.*

 c) *Use a new pipe connection O-ring, and reconnect the fluid pipe securely.*

 d) *Top-up the fluid reservoir, and bleed the system as described in Section 4.*

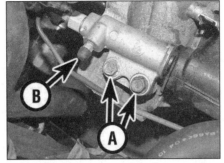

3.5 Unscrew the slave cylinder mounting bolts (A) – also note bleed screw (B)

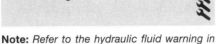

4 Hydraulic system – bleeding

Note: *Refer to the hydraulic fluid warning in Section 1 before proceeding.*

1 The correct operation of any hydraulic system is only possible after removing all air from the components and circuit; this is achieved by bleeding the system.

2 During the bleeding procedure, add only clean, unused hydraulic fluid of the recommended type; never re-use fluid that has already been bled from the system. Ensure that sufficient fluid is available before starting work.

3 If there is any possibility of incorrect fluid being already in the system, the hydraulic circuit must be flushed completely with uncontaminated, correct fluid.

4 If hydraulic fluid has been lost from the system, or air has entered because of a leak, ensure that the fault is cured before continuing further.

5 Check that all pipes and hoses are secure, unions tight and the bleed screw is closed. The bleed screw is located on the end of the slave cylinder, on the front of the transmission casing **(refer to illustration 3.5)**.

6 Remove the air cleaner as described in Chapter 4A.

7 Remove the battery and its tray as described in Chapter 5A.

8 To improve access to the clutch (and brake) reservoirs, a removable panel is provided in the windscreen cowl panel. Pull back the rubber strip on the driver's side, then unclip and remove the panel section provided **(see illustrations)**.

9 Unscrew the master cylinder fluid reservoir cap (the smaller of the two reservoirs), then take out the filter and the rubber baffle – place them on a clean piece of cloth or towel **(see illustrations)**.

10 Top the level up to the upper (MAX) line **(see illustration)**. Refit the cap loosely, and remember to maintain the fluid level at least above the lower (MIN) level line throughout the procedure, or there is a risk of further air entering the system.

11 Clean any dirt from around the bleed screw (which is on the slave cylinder), and remove the dust cap.

12 The procedure for bleeding is much the same as that for bleeding the brakes as described in Chapter 9. It is recommended

4.8a Pull back the rubber strip . . .

4.8b . . . and unclip the access panel

4.9a Unscrew the reservoir cap and lift out the filter . . .

4.9b . . . then remove the rubber baffle

4.10 Top-up the clutch fluid level to the MAX line

5.5 Mark the pressure plate and flywheel

5.6a Unscrew the six pressure plate bolts . . .

that either the basic (two-man) or one-way valve method is used, for simplicity.

13 When bleeding is complete, and correct pedal feel is restored, tighten the bleed screw securely and wash off any spilt fluid. Refit the dust cap to the bleed screw. Refit any components removed for access.

14 Check the hydraulic fluid level in the master cylinder reservoir, and top-up if necessary (see *Weekly checks*).

15 Discard any hydraulic fluid that has been bled from the system; it will not be fit for re-use.

16 Check the operation of the clutch pedal. If the clutch is still not operating correctly, air may still be present in the system, and further bleeding is required. Failure to bleed satisfactorily after a reasonable repetition of the bleeding procedure may be due to worn master cylinder/slave cylinder seals.

5 Clutch components – removal, inspection and refitting

Note: *Refer to the clutch dust warning in Section 1 before proceeding.*

Removal

1 Access to the clutch components is normally accomplished by removing the transmission, leaving the engine in the car. However, note that this does not actually save much work over removing the engine and transmission together.

2 If the engine is being removed for major overhaul, check the clutch for wear, and renew worn components as necessary. However, the relatively low cost of the clutch components compared to the time and trouble spent gaining access to them warrants their renewal anytime the engine or transmission is removed, unless they are new or in near-perfect condition. The following procedures are based on the assumption the engine will stay in place.

3 Remove the transmission from the car

(see Chapter 7A). Support the engine while the transmission is out. Preferably, an engine hoist should be used to support it from above. However, if a jack is used underneath the engine, make sure a piece of wood is positioned between the jack and engine sump to spread the load.

4 The clutch fork and release bearing can remain attached to the transmission housing for the time being.

5 If the pressure plate is to be refitted, scribe or paint marks so the pressure plate and the flywheel will be in the same alignment during refitting **(see illustration)**.

6 Turning each bolt a little at a time, loosen the six pressure plate-to-flywheel bolts (note that they have bi-hex heads – an ordinary splined socket will undo them). Work in a diagonal pattern until all spring pressure is relieved. Then hold the pressure plate securely and completely remove the bolts, followed by the pressure plate and friction disc **(see illustrations)**.

Inspection

7 Ordinarily, when a problem occurs in the clutch, it can be attributed to wear of the clutch friction disc. However, all components should be inspected at this time.

8 Inspect the flywheel for cracks, heat distortion, grooves and other obvious defects.

5.6b . . . until the pressure plate and friction disc can be removed

If the imperfections are slight, a engineering workshop can machine the surface flat and smooth, which is highly recommended regardless of the surface appearance. Refer to Chapter 2A for the flywheel removal and refitting procedure.

9 Inspect the lining on the clutch disc, and in particular, the amount of lining above the rivet heads. Check for loose rivets, distortion, cracks, broken springs and other obvious damage. As mentioned above, ordinarily the clutch friction disc is routinely renewed, so if in doubt about the condition, renew it.

10 If the clutch lining is blackened or oil-soaked, this indicates that the clutch has been slipping, or that oil is leaking onto it (most likely from the crankshaft oil seal). Both these conditions need investigating, or they will recur when the new disc is fitted.

11 The release bearing should also be renewed along with the clutch friction disc (see Section 7). Typically, the release bearing, friction disc and pressure plate will be available as a three-part clutch 'kit' from dealers and other parts suppliers. This is also a good time to check the condition of the pilot bearing (see Section 6).

12 Check the machined surfaces and the diaphragm spring fingers of the pressure plate. If the surface is grooved or otherwise damaged, renew the pressure plate. Also check for obvious damage, distortion, cracking, etc. Light glazing can be removed with emery cloth or sandpaper. If a new pressure plate is required, new and reconditioned units are available.

Refitting

13 Before refitting, clean the flywheel and pressure plate machined surfaces with brake cleaner or degreaser. It's important that no oil or grease is on these surfaces or the lining of the clutch friction disc. Handle the parts only with clean hands.

14 Position the clutch friction disc against the flywheel. Make sure the disc is installed properly (most new clutch discs will be marked 'flywheel side' or something similar – if not marked, fit the clutch friction disc with the damper springs towards the transmission).

15 Centre the clutch disc by ensuring the alignment tool extends through the splined hub and into the pocket in the crankshaft. Wiggle the tool up, down or side-to-side as needed to centre the disc **(see illustrations)**.

16 Offer the pressure plate into position over the tool, and tighten the pressure plate-to-flywheel bolts a little at a time, working in a criss-cross pattern to prevent distorting the cover **(see illustrations)**. When all of the bolts are snug, tighten them to the torque listed in this Chapter's Specifications. Remove the alignment tool.

17 Using clutch assembly grease (copper grease will do as a substitute), lubricate the inside of the release bearing. Also apply a little grease on the release lever contact areas and the transmission input shaft bearing retainer.

18 Fit the clutch release bearing (see Section 7).

19 Fit the transmission and all components removed previously.

6 Pilot bearing –
inspection and renewal

Refer to Chapter 2A, Section 16.

7 Release bearing and fork –
removal, inspection and refitting

Removal

1 Unbolt the clutch slave cylinder (see Section 3), but don't disconnect the fluid line. Suspend the release cylinder out of the way with a piece of wire or string.

2 Remove the transmission (see Chapter 7A). Slide out the release fork dust boot, noting how it is fitted **(see illustration)**.

3 Release the spring from the ball-stud, then pull the release fork out from inside the bellhousing. Recover the spring **(see illustrations)**.

4 Lift the release fork, and slide the release bearing off the end **(see illustration)**.

5.15a Offer in the friction disc with the alignment tool . . .

5.15b . . . then move the tool until the disc is centred

5.16a Fit the pressure plate over the tool . . .

5.16b . . . and fit the bolts to grip the friction disc

Inspection

5 Hold the bearing by the outer race and rotate the inner race while applying pressure. If the bearing doesn't turn smoothly or if it's noisy, renew the bearing/hub assembly.

6 Wipe the bearing with a clean rag and inspect it for damage, wear and cracks. It's common practice to renew the bearing whenever a clutch overhaul is performed, to decrease the possibility of a bearing failure in the future.

7.2 Unclip and remove the release fork dust boot

7.3a Use a screwdriver to release the spring from the ball-stud . . .

7.3b . . . and remove the release fork with bearing

7.3c Recover the spring from inside the bellhousing

7.4 Slide the release bearing off the fork

7.8 Fitting the spring to the release fork

7.10 Lightly grease the shaft splines and the release bearing guide

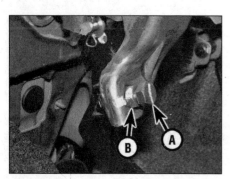

8.2 Clutch pedal height adjuster bolt (A) and locknut (B)

8.5 Clutch pedal pushrod locknut

Don't immerse the bearing in solvent – it's sealed for life and to do so would ruin it. Also check the release lever for cracks and bends.

Refitting

7 Fill the inner groove of the release bearing with clutch assembly grease (copper grease will suffice). Lubricate the release fork ball socket, fork ends and slave cylinder pushrod socket with the same grease.

8 Attach the release bearing to the release fork. Slide the curved end of the spring through the hole in the fork, then squeeze the ends together and attach it to the inside of the fork **(see illustration)**.

9 Slide the release bearing onto the transmission input shaft front bearing retainer while passing the end of the release fork through the opening in the clutch housing. Push the clutch release fork onto the ball-stud until the spring clicks home.

10 Apply a light coat of the clutch assembly grease to the transmission input shaft splines and release bearing guide **(see illustration)**.

Also apply a little grease to the face of the release bearing where it contacts the pressure plate diaphragm fingers.

11 The remainder of refitting is the reverse of the removal procedure.

8 Clutch pedal adjustment

Pedal height

1 The height of the clutch pedal is the distance the pedal sits off the floor, measured from the top surface of the pedal. If the pedal height is not as specified, it must be adjusted. Remove the driver's floor mat before making the check.

2 To adjust the clutch pedal, loosen the locknut on the adjuster bolt and back the bolt out until it no longer touches the pedal, then loosen the locknut on the clutch pushrod **(see illustration)**. Turn the pushrod to adjust the pedal height. Also check the pedal stroke, which is the distance from the fully-depressed to fully-released position. When both adjustments are correct, tighten the locknut.

3 Turn the switch/bolt clockwise until it just contacts the pedal arm, then turn it in an additional 3/4 to 1 turn. Tighten the locknut.

Pedal freeplay

4 The freeplay is the pedal slack, or the distance the pedal can be depressed before it begins to have any effect on the clutch system. If the pedal freeplay is not within the specified range, it must be adjusted.

5 To adjust the pedal freeplay, loosen the locknut on the clutch pushrod **(see illustration)**. Back off the pushrod to adjust the pedal freeplay to the specified range, and retighten the locknut.

Chapter 7 Part A:
Manual transmission

Contents

Degrees of difficulty

Easy, suitable for novice with little experience	**Fairly easy,** suitable for beginner with some experience	**Fairly difficult,** suitable for competent DIY mechanic	**Difficult,** suitable for experienced DIY mechanic	**Very difficult,** suitable for expert DIY or professional

Specifications

General
Type . . . . Manual, five forward speeds and reverse. Synchromesh on all forward speeds

Gear ratios (typical)
1st 3.142
2nd 1.750
3rd 1.241
4th 0.969
5th 0.805
Reverse 3.230
Final drive 4.111

Lubrication
Oil type . . . . See Lubricants and fluids on page 0•17
Oil capacity . . . . See Chapter 1

Torque wrench settings	Nm	lbf ft
Air cleaner support bracket bolts	22	16
Engine/transmission mountings:		
Front mounting bracket bolts	39	29
Left-hand mounting**:		
Adjustment nut	74	55
Mounting bracket nuts/bolt	49	36
Through-bolt	44	32
Rear mounting:		
Subframe and rear bracket bolts	44	32
Through-bolt	59	44
Gearchange cable mounting bracket bolts	27	20
Gearchange mechanism mounting bolts	22	16
Reversing light switch	29	21
Roadwheel nuts	108	80
Starter motor mounting bolts:		
Lower bolt	64	47
Upper bolt	44	32
Subframe mounting bolts*	93	69
Transmission-to-engine bolts	64	47

* Use new bolts

** Left and right are as seen from the driver's seat

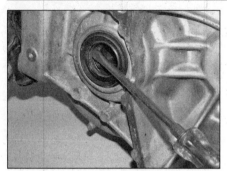

2.4 Prise out the old seal with a screwdriver

1 General information

The transmission is contained in a cast-aluminium alloy casing bolted to the engine's left-hand end, and consists of the gearbox and final drive differential.

Drive is transmitted from the crankshaft via the clutch to the input shaft, which has a splined extension to accept the clutch friction disc, and rotates in tapered roller bearings. From the input shaft, drive is transmitted to the output shaft, which also rotates in tapered roller bearings. From the output shaft, the drive is transmitted to the differential crownwheel, which rotates with the differential case and planetary gears, thus driving the sun gears and driveshafts. The rotation of the planetary gears on their shaft allows the inner

roadwheel to rotate at a slower speed than the outer roadwheel when the car is cornering.

The input and output shafts are arranged side-by-side, parallel to the crankshaft and driveshafts, so that their gear pinion teeth are in constant mesh. In the neutral position, the output shaft gear pinions rotate freely, so that drive cannot be transmitted to the crownwheel.

Gear selection is via a floor-mounted lever with a cable linkage. The selector linkage causes the appropriate selector fork to move its respective synchro-sleeve along the shaft, to lock the gear pinion to the synchro-hub. Since the synchro-hubs are splined to the output shaft, this locks the pinion to the shaft, so that drive can be transmitted. To ensure that gearchanging can be made quickly and quietly, a synchromesh system is fitted to all forward gears, consisting of baulk rings and spring-loaded fingers, as well as the gear pinions and synchro-hubs. The synchromesh cones are formed on the mating faces of the baulk rings and gear pinions.

2 Driveshaft oil seals – renewal

1 Oil leaks frequently occur due to wear of the driveshaft oil seals. Renewal of these seals is relatively easy, since the repair can usually be performed without removing the transmission from the car.
2 Driveshaft oil seals are located at the sides of the transmission, where the driveshafts are attached. If leakage at the seal is suspected,

raise the car and support it securely on axle stands (see *Jacking and vehicle support*). If the seal is leaking, lubricant will be found on the sides of the transmission, below the seals.
3 Refer to Chapter 8 and remove the driveshaft(s).
4 Use a screwdriver or lever bar to carefully prise the oil seal out of the transmission casing **(see illustration)**.
5 Using a large section of pipe or a large deep socket (slightly smaller than the outside diameter of the seal) as a drift, fit the new oil seal. Ensure that the spring side of the seal faces into the transmission casing. Drive it into the bore squarely and make sure it's completely seated. Coat the seal lip with transmission fluid.
6 Refit the driveshaft(s). Be careful not to damage the lip of the new seal.

3 Gearchange mechanism and cables – removal and refitting

Removal

Gearchange mechanism

1 Remove the centre console as described in Chapter 11.
2 At the front, prise out the clip securing the wiring harness to the heater floor duct, then slide the duct downwards to free it from the heater unit. Prise up the single clip either side of the gear lever, then slide the black plastic heater floor duct into the car, and lift it out **(see illustrations)**.
3 The left-hand inner cable is secured by a split pin and washer – pull out the pin, recover the washer, and separate the cable end fitting from the lever **(see illustrations)**. Note that a new split pin should be used when refitting.
4 To remove the right-hand inner cable, spread apart the legs of the spring clip, then prise down the cable end to release it from the ball fitting **(see illustration)**.
5 At the front of the gearchange mechanism, use a pair of slip-joint ('water pump') pliers to twist the left-hand cable anti-clockwise, and release it upwards from its fitting. The right-hand cable is secured using a horseshoe clip – prise it upwards to remove. Unhook the

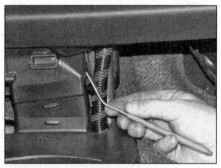

3.2a To remove the heater floor duct, first prise off the wiring harness . . .

3.2b . . . then slide it down off the heater unit . . .

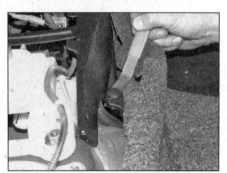

3.2c Prise up the floor clip either side . . .

3.2d . . . then slide the duct back and lift it out

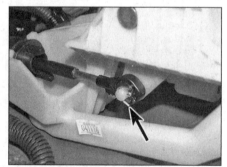

3.3a The left-hand cable is secured by a split pin and washer

3.3b Pull out the split pin . . .

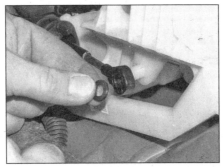

3.3c . . . then take off the washer and pull off the cable

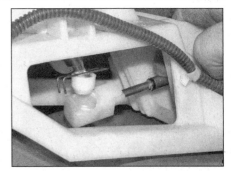

3.4 Prise apart the spring clip legs, then pull down the right-hand cable

3.5a Twist the left-hand cable anti-clockwise, and lift it out

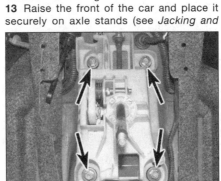

3.5b Prise up the horseshoe clip from the right-hand cable

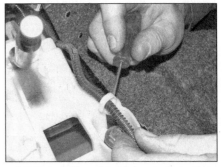

3.6 Detach the wiring harness from the mechanism

cable fittings from the gearchange housing **(see illustrations)**. A new horseshoe clip should be obtained for refitting.

6 Unclip the wiring harness from the right-hand side of the gearchange mechanism **(see illustration)**.

7 Unscrew the four gearchange mechanism bolts, then lift the assembly out of the car **(see illustration)**.

Gearchange cables

8 Proceed as described in paragraphs 1 to 5.

9 Remove the air cleaner as described in Chapter 4A.

10 Remove the battery and its tray as described in Chapter 5A.

11 Disconnect the shift and selector cables from their levers on the transmission – each is secured by a split pin, and there are two washers. Unhook the cables from the levers **(see illustrations)**. Mark the cables for identification purposes if they are to be refitted.

12 Pull up the horseshoe clip securing the cable outers, and detach the cables **(see illustration)**. New horseshoe clips should be obtained for refitting.

13 Raise the front of the car and place it securely on axle stands (see *Jacking and*

vehicle support). Trace the gearchange cables under the car, to the point where they enter through the floorpan – depending on model, it may be necessary to unbolt and remove the exhaust system heat shields for access.

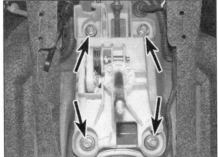

3.7 Unscrew the four mechanism mounting bolts, and lift it out

3.11a Pull out the split pin . . .

3.11b . . . then take off the washers . . .

3.11c . . . and lift off each cable from the transmission lever

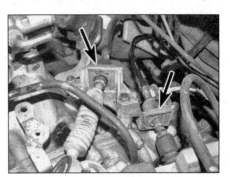

3.12 Slide up the horseshoe clips to disconnect the cable outers

4.10 Disconnect the reversing light switch wiring plug

4.11a Using a large spanner or deep socket . . .

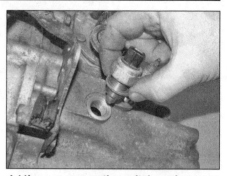

4.11b . . . unscrew the switch, and recover its sealing washer

14 Trace the cables back to the support bracket at the rear of the engine compartment. Remove the clamp bolt and detach the cable clamp (alternatively, undo the two bracket nuts, and release the bracket first).

15 With the help of an assistant inside the car, feed the cables through the floor grommet, and withdraw them into the engine compartment for removal.

Refitting

16 Refitting is a reversal of removal, noting the following points:
  a) *Lightly grease the cable end fittings, at the transmission and gearchange mechanism ends, when refitting.*
  b) *Honda state that new split pins and horseshoe clips should be used when refitting the cables.*
  c) *Ensure that the cables are correctly refitted, and routed as before, with no sharp bends.*
  d) *Tighten the gearchange mechanism mounting bolts to the specified torque.*
  e) *On completion, check that all gears can be selected properly before taking the car out on the road.*

4 Reversing light switch – testing and renewal

Testing

1 Before testing the reversing light switch, check the fuse in the passenger compartment

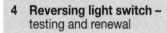

5.3a Disconnect the radiator top hose from the thermostat housing

fuse/relay box (refer to the wiring diagrams in Chapter 12).

2 Put the gear lever in reverse, and turn the ignition switch to the on position (warning lights on). The reversing lights should go on. Turn off the ignition switch.

3 If the reversing lights don't go on, check the light bulbs in the tail light assembly (see Chapter 12). It's unlikely that both bulbs would fail at once, but it's still a possibility.

4 If the fuse and bulbs are both okay, the reversing light switch on top of the transmission should be checked. Gain access to the switch by removing the air cleaner, battery and battery tray, as described in Chapters 4A and 5A.

5 The reversing light switch should not be confused with the vehicle speed sensor, which is also screwed into the top of the transmission, but unlike the reversing light switch, has a separate mounting bolt. Disconnect the switch wiring plug.

6 With the gear lever in reverse, there should be continuity; with the lever in any other gear, there should be no continuity.

7 If the switch fails this test, renew it (see below).

8 If the switch is OK, but the reversing lights aren't coming on, check for power to the switch. If voltage is not available, trace the circuit between the switch and the fusebox. If power is present, trace the circuit between the switch and the reversing lights for an open-circuit condition.

Renewal

9 If not already done, gain access to the

5.3b Disconnect the bottom hose from the front of the housing . . .

switch by removing the air cleaner, battery and battery tray, as described in Chapters 4A and 5A.

10 The reversing light switch should not be confused with the vehicle speed sensor, which is also screwed into the top of the transmission, but unlike the reversing light switch, has a separate mounting bolt. Disconnect the switch wiring plug **(see illustration)**.

11 A large deep socket or spanner will be needed to unscrew the switch – recover the sealing washer **(see illustrations)**.

12 Refitting is a reversal of removal. Use a new sealing washer, and tighten the switch to the specified torque. Test the operation of the lights on completion.

5 Transmission – removal and refitting

Removal

1 Remove the air cleaner as described in Chapter 4A.

2 Remove the battery and its tray as described in Chapter 5A.

3 Drain the cooling system as described in Chapter 1. Disconnect the radiator top hose from the side of the thermostat housing, then unclip it from the support bracket on top of the transmission. Similarly, disconnect the bottom hose from the front of the housing, and unclip it from the front of the engine **(see illustrations)**.

4 Slide the wiring harness at the front of the

5.3c . . . and unclip it from the front of the engine

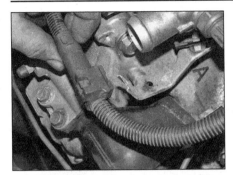

5.4 Unclip the wiring harness from the front of the transmission

5.5 Unclip the breather hose from the bracket

5.6a Unbolt the clutch pipe/union mounting bracket . . .

5.6b . . . then unclip the pipe from the top of the transmission

5.6c Unbolt the slave cylinder . . .

5.6d . . . then move it clear without bending the pipe

transmission upwards off its support clip (see illustration).

5 Unclip the gearbox breather hose from the bracket on top of the transmission (see illustration).

6 Trace the clutch slave cylinder fluid pipe back

from the cylinder to the fluid hose union, and unbolt the pipe/union support bracket. Unclip the pipe from the top of the transmission. Remove the two slave cylinder mounting bolts, and move the cylinder clear of the transmission, if possible without bending the pipe (see illustrations).

Caution: Be careful not to bend or kink the clutch hydraulic pipe, and don't depress the clutch pedal while the slave cylinder is removed.

7 Disconnect the wiring plugs from the reversing light switch and vehicle speed sensor. Release the wiring harness clips and move the wiring clear.

8 Release the clip securing the primary oxygen sensor wiring plug support bracket (at the back of the transmission cable support bracket), and move the wiring clear of the transmission.

9 Remove the split pin and washers securing the cable ends to the transmission levers, and disconnect the cables. Unscrew the three bolts securing the gearchange cable bracket to the top of the transmission, then move the whole assembly to one side, taking care not to bend the cables (see illustrations).

10 Remove the starter motor as described in Chapter 5A.

5.9a Pull out the split pin . . .

5.9b . . . then take off the washers . . .

5.9c . . . and lift off each cable from the transmission lever

5.9d Unscrew the three gearchange cable bracket bolts . . .

5.9e . . . noting that one secures the oxygen sensor wiring bracket . . .

5.9f . . . and lift the bracket and cables clear

5.12 One of the transmission-to-engine bolts

5.13 Unbolt the radiator hose support bracket

11 Support the transmission end of the engine. Preferably, this should be done from above, either with an engine hoist/crane or an engine support bar – supporting from below will be awkward, as the subframe must be removed later.

12 Loosen the transmission-to-engine bolts which are accessible from above (see illustration).

13 Unbolt the radiator hose support bracket from the left-hand (transmission) mounting (see illustration).

14 Unbolt the earth strap in front of the left-hand mounting, and move it clear. Unscrew and remove the mounting through-bolt, then unscrew the two mounting nuts and single bolt, and lift off the mounting bracket (see illustrations).

15 Loosen the front wheel nuts, and if possible, also loosen both driveshaft nuts while the car is still on the ground. Jack up the

front of the car, and support it on axle stands (see Jacking and vehicle support). Note that the car must be raised sufficiently high for the transmission to be lowered out and withdrawn from underneath. Remove the front wheels and the engine undertray.

16 Remove the left-hand front wheel arch liner (refer to Chapter 11, Section 23, if necessary).

17 Remove the two bolts securing the air cleaner support bracket to the end of the transmission, and take off the bracket (see illustration).

18 Drain the transmission fluid as described in Chapter 1.

19 Remove the driveshafts as described in Chapter 8.

20 Remove the subframe as described in Chapter 10.

21 At the sump-to-transmission joint, remove three bolts and take off the small cover plate from below the flywheel. Also remove the

two larger sump-to-transmission bolts (see illustration).

22 Remove the engine front and rear mountings as described in Chapter 2A.

23 Support the transmission from below, using a jack and a flat piece of wood. Have an assistant ready to support the transmission as the jack is lowered.

 Paint or scribe an alignment mark across the transmission and engine faces. This is simply to make refitting easier – the transmission has two locating dowels, but an alignment mark will be helpful in eliminating guesswork when offering the unit into position.

24 Unscrew the remaining transmission-to-engine bolts, then carefully pull the trans-

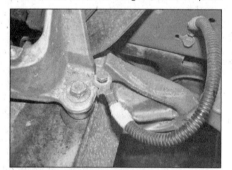

5.14a Unbolt the earth strap in front of the left-hand mounting

5.14b Unscrew the through-bolt . . .

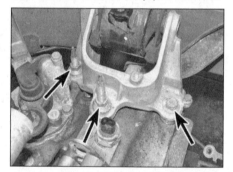

5.14c . . . then unscrew the bracket's two nuts and bolt . . .

5.14d . . . and lift off the mounting bracket

5.17 Unbolt the air cleaner support bracket from the end of the transmission

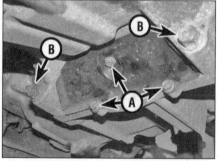

5.21 Remove the cover plate bolts (A) and the sump-to-transmission bolts (B)

mission away from the engine until the transmission shaft is clear of the clutch pressure plate. If necessary, carefully prise the transmission away at first, to release the alignment dowels. Do not allow the weight of the transmission to hang on the input shaft (support the unit until it is completely clear of the engine).

25 Check round the transmission that everything has been disconnected from it, and that there is nothing in the way which might hinder its removal.

26 With the help of an assistant to guide the unit out, lower the transmission on the jack until it can be removed from under the car **(see illustration)**. Recover the two dowel pins, noting their fitted locations, and store them for safekeeping.

Refitting

27 If removed, fit the clutch components (see Chapter 6). It is recommended that the clutch components are at least inspected, if not renewed, while the transmission is removed.

28 If the clutch components were not removed, apply a little grease (such as copper grease) to the transmission input shaft splines.

29 Make sure the two locating dowels are installed in the transmission mating face.

30 Raise the transmission on the jack, then use the alignment marks made on dismantling to align it with the engine.

31 Make sure the transmission is at the right height, then slide it onto the engine so that the transmission shaft enters the clutch. It may be necessary to 'wiggle' the transmission slightly, to align the shaft splines with those of the clutch – if great difficulty is experienced when new clutch components have been fitted, it may mean that the clutch disc has not been centred (see Chapter 6). With the splines aligned, the transmission should slide onto the two dowels, and fully up to the engine.

32 While your assistant holds the transmission in place, insert two or three transmission-to-

5.26 Lower the transmission to the floor

engine bolts initially, and tighten them fully by hand to hold the unit fully onto the dowels.

33 Further refitting is a reversal of removal, noting the following points:

a) As far as possible, fit all engine/ transmission mounting bolts hand-tight only at first. Delay fully tightening the engine/transmission mounting bolts until the weight of the engine is resting on its mountings.

b) Tighten all nuts/bolts to the specified torque. Note that one of the transmission-to-engine bolts also secures the starter motor.

c) Refer to Chapter 10 when refitting the subframe – new subframe bolts must be used. Also, ensure that the appropriate new nuts and locking/split pins are used when reconnecting the steering/ suspension components.

d) Lightly grease the gearchange cable end fittings and slave cylinder pushrod end when refitting.

e) Honda state that new split pins and horseshoe clips should be used when refitting the cables.

f) Refill the transmission with fluid as described in Chapter 1.

g) Check the operation of the clutch, and bleed the system if necessary as described in Chapter 6.

h) Refill the cooling system as described in Chapter 1.

i) As the subframe was removed, have the front wheel alignment checked at the earliest opportunity.

6 Transmission overhaul – general information

Overhauling a manual transmission is a difficult and involved job for the DIY home mechanic. In addition to dismantling and reassembling many small parts, clearances must be precisely measured and, if necessary, changed by selecting shims and spacers. Internal transmission components are also often difficult to obtain, and in many instances, extremely expensive. Because of this, if the transmission develops a fault or becomes noisy, the best course of action is to have the unit overhauled by a specialist repairer, or to obtain an exchange reconditioned unit.

Nevertheless, it is not impossible for the more experienced mechanic to overhaul the transmission, provided the special tools are available, and the job is done in a deliberate step-by-step manner, so that nothing is overlooked.

The tools necessary for an overhaul include internal and external circlip pliers, bearing pullers, a slide hammer, a set of pin punches, a dial test indicator, and possibly a hydraulic press. In addition, a large, sturdy workbench and a vice will be required.

During dismantling of the transmission, make careful notes of how each component is fitted, to make reassembly easier and more accurate.

Before dismantling the transmission, it will help if you have some idea what area is malfunctioning. Certain problems can be closely related to specific areas in the transmission, which can make component examination and renewal easier. Refer to the *Fault finding* Section of this manual for more information.

Notes

Chapter 7 Part B:
Automatic transmission

Contents

Degrees of difficulty

Easy, suitable for novice with little experience	Fairly easy, suitable for beginner with some experience	Fairly difficult, suitable for competent DIY mechanic	Difficult, suitable for experienced DIY mechanic	Very difficult, suitable for expert DIY or professional

Specifications

General

Type	Continuously Variable automatic Transmission (CVT), multi-mode operation, with up to 7 selectable speeds, 1 reverse, electronic control by powertrain control module (PCM)
Designation	CVT-7

Gear ratios (typical)

Low to High	2.367 to 0.407
Reverse	2.367 to 1.326
Final drive	4.714

Torque wrench settings

	Nm	lbf ft
Driveplate-to-flywheel bolts	12	9
Engine/transmission mountings:		
Left-hand mounting**:		
Adjustment nut	74	55
Mounting bracket nuts/bolt	49	36
Through-bolt	44	32
Rear mounting:		
Subframe and rear bracket bolts	44	32
Through-bolt	59	44
Front subframe mounting bolts*	93	69
Roadwheel nuts	108	80
Starter motor mounting bolts:		
Lower bolt	64	47
Upper bolt	44	32
Transmission-to-engine bolts	64	47

* Use new bolts
** Left and right are as seen from the driver's seat

1 General information

The automatic transmission fitted to the Jazz is of continuously variable type (also known as CVT), which would normally mean it has no fixed gear ratios. However, it also offers a manual mode, with seven selectable gears. There are also three selectable positions for forward gears on the selector lever, making this a very fully-featured transmission.

When D (Drive) is selected, the transmission is in full 'CVT' mode. In this position, the gear ratio varies all the time, seamlessly moving around between the maximum and minimum ratios permitted by the design. This is achieved using two pulleys and a steel belt which transmits the drive, in a similar way to the sprockets and chain on a bicycle. If the sprockets on a bicycle could change size, the gearing would be altered. In this case, the cone-shaped halves of each pulley can move under fluid pressure, which effectively alters their working diameter, and hence, the gear ratio. The two pulleys are controlled by the powertrain control module (PCM), which takes into account several influencing factors before deciding the correct gear ratio. These factors include engine and vehicle speed, engine load, brake pedal position, throttle position, and the rate at which the throttle pedal position is changed. The result is a near-infinite number of ratios (within the upper and lower limits), which the PCM can tailor to match driving style, from sporting to economical. The PCM on automatic transmission models is, however, all but identical to the ECM which controls the fuel and ignition systems, and differs only in its transmission control functions.

When the selector lever is in the S (Second) position, a lower range of gear ratios is available. This position offers more responsive driving, especially on twisty roads, and could almost be considered a sport mode.

Similarly, in position L (Low), only the lowest ratios are available, giving better response in hilly areas, either for climbing hills or descending using engine braking.

The manual 7-speed mode can be used when the selector lever is in positions D or S. Manual mode is selected using a button on the steering wheel, and two further buttons or paddles are then used to change up or down the seven 'fixed' ratios provided. Since D or S offer different ranges of gearing anyway, there are effectively two sets of seven predetermined ratios to choose from. A transmission display on the instrument panel indicates the selector lever position, and which ratio has been selected when in manual mode.

A safety interlock system is fitted, which requires that the transmission is placed in P before leaving the car – the system prevents the ignition key being removed until P is selected. On next entering the car, the transmission cannot be shifted out of P unless

the brake pedal is pressed (the accelerator pedal must be completely released), and the ignition switch is in positions II or III. An emergency override procedure is provided in the car's handbook. Similarly, a reverse interlock prevents R being selected at speeds above 9 mph.

When the engine is cold, the PCM allows the engine to rev higher, to promote a faster warm-up.

Transmission control is made through several sets of solenoid valves, which control the flow of fluid inside the unit – fluid pressure is derived from an internal pump. It is vital, both for correct operation and for long life, that the transmission fluid level is maintained, and that the fluid is changed regularly (see Chapter 1).

Because of the need for special test equipment, the complexity of many parts, and the need for scrupulous cleanliness when servicing the transmission, the amount which the owner can do is limited. Repairs to the final drive differential are also not recommended. Most major repairs and overhaul operations should be left to a Honda dealer or specialist, who will have the necessary equipment for fault diagnosis and repair. The information in this Chapter is therefore limited to removal and refitting of the transmission as a complete unit.

In the event of a transmission problem occurring, consult a Honda dealer or transmission specialist before removing the transmission from the car, since the majority of fault diagnosis is carried out with the transmission in situ.

2 Fault finding – general

Note: *Automatic transmission malfunctions may be caused by five general conditions: poor engine performance, improper adjustments, hydraulic malfunctions, mechanical malfunctions, or malfunctions in the computer or its signal network. Diagnosis of these problems should always begin with a check of the easily-repaired items: fluid level and condition (see Chapter 1), and selector cable adjustment (Section 3). Next, perform a road test to determine if the problem has been corrected or if more diagnosis is necessary. If the problem persists after the preliminary tests and corrections are completed, additional diagnosis should be done by a dealer service department or transmission specialist.*

Preliminary checks

1 Drive the car to warm the transmission to normal operating temperature.
2 Check the fluid level as described in Chapter 1:
a) *If the fluid level is unusually low, add enough fluid to bring the level within the designated area of the dipstick, then check for external leaks (see below).*

b) *If the fluid level is abnormally high, drain off the excess, then check the drained fluid for contamination by coolant. The presence of engine coolant in the automatic transmission fluid indicates that a failure has occurred in the internal radiator walls that separate the coolant from the transmission fluid.*
c) *If the fluid is foaming, drain it and refill the transmission, then check for coolant in the fluid, or a high fluid level.*
3 Check the engine idle speed. **Note:** *If the engine is malfunctioning, do not proceed with the preliminary checks until it has been repaired and runs normally.*
4 Inspect the selector cable linkage (see Section 3). Make sure that it's properly adjusted and that the linkage operates smoothly.

Fluid leak diagnosis

5 Most fluid leaks are easy to locate visually. Repair usually consists of renewing a seal or gasket. If a leak is difficult to find, the following procedure may help.
6 Identify the fluid. Make sure it's transmission fluid and not engine oil or brake fluid (automatic transmission fluid is typically a deep red colour).
7 Try to pinpoint the source of the leak. Drive the car several miles, then park it over a large sheet of cardboard. After a minute or two, you should be able to locate the leak by determining the source of the fluid dripping onto the cardboard.
8 Make a careful visual inspection of the suspected component and the area immediately around it. Pay particular attention to gasket mating surfaces. A mirror is often helpful for finding leaks in areas that are hard to see.
9 If the leak still cannot be found, clean the suspected area thoroughly with a degreaser, then dry it.
10 Drive the car for several miles at normal operating temperature and varying speeds. After driving the car, inspect the suspected component again.
11 Once the leak has been located, the cause must be determined before it can be properly repaired. If a gasket is renewed but the sealing flange is bent, the new gasket will not stop the leak. The bent flange must be straightened.
12 Before attempting to repair a leak, check to make sure that the following conditions are corrected or they may cause another leak. **Note:** *Some of the following conditions cannot be fixed without highly specialised tools and expertise. Such problems must be referred to a transmission specialist or a dealer service department.*
13 If a transmission seal is leaking, the fluid level or pressure may be too high, the vent may be blocked, the seal bore may be damaged, the seal itself may be damaged or improperly installed, the surface of the shaft protruding through the seal may be damaged

or a loose bearing may be causing excessive shaft movement.

14 The driveshaft fluid seals are renewed in much the same way as those on manual transmissions – refer to Chapter 7A.

15 If the housing itself appears to be leaking, the casting is porous and will have to be repaired or renewed.

16 Make sure the fluid cooler hose fittings are tight and in good condition.

Fault diagnosis

17 Should a fault be recognised by the PCM, a fault code will be generated and stored in the module's memory, and the D warning light on the instrument panel's transmission display will flash.

18 First ensure that all the system wiring connectors are securely connected and free of corrosion.

19 If these checks fail to reveal the cause of the problem, the car should be taken to a suitably-equipped Honda dealer for testing. A diagnostic connector is incorporated in the wiring harness, into which dedicated electronic test equipment can be plugged – the connector is located under the steering column. The test equipment is capable of 'interrogating' the PCM electronically and accessing its internal fault log (reading fault codes).

20 Fault codes can only be extracted from the PCM using a dedicated fault code reader. A Honda dealer will obviously have such a reader, but they are also available from other suppliers. It is unlikely to be cost-effective for the private owner to purchase a fault code reader, but a well-equipped local garage or auto-electrical specialist will have one.

21 Using this equipment, faults can be pinpointed quickly and simply, even if their occurrence is intermittent. Testing all the system components individually in an attempt to locate the fault by elimination is a time-consuming operation that is unlikely to be fruitful (particularly if the fault occurs dynamically), and carries a high risk of damage to the PCM's internal components.

Clearing fault codes

22 Once the fault has been identified and the problem corrected (usually by fitting a new component), the fault code must be cleared. In some cases, this will happen automatically once the ignition has been switched on and off enough times – if the fault does not recur, it may clear itself.

23 To clear fault codes manually requires the use of a fault code reader tool as described at the start of this Section. However, codes may also be cleared by the DIY mechanic, as follows.

24 It appears that it may be sufficient to simply disconnect the battery negative lead for a few minutes to clear any stored codes. Alternatively, with the ignition off, remove fuse No 14 from the interior fusebox for at least 10 seconds, then refit it. Switch the ignition on, and the fault should have cleared.

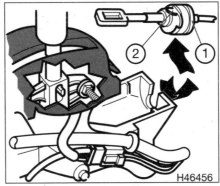

3.4 Twist the cable moulded fitting (1) so that the tab (2) is at the top, and remove

25 If the warning light remains on (or comes back on later), either the same fault still exists, or there is another faulty component triggering a different fault code. Check that any new components have been correctly fitted, and especially, that their wiring plugs are clean and secure.

3 Selector cable – renewal and adjustment

Renewal

1 Remove the centre console as described in Chapter 11. Also unclip the heater duct from the right-hand side of the selector lever.

2 Move the selector lever to the N position.

3 Unscrew the nut, and slide off the selector cable end fitting from the selector lever.

4 Further down the cable, twist the moulded fitting anti-clockwise so that the projecting tab is at the top, then lift it out of the cable mounting bracket on the selector lever housing **(see illustration)**.

5 Raise the front of the car and support it securely on axle stands (see *Jacking and vehicle support*). Remove the engine undertray.

6 Gain access to the cable where it comes through the floor – it may be necessary to unbolt and remove one or more of the exhaust heat shields. Unscrew the two cable support bracket nuts, then unclip the selector cable grommet from the floor **(see illustration)**.

7 Remove the air cleaner as described in Chapter 4A.

8 Remove the battery and its tray as described in Chapter 5A.

9 Note the position of the transmission control lever, which should be in the N position. Disconnect the selector cable from the transmission control lever – the cable end is secured by a split pin, and there are two washers. Unhook the cable from the lever **(see illustration)**. Note that a new split pin should be used when refitting.

10 Unscrew the two bolts securing the cable plate to the support bracket on the transmission, and the cable is free to be removed.

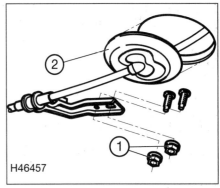

3.6 Remove the support bracket nuts (1), then unclip the cable grommet (2)

11 Withdraw the cable from the car, freeing it from any further support clips or brackets.

12 Refitting is a reversal of removal, noting the following points:

a) Ensure that the transmission control lever is still in the N position, then refit the cable using a new split pin.

b) Refit and tighten the cable plate bolts securing the cable to the transmission support bracket.

c) Once the cable is fully refitted at the transmission end, feed the cable back into the car. Refit the underbody support bracket, then ensure that the floor grommet is clipped back in place.

d) Adjust the cable as described later in this Section.

Adjustment

13 If not already done, proceed as described in paragraphs 1 to 4.

14 Grip the end of the cable (not the guide sleeve), and push it in until it stops.

15 Now pull the cable out by two 'clicks', which should be the N position again. Switch on the ignition, and check that the instrument panel display shows N. Switch the ignition off.

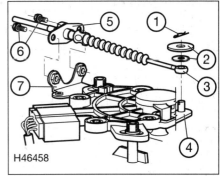

3.9 Removing the selector cable at the transmission end

1 Split pin
2 Washers
3 Selector cable
4 Transmission control lever
5 Cable plate
6 Bolts
7 Support bracket

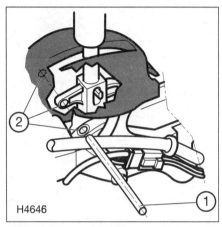

3.16 Fit a 6 mm pin (1) through the holes (2) in the selector lever and housing

16 Insert a 6.0 mm pin (such as a drill bit) into the hole on the right-hand side at the base of the selector lever housing, and out of the corresponding hole on the opposite side, to lock the selector lever in the N position **(see illustration)**.

17 Offer the cable's moulded fitting into the cable mounting bracket, with the projecting tab at the top. When the cable is slotted in correctly, twist the moulded fitting a quarter-turn clockwise to secure it.

18 Refit the cable end fitting onto the selector lever, noting that the rectangular end fitting must locate over the square section on the lever, and secure with the nut **(see illustration)**.

19 Remove the 6.0 mm pin or drill bit.

20 Switch on the ignition and move the selector lever to each position in turn. Check that the instrument panel display corresponds to the position selected in each case.

21 If all is well, press the brake pedal, then start the engine and repeat the check. Also ensure that the lever locks when returned to the P position.

22 On completion, refit the heater duct and the centre console. Take the car for a road test.

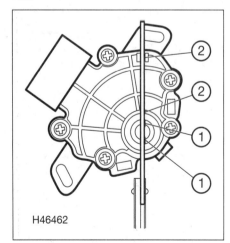

4.8 Use a feeler blade to align the switch centre slots (1) with those on the body (2)

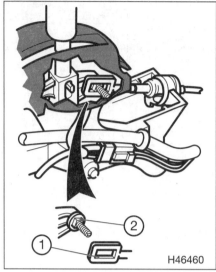

3.18 Selector cable rectangular fitting (1) must locate over square fitting (2) on lever

---

4 Transmission range switch – renewal and adjustment

Renewal

1 Remove the air cleaner as described in Chapter 4A.

2 Remove the battery and its tray as described in Chapter 5A.

3 Move the selector lever to the N position.

4 The transmission range switch is located on top of the transmission, next to the selector cable. Disconnect the switch wiring plug.

5 If the same switch is to be refitted, mark its fitted position relative to the transmission – this will make refitting and adjustment easier.

6 Unscrew the two switch mounting bolts, and lift it off its shaft.

7 Before refitting the switch, ensure that the shaft on the transmission is in the N position – this should be the case if the selector lever inside the car is also in the N position.

8 Unclip the round cover from the switch. The switch has to be 'aligned with itself' before fitting – the centre part (which turns) has to align with the switch body. Using a 2.0 mm thick feeler blade across the face of the switch, align the two slots in the centre of the switch with the slots on the edge of the switch body, just above one of the slotted mounting holes **(see illustration)**.

9 Keeping the switch aligned in this position, offer it carefully onto the transmission shaft **(see illustration)**.

10 With the feeler blade still holding the switch aligned, tighten the two switch mounting bolts securely.

11 Reconnect the wiring plug, then clip on the switch cover.

12 Refit the components removed for access.

13 Turn the ignition on, then move the selector lever through all positions, and check that the instrument panel display follows the selected gear.

14 Check that the engine can only be started in positions P or N, and that the reversing lights come on when R is selected.

Adjustment

15 To adjust the switch, follow the renewal procedure, with the exception that the switch does not have to be removed – for adjustment only, the switch mounting bolts need only be loosened.

---

5 Selector lever and related components – removal and refitting

Selector lever

1 Proceed as described in Section 3, paragraphs 1 to 4 inclusive.

2 Disconnect the two wiring plugs – one at the side, one at the rear – from the selector lever assembly.

3 Unscrew the four lever assembly mounting bolts, then lift it out of its location.

4 Refitting is a reversal of removal, noting the following points:
a) Tighten the selector lever mounting bolts securely.
b) Reconnect and adjust the selector cable as described in Section 3.

Selector illumination bulb

5 Remove the centre console as described in Chapter 11.

6 Remove the two small screws at the front, and lift off the selector lever knob.

7 Carefully prise up the selector lever surround panel, which is secured by four clips (one at each 'corner') **(see illustration)**.

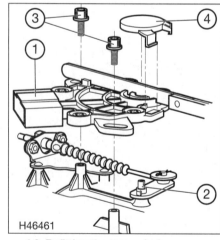

4.9 Refitting the transmission range switch

1 Switch	3 Mounting
2 Transmission	bolts
shaft	4 Switch cover

8 The illumination bulbholder is clipped into the underside of the lever surround panel. Pull out the bulbholder, then withdraw the wedge-base bulb.

9 Fit the new bulb, then clip the bulbholder back into place.

10 Refit the selector lever surround panel, ensuring that it is fully seated all round.

11 Refit the selector lever knob and the centre console to complete.

Shift lock solenoid

12 Remove the centre console as described in Chapter 11.

13 Remove the two small screws at the front, and lift off the selector lever knob.

14 Carefully prise up the selector lever surround panel, which is secured by four clips (one at each 'corner').

15 Unclip the illumination bulbholder from the underside of the lever surround panel.

16 Disconnect the two wiring plugs – one at the side, one at the rear – from the selector lever assembly.

17 Unhook the solenoid plunger from the operating lever at the front. The main body of the solenoid is clipped into a housing on the side of the selector lever assembly, and slides out to the side.

18 It appears at the time of writing that the shift lock solenoid is only available with the selector illumination bulbholder, as it shares a common wiring harness and wiring connector plug. If a new (or secondhand) solenoid can be obtained separately, it will be necessary to splice the solenoid wires into the existing ones – ensure that good soldered connections

are made, and that the wires are properly insulated afterwards.

19 Refitting is a reversal of removal.

Park pin switch

20 The Park pin switch is fitted at the front of the selector assembly, on the left-hand side. It appears that the pin switch is not available separately.

---

6 Steering wheel switches – removal and refitting

Up to October 2004 (shift buttons)

1 Remove the driver's airbag as described in Chapter 12.

2 Disconnect the switch wiring plug in the centre of the wheel, at the bottom. Unclip the wiring from its guide channels in the wheel.

3 Carefully prise out the screw covers from the back of the wheel (one each side, at the top).

4 Remove a total of three screws, then withdraw the left and right-hand switches from the front of the wheel.

5 It appears that the button-type switches are only available as a complete assembly (ie, both shift buttons and the main mode switch). The only way to renew one of the two switch assemblies would be to cut the wiring harness, and splice in the new switch – ensure that all connections are soldered and insulated.

6 Refitting is a reversal of removal.

October 2004 onwards (shift paddles)

7 Remove the steering wheel as described in Chapter 10.

8 From the front of the wheel, remove the four screws securing the wheel's rear cover (note that one of these screws also secures the 7-speed main mode switch). Withdraw the cover from the wheel.

Main mode switch

9 Remove the 'plus' switch as described later in this Section.

10 The main switch securing screw is also one of the four screws securing the steering wheel rear cover. All that remains is to disconnect the main switch wiring plug, and remove the switch. The switch is part of the steering wheel right-hand front trim panel, and is not available separately.

11 Refitting is a reversal of removal.

'Plus' shift switch

12 Unclip the switch wiring plug from the back of the wheel, and disconnect it.

13 Remove the single securing screw, and remove the switch.

14 Refitting is a reversal of removal.

'Minus' shift switch

15 Unclip and remove the steering wheel left-hand front trim panel (this panel is also secured by one of the four screws securing the rear cover, which were previously removed).

16 Unclip the switch wiring plug from the back of the wheel, and disconnect it.

17 Remove the single securing screw, and remove the switch.

18 Refitting is a reversal of removal.

---

7 Shift lock system – description and component renewal

1 The main components of the interlock system are as follows:

a) *The powertrain control module (PCM) – see Chapter 4A, where this component is referred to as the ECM. Through its control of the ignition system, it is able to prevent the engine being started when this is inappropriate. The information it receives from the vehicle speed sensor enables it to control the reverse gear interlock, and it also receives a signal from the brake pedal position switch for the Park interlock system.*

b) *The brake pedal position switch – see Chapter 4A. This informs the PCM when the brake pedal is being pressed, for the Park interlock system.*

c) *The ignition switch/steering lock assembly – see Chapter 10. This contains the ignition key interlock and solenoid, which prevents the key being removed, and which only allows the selector lever to be moved out of P in switch positions II and III.*

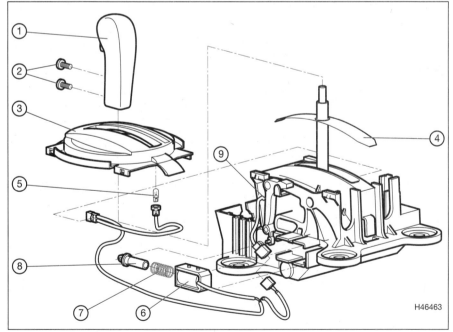

5.7 Exploded view of the selector lever assembly

1 *Selector lever knob*	4 *Lever inner cover*	7 *Solenoid plunger spring*
2 *Knob securing screws*	5 *Illumination bulbholder*	8 *Solenoid plunger*
3 *Lever surround panel*	6 *Shift lock solenoid body*	9 *Park pin switch*

d) *The shift lock solenoid and Park pin switch – refer to Section 5. Fitted to the selector lever assembly, these two items are what physically prevent the lever being moved into or out of P.*

8 Powertrain control module (PCM) – removal and refitting

The procedure is identical to that for the engine control module (ECM), described in Chapter 4A, Section 11.

9 Automatic transmission – removal and refitting

Removal

1 Remove the air cleaner as described in Chapter 4A.
2 Remove the battery and its tray as described in Chapter 5A.
3 Loosen the front wheel nuts, and if possible, also loosen both driveshaft nuts while the car is still on the ground. Jack up the front of the car, and support it on axle stands (see *Jacking and vehicle support*). Note that the car must be raised sufficiently high for the transmission to be lowered out and withdrawn from underneath. Remove the front wheels and the engine undertray.
4 Drain the transmission fluid as described in Chapter 1.
5 Remove the starter motor as described in Chapter 5A.
6 Work methodically round the transmission, and disconnect a total of eight wiring plugs, labelling each one to ensure correct refitting. These plugs are for the various transmission control solenoids, speed sensors, and the transmission range switch. Unclip and unbolt the wiring harness from the transmission as the plugs are disconnected, noting how the harness is routed.
7 Release the battery wiring harness from the support brackets on the transmission, then unbolt and remove the brackets.
8 Release the radiator hose from the transmission support clip.
9 Unbolt the primary oxygen sensor wiring plug support bracket from the transmission, and move it clear – it does not have to be disconnected.

10 Disconnect the selector cable from the transmission control lever – the cable end is secured by a split pin, and there are two washers. Unhook the cable from the lever. Note that a new split pin should be used when refitting.
11 Unscrew the two bolts securing the cable plate to the support bracket on the transmission, and move the cable to one side.
12 At the front of the transmission, release the hose clips and disconnect the fluid hoses from the pipes. Anticipate some fluid spillage as this is done – keep the hose ends turned upwards to reduce this, and either plug or tape over the open connections.
13 Remove the driveshafts as described in Chapter 8.
14 Support the transmission end of the engine. Preferably, this should be done from above, either with an engine hoist/crane or an engine support bar – supporting from below will be awkward, as the front subframe must be removed later.
15 Referring to Chapter 10 if necessary, remove the front subframe.
16 At the transmission-to-engine joint, remove the three bolts and take off the small cover plate. There are six driveplate-to-flywheel bolts to remove – one should be visible, but the engine will have to be turned (use the crankshaft pulley bolt) to access all six.
17 Support the transmission from below, using a jack and a flat piece of wood. Have an assistant ready to support the transmission as the jack is lowered.

 Paint or scribe an alignment mark across the transmission and engine faces. This is simply to make refitting easier – the transmission has two locating dowels, but an alignment mark will be helpful in eliminating guesswork when offering the unit into position.

18 Unscrew and remove the right-hand mounting through-bolt, then lower the transmission slightly on the jack, to separate the mounting. Unscrew the two mounting nuts and single bolt on top of the transmission, and take off the upper bracket.
19 Unscrew the transmission-to-engine bolts, then carefully pull the transmission away from the engine until the transmission is clear of the locating dowels. If necessary, push the flywheel back into the transmission – take care

that it does not fall out as the transmission is lowered.
20 Check round the transmission that everything has been disconnected from it, and that there is nothing in the way which might hinder its removal.
21 With the help of an assistant to guide the unit out, lower the transmission on the jack until it can be removed from under the car. Recover the two dowel pins, noting their fitted locations, and store them for safekeeping. Remove the flywheel, and store it safely until the transmission is to be refitted.

Refitting

22 Check the condition of the transmission input shaft fluid seal, and if necessary, fit a new one. The new seal should be fitted flush in its housing.
23 Make sure the two locating dowels are installed in the transmission mating face.
24 Lightly grease the input shaft splines, then refit the flywheel.
25 Raise the transmission on the jack, then use the alignment marks made on dismantling to align it with the engine.
26 Make sure the transmission is at the right height, then slide it onto the two dowels, and fully up to the engine.
27 While your assistant holds the transmission in place, insert two or three transmission-to-engine bolts initially, and tighten them fully by hand to hold the unit fully onto the dowels.
28 Further refitting is a reversal of removal, noting the following points:
a) *As far as possible, fit all engine/transmission mounting bolts hand-tight only at first. Delay fully tightening the engine/transmission mounting bolts until the weight of the engine is resting on its mountings.*
b) *Tighten all nuts/bolts to the specified torque.*
c) *Refer to Section 3 when reconnecting the selector cable at the transmission end, and adjust the cable if necessary.*
d) *Refill the transmission with fluid as described in Chapter 1. If a new transmission has been fitted, more fluid will be needed than at a normal fluid change.*
e) *On completion, start the engine. Allow the engine to reach its proper operating temperature with the transmission in P or N, then switch it off and check the fluid level. Road test the car and check for fluid leaks.*
f) *As the front subframe was removed, have the front wheel alignment checked at the earliest opportunity.*

Chapter 8
Driveshafts

Contents

Degrees of difficulty

Easy, suitable for novice with little experience	Fairly easy, suitable for beginner with some experience	Fairly difficult, suitable for competent DIY mechanic	Difficult, suitable for experienced DIY mechanic	Very difficult, suitable for expert DIY or professional

Specifications

General

Driveshaft type	Unequal-length, solid shaft, ball-and-cage outer CV joint, tripod inner joint, dynamic damper fitted to right-hand driveshaft
Driveshaft 'length' (from the outer ends of the CV joints):	
Left-hand driveshaft	501 to 506 mm
Right-hand driveshaft	787 to 792 mm
Dynamic damper fitted position (from outer end of outer CV joint)	516 to 520 mm

Torque wrench settings

	Nm	lbf ft
Bottom balljoint nut:		
Stage 1 (or minimum setting)	49	36
Stage 2 (or maximum setting)	59	44
Driveshaft hub nut*	181	134
Roadwheel nuts	108	80

Use a new nut

1 General information

Drive is transmitted from the differential to the front wheels by means of two steel driveshafts of solid construction. Both driveshafts are splined at their outer ends, to accept the wheel hubs, and are secured to the hub by a large nut. The inner end of each driveshaft is a push-fit, secured by a circlip.

Constant velocity (CV) joints are fitted to each end of the driveshafts, to ensure the smooth and efficient transmission of drive at all the angles possible as the roadwheels move up and down with the suspension, and as they turn from side to side under steering. On all models, the outer joint is of the ball-and-cage type, but the inner joint is of the tripod type.

Rubber or plastic gaiters are secured over both CV joints with steel clips. The gaiters contain the grease which lubricates the joints, and also protect the joints from the entry of dirt and debris.

2 Driveshafts – removal and refitting

Removal

1 The driveshaft nut is tightened to an extremely high torque, and for this reason, it is preferable if possible to loosen the nut with the wheel on the ground. Remove either the wheel trim or alloy wheel centre cap (where possible) for access to the nut **(see illustration)**.

2 The driveshaft nut has a locking tab (or a raised collar) which is punched into the driveshaft groove to stop the nut loosening accidentally. Using a sturdy flat-bladed screwdriver, or preferably a punch or chisel, bend the tab/collar back so the nut can be unscrewed **(see illustration)**.

2.1 To loosen the driveshaft nut with the wheel on, take out the wheel centre cap

2.2 Use a punch or chisel to knock back the driveshaft nut's collar

2.8 Removing the right-hand driveshaft's heat shield

2.9 Unbolt the lower end of the anti-roll bar drop link

2.10 Tap the end of the driveshaft to release the hub splines

2.12a Unscrew the two nuts from the back of the strut-to-hub pinch-bolts . . .

2.12b . . . then tap the bolts through and remove them

3 Significant force will be required to loosen the nut, so be sure to use only good-quality, close-fitting tools. A long-handled 'breaker bar' will be needed, to provide the necessary leverage – if this is not available, slip a strong piece of metal pipe over the end of the socket handle. Wear gloves to protect your hands, should something slip.

4 Chock the front wheel, and have an assistant apply the footbrake firmly, while you slacken the nut. It is not necessary at this stage to remove the nut completely.

5 If the nut has to be loosened with the car raised, ensure that it is very well supported, using well-placed, good-quality axle stands (see *Jacking and vehicle support*). Have an assistant firmly depress the brake pedal to prevent the disc from turning, whilst you slacken and remove the driveshaft retaining nut. Alternatively, a tool can be fabricated from two lengths of steel strip (one long, one short)

and a nut and bolt; the nut and bolt forming the pivot of a forked tool which fits over the wheel studs.

6 Once the nut has been loosened, (if not already done) jack up the front of the car and support it on axle stands (see *Jacking and vehicle support*). Remove the front wheel.

7 Drain the transmission fluid as described in Chapter 1. If this is not done, be prepared for significant fluid spillage when the driveshafts are removed.

8 On the right-hand driveshaft there is a curved heat shield which is fitted over the inner CV joint, secured by three bolts (two above, one below). We found that the driveshaft could be removed without taking off this heat shield, but it can be unbolted and removed if preferred (where applicable, the shield has to be removed before dropping the front subframe) **(see illustration)**.

9 Unbolt the lower end of the anti-roll bar

drop link, using an Allen key to hold the 'bolt' as the nut is loosened **(see illustration)**. Move the link to one side, to allow room for the driveshaft to pass.

10 The splined end of the driveshaft now has to be released from its location in the hub. It's likely that the splines will be very tight (corrosion may even be a factor, if the driveshaft has not been disturbed for some time), and considerable force may be needed. Tap the end of the shaft with a plastic or hide mallet only – if an ordinary hammer is used, place a small piece of wood over the end of the driveshaft – and leave the old nut loosely in place on the end to avoid damaging the splines **(see illustration)**.

11 Once the splines have been released, remove the driveshaft nut and discard it – the nut is only intended to be used once.

12 Unscrew the two nuts from the pinch-bolts securing the lower end of the suspension strut to the hub. Support the hub, then tap the bolts through using a pin punch, noting that they are fitted from the front **(see illustrations)**. Also note that these two bolts are used to secure the brake hose support plate.

13 Separate the hub from the base of the strut. Tilt the hub outwards on the lower balljoint, and slide out the driveshaft to the inside **(see illustration)**.

14 When the driveshaft has been withdrawn from the hub, temporarily refit the two strut-to-hub bolts by hand, to keep the hub upright – this also prevents straining the brake hose.

15 Carefully lever the inner end of the driveshaft from the transmission, using a large screwdriver or lever bar positioned between the transmission and the CV joint housing. The inner end of the shaft is secured with a circlip, which must be released – do not pull on the shaft, as the inner joint may separate. Support the CV joints and carefully remove the driveshaft from the car. To prevent damage to the driveshaft oil seal, hold the inner CV joint horizontal until the driveshaft is clear of the transmission **(see illustrations)**.

16 Lever the old circlip from the inner end of the driveshaft, and fit a new one **(see illustrations)**.

Refitting

17 Lubricate the differential with multi-

2.13 Tilt the hub outwards at the top, and pull out the driveshaft

2.15a Prise the inner end of the driveshaft out of the transmission . . .

2.15b ... then withdraw the (right-hand) shaft, keeping it as straight as possible

2.15c Removing the left-hand driveshaft

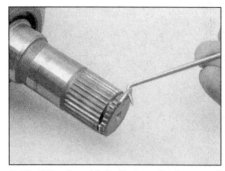
2.16a Prise the old circlip from the inner end of the driveshaft with a small screwdriver

purpose grease, and raise the driveshaft into position while supporting the CV joints.
18 Insert the splined end of the inner CV joint into the differential side gear, and make sure the circlip locks in its groove. Grasp the inner CV joint housing (not the driveshaft) and pull out to make sure the driveshaft has seated securely in the transmission.
19 Lightly grease the splined end of the driveshaft. Remove the strut-to-hub bolts once more, tilt the hub outwards on the lower balljoint, and fit the driveshaft into the hub.
20 Refit the strut-to-hub bolts and nuts, and tighten to the specified torque.
21 Lightly oil the new hub nut, and tighten it by hand to draw the driveshaft into position.
22 Reconnect the anti-roll bar drop link, using a new nut. Refer to Chapter 10, Section 5, for the procedure to be followed when tightening the drop link nuts.
23 On the right-hand driveshaft, if the heat shield was removed, secure it with the three bolts – tighten the top two before the lower one.
24 Refit the wheel, then lower the car to the ground and tighten the wheel nuts to the specified torque.
25 With the car resting on its wheels, tighten the hub nut to the specified torque. Stake the hub nut collar into the driveshaft groove **(see illustrations)**.
26 Refill the transmission with the recommended type and amount of lubricant (see Chapter 1).

3 Driveshaft gaiters – renewal

1 Remove the driveshaft from the car (see Section 2).
2 Mount the driveshaft in a vice. The jaws of the vice should be lined with wood or rags to prevent damage to the driveshaft.

Inner CV joint and gaiter

Dismantling

3 If you have any doubts about the condition of the outer gaiter, this would be a good time to renew it as well. Cut off both gaiter clamps, and slide the gaiter towards the centre of the driveshaft **(see illustrations)**.

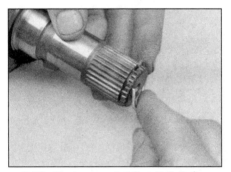
2.16b Start one end of the circlip in the groove, then work it over the end of the shaft

2.25b ... then stake the nut's collar ...

3.3a Cut off the gaiter clamps and discard them

2.25a Tighten the nut with the wheel on the ground ...

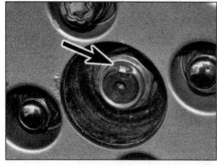
2.25c ... into the driveshaft groove

3.3b Slide the gaiter towards the centre of the driveshaft

4 Scribe or paint alignment marks on the outer race and the tripod bearing assembly so they can be returned to their original position, then slide the outer race off the tripod bearing assembly.
5 Remove the circlip from the end of the driveshaft.
6 Secure the bearing rollers with tape, then remove the tripod bearing assembly from the driveshaft with a brass drift and a hammer. Remove the tape, but don't let the rollers fall off and get mixed up.
7 Remove the stop-ring (if equipped), slide the old gaiter off the driveshaft and discard it.

3.10 Slide the inner gaiter onto the driveshaft

3.11a Slide the tripod onto the shaft . . .

3.11b . . . and tap it home on the splines

3.12 Fit the outer circlip

Inspection

8 Clean the old grease from the outer race and the tripod bearing assembly. Carefully dismantle each section of the tripod assembly, one at a time so as not to mix up the parts, and clean the needle bearings with degreaser.
9 Inspect the rollers, tripod, bearings and outer race for scoring, pitting or other signs of abnormal wear, which will warrant the renewal of the inner CV joint.

Reassembly

10 Wrap the splines of the driveshaft with tape to avoid damaging the new gaiter, then slide the gaiter onto the driveshaft **(see illustration)**. Remove the tape and slide the inner stop-ring (if equipped) into place.
11 Slide the tripod assembly onto the driveshaft, and tap it home with a soft-faced mallet **(see illustrations)**.
12 Fit the outer circlip **(see illustration)**.
13 Apply a little CV joint grease to the inner bearing surfaces to hold the needle bearings in place when reassembling the tripod assembly **(see illustration)**. Make sure each roller is refitted on the same post as before.
Note: *If the rollers are equipped with a flat, rectangular-shaped surface, make sure the flat sides are positioned closest to the driveshaft.*
14 Pack the outer race with half of the grease supplied with the new gaiter, and place the remainder in the gaiter. Refit the outer race – we found it easier to fit the outer race in a vice, and offer in the shaft **(see illustrations)**. Make sure the marks you made on the tripod assembly and the outer race are aligned.
15 Seat the gaiter in the grooves in the outer race and the driveshaft, then lift the gaiter edges to release any trapped air **(see illustration)**.
16 Fit and tighten the new gaiter clamps **(see illustrations)**.
17 Refit the driveshaft assembly (see Section 2).

3.13 Use grease to hold the roller's needle bearings in place during fitting

3.14a Fill the outer race with half the supplied grease . . .

3.14b . . . then fit the shaft into the outer race

3.15 Fit the gaiter into its grooves, then lift the edge to equalise pressure

3.16a Adjust the driveshaft length to that specified before tightening the gaiter clips

3.16b Fit the clip, and thread the end through the loop . . .

3.16c . . . then pull tight using pliers and a screwdriver as shown . . .

3.16d . . . fold over the end . . .

3.16e . . . and flatten down to secure

3.16f Repeat the process on the larger clip

3.16g Some clips need special crimping pliers, but side-cutters can be used with care

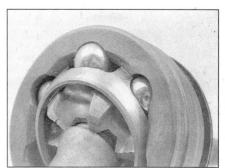

3.23 Inspect the bearing surfaces for signs of wear

Outer CV joint and gaiter

Dismantling

18 Cut the gaiter clamps from the outer CV joint. Slide the gaiter back down the shaft.

19 The outer joint is secured on the shaft by a small circlip at the outer end. Mount the shaft in a vice, then, using a soft-headed mallet (or a hammer and block of wood), tap the outer joint off the shaft. Remove the old gaiter.

20 If the driveshaft is equipped with a dynamic damper, it should not need to be removed for this operation. However, if the shaft is being stripped, scribe or paint a location mark on the driveshaft along the outer edge of the damper (the side facing the outer CV joint), cut the retaining clamp and slide the damper off.

21 Remove the circlip from the driveshaft outer groove – a new one should always be

used when refitting (and will probably be supplied in the gaiter repair kit).

Inspection

22 Thoroughly wash the inner and outer CV joints in degreaser and blow them dry with compressed air, if available. **Note:** *Because the outer joint can't be dismantled, it is difficult to wash away all the old grease and to rid the bearing of degreaser once it's clean. But it is imperative that the job be done thoroughly.*

 Warning: Wear eye protection when using compressed air.

23 Bend the outer CV joint housing at an angle to the driveshaft to expose the bearings, inner race and cage. Inspect the bearing surfaces for signs of wear **(see illustration)**. If the bearings are damaged or worn, a new driveshaft will probably be needed – check

the availability of spare parts, or try to source a good secondhand item.

Reassembly

24 Slide the dynamic damper, if removed, onto the shaft. Make sure its outer edge is aligned with the previously-applied mark. Fit a new retaining clamp.

25 Slide the inner clip, then the new outer gaiter, onto the driveshaft **(see illustrations)**. It's a good idea to wrap tape around the splines of the shaft to prevent damage to the gaiter.

26 Fit a new circlip into the groove at the end of the shaft, and fit the larger gaiter clip to the boot **(see illustrations)**.

27 Add the grease from the repair kit to the outer joint – try to 'squirt' the grease into the centre, as this will distribute it around the ball-bearings. Work the grease around the

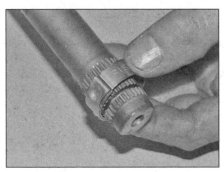

3.25a Slide the inner clip . . .

3.25b . . . then the new gaiter onto the shaft

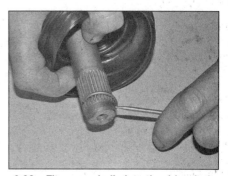

3.26a Fit a new circlip into the driveshaft groove . . .

3.26b . . . and the larger clip to the gaiter

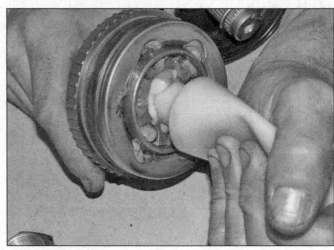

3.27a Squirt the grease into the centre of the outer joint . . .

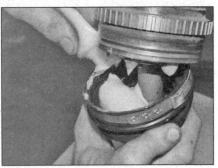

3.27b . . . and out any left over into the gaiter

3.28 Slide the outer joint onto the shaft, and locate onto the circlip

joint's insides. Put most of the grease into the joint, and any left over into the gaiter (see illustrations).

28 Slide the joint on to the end of the driveshaft, and locate it onto the circlip (see illustration). When the joint is secure on the shaft, fit the gaiter onto the joint, and sit it into the grooves.

29 Tighten the gaiter clips as described in paragraph 16.

30 Refit the driveshaft assembly (see Section 2).

Chapter 9
Braking system

Contents

Degrees of difficulty

Easy, suitable for novice with little experience 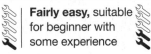	**Fairly easy,** suitable for beginner with some experience	**Fairly difficult,** suitable for competent DIY mechanic	**Difficult,** suitable for experienced DIY mechanic	**Very difficult,** suitable for expert DIY or professional

Specifications

General

Brake pedal:	
Freeplay	1.0 to 5.0 mm
Height (with carpet pulled back):	
Manual transmission models	141 mm
Automatic transmission models	145 mm
Handbrake lever travel	7 to 10 clicks
Brake pad minimum thickness (excluding backing plate)	1.6 mm
Brake shoe lining minimum thickness	1.0 mm
Brake disc minimum thickness:	
Front	19.0 mm
Rear	8.0 mm
Disc thickness variation (parallelism)	0.015 mm
Disc run-out limit	0.10 mm
Drum inside diameter:	
New	180 mm
Wear limit	181 mm

Torque wrench settings

	Nm	lbf ft
ABS wheel sensor retaining bolt	10	7
Brake disc retaining screws	10	7
Brake pipe unions to master cylinder:		
Models without Vehicle Stability Assist (VSA)	15	11
Models with Vehicle Stability Assist (VSA)	22	16
Front caliper:		
Brake hose support bracket bolt	22	16
Brake hose union bolt	34	25
Guide pin bolts	22	16
Mounting bracket bolts	108	80
Master cylinder mounting nuts	15	11
Rear brake backplate/splash shield bolts	64	47
Rear caliper:		
Brake hose union bolt	34	25
Guide pin bolts	23	17
Handbrake linkage retaining nut	27	20
Mounting bracket bolts	55	41
Rear hub nut*	162	120
Rear wheel cylinder mounting bolts	11	8
Roadwheel nuts	108	80
Servo mounting nuts	13	10

* Use new nut

1 General information

The braking system is of the servo-assisted, dual circuit hydraulic type, with ventilated front disc brakes. Models up to early 2004 use rear drum brakes, with later models having solid rear discs. An anti-lock braking system (ABS) is fitted to most models – refer to Section 20 for further information on ABS operation.

The front and rear disc brakes are actuated by single-piston sliding type calipers, which ensure that equal pressure is applied to each disc pad.

The rear disc brake calipers incorporate mechanical handbrake mechanisms, providing an independent mechanical means of rear brake application.

The rear drums are of standard type, with leading and trailing shoes operated by a hydraulic wheel cylinder. The handbrake cable is attached to the trailing shoe.

The vacuum servo unit uses inlet manifold depression (generated only when the engine is running) to boost the effort applied by the driver at the brake pedal and transmits this increased effort to the master cylinder pistons.

Precautions

The car's braking system is one of its most important safety features. When working on the brakes, there are a number of points to be aware of, to ensure that your health (or even your life) is not being put at risk.

⚠ *Warning: Brake fluid is poisonous. Take care to keep it off bare skin, and in particular not to get splashes in your eyes. The fluid also attacks paintwork and plastics – wash off spillages immediately with cold water. Finally, brake fluid is highly flammable, and should be handled with the same care as petrol.*

• *Make sure the ignition is off (take out the key) before disconnecting any braking system hydraulic union, and do not switch it on until after the hydraulic system has been bled. Failure to do this could lead to air entering the ABS hydraulic unit. If air enters the hydraulic unit pump, it will prove very difficult (in some cases impossible) to bleed the unit (see Section 5).*

• *When servicing any part of the system, work carefully and methodically – do not take short-cuts; also observe scrupulous cleanliness when overhauling any part of the hydraulic system.*

• *Always renew components in axle sets, where applicable – this means renewing brake pads, shoes, etc, on BOTH sides, even if only one set of pads is worn, or one wheel cylinder is leaking (for example). In the instance of uneven brake wear, the cause should be investigated and fixed (on disc brakes, sticking caliper pistons is a likely problem).*

• *Use only genuine Honda parts, or at least those of known good quality.*

• *Although genuine Honda brake pads and shoes are asbestos-free, the dust created by wear of non-genuine parts may contain asbestos, which is a health hazard. Never blow it out with compressed air, and don't inhale any of it.*

• *DO NOT use petroleum-based solvents to clean brake parts; use brake cleaner or methylated spirit only.*

• *DO NOT allow any brake fluid, oil or grease to contact the brake pads or disc.*

2 Brake pedal – removal, refitting and adjustment

Removal

1 Remove the pedal position switch as described in Section 18.

2 On the right-hand side of the pedal, pull out the spring clip, then withdraw the clevis pin from the left-hand side (see illustration).

3 Unhook the return spring from the top of the pedal, and remove it.

4 If required, the pedal bracket can also be removed, by unscrewing the two mounting

2.2 Pull down the brake pedal clevis pin's spring clip

2.4 Two of the four brake pedal bracket nuts

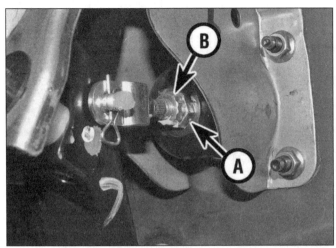

2.8 Brake pedal height adjuster nut (A) and locknut (B)

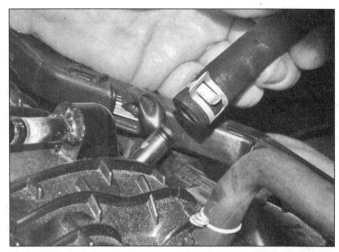

3.7 Disconnect the brake servo hose from the inlet manifold

nuts either side **(see illustration)**. Note that these are also the mounting nuts for the brake servo – take care when removing the bracket that the servo is not disturbed.

5 Check the condition of the clevis pin and its spring clip – these are vital components connecting the brake pedal to the master cylinder, and if their condition is at all suspect, new parts should be fitted.

Refitting

6 Refitting is a reversal of removal, noting the following points:
a) If removed, tighten the pedal mounting bracket nuts securely.
b) Ensure that the pedal-to-cross-shaft clevis pin's spring clip is securely refitted.
c) Check the operation of the brakes before taking the car out on the road.

Adjustment

Pedal height

7 The height of the brake pedal is the distance the pedal sits off the floor, measured from the top surface of the pedal. If the pedal height is not as specified, it must be adjusted.
8 To adjust the brake pedal, twist the pedal position switch anti-clockwise and back the switch out until it no longer touches the pedal, then loosen the locknut on the brake pushrod (note that this is a special splined nut, and in the absence of a proper tool, pliers may have to be used). Turn the adjuster nut behind to adjust the pedal height. When the adjustment is correct, tighten the locknut against the adjuster nut to lock it **(see illustration)**.
9 Push the switch up to the pedal until it just contacts the pedal arm, then turn it clockwise to lock it in position.

Pedal freeplay

10 The freeplay is the pedal slack, or the distance the pedal can be depressed before it begins to have any effect on the brake system. If the pedal freeplay is not within the specified range, it must be adjusted.

11 Pedal freeplay is adjusted using the brake pedal position switch. Turn the switch anti-clockwise to unlock it, then slide it up to the pedal until it just contacts it. Without moving the switch in or out, turn it clockwise to lock it.

3 Vacuum servo unit – testing, removal and refitting

Testing

1 To test the operation of the servo unit, depress the footbrake several times to exhaust the vacuum, then start the engine whilst keeping the pedal firmly depressed.
2 As the engine starts, there should be a noticeable 'give' in the brake pedal as the vacuum builds-up. Allow the engine to run for at least two minutes, then switch it off. If the brake pedal is now depressed it should feel normal, but further applications should result in the pedal feeling firmer, with the pedal stroke decreasing with each application.
3 If the servo does not operate as described, inspect the servo unit check valve as described in Section 4.
4 If the servo unit still fails to operate satisfactorily, the fault lies within the unit itself. Apart from external components, no spares are available, so a defective servo must be renewed.

Removal

5 Servo units should not be dismantled. They require special tools not normally found in most repair workshops. They are fairly complex and because of their critical relationship to brake performance it is best to renew a defective servo unit or fit a rebuilt one.
6 To remove the servo, first remove the brake master cylinder as described in Section 7.
7 Trace the servo vacuum hose from the servo to the fitting on the engine, and disconnect it – this is simpler, and less likely to cause damage, than trying to prise out the hose

fitting from the servo itself. The hose runs to the centre on the inlet manifold, at the rear **(see illustration)**.
8 Remove the driver's side facia lower trim panels as described in Chapter 11, Section 27.
9 Remove the two bolts and take out the facia panel support strut next to the brake pedal **(see illustration)**.
10 Locate the pushrod clevis pin connecting the servo to the brake pedal. Remove the spring clip with pliers and pull out the clevis pin **(refer to illustration 2.2)**.
11 Remove the four nuts in front of the brake pedal holding the brake servo to the bulkhead **(refer to illustration 2.4)**.
12 Slide the servo straight out from the bulkhead until the studs clear the holes and pull the servo, brackets and gaskets from the engine compartment area.

Refitting

13 If a new servo is being installed, the servo pushrod clearance must be set. This requires the use of special tools, so should be entrusted to a Honda dealer. If the same servo is being refitted, it can be assumed that the pushrod clearance is still correct.
14 Refitting is a reversal of removal, noting the following points:
a) Tighten the servo mounting nuts to the specified torque.

3.9 Unscrew the two bolts, and take out the support strut next to the brake pedal

b) Use a new split pin when reconnecting the servo pushrod to the brake pedal.
c) After the final refitting of the master cylinder and brake hoses and pipes, bleed the brakes as described in Section 5.
d) Check and if necessary adjust the brake pedal height as described in Section 2.

4 Vacuum servo unit check valve – removal, testing and refitting

Removal

1 Trace the servo vacuum hose from the centre on the inlet manifold, at the rear, back to the servo itself, and disconnect it. Be careful not to damage the hose when removing it from the servo fitting.
2 The check valve is an integral part of the hose. Disconnect the other end from the inlet manifold. Remove the hose from the engine compartment, freeing it from any securing clips, and noting how it is routed.

Testing

3 Examine the hose for signs of damage, such as splits at the ends, and renew if necessary. The valve may be tested by blowing through it in both directions. Air should flow through the valve in one direction only – when blown through from the servo unit end of the valve. Renew the valve if this is not the case.

Refitting

4 Refitting is a reversal of removal. Ensure that the hose clips are secure, to prevent leaks. Check the operation of the brakes before taking the car onto the road.

5 Hydraulic system – bleeding

Note: Refer to the precautions in Section 1 before proceeding.
Caution: On models with ABS, make sure the ignition is off (take out the key) before bleeding the system.

General

1 The correct operation of any hydraulic system is only possible after removing all air from the components and circuit; this is achieved by bleeding the system.
2 During the bleeding procedure, add only clean, unused hydraulic fluid of the recommended type; never re-use fluid that has already been bled from the system. Ensure that sufficient fluid is available before starting work.
3 If there is any possibility of incorrect fluid being already in the system, the system must be flushed completely with uncontaminated, correct fluid, and new seals should be fitted to the various components.
4 If air has entered the hydraulic system

because of a leak, ensure that the fault is cured before proceeding further.
5 Park the car on level ground, switch off the engine, remove the key, and select first or reverse gear (or P on automatic transmission models). Chock the wheels and release the handbrake.
6 Check that all pipes and hoses are secure, unions tight and bleed screws closed. Clean any dirt from around the bleed screws – if they have not been opened for some time, use a small wire brush to clean the threads, then apply a maintenance spray such as WD-40, and allow time for it to soak in. If a bleed screw has seized, do not apply heat to it, as brake fluid is highly flammable.
7 Unscrew the master cylinder reservoir cap and top the master cylinder reservoir up to the MAX level line; refit the cap loosely. Remember to maintain the fluid level at least above the MIN level line throughout the procedure, or there is a risk of further air entering the system.
8 There is several one-man, do-it-yourself brake bleeding kits currently available from motor accessory shops. It is recommended that one of these kits is used whenever possible, as they greatly simplify the bleeding operation, and also reduce the risk of expelled air and fluid being drawn back into the system. If such a kit is not available, the basic (two-man) method must be used, which is described in detail below.
9 If a kit is to be used, prepare the car as described previously, and follow the kit manufacturer's instructions. The procedure may vary slightly according to the type of kit being used; general procedures are as outlined below in the relevant sub-section.
10 Whichever method is used, the same sequence must be followed (paragraphs 11 and 12) to ensure the removal of all air from the system.

Bleeding sequence

11 If the system has been only partially disconnected, and the correct precautions were taken to minimise fluid loss, it should be necessary only to bleed that part of the system (ie, the primary or secondary circuit).
12 If the complete system is to be bled, then it should be done working in the following sequence:

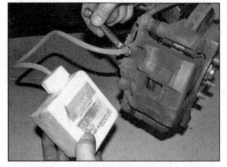

5.22 Bleeding the brakes with a one-way valve kit

a) Left-hand front brake.
b) Right-hand front brake.
c) Right-hand rear brake.
d) Left-hand rear brake.

Bleeding

Basic (two-man) method

13 Collect a clean glass jar, a length of plastic or rubber tubing which is a tight fit over the bleed screw, and a ring spanner to fit the screw. The help of an assistant will also be required.
14 Remove the dust cap from the first screw in the sequence. Fit the spanner and tube to the screw, place the other end of the tube in the jar, and pour in sufficient fluid to cover the end of the tube.
15 Ensure that the master cylinder reservoir fluid level is maintained at least above the MIN level line throughout the procedure.
16 Have the assistant fully depress the brake pedal several times to build-up pressure, then maintain it on the final stroke.
17 While pedal pressure is maintained, unscrew the bleed screw (approximately one turn) and allow the compressed fluid and air to flow into the jar. The assistant should maintain pedal pressure, following it down to the floor if necessary, and should not release it until instructed to do so. When the flow stops, tighten the bleed screw again. Have the assistant release the pedal slowly.
18 Repeat the steps given in paragraphs 16 and 17 until the fluid emerging from the bleed screw is free from air bubbles. Remember to recheck the fluid level in the master cylinder reservoir every five strokes or so. If the master cylinder has been drained and refilled, and air is being bled from the first screw in the sequence, allow approximately five seconds between strokes for the master cylinder passages to refill.
19 When no more air bubbles appear, tighten the bleed screw securely, remove the tube and spanner, and refit the dust cap. Do not overtighten the bleed screw.
20 Repeat the procedure on the remaining screws in the sequence until all air is removed from the system and the brake pedal feels firm.

Using a one-way valve kit

21 As their name implies, these kits consist of a length of tubing with a one-way valve fitted to prevent expelled air and fluid being drawn back into the system; some kits include a translucent container, which can be positioned so that the air bubbles can be more easily seen flowing from the end of the tube.
22 The kit is connected to the bleed screw, which is then opened (see illustration). The user returns to the driver's seat and depresses the brake pedal with a smooth, steady stroke and slowly releases it; this is repeated until the expelled fluid is clear of air bubbles.
23 Note that these kits simplify work so much that it is easy to forget the master cylinder reservoir fluid level; ensure that this is maintained at least above the MIN level line at all times.

Using a pressure-bleeding kit

24 These kits are usually operated by the reservoir of pressurised air contained in the spare tyre, although it may be necessary to reduce the pressure in the tyre to lower than normal; refer to the instructions supplied with the kit.

25 By connecting a pressurised, fluid-filled container to the master cylinder reservoir, bleeding can be carried out simply by opening each screw in turn (in the specified sequence) and allowing the fluid to flow out until no more air bubbles can be seen in the expelled fluid.

26 This method has the advantage that the large reservoir of fluid provides an additional safeguard against air being drawn into the system during bleeding.

27 Pressure-bleeding is particularly effective when bleeding 'difficult' systems, or when bleeding the complete system at the time of routine fluid renewal.

All methods

28 When bleeding is complete and firm pedal feel is restored, wash off any spilt fluid, tighten the bleed screws securely and refit their dust caps.

29 Check the hydraulic fluid level, and top-up if necessary (see *Weekly checks*).

30 Discard any hydraulic fluid that has been bled from the system; it will not be fit for re-use.

31 Check the feel of the brake pedal. If it feels at all spongy, air must still be present in the system, and further bleeding is required. Failure to bleed satisfactorily after several repetitions of the bleeding procedure may be due to worn master cylinder seals.

6 Brake pipes and hoses – renewal

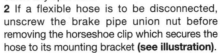

Note: *Refer to the precautions in Section 1 before proceeding.*

1 If any pipe or hose is to be renewed, minimise fluid loss by removing the master cylinder reservoir cap and then tightening it down onto a piece of polythene (taking care not to damage the sender unit) to obtain an airtight seal. Alternatively, flexible hoses can be sealed, if required, using a proprietary

7.2a Pull back the rubber strip . . .

brake hose clamp; metal brake pipe unions can be plugged (if care is taken not to allow dirt into the system) or capped immediately they are disconnected. Place a wad of rag under any union that is to be disconnected, to catch any spilt fluid.

2 If a flexible hose is to be disconnected, unscrew the brake pipe union nut before removing the horseshoe clip which secures the hose to its mounting bracket **(see illustration)**.

3 To unscrew the union nuts, it is preferable to obtain a brake pipe spanner of the correct size (split ring); these are available from motor accessory shops. Failing this, a close-fitting open-ended spanner will be required, though if the nuts are tight or corroded, their flats may be rounded off if the spanner slips. In such a case, a self-locking wrench is often the only way to unscrew a stubborn union, but it follows that the pipe and the damaged nuts must be renewed on reassembly. Always clean a union and surrounding area before disconnecting it. If disconnecting a component with more than one union, make a careful note of the connections before disturbing any of them.

4 If a brake pipe is to be renewed, it can be obtained, cut to length and with the union nuts and end flares in place, from Honda dealers. All that is then necessary is to bend it to shape, following the line of the original, before fitting it to the car. Alternatively, most motor accessory shops can make up brake pipes from kits, but this requires very careful measurement of the original to ensure that the new pipe is of the correct length. The safest answer is usually to take the original to the shop as a pattern.

5 On refitting, do not overtighten the union nuts – it is not necessary to exercise brute force to obtain a sound joint.

6 Ensure that the pipes and hoses are correctly routed with no kinks, and that they are secured in the clips or brackets provided. In the case of flexible hoses, make sure that they cannot contact other components during movement of the steering and/or suspension assemblies.

7 After fitting, remove the polythene from the reservoir (or remove the plugs or clamps, as applicable), and bleed the hydraulic system as described in Section 5. Wash off any spilt fluid, and check carefully for fluid leaks.

7.2b . . . and unclip the access panel

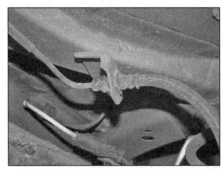

6.2 Loosen the brake pipe union nut before releasing the brake hose from its bracket

7 Master cylinder – removal, overhaul and refitting

Note: *Refer to the precautions in Section 1 before proceeding.*

Removal

1 The master cylinder is located on the driver's side of the engine compartment, mounted on the servo unit.

2 To improve access to the brake (and clutch) reservoirs, a removable panel is provided in the windscreen cowl panel. Pull back the rubber strip on the driver's side, then unclip and remove the panel section provided **(see illustrations)**.

3 Remove the clutch fluid reservoir mounting bracket, which is secured by a single bolt at the top. Move the reservoir to one side, without disconnecting the fluid hose.

4 Remove as much fluid as you can from the brake fluid reservoir before starting, using a syringe. If a syringe is not available, the fluid can be soaked out with clean paper towel. Take care not to drip hydraulic fluid onto paintwork or hot engine components.

5 Disconnect the brake fluid level sensor wiring plug at the driver's side of the reservoir **(see illustration)**.

6 Loosen the two brake pipe union nuts on the side of the master cylinder. To prevent rounding off the corners on these nuts, the use of a brake pipe nut spanner, which wraps around the nut, is preferred. Place some

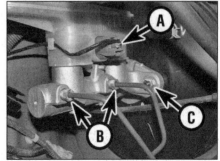

7.5 Level sensor plug (A), brake unions (B), and one of the cylinder mounting nuts (C)

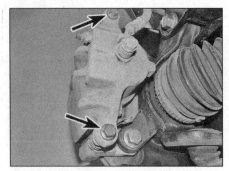

8.4a Brake caliper guide pin bolts

8.4b If the caliper is removed completely, suspend it using wire or cable-ties

system as described in Section 5. Check the operation of the brakes before taking the car out on the road.

8 Brake pads – renewal

Note: *Refer to the precautions in Section 1 before proceeding.*

Front pads

absorbent rag or towel underneath, pull the brake pipes away slightly from the master cylinder. Either plug or tape over the open connections to prevent contamination.
7 Unscrew and remove the two nuts attaching the master cylinder to the servo. Pull the master cylinder off the studs and out of the engine compartment. Again, be careful not to spill the fluid as this is done. Recover the master cylinder pushrod seal – a new one should be obtained for refitting.

Overhaul

Note: *Check availability of overhaul kits prior to dismantling the cylinder.*
8 Unscrew the reservoir front mounting bolt. Wrap some clean rag or paper towel around the reservoir, then release the hose clips, disconnect the two hoses, and remove the reservoir from the cylinder.
9 Push the rear piston into the cylinder body, and extract the circlip.
10 Remove the screw which secures the reservoir to the top of the cylinder, and withdraw it. Recover the two grommets – new ones must be used on reassembly.
11 Push the rear piston inwards, then extract the stop pin through the cylinder front port.
12 Remove the stopper, then ease out the piston assemblies. If necessary, use compressed air to force the piston from the cylinder body.
13 Carefully examine the bore of the cylinder for rust, scratches, gouges and general wear. If the bore is damaged, the complete cylinder must be renewed. If the bore is in good condition, thoroughly clean the assembly, and renew the seals as described below.

14 Take note of the seal orientation on the piston, and using a small screwdriver, lever the seals from the grooves on the piston.
15 Smear the new seals with clean brake fluid, then fit them to the piston as noted on removal.
16 Apply a little of the assembly grease (which should be supplied in the overhaul kit) to the piston bodies and O-rings.
17 Insert the primary piston assembly into the cylinder, spring end first. Ensure the seal lips enter the cylinder bore without catching or folding back. Align the piston slot with the stop pin hole at the top of the cylinder.
18 Fit the secondary piston, and use it to push the primary piston in far enough to refit the stop pin, though the cylinder front port.
19 Push the rear piston inwards, fit the stopper, then secure with the circlip.
20 Using two new grommets, refit the reservoir, and secure with the screw.

Refitting

21 Apply some of the overhaul kit's assembly grease to a new pushrod seal, and fit it to the rear of the cylinder.
22 Fit the master cylinder over the studs on the servo, and tighten the attaching nuts only finger-tight at this stage.
23 Thread the brake pipe fittings into the master cylinder. Since the master cylinder is still loose, it can be moved slightly in order for the fittings to thread in easily. Do not strip the threads as the fittings are tightened.
24 Fully tighten the mounting nuts and pipe unions to the specified torque.
25 Fill the master cylinder reservoir with fluid, then bleed the master cylinder and the brake

1 Loosen the roadwheel nuts, then raise the front of the car and support it securely on axle stands (see *Jacking and vehicle support*).
2 Remove the front wheels. Work on one brake assembly at a time, using the assembled brake for reference if necessary.
3 First, inspect the brake disc carefully as outlined in Section 10. If renewal is necessary, follow the information in that Section to remove the disc, at which time the calipers and pads can be removed as well.
4 Unscrew and remove the caliper lower guide pin bolt, then swing the caliper upwards off the pads. For better access (and to make pushing the piston back easier), unscrew both guide pin bolts, and lift the caliper off completely – suspend it on a piece of wire to avoid straining the brake hose **(see illustrations)**.
5 Noting their order of fitting, unclip and remove the pad shims. Two shims are used on the inner pad (the larger one fits next to the pad), with one shim on the outer pad.
6 Unclip the pads from the caliper mounting bracket, and remove them **(see illustration)**. Note that the inner pad has a metal tab attached – this tab rubs against the disc when the friction material is wearing low.

> **HAYNES HINT** *If the pads are wearing unevenly, the calipers are probably seized, which will also wear the discs prematurely. Just removing the pads and pushing the piston fully back into its bore (see paragraph 10) may unseize the piston enough to restore correct operation. If not, remove and overhaul the calipers as described in Section 9.*

7 Release the pad retaining clips from the top and bottom of the caliper bracket, noting how they are fitted **(see illustration)**. If the clips are in poor condition, it is recommended that new clips are used when refitting.
8 While the pads are removed, clean the caliper and mounting bracket. This is best done using a brush together with spray or liquid brake cleaner, rather than dry brushing, which carries a greater risk of inhaling brake dust. Though the chance of any pads containing harmful asbestos is greatly reduced nowadays, it still pays to take care on this point.
9 Check the disc and caliper, brake hose, piston dust seals and guide pin boots for any

8.6 Unclip the pads from the caliper mounting bracket

8.7 Removing a pad retaining clip – caliper bracket removed

8.10 Retracting the caliper piston with the hose clamped and bleed screw open

8.13a Fit the two shims to the inner pad (with the metal tab) . . .

8.13b . . . then apply a little copper grease to the shims . . .

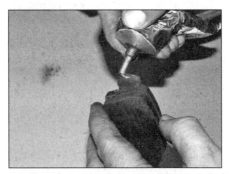

8.13c . . . and to the pad locating 'ears'

8.13d The outer pad only has one shim to fit

signs of damage. Caliper overhaul is covered in Section 9.

10 The caliper piston must be pushed back into the caliper to make room for the new pads – this may require considerable effort. Either use a G-clamp, sliding-jaw (water pump) pliers, or suitable pieces of wood as levers **(see illustration)**.

Caution: Pushing back the piston causes a reverse-flow of brake fluid, which has been known to 'flip' the master cylinder rubber seals, resulting in a total loss of braking. To avoid this, clamp the caliper flexible hose and open the bleed screw – as the piston is pushed back, the fluid can be directed into a suitable container using a hose attached to the bleed screw. Close the screw just before the piston is pushed fully back, to ensure no air enters the system.

11 If the recommended method of opening a bleed screw before pushing back the piston is not used, the fluid level in the reservoir will rise, and possibly overflow. Make sure that there is sufficient space in the brake fluid reservoir to accept the displaced fluid, and if necessary, syphon some off first. Any brake fluid spilt on paintwork should be washed off with clean water without delay – brake fluid is also a highly-effective paint-stripper.

12 Begin refitting by applying a little copper brake grease to the mating surfaces of the

pad retaining clips, before clipping them into the caliper bracket.

13 Clip the pad shims onto the new pads, then apply a little of the same grease to the shims, and to the edges of the brake pad backing plates – in particular the 'ears' which locate in the caliper bracket. Don't get any grease on the pad friction material **(see illustrations)**.

14 Fit the pads into the caliper mounting bracket, clipping them firmly into place, with the friction material facing the disc **(see illustration)**.

15 Fit the caliper back over the pads, then refit and tighten the guide pin bolt(s) to the specified torque. If the caliper will not fit over the new pads, the caliper piston has not been pushed back far enough – see paragraph 10.

16 Depress the brake pedal several times to bring the pads into firm contact with the brake disc.

17 Repeat the above procedure on the other front brake caliper.

18 Refit the roadwheels, then lower the car to the ground and tighten the wheel nuts to the specified torque.

19 Check the hydraulic fluid level as described in *Weekly checks*.

20 If new pads have been fitted, full braking efficiency will not be obtained until the linings have bedded-in. Be prepared for longer stopping distances, and avoid harsh braking

as far as possible for the first hundred miles or so after fitting new pads.

Rear pads

21 Chock the front wheels, loosen the road-wheel nuts, then raise the rear of the car and support it securely on axle stands (see *Jacking and vehicle support*).

22 Remove the rear wheels. Work on one brake assembly at a time, using the assembled brake for reference if necessary.

23 Release the handbrake fully.

24 First, inspect the brake disc carefully as outlined in Section 10. If renewal is necessary, follow the information in that Section to

8.14 Clip the pads back into the caliper bracket

8.25a Unscrew the nut . . .

8.25b . . . and separate the handbrake cable from the trailing arm

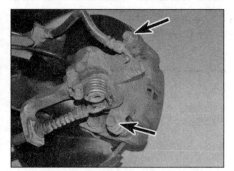

8.26a Rear caliper guide pin bolts

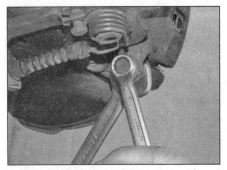

8.26b Hold the pin with a spanner while the bolt is loosened . . .

8.26c . . . and then removed

remove the disc, at which time the calipers and pads can be removed as well.

25 Trace the handbrake cable back from the caliper, and remove the single nut securing the cable support bracket to the trailing arm **(see illustrations)**.

26 Unscrew and remove the two caliper guide pin bolts, and remove the caliper body from its mounting bracket for access to the pads. Support the caliper while it is removed, either by suspending it on a piece of wire (or cable-ties), or by resting it on an axle stand

– do not let it hang down on its brake hose **(see illustrations)**. Also, do not bend the handbrake cable excessively.

27 Unclip the pads from the caliper mounting bracket, and remove them **(see illustration)**. Note that the inner pad has a metal tab attached – this tab rubs against the disc when the friction material is wearing low. The inner pad also has a raised tab on the backplate, which engages in a slot in the caliper piston.

28 Where applicable, unclip and remove the pad shims – different shims are used on the inner and outer pads **(see illustration)**.

29 Release the pad retaining clips from the top and bottom of the caliper bracket, noting how they are fitted. If the clips are in poor condition, it is recommended that new clips are used when refitting.

30 While the pads are removed, clean the caliper and mounting bracket. This is best done using a brush together with spray or liquid brake cleaner, rather than dry brushing, which carries a greater risk of inhaling brake dust. Though the chance of any pads containing harmful asbestos is greatly reduced nowadays, it still pays to take care on this point.

31 Check the disc and caliper, brake hose, piston dust seals and guide pin boots for any signs of damage. Caliper overhaul is covered in Section 9.

32 If new brake pads are to be fitted, it will be necessary to retract the piston fully into the caliper bore by rotating it in a clockwise direction. This can be achieved using sturdy circlip pliers, but note that as well as being turned, the piston has to be pressed in

8.26d Lift the caliper off the pads . . .

8.26e . . . and hang it from the rear spring using a cable-tie

8.27 Unclip the pads from the caliper mounting bracket (this is the inner pad)

8.28 Unclip the pad shims – the smaller shim fits the inner pad (with the metal tab)

8.32 Retracting the caliper piston with the hose clamped and bleed screw open

very firmly. Special tools are available from companies such as Draper to achieve this with less effort **(see illustration)**.

Caution: Pushing back the piston causes a reverse-flow of brake fluid, which has been known to 'flip' the master cylinder rubber seals, resulting in a total loss of braking. To avoid this, clamp the caliper flexible hose and open the bleed screw – as the piston is pushed back, the fluid can be directed into a suitable container using a hose attached to the bleed screw. Close the screw just before the piston is pushed fully back, to ensure no air enters the system.

33 Lubricate the piston dust seal with rubber grease (a little washing-up liquid will serve as a substitute) before turning the piston. If the seal gets twisted, turn the piston the opposite way to un-twist the seal, then try again. When the piston is fully retracted, turn it so that one of its grooves is vertical in the caliper body, to accept the raised tab on the back of the inner pad **(see illustration)**.

34 If the recommended method of opening a bleed screw before pushing back the piston is not used, the fluid level in the reservoir will rise, and possibly overflow. Make sure that there is sufficient space in the brake fluid reservoir to accept the displaced fluid, and if necessary, syphon some off first. Any brake fluid spilt on paintwork should be washed off with clean water without delay – brake fluid is also a highly-effective paint-stripper.

35 Clip the pad shims onto the new pads, then apply a little of the same grease to the shims, and to the edges of the brake pad backing plates – in particular the 'ears' which locate in the caliper bracket. Don't get any grease on the pad friction material **(see illustration)**.

36 The caliper has a pad retaining clip incorporated. This should not need to be disturbed, but if loose, clip it back into place **(see illustration)**.

37 Offer the caliper into position over the pads, then refit and tighten the guide pin bolts to the specified torque. If the caliper will not fit over the new pads, the caliper piston has either not been retracted far enough, or the piston's groove is not in the correct alignment – see paragraphs 32 and 33.

38 Refit the handbrake cable support bracket to the trailing arm, and tighten the nut securely.

39 Depress the brake pedal, and operate the handbrake, several times to bring the pads into firm contact with the brake disc.

40 Repeat the above procedure on the other rear brake caliper.

41 Refit the roadwheels, then lower the car to the ground and tighten the wheel nuts to the specified torque.

42 Check the hydraulic fluid level as described in *Weekly checks*.

43 Check the handbrake operation as described in Chapter 1, and adjust if necessary as described in Section 15.

44 If new pads have been fitted, full braking efficiency will not be obtained until the linings have bedded-in. Be prepared for longer

8.33 Align the piston grooves as shown

stopping distances, and avoid harsh braking as far as possible for the first hundred miles or so after fitting new pads.

9 Brake caliper – removal, overhaul and refitting

Note: *Refer to the precautions in Section 1 before proceeding.*

Front caliper

Removal

1 Loosen the roadwheel nuts, then raise the front of the car and support it securely on axle stands (see *Jacking and vehicle support*). Remove the front wheel.

2 If the caliper is being removed as part of another operation (such as removing the brake disc), the brake hose union does not have to be disturbed.

9.3a Hold the guide pin with a spanner while the bolt is loosened . . .

9.3c . . . and lift off the caliper

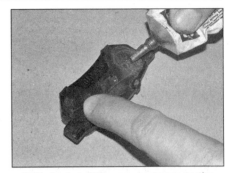

8.35 Apply a little copper grease to the pad shims

8.36 Clip the caliper's pad retaining clip back inside if loose

3 Unscrew and remove both caliper guide pin bolts, then lift the caliper off the pads. Hang the caliper up using a piece of wire, or rest it on an axle stand – do not allow it to hang down on the brake hose **(see illustrations)**.

9.3b . . . then remove the bolts . . .

9.3d Suspend the caliper using wire or cable-ties

Removal (for overhaul)

4 Loosen the roadwheel nuts, then raise the front of the car and support it securely on axle stands (see *Jacking and vehicle support*). Remove the front wheel.

5 Trace the brake hose back from the caliper, and remove the single bolt securing the hose support bracket to the strut.

6 Clamp the brake hose, using a proper brake hose clamp if available (these are not expensive, and greatly reduce the risk of damaging the hose). In the absence of a proper clamp, use some self-locking pliers, but protect the hose by placing a couple of pieces of card in the plier jaws.

7 Wrap some clean rag or paper towel around the brake hose union on the caliper, then just loosen the bolt.

8 Unscrew and remove both caliper guide pin bolts, then lift the caliper off the pads.

9 Fully unscrew the union bolt, and disconnect the brake hose from the caliper – anticipate a small amount of fluid spillage as this is done. Recover the copper sealing washers fitted either side of the hose end fitting – new washers should be used when reassembling.

Overhaul

Note: *Ensure that an appropriate caliper overhaul kit is obtained before starting work.*

10 With the caliper on the bench, wipe away all traces of dust and dirt, but avoid inhaling the dust, as it is may be a health hazard.

11 Using a small flat-bladed screwdriver, carefully prise the dust seal retaining clip out of the caliper bore **(see illustration)**.

12 Withdraw the partially-ejected piston from the caliper body and remove the dust seal. The piston can be withdrawn by hand, or if

necessary forced out by applying compressed air to the union bolt hole.

Caution: The piston may be ejected with some force. Only low pressure should be required, such as is generated by a foot pump.

13 Extract the piston hydraulic seal using a blunt instrument such as a knitting needle or a crochet hook, taking care not to damage the caliper bore.

14 Withdraw the guide sleeves or pins from the caliper body or mounting bracket (as applicable) and remove the rubber gaiters.

15 Thoroughly clean all components, using only methylated spirit, isopropyl alcohol or clean hydraulic fluid as a cleaning medium. Never use mineral-based solvents, such as petrol or paraffin, which will attack the hydraulic system rubber components. Dry the components immediately, using compressed air or a clean, lint-free cloth. Use compressed air to blow clear the fluid passages.

16 Check all components and renew any that are worn or damaged. Check particularly the cylinder bore and piston; if they are scratched, worn or corroded in any way, they must be renewed (note that this means the renewal of the complete body assembly). Similarly check the condition of the guide sleeves or pins and their bores; they should be undamaged and (when cleaned) a reasonably tight sliding fit in the body or mounting bracket bores. If there is any doubt about the condition of a component, renew it.

17 If the assembly is fit for further use, obtain the appropriate repair kit.

18 Renew all rubber seals, dust covers and caps disturbed on dismantling as a matter of course; these should never be re-used.

19 Before commencing reassembly, ensure that all components are absolutely clean and dry.

20 Dip the piston and the new piston (fluid) seal in clean hydraulic fluid. Smear clean fluid on the cylinder bore surface.

21 Fit the new piston (fluid) seal, using only the fingers to manipulate it into the cylinder bore groove. Fit the new dust seal to the piston. Refit the piston to the cylinder bore using a twisting motion, ensuring that the piston enters squarely into the bore. Press the piston fully into the bore, then press the dust seal into the caliper body.

22 Install the dust seal retaining clip, ensuring that it is correctly seated in the caliper groove.

23 Apply the grease supplied in the repair kit (or copper brake grease) to the guide sleeves or pins. Fit the sleeves or pins to the caliper body or mounting bracket. Fit the new rubber gaiters, ensuring that they are correctly located in the grooves on both the sleeve or pin, and body or mounting bracket (as applicable).

24 As with all other work on the braking system, it is recommended that the calipers are overhauled in axle pairs – in other words, it is not advisable to only overhaul one caliper at a time, as this may result in uneven braking.

Refitting (after overhaul)

25 Using new copper sealing washers either side of the hose end fitting, reconnect the brake hose to the caliper, tightening the bolt only hand-tight at this stage.

26 Offer the caliper into position over the pads, then refit the guide pin bolts and tighten them to the specified torque.

27 Tighten the brake hose union bolt to the specified torque, then remove the brake hose clamp.

28 Bleed the brakes as described in Section 5. If the brake hose was clamped throughout, then only the disturbed caliper should require bleeding.

29 On completion, refit the wheel and lower the car to the ground. Tighten the wheel nuts to the specified torque.

Refitting

30 Offer the caliper into position over the pads, then refit the guide pin bolts and tighten them to the specified torque.

31 On completion, refit the wheel and lower the car to the ground. Tighten the wheel nuts to the specified torque.

Rear caliper

Removal

32 Chock the front wheels, loosen the roadwheel nuts, then raise the rear of the car and support it securely on axle stands (see *Jacking and vehicle support*). Remove the rear wheel.

33 Trace the handbrake cable back from the caliper, and remove the nut securing the cable

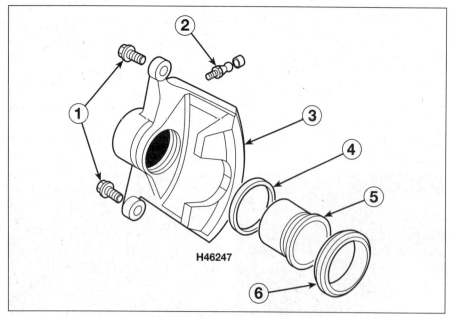

9.11 Front brake caliper exploded view

| 1 | Guide pin bolts | 3 | Caliper body | 5 | Piston |
| 2 | Bleed screw | 4 | Piston seal | 6 | Dust seal |

9.33a Unscrew the nut . . .

9.33b . . . and separate the handbrake cable from the trailing arm

9.35 Hang the caliper from the rear spring using a cable-tie

9.38a Pull out the horseshoe clip securing the handbrake cable to the caliper bracket

9.38b Using pliers (or in this case, the tip of a large screwdriver), turn the lever . . .

support bracket from the trailing arm (see illustrations).

34 If the caliper is being removed as part of another operation (such as removing the brake disc), the brake hose union does not have to be disturbed.

35 Unscrew and remove both caliper guide pin bolts, then slide the caliper off the pads. Hang the caliper up using a piece of wire (or cable-ties), or rest it on an axle stand – do not allow it to hang down on the brake hose (see illustration).

Removal (for overhaul)

36 Chock the front wheels, loosen the roadwheel nuts, then raise the rear of the car and support it securely on axle stands (see *Jacking and vehicle support*). Remove the rear wheel.

37 Trace the handbrake cable back from the caliper, and remove the nut securing the cable support bracket from the trailing arm.

38 Pull out the horseshoe clip securing the outer cable to its bracket on the caliper body. Turn the caliper handbrake lever using pliers, and unhook the handbrake cable end fitting from it (see illustrations).

39 Clamp the brake hose, using a proper brake hose clamp if available (these are not expensive, and greatly reduce the risk of damaging the hose). In the absence of a

proper clamp, use some self-locking pliers, but protect the hose by placing a couple of pieces of card in the plier jaws.

40 Wrap some clean rag or paper towel around the brake hose union on the caliper, then just loosen the bolt.

41 Unscrew and remove both caliper guide pin bolts, then slide the caliper off the pads.

42 Fully unscrew the union bolt, and disconnect the brake hose from the caliper – anticipate a small amount of fluid spillage as this is done. Recover the copper sealing washers fitted either side of the hose end fitting – new washers should be used when reassembling.

9.38c . . . and unhook the cable end fitting

Overhaul

Note: *Ensure the correct caliper overhaul kit is obtained before starting work.*

43 With the caliper on the bench, wipe away all traces of dust and dirt, but avoid inhaling the dust, as it is may be a health hazard.

44 Using a small screwdriver, carefully prise out the dust seal from the caliper bore, taking care not to damage the piston.

45 Remove the piston from the caliper bore by rotating it in an anti-clockwise direction (see illustration). This can be achieved by using a square-section bar, such as the shaft of a screwdriver, which locates snugly in the caliper piston slots. Once the piston turns freely but

9.38d Removing the handbrake cable from the caliper bracket

does not come out any further, the piston can be withdrawn by hand, or if necessary pushed out by applying compressed air to the union bolt hole.

Caution: The piston may be ejected with some force – only low pressure should be required, such as is generated by a foot pump.

46 Using a blunt instrument such as a knitting needle or a crochet hook, extract the piston hydraulic seal, taking care not to damage the caliper bore.

47 Withdraw the guide sleeves from the caliper body, and remove the guide sleeve gaiters.

48 Inspect the caliper components as described previously in this Section for the front calipers. Renew as necessary, noting that the inside of the caliper piston must not be dismantled. If necessary, the handbrake mechanism can be overhauled as described in the following paragraphs. If it is not wished to overhaul the handbrake mechanism, proceed to paragraph 54.

49 Before dismantling the handbrake mechanism, note carefully how it is assembled. If possible, take some digital photos from various angles, as a guide for refitting – the other rear caliper may also be used for guidance.

50 Remove the nut and bolt securing the handbrake cable support bracket, and take off the bracket. Recover the washer fitted under the nut.

51 Take off the return spring, cam lever, boot and the cam, noting their fitted sequence.

52 Clean all the handbrake components in brake cleaner or methylated spirit, and examine them for wear. If there is any sign of wear or damage, the complete handbrake mechanism assembly should be renewed.

53 Ensure that all components are clean and dry. Apply some copper brake grease to the cam and its boot, then fit them, followed by the cam lever and return spring. Refit the cable support bracket, secured with the washer, nut and bolt – tighten the nut and bolt securely.

54 Soak the piston and the new piston (fluid) seal in clean hydraulic fluid. Smear clean fluid on the cylinder bore surface.

55 Fit the new piston (fluid) seal, using only the fingers to manipulate it into the cylinder bore groove, and refit the piston assembly. Turn the piston in a clockwise direction, using the method employed on dismantling, until it is fully retracted into the caliper bore. When the piston is fully retracted, turn it so that its tapered cut-out will align with the raised tab on the back of the inner pad, when both are refitted.

56 Fit the dust seal to the caliper, ensuring that it is correctly located in the caliper and also the groove on the piston.

57 Apply the grease supplied in the repair kit (or copper brake grease) to the guide sleeves or pins. Fit the sleeves or pins to the caliper body or mounting bracket. Fit the new rubber

gaiters, ensuring that they are correctly located in the grooves on both the sleeve or pin, and body or mounting bracket (as applicable).

58 As with all other work on the braking system, it is recommended that the calipers are overhauled in axle pairs – in other words, it is not advisable to only overhaul one caliper at a time, as this may result in uneven braking.

Refitting (after overhaul)

59 Using new copper sealing washers either side of the hose end fitting, reconnect the brake hose to the caliper, tightening the bolt only hand-tight at this stage.

60 Offer the caliper into position over the pads, then refit the guide pin bolts and tighten them to the specified torque.

61 Tighten the brake hose union bolt to the specified torque, then remove the brake hose clamp.

62 Reconnect the handbrake cable support bracket to the trailing arm, and secure with the nut.

63 Hook the handbrake inner cable into the caliper handbrake operating lever, then clip the outer cable into its bracket on the caliper body.

64 Bleed the brakes as described in Section 5. If the brake hose was clamped throughout, then only the disturbed caliper should require bleeding.

65 On completion, refit the wheel and lower the car to the ground. Tighten the wheel nuts to the specified torque.

Refitting

66 Offer the caliper into position over the pads, then refit the guide pin bolts and tighten them to the specified torque.

67 Reconnect the handbrake cable support bracket to the trailing arm, and secure with the nut.

68 On completion, refit the wheel and lower the car to the ground. Tighten the wheel nuts to the specified torque.

10 Brake discs –
inspection, removal
and refitting

Note: *Refer to the precautions in Section 1 before proceeding.*

Inspection

1 Loosen the relevant wheel nuts, chock the wheels, then jack up either the front or rear of the car and support on axle stands (see *Jacking and vehicle support*). Remove the appropriate roadwheel.

2 Slowly rotate the brake disc so that the full area of both sides can be checked; remove the brake pads, as described in Section 8, if better access is required to the inboard surface. Light scoring is normal in the area swept by the brake pads, but if heavy scoring is found, the disc must be renewed.

3 It is normal to find a lip of rust and brake dust around the disc's perimeter; this can be

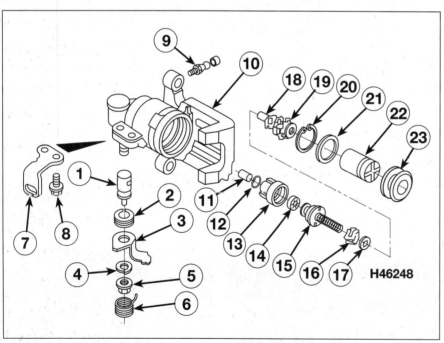

9.45 Rear brake caliper exploded view

1 Cam	7 Handbrake cable	12 O-ring	18 Adjusting spring
2 Boot	support bracket	13 Slave piston	19 Spring cover
3 Cam lever	8 Bolt	14 Clip	20 Circlip
4 Spring washer	9 Bleed screw	15 Adjusting bolt	21 Piston seal
5 Nut	10 Caliper body	16 Bearing	22 Piston
6 Return spring	11 Pin	17 Spacer	23 Dust seal

scraped off if required. If, however, a lip has formed due to wear of the brake pad swept area, the disc thickness must be measured using a micrometer. Take measurements at several places around the disc at the inside and outside of the pad swept area; if the disc has worn at any point to the specified minimum thickness or less, it must be renewed.

4 If the disc is thought to be warped, it can be checked for run-out, ideally by using a dial gauge mounted on any convenient fixed point, while the disc is slowly rotated. In the absence of a dial gauge, use feeler blades to measure (at several points all around the disc) the clearance between the disc and a fixed point such as the caliper mounting bracket.

5 If the measurements obtained are at the specified maximum or beyond, the disc is excessively warped, and must be renewed; however, it is worth checking first that the wheel bearing is in good condition (Chapters 1 and 10). Also try the effect of removing the disc and turning it through 180° to reposition it on the hub; if run-out is still excessive, the disc must be renewed.

6 Check the disc for cracks (especially around the wheel bolt holes), and for any other wear or damage. Renew the disc if necessary.

Removal

7 Remove the brake caliper and pads as described in Sections 8 and 9.

8 Unscrew the two bolts securing the brake caliper mounting bracket to the hub, and slide the bracket off the disc **(see illustrations)**.

9 If the same disc is to be refitted, use chalk or paint to mark the relationship of the disc to the hub.

10 Remove the two disc retaining screws – these may be tight, due to corrosion. If available, use an impact driver to remove the screws, or try tapping the end of the screwdriver to break the screw free. Sometimes, using a close-fitting screwdriver bit in a socket handle can provide greater leverage on a difficult screw than a screwdriver will **(see illustration)**.

11 With the screws removed, pull the brake disc from the hub – if it is tight, lightly tap its rear face with a hide or plastic mallet. If the disc is stuck, two M8 threaded holes are provided in the disc face – screw two M8 bolts

10.8a Unscrew the front caliper bracket mounting bolts . . .

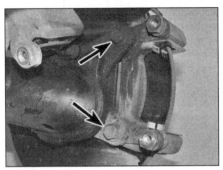

10.8c Unscrew the rear caliper mounting bracket bolts . . .

into these, and tighten them evenly to draw off the disc **(see illustrations)**.

Refitting

12 Refitting is the reverse of the removal procedure, noting the following points:

10.10 The two brake disc screws should not be tight, but use a good tool

10.8b . . . and lift the bracket off the disc

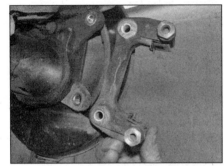

10.8d . . . and take out the bracket

a) *Ensure that the mating surfaces of the disc and hub are clean and flat. To reduce the risk of corrosion, apply copper grease to the hub before fitting the disc (ensure that the grease does not get on the disc friction surfaces)* **(see illustration)**.

10.11a If the brake disc will not simply pull off (or tap off) . . .

10.11b . . . screw in a pair of M8 bolts into the holes provided . . .

10.11c . . . and tighten them equally to press off the disc

10.12 Apply a little copper grease to the hub flange before fitting the disc

11.2 Removing the brake drum

11.3 Use a pair of 8 mm bolts into the holes provided to press the drum off

11.8 Lift the wheel cylinder boots and check for wetness

b) If applicable, align the marks made on removal.
c) If a new disc has been fitted, use a suitable solvent to wipe any preservative coating from the disc before refitting the caliper.
d) If the disc retaining screws suffered damage during removal, use new ones when reassembling. Apply a little copper grease to their threads, to prevent future corrosion problems.
e) Tighten the brake caliper mounting bracket bolts to the specified torque.
f) Refit the pads and caliper as described in Sections 8 and 9.
g) Refit the roadwheel, then lower the car to the ground and tighten the wheel nuts to the specified torque. On completion, depress the brake pedal several times to bring the brake pads into contact with the disc.

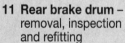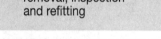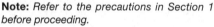
11 Rear brake drum –
removal, inspection
and refitting

Note: *Refer to the precautions in Section 1 before proceeding.*

Removal

1 Loosen the relevant wheel nuts, chock the wheels, then jack up either the front or rear of the car and support on axle stands (see *Jacking and vehicle support*). Remove the appropriate roadwheel.

2 Ensure that the handbrake is fully released, and remove the brake drum **(see illustration)**. It should simply pull straight off the hub, but if necessary, a few sharp blows with a soft-faced mallet may be required to free it.
3 If the drum is tight, screw a couple of 8.0 mm bolts into the tapped holes, and tighten them to free the drum **(see illustration)**.
4 If the drum is catching on the shoes, it may be possible to get the drum off by repeatedly pushing the drum back on, turning it a little, and carefully trying to withdraw it squarely over the shoes – getting the 'alignment' right is critical, and can only be achieved by trial-and-error.

Inspection

5 Brush the dirt and dust from the drum, taking care not to inhale it.
6 Examine the internal friction surface of the drum. If deeply scored, or so worn that the drum has become ridged to the width of the shoes, then both drums must be renewed.
7 Regrinding of the friction surface may be possible, provided the maximum diameter given in the Specifications is not exceeded, but note that both rear drums should be reground to the identical diameter.
8 While the drum is removed, check the condition of the shoes. Also look for signs of fluid leakage from the wheel cylinder – one sign is a build-up of brake dust on either end of the cylinder body (gently pull back the cylinder rubber boots, and look for wetness) **(see illustration)**.

Refitting

9 If necessary, back off the adjuster wheel on the strut until the drum will pass over the shoes, then slip the drum into position.
10 Adjust the brakes by operating the footbrake a number of times. A clicking noise may be heard from the drum as the automatic adjuster operates. When the clicking stops, or normal pedal feel is restored, adjustment is complete.
11 Check the operation of the handbrake, then refit the roadwheel and lower the car to the ground. Tighten the wheel nuts to the specified torque.

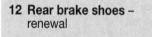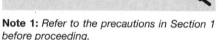
12 Rear brake shoes –
renewal

Note 1: *Refer to the precautions in Section 1 before proceeding.*
Note 2: *All four rear brake shoes must be renewed at the same time, but to avoid mixing up parts, work on only one brake assembly at a time.*

1 Remove the brake drum on the side concerned, as described in Section 11. Since both sets of shoes must be renewed, it is helpful to remove both drums, so that the undisturbed shoes can be referred to as a guide.
2 Follow **illustrations 12.3a to 12.3r** for the brake shoe renewal procedure **(see illustrations)**. Be sure to stay in order and read the caption under each illustration.

12.3a Turn the end of each shoe retainer pin with pliers . . .

12.3b . . . then withdraw the pin from the rear, and take off the spring

12.3c Pull out the shoes from the anchor plate . . .

12.3d . . . and unhook the return spring

12.3e Remove the shoes from the backplate . . .

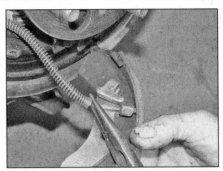

12.3f . . . then pull back the spring and unhook the handbrake cable

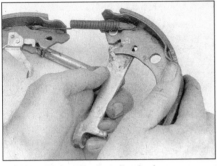

12.3g Swing the handbrake lever away from the trailing shoe, which will force the adjuster bolt clevis out of its groove in the shoe; the two shoes can now be separated

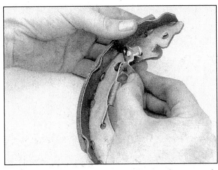

12.3h Remove the self-adjuster lever and spring from the leading shoe

12.3i Prise open the handbrake lever retaining clip and separate the lever from the shoe; don't lose the wave washer under the clip

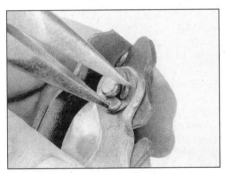

12.3j Put the new trailing shoe on the lever, place the wave washer over the pin, then fit the retaining clip; crimp the ends of the clip together with thin-nose pliers

12.3k Clean the adjuster bolt and clevis, then apply copper grease to the threads and ends

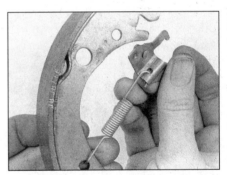

12.3l Connect the self-adjuster lever spring to the leading brake shoe, then insert the pin on the lever into its hole in the shoe

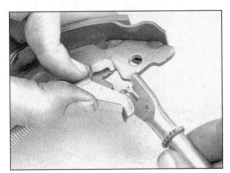

12.3m Insert the short clevis of the adjuster bolt into its slot in the leading shoe, making sure it catches the self-adjuster lever

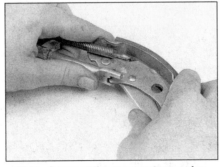

12.3n Connect the upper return spring, prise the shoe lower ends apart, and fit the adjuster into the other shoe; note how the clevis stepped portion fits

12.3o Lubricate the brake shoe contact areas on the backplate with copper grease

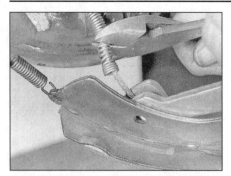

12.3p Compress the handbrake cable spring, hold it in position and connect the cable end to the handbrake lever

12.3q Offer up the brake shoes to the backplate, engaging the shoe upper ends in the wheel cylinder piston slots. Connect the shoe lower return spring

12.3r Secure the shoes with the retainer pins and spring plates – make sure the handbrake cable spring and lower return spring are behind the anchor plate

3 When refitting the brake drum, adjust the brake shoes by turning the star wheel on the adjuster bolt until the drum just slips over the shoes. When turning the drum, the shoes should not rub; if they do, remove the drum and back off the star wheel a little bit so they don't.
4 Refit the drum as described in Section 11.
5 Check the brake operation before taking the car out on the road – remember that the new shoes will need several hundred miles before they bed-in fully and give proper performance..

13 Rear brake backplate (drum brake models) – removal and refitting

Removal

1 Remove the brake drum as described in Section 11.
2 Remove the rear hub assembly as described in Chapter 10.
3 If the backplate is being removed purely for access to the rear suspension, and no work is required on the brake shoes or wheel cylinder, the backplate can be removed with the shoes and wheel cylinder attached, which makes less work when refitting; otherwise, remove the shoes as described in Section 12.
4 Clamp the rear brake hose, then unscrew the brake pipe union from the rear wheel cylinder – anticipate a small amount of brake fluid loss as this is done.

14.2a Wheel cylinder mounting bolts

5 If the brake shoes have been removed, and the backplate is to be removed completely, unscrew the two small bolts securing the handbrake cable to the backplate, and withdraw the cable through it.
6 Remove the four brake backplate mounting bolts, and withdraw the backplate from the stub axle.

Refitting

7 Refitting is a reversal of removal, noting the following points:
  a) Before refitting the backplate, clean up the stub axle and backplate mating surfaces.
  b) Tighten the backplate mounting bolts to the specified torque.
  c) Tighten the wheel cylinder pipe union securely.
  d) If removed, refit the shoes as described in Section 12.
  e) Refit the rear hub as described in Chapter 10.
  f) On completion, once the drum has been refitted, bleed the brakes as described in Section 5, and if necessary adjust the handbrake as described in Section 15.

14 Rear wheel cylinder (drum brake models) – renewal

1 Remove the brake drum as described in Section 11.

14.2b Removing the wheel cylinder from the backplate

2 Unscrew the two wheel cylinder bolts, and withdraw the cylinder from the backplate (see illustrations). Gently pull the shoes apart at the top, to release the cylinder.
3 If a wheel cylinder is leaking, usually the only course of action is to fit a new one complete, though repair kits may be available – check with your Honda dealer or parts supplier. Unlike other brake components, it is not essential to renew both rear cylinders at the same time, but if one has gone, it is likely the other will soon follow, and it may be wise to renew them in pairs for peace of mind.
4 When refitting, check that the mating faces are clean, and tighten the wheel cylinder mounting bolts to the specified torque.
5 Refit the brake drum as described in Section 11.

15 Handbrake – adjustment

1 If the handbrake check in Chapter 1 reveals a need for handbrake adjustment, proceed as follows.
2 Chock the front wheels, then jack up the rear of the car, and support it on axle stands (see Jacking and vehicle support).
3 Release the handbrake lever fully.
4 On rear disc brake models, check to see whether the rear brake caliper's handbrake lever is in contact with the caliper stop pin (see illustration). If not, this suggests that

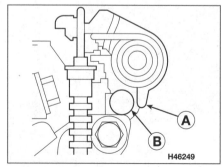

15.4 When fully released, handbrake lever (A) should contact caliper stop pin (B)

15.7 Adjusting the handbrake

the cable on that side may be seized (not releasing properly), or that the handbrake is over-adjusted (being held off the rest position).

5 Remove the centre console as described in Chapter 11, Section 28.

16.5a Pull out the horseshoe clip securing the handbrake cable to the caliper bracket

16.5c . . . and unhook the cable end fitting

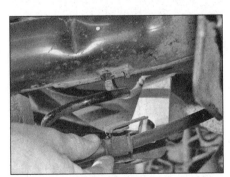

16.7b . . . and separate the handbrake cable from the trailing arm

6 Apply the handbrake lever by one click.
7 Tighten the handbrake adjuster nut at the rear of the handbrake lever, until the rear wheels just start to drag **(see illustration)**.
8 Release the handbrake lever completely, and verify that the rear wheels are free to turn. Reset the adjuster nut accordingly if this is not the case.
9 Ensure that, by the time the handbrake lever is applied by 7 to 10 clicks, the rear wheels are completely locked.
10 Failure to adjust properly suggests that one or more of the handbrake cables may be binding. Examine and lubricate the cables and linkages as far as possible first. If necessary, new cables should be fitted as described in Section 16.
11 On completion, refit the centre console. Refit the rear wheels (where applicable) then lower the car to the ground and tighten the wheel nuts to the specified torque.

16.5b Using pliers (or in this case, the tip of a large screwdriver), turn the lever . . .

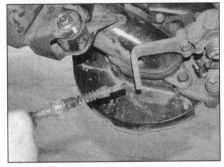

16.5d Removing the handbrake cable from the caliper bracket

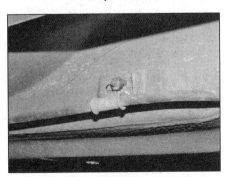

16.7c Unbolt the handbrake cable support brackets

16 Handbrake cables – renewal

1 Chock the front wheels, loosen the rear wheel nuts, then jack up the rear of the car, and support it on axle stands (see *Jacking and vehicle support*). Remove the rear wheels.
2 Release the handbrake lever fully.
3 Remove the centre console as described in Chapter 11, Section 28.
4 Fully slacken the handbrake adjuster nut at the rear of the handbrake lever.
5 On rear disc brake models, pull off the spring clip securing each outer cable to its bracket on the caliper body, then turn the caliper handbrake lever against the spring, and unhook the handbrake inner cable **(see illustrations)**.
6 On rear drum brake models, remove the brake shoes as described in Section 12. With the handbrake cable unhooked from the shoe, unscrew the two small bolts securing the cable to the backplate, and feed the cable through the backplate.
7 Working from the rear of the car forwards, trace the cables along the underside, unbolting the support brackets and releasing the cables from any clips or ties **(see illustrations)**. Note how the cables are arranged and routed, for refitting.
8 Inside the car, unhook the cable ends from the equaliser plate, and then from the floor bracket, at the rear of the handbrake lever **(see illustrations)**. Feed the cables down

16.7a Unscrew the nut . . .

16.8a Unhook the cable ends from the equaliser plate . . .

through the floor grommet, and remove them from under the car.

9 Refitting is a reversal of removal, noting the following points:
- a) *Apply grease to all accessible handbrake pivots and linkages.*
- b) *Ensure that the cables are correctly routed, and secured using all of the support brackets to the underside of the car.*
- c) *On rear drum brake models, refit the brake shoes as described in Section 12.*
- d) *Adjust the handbrake as described in Section 15.*

17 Handbrake lever – removal and refitting

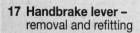

Removal

1 For preference, park the car on level ground before starting. Chock the front wheels, engage a gear (or P) and release the handbrake.
2 Though not essential, access to the handbrake is greatly improved by removing one of the front seats (see Chapter 11).
3 Remove the centre console as described in Chapter 11, Section 28.
4 To make adjusting the handbrake easier, measure and note down the length of adjuster bolt behind the adjuster nut – on completion, the nut can be tightened to the same position **(see illustration)**.
5 Loosen and remove the handbrake adjuster nut **(see illustration)**.
6 On the right-hand side of the lever, disconnect

16.8b ... and from the floor bracket

the wiring plug from the handbrake warning light switch **(see illustration)**.
7 Unscrew the three handbrake lever mounting bolts, and lift the lever assembly out of the car **(see illustration)**.

Refitting

8 Refitting is a reversal of removal. Adjust the handbrake as described in Section 15. Check the operation of the handbrake warning light switch before refitting the handbrake lever cover.

18 Brake pedal position switch – testing and renewal

1 The brake pedal position switch has a dual role – it informs the engine management ECM when the brakes are applied (which among other things, allows the ECM to implement

fuel injection cut-off, where applicable), and also switches on the brake lights.

Testing

2 To check the brake light switch, push on the brake pedal and verify that the brake lights come on.
3 If they don't, check the brake light fuse (refer to the wiring diagrams at the end of Chapter 12). Also check the brake light bulbs in both tail light assemblies – don't forget to check the high-mounted brake light (also Chapter 12).
4 If the fuse and the bulbs are okay, locate the brake light switch at the top of the brake pedal.
5 Disconnect the switch wiring plug **(see illustration)**.
6 Check for continuity across the switch terminals. When the brake pedal is depressed, there should be continuity; when it's released, there should be no continuity. If the switch doesn't operate as described, renew it.

Renewal

7 The brake pedal position switch is fitted above and behind the top of the brake pedal itself – access is from the driver's footwell.
8 Reach up under the facia to the switch mounting bracket, and disconnect the wiring plug from the top of the switch.
9 Turn the switch body anti-clockwise to remove it from the bracket **(see illustration)**.
10 To refit and set the switch, offer the switch into its bracket, so that the switch plunger touches the pedal. Without moving the switch in or out, turn it clockwise to lock it.
11 Reconnect the switch wiring plug to complete.

17.4 Note the length of thread behind the adjuster nut ...

17.5 ... then unscrew and remove it

17.6 Disconnect the warning light switch – also note two lever mounting bolts (arrowed)

17.7 Removing the handbrake lever

18.5 Disconnect the brake light/pedal position switch wiring plug

18.9 Turn the switch anti-clockwise to remove it from the pedal bracket

19.1a Pull back the rubber strip . . .

19.1b . . . and unclip the access panel

19.2 Disconnect the level switch wiring plug

19 Brake fluid level switch – testing and renewal

1 To improve access to the brake (and clutch) reservoirs, a removable panel is provided in the windscreen cowl panel. Pull back the rubber strip on the driver's side, then unclip and remove the panel section provided **(see illustrations)**.

Testing

2 Disconnect the wiring plug from the switch, which is located next to the reservoir mounting bolt **(see illustration)**.
3 Unscrew the reservoir cap for access to the fluid level float.
4 Connect a multimeter across the switch terminals, and check for continuity.
5 When the float is up, there should be no continuity. Now press the float down – continuity should be indicated. If this is not the case, the switch is faulty.
6 The brake fluid level float and switch are integral with the brake fluid reservoir, and are not available separately.

Renewal

7 Remove as much fluid as you can from the reservoir before starting, using a syringe. If a syringe is not available, the fluid can be soaked out with clean paper towel. Take care not to drip hydraulic fluid onto the paintwork or hot engine components.
8 If not already done, disconnect the brake fluid level sensor wiring plug at the side of the reservoir, next to the reservoir mounting bolt.
9 Unscrew the reservoir front mounting bolt. Wrap some clean rag or paper towel around the reservoir, then release the hose clips, disconnect the two hoses, and remove the reservoir from the cylinder.
10 Refitting is a reversal of removal, noting the following points:
  a) *Ensure the reservoir hose connections are securely remade.*
  b) *On completion, refill the reservoir with fresh fluid, and bleed the brakes as described in Section 5.*

20 Anti-lock braking system (ABS) – general information

Virtually all Jazz models are equipped with ABS. The purpose of the system is to prevent the wheel(s) locking during heavy braking. This is achieved by automatic release of the brake on the relevant wheel before it can lock up, followed by rapid reapplication of the brake.

The main components of the system are four wheel sensors (one per wheel), and the hydraulic unit, which contains the ABS computer, the hydraulic solenoid valves and accumulators, and an electrically-driven return pump.

The solenoids are controlled by the computer, which receives signals from the wheel sensors. The sensors detect the speed of rotation of a reluctor ring, attached to the wheel hub. By comparing the speed signals from the four wheels, the computer can determine when a wheel is decelerating at an abnormal rate, and can therefore predict when a wheel is about to lock. During normal operation, the system functions in the same way as a non-ABS braking system does.

If the computer senses that a wheel is about to lock, the ABS system enters the 'pressure-maintain' phase. The computer operates the relevant solenoid valve in the hydraulic unit; this isolates the brake on the wheel in question from the master cylinder, effectively sealing-in the hydraulic pressure.

If the speed of rotation of the wheel continues to decrease at an abnormal rate, the ABS system then enters the 'pressure-decrease' phase. The return pump operates and pumps the hydraulic fluid back into the master cylinder, releasing pressure on the brake. When the speed of rotation of the wheel returns to an acceptable rate, the pump stops and the solenoid valve opens, allowing hydraulic pressure to return and reapply the brake. This cycle can be carried out at up to 10 times a second.

The action of the solenoid valves and return pump creates pulses in the hydraulic circuit. When the ABS system is functioning, these pulses can be felt through the brake pedal.

The Jazz is also equipped with an additional safety feature built into the ABS system, called EBD (Electronic Brake force Distribution), which automatically apportions braking effort between the front and rear wheels. On any car, whether fitted with ABS or not, 90% of the actual braking is done by the front wheels, and under heavy braking, there is significant weight transfer to the front wheels. This situation is compounded if the car is lightly-loaded (without rear seat passengers or luggage), as the rear wheels will have very little weight over them. The EBD function is built into the system's software, and the intention is to limit braking effort (fluid pressure) to the rear wheels, to prevent them locking prematurely under heavy braking, which might otherwise lead to the driver losing control of the rear of the car.

Certain models also feature Brake Assist, which monitors how rapidly the brake pedal is pressed, and determines whether an emergency stop is required – in this case, maximum braking effort is applied more quickly than the driver would normally be able to unaided.

Later models may also feature a Traction Control System (TCS) and Vehicle Stability Assist (VSA). Both of these systems use the ABS to brake wheels which are spinning under power, or to brake one or more wheels to steer the car in the event of a skid. When the traction control system detects wheel spin, the brakes are applied gently on that wheel to reduce its speed, and the throttle actuator closes the throttle valve slightly, reducing engine power. Vehicle stability assist detects when the car is sliding off its intended course, and uses the ABS to correct it. Sensors measure the position of the steering wheel, the pressure in the brake master cylinder, the yaw velocity/rate (body roll), and the lateral (sideways) acceleration. With this information, the system can compare the driver's intention with the car's movement, and apply the appropriate corrective action – this might be to apply or release an individual brake to steer the car, or to reduce engine power via the engine management system.

The operation of the ABS system is entirely dependent on electrical signals. To prevent the system responding to any inaccurate signals, a built-in safety circuit monitors all signals

21.3 ABS hydraulic unit wiring plug clip (A) and mounting nuts (B)

21.12a Unscrew the single bolt . . .

received by the computer. If an inaccurate signal or low battery voltage is detected, the ABS system is automatically shut down, and the warning light on the instrument panel is illuminated to inform the driver that the ABS system is not operational. Normal braking is unaffected, apart from the loss of the Electronic Brake force Distribution function (which may result in premature rear wheel lock-up under braking).

If a fault does develop in the ABS system, the car must be taken to a Honda dealer for fault diagnosis and repair. Check first, however, that the problem is not due to loose or damaged wiring connections, or badly-routed wiring picking up spurious signals from the ignition system.

21 Anti-lock braking system (ABS) components – removal and refitting

Note: *Refer to the precautions in Section 1 before proceeding.*

Hydraulic unit

Removal

1 The hydraulic unit is located behind the screen washer reservoir filler neck. On models with air conditioning, one of the refrigerant hoses passes over the unit, and is secured to the inner wing by a support bracket. It may be useful to remove the hose support bracket bolt, to give some movement in the hose.

2 Disconnect the battery negative lead (refer to *Disconnecting the battery* in the Reference Section).

3 Release the unit's wiring connector plug by pulling up the locking clip on top, then disconnect the plug and move the harness to one side **(see illustration)**.

4 Before removing the hydraulic unions from the unit, it may be advisable to mark them for position, perhaps by attaching labels, or marked pieces of tape, to each pipe.

5 Loosen the hydraulic unions, then disconnect and unclip the pipes from the unit – avoid bending the pipes at all costs.

6 Unscrew the two upper nuts securing the unit to its mounting bracket, and lift it out.

Caution: Do not attempt to dismantle the hydraulic unit assembly. Overhaul of the unit is a complex job, and should be entrusted to a Honda dealer.

Refitting

7 Refitting is the reverse of the removal procedure, noting the following points:

 a) *Refit the brake pipes to the correct unions, and tighten the union nuts securely.*

 b) *Reconnect the wiring plug securely.*

 c) *Before reconnecting the battery, bleed the complete braking system as described in Section 5. Ensure the system is bled in the correct order, to prevent air entering the return pump.*

ABS computer

8 The computer is an integral part of the hydraulic unit assembly, and cannot be renewed separately. If renewal is necessary, the hydraulic unit must be renewed as a complete assembly, as described in this Section.

Wheel sensors

9 The wheel sensors are subject to extreme operating conditions, and many faults are due to corrosion resulting from water ingress. In the event of a fault arising with a sensor, its wiring plug should first be disconnected and sprayed with a maintenance spray such as WD-40 (the wiring to the sensor should also be checked for damage).

10 If there is any evidence of corrosion on the plug terminals (which will typically appear as a green or white powdery deposit), it may be possible to clean the terminals carefully with a narrow file, or a folded piece of emery paper.

Front wheel sensor

11 Loosen the front wheel nuts, then jack up the front of the car and support it on axle stands (see *Jacking and vehicle support*). Remove the front wheel.

12 The wheel sensor is located at the rear of the swivel hub assembly. Unscrew the single mounting bolt (next to the steering arm), and carefully prise the sensor from the hub. It is likely that the sensor and its mounting bolt will have suffered from its exposed position – use plenty of penetrating fluid, and clean around the bolt and sensor before attempting removal. If the sensor is being re-used, take care when removing it, or it will suffer damage **(see illustrations)**.

13 Trace the sensor wiring back from the

21.12b . . . and withdraw the ABS sensor

21.12c We removed the front hub, and tapped out the sensor with a block of wood

21.13a Trace the sensor wiring back, and release the first clip . . .

21.13b . . . the second clip has a 'cover' which is released . . .

21.13c . . . to free the wiring from the strut

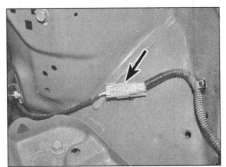

21.13d The sensor wiring connector is inside the engine bay, on the inner wing

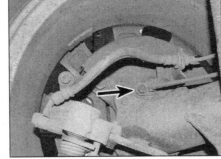

21.16 Rear wheel sensor location

21.17a With the rear hub removed, the tip of the sensor can be seen

hub, freeing the wiring from any clips or ties. The wiring feeds up the strut, and finally through an inner wing grommet into the engine compartment **(see illustrations)**. Note how the wiring is routed, for refitting. Once all the wiring has been detached, disconnect the wiring plug and remove the sensor.

14 Refitting is a reversal of removal, noting the following points:

a) *Clean the sensor location in the hub, and apply a little copper grease to make future removal easier.*

b) *Ensure that the wiring is routed as noted before removal, and secured with all necessary brackets, clips and ties.*

c) *Reconnect the wiring plug securely.*

Rear wheel sensor

15 Chock the front wheels, loosen the rear wheel nuts, then jack up the rear of the car and support it on axle stands (see *Jacking and vehicle support*). Remove the rear wheel.

16 The wheel sensor is located on the inside of the hub assembly, just above the rear axle **(see illustration)**.

17 Unscrew the single mounting bolt, and carefully prise the sensor from the hub. It is likely that the sensor and its mounting bolt will have suffered from its exposed position – use plenty of penetrating fluid, and clean around the bolt and sensor before attempting removal. If the sensor is tight, we found that removing the hub (Chapter 10, Section 9) allowed us to tap the sensor through from the other side, using a piece of wood to protect the sensor **(see illustrations)**.

18 Trace the sensor wiring back from the hub,

freeing the wiring from any clips or ties. Unbolt the wiring support brackets as necessary. The wiring runs along the rear axle, and passes through a grommet in the floor, into the car **(see illustration)**.

21.17b Using a block of wood, we tapped out the sensor

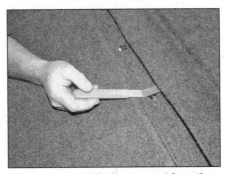

21.19 Prise up the boot carpet from the base of the rear seats

19 Detach the boot floor carpet behind the rear seats **(see illustration)**.

20 With all the wiring detached under the car, disconnect the wiring plug and remove the sensor **(see illustration)**.

21.18 The rear wheel sensor wiring passes up through the floor

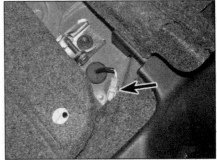

21.20 The rear wheel ABS sensor plug is behind the rear seat, either side

21 Refitting is a reversal of removal, noting the following points:

a) *Clean the sensor location in the hub, and apply a little copper grease to make future removal easier.*

b) *Ensure that the wiring is routed as noted before removal, and secured with all necessary brackets, clips and ties.*

c) *Reconnect the wiring plug securely.*

22 Vehicle Stability Assist components – removal and refitting

1 As already discussed in Section 20, the VSA system is a further function of the ABS, and therefore uses all of the components mentioned in Sections 20 and 21. However, for the VSA system to function, it requires input from the yaw rate/lateral acceleration sensor, and the steering angle sensor – their removal is described below.

Yaw rate sensor

2 This sensor measures the car's lateral (sideways) acceleration and its yaw rate (body roll) – both of these give a clear indication of the speed and direction of cornering. The sensor is mounted in the centre of the car, under the centre console.

3 Remove the centre console as described in Chapter 11, and pull the carpet clear for access to the sensor.

4 Ensure that the ignition is switched off (take out the key). Disconnect the sensor wiring plug, then remove the two mounting bracket bolts and withdraw the sensor from the car. Do not confuse the sensor with the airbag control unit, which is much larger, and has a yellow wiring plug.

5 Honda do not suggest removing the sensor from its mounting bracket, and its orientation on the bracket may be important for it to work properly.

6 Refitting is a reversal of removal. Ensure that the sensor is mounted the same way round as before, and that its mounting bracket bolts are secure – both are necessary to ensure correct operation.

Steering angle sensor

7 Remove the steering column switches as described in Chapter 12. The steering angle sensor is mounted on the steering column switch assembly, but is not intended to be removed – Honda state that the switch assembly and sensor must be renewed as a complete unit.

VSA off switch

8 The switch is mounted to the left of the steering wheel. Taking care not to mark the trim (use a small piece of card behind any prising tool), prise the switch surround out of its location, then disconnect the wiring plug and remove the switch. Take care that the wiring plug does not disappear back into the facia – tape it down temporarily if necessary.

9 If the switch proves difficult to remove, rather than risk damage, remove the instrument panel as described in Chapter 12, and see if the switch can be pushed out from behind.

10 Refitting is a reversal of removal.

23 Traction control system (TCS) components – general

Apart from the software in the ABS control unit and ECM, there are no components specific to the traction control system – the system is a further function of the ABS (refer to Sections 20 and 21). In addition to the ABS components, the system uses the throttle actuator fitted to the throttle body, to close the throttle valve – however, the actuator is part of the throttle body, and should not be removed (see Chapter 4A, Section 11).

Chapter 10
Suspension and steering

Contents

Degrees of difficulty

| Easy, suitable for novice with little experience | 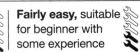 | Fairly easy, suitable for beginner with some experience | | Fairly difficult, suitable for competent DIY mechanic | | Difficult, suitable for experienced DIY mechanic | | Very difficult, suitable for expert DIY or professional | |

Specifications

Front suspension

Type . . . . Independent with MacPherson strut, lower control arm, anti-roll bar, front subframe

Rear suspension

Type . . . . Beam axle, compact rear spring, separate shock absorber

Steering

Type . . . . Rack and pinion, electrically power-assisted

Wheel alignment and steering angles

Total toe:
  Front. . . . . 0 ± 3.0 mm
  Rear:
    Inspection values (toe-in) . . . . 2.0 ± 3.0 mm
    Setting values (toe-in). . . . . 2.0 +4.0 -2.0 mm
Camber angle:
  Front. . . . . 0° 00' ± 1°
  Rear . . . . -1° 00' ± 1°
Castor angle. . . . . 2° 10' ± 1°

Roadwheels

Type . . . . Pressed-steel or aluminium alloy
Size. . . . . 14 x 5.5 or 15 x 6

Tyres

Pressures . . . . Refer to the label on the driver's door aperture
Size. . . . . 175/65 R14 or 185/55 R15

Torque wrench settings

	Nm	lbf ft
Front suspension		
Anti-roll bar clamp bolts...................................	22	16
Anti-roll bar drop link nuts*:		
Lower nut	38	28
Upper nut	29	21
Driveshaft/hub nut*...	181	134
Lower arm:		
Balljoint nut:		
Stage 1 (or minimum setting)	49	36
Stage 2 (or maximum setting)...........................	59	44
Front pivot bolt.....................................	69	51
Rear bolt..	93	69
Strut piston rod (inner) nut*	34	25
Strut-to-hub pinch-bolt/nut	69	51
Strut upper mounting nut...................................	44	32
Subframe bolts*	93	69
Rear suspension		
Axle pivot bolts*	69	51
Hub nut*...	162	120
Rear brake backplate/splash shield bolts	64	47
Shock absorber:		
Lower mounting bolt..................................	54	40
Upper mounting nut	29	21
Steering		
Steering column mounting nuts/bolts	16	12
Steering column pinch-bolts	28	21
Steering motor mounting bolts..............................	20	15
Steering rack mounting bracket bolts*.......................	49	36
Steering wheel:		
Mounting bolt......................................	39	29
Mounting nut	49	36
Track rod end balljoint nut	43	32
Roadwheels		
Wheel nuts	108	80

* Use new nuts/bolts

1 General information

The front suspension is of independent type, with MacPherson struts, lower arms, and an anti-roll bar mounted onto a subframe. The struts, which incorporate coil springs and integral shock absorbers, are attached at their upper ends to the reinforced strut mountings on the body shell. The lower end of each strut is clamped to the swivel hub assembly, which carries the hub, and the brake disc and caliper. The hubs run within non-adjustable bearings in the swivel hubs. The lower end of each swivel hub is attached, via a balljoint, to a pressed-steel lower arm assembly. The lower balljoint is integral with the lower arm. Each lower arm is attached at its inboard end to the subframe, via flexible rubber bushes, and controls both lateral and fore and aft movement of the front wheels. The anti-roll bar is mounted on the subframe, and is connected to the struts via vertical drop links.

The rear suspension is a semi-independent beam axle, with compact springs fitted between the axle and the rear floor. Separate shock absorbers are bolted to the 'trailing arm' ends of the axle, and to the body shell. The rear hubs are also mounted directly to the ends of the axle. The axle pivots on two bushed mountings attached to the rear floor – these mountings have the ability to flex, and provide a degree of rear steering, when appropriate.

All models have power-assisted rack-and-pinion steering, but the Jazz has an electric motor at the base of the steering column to provide the turning assistance, rather than an engine-driven hydraulic system. The advantage of the EPS (electric power steering) system is that it only operates when the wheels are turned – a torque sensor signals the motor – whereas on a hydraulic steering system, the pump runs at all times, taking power from the engine. Not having an engine-driven power steering pump also simplifies the auxiliary drivebelt arrangement and engine installation. The system has an electronic control unit mounted behind the facia. The vehicle speed sensor (see Chapter 4A) signals the steering system to provide extra assistance at low speeds.

Seized nuts/bolts

When working on the suspension or steering system components, you may come across fasteners which seem impossible to loosen. These fasteners on the underside of the car are continually subjected to water, road grime, mud, etc, and can become rusted or 'seized,' making them extremely difficult to remove.

In order to unscrew these stubborn fasteners without damaging them (or other components), first use a wire brush to clean exposed threads. Afterwards, use lots of penetrating oil or a maintenance spray such as WD-40, and allow it to soak in for a while.

On stubborn screws, using a close-fitting screwdriver bit in a socket handle can provide greater leverage on a difficult screw than a screwdriver will, reducing the chance of chewing-up the screw head.

With nuts or bolts, hex sockets (ones with six 'sides') are preferable to bi-hex ones, as they are less likely to round off the corners – 'surface-drive' sockets are also available, which grip on the flats, not the corners. With spanners, use the open end rather than the ring end, for the same reason. In any case, don't use any tool which isn't a close fit, as it will slip if enough force is applied. If the nut/bolt corners have already gone, it can help to use a socket one size smaller (or try an imperial size), and tap it on using a hammer, to make a tight fit – in this case, a new nut or bolt will clearly be needed.

Try turning the nut or bolt in the tightening (usually clockwise) direction first – this will help to break it loose. If this produces a little movement, loosen then tighten the nut or bolt several times, and slowly try to increase the range of movement, until it will unscrew completely. Beware, however, that this approach may cause the nut or bolt to shear off.

Sometimes a sharp blow with a hammer and punch is effective in breaking the bond between a nut and bolt threads, but care must be taken to prevent the punch from slipping off the fastener and ruining the threads. Impact drivers can also be successful in freeing a stubborn fastener, but make sure a close-fitting socket is used.

Heating the stuck fastener and surrounding area sometimes helps too, but isn't always recommended because of the obvious dangers associated with fire – take care if rubber or plastic components, or fuel/brake pipes, are close by. Heat may also ignite the penetrating oil or maintenance spray.

Long breaker bars and extension pipes will increase leverage (an extension pipe is any strong piece of metal tube, slipped over a socket handle, to make it 'longer'). Don't use an extension pipe on a ratchet handle – the ratchet mechanism could be damaged. Wear gloves if a great amount of force is being applied – these will protect your hands if something 'lets go'.

In extreme cases, the nut or bolt head may have to be cut off, if there's sufficient access. Fasteners that require drastic measures to remove should always be renewed.

> ⚠ **Warning: Since most of the procedures that are dealt with in this Chapter involve jacking up the car and working underneath it, a good pair of axle stands will be needed. A trolley jack is the preferred type of jack to lift the car, and it can also be used to support other components during certain operations. Do not rely on a trolley jack alone to support the car, as they can 'creep' down – once the car is raised on the jack, place at least one axle stand underneath as a precaution.**

2 Front swivel hub – removal and refitting

Removal

1 To remove the hub, the driveshaft nut first has to be loosened. The nut is tightened to an extremely high torque, and for this reason, it is preferable if possible to loosen the nut with the wheel on the ground. Remove either the wheel trim or alloy wheel centre cap (where possible) for access to the nut.

2.2 Use a punch or chisel to knock back the driveshaft nut's collar

2 The driveshaft nut has a locking tab (or a raised collar) which is punched into the driveshaft groove to stop the nut loosening accidentally. Using a sturdy flat-bladed screwdriver, or preferably a punch or chisel, bend the tab/collar back so the nut can be unscrewed **(see illustration)**.

3 Significant force will be required to loosen the nut, so be sure to use only good-quality, close-fitting tools. A long-handled 'breaker bar' will be needed, to provide the necessary leverage – if this is not available, slip a strong piece of metal pipe over the end of the socket handle. Wear gloves to protect your hands, should something slip.

4 Chock the front wheel, and have an assistant apply the footbrake firmly, while you slacken the nut. It is not necessary at this stage to remove the nut completely.

5 If the nut has to be loosened with the car raised, ensure that it is very well supported, using well-placed, good-quality axle stands (see *Jacking and vehicle support*). Have an assistant firmly depress the brake pedal to prevent the disc from turning, whilst you slacken and remove the driveshaft retaining nut. Alternatively, a tool can be fabricated from two lengths of steel strip (one long, one short) and a nut and bolt; the nut and bolt forming the pivot of a forked tool which fits over the wheel studs.

6 Once the nut has been loosened, (if not already done) jack up the front of the car and support it on axle stands (see *Jacking and vehicle support*). Remove the front wheel.

7 Remove the brake disc as described in Chapter 9.

8 Unscrew the ABS wheel sensor mounting

2.10 Split the balljoint taper, then remove the nut and separate the track rod

2.9 Remove the split pin from the track rod end balljoint nut

bolt (next to the steering arm), and carefully remove the wheel sensor from the front of the hub. Move the sensor clear of the hub – unclip the wiring harness as necessary. Alternatively, if the sensor will not come out, unclip the sensor wiring, disconnect it at the inner wing, and pull it through (see Chapter 9, Section 21).

9 Extract the split pin, then unscrew the track rod end balljoint nut – note that a new split pin will be needed for refitting **(see illustration)**.

10 The track rod balljoint's taper can be released using a balljoint separator tool, but this carries the risk of damaging the balljoint's rubber boot. It is possible to release the taper by tapping the track rod upwards with a soft-faced mallet, but refit the balljoint nut by a few threads first, so that the threads are protected from damage. Disconnect the track rod from the swivel hub **(see illustration)**.

11 The splined end of the driveshaft now has to be released from its location in the hub. It's likely that the splines will be very tight (corrosion may even be a factor, if the driveshaft has not been disturbed for some time), and considerable force may be needed. Tap the end of the shaft with a plastic or hide mallet only – if an ordinary hammer is used, place a small piece of wood over the end of the driveshaft – and leave the old nut loosely in place on the end to avoid damaging the threads **(see illustration)**.

12 Once the splines have been released, remove the driveshaft nut and discard it – the nut is only intended to be used once.

13 Unscrew the two nuts from the pinch-bolts securing the lower end of the suspension strut to the hub. Support the hub, then tap the

2.11 Tap the end of the driveshaft to release the splines from the hub

2.13a Unscrew the nuts from the two strut-to-hub pinch-bolts . . .

2.13b . . . and pull off the brake hose support plate from the top one

2.13c Tap the bolts through and remove them

bolts through using a pin punch, noting that they are fitted from the front. Also note that one of these two bolts is used to secure the brake hose support plate **(see illustrations)**.

14 Tilt the hub outwards on the lower balljoint, and slide out the driveshaft to the inside **(see illustrations)**. Either rest the driveshaft on the lower arm, or tie it up – do not let it hang down unsupported.

15 When the driveshaft has been withdrawn from the hub, temporarily refit the two strut-to-hub bolts by hand, to keep the hub upright.

16 To release the locking clip on the lower balljoint nut, first push the clip into the nut, and unhook the clip's spring leg at the side – only then can the clip be pulled out (a new clip should be used when refitting). Unscrew and remove the balljoint nut **(see illustrations)**.

17 The balljoint's taper can be released using a balljoint separator tool, but this carries the risk of damaging the balljoint's rubber boot,

or the balljoint threads **(see illustration)**. If preferred, release the taper by tapping the end of the lower arm with a soft-faced mallet (or a hammer and block of wood). Use a suitable lever to prise down the arm, and disconnect the lower arm from the swivel hub. Take care not to damage the driveshaft outer CV joint rubber boot. Once the lower arm has been released, fit the nut back onto the balljoint.

18 Remove the strut-to-hub bolts (if refitted), and remove the hub from the car **(see illustration)**.

Refitting

19 Refitting is a reversal of removal, bearing in mind the following points:

a) *Reconnect the lower balljoint first. Once the driveshaft has been refitted to the hub, there is insufficient room to refit the lower balljoint nut.*

b) *Clean the lower balljoint and its seat in the*

hub before fitting – it must be fitted dry. Tighten the lower balljoint nut initially to the Stage 1 (minimum) setting. From this point, tighten the nut as required to align the locking pin holes (do not loosen to align), then fit a new pin to secure.

c) *Similarly, reconnect the track rod end balljoint to the hub steering arm. Tighten the track rod end balljoint nut to the specified torque, then tighten the nut slightly as required to align the split pin holes (do not loosen to align). Fit a new split pin, and bend the ends over the nut to secure.*

d) *Lightly oil the new driveshaft nut before fitting. Do not fully tighten the hub nut until the car is resting on its wheels. Stake the nut collar into the driveshaft groove (or bend over the locktabs).*

e) *Tighten all fixings to the specified torque.*

f) *On completion, have the front wheel alignment checked.*

2.14a Tilt the hub outwards . . .

2.14b . . . and pull the driveshaft out to the inside

2.16a Unhook the locking clip from the lower balljoint's castellated nut . . .

2.16b . . . then unscrew the nut

2.17 If used with care, a conventional balljoint splitter can be used

2.18 Removing the front hub assembly

3.2a We fitted a large bolt, packed out with a nut, then used a hammer . . .

3.2b . . . to drive out the hub flange

3.3a Mount the flange in a vice, then use a chisel . . .

3.3b . . . to start moving the inner race . . .

3.3c . . . until it can be removed

3.3d A knife-edge puller can be used if available

3 Front wheel bearings – renewal

Note: *A press, a suitable puller, or a selection of large bolts, washers and other improvised tools will be required for this operation. Obtain a bearing kit before proceeding.*

1 With the swivel hub removed as described in Section 2, proceed as follows.

2 Securely support the hub carrier, on two metal bars for instance, with the inner face uppermost then, using a metal bar or tube of suitable diameter, press or drive out the hub flange – we used a large bolt and nut (the same diameter as the end of the hub's splined end) and a hammer **(see illustrations)**. Alternatively, use the puller to separate the hub from the bearing. Note that the bearing inner race will remain on the hub. Take care not to damage the brake disc splash shield.

3 The bearing inner race left on the hub flange must now be removed. To do this, grip the edge of the flange in a vice, and drive the race off with a chisel, then a punch. Tap the race at the top and both sides (even turn the flange over in the vice) to stop it jamming as it comes off. Take care not to mark the hub flange bearing surface. Alternatively, if available, use a knife-edge puller **(see illustrations)**.

4 Take off the disc shield, which is secured by three screws **(see illustrations)**.

5 Preferably using circlip pliers (two small screwdrivers could be used as a substitute), extract the bearing circlip **(see illustrations)**.

6 Now the bearing itself must be removed. Apply a generous amount of spray lubricant to start with. We mounted the hub in a vice, then used a threaded bar, an old bearing and some washers, with a nut fitted on either end of the bar. With this arrangement, we were able to drive out the old bearing **(see illustration)**.

3.4a Remove the three screws . . .

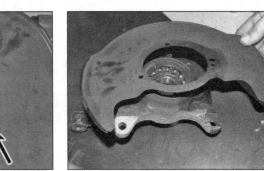

3.4b . . . and take off the disc shield

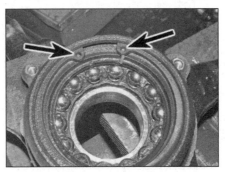

3.5a The bearing circlip has two holes . . .

3.5b . . . into which circlip pliers are inserted and compressed . . .

3.5c . . . to remove the circlip from its groove

3.6 Driving out the old bearing

3.7 Clean up the bearing surface in the hub carrier

3.8 Lubricate the hub carrier and the new bearing

3.9 Fit the new bearing the right way round, and tap it in squarely to start

3.11a Fit a threaded bar, collar, nuts and washers . . .

7 Using emery paper, clean off any burrs or raised edges from the hub flange and hub carrier which might stop the components going back together (see illustration).

8 Apply a light coat of lubricant to the inside of the hub carrier, and to the outside of the new bearing (see illustration).

9 Note that the new bearing should be marked in some way to indicate its direction of fitting – genuine Honda bearings should have a brown side, which is fitted into the hub first (see illustration).

10 Start fitting the bearing by offering it squarely into the carrier, then give it a few light taps with the hammer all round to locate it –

3.11b . . . then tighten the nut and tap the bearing home

3.12 Fit the bearing circlip into its groove

3.13 Refit the disc splash shield

3.14a Mount the flange in a vice, then lubricate it . . .

3.14b . . . fit the hub assembly over a threaded rod . . .

3.14c . . . then tighten the nuts on the rod to pull in the flange

keep the bearing square as this is done, or it will jam.

11 Fitting the bearing by tapping it in all the way with a hammer will likely damage it. We used a length of threaded bar (available from motor factors, DIY stores, etc), with a nut, some large washers and a drilled plate on the inside of the hub carrier. With a drilled collar, another washer, and a nut on the outside, the whole assembly was mounted in a vice, and the nut tightened to press the new bearing in place. The actual method was to tighten the nut slightly, give the old bearing a few taps round its edge, tighten the nut some more, and so on until the bearing was fully home **(see illustrations)**.

12 Fit the bearing circlip, ensuring that it locates fully into its groove all round **(see illustration)**. The old circlip can be re-used if it is undamaged, but if a new one is supplied with the bearing kit, it makes sense to use it.

13 Refit the brake disc shield, tightening its three screws securely **(see illustration)**.

14 The hub flange can be pressed into the new bearing using a very similar method to the one just used for the bearing **(see illustrations)**.

 HAYNES HiNT *There is a distinct change in the sound produced by the hammer when the bearing and flange are fully home – this may otherwise be hard to judge.*

15 On completion, refit the swivel hub as described in Section 2.

4.2 Disconnect the top end of the anti-roll bar drop link from the strut

4 Front strut – removal, overhaul and refitting

Removal

1 Slacken the relevant front wheel nuts, then jack up the front of the car, and support securely on axle stands (see *Jacking and vehicle support*). Remove the roadwheel.

2 Unscrew the nut securing the upper end of the anti-roll bar drop link to the strut – while this is done, use an Allen key in the drop link balljoint to stop it turning. Disconnect the drop link from the strut **(see illustration)**.

3 Where applicable, release the ABS sensor wiring from the support clip on the strut, and move it clear – the wiring does not have to be disconnected **(see illustrations)**.

4.3a The ABS sensor clip has a 'cover' which is released . . .

4 Unscrew the two nuts from the pinch-bolts securing the lower end of the suspension strut to the hub. Support the hub, then tap the bolts through using a pin punch, noting that they are fitted from the front. Also note that the top bolt is used to secure the brake hose support plate **(see illustrations)**.

5 Release the base of the strut from the hub (it may have to be prised free) **(see illustration)**.

6 Under the bonnet, prise off the cap fitted over the strut piston rod's exposed threads. Unscrew the strut top mounting nut, while holding the strut piston using an Allen key. Recover the strut's upper rubber mounting **(see illustrations)**.

7 Withdraw the strut down into the wheel arch, and remove it from under the car **(see illustration)**.

4.3b . . . to free the wiring from the strut

4.4a Unscrew the nuts from the two strut-to-hub pinch-bolts . . .

4.4b . . . and pull off the brake hose support plate from the top one

4.4c Tap the bolts through and remove them

4.5 Separate the base of the strut from the hub

4.6a Take off the cap fitted over the piston rod . . .

4.6b . . . then use an Allen key to hold the rod while the nut is loosened . . .

4.6c . . . and removed

4.6d Take off the strut's upper mounting

4.7 Withdraw the strut from under the wheel arch

Overhaul

Note: *A spring compressor tool will be required for this operation.*

8 If not already done, take off the strut upper mounting rubber **(see illustration)**.

4.8 Take off the strut upper mounting rubber

9 With the suspension strut resting on a bench, or clamped in a vice, fit a spring compressor tool, and compress the coil spring to relieve the pressure on the spring seats **(see illustrations)**. Ensure that the compressor

tool is securely located on the spring, in accordance with the tool manufacturer's instructions.

10 Counterhold the strut piston rod with the Allen key or hexagon bit used during removal, and unscrew the piston rod nut **(see illustration)**.

11 Remove the piston rod nut, followed by the strut bearing, the spring and upper seat (with compressor tool still fitted), and the rubber gaiter **(see illustrations)**. If only the strut (shock absorber) is being renewed, the spring assembly need not be dismantled.

12 Examine all the components for wear, damage or deformation, and check the strut bearing for smoothness of operation. Renew any of the components as necessary.

13 Examine the strut for signs of fluid leakage. Check the strut piston for signs of pitting along its entire length, and check the

4.9a Fit the spring compressor tool . . .

4.9b . . . and compress the spring

4.10 Unscrew the piston rod nut

4.11a Take off the piston rod nut . . .

4.11b . . . followed by the strut bearing . . .

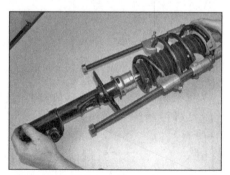

4.11c . . . and the spring, upper seat, and gaiter

strut body for signs of damage. While holding it in an upright position, test the operation of the strut by moving the piston through a full stroke, and then through short strokes of 50 to 100 mm. In both cases, the resistance felt should be smooth and continuous. If the resistance is jerky or uneven, or if there is any visible sign of wear or damage to the strut, renewal is necessary.

14 If any doubt exists as to the condition of the coil spring, carefully remove the spring compressors, and check the spring for distortion or signs of cracking. Renew the spring if it is damaged or distorted, or if there is any doubt as to its condition.

15 If the strut top bearing is worn, this can be pressed out of the spring upper seat, and a new one fitted. Note that the new bearing should also be pressed home, not tapped in.

16 Slide the rubber bump stop/gaiter onto the strut piston.

17 If the spring compressor tool has been removed from the spring, refit it and compress the spring sufficiently to enable it to be refitted to the strut.

18 Slide the spring over the strut, and position it so that the lower end of the spring is resting against the stop on the lower seat (see illustration).

19 Apply a little silicone grease around the inner rim of the spring upper seat, where it meets the rubber bump stop. Refit the spring upper seat, making sure the rubber part is aligned on the spring end correctly.

20 Fit the piston rod nut, and tighten it securely, using the specified torque as a guide. Counterhold the piston rod using an Allen key or hexagon bit as during removal.

21 Slowly slacken the spring compressor tool to relieve the tension in the spring. Check that the ends of the spring locate correctly against the stops on the spring seats. If necessary, turn the spring and the upper seat so that the components locate correctly before the compressor tool is removed. Remove the compressor tool when the spring is fully seated.

Refitting

22 Refitting is a reversal of removal, bearing in mind the following points:
a) Tighten the strut upper mounting nut,

5.6 Use an Allen key to hold the drop link balljoints as the nut is undone

4.18 Ensure that the spring lower end is against the stop on the lower seat

using the specified torque as a guide, and using an Allen key to stop the piston rod turning.
b) Use a new self-locking nut when reconnecting the anti-roll bar drop link to the strut, and observe the instructions in Section 5 when tightening it.
c) Tighten all fixings to the specified torque.

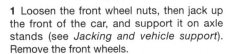

5 Front anti-roll bar, bushes and drop links – removal and refitting

1 Loosen the front wheel nuts, then jack up the front of the car, and support it on axle stands (see *Jacking and vehicle support*). Remove the front wheels.

Bushes

2 If the bushes alone are to be renewed, working on one side at a time, unscrew the two bolts and remove the anti-roll bar mounting clamp. The bar can then be lifted slightly, and the bush removed (the bush is split for easy removal).

3 Slip the new bush into place around the roll bar – if necessary, lubricate the bush with a little washing-up liquid first. Also note that the roll bar has a painted mark to indicate the fitted position of the bushes, to make initial fitting more accurate.

4 Refit the clamp, noting that it has an arrow marking which indicates the front of the car. Slide the bush along the bar slightly if required, to bring the clamp bolt holes into alignment. Tighten the clamp bolts to the specified torque, then repeat the procedure on the other side.

5 On completion, refit the wheels, then lower the car to the ground and tighten the wheel nuts to the specified torque.

Drop links

6 Unscrew the nut at each end of the link – use an Allen key to stop the drop link balljoints turning as this is done (see illustration). Remove the drop link from the strut and anti-roll bar, noting how it is fitted. Discard the nuts – new ones should be used when refitting.

7 Refitting is a reversal of removal, noting the following points:

a) Use new self-locking nuts on the anti-roll bar drop links.
b) Position a jack under the lower arm, and raise it to load the front suspension before tightening the nuts to the specified torque. Since an Allen key must also be used when tightening, a torque wrench can only be used with a special adapter, so use the specified torque as a guide.
c) On completion, refit the wheels, then lower the car to the ground and tighten the wheel nuts to the specified torque.
d) Honda state that the car should be driven for approximately 5 minutes, and the tightness of the drop link nuts should then be rechecked.

Anti-roll bar

8 Unscrew the nut securing each of the two drop links to the anti-roll bar – use an Allen key to stop the drop link balljoint turning as this is done. Unhook the drop links from the roll bar. Discard the two nuts – new ones should be used when refitting.

9 Unscrew the two bolts from each of the two anti-roll bar outer clamps, then remove the clamps (see illustration).

10 Withdraw the anti-roll bar from under the car, working it out from above the subframe and around the steering gear. With care, it should not be necessary to unbolt the subframe or the steering gear, but if either is necessary, refer to the relevant Sections of this Chapter.

11 Refitting is a reversal of removal, noting the following points:
a) Ensure that the clamps are refitted with their arrow markings facing forwards, and tighten the bolts to the specified torque.
b) When reconnecting the drop links, refer to paragraph 7.
c) On completion, refit the wheels, then lower the car to the ground and tighten the wheel nuts to the specified torque.

6 Front lower arm – removal and refitting

Removal

1 To remove the lower arm, the driveshaft nut

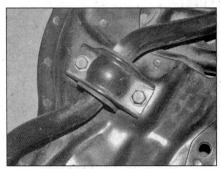

5.9 One of the anti-roll bar clamps (seen with the subframe removed)

6.2 Use a punch or chisel to knock back the driveshaft nut's collar

6.7 Remove the split pin from the track rod end balljoint nut

6.8 Split the balljoint taper, then remove the nut and separate the track rod

first has to be loosened. The nut is tightened to an extremely high torque, and for this reason, it is preferable if possible to loosen the nut with the wheel on the ground. Remove either the wheel trim or alloy wheel centre cap (where possible) for access to the nut.

2 The driveshaft nut has a locking tab (or a raised collar) which is punched into the driveshaft groove to stop the nut loosening accidentally. Using a sturdy flat-bladed screwdriver, or preferably a punch or chisel, bend the tab/collar back so the nut can be unscrewed **(see illustration)**.

3 Significant force will be required to loosen the nut, so be sure to use only good-quality, close-fitting tools. A long-handled 'breaker bar' will be needed, to provide the necessary leverage – if this is not available, slip a strong piece of metal pipe over the end of the socket handle. Wear gloves to protect your hands, should something slip.

4 Chock the front wheel, and have an assistant apply the footbrake firmly, while you slacken the nut. It is not necessary at this stage to remove the nut completely.

5 If the nut has to be loosened with the car raised, ensure that it is very well supported, using well-placed, good-quality axle stands (see *Jacking and vehicle support*). Have an assistant firmly depress the brake pedal to prevent the disc from turning, whilst you slacken and remove the driveshaft retaining nut. Alternatively, a tool can be fabricated from two lengths of steel strip (one long, one short) and a nut and bolt; the nut and bolt forming the pivot of a forked tool which fits over the wheel studs.

6 Once the nut has been loosened, (if not already done) jack up the front of the car and support it on axle stands (see *Jacking and vehicle support*). Remove the front wheel.

7 Extract the split pin, then unscrew the track

rod end balljoint nut – note that a new split pin will be needed for refitting **(see illustration)**.

8 The track rod balljoint's taper can be released using a balljoint separator tool, but this carries the risk of damaging the balljoint's rubber boot. It is possible to release the taper by tapping the track rod upwards with a soft-faced mallet, but refit the balljoint nut by a few threads first, so that the threads are protected from damage. Disconnect the track rod from the swivel hub **(see illustration)**.

9 The splined end of the driveshaft now has to be released from its location in the hub. It's likely that the splines will be very tight (corrosion may even be a factor, if the driveshaft has not been disturbed for some time), and considerable force may be needed. Tap the end of the shaft with a plastic or hide mallet only – if an ordinary hammer is used, place a small piece of wood over the end of the driveshaft – and leave the old nut loosely in place on the end to avoid damaging the threads **(see illustration)**.

10 Once the splines have been released, remove the driveshaft nut and discard it – the nut is only intended to be used once.

11 Unscrew the two nuts from the pinch-bolts securing the lower end of the suspension strut to the hub. Support the hub, then tap the bolts through using a pin punch, noting that they are fitted from the front. Also note that the top bolt is used to secure the brake hose support plate **(see illustrations)**.

12 Tilt the hub outwards on the lower balljoint, and slide out the driveshaft to the inside **(see illustrations)**.

6.9 Tap the end of the driveshaft to release the splines from the hub

6.11a Unscrew the nuts from the two strut-to-hub pinch-bolts . . .

6.11b . . . and pull off the brake hose support plate from the top one

6.11c Tap the bolts through and remove them

6.12a Tilt the hub outwards . . .

6.12b ...and pull the driveshaft out to the inside

6.14a Unhook the locking clip from the lower balljoint's castellated nut ...

6.14b ...then unscrew the nut

6.15 If used with care, a conventional balljoint splitter can be used

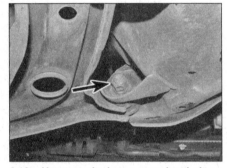

6.16a Unscrew the lower arm pivot bolt ...

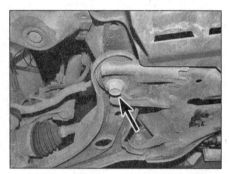

6.16b ...and the rear mounting bolt

13 When the driveshaft has been withdrawn from the hub, temporarily refit the two strut-to-hub bolts by hand, to keep the hub upright – this also prevents straining the brake hose.

14 To release the locking clip on the lower balljoint nut, first push the clip into the nut, and unhook the clip's spring leg at the side – only then can the clip be pulled out (a new clip should be used when refitting). Unscrew and remove the balljoint nut **(see illustrations)**.

15 The balljoint's taper can be released using a balljoint separator tool, but this carries the risk of damaging the balljoint's rubber boot, or the balljoint threads **(see illustration)**. If preferred, release the taper by tapping the end of the lower arm with a soft-faced mallet (or a hammer and block of wood). Use a suitable lever to prise down the arm, and disconnect the lower arm from the swivel hub. Take care not to damage the driveshaft outer CV joint rubber boot. Once the lower arm has been released, fit the nut back onto the balljoint.

16 Unscrew and remove the lower arm pivot bolt and the rear mounting bolt, then remove the arm from under the car **(see illustrations)**.

Overhaul

17 Examine the rubber bushes for wear and damage, and check the arm for straightness, as it could have been bent by careless jacking-up. At the time of writing, the rubber bushes could not be renewed separately. Renew the complete lower arm if there is any wear or damage.

Refitting

18 Check the lower balljoint rubber boot condition while the lower arm is removed (see Section 7).

19 Clean the balljoint and its seat in the hub before fitting – it must be fitted dry. Offer the lower arm into position, taking care not to damage the balljoint boot as the lower arm is refitted.

20 Refit the two lower arm bolts, and tighten them by hand only at this stage.

21 Tighten the lower balljoint nut initially to the Stage 1 (minimum) setting. From this point, tighten the nut as required to align the locking clip holes (do not loosen to align), then fit a new clip to secure.

22 Lightly grease the splined end of the driveshaft. Remove the strut-to-hub bolts once more, tilt the hub outwards on the lower balljoint, and fit the driveshaft into the hub.

23 Refit the strut-to-hub bolts and nuts, and tighten to the specified torque.

24 Lightly oil the new hub nut, and tighten it by hand to draw the driveshaft into position.

25 Reconnect the track rod end balljoint to the hub steering arm. Tighten the track rod end balljoint nut to the specified torque, then tighten the nut slightly as required to align the split pin holes (do not loosen to align). Fit a new split pin, and bend the ends over the nut to secure.

26 Refit the wheel, then lower the car to the ground and tighten the wheel nuts to the specified torque.

27 With the car resting on its wheels, tighten the hub nut and the two lower arm bolts to the specified torque. Stake the hub nut collar into the driveshaft groove.

28 On completion, have the front wheel alignment checked.

7 Front lower balljoint – renewal

If the lower balljoint rubber boot is damaged, a new one can be obtained from Honda dealers. Once the lower arm has been disconnected (refer to Section 6 for details), the old boot can be unclipped. Wipe the balljoint clean (do not use excessive amounts of solvent), then pack it with fresh grease and fit the new boot. However, bear in mind that if the boot has been damaged for some time, it is likely that dirt will have got into the balljoint, and a new balljoint may soon be needed.

If the lower balljoint itself is worn, the balljoint is available separately, but a press and various special tools are needed to fit it. If possible, remove the lower arm as described in Section 6, and take it to a Honda dealer for the new balljoint to be fitted.

8 Front subframe – removal and refitting

Removal

1 Using the information in Section 6, disconnect both front lower arms – note that

8.3a Prise out the clips . . .

8.3b . . . and remove the plastic shields behind the subframe

8.4 Use an Allen key to hold the drop link balljoints as the nut is undone

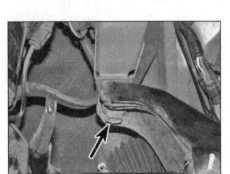

8.8 The subframe front bolts are accessed through a hole in the lower arm

8.9 Removing the subframe rear bolt

the driveshafts must be withdrawn to gain sufficient access to the lower arm balljoint nuts. The arms themselves do not, however, have to be removed completely.

2 Unbolt and remove the engine undertray (refer to Chapter 11, Section 23, if necessary).

3 Just behind the subframe, remove the clips each side securing the plastic undershields, and take the shields off **(see illustrations)**.

4 Unscrew the nut at the lower end of each anti-roll bar drop link – use an Allen key to stop the drop link balljoints turning as this is done **(see illustration)**. Disconnect the drop links from the anti-roll bar. Discard the nuts – new ones should be used when refitting.

5 Referring to Section 15 if necessary, unbolt and remove the three mounting brackets securing the steering gear to the subframe (each small bracket has two bolts). Also remove the three steering gear mounting bolts (two above, one below) on the driver's side. Use wire or cable-ties to support the steering gear, from a convenient point on the bulkhead, for when the subframe is lowered out.

6 Referring to Chapter 2A if necessary, unbolt the front (manual transmission models only) and rear engine mountings. Provided the left- and right-hand mountings have not been disturbed, this will result in increased movement of the engine.

7 Check around the subframe to ensure that there are no brackets, hoses or wiring harnesses still attached, or anything in the way which would prevent it from being lowered.

8 The subframe is secured to the body by four bolts **(see illustration)**. By the two rear bolts, there are alignment markings to indicate

the subframe's relative position to the body – if these are not clear, clean the area and make your own subframe-to-body marks with paint. However, there appears to be no requirement to align the subframe during refitting.

9 Support the subframe, either with two jacks, or (preferably) with the help of an assistant, then progressively loosen and remove the bolts **(see illustration)**.

10 Lower the subframe to clear the engine mounting(s), then withdraw it from under the car.

11 Note that the four subframe bolts are only intended to be used once, and new ones should be obtained for refitting.

Refitting

12 With the help of an assistant, position the subframe on the jacks, then raise the jack to lift the subframe into position under the car. Ensure that the subframe is securely supported.

9.5 Prise off the dust cap over the rear hub nut

13 Where applicable, align the marks made prior to removal. Fit the four new subframe bolts, and tighten them to the specified torque.

14 The remainder of refitting is a reversal of removal, noting the following points:
a) Tighten all fixings to the specified torque.
b) Reconnect the lower arms as described in Section 6.
c) Use new nuts on the anti-roll bar drop links, and refer to Section 5 when tightening them.
d) Use new split pins on the track rod end nuts.
e) Have the front wheel alignment checked on completion.

9 Rear hub and wheel bearing – inspection and renewal

Inspection

1 The rear wheel bearings are non-adjustable.

2 To check the bearings for excessive wear, chock the front wheels, then jack up the rear of the car and support it on axle stands. Fully release the handbrake.

3 Grip the rear wheel at the top and bottom, and attempt to rock it. A small amount of play is acceptable, but if excessive movement is noted, or if there is any rumbling noise heard when the wheel is spun, it is indicative that the wheel bearings are worn. Worn wheel bearings can usually be heard from inside the car at certain speeds.

Renewal

4 The rear hub nut first has to be loosened. The nut is tightened to an extremely high torque, and for this reason, it is preferable if possible to loosen the nut with the wheel on the ground. Either remove the wheel trim or prise out the alloy wheel centre cap (where possible) for access to the nut.

5 Prise off the dust cap to access the hub nut **(see illustration)**. Note that Honda recommend a new dust cap is used when refitting, though in practice, provided the old cap is in good condition and still a tight fit, it can be re-used.

6 The hub nut has a locking tab (or a raised collar) which is punched into the stub axle groove to stop the nut loosening accidentally. Using a sturdy flat-bladed screwdriver, or preferably a punch or chisel, bend the tab/collar back so the nut can be unscrewed **(see illustration)**.
7 Significant force will be required to loosen the nut, so be sure to use only good-quality, close-fitting tools. A long-handled 'breaker bar' will be needed, to provide the necessary leverage – if this is not available, slip a strong piece of metal pipe over the end of the socket handle. Wear gloves to protect your hands, should something slip.
8 Chock the rear wheel, and have an assistant apply the footbrake firmly, while you slacken the nut. Unscrew the nut completely, and discard it – a new nut must be used when refitting **(see illustration)**.
9 If the nut has to be loosened with the car raised, ensure that it is very well supported, using well-placed, good-quality axle stands (see *Jacking and vehicle support*). Have an assistant firmly depress the brake pedal to prevent the disc from turning, whilst you slacken and remove the hub nut. Alternatively, a tool can be fabricated from two lengths of steel strip (one long, one short) and a nut and bolt; the nut and bolt forming the pivot of a forked tool which fits over the wheel studs.
10 Once the nut has been loosened, (if not already done) jack up the rear of the car and support it on axle stands (see *Jacking and vehicle support*). Remove the rear wheel.
11 Remove the brake drum or disc as described in Chapter 9.
12 Pull off the rear hub from the stub axle **(see illustration)**. Note that the wheel bearing is an integral part of the hub flange, and is not available separately – to renew the wheel bearing, a new hub flange will have to be fitted.

Refitting

13 Clean the stub axle, then slide the hub flange into position and secure with a new hub nut, lightly oiled, and tightened by hand only at this stage. It is preferable to tighten the hub nut with the wheel refitted and the car lowered to the ground.

9.6 Bend back the staking on the rear hub nut's collar

9.12 Pull off the rear hub

14 Refit the brake drum or disc as described in Chapter 9.
15 Refit the wheel, then lower the car to the ground and tighten the wheel nuts to the specified torque.
16 Tighten the hub nut to the specified torque when the car is resting on its wheels. Stake the nut collar into the stub axle groove (or bend over the locktabs), then refit the dust cap, tapping it squarely into place **(see illustration)**.

10 Rear shock absorber – removal and refitting

Removal

1 Slacken the relevant rear wheel nuts.

9.8 Unscrew and discard the old hub nut

9.16 Stake the new nut's collar into the stub axle groove

Chock the front wheels, select 1st gear (or P), then jack up the rear of the car, and support securely on axle stands (see *Jacking and vehicle support*). Remove the rear roadwheel.
2 Position a jack under the 'trailing arm' end of the rear axle, and raise it slightly to take the pressure off the lower end of the shock absorber **(see illustration)**.
3 Unscrew the shock absorber lower mounting bolt. If necessary, use a pin punch to tap the bolt out to the inside. Separate the shock absorber from the rear axle mounting bracket **(see illustrations)**.
4 Inside the boot, fold the backrest forwards and unclip the access cover in the side trim panel for access to the strut upper mounting nut **(see illustration)**.
5 Hold the shock absorber piston rod with a 5 mm Allen key to stop it turning, then

10.2 Support the rear axle under the shock absorber

10.3a Remove the shock absorber lower mounting bolt . . .

10.3b . . . and separate the shock absorber from the rear axle

10.4 Unclip the side trim panel access cover inside the boot

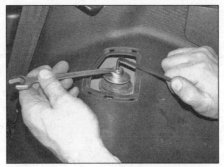

10.5a Hold the piston rod with an Allen key, then loosen . . .

10.5b . . . and remove the nut

10.6a Take off the upper mounting washer . . .

10.6b . . . and the mounting rubber . . .

10.6c . . . then lower the shock absorber into the wheel arch

unscrew the 10 mm upper mounting nut **(see illustrations)**. If the nut is of self-locking type (with a coloured plastic insert), a new one should be used when refitting.

6 Take off the upper mounting washer and mounting rubber, then withdraw the shock absorber into the rear wheel arch **(see illustrations)**.

7 Recover the lower mounting rubber, which may still be stuck to the top of the rear wheel arch.

Refitting

8 Fit the lower mounting rubber to the top of the shock absorber, then offer it up into the rear wheel arch **(see illustration)**.

9 Fit the lower end of the shock absorber into the rear axle bracket. If the rear axle is still being supported on a jack, it may be necessary to adjust the height of the jack to line up the shock absorber. Refit the lower

10.8 Fit the lower mounting rubber to the shock absorber before fitting

mounting bolt – tap it in if necessary, then tighten it by hand at this stage.

10 Inside the boot, refit the upper mounting rubber and the top washer, then screw on the (new) upper mounting nut by hand.

11 Raise the jack under the rear axle, so that the suspension is compressed, approximately the same as if the car were resting on its wheels. Tighten the shock absorber lower mounting bolt to the specified torque.

12 With the axle still raised on the jack, tighten the upper mounting nut fully. Since the piston rod must again be held with a 5 mm Allen key, it will not be possible to use a torque wrench, but use the specified torque as a guide for tightening. Refit the access cover to the side trim panel.

13 Lower the jack from under the rear axle.

14 Refit the rear wheel, then lower the car to the ground and tighten the wheel nuts to the specified torque.

11.6 Lift the spring out of the lower seat in the axle

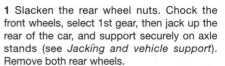

11 Rear spring – removal and refitting

Removal

1 Slacken the rear wheel nuts. Chock the front wheels, select 1st gear, then jack up the rear of the car, and support securely on axle stands (see *Jacking and vehicle support*). Remove both rear wheels.

2 Position a jack under the 'trailing arm' end of the rear axle, and raise it slightly to take the pressure off the lower end of the shock absorber.

3 Unscrew the shock absorber lower mounting bolt. If necessary, use a pin punch to tap the bolt out to the inside. Separate the shock absorber from the rear axle mounting bracket.

4 Repeat the procedure and disconnect the other shock absorber from the rear axle.

5 Lower the rear axle completely on the jack, but do not allow it to hang down, as this may strain the brake pipes/hoses.

6 Lift each spring out of its lower seat in the axle, and recover the upper mounting rubber **(see illustration)**.

7 Check the condition of the upper mounting rubbers, and if necessary, obtain new ones for reassembly.

Refitting

8 Fit the upper mounting rubber onto each spring, aligning the stepped part with the end of the spring **(see illustration)**.

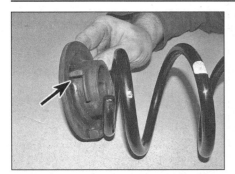

11.8 Align the stepped part of the upper rubber with the spring end

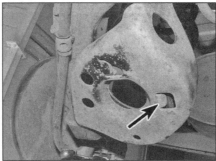

11.9 Turn the spring so the lower end hits the stop on the seat

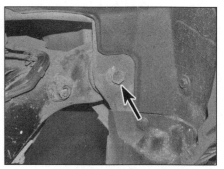

12.9 Rear axle pivot bolt

9 Offer each spring onto its lower seat in the rear axle, and align the spring end with the stop on the seat **(see illustration)**.
10 Raise each end of the axle in turn, and refit the shock absorber lower mounting bolt. Raise the axle further to compress the suspension, then tighten the bolt to the specified torque. Repeat this procedure on the other rear shock absorber.
11 Refit the rear wheels, then lower the car to the ground and tighten the wheel nuts to the specified torque.

12 Rear axle –
removal and refitting

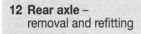

Removal

1 Remove the rear hub assemblies as described in Section 9.
2 On models with rear drum brakes, remove the brake backplates as described in Chapter 9.
3 On models with rear disc brakes, remove the brake splash shields – these are secured with four bolts.
4 Remove the rear springs as described in Section 11.
5 On models with ABS, unbolt and remove the rear wheel sensors from the axle. Trace the wiring back from the sensors, and unclip it from the axle. Tie the sensors and wiring up, clear of the axle – there is no need to disconnect them.

> **HAYNES HINT** *If the ABS sensors prove difficult to remove, and the same axle is being refitted, the wiring plugs inside the car (under the carpet behind the rear seat) can be disconnected instead, and the sensors removed with the axle.*

6 Slide out the retaining clip, and release the rear brake hoses from the axle. Clamp the rear brake hoses, then unscrew the pipe-to-hose union nut and disconnect the union. Plug or tape over the pipe ends, to reduce fluid loss.
7 Trace the handbrake cables back from the rear brakes, and unbolt the cable support brackets as necessary to release the cables from the rear axle.
8 If not already done, support the weight of the axle on a pair of trolley jacks (or axle stands). Preferably, an assistant should be available to help lower out the axle.
9 Unscrew the axle pivot bolt either side, then lower the axle to the ground **(see illustration)**. Note that the axle pivot bolts should not be re-used. Remove the axle from under the car.

Refitting

10 Refitting is a reversal of removal, noting the following points:
a) *Use new axle pivot bolts, tightened by hand initially. Raise the axle to its approximate 'working' position, then tighten the bolts to the specified torque.*
b) *Refit the springs as described in Section 11, and the rear hubs as described in Section 9.*

c) *Where applicable, ensure that the ABS wiring is correctly routed, and secured with the clips.*
d) *On completion, top-up the brake fluid level, then bleed the brakes as described in Chapter 9.*

13 Steering wheel –
removal and refitting

Removal

1 Disconnect the battery negative lead, and position the lead away from the battery (also see *Disconnecting the battery*). Wait at least one minute before proceeding. If this waiting period is not observed, there is a danger of accidentally activating the airbag(s).
2 Remove the airbag unit from the steering wheel as described in Chapter 12.
3 Ensure that the front wheels are pointing in the straight-ahead position.
4 Prevent the steering wheel turning by grasping the rim firmly, then unscrew and remove the steering wheel securing bolt (some models may have a nut) **(see illustrations)**. Do not rely on the steering column lock to prevent the wheel turning, as this may damage the lock.
5 As applicable, disconnect the wiring plugs inside the wheel **(see illustration)**. Typically, there will be a plug on the left for the audio remote controls, and on models with automatic transmission one or more further wiring plugs for the shift buttons or paddles.

13.4a Hold the wheel rim while loosening the steering wheel bolt

13.4b Removing the steering wheel bolt

13.5 Disconnect the wiring plugs inside the wheel

13.7 Pull the wheel off its splines

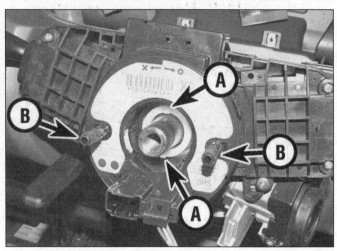

13.11 Self-cancelling tabs (A) are vertical, clock spring pins (B) are horizontal

6 If one is not already present, make an alignment mark between the steering wheel and the column, to make refitting easier.

> **HAYNES HiNT** *Before pulling off the wheel, refit the wheel bolt/nut by a couple of threads. This way, if excess effort is needed to pull the wheel off its splines, the wheel won't suddenly fly off and cause injury.*

7 Grip the steering wheel on each side (or top and bottom), then pull and withdraw it from the splines on the end of the column

(see illustration). If it was refitted, remove the wheel bolt/nut completely.
8 If the wheel proves difficult to remove, use a puller to release it from the splines. Two threaded holes are provided, which may be used with two bolts, a strong metal plate and a socket as a spacer, to free the wheel.
Caution: Do not allow the bolts to protrude through by more than five threads, or the airbag clockspring unit will be damaged.

Refitting

9 Make sure that the front wheels are pointing in the straight-ahead position.
10 If not already done, set the airbag clock-

spring to its central position, as described in Chapter 12.
11 The two direction indicator self-cancelling tabs should be in the vertical position, and the airbag clock spring's two locating pins should be horizontal (see illustration).
12 Offer the steering wheel into position, ensuring that the recesses on the back of the wheel fit over the airbag clock spring's two pins.
13 Refit the steering wheel bolt/nut, and tighten to the specified torque – again, do not rely on the steering column lock to hold the wheel as it is tightened.
14 The remainder of the refitting procedure is a reversal of removal. Ensure that the battery is still disconnected before refitting the airbag unit as described in Chapter 12.

14 Steering column – removal and refitting

Removal

1 Disconnect the battery negative lead, and position the lead away from the battery (also see *Disconnecting the battery*). Wait at least one minute before proceeding. If this waiting period is not observed, there is a danger of accidentally activating the airbag(s).
2 Remove the steering wheel as described in Section 13.
3 Move the driver's seat fully to the rear, to allow maximum working area.
4 Remove the driver's side lower facia panels as described in Chapter 11, Section 27.
5 Remove the three screws from the steering column lower shroud, unclip the upper shroud from it, then work off the lower shroud (see illustrations).
6 Disconnect the three wiring plugs from the ignition switch and related components, as described in Chapter 12, Section 4.
7 Remove the airbag clockspring as described in Chapter 12, Section 21.

14.5a Unscrew the lower shroud's three screws . . .

14.5b . . . then unclip the upper shroud . . .

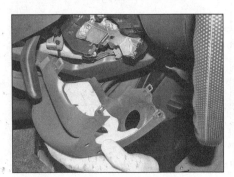

14.5c . . . and drop the lower shroud

14.8a Loosen the steering column switch clamp screw on top . . .

14.8b . . . disconnect the large wiring plugs behind . . .

14.8c . . . then remove the two front screws . . .

14.8d . . . and slide off the switch assembly

8 The steering column switches are removed as an assembly. First, loosen the switch clamp screw on top. Disconnect both the large wiring plugs from behind the switches, then remove the two screws at the front, and slide the switch assembly off the column **(see illustrations)**.

9 Working in the footwell, remove the two push-fit plugs and take off the plastic cover fitted at the base of the column – the cover is split at the top for removal **(see illustration)**.

10 Mark the fitted position of the column shaft to the universal joint, using a dab of paint. Unscrew the upper pinch-bolt securing the column shaft to the universal joint. The column shaft has a flattened side, so in theory the bolt will only fit in one position, but we found the painted mark was useful for alignment **(see illustrations)**.

11 Unscrew the steering column's two upper mounting nuts and two lower mounting

bolts, and lower the column assembly into the footwell. Pull the column rearwards to separate it from the universal joint, and it can be removed from the car **(see illustrations)**.

Inspection

12 Check the column for obvious signs of damage, then check the upper and lower bearings for play. Check the condition of the sliding bushes on the column adjustment linkage. The column is only available as a complete assembly.

Refitting

13 Refitting is a reversal of removal, noting the following points:
a) Align the previously-made marks when refitting the column to the universal joint.
b) Tighten all fixings to the specified torque.
c) Ensure that the column wiring harness is routed correctly, and securely

re-attached. Also ensure that all wiring connections are properly remade.
d) Refit the airbag clockspring as described in Chapter 12, Section 21.
e) Refit the steering wheel as described in Section 13.

15 Steering rack – removal and refitting

Removal

1 Set the front wheels to the straight-ahead position, and engage the steering lock. The lock must be engaged, to prevent the column from turning during rack removal – which might otherwise cause damage to the airbag clockspring. Honda recommend that the steering wheel is removed, to prevent unwanted turning.

14.9 Take off the plastic cover at the base of the column

14.10a The pinch-bolt fits in a flattened side of the shaft . . .

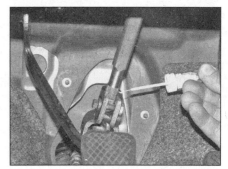

14.10b . . . but making a paint mark is useful . . .

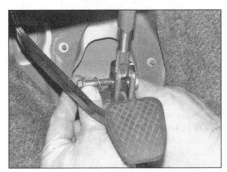

14.10c . . . before removing the bolt

14.11a Steering column upper mounting nuts

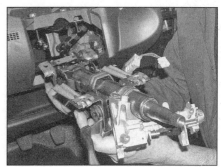

14.11b Removing the steering column

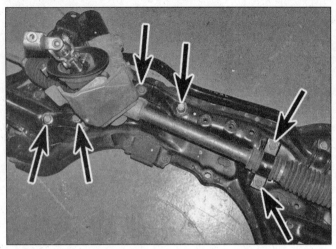

15.19a Steering rack mounting brackets (seen removed with subframe)

15.19b Unbolt the rack mounting brackets . . .

2 Move the driver's seat fully to the rear, to allow maximum working area.

3 Remove the driver's side lower facia panels as described in Chapter 11, Section 27.

4 Working in the footwell, remove the two fasteners and take off the boot fitted at the base of the column – the boot is split at the top for removal.

5 Make alignment marks at either end of the universal joint for easier refitting. Unscrew the upper and lower pinch-bolt from the universal joint, then pull the joint back into the car, to free it from the rack pinion.

6 Using the information in Section 6, disconnect both front lower arms – note that the driveshafts must be withdrawn to gain sufficient access to the lower arm balljoint nuts. The arms themselves do not, however, have to be removed completely.

7 Unbolt and remove the engine undertray (refer to Chapter 11, Section 23, if necessary).

8 Just behind the subframe, remove the clips each side securing the plastic undershields, and remove the shields.

9 Unscrew the nut at the lower end of each anti-roll bar drop link – use an Allen key to stop the drop link balljoints turning as this is done. Disconnect the drop links from the anti-roll bar. Discard the nuts – new ones should be used when refitting.

10 Extract the split pin, then unscrew the

15.19c . . . note that new bolts should be used when refitting

track rod end balljoint nut each side – note that a new split pin will be needed for refitting. The track rod balljoint's taper can be released using a balljoint separator tool, but this carries the risk of damaging the balljoint's rubber boot. It is possible to release the taper by tapping the track rod upwards with a soft-faced mallet, but refit the balljoint nut by a few threads first, so that the threads are protected from damage. Disconnect both track rods from the swivel hubs.

11 Unclip the primary oxygen sensor wiring harness from the transmission support bracket.

12 Disconnect the three wiring plugs from the electric power steering (EPS) motor, which is behind the steering rack, next to the bulkhead. Honda recommend taping over the 'open' connections, to prevent dirt entry.

13 Referring to Chapter 2A if necessary, unbolt the front (manual transmission models only) and rear engine mountings. Provided the left- and right-hand mountings have not been disturbed, this will only result in increased movement of the engine.

14 Check around the subframe to ensure that there are no brackets, hoses or wiring harnesses still attached, or anything in the way which would prevent it from being lowered with the steering rack.

15 The subframe is secured to the body by four bolts. By the two rear bolts, there are alignment markings to indicate the subframe's relative position to the body – if these are not clear, clean the area and make your own subframe-to-body marks with paint. However, there appears to be no requirement to align the subframe during refitting.

16 Support the subframe, either with two jacks, or (preferably) with the help of an assistant, then progressively loosen and remove the bolts.

17 Lower the subframe to clear the engine mounting(s), then withdraw it from under the car.

18 Note that the four subframe bolts are

only intended to be used once, and new ones should be obtained for refitting.

19 Unbolt and remove the three steering rack mounting brackets – each is secured by two bolts, and all six bolts should be renewed when refitting **(see illustrations)**. Note which way round each bracket is fitted, and which bolts are used, as they are of different lengths – store the old bolts with the brackets as a guide. Lift off the steering rack, and remove it from the subframe.

20 Check the condition of the grommet fitted to the pinion shaft, and if necessary, obtain a new one for refitting.

Refitting

21 Refitting is a reversal of removal, noting the following points:

a) *Check that the rack is in the centre of its stroke, as far as possible. If the same rack is being refitted, and was centralised (wheels pointing straight-ahead) on removal, it should still be in the centred position.*

b) *If removed, refit the grommet to the pinion shaft, noting that it has a tab which locates in a recess on top of the EPS motor.*

c) *Offer the rack into position on the subframe, then refit the brackets with new bolts, and tighten them to the specified torque.*

d) *Lubricate the pinion shaft grommet with a little washing-up liquid. As the subframe is raised, check that the grommet fits into the floor properly – have an assistant 'help' the lips of the grommet into place from inside the car.*

e) *Use new subframe bolts, tightened to the specified torque.*

f) *Ensure that the three EPS motor wiring plugs are securely reconnected.*

g) *Reconnect the lower arms as described in Section 6.*

h) *Use new nuts on the anti-roll bar drop links, and refer to Section 5 when tightening them.*

i) *Use new split pins on the track rod end nuts.*

j) *When reconnecting the pinion to the column inside the car, align the bolt holes with the groove in the shaft, or the flat on the shaft.*

k) *When the car is back on the ground, start the engine and let it idle – check that the EPS warning light goes off correctly. Turn the steering from lock-to-lock several times, and check that the EPS light stays off. Finally, take the car on a short test-drive.*

l) *Have the front wheel alignment checked on completion.*

16 Steering rack rubber gaiters – renewal

1 Remove the track rod end as described in Section 18. The locknut must be removed, however, to allow the gaiter to pass along the track rod – if wished, the locknut's position could be marked with paint (or count the number of turns required to remove it).

2 Release the clips at each end of the gaiter, then slide it off the track rod and remove it.

3 Clean the 'gaiter section' of the track rod and rack, then apply a little grease around the housing on the end of the rack, where the track rod fits. Also apply a little grease to the wider groove at the inner end of the track rod – do not grease the narrower groove where the gaiter outer clip will locate.

4 Clean the gaiter inner clip groove on the rack.

5 Slide the new gaiter into position, and secure with the inner and outer clips.

6 Refit the track rod end locknut, screwing it onto the track rod to the position noted when the nut was removed.

7 Refit the track rod end as described in Section 18.

17 Steering rack guide – adjustment

The Jazz has an adjustable guide (sometimes known as the 'slipper') fitted

at the front of the steering rack, at the passenger-side end. If any unusual rattling or vibration is felt through the steering wheel when travelling over rough roads, it is possible that the noise could be the rack, rattling up and down inside the steering rack housing. The rack guide can be adjusted, to take out this vertical movement. This is not in itself a difficult operation, but special tools are required, and the job must be performed to a high level of accuracy – overtightening the adjuster will lead to stiff steering, which could be dangerous. It is therefore recommended that this job is entrusted to a Honda dealer.

18 Track rod end – removal and refitting

1 If the track rod end rubber boot is damaged, a new one can be obtained from Honda dealers. Once the track rod end has been disconnected (as described later in this Section), the old boot can be unclipped. Wipe the balljoint clean (do not use excessive amounts of solvent), then pack it with fresh grease and fit the new boot. However, bear in mind that if the boot has been damaged for some time, it is likely that dirt will have got into the balljoint, and a new track rod end may soon be needed.

2 If the complete track rod end is to be renewed, proceed as follows.

Removal

3 Set the front wheels to the straight-ahead position.

4 Slacken the relevant front wheel nuts. Apply the handbrake, then jack up the front of the car, and support securely on axle stands (see *Jacking and vehicle support*). Remove the wheel.

5 Extract the split pin from the track rod balljoint nut (a new split pin will be needed when refitting). Unscrew the nut, but leave it attached by a couple of threads for now **(see illustration)**.

6 Disconnect the track rod end from the strut, either using a balljoint separator tool, or by tapping the end of the balljoint stud (use a block of wood and the still-fitted nut to protect the threads). When the balljoint separates,

unscrew the nut completely, and move the track rod clear **(see illustration)**.

7 Just slacken the track rod end locknut (move it as little as possible) **(see illustration)**. Once the locknut is slackened, gently turn it back up against the track rod end. If the locknut is left in this position, it can be used as a guide to the correct fitted position of the track rod end.

8 Without disturbing the locknut, unscrew the track rod end from the track rod, counting the number of turns necessary to remove it.

Refitting

9 Screw the track rod end onto the track rod the number of turns noted during removal (or up to the locknut), then tighten the locknut while holding the track rod in position (the track rod has flats to accept a spanner).

10 Clean the balljoint and its seat in the steering arm before fitting – it must be fitted dry. Offer the balljoint into position, taking care not to damage the boot.

11 Tighten the balljoint nut to the specified torque. From this point, tighten the nut slightly as required to align the split pin holes (do not loosen to align), then fit a new pin to secure.

12 Refit the roadwheel, then lower the car to the ground, and tighten the wheel nuts to the specified torque.

13 Have the front wheel alignment checked (see Section 20) at the earliest opportunity.

19 Electric power steering components – removal and refitting

Motor

1 Disconnect the battery negative lead, and position the lead away from the battery (also see *Disconnecting the battery*).

2 The motor is located in the engine compartment, at the pinion end (driver's side) of the steering rack. Access is not easy, but is probably best from below. The only alternative if accessed cannot be gained is to remove the steering rack, as described in Section 15.

3 Apply the handbrake, then jack up the front of the car, and support securely on axle stands (see *Jacking and vehicle support*).

4 Disconnect the motor wiring plug – this is

18.5 Remove the split pin from the track rod end balljoint nut

18.6 Split the balljoint taper, then remove the nut and separate the track rod

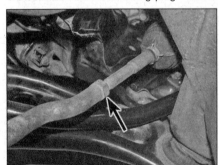
18.7 Slacken the track rod end locknut

19.13 Electric power steering control unit location

the largest of the three on top of the steering rack. Note which way round the motor wiring harness sits, to ensure correct refitting of the motor.
5 Remove the two mounting bolts, and withdraw the motor from the steering rack. Recover the large O-ring – a new one should be used when refitting.
6 Clean the mating surfaces of the motor and steering rack.
7 Lightly grease the steering motor drive components on the motor and inside the steering rack.
8 Apply a little silicone grease to the new motor O-ring, then fit it to the motor. Offer the motor into position, ensuring it is the right way round (as noted prior to removal). Fit the mounting bolts, and tighten them to the specified torque.
9 Reconnect the motor wiring plug securely.
10 Further refitting is a reversal of removal. On completion, start the engine and let it idle. Turn the steering from lock-to-lock several times, and make sure that the EPS warning light on the instrument panel does not come on.

Torque sensor

11 The torque sensor is part of the steering rack housing, and is not available separately.

Control unit

12 Disconnect the battery negative lead, and position the lead away from the battery (also see *Disconnecting the battery*). It is **essential** that this is done, to prevent possible damage to the EPS control unit when its plug is disconnected.
13 The control unit is located directly above the pedals, and can be accessed working in the driver's footwell **(see illustration)**.
14 Remove the driver's side facia closing panel as described in Chapter 11, Section 27.
15 Disconnect the wiring plug from the EPS motor relay at the back of the control unit, then unbolt the relay mounting bracket and remove it.
16 Disconnect the two wiring plugs from the control unit, then unscrew the nut and bolt, and remove the control unit from its location.
17 Refitting is a reversal of removal, noting the following points:
a) Ensure that the control unit wiring plugs are correctly and securely refitted.

19.21 EPS 2-pin connector (arrowed) is to the right of the diagnostic plug

b) On completion, start the engine and let it idle. Turn the steering from lock-to-lock several times, and make sure that the EPS warning light on the instrument panel does not come on.

Clearing EPS fault codes

18 If the system detects a fault, a fault code will be logged in the system control unit. In normal operation, the EPS warning light on the instrument panel will come on with the ignition, then go out after the engine is started. If the light stays on, it means a fault has been logged.
19 In some cases, just driving the car (with care, as the steering will be very heavy) will be enough to clear the fault, and put the warning light out. Where this does not work, the system can be cleared as follows.
20 Remove the driver's side facia closing panel as described in Chapter 11, Section 27.
21 Looking up under the facia from the driver's footwell, the 16-pin diagnostic connector can be seen, clipped into a metal bracket. Next to this is a smaller 2-pin connector, which is for the EPS – unclip it from the metal panel **(see illustration)**.
22 Make sure the ignition is switched off, and the front wheels are pointing straight-ahead.
23 Bridge the two pins on the EPS connector, using a short piece of wire.
24 Turn the steering wheel 45 degrees to the left, and hold it in this position.
25 Switch on the ignition. The EPS warning light should come on, then go out after four seconds.
26 Within four seconds of the light going out, turn the wheel back to the straight-ahead position. The EPS light should come on again after four seconds.
27 Within four seconds of the light coming on, turn the wheel 45 degrees to the left, and hold it. The light should again go off.
28 Within four seconds of the light going off, turn the wheel back to the straight-ahead position. The EPS light should now blink twice, indicating that the codes have been cleared. Turn the ignition off, then remove the bridging wire from the connector.
29 Confirm that the codes have been cleared by switching on the ignition once more – if all is well, the EPS light should come on and then go off. If not, try repeating the code-clearing procedure from the start.

30 On completion, clip the 2-pin connector back into place, then refit the facia closing panel.

20 Wheel alignment and steering angles – general information

Definitions

1 A car's steering and suspension geometry is defined in four basic settings – the angles are expressed in degrees or mm; the steering axis is defined as an imaginary line drawn through the axis of the suspension strut, extended where necessary to contact the ground.
2 Camber is the angle between each roadwheel and a vertical line drawn through its centre and tyre contact patch, when viewed from the front or rear of the car. Positive camber is when the roadwheels are tilted outwards from the vertical at the top; negative camber is when they are tilted inwards.
3 The camber angle is not adjustable, and is given for reference only (see paragraph 5).
4 Castor is the angle between the steering axis and a vertical line drawn through each roadwheel's centre and tyre contact patch, when viewed from the side of the car. Positive castor is when the steering axis is tilted so that it contacts the ground ahead of the vertical; negative castor is when it contacts the ground behind the vertical.
5 Castor is not adjustable, and is given for reference only; while it can be checked using a castor checking gauge, if the figure obtained is significantly different from that specified, the car must be taken for careful checking by a professional, as the fault can only be caused by wear or damage to the body or suspension components.
6 Steering axis inclination/SAI – also known as **kingpin inclination/KPI** – is the angle between the steering axis and a vertical line drawn through each roadwheel's centre and tyre contact patch, when viewed from the front or rear of the car.
7 SAI/KPI is not adjustable, and is given for reference only.
8 Toe is the difference, viewed from above, between lines drawn through the roadwheel centres and the car's centre-line. 'Toe-in' is when the roadwheels point inwards, towards each other at the front, while 'toe-out' is when they splay outwards from each other at the front.
9 The front wheel toe setting is adjusted by screwing the track rods in or out of their balljoint, to alter the effective length of the track rod assembly.
10 Rear wheel toe setting is not adjustable, and is given for reference only.

Checking – general

11 Due to the special measuring equipment necessary to check the wheel alignment, and the skill required to use it properly, the checking and adjustment of these settings is best left to an expert. Most tyre-fitting centres now possess sophisticated checking equipment.

12 For accurate checking, the car must be unloaded. Also note that the results may be inaccurate if the car has been modified, including by fitting non-standard wheels or tyres.

13 Check the tyre pressures, and ensure that the roadwheels are undamaged. Also check the condition of the front suspension and steering components (Chapter 1). Correct any faults.

14 Park the car on level ground, with the front roadwheels in the straight-ahead position. Rock both ends to settle the suspension. Release the handbrake and roll the car backwards 1 metre (3 feet), then forwards again, to relieve any stresses in the steering and suspension components.

Front wheel toe setting

Checking

15 Two methods are available to the home mechanic for checking the front wheel toe setting. One method is to use a gauge to measure the distance between the front and rear inside edges of the roadwheels. The other method is to use a scuff plate, in which each front wheel is rolled across a movable plate which records any deviation, or scuff, of the tyre from the straight-ahead position as it moves across the plate. Such gauges are available in relatively-inexpensive form from accessory outlets. It is up to the owner to decide whether the expense is justified, in view of the small amount of use such equipment would normally receive. Also note that Honda only quote the toe setting in millimetres, so ensure that there is some means of converting the angle recorded into a measurement.

16 Prepare the car as described previously in paragraphs 12 to 14.

17 If the measurement procedure is being used, carefully measure the distance between the front edges of the roadwheel rims and the rear edges of the rims. Subtract the rear measurement from the front measurement, and check that the result is within the specified range. If not, adjust the toe setting as described in paragraph 19.

18 If scuff plates are to be used, roll the car backwards, check that the roadwheels are in the straight-ahead position, then roll it across the scuff plates so that each front roadwheel passes squarely over the centre of its respective plate. Note the angle recorded by the scuff plates. To ensure accuracy, repeat the check three times, and take the average of the three readings. If the roadwheels are running parallel, there will of course be no angle recorded; if a deviation value is shown on the scuff plates, compare the reading obtained for each wheel with that specified. If the value recorded is outside the specified tolerance, the toe setting is incorrect, and must be adjusted as follows.

Adjustment

19 Apply the handbrake, jack up the front of the car and support it securely on axle stands (see *Jacking and vehicle support*). Turn the steering wheel onto full-left lock, and record the number of exposed threads on the right-hand track rod end. Now turn the steering onto full-right lock, and record the number of threads on the left-hand side. If there are the same number of threads visible on both sides, then subsequent adjustment should be made equally on both sides. If there are more threads visible on one side than the other, it will be necessary to compensate for this during adjustment. **Note:** *It is important that, after adjustment, the same number of threads be visible on each track rod end.*

20 First clean the track rod threads; if they are corroded, apply penetrating fluid before starting adjustment.

21 Use a straight-edge and a scriber or similar to mark the relationship of each track rod to its balljoint. Holding each track rod in turn, unscrew its locknut fully.

22 Alter the length of the track rods, bearing in mind the note in paragraph 19, by screwing them into or out of the balljoints. Rotate the track rod using an open-ended spanner fitted to the flats provided. Shortening the track rods (screwing them onto their balljoints) will reduce toe-in and increase toe-out. Each complete turn of the track rod effectively adjusts the toe setting by 30' or 3 mm (depending on the method being used).

23 When the setting is correct, hold the track rods and securely tighten the balljoint locknuts. Count the exposed threads – if the number of threads exposed is not the same on both sides, then the adjustment has not been made equally, and problems will be encountered with tyre scrubbing in turns; also, the steering wheel will no longer sit straight when the wheels are in the straight-ahead position.

24 When the track rod lengths are the same, lower the car to the ground and recheck the toe setting; readjust if necessary.

Chapter 11
Bodywork and fittings

Contents

Degrees of difficulty

Easy, suitable for novice with little experience	**Fairly easy,** suitable for beginner with some experience	**Fairly difficult,** suitable for competent DIY mechanic	**Difficult,** suitable for experienced DIY mechanic	**Very difficult,** suitable for expert DIY or professional

Specifications

Torque wrench settings	Nm	lbf ft
Door hinge bolts (all)*	29	21
Facia mounting bolts	22	16
Front seat bolts	34	25
Rear seat hinge bolts	34	25
Seat belt bolts:		
Front/rear seat belt inertia reel smaller mounting bolt	4	3
Front seat belt height adjuster bolts.	22	16
All other seat belt mounting bolts.	32	24
Tailgate hinge nuts/bolts	22	16
Tailgate lock striker bolts	22	16

* Use new bolts

1 General information

The body shell is made of pressed-steel sections, and is available only in five-door Hatchback form. Most body panel components are welded together. The front wings are bolted on, for easier accident repair.

Though the body is not 'fully' galvanised, all the outer panels and floor are, and high-strength steel is used extensively, giving a high degree of strength to the shell. Extensive use is made of plastic materials, mainly in the interior, but also in exterior components. The front and rear bumpers, and front grille, are injection-moulded from a synthetic material that is very strong and yet light. Plastic components such as wheel arch liners are fitted to the underside of the car, to improve the body's resistance to corrosion.

2 Maintenance – bodywork and underside

The general condition of a car's bodywork is the one thing that significantly affects its value. Maintenance is easy, but needs to be regular. Neglect, particularly after minor damage, can lead quickly to further deterioration and costly repair bills. It is important also to keep watch on those parts of the car not immediately visible, for instance the underside, inside all the wheel arches, and the lower part of the engine compartment.

The basic maintenance routine for the bodywork is washing – preferably with a lot of water, from a hose. This will remove all the loose solids which may have stuck to the car. It is important to flush these off in such a way as to prevent grit from scratching the finish. The wheel arches and underside need washing in the same way, to remove any accumulated mud which will retain moisture and tend to encourage rust. Strange as it sounds, the best time to clean the underside and wheel arches is in wet weather, when the mud is thoroughly wet and soft. In very wet weather, the underside is usually cleaned of large accumulations automatically, and this is a good time for inspection.

Periodically, except on cars with a wax-based underbody protective coating, it is a good idea to have the whole of the underside of the car steam-cleaned, so that a thorough inspection can be carried out to see what minor repairs are necessary. Steam-cleaning is available at many garages, and is necessary for the removal of the accumulation of oily grime, which sometimes is allowed to become thick in certain areas. If steam-cleaning facilities are not available, grease solvents are available which can be brush-applied; the dirt can then be simply hosed off. Note that these methods should not be used on cars with wax-based underbody protective coating, or the coating will be removed. Such cars should be inspected annually, preferably just prior to Winter, when the underbody should be washed down, and any damage to the wax coating repaired. Ideally, a completely fresh coat should be applied. It would also be worth considering the use of such wax-based protection for injection into door panels, sills, box sections, etc, as an additional safeguard against rust damage, where such protection is not provided by the car manufacturer.

After washing the paintwork, wipe off with a chamois leather to give an unspotted clear finish. A coat of clear protective wax polish will give added protection against chemical pollutants in the air. If the paintwork sheen has dulled or oxidised, use a cleaner/polisher combination to restore the brilliance of the shine. This requires a little effort, but such dulling is usually caused because regular washing has been neglected. Care needs to be taken with metallic paintwork, as special non-abrasive cleaner/polisher is required to avoid damage to the lacquer finish – also note that many 'solid' colours are in fact lacquered ('clear over base') these days. Always check that the door and ventilator opening drain holes and pipes are completely clear, so that water can be drained out. Brightwork should be treated in the same way as paintwork. Windscreens and windows can be kept clear of the smeary film which often appears, by the use of proprietary glass cleaner. Never use wax polish on the windscreen.

Mats and carpets should be brushed or vacuum-cleaned regularly, to keep them free of grit. If they are badly stained, remove them from the car for scrubbing or sponging, and make quite sure they are dry before refitting.

Cloth or velour seats and interior trim panels can be kept clean by wiping with a damp cloth. If they do become stained (which can be more apparent on light-coloured cloth or velour upholstery), use a little liquid detergent and a soft nail brush to scour the grime out of the grain of the material. Keep the headlining clean in the same way as the upholstery.

In the case of leather upholstery, a whole range of different products exist to clean, feed and generally restore the leather, and it is

recommended that these are used exclusively. Ordinary detergents should be avoided, as they will prematurely dry out leather, causing it to crack and split.

When using liquid cleaners inside the car, do not over-wet the surfaces being cleaned. Excessive damp could get into the seams and padded interior, causing stains, offensive odours or even rot. If the inside of the car gets wet accidentally, it is worthwhile taking some trouble to dry it out properly, particularly where carpets are involved. *Do not leave oil or electric heaters inside the car for this purpose.*

4   Minor body damage –
repair

Minor scratches

If the scratch is very superficial, and does not penetrate to the metal of the bodywork, repair is very simple. Lightly rub the area of the scratch with a paintwork renovator, or a very fine cutting paste, to remove loose paint from the scratch, and to clear the surrounding bodywork of wax polish. Rinse the area with clean water.

In the case of metallic paint, the most commonly-found scratches are not in the paint, but in the lacquer top coat, and appear white. If care is taken, these can sometimes be rendered less obvious by very careful use of paintwork renovator (which would otherwise not be used on metallic paintwork); otherwise, repair of these scratches can be achieved by applying lacquer with a fine brush. Also note that damage to the lacquer coat will show up worse if (white) polish residue collects in the chip or scratch – clean any suspected area thoroughly.

Apply touch-up paint to the scratch using a fine paint brush; continue to apply fine layers of paint (allowing each one time to dry) until the surface of the paint in the scratch is level with the surrounding paintwork. Allow the new paint at least two weeks to harden, then blend it into the surrounding paintwork by rubbing the scratch area with a paintwork renovator or a very fine cutting paste. Finally, apply wax polish.

Where the scratch has penetrated right through to the metal of the bodywork, causing the metal to rust, a different repair technique is required. Remove any loose rust from the bottom of the scratch with a penknife, then apply rust-inhibiting paint, to prevent the formation of rust in the future. Using a rubber or nylon applicator, fill the scratch with bodystopper paste. If required, this paste can be mixed with cellulose thinners, to provide a very thin paste which is ideal for filling narrow scratches. Before the stopper-paste in the scratch hardens, wrap a piece of smooth cotton rag around the top of a finger. Dip the finger in cellulose thinners, and quickly sweep it across the surface of the stopper-paste in

the scratch; this will ensure that the surface of the stopper-paste is slightly hollowed. The scratch can now be painted over as described earlier in this Section.

Dents

If the dent is shallow, and the paint has not been broken, it may be possible to have the dent repaired professionally, by one of the specialist mobile dent repair companies.

When deep denting of the car's bodywork has taken place, the first task is to pull the dent out, until the affected bodywork almost attains its original shape. There is little point in trying to restore the original shape completely, as the metal in the damaged area will have stretched on impact, and cannot be reshaped fully to its original contour. It is better to bring the level of the dent up to a point which is about 3 mm below the level of the surrounding bodywork. In cases where the dent is very shallow anyway, it is not worth trying to pull it out at all. If the underside of the dent is accessible, it can be hammered out gently from behind, using a mallet with a wooden or plastic head. Whilst doing this, hold a block of wood firmly against the outside of the panel, to absorb the impact from the hammer blows and thus prevent a large area of the bodywork from being 'belled-out'.

Should the dent be in a section of the bodywork which has a double skin, or some other factor making it inaccessible from behind, a different technique is called for. Drill several small holes through the metal inside the area – particularly in the deeper section. Then screw long self-tapping screws into the holes, just sufficiently for them to gain a good purchase in the metal. Now the dent can be pulled out by pulling on the protruding heads of the screws with a pair of pliers.

The next stage of the repair is the removal of the paint from the damaged area, and from an inch or so of the surrounding 'sound' bodywork. This is accomplished most easily by using a wire brush or abrasive pad on a power drill, although it can be done just as effectively by hand, using sheets of abrasive paper. To complete the preparation for filling, score the surface of the bare metal with a screwdriver or the tang of a file, or alternatively, drill small holes in the affected area. This will provide a really good 'key' for the filler paste.

To complete the repair, see the Section on filling and respraying.

Rust holes or gashes

Remove all paint from the affected area, and from an inch or so of the surrounding 'sound' bodywork, using an abrasive pad or a wire brush on a power drill. If these are not available, a few sheets of abrasive paper will do the job most effectively. With the paint removed, you will be able to judge the severity of the corrosion, and therefore decide whether to renew the whole panel (if this is possible) or to repair the affected area. New body panels are not as expensive as most people think, and it is often quicker and more satisfactory to fit a new panel than to attempt to repair large areas of corrosion.

Remove all fittings from the affected area, except those which will act as a guide to the original shape of the damaged bodywork (e.g. light units). Then, using tin snips or a hacksaw blade, remove all loose metal and any other metal badly affected by corrosion. Hammer the edges of the hole inwards, in order to create a slight depression for the filler paste.

Wire-brush the affected area to remove the powdery rust from the surface of the remaining metal. Paint the affected area with rust-inhibiting paint; if the back of the rusted area is accessible, treat this also.

Before filling can take place, it will be necessary to block the hole in some way. This can be achieved by the use of aluminium or plastic mesh, or aluminium tape.

Aluminium or plastic mesh, or glass-fibre matting is probably the best material to use for a large hole. Cut a piece to the approximate size and shape of the hole to be filled, then position it in the hole so that its edges are below the level of the surrounding bodywork. It can be retained in position by several blobs of filler paste around its periphery.

Aluminium tape should be used for small or very narrow holes. Pull a piece off the roll, trim it to the approximate size and shape required, then pull off the backing paper (if used) and stick the tape over the hole; it can be overlapped if the thickness of one piece is insufficient. Burnish down the edges of the tape with the handle of a screwdriver or similar, to ensure that the tape is securely attached to the metal underneath.

Filling and respraying

Before using this Section, see the Sections on dent, deep scratch, rust holes and gash repairs.

Many types of bodyfiller are available, but generally speaking, those proprietary kits which contain a tin of filler paste and a tube of resin hardener are best for this type of repair. A wide, flexible plastic or nylon applicator will be found invaluable for imparting a smooth and well-contoured finish to the surface of the filler.

Mix up a little filler on a clean piece of card or board – measure the hardener carefully (follow the maker's instructions on the pack), otherwise the filler will set too rapidly or too slowly. Using the applicator, apply the filler paste to the prepared area; draw the applicator across the surface of the filler to achieve the correct contour and to level the surface. As soon as a contour that approximates to the correct one is achieved, stop working the paste – if you carry on too long, the paste will become sticky and begin to 'pick-up' on the applicator. Continue to add thin layers of filler paste at 20-minute intervals, until the level of the filler is just proud of the surrounding bodywork.

Once the filler has hardened, the excess can be removed using a metal plane or file. From then on, progressively-finer grades of abrasive paper should be used, starting with a 40-grade production paper, and finishing with a 400-grade wet-and-dry paper. Always wrap the abrasive paper around a flat rubber, cork, or wooden block – otherwise the surface of the filler will not be completely flat. During the smoothing of the filler surface, the wet-and-dry paper should be periodically rinsed in water. This will ensure that a very smooth finish is imparted to the filler at the final stage.

At this stage, the 'dent' should be surrounded by a ring of bare metal, which in turn should be encircled by the finely 'feathered' edge of the good paintwork. Rinse the repair area with clean water, until all of the dust produced by the rubbing-down operation has gone.

Spray the whole area with a light coat of primer – this will show up any imperfections in the surface of the filler. Repair these imperfections with fresh filler paste or bodystopper, and once more smooth the surface with abrasive paper. If bodystopper is used, it can be mixed with cellulose thinners, to form a really thin paste which is ideal for filling small holes. Repeat this spray-and-repair procedure until you are satisfied that the surface of the filler, and the feathered edge of the paintwork, are perfect. Clean the repair area with clean water, and allow to dry fully.

The repair area is now ready for final spraying. Paint spraying must be carried out in a warm, dry, windless and dust-free atmosphere. This condition can be created artificially if you have access to a large indoor working area, but if you are forced to work in the open, you will have to pick your day very carefully. If you are working indoors, dousing the floor in the work area with water will help to settle the dust which would otherwise be in the atmosphere. If the repair area is confined to one body panel, mask off the surrounding panels; this will help to minimise the effects of a slight mis-match in paint colours. Bodywork fittings (e.g. chrome strips, door handles etc) will also need to be masked off. Use genuine masking tape, and several thicknesses of newspaper, for the masking operations.

Before commencing to spray, agitate the aerosol can thoroughly, then spray a test area (an old tin, or similar) until the technique is mastered. Cover the repair area with a thick coat of primer; the thickness should be built up using several thin layers of paint, rather than one thick one. Using 400-grade wet-and-dry paper, rub down the surface of the primer until it is really smooth. While doing this, the work area should be thoroughly doused with water, and the wet-and-dry paper periodically rinsed in water. Allow to dry before spraying on more paint.

Spray on the top coat, again building up the thickness by using several thin layers of paint. Start spraying at the top of the repair area, and then, using a side-to-side motion, work downwards until the whole repair area

and about 2 inches of the surrounding original paintwork is covered. Remove all masking material 10 to 15 minutes after spraying on the final coat of paint.

Allow the new paint at least two weeks to harden, then, using a paintwork renovator or a very fine cutting paste, blend the edges of the paint into the existing paintwork. Finally, apply wax polish.

Plastic components

With the use of more and more plastic body components by the car manufacturers (e.g. bumpers, spoilers, and in some cases major body panels), rectification of more serious damage to such items has become a matter of either entrusting repair work to a specialist in this field, or renewing complete components. Repair of such damage by the DIY owner is not really feasible, owing to the cost of the equipment and materials required for effecting such repairs. The basic technique involves making a groove along the line of the crack in the plastic, using a rotary burr in a power drill. The damaged part is then welded back together, using a hot-air gun to heat up and fuse a plastic filler rod into the groove. Any excess plastic is then removed, and the area rubbed down to a smooth finish. It is important that a filler rod of the correct plastic is used, as body components can be made of a variety of different types (e.g. polycarbonate, ABS, polypropylene).

Damage of a less serious nature (abrasions, minor cracks etc) can be repaired by the DIY owner using a two-part epoxy filler repair. Once mixed in equal, this is used in similar fashion to the bodywork filler used on metal panels. The filler is usually cured in twenty to thirty minutes, ready for sanding and painting.

If the owner is renewing a complete component himself, or if he has repaired it with epoxy filler, he will be left with the problem of finding a suitable paint for finishing which is compatible with the type of plastic used. At one time, the use of a universal paint was not possible, owing to the complex range of plastics encountered in body component applications. Standard paints, generally speaking, will not bond to plastic or rubber satisfactorily, but suitable paints to match any plastic or rubber finish, can be obtained from dealers. However, it is now possible to obtain a plastic body parts finishing kit which consists of a pre-primer treatment, a primer and coloured top coat. Full instructions are normally supplied with a kit, but basically, the method of use is to first apply the pre-primer to the component concerned, and allow it to dry for up to 30 minutes. Then the primer is applied, and left to dry for about an hour before finally applying the special-coloured top coat. The result is a correctly-coloured component, where the paint will flex with the plastic or rubber, a property that standard paint does not normally possess.

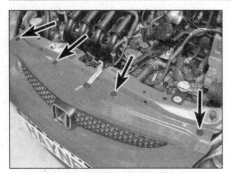

6.1a There are four clips along the top edge of the grille . . .

6.1b . . . which have to be prised out

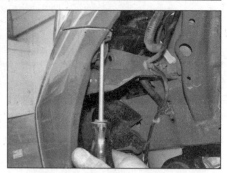

6.2 Remove the single vertical screw inside each wheel arch at the top

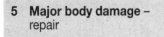

5 Major body damage – repair

Where serious damage has occurred, or large areas need renewal due to neglect, it means that complete new panels will need welding-in, and this is best left to professionals. If the damage is due to impact, it will also be necessary to check completely the alignment of the body shell, and this can only be carried out accurately by a Honda dealer using special jigs. If the body is left misaligned, it is primarily dangerous, as the car will not handle properly, and secondly, uneven stresses will be imposed on the steering, suspension and possibly transmission, causing abnormal wear, or complete failure, particularly to such items as the tyres.

6 Front bumper and crossmember – removal and refitting

Front bumper

Removal

1 Open the bonnet, and carefully prise out the four clips securing the top edge of the grille to the front crossmember ('slam panel') **(see illustrations)**.
2 Remove the single (vertical) bumper retaining screw at the top of each front wheel arch **(see illustration)**.
3 On the underside of the bumper, remove two clips and two screws along the bottom edge.
4 Where applicable, disconnect the wiring plugs from the front foglights.
5 With the help of an assistant, unclip the ends of the bumper (the clips are stiff to release,

and a small screwdriver may help), then slide it forwards to release the clips under the headlights, and remove it **(see illustrations)**.

Refitting

6 Refitting is a reversal of removal. Again, the help of an assistant will be required, to line up the bumper clips as the bumper is refitted.

Front bumper crossmember

Removal

7 Remove the front bumper as described previously in this Section.
8 Reach up behind the crossmember, and unclip the external air temperature sensor from its location. Detach the sensor wiring harness from the front of the crossmember **(see illustrations)**.
9 At each end of the crossmember, remove the two bolts and withdraw the crossmember from the front of the car **(see illustrations)**.

6.5a Unclip the ends of the bumper . . .

6.5b . . . then slide it forwards and remove it

6.8a Unclip the air temperature sensor from behind . . .

6.8b . . . and release the wiring harness from in front

6.9a Remove the two bolts at each end . . .

6.9b . . . and withdraw the crossmember from the front of the car

Refitting

10 Refitting is a reversal of removal.

7 Rear bumper – removal and refitting

Removal

1 Remove the four bumper retaining screws at the rear of each rear wheel arch (one screw is fitted vertically, at the front corner of the bumper) **(see illustrations)**. On models with rear mudflaps, two of these screws are used to secure the mudflaps.

2 Working underneath, carefully prise out the four clips along the bottom edge of the bumper **(see illustration)**.

3 Open the tailgate, then using an Allen key, unscrew the bumper retaining bolt from the bottom corners of the tailgate aperture **(see illustration)**.

4 With the help of an assistant, unclip the bumper ends by pulling them slightly outwards (the clips are stiff to release), and withdraw the bumper from the car **(see illustrations)**.

Refitting

5 Refitting is a reversal of removal. Again, the help of an assistant will be required, to line up the bumper clips as the bumper is refitted.

8 Radiator grille – removal and refitting

The radiator grille is part of the front bumper assembly – refer to Section 6.

9 Bonnet – removal, refitting and adjustment

Removal

1 Open the bonnet, then using a pencil or felt tip pen, mark the outline of each bonnet hinge relative to the bonnet, to use as a guide on refitting **(see illustration)**.

2 Have an assistant support the bonnet in its open position.

3 Unscrew the bonnet retaining bolts and carefully lift the bonnet clear. Store the bonnet out of the way in a safe place.

4 Inspect the bonnet hinges for signs of wear and free play at the pivots, and if necessary renew them. Each hinge is secured to the body by two bolts; mark the position of the hinge on the body then undo the retaining bolts and remove it from the car.

Refitting and adjustment

5 Where removed, refit the bonnet hinges, and align them with the previously-made marks. Tighten the bolts securely.

6 With the aid of an assistant, offer up the bonnet and loosely fit the retaining bolts. Align the hinges with the marks made on removal, then tighten the retaining bolts securely.

7 Close the bonnet, and check for alignment with the adjacent panels. If necessary, slacken the hinge bolts and re-align the bonnet. Adjust the height of the bonnet so that it is level with the surrounding front wings, by turning the rubber buffer at each front corner of the front crossmember. Once the bonnet is correctly aligned, tighten the hinge bolts. Check that the bonnet fastens and releases satisfactorily.

7.1a Three of the four screws at the rear of each wheel arch . . .

7.1b . . . with the fourth fitted vertically . . .

7.1c . . . all must be unscrewed

7.2 Prise out the four plastic clips along the bumper's bottom edge

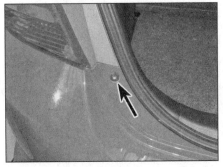
7.3 Remove the Allen bolt from each lower 'corner' of the tailgate aperture

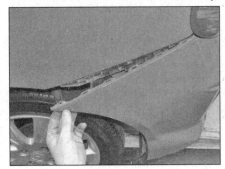
7.4a Unclip the bumper ends . . .

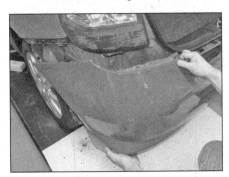
7.4b . . . and slide the bumper rearwards to remove

9.1 Mark around the bonnet hinge bolts before unscrewing them

10.3a Unscrew the two bonnet release lever bolts . . .

10.3b . . . then prise up the cable outer to release it . . .

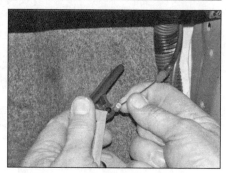

10.3c . . . and unhook the cable inner

10 Bonnet release cable – removal and refitting

Removal

1 Remove the right-hand front wheel arch liner as described in Section 23.

2 Remove the kick panel from the driver's footwell as described in Section 27.

3 Unscrew the two bolts securing the bonnet release lever to the car. With the lever removed, prise up the cable outer's end fitting to release it from the lever, then unhook the cable inner end fitting to free it completely **(see illustrations)**.

4 At the bonnet lock, lift the cable to release it from the locating slot, then unhook the cable end fitting. Take care not to bend the cable as this is done.

5 Trace the cable back from the bonnet lock,

releasing it from its retaining clips and ties, and noting how it is routed. The cable is taped to the wiring harness running under the inner wing.

6 Release the bulkhead grommet around the cable, then withdraw the cable into the car and remove it.

Refitting

7 Refitting is a reversal of removal. Ensure the cable is correctly routed and secured to all the relevant retaining clips. Before closing the bonnet, check the operation of the release lever and cable.

11 Bonnet lock – removal and refitting

Removal

1 Open the bonnet, and carefully prise out the

four clips securing the top edge of the grille to the front crossmember ('slam panel'). Release the top of the radiator grille for access to the bonnet lock.

2 Disconnect the alarm switch wiring plug from the bonnet lock, then unclip the alarm wiring harness from the back of the lock assembly.

3 Lift the bonnet release cable to free it from the locating slot, then unhook the cable end fitting. Take care not to bend the cable as this is done.

4 If possible, make alignment marks between the lock and the body, to make refitting easier.

5 Unscrew and remove the three bonnet lock mounting bolts, and withdraw the lock assembly from the car **(see illustration)**.

Refitting

6 Refitting is a reversal of removal. Align the lock using the marks made on removal, and tighten the three bolts securely. Before closing the bonnet fully, check that the bonnet striker appears to be entering the lock centrally, and if necessary, adjust the lock position (by loosening the three mounting bolts) to achieve satisfactory bonnet closing

12 Door – removal, refitting and adjustment

Removal

Front door

1 Remove the footwell kick panel on the side concerned, as described in Section 27.

2 Locate the door wiring connector plugs, and disconnect them **(see illustration)**.

3 Unbolt the door check strap from the door pillar **(see illustration)**.

4 Have an assistant support the door, or rest it on an axle stand – pad the top of the stand with cloth, to prevent damage to the paint.

5 Unscrew the two upper and lower door-to-hinge bolts, and remove the door from the car **(see illustration)**. Unclip the door wiring boot as the door is removed. Discard the hinge bolts – new ones should be used when refitting.

6 Examine the hinges for signs of wear

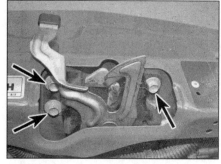

11.5 Unscrew the bonnet lock mounting bolts

12.2 Trace the door wiring back, and disconnect it

12.3 Unbolt the door check strap

12.5 With the door supported, unbolt the door hinges

or damage. If renewal is necessary, mark the position of the hinge, then unscrew the retaining bolts and remove the hinge from the car. Fit the new hinge, aligning it with the marks made before removal, then tighten the retaining bolts to the specified torque.

Rear door

7 Remove the front seat belt as described in Section 26.
8 Locate the door wiring plug inside the B-pillar, then disconnect it.
9 Unbolt the door check strap from the door pillar.
10 Have an assistant support the door, or rest it on an axle stand – pad the top of the stand with cloth, to prevent damage to the paint.
11 Unscrew the two upper and lower door-to-hinge bolts, and remove the door from the car. Unclip the door wiring boot as the door is removed. Discard the hinge bolts – new ones should be used when refitting.
12 Examine the hinges for signs of wear or damage. If renewal is necessary, mark the position of the hinge, then unscrew the retaining bolts and remove the hinge from the car. Fit the new hinge, aligning it with the marks made before removal, then tighten the retaining bolts to the specified torque.

Refitting

13 Refitting is a reversal of removal, noting the following points:
 a) *Use new hinge bolts, and tighten them to the specified torque.*
 b) *Check the door alignment and if*

12.14 Loosen the striker screws slightly, and adjust its position

necessary adjust as described later in this Section.
 c) *If the paintwork around the hinges has been damaged, paint the area with a suitable touch-in brush to prevent corrosion.*

Adjustment

14 To adjust the door to compensate for general wear in the hinges, this is best done by adjusting the position of the lock striker **(see illustration)**.
15 If adjusting the door after removal, close the door and check that the gap between the door and surrounding bodywork is equal around the complete perimeter. If necessary, slight adjustment of the door position can be made by slackening the hinge retaining bolts and repositioning the hinge/door as necessary. Once the door is correctly positioned, tighten the hinge bolts to their specified torque. Check

that the door striker engages centrally with the lock, and if necessary, adjust the position of the striker.

13 Door trim panel – removal and refitting

Removal

Front door

1 Pull open the door lock handle, then remove the cross-head screw at the top. Slide the whole handle forwards, and unhook it by pulling out the rear edge. Unhook the door lock operating rod, noting how it fits **(see illustrations)**.
2 Carefully prise off the side cover from the armrest, using a flat-bladed screwdriver to push up and release the three clips along the base of the armrest, at the front. Pull the armrest cover away from the door at the front, then work along the armrest, releasing the side clips; finally, pull the cover forwards to release the rear hooked clip **(see illustrations)**.
3 Disconnect the window switch wiring plug(s), then remove the three screws from the armrest inner section **(see illustrations)**.
4 Starting at the bottom of the door trim panel, either prise behind it or simply pull the panel itself, to release the clips holding it to the door (there are three clips along the base, and two up each side). When the panel is free, it must be pulled upwards, to disengage the window

13.1a Remove the cross-head screw from the door lock handle . . .

13.1b . . . then slide the handle forward and unhook the operating rod

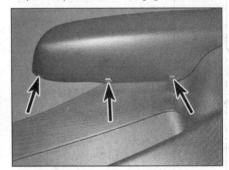

13.2a Push up with a screwdriver in the slots at the base of the armrest . . .

13.2b . . . then pull the cover away at the front, and release at the rear

13.3a Disconnect the window switch wiring plugs . . .

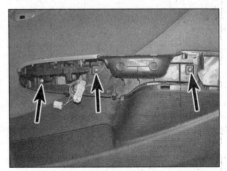

13.3b . . . then remove the three armrest screws

13.4 Start unclipping the door panel at the base, then lift it to remove

13.6a Remove the screw from the door lock handle . . .

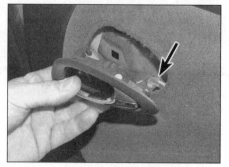

13.6b . . . then slide the handle forwards, and unhook the operating rod

> **HAYNES HiNT**
>
> *Prise the regulator handle to open a gap between it and the circular disc behind. Work the edge of a piece of (clean) cloth/rag into the gap behind the handle, either from the top or underneath. Using a 'sawing' action, work the cloth side-to-side, and also pull the ends of the cloth up (or down). It may take some time, but what you're trying to do is snag the ends of the spring clip holding the handle in place – when you do, the sawing action should work the clip off, allowing the handle to be pulled from the splines. A little patience is required, but it will work. Keep an eye on where the spring clip goes, though – it will release with some force.*

channel sealing strip – this is best done by lifting the panel at the rear, and working the strip out gradually. Remove the panel from the car, over the door lock knob **(see illustration)**.

Rear door

5 On models with manual rear windows, use a hooked piece of wire or a commercially-available tool to release the window regulator handle securing clip from the shaft – if neither of these is available, see the **Haynes Hint**. Pull off the regulator handle, and recover the spring clip and the trim disc. Note the angle the handle is fitted at, so that it can be refitted in the same position.
6 Pull open the door lock handle, then remove the cross-head screw at the top. Slide the whole handle forwards, and unhook it by pulling out the rear edge. Unhook the door lock operating rod, noting how it fits **(see illustrations)**.

7 Carefully prise off the side cover from the armrest, using a flat-bladed screwdriver to push up and release the three clips along the base of the armrest, at the front. Pull the armrest cover away from the door at the front, then work along the armrest, releasing the side clips; finally, pull the cover forwards to release the rear hooked clip **(see illustrations)**.
8 On models with electric rear windows, disconnect the window switch wiring plug **(see illustration)**.
9 Remove the two screws from the centre of the armrest inner section **(see illustration)**.
10 Pull out the rear edge of the triangular trim panel at the rear of the door, and remove the trim panel **(see illustration)**.
11 Starting at the bottom of the door trim panel, either prise behind it or simply pull the panel itself, to release the clips holding it to the door (there are three clips along the base,

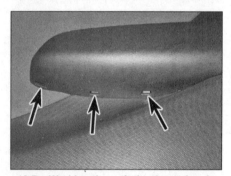

13.7a Working through the three slots in the base of the armrest . . .

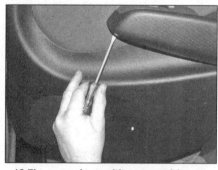

13.7b . . . push up with a screwdriver to release the clips . . .

13.7c . . . and remove the armrest cover

13.8 Where applicable, disconnect the electric rear window switch

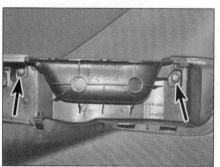

13.9 Remove the two armrest screws

13.10 Unclip and remove the triangular trim panel at the rear

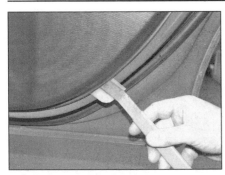

13.11a Take care to protect the paint when prising the trim panel

13.11b Removing the trim panel from the door

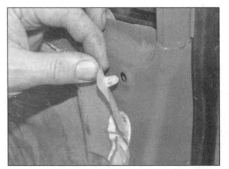

13.14a Prise out the membrane securing clips . . .

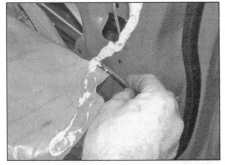

13.14b . . . then carefully slice along the bead of mastic to remove it

13.15a If any trim panel clips were 'left behind', prise them out of the door . . .

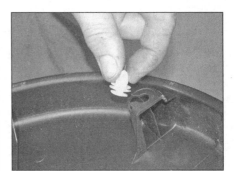

13.15b . . . and refit to the slots in the trim panel

and two up each side). When the panel is free, it must be pulled upwards, to disengage the window channel sealing strip – this is best done by lifting the panel at the rear, and working the strip out gradually. Remove the panel from the car, over the door lock knob **(see illustrations)**.

Door membrane

12 To access the door internal components, the plastic membrane must be removed.
13 On models with deadlocking ('super-locking'), disconnect the wiring plug then remove the screw securing the deadlocking control unit from the centre of the panel.
14 Prise out the clips, then carefully peel back the membrane. This sheet will be stuck on with a bead of mastic, which can be sliced though 'vertically' with a sharp knife, so that the membrane can be re-attached afterwards **(see illustrations)**. Pull off the membrane and move it to a safe place, where it can be kept clean.

Refitting

15 Refitting is a reversal of removal, noting the following points:
  a) *Check the door for any trim clips which might have been left behind by the panel as it was removed. If necessary, carefully prise these clips out of the door, and refit them to the panel – if this is not done, they will not re-engage properly when refitting the panel (see illustrations). If any clips have been broken, obtain new ones for refitting – take one of the good clips along to the dealer for matching.*

  b) *Once the trim panel wiring has been reconnected, check the operation of the door electrical equipment as applicable, before clipping the panel back in place.*
  c) *Similarly, check the operation of the interior lock handle, once the operating rod has been reconnected.*
  d) *On models with manual rear windows, refit the regulator handle trim disc, then slot the spring clip into the handle. With the window fully closed, offer the handle onto the splines – the handle should be set to face forwards and upwards at 45°. Push the handle home until the spring clip clicks into place.*

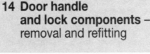

14 Door handle and lock components – removal and refitting

Removal

Interior door handle

1 The interior door handle is removed as part of the door trim panel procedure – refer to Section 13.

Front door handle and lock cylinder

2 Remove the door trim panel and membrane as described in Section 13, then temporarily reconnect the door window switch and close the window.
3 Where applicable, unclip the plastic cover fitted over the lock rods, then unhook the handle operating mechanism from the lock assembly at the rear of the door.

4 Pull out the guide rubber from the window channel at the rear of the door, then unscrew the two guide channel bolts and withdraw the channel from the door **(see illustrations)**.
5 On the inside of the handle, remove the

14.4a Pull out the guide rubber from the window channel at the rear . . .

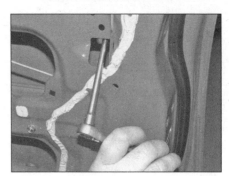

14.4b . . . then unscrew the upper and lower bolts . . .

14.4c . . . and remove the guide channel from the door

14.5a Remove the smallest (middle) cross-head screw . . .

14.5b . . . then unclip the wiring harness lower down . . .

14.5c . . . and pull off the lock cylinder switch

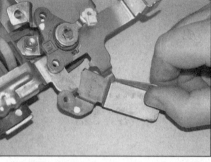
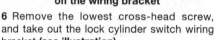
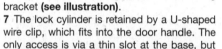

14.6 Remove the lowest screw, and take off the wiring bracket

this gives insufficient leverage to pull the clip down and release it. After several attempts, we accidentally broke the thin metal bar which forms the base of this slot, and found that this gave the leverage needed (the slot appears to serve no useful purpose). Once the cylinder is released, withdraw it into the door, and disconnect its operating rod (see illustrations).

8 If the lock cylinder cannot be removed as described, disconnect its operating rod, then continue and remove the handle.

9 Release the operating rod from the handle – this is a stiff fit, and we had to use a pair of thin-nosed pliers through the top of the door to press the rod out.

10 Support the handle from outside, perhaps by taping it temporarily to the door. Remove the two bolts from the handle's inner metal plate, then unclip and remove the plate inside the door. Take off the handle from the outside of the door (see illustrations).

smallest of the three cross-head screws visible, securing the (round, black) lock cylinder switch. Trace the lock cylinder switch wiring downwards, and unclip it from the bracket. Pull the switch body off the lock cylinder, and remove it completely (see illustrations).

6 Remove the lowest cross-head screw, and take out the lock cylinder switch wiring bracket (see illustration).

7 The lock cylinder is retained by a U-shaped wire clip, which fits into the door handle. The only access is via a thin slot at the base, but

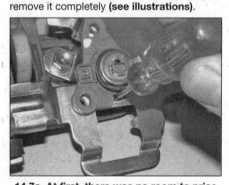

14.7a At first, there was no room to prise down the clip . . .

14.7b . . . but when the thin metal bar broke, the clip could be prised down . . .

14.7c . . . and removed, which allows the lock cylinder itself . . .

14.7d . . . to be withdrawn from the door

14.10a Remove the two handle-to plate bolts . . .

14.10b . . . then withdraw the metal plate inside the door

14.10c Unclip and remove the handle from the outside

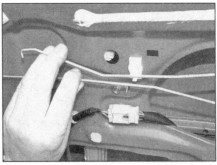

14.12 Unclip the two lock rods from the door

14.13a Remove the two bolts . . .

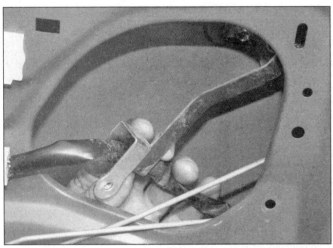

14.13b . . . and take out the harness plate inside the door

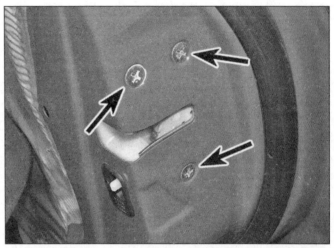

14.14 Remove the three lock screws at the rear edge of the door

Rear door handle

11 Remove the door trim panel and membrane as described in Section 13, then temporarily reconnect the door window switch (or refit the regulator handle) and close the window.

12 Noting their fitted positions, unclip the two lock operating rods from the holder on the door **(see illustration)**.

13 Remove the two bolts and take off the wiring harness protector plate inside the door – separate the plate from the harness and remove it completely **(see illustrations)**.

14 Unscrew and remove the three lock securing screws at the rear of the door, then move the lock down slightly, without bending any of the operating rods – the lock must be lowered to gain access to the door handle's rear bolt **(see illustration)**.

15 Unscrew the two door handle retaining bolts – these bolts also secure the handle's inner plate. Unhook the inner plate from the tab on the handle **(see illustrations)**.

16 From inside the door, use a small screwdriver to press upwards on the handle's plastic retaining tab, then from outside the car, lift the handle and pull it outwards to remove **(see illustrations)**.

Front door lock

17 Proceed as described in paragraphs 2 to 4 inclusive.

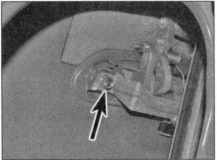

14.15a Unscrew the front . . .

14.15b . . . and rear door handle/inner plate bolt . . .

14.15c . . . and remove the inner plate

14.16a Press upwards on the retaining tab at the base of the handle . . .

14.16b . . . and remove the handle from outside the door

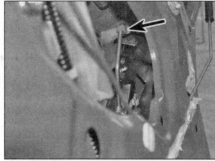

14.18a Unclip the handle operating rod from its (blue, plastic) clip . . .

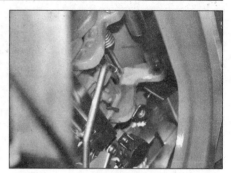

14.18b . . . and withdraw the rod from the handle

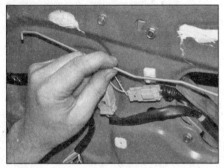

14.19 Unclip the handle rod from the door

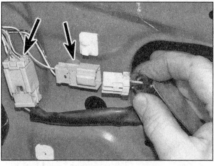

14.20 Disconnect the two lock wiring plugs

wiring harness protector plate inside the door – separate the plate from the harness and remove it completely **(see illustrations)**.

22 Remove the three lock securing screws from the rear edge of the door, then move the lock assembly forwards and withdraw it from the door, taking care not to bend the still-attached operating rods **(see illustrations)**.

Rear door lock

23 Proceed as described in paragraphs 11 to 13 inclusive.

24 Disconnect the operating rod from the door lock knob linkage at the front of the door **(see illustration)**.

25 Disconnect the lock wiring plug. On some models, the plug is at the lock itself, while on others, the plug is in the centre of the door (on these models, unclip the plug from the door panel) **(see illustrations)**.

18 Release the clips, and disconnect the operating rods from the handle and lock cylinder **(see illustrations)**.

19 Unclip the interior handle operating rod from the holder on the door **(see illustration)**.

20 Disconnect the lock wiring plug(s). On some models, there are two plugs at the lock itself, while others have a single plug at the top of the door **(see illustration)**.

21 Remove the two bolts and take off the

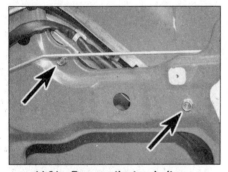

14.21a Remove the two bolts . . .

14.21b . . . take out the wiring harness plate from inside the door . . .

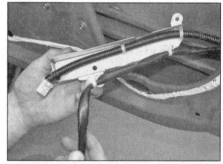

14.21c . . . and unclip the wiring from it

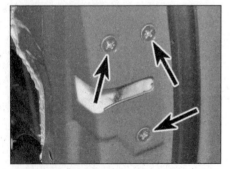

14.22a Remove the three lock screws at the back edge of the door . . .

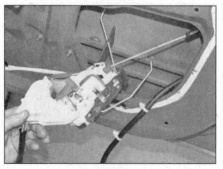

14.22b . . . then withdraw the lock into the door, without bending the rods

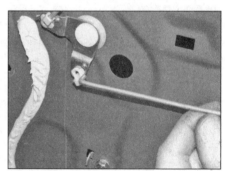

14.24 Unhook the rod from the door knob linkage

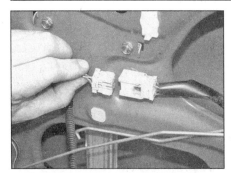

14.25a Disconnect the lock wiring plug . . .

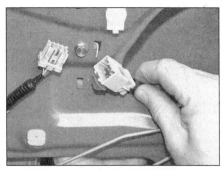

14.25b . . . and unclip the plug from the door

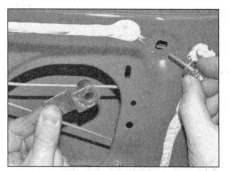

14.26a The window guide channel top bolt also secures this stepped spacer

14.26b Remove the guide channel lower bolt

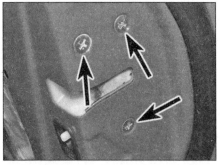

14.27 Remove the three lock screws from the rear edge of the door

14.28 Unhook the operating rods from the lock

26 Remove the two window rear guide channel bolts. Note that the (longer) upper bolt also secures a stepped spacer plate – this plate should also be removed, noting how it fits **(see illustrations)**.

27 Remove the three lock securing screws from the rear edge of the door, then move the lock assembly forwards for access **(see illustration)**.

28 Disconnect the interior handle and lock knob operating rods from the lock – mark the rods with tape to identify them for refitting **(see illustration)**.

29 Slide the lock down inside the door, work it round the base of the window rear guide channel, then withdraw it from the door **(see illustration)**.

Refitting

30 Refitting is a reversal of removal, noting the following points:
a) *When refitting the front door lock cylinder/handle, just locate the wire clip into the handle before fitting to the door* ***(see illustration)***. *Offer in the inner plate and lock cylinder, then push the clip upwards to secure – we found this to be easier than trying to fit the wire clip into the door afterwards.*
b) *Ensure that all operating rods and wiring plugs are correctly and securely reconnected.*
c) *Lightly grease the operating rod sliding surfaces and pivots as necessary.*

d) *Check the operation of all components before refitting the membrane and door trim panel.*

15 Door window glass and regulator – removal and refitting

Removal

1 Remove the door trim panel and membrane as described in Section 13.

Front glass

2 Temporarily reconnect the window switch, and lower the glass until the two securing bolts are visible in the door frame **(see illustration)**.

14.29 Removing the rear door lock

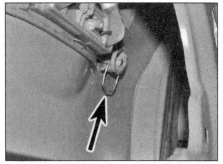

14.30 Fit the lock cylinder clip to the handle as shown when refitting

15.2 Lower the window until the two bolts can be seen

15.3 Tilt the glass forwards to remove it from the door

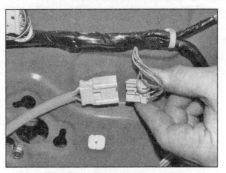

15.5a Disconnect the window motor wiring plug . . .

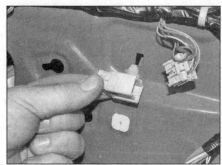

15.5b . . . then release the plug from the door . . .

15.5c . . . and unclip the harness from inside

15.6a Unscrew one top bolt, loosen the other . . .

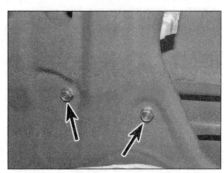

15.6b . . . and unscrew the two regulator lower bolts

3 Have an assistant support the glass (take care – it's heavy), then unscrew and remove the bolts. Tilt the glass forwards, then lift and withdraw it from the door **(see illustration)**.

Front regulator/motor

4 To remove the regulator, first remove the glass as described previously in this Section.
5 Disconnect the motor wiring plug. Trace the

wiring back towards the motor, and release the harness clip **(see illustrations)**.
6 Unscrew and remove three of the four regulator bolts – the other bolt is on a slotted mounting, and need only be loosened **(see illustrations)**.
7 Similarly, the three motor mounting bolts need only be loosened, as they sit in slotted mountings. Withdraw the regulator and motor assembly through the door frame **(see illustrations)**.

Rear glass

8 Reconnect the switch (or refit the handle), and move the glass until the two securing bolts are visible in the door frame **(see illustration)**.
9 Have an assistant support the glass (take care – it's heavy), then unscrew and remove the bolts. Lower the glass as far as it will go, noting that it cannot be removed for the moment **(see illustration)**.
10 Remove the screw in the centre of the triangular plate at the rear of the door frame – this secures the door's rear outer trim panel. From the outside of the door, pull upwards then rearwards on the door's rear trim panel, and remove it **(see illustrations)**.
11 Pull out the rubber from the window guide channel, at the top rear corner of the window frame – this will make it easier to move the guide channel itself forwards in a moment **(see illustration)**.
12 Loosen the guide channel's upper nut, which is on the triangular plate at the rear of the door frame **(see illustration)**.
13 Remove the two window rear guide

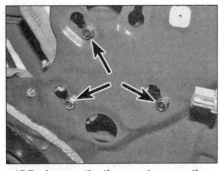

15.7a Loosen the three motor mounting bolts . . .

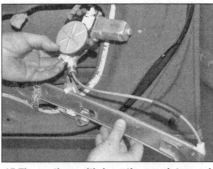

15.7b . . . then withdraw the regulator and motor from the door

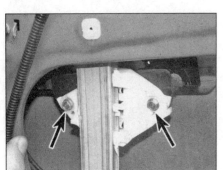

15.8 Lower the rear window until the two bolts can be seen

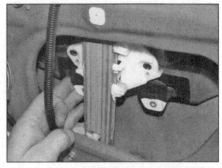

15.9 Remove the two bolts, and lower the glass into the door for now

15.10a Remove the screw in the triangular section at the back of the door . . .

15.10b . . . then unclip the door's rear outer trim panel

15.11 Pull out the window guide channel rubber at the top of the triangular section

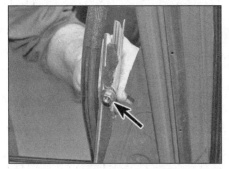

15.12 Loosen the guide channel upper nut, and pull out the guide

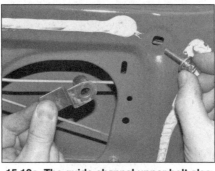

15.13a The guide channel upper bolt also secures a spacer inside

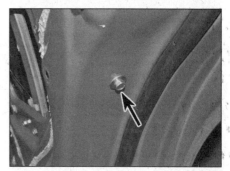

15.13b Remove the guide channel lower bolt

channel bolts. Note that the (longer) upper bolt also secures a stepped spacer plate – this plate should also be removed, noting how it fits (see illustrations).

14 Move the rear guide channel forwards, sliding the section secured by the upper nut out of the door. Release the channel from the back edge of the glass by pulling it upwards – pull out more of the channel trim as necessary. Finally, twist the channel so that it will pass out through the top of the door, and remove it (see illustration).

15 Lift the glass from the bottom of the door, and withdraw it completely (see illustration).

Rear regulator/motor

16 To remove the regulator, first remove the glass as described previously in this Section.

17 On models with electric rear windows,

disconnect the motor wiring plug and unclip the wiring harness from the door (see illustrations).

18 Unscrew and remove the four regulator bolts, and the three regulator spindle (or motor) bolts (see illustrations).

15.15 Lift out the glass from the door

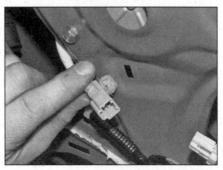

15.14 Removing the rear guide channel from the top of the door

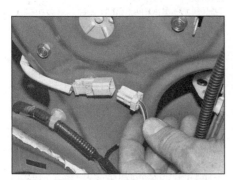

15.17a Where applicable, disconnect the motor wiring plug . . .

15.17b . . . and unclip the wiring from the door

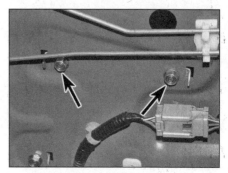

15.18a Unscrew the two regulator upper . . .

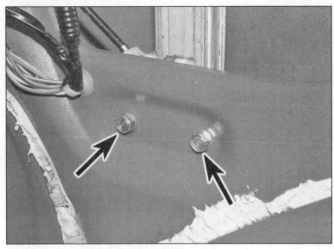

15.18b . . . and two lower bolts . . .

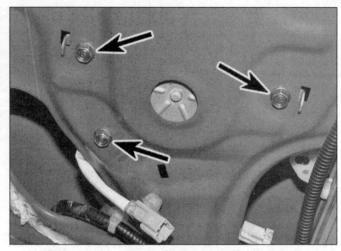

15.18c . . . then remove the three spindle/motor bolts

15.19 Removing the regulator/motor assembly out of the door

19 Lift the regulator and spindle/motor assembly to unhook the two pairs of mounting lugs, then remove the assembly through the door frame **(see illustration)**.

Refitting

20 Refitting is a reversal of removal, noting the following points:
a) Tighten all mounting bolts securely.
b) Lightly grease the regulator sliding surfaces as necessary.
c) Check the operation of all components before refitting the membrane and door trim panel.

16 Tailgate and support struts – removal and refitting

Tailgate

Removal

1 Remove all the tailgate trim panels, the C-pillar trim panels, and the rear grab handles, as described in Section 27. Also remove the cover from the centre rear seat belt's inertia reel, referring to Section 26 if necessary.
2 Disconnect all wiring connectors from inside the tailgate, and disconnect the washer tube from the rear wiper motor (refer to Chapter 12 if necessary). Also, prise the washer tube and wiring grommets from the tailgate **(see illustrations)**.
3 Tie a piece of string to each end of the wiring then, noting the correct routing of the wiring harness, release the harness rubber grommets from the tailgate and withdraw the wiring. When the end of the wiring appears, untie the string and leave it in position in the tailgate; it can then be used on refitting to draw the wiring into position.
4 Release the headlining at the rear edge, and carefully pull it down for access to the tailgate hinges.
5 Remove the two nuts, and take off the adapters for fitting child seats from the hinge studs.
6 Using a suitable marker pen, draw around the outline of each hinge, marking its correct position on the tailgate **(see illustration)**. Protect the paintwork surrounding the hinges with masking tape.
7 With the help of an assistant to support the tailgate, remove the support struts as described below.
8 With the tailgate still supported, unscrew the two nuts and bolts from each hinge, then lift the tailgate from the car.
9 Inspect the hinges for signs of wear or damage and renew if necessary.

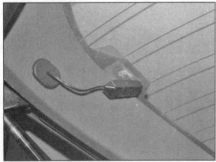

16.2a Disconnect the heated rear window wiring plugs . . .

16.2b . . . release the wiring grommets . . .

16.2c . . . and the washer tube

16.6 Mark around the tailgate hinges before removing them

16.12a Unscrew the two upper . . .

16.12b . . . and two lower bolts for the tailgate strut

Refitting

10 Refitting is a reversal of removal, but tighten the tailgate mounting nuts and bolts to the specified torque. Check the tailgate alignment with the surrounding panels. If necessary, slight adjustment can be made by slackening the hinge fasteners and repositioning the tailgate on its hinges – adjustable tailgate rubbers are also fitted on either side, and the tailgate lock striker is also adjustable.

Support struts

 Warning: The support struts are filled with gas, and must be disposed of safely.

Removal

11 With the help of an assistant (or a suitable wooden prop), support the tailgate in the open position.
12 Unscrew and remove the two strut mounting bolts at either end, then withdraw the strut from the car **(see illustrations)**.

Refitting

13 Refitting is a reversal of removal. Attach the strut to the tailgate first, then to the body, and tighten the bolts securely.

17 Tailgate lock components – removal and refitting

Lock

1 Remove the tailgate inner trim panel as described in Section 27.
2 Unscrew the three lock mounting bolts, and withdraw the lock from the tailgate **(see illustrations)**.
3 Unhook the tailgate handle operating cable from the lock, and disconnect the lock motor wiring plugs **(see illustration)**.
4 Trace the remaining wiring back into the

tailgate, and disconnect the lock switch wiring plug **(see illustration)**.
5 Refitting is a reversal of removal. Check the operation of the lock before refitting the tailgate trim panel.

Lock cylinder

Note: *Not all models have a tailgate lock cylinder.*
6 Remove the tailgate inner trim panel as described in Section 27.
7 Either unhook the lock cylinder operating rod, or disconnect the lock cylinder switch wiring plug and detach the wiring from the tailgate.

8 Remove the lock cylinder mounting bolt on the outside of the tailgate, then twist the lock cylinder through 90° and withdraw it to the inside of the tailgate.
9 Refitting is a reversal of removal. Check the operation of the lock before refitting the tailgate inner trim panel.

Tailgate handle

10 Remove the tailgate outer trim panel as described in Section 27.
11 Working inside the tailgate, disconnect the operating cable from the tailgate handle, by sliding the cable end fitting sideways out

17.2a Unscrew the three tailgate lock mounting bolts . . .

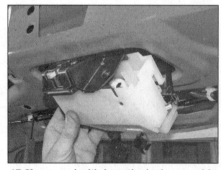

17.2b . . . and withdraw the lock assembly from the tailgate

17.3 Disconnecting the lock motor wiring plugs

17.4 Disconnect the lock switch wiring plug

17.11 Unhook the handle cable end fitting sideways

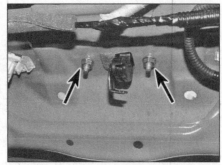

17.12a Unscrew the handle nuts inside . . .

17.12b . . . then withdraw the handle from outside the tailgate

of the arm on the inside of the handle (see illustration).

12 Unscrew the two handle mounting nuts from the inside, then withdraw the handle from the outside of the tailgate (see illustration).

13 Refitting is a reversal of removal. Check the operation of the handle before refitting the tailgate trim panels.

Lock striker

14 Remove the luggage area rear panel as described in Section 27.

15 Mark around the striker with paint (such as typist's correction fluid) to ensure it is accurately refitted.

16 Unscrew the two mounting bolts, and withdraw the striker from the tailgate aperture (see illustration).

17 Refitting is a reversal of removal. Align the striker with the previously-made marks, and tighten the bolts to the specified torque.

17.16 Unscrew the tailgate striker mounting bolts

18 Central locking components – general

Central locking switches

1 The central locking switches fitted to the two front door lock cylinders are removed as described in Section 14. Some models have a separate switch fitted to the tailgate lock cylinder, which is described in Section 17.

Remote locking/ keyless entry receiver

2 The remote central locking receiver unit is mounted behind the facia, on the right-hand side, above the interior fusebox. Where fitted, this same unit provides the keyless entry function. Remove the driver's side facia panels as described in Section 27 for access.

Disconnect the wiring plug, then unscrew the mounting bolt and remove the receiver unit.

Deadlocking control units

3 When the deadlocking feature is activated, the interior door handles are effectively disconnected, meaning that a thief will still not be able to open a door, even after breaking a window. Each of the doors has a separate deadlocking (or 'superlocking') unit fitted – this is part of each door lock assembly (see Section 14).

Control unit

4 The central locking system control unit is part of the instrument panel, which is removed as described in Chapter 12, Section 10.

19 Electric window components – removal and refitting

Window switch

1 Refer to Chapter 12.

Window motor

2 The window motor is removed with the regulator assembly, as described in Section 15.

20 Mirrors and associated components – removal and refitting

Interior mirror

1 See Section 27.

Door mirror assembly

2 Raise the window glass fully.

3 Remove the door trim panel as described in Section 13. It will also be necessary to peel back the front part of the door membrane.

4 Disconnect the mirror wiring plug at the front of the door, then trace the wiring back into the door frame, and release the clip (see illustration).

5 Prise out the access cap from the door, then unscrew the three mirror mounting nuts (it's quite likely the nuts will drop into the door as this is done – a magnetic pick-up tool is ideal for retrieving them). Withdraw the mirror from the outside of the door, with its wiring harness (see illustrations).

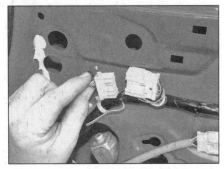

20.4 Disconnect the mirror wiring plug at the front of the door

20.5a The front mounting nut is hidden under this cap

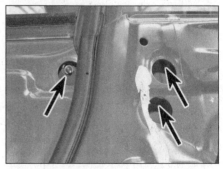

20.5b The three mirror mounting nuts are now accessible . . .

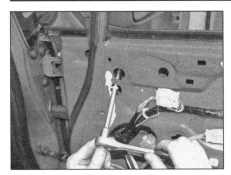

20.5c . . . working at an angle, through the door access holes

20.5d Remove the mirror from the door, and pull through the wiring plug

20.7a Prise the mirror glass out at the bottom . . .

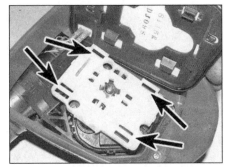

20.7b . . . and release the glass from the clips on the pivot plate

20.8 Disconnect the wiring plug from the heating element

20.11 Door mirror completely dismantled

6 Refitting is a reversal of removal. Feed the mirror wiring into the door, and route it so that it will be clear of the window glass. Check the mirror operation before refitting the door trim panel.

Door mirror glass

7 Push the glass fully into the housing at the top, so that the lower edge is sticking out. Insert a wide, flat-bladed tool (wrapped with tape to protect the housing) into the gap between the glass and mirror housing, and release the glass, which is secured to the centre pivot plate with two hooked clips **(see illustrations)**.
8 Disconnect the wiring connector from the mirror heating element, and remove the glass **(see illustration)**.
9 When refitting, align the glass with the two mounting clips, and push it evenly onto them – use a wad of cloth, and take care not to use excessive force, as the glass is easily broken.

Door mirror switch

10 Refer to Chapter 12.

Door mirror motor

11 With the mirror glass removed as described previously in this Section, separate the motor by removing the three screws, and disconnect the two wiring plugs **(see illustration)**.
12 Refitting is a reversal of removal. Tighten the screws securely, and ensure that the wiring plugs are correctly reconnected. Test the mirror operation before refitting the glass.

21 Windscreen, tailgate and fixed side window glass – general information

These areas of glass, which include the front quarter-light, are bonded in position with a special adhesive. Renewal of such fixed glass is a difficult, messy and time-consuming task, which is beyond the scope of the home mechanic. It is difficult, unless one has plenty of practice, to obtain a secure, waterproof fit. In view of this, owners are strongly advised to have this work carried out by one of the many specialist windscreen fitters.

22 Sunroof – general information

Due to the complexity of the sunroof mechanism, considerable expertise is needed to repair, renew or adjust the sunroof components successfully. Removal of the roof first requires the headlining to be removed, which is a complex and tedious operation, and not a task to be undertaken lightly. Therefore, any problems with the sunroof should be referred to a Honda dealer.

On models with an electric sunroof, if the sunroof motor fails to operate, first check the relevant fuse. If the fault cannot be traced and rectified, the sunroof can be opened and closed manually using a special cranked tool to turn the motor spindle (this tool is supplied with the car, in the toolkit which is in the

boot). To gain access to the motor, unclip the small round trim cover in front of the rear interior light. Insert the tool fully into the motor opening, and turn it to open or close the sunroof.

23 Exterior fittings – removal and refitting

Engine undertray

1 Jack up the front of the car, and support it on axle stands (see *Jacking and vehicle support*).
2 The undertray is secured by a total of ten fasteners – six from below, and two from the sides, accessed within the front wheel arches. Most of these are plastic plug-type clips, which can be prised out, but at each front corner, there is a single cross-head screw to remove **(see illustrations)**.

23.2a The engine undertray has plastic plugs along the front . . .

23.2b . . . at the rear . . .

23.2c . . . and at the side, in the wheel arches

23.2d There's a single cross-head screw to remove at the front . . .

23.2e . . . and the undertray can be removed

23.5a Prise out the clips . . .

23.5b . . . and remove the front under shields

3 Refitting is a reversal of removal.

Front under shields

4 Jack up the front of the car, and support it on axle stands (see *Jacking and vehicle support*).
5 The Jazz has two more plastic shields fitted behind the main undertray at the front. The left-hand shield is smaller, and is secured with three clips, while the larger right-hand shield has five clips. Release the clips and remove the shields as required **(see illustrations)**.
6 Refitting is a reversal of removal.

Wheel arch liners

7 Removing the wheel arch liners is much easier with the relevant wheel removed. Loosen the relevant wheel nuts, then jack up the front or rear of the car, and support it on axle stands (see *Jacking and vehicle support*). Remove the wheel.

Front

8 Where applicable, remove the two screws and one clip from the mudflap at the rear of the wheel arch, and a further single screw underneath at the front. If mudflaps aren't fitted, there are three clips at the rear – these are easily broken, so take care when prising them out **(see illustration)**.
9 Work around the inside of the arch liner, and prise out the clips (approximately six in total) securing the liner to the wheel arch **(see illustration)**. It may be necessary to wipe the liner clean, to see them clearly. Again, take care, as the clips are easily broken – special forked tools are available for removing these clips, and these are preferable to using a flat-bladed screwdriver.
10 At the top of the liner inside, remove the single retaining bolt.

11 Release the liner and withdraw it from under the wheel arch **(see illustration)**.
12 On refitting, renew any retaining clips that may have been broken on removal, and ensure that the panel is securely retained.

Rear 'half liner'

13 Remove the three screws securing the liner to the edge of the rear bumper, then prise out the clip securing it to the inner wing, and withdraw the liner.
14 Refitting is a reversal of removal.

Rear 'full liner'

15 To remove the full rear wheel arch liner fitted to some models, the rear shock absorber must first be removed, as described in Chapter 10.
16 Work around the inside of the arch liner, and prise out the clips (approximately six

23.8 Take care when prising the clips at the rear of the arch

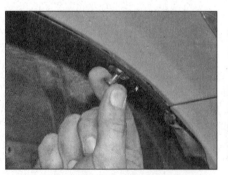

23.9 Remove the clips around the arch liner

23.11 Removing a front wheel arch liner

in total) securing the liner to the wheel arch. It may be necessary to wipe the liner clean, to see them clearly. Take care, as the clips are easily broken – special forked tools are available for removing these clips, and these are preferable to using a flat-bladed screwdriver.

17 Remove the three screws securing the liner to the edge of the rear bumper. In addition, there are four bolts to remove – two at the top, one into the inner wing near the front, and one right at the front.

18 Release the liner and withdraw it from under the wheel arch.

19 On refitting, renew any retaining clips that may have been broken on removal, and ensure that the panel is securely retained.

Body trim strips and badges

20 The various body trim strips and badges are held in position with a special adhesive tape and locating lugs. Removal requires the trim/badge to be heated, to soften the adhesive, and then carefully lifted away from the surface. Due to the high risk of damage to the paintwork during this operation, it is recommended that this task should be entrusted to a Honda dealer.

24 Seats – removal and refitting

Note: *Refer to the airbag warnings in Chapter 12 if removing front seats with side airbags. Before disconnecting the battery, refer to Disconnecting the battery at the rear of this manual.*

Removal

Front seats

1 On models with side airbags (identifiable by having an AIRBAG label on the side of the front seat), disconnect the battery negative lead, and wait for at least 3 minutes before proceeding (refer to *Disconnecting the battery*). If this precaution is not taken, there is a risk that the side airbags will fire when the seat wiring plug is disconnected.

2 Slide the seat fully to the front. Unclip and remove the plastic end caps from the rear of each seat rail (these wrap around the seat rail, and have slots which fit over locating tabs – splay the sides outwards to remove). Unscrew and remove the two seat rear mounting bolts **(see illustration)**.

3 Slide the seat fully rearwards. Remove the plastic end caps from the front of each seat rail (like those at the rear, these locate over tabs on the seat rail, and should be folded outwards to remove) **(see illustration)**. Unscrew and remove the two seat front mounting bolts.

4 Tilt the seat backwards and disconnect the wiring plugs underneath for the side airbag, seat heating and seat belt buckle signalling, as applicable **(see illustrations)**.

24.2a Unclip the seat rail rear covers . . .

5 Carefully remove the seat from inside the car, taking care not to damage the surrounding trim panels. The help of an assistant may be necessary, as the seat is heavy.

Rear seats

6 First, lift each seat cushion and detach the footwell carpet from the base of the seat – the carpet is attached with Velcro **(see illustration)**. Lower the seat into its normal position once this is done.

7 Fold each backrest forwards about halfway, to create a gap between the backrest and cushion, then feed the seat belt buckles through. Each buckle has an elasticated loop which it must be pulled through **(see illustration)**.

8 Fold both backrests fully forwards (remove the rear headrests if necessary). Prise out the row of clips securing the front edge of

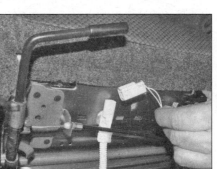

24.4a Disconnect the seat side airbag wiring plug underneath . . .

24.6 Detach the footwell carpet from the front of the seat

24.2b . . . and remove the seat rear mounting bolts

24.3 Removing the seat rail cover at the front

the boot carpet to the back of the seat, and remove the boot carpet/spare wheel cover **(see illustration)**.

9 Unscrew and remove the four seat hinge

24.4b . . . and the seat belt signalling plug

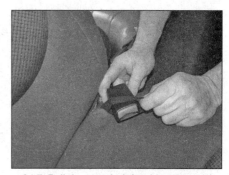

24.7 Pull the seat belt buckles through their loops, and through the seat

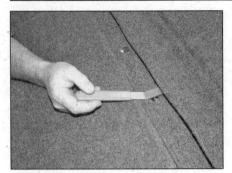

24.8 Prise up the clips securing the boot carpet to the seat backs

24.9a Unscrew and remove the seat hinge bolts ...

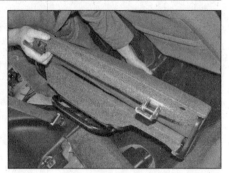

24.9b ... and remove the rear seats from the car

bolts from the floor, then lift the seats and remove them from the car **(see illustrations)**

Refitting

10 Refitting is a reversal of removal, noting the following points:

a) *Before reconnecting the front seat wiring, on models with side airbags, ensure that the battery is still disconnected.*

b) *Tighten the seat mounting bolts (or seat hinge bolts) to the specified torque.*

25 Front seat belt tensioners – general information and precautions

The front seat belt inertia reels are fitted with integral automatic belt tensioners (the rear seat belt inertia reels are not fitted with tensioners). The system is designed to instantaneously take up any slack in the seat

belt in the case of a sudden frontal impact, therefore reducing the possibility of injury to the front seat occupants.

The seat belt tensioner is triggered by a frontal impact above a predetermined force. Lesser impacts, including impacts from behind, will not trigger the system. If the impact is sufficient to trigger the airbags, the seat belt tensioners will also be deployed.

When the system is triggered, the explosive gas in the tensioner mechanism retracts and locks the seat belt through a cable which acts on the inertia reel. This prevents the seat belt moving and keeps the occupant firmly in position in the seat. Once the tensioner has been triggered, the seat belt will be permanently locked and the assembly must be renewed.

Note the following warnings before contemplating any work on the front seat belts.

⚠️ *Warning: Do not expose the tensioner mechanism to temperatures in excess of 100°C.*

• *If the tensioner mechanism is dropped, it must be renewed, even it has suffered no apparent damage.*

• *Do not allow any solvents to come into contact with the tensioner mechanism.*

• *Do not attempt to open the tensioner mechanism as it contains explosive gas.*

• *Tensioners must be discharged before they are disposed of, but this task should be entrusted to a Honda dealer.*

• *Before removing the front seat belt inertia reels, the battery negative lead must be disconnected. Once disconnected, wait at least 3 minutes before proceeding, otherwise there is a risk that the tensioners will fire when the inertia reel wiring plug is disconnected. The battery must remain disconnected until after the tensioner wiring plug is reconnected.*

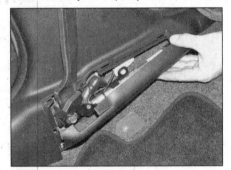

26.3a Unclip the trim panel upwards for access to ...

26.3b ... the lower anchor bolt

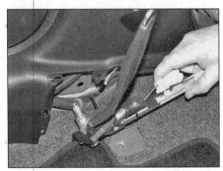

26.3c Unscrew the anchor bolt, withdraw the belt ...

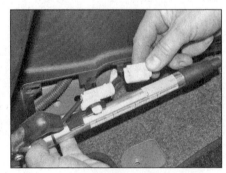

26.3d ... and disconnect the tensioner wiring plug

26 Seat belt components – removal and refitting

Front seat belt

Note: *Refer to the warnings in Section 25.*

1 Disconnect the battery negative lead (refer to *Disconnecting the battery* in the *Reference* Chapter at the end of this manual). Wait at least 3 minutes before proceeding.

2 Slide the front seat fully forwards.

3 On some models, the lower anchor bolt can be accessed directly. On others, a trim panel at the base of the B-pillar must be unclipped upwards first. Unscrew the lower anchor bolt, noting carefully how the washers and bushes are arranged, and move the belt clear. Disconnect the wiring plug from the seat belt tensioner **(see illustrations)**.

4 Unclip the seat belt upper anchor's plastic cover by pressing the sides inwards with a small screwdriver, then pulling the cover upwards and forwards. Unscrew and remove the upper anchor bolt, again noting carefully how the washers and bushes are arranged **(see illustrations)**.

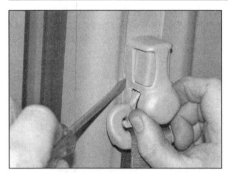

26.4a Unclip the cover using a small screwdriver . . .

26.4b . . . for access to the upper anchor bolt

26.4c Remove the upper bolt, and withdraw the belt

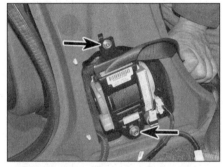

26.6a Unscrew the reel upper and lower bolts . . .

26.6b . . . then withdraw the reel from its location . . .

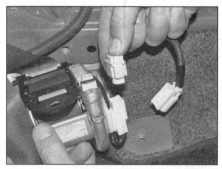

26.6c . . . and disconnect the reel tensioner wiring plug

5 Remove the rear sill and B-pillar lower trim panels as described in Section 27.
6 Unscrew the upper mounting bolt and (larger) lower bolt, withdraw the inertia reel and belt, then disconnect the reel tensioner wiring plug (note that this has a spring-loaded locking collar) (see illustrations).
7 Refitting is a reversal of removal, noting the following points:
a) Apply thread-locking fluid to the upper anchor bolt.
b) Tighten all bolts to the specified torque, where given.
c) Ensure that the battery is still disconnected before reconnecting the tensioner wiring plug.

Front height adjuster

8 Unclip the seat belt upper anchor's plastic cover by pressing the sides inwards with a small screwdriver, then pulling the cover upwards and forwards. Unscrew and remove the upper anchor bolt, again noting carefully how the washers and bushes are arranged.
9 Remove the B-pillar upper trim panel as described in Section 27.
10 Unscrew the height adjuster upper and lower mounting bolts (only one bolt is accessible at a time – slide the adjuster up or down as required), and remove the adjuster from the B-pillar (see illustration).
11 Refitting is a reversal of removal, noting the following points:
a) Apply thread-locking fluid to the upper anchor bolt.
b) Tighten all bolts to the specified torque, where given.

Front belt stalk

12 Remove the front seat as described in Section 24.
13 Unclip and remove the plastic cover from the inner side of the seat (see illustration).
14 Disconnect the wiring from the seat occupancy monitor and stalk buckle indicator (where applicable), and unclip the wiring from under the seat.
15 Unscrew the stalk mounting bolt, noting carefully how the washers are arranged, and remove the stalk from the seat (see illustration).
16 Refitting is a reversal of removal. Engage the stalk's mounting lug into the hole on the seat frame, and tighten the mounting bolt to the specified torque.

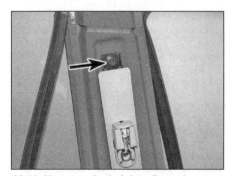

26.10 Unscrew the height adjuster's upper and lower bolts

26.13 Unclip the seat's side plastic cover

26.15 Front belt stalk mounting bolt

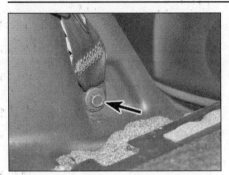

26.17a Unscrew the seat lower anchor bolt . . .

26.17b . . . noting how the washers and bushes are arranged

26.18a Unclip the cover from the upper anchor arm . . .

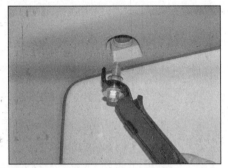

26.18b . . . then remove the upper anchor bolt, and remove the arm

Rear side belts

Outer belts

17 Lift up the rear seat cushion, and unscrew the seat belt lower anchor bolt, noting carefully

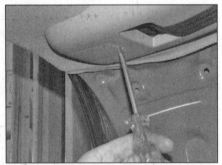

26.21a Prise down the hinged cover at the rear . . .

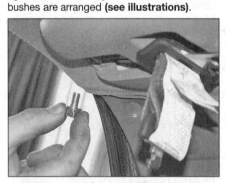

26.20 Remove the two inertia reel bolts, and remove the belt

how the washers and bushes are arranged (see illustrations).

18 Unclip the cover from the upper anchor arm, then unscrew the upper anchor bolt – again, note carefully how the washers and bushes are arranged (see illustrations).

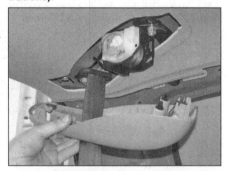

26.21b . . . and remove the bolt inside

19 Remove the luggage area side trim panel as described in Section 27.

20 Unscrew the upper mounting bolt and (larger) lower bolt, and remove the inertia reel and belt from the car (see illustration).

Centre belt

21 Unclip the belt end from the front of the belt cover on the headlining. Using a screwdriver in the slot provided, prise down the rear hinged cover, then unscrew the bolt inside. Release the two clips at the front, and take down the centre belt cover (see illustrations).

22 Remove the C-pillar trim panel as described in Section 27.

23 Remove the large bolt behind the inertia reel, and the smaller bolt at the end of the mounting arm. Carefully withdraw the inertia reel from the headlining (see illustrations).

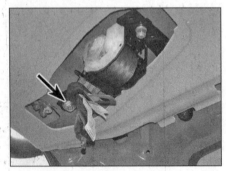

26.23a Remove the bolt behind the inertia reel . . .

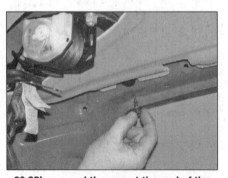

26.23b . . . and the one at the end of the mounting arm . . .

26.21c Unclip the cover at the front, and remove it from the headlining

26.23c . . . then withdraw the centre belt reel from the headlining

26.25 Pull the buckles through their elastic loops, and through the seat

26.26 Prise up the row of clips securing the boot carpet to the rear seats

26.27 Unscrew the rear seat belt buckle mounting bolt

24 Refitting is a reversal of removal. Tighten all bolts to the specified torque.

Rear belt buckles

25 Fold each backrest forwards about halfway, to create a gap between the backrest and cushion, then feed the seat belt buckles through. Each buckle has an elasticated loop which it must be pulled through **(see illustration)**.
26 Fold both backrests fully forwards (remove the rear headrests if necessary). Prise out the row of clips securing the front edge of the boot carpet to the back of the seat, and remove the boot carpet/spare wheel cover **(see illustration)**.
27 Unscrew the buckle mounting bolts as required, and remove the buckles from the car **(see illustration)**.
28 Refitting is a reversal of removal. Tighten all bolts to the specified torque.

27 Interior trim and fittings – removal and refitting

General

1 The interior trim panels are secured by a combination of clips and screws, with plastic clips featuring heavily – these clips often get 'left behind' in the bodywork when the panels are removed, and should be prised out for refitting to the panels. Removal and refitting is generally self-explanatory, noting that it may be necessary to remove or loosen surrounding panels to allow a particular panel to be removed. The following paragraphs describe the removal and refitting of the major panels in more detail.

Door trim panels

2 Refer to Section 13.

Steering column shrouds

3 Working in the driver's footwell, remove the three screws from the lower shroud **(see illustration)**.
4 Unclip the upper shroud from the lower one, and withdraw it **(see illustration)**.
5 Remove the lower shroud, manoeuvring it out past the column height adjuster lever, and over the ignition switch **(see illustration)**.
6 Refitting is a reversal of removal.

Driver's lower facia trim panels

Fusebox surround

7 Pull out the fusebox cover, and remove it **(see illustration)**.
8 Remove the two screws at the top of the panel, then release the row of four clips along the bottom. Pull back the driver's tray to free the hooks on the left-hand side of the panel, and remove it **(see illustrations)**.

27.3 Remove the three screws from the column lower shroud

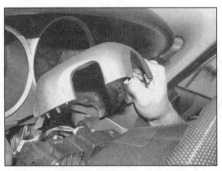

27.4 Unclip the upper shroud from the lower one

27.5 Work the lower shroud down over the column adjuster and ignition switch

27.7 Pull out the fusebox cover

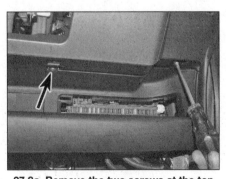

27.8a Remove the two screws at the top of the panel . . .

27.8b . . . then release the lower clips and hooks, and remove it

27.10 Turn the fastener on the left to release the closing panel

9 Refitting is a reversal of removal.

Facia closing panel

10 Release the turn-buckle fastener on the left side of the panel by turning it through 90° **(see illustration)**.

11 Pull the front edge of the panel down to release the two clips, then pull the panel away from the facia, to release the inner rear clip from its guide, and the outer rear peg from the footwell kick panel **(see illustration)**.

12 Refitting is a reversal of removal. Line up the rear clip and pin when offering the panel into place.

Facia centre control panel

13 Refer to the heater control panel removal procedure, in Chapter 3, Section 9.

Passenger's facia closing panel

14 Pull the panel down at the front to release the two clips securing it to the facia, then

27.11 Removing the driver's-side facia closing panel

pull the panel away from the facia, to release the two rear clips from their guides **(see illustration)**.

15 Refitting is a reversal of removal.

Storage trays

16 The storage trays running along the base of the facia can only be removed once the main facia panel has been removed, as described in Section 29.

Glovebox

17 To remove the glovebox inner section, open the lid. If the glovebox is full, it may be advisable to empty it now. Gently pull the glovebox 'liner' towards you, and withdraw it from the glovebox – note that it has a protruding tab on the back, which locates in a slot in the crossmember behind the facia **(see illustration)**.

18 To remove the glovebox lid, close the lid,

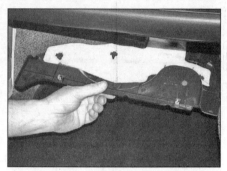

27.14 Removing the passenger-side facia closing panel

then unscrew and remove the two glovebox hinge bolts from below **(see illustrations)**.

19 Refitting is a reversal of removal.

A-pillar trim panels

20 Pull back the rubber weatherstrip along the edge of the panel. The A-pillar trim panels are held in place by two clips along their length, and there are locating lugs along the bottom edge. Start at the top of the panel, and pull the panel towards the facia to release the clips **(see illustrations)**.

21 Lift the panel to free the lugs at the base from the facia, and remove it **(see illustration)**.

22 Refitting is a reversal of removal. Transfer any clips back onto the panel as necessary before refitting.

Front footwell kick panels

23 Remove the facia closing panel on the

27.17 Pull out the glovebox 'liner'

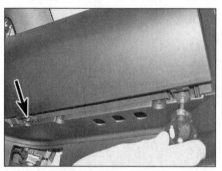

27.18a Unscrew the two glovebox hinge bolts from below . . .

27.18b . . . and withdraw the glovebox from the facia

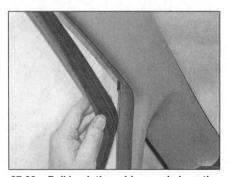

27.20a Pull back the rubber seal along the panel edges . . .

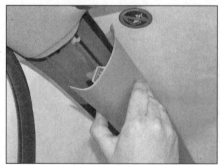

27.20b . . . then start by unclipping the A-pillar trim panel at the top

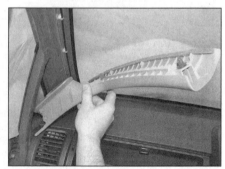

27.21 Lift the A-pillar trim panel to free it from the facia

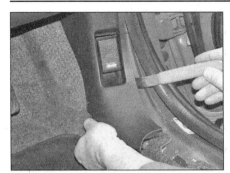

27.24a On the driver's side, prise the kick panel to release the clips . . .

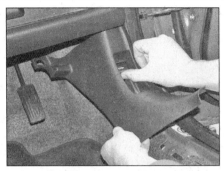

27.24b . . . then work the panel around the bonnet release lever . . .

27.24c . . . and remove it

27.24d On the passenger side, pull back the rubber seal . . .

27.24e . . . and unclip the kick panel

27.26 Unclip the front of the B-pillar trim panel from the sill trim panel

side concerned, as described previously in this Section.

24 The panel is secured by two clips. Pull the panel into the car to release the clips, then ease the surrounding panels clear so that the kick panel can be removed. If working on the driver's side, twist the kick panel to free it from the bonnet release lever **(see illustrations)**.

25 Refitting is a reversal of removal. Transfer any clips back onto the panel as necessary before refitting.

Sill trim panels

Front

26 Pull up the rubber weather strip to free the edge of the panel, then unclip the front of the B-pillar trim panel inwards where it meets the sill panel **(see illustration)**.

27 Starting at one end, pull upwards on the sill panel to release the three clips, then unhook

the carpet from the clips inside the panel, and remove it from the car **(see illustrations)**.

28 Refitting is a reversal of removal.

Rear

29 Pull up the rubber weather strip to free the

edge of the panel, then unclip the rear of the B-pillar trim panel inwards where it meets the sill panel **(see illustration)**.

30 Carefully prise the sill panel upwards and inwards to release the three clips, and remove the panel from the car **(see illustration)**.

27.27a Prise the sill trim panel upwards . . .

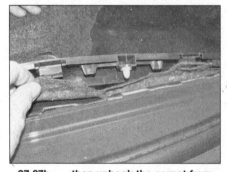

27.27b . . . then unhook the carpet from the clips inside . . .

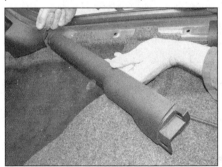

27.27c . . . and remove the panel

27.29 Unclip the back of the B-pillar trim panel inwards

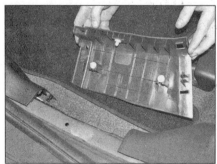

27.30 Pull the sill trim panel up and inwards to release the clips

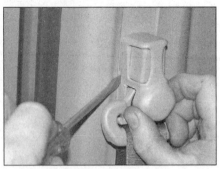

27.33a Unclip the seat belt anchor cover using a small screwdriver . . .

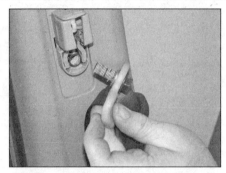

27.33b . . . then unscrew the anchor bolt, and remove the seat belt

27.34 Removing the B-pillar upper trim panel

27.36 Pull upwards to remove the access panel at the base of the B-pillar

31 Refitting is a reversal of removal.

B-pillar trim panels

32 Detach the rubber weatherstrip from the B-pillar as necessary to free the edges of the trim panel.

27.37a Pull the rubber seals away from the panel sides

Upper panel

33 Unclip the seat belt upper anchor's plastic cover by pressing the sides inwards with a small screwdriver, then pulling the cover upwards and forwards. Unscrew and remove

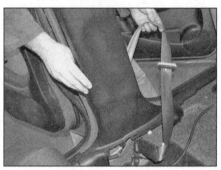

27.37b Removing the B-pillar lower trim panel

the upper anchor bolt, noting carefully how the washers and bushes are arranged (see illustrations).

34 Pull the panel out at the top to release the clip, then lift it to free the lower mounting lugs, and remove it from the car (see illustration).

35 Refitting is a reversal of removal. Apply thread-locking fluid to the seat belt upper anchor bolt, then tighten it to the specified torque.

Lower panel

36 Where applicable, unclip the seat belt access panel at the base first, by sliding it upwards (see illustration).

37 Pull back the rubber weatherseals from the sides of the panel. At the top of the panel, pull both sides outwards to release them. Pull the panel out at the top to release the clip, then release it from the sill trim panels, and remove it from the car (see illustrations).

38 Refitting is a reversal of removal.

Rear trim panels

C-pillar trim panel

39 Open the rear door and tailgate, and pull the rubber weatherstrips off the edges of the trim panel (see illustration).

40 Unclip the cover from the seat belt upper anchor arm, then unscrew the upper anchor bolt – note carefully how the washers and bushes are arranged (see illustrations).

41 Take out the parcel shelf/load cover, then remove the two screws at the top of the luggage area trim panel (see illustration). Note that these two screws secure both the C-pillar and luggage area side panels.

27.39 Pull the rubber seals off the edges of the C-pillar trim panel

27.40a Unclip the seat belt arm's cover . . .

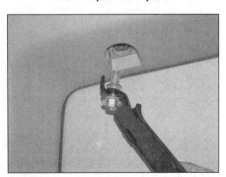

27.40b . . . then unscrew the upper anchor bolt

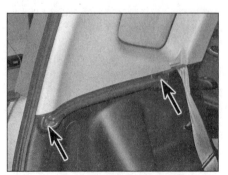

27.41 Remove the two screws from the side trim panel

27.42 Removing the C-pillar trim panel

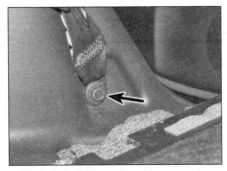

27.46 Unbolt the seat belt lower anchor bolt from the trim panel

27.47 Unclip the side panel from the sill panel

27.49 Unbolt and remove the tie-down hooks

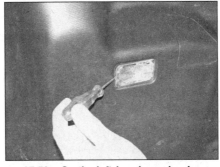

27.50a On the left-hand panel, prise out . . .

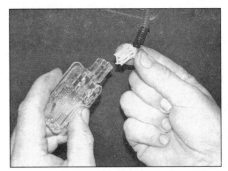

27.50b . . . and disconnect the boot light

42 Starting at the bottom, pull the panel into the car to release the clips around its edge, and remove it. Pull the top of the luggage area side panel out slightly, as the C-pillar panel fits behind it (see illustration).

43 Refitting is a reversal of removal. Tighten the seat belt anchor bolt to the specified torque.

Luggage area side panel

44 Remove the luggage area rear panel as described later in this Section.

45 Open the rear door, and pull the rubber weatherstrip forward to free the front edge of the trim panel.

46 Unscrew the seat belt lower anchor bolt, noting carefully how the washers and bushes are arranged (see illustration).

47 Release the side panel from the sill trim panel, then fold forwards the rear seat backrest on the side concerned (see illustration).

48 Take out the parcel shelf/load cover, then remove the two screws at the top of the luggage area trim panel (see illustration 27.41).

49 Remove the single screw from each of the two tie-down hooks, and lift them off the base of the panel (see illustration).

50 If working on the left-hand panel, prise out the boot light, and disconnect the wiring plug (see illustrations).

51 Starting at the top, pull the panel into the car to release the clips, and remove it (see illustration).

52 Refitting is a reversal of removal. Tighten the seat belt anchor bolt to the specified torque.

Luggage area rear panel

53 The trim panel has a row of four clips along its top edge, and two hooked lugs at each side, further down. Starting at one end, carefully prise the panel upwards to free the clips, then lift it off the two hooked lugs and remove it (see illustration).

54 Refitting is a reversal of removal.

Tailgate trim panels

Inner trim panel

55 Open the tailgate, then prise out the pull handle from the main panel – the pull handle is secured by two clips (see illustration).

56 Next to the handle, there is another clip to remove. This type of clip is released by pushing the centre pin inwards, then prising

27.51 Removing the luggage area side trim panel

27.53 Removing the luggage area rear trim panel

27.55 Prise out the tailgate pull handle

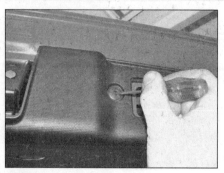

27.56a Gently push in the clip's centre pin . . .

27.56b . . . then prise out the clip's outer body

27.57 Removing the tailgate inner trim panel

the body of the clip out. To 'reset' the clip for refitting, push the pin back through so it is proud of the top, then insert the clip and press the pin in so it is flush (see illustrations).

57 Starting at one corner, pull the panel downwards to release the clips, and remove it from the car (see illustration).

58 Refitting is a reversal of removal.

Outer trim panel (handle cover)

59 Remove the inner trim panel from the inside of the tailgate, as described previously in this Section.

60 Remove the tailgate wiper motor as described in Chapter 12.

61 Working inside the tailgate, remove the single outer trim panel bolt on the left, then use pliers to squeeze and release the black and white plastic panel retaining clips, and withdraw the panel from the outside (see illustrations).

62 Refitting is a reversal of removal.

Carpets

63 The passenger compartment floor carpet is in several pieces, and is secured along the edges by various types of clips.

64 Carpet removal and refitting is reasonably straightforward, but time-consuming, due to the fact that all adjoining trim panels must be released, and the seats and centre console must be removed.

Grab handles

65 Carefully prise out the screw covers using a small screwdriver (see illustration).

66 Unscrew and remove the single screw at each end of the handle, and remove it from the roof.

67 Refitting is a reversal of removal.

Sun visors

68 Unclip the visor from the inner support,

then move it for the best access to the outer mounting.

69 Remove the two screws from the outer mounting and remove the visor from the headlining (see illustration).

70 If required, the inner support can be removed by twisting it 90° anti-clockwise (see illustration).

71 Refitting is a reversal of removal.

Headlining

72 The headlining is clipped to the roof, and can be withdrawn only once all fittings such as the grab handles, sun visors, sunroof, A-, B- and C-pillar trim panels, and associated components have been removed. The door, tailgate and sunroof aperture weatherseals will also have to be prised clear.

73 Note that headlining removal requires considerable skill and experience if it is to be

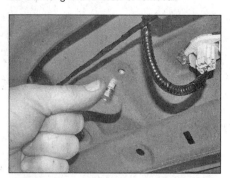

27.61a Remove the trim panel bolt on the left . . .

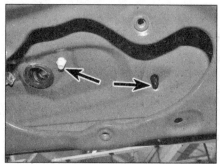

27.61b . . . then squeeze the tabs on the black and white plastic clips . . .

27.61c . . . and remove the tailgate outer trim panel

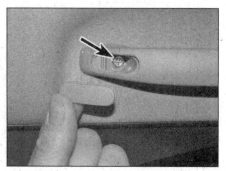

27.65 Prise out the grab handle end covers to access the screws

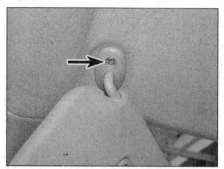

27.69 Remove the two screws from the sun visor outer mounting

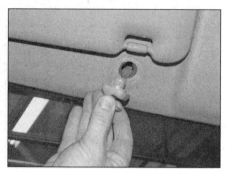

27.70 The sun visor inner support twists through 90° for removal

carried out without damage, and is therefore best entrusted to an expert.

Interior mirror

74 Starting at the front edge, carefully prise down the mirror trim panel from the headlining, and remove it **(see illustration)**.

75 Remove the three mirror mounting screws, then unclip the mirror from the holder on the windscreen, and remove it completely.

76 Refitting is a reversal of removal. Tighten the mirror screws securely.

28 Centre console – removal and refitting

Removal

1 Slide both front seats fully forwards. Although not essential, access is greatly improved if one or both front seats are removed as described in Section 24.

2 Taking care not to mark the trim, use a flat-bladed screwdriver to prise out the curved trim panel in front of the handbrake lever **(see illustration)**.

3 On manual transmission models, unscrew the gear lever knob **(see illustration)**.

4 Locate the clip on either side of the console, at the front. Push in each clip's centre pin, then prise out the clip body **(see illustration)**.

5 Remove the screw on either side of the console, at the rear **(see illustration)**.

6 Lift the console at the back, then slide it

rearwards to release it from the floor clip in the centre of its length **(see illustration)**.

7 Lift the console at the front, disconnect the cigar lighter wiring plug from below, and remove the console completely **(see illustration)**.

Refitting

8 Refitting is a reversal of removal. Note that the console has a slot under the rear storage pocket, which locates over the handbrake lever bracket.

29 Facia panel assembly – removal and refitting

Removal

Facia panel

Note: *This is a complicated procedure – it is strongly recommended that this Section is read through thoroughly before starting work. The plastic facia panel is removed WITH the metal crossmember underneath it – if required, the panel can be separated from the crossmember after removal.*

⚠ *Warning: Remove the ignition key, disconnect both battery leads, negative first (see Disconnecting the battery). Wait at least 3 minutes before starting work. If this precaution is not observed, there is danger of activating the airbags and seat belt tensioners.*

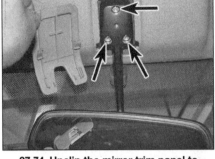

27.74 Unclip the mirror trim panel to access the three mounting screws

1 Disconnect the battery negative lead (refer to *Disconnecting the battery* in the *Reference* Chapter at the end of this manual).

2 Remove the centre console as described in Section 28.

3 Referring to Section 27, remove the following trim panels:
a) *Driver's lower facia panels.*
b) *Glovebox.*
c) *A-pillar trim panels.*
d) *Front footwell kick panels.*

4 Working in the passenger's footwell, remove the single screw/clip and take out the lower heater duct from the base of the facia **(see illustration)**.

5 Unclip the wiring harness from the central heater duct, then slide the duct downwards off the heater assembly. Release the two clips

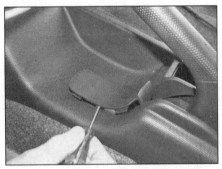

28.2 Prise up the curved panel in front of the handbrake lever

28.3 Unscrew the gear lever knob

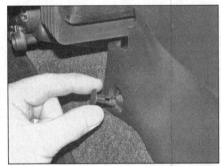

28.4 Remove the clip on either side at the front of the console

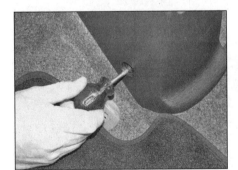

28.5 Remove the screw either side at the rear

28.6 Lift the console at the back, and slide it rearwards

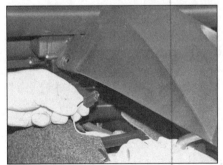

28.7 Unplug the cigar lighter, and remove the console

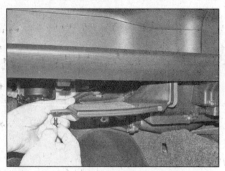

29.4 Remove the screw/clip and take out the passenger footwell heater duct

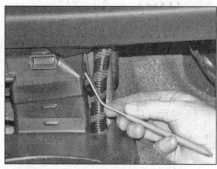

29.5a Prise off the wiring harness . . .

29.5b . . . then slide the duct down off the heater unit . . .

29.5c Prise up the floor clip either side . . .

29.5d . . . then slide the duct back and lift it out

(if necessary, attach labels for easier refitting):
a) *Driver's door wiring harness plugs at the right-hand end. Unclip the wiring plugs from the body* **(see illustrations)**.
b) *Brake pedal position switch* **(see illustration)**.
c) *Fusebox wiring plugs* **(see illustrations)**.
d) *On models with automatic air conditioning, disconnect the cabin temperature sensor, and pull off the air hose from behind the small facia grille.*

9 Working around the centre console area, disconnect all the wiring plugs – there may be up to six of these, depending on model and equipment:
a) *Remove the fuel tank sender unit cover (four screws), and disconnect the wiring plug inside. Release the wiring grommet from the cover, and feed the wiring through it* **(see illustration)**.

securing it to the floor either side of the gear lever, and remove it **(see illustrations)**.
6 Remove the steering column as described in Chapter 10.

7 Remove the heater control panel as described in Chapter 3.
8 Working in the driver's footwell, look up under the facia, and disconnect the following

29.8a Disconnect the door harness plugs . . .

29.8b . . . and unclip them from the body

29.8c Disconnect the brake pedal position switch

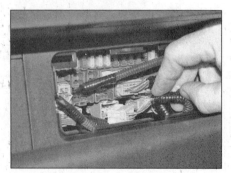

29.8d Unplug the fusebox wiring . . .

29.8e . . . and pull the fusebox harness down under the facia

29.9a Disconnect the wiring plug under the sender unit cover

29.9b Unplug the airbag control unit

29.9c Disconnect the oxygen sensor wiring plug

29.9d Unplug the handbrake warning light switch

29.9e Unscrew the bolt and remove the multi-earth lead

29.11 Remove the two bolts from the brake pedal support bracket

29.12 Remove the floor support bracket bolts

b) *Airbag control unit wiring plugs (see illustration).*
c) *Oxygen sensor wiring plug (see illustration).*
d) *Handbrake warning light switch plug (see illustration).*
e) *Remove the multi-terminal earth lead in this area, which is secured by a single T30 Torx screw (see illustration).*
f) *Unclip the wiring harness from the floor bracket, and feed it back towards the facia.*

10 From the passenger footwell, reach up behind the facia as necessary, and disconnect all the wiring plugs, including the ECM wiring connector, inertia switch, and the aerial lead. Attach labels as required, to ensure correct refitting. Unclip the additional wiring plugs from the ECM bracket.

11 Above the brake pedal, remove the two bolts securing the brake pedal support bracket, and take it off **(see illustration)**.
12 Remove the two small floor support bracket bolts in the centre, from the driver's footwell **(see illustration)**.
13 If not already done, release all the disconnected wiring harnesses from the facia securing clips and ties – note how it is routed, for refitting.
14 Open the passenger front door, and prise off the caps from the three bolts on the end of the facia **(see illustration)**.
15 Unscrew the first bolt until it is felt to be free of the threads, then pull it outwards and continue turning it in a loosening direction. Keep turning the bolt until it can be removed completely **(see illustration)**. Repeat this process for the other two bolts. **Note:** *The*

bolt which is furthest to the front cannot be removed completely as it hits the door – remove it as far as possible for now.
16 The three large nuts now visible at the end of the facia have a **left-hand thread**, meaning they tighten by turning in the unscrewing direction (anti-clockwise, or spanner moving 'upwards'). Using a 21 mm spanner, turn the three nuts gently anti-clockwise – do not use any force, just ensure they are turned fully anti-clockwise **(see illustration)**.
17 Open the driver's door, and prise off the caps from the three bolts on the end of the facia. Unscrew and remove the bolts **(see illustrations)**.
18 The facia panel now rests on five locating pins – one each side, and three along the windscreen. With the help of an assistant, lift the facia evenly both sides to clear the pins.

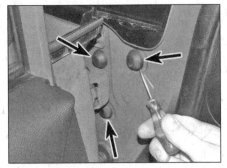

29.14 Prise off the caps from the three facia bolts at the passenger's end

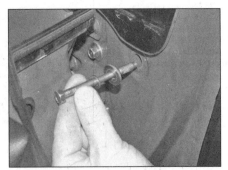

29.15 Unscrew the bolt, pull it out, then unscrew until it can be removed

29.16 Gently turn the three facia end nuts fully anti-clockwise

29.17a Prise off the caps from the driver's-side facia end bolts . . .

29.17c . . . and remove them

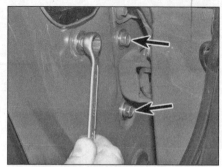

29.17b . . . then unscrew all three . . .

29.18 Removing the facia panel

Check that nothing is still attached to the facia to prevent its removal, then take the facia out through one of the doors **(see illustration)**.

Crossmember

19 With the facia removed, the metal crossmember can be separated from the facia panel if required, as follows.
20 Remove the instrument panel and passenger airbag as described in Chapter 12.
21 Remove the two screws securing the driver's side heater duct, and take off the duct.

22 Remove a total of seven screws, and take off the driver's storage tray from the back of the facia.
23 Similarly, remove a total of eight screws, and take off the passenger storage tray from the back of the facia.
24 Unclip the aerial lead from the facia, noting how it is routed.
25 The crossmember is secured to the facia by two bolts and eight screws along its length. Remove the bolts and screws.
26 Disconnect the wiring plugs from the following facia switches (if not already done):

a) *Hazard warning light switch.*
b) *Headlight adjuster switch.*
c) *Mirror adjuster switch.*
d) *VSA 'off' switch.*

27 Unclip the switch wiring harness from the facia as necessary.
28 On models with satellite navigation, unclip the GPS aerial in the centre of the facia.
29 Lift the crossmember away from the facia panel, taking care that none of the wiring harness gets caught up, and remove it.
30 Refitting is a reversal of removal. Ensure that the wiring doesn't get trapped as the crossmember is offered into position.

Refitting

31 With the help of an assistant, offer the facia into position, and locate it onto the five guide pins. Take care that none of the wiring gets trapped as this is done.
32 Tighten the three bolts on the driver's side, and the two floor bracket bolts in the driver's footwell, to the specified torque.
33 Fit the first of the special passenger-side facia bolts, and tighten it (clockwise) until the bolt threads are fully engaged with the large nut. Push the bolt inwards, and continue tightening it. Tighten the bolt to the specified torque. Repeat this process on the other two bolts.
34 Further refitting is a reversal of the removal procedure, noting the following points:
a) *Make sure the wiring is correctly routed and connected, and secure where necessary with cable-ties. Do not allow the wiring harness to get trapped or pinched during refitting.*
b) *On completion, check that all the electrical components and switches function correctly. As a precaution against the airbags being activated, make sure no one is sitting in the car as the battery is being reconnected.*

Chapter 12
Body electrical system

Contents

Degrees of difficulty

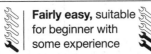

Easy, suitable for novice with little experience	**Fairly easy,** suitable for beginner with some experience	**Fairly difficult,** suitable for competent DIY mechanic	**Difficult,** suitable for experienced DIY mechanic	**Very difficult,** suitable for expert DIY or professional

Specifications

General
System type . . . .   12 volt, negative earth

Fuses
Refer to labels on fusebox lids

Bulbs

	Type	Wattage
Courtesy light:		
Front.	Festoon	5
Rear	Festoon	8
Front direction indicator light*	Push-fit	21
Front direction indicator side repeater light*	Push-fit	5
Front foglight	H11	55
Front sidelight.	Push-fit	5
Headlight:		
Conventional type.	H4	60/55
HID type	-	35
High-level stop-light.	Push-fit	21
Luggage compartment light.	Push-fit	5
Map reading lights	Festoon	8
Number plate light	Push-fit	5
Rear direction indicator light*	Push-fit	21
Rear foglight	Push-fit	21
Reversing light	Push-fit	21
Stop/tail light	Push-fit	21/5

* *Amber bulb*

1 General information and precautions

⚠️ *Warning: Before carrying out any work on the electrical system, read through the precautions given in Safety first! at the beginning of this manual.*

The electrical system is of 12 volt negative-earth type. Power for the lights and all electrical accessories is supplied by a lead-acid battery which is charged by the alternator.

This Chapter covers repair and service procedures for the various electrical components not associated with the engine. Information on the battery, alternator, and starter motor can be found in Chapter 5A; the ignition system is covered in Chapter 5B.

All UK models are fitted with an engine immobiliser. A transponder chip fitted to the ignition key automatically disarms the immobiliser when it is inserted into the ignition switch. Various different alarm systems were also available as an option. For more information, refer to Section 19.

All models are fitted with airbags for the driver and front seat passenger, which are designed to prevent serious chest and head injuries during a frontal accident. Some Jazz models also have side airbags, fitted into the front seat side cushions. For more information, refer to Section 20.

All models are fitted with a manually-controlled headlight levelling system, with a facia-mounted control. On position 0, the headlights are in their base (normal) position – from here, turn the control to lower the aim of the headlights according to the load being carried.

It should be noted that, when portions of the electrical system are serviced, the lead should be disconnected from the battery negative terminal, to prevent electrical shorts and fires (refer to *Disconnecting the battery* at the end of this manual).

2 Electrical fault finding – general information

Note: *Refer to the precautions given in Safety first! and at the beginning of Chapter 5A before starting work. The following tests relate to testing of the main electrical circuits, and should not be used to test delicate electronic circuits (such as the airbag or anti-lock braking systems), particularly where an electronic control module is used.*

General

1 A typical electrical circuit consists of an electrical component, any switches, relays, motors, fuses, fusible links or circuit breakers related to that component, and the wiring and connectors which link the component to both the battery and the chassis. To help to pinpoint a problem in an electrical circuit, wiring diagrams are included at the end of this Chapter.

2 Before attempting to diagnose an electrical fault, first study the appropriate wiring diagram, to obtain a more complete understanding of the components included in the particular circuit concerned. The possible sources of a fault can be narrowed down by noting whether other components related to the circuit are operating properly. If several components or circuits fail at one time, the problem is likely to be related to a shared fuse or earth connection.

3 Electrical problems usually stem from simple causes, such as loose or corroded connections, a faulty earth connection, a blown fuse, a melted fusible link, or a faulty relay (refer to Section 3 for details of testing relays). Visually inspect the condition of all fuses, wires and connections in a problem circuit before testing the components. Use the wiring diagrams to determine which terminal connections will need to be checked, in order to pinpoint the trouble-spot.

4 The basic tools required for electrical fault finding include a circuit tester or voltmeter (a 12 volt bulb with a set of test leads can also be used for certain tests); a self-powered test light (sometimes known as a continuity tester); an ohmmeter (to measure resistance); a battery and set of test leads; and a jumper wire, preferably with a circuit breaker or fuse incorporated, which can be used to bypass suspect wires or electrical components. Before attempting to locate a problem with test instruments, use the wiring diagram to determine where to make the connections.

5 To find the source of an intermittent wiring fault (usually due to a poor or dirty connection, or damaged wiring insulation), a 'wiggle' test can be performed on the wiring. This involves wiggling the wiring by hand, to see if the fault occurs as the wiring is moved. It should be possible to narrow down the source of the fault to a particular section of wiring. This method of testing can be used in conjunction with any of the tests described in the following sub-Sections.

6 Apart from problems due to poor connections, two basic types of fault can occur in an electrical circuit – open-circuit, or short-circuit.

7 Open-circuit faults are caused by a break somewhere in the circuit, which prevents current from flowing. An open-circuit fault will prevent a component from working, but will not cause the relevant circuit fuse to blow.

8 Short-circuit faults are caused by a 'short' somewhere in the circuit, which allows the current flowing in the circuit to 'escape' along an alternative route, usually to earth. Short-circuit faults are normally caused by a breakdown in wiring insulation, which allows a feed wire to touch either another wire, or an earthed component such as the bodyshell. A short-circuit fault will normally cause the relevant circuit fuse to blow.

Finding an open-circuit

9 To check for an open-circuit, connect one lead of a circuit tester or voltmeter to either the negative battery terminal or a known good earth.

10 Connect the other lead to a connector in the circuit being tested, preferably nearest to the battery or fuse.

11 Switch on the circuit, bearing in mind that some circuits are live only when the ignition switch is moved to a particular position.

12 If voltage is present (indicated either by the tester bulb lighting or a voltmeter reading, as applicable), this means that the section of the circuit between the relevant connector and the battery is problem-free.

13 Continue to check the remainder of the circuit in the same fashion.

14 When a point is reached at which no voltage is present, the problem must lie between that point and the previous test point with voltage. Most problems can be traced to a broken, corroded or loose connection.

Finding a short-circuit

15 To check for a short-circuit, first disconnect the load(s) from the circuit (loads are the components which draw current from a circuit, such as bulbs, motors, heating elements, etc).

16 Remove the relevant fuse from the circuit, and connect a circuit tester or voltmeter to the fuse connections.

17 Switch on the circuit, bearing in mind that some circuits are live only when the ignition switch is moved to a particular position.

18 If voltage is present (indicated either by the tester bulb lighting or a voltmeter reading, as applicable), this means that there is a short-circuit.

19 If no voltage is present, but the fuse still blows with the load(s) connected, this indicates an internal fault in the load(s).

Finding an earth fault

20 The battery negative terminal is connected to 'earth' – the metal of the engine/transmission unit and the car body – and most systems are wired so that they only receive a positive feed, the current returning via the metal of the car body. This means that the component mounting and the body form part of that circuit. Loose or corroded mountings can therefore cause a range of electrical faults, ranging from total failure of a circuit, to a puzzling partial fault.

21 In particular, lights may shine dimly (especially when another circuit sharing the same earth point is in operation), motors (eg, wiper motors or the radiator cooling fan motor) may run slowly, and the operation of one circuit may have an apparently-unrelated effect on another.

22 Note that on many vehicles, earth straps are used between certain components, such as the engine/transmission and the body, usually where there is no metal-to-metal contact between components, due to flexible rubber mountings, etc.

23 To check whether a component is properly earthed, disconnect the battery, and connect one lead of an ohmmeter to a known good earth point. Connect the other lead to the wire or earth connection being tested. The resistance reading should be zero; if not, check the connection as follows.

24 If an earth connection is thought to be faulty, dismantle the connection, and clean back to bare metal both the bodyshell and the wire terminal or the component earth connection mating surface. Be careful to remove all traces of dirt and corrosion, then use a knife to trim away any paint, so that a clean metal-to-metal joint is made.

25 On reassembly, tighten the joint fasteners securely; if a wire terminal is being refitted, use serrated washers between the terminal and the bodyshell, to ensure a clean and secure connection.

26 When the connection is remade, prevent the onset of corrosion in the future by applying a coat of petroleum jelly or silicone-based grease, or by spraying on (at regular intervals) a proprietary maintenance spray such as WD-40.

3 Fuses and relays – general information

Fuses

1 Fuses are designed to break a circuit when a predetermined current is reached, in order to protect the components and wiring which could be damaged by excessive current flow. Any excessive current flow will be due to a fault in the circuit, usually a short-circuit (see Section 2).

2 The main fuses are located in the fusebox, below and to the right of the steering column.

3 To access the fuses, use the pull handle built into the cover, and pull out the cover, which has clips along its upper and lower edges **(see illustration)**.

4 A blown fuse can be recognised from its melted or broken wire.

5 To remove a fuse, first ensure that the relevant circuit is switched off – for maximum safety, disconnect the battery (see *Disconnecting the battery*).

6 Pull the fuse from its location, using the plastic 'tweezer' tool provided inside the fusebox **(see illustration)**.

7 Before renewing a blown fuse, trace and rectify the cause, and always use a fuse of the correct rating. Never substitute a fuse of a higher rating, or make temporary repairs using wire or metal foil; more serious damage, or even fire, could result.

8 Note that the fuses are colour-coded as follows. Refer to the markings on the back of the glovebox for details of the circuits protected. Also note that the Jazz uses the later-type 'mini' fuses.

Colour	Rating
Orange	5A
Red	10A
Blue	15A
Yellow	20A
Clear or white	25A
Green	30A

9 Additional fuses are located the engine fusebox, behind the battery in the engine compartment. Some of these are rated at 60 amps – if any of these have blown, it indicates a serious wiring fault, which should be investigated. Just fitting a new fuse may cause further problems.

Relays

10 A relay is an electrically-operated switch, which is used for the following reasons:

a) *A relay can switch a heavy current remotely from the circuit in which the current is flowing, allowing the use of lighter-gauge wiring and switch contacts.*

b) *A relay can receive more than one control input, unlike a mechanical switch.*

c) *A relay can have a timer function – for example, the intermittent wiper relay.*

3.3 Unclip the fusebox cover below the steering column to access the fuses

11 Most of the relays are located under the facia, above the main fusebox. Additional relays are located in the engine fusebox, next to the battery in the engine compartment **(see illustration)**.

12 If a circuit or system controlled by a relay develops a fault, and the relay is suspect, operate the system. If the relay is functioning, it should be possible to hear it 'click' as it is energised. If this is the case, the fault lies with the components or wiring of the system. If the relay is not being energised, then either the relay is not receiving a main supply or a switching voltage, or the relay itself is faulty. Testing is by the substitution of a known good unit, but be careful – while some relays are identical in appearance and in operation, others look similar but perform different functions.

13 To remove a relay, first ensure that the relevant circuit is switched off. The relay can then simply be pulled out from the socket, and pushed back into position.

4 Switches – removal and refitting

Note: *Before removing any switch, disconnect the battery negative lead, and position the lead*

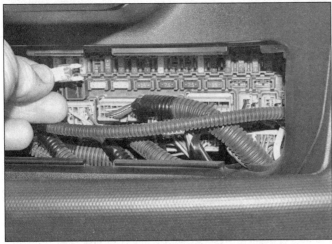

3.6 Pull out the fuse using the tool provided

3.11 Several relays are to be found in the engine compartment fusebox

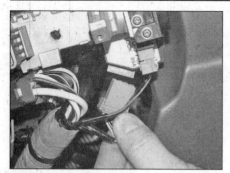

4.2a Disconnect the immobiliser reader coil wiring plug . . .

4.2b . . . remove the screw at the back . . .

4.2c . . . and the lower one of the two in front . . .

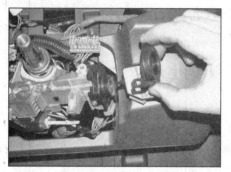

4.2d . . . then withdraw the coil from the ignition barrel

4.3a Disconnect the other green plug from the ignition key switch . . .

the lower one of the two in front, then take off the immobiliser reader coil (see illustrations).

3 Disconnect the second (green) wiring plug underneath, then remove the two screws (again, in front and behind) and take off the ignition key switch (see illustrations).

4 Disconnect the (brown) wiring plug from underneath the ignition switch (see illustration).

5 The ignition switch has two cross-head mounting screws – the one on the front is easy to reach, but the left one requires the use of a cranked tool or a socket bit. Remove the screws and withdraw the ignition switch (see illustrations).

6 Refitting is a reversal of removal. Ensure that all wiring plugs are securely reconnected.

Steering column lock

7 Remove the ignition switch as described previously in this Section.

8 Referring to Chapter 10, unscrew the

away from the battery (also see Disconnecting the battery).

Ignition switch/steering lock

Ignition switch

1 Remove the three screws from the steering column lower shroud, unclip the upper shroud from it, then work off the lower shroud (refer to Chapter 11, Section 27. if necessary).

2 The immobiliser reader coil is removed first. Disconnect the larger (green) wiring plug visible from below. Remove one screw from behind, and

4.3b . . . then remove the remaining front screw . . .

4.3c . . . and one more from above/ behind . . .

4.3d . . . and remove the ignition key switch

4.4 Disconnect the ignition switch wiring plug

4.5a The switch right-hand screw is easy to access . . .

4.5b . . . but the left-hand one needs a cranked screwdriver or bit

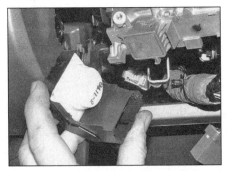

4.5c Removing the ignition switch

4.18a Loosen the screw on top of the switch assembly

4.18b Disconnect the two wiring plugs from the switch assembly

steering column mounting nuts/bolts, and lower the column into the driver's footwell.

9 The lock assembly is clamped to the column by two shear-bolts, which must be drilled out using a 5 mm drill bit, after centre-punching them.

10 Place the new lock assembly in position without the key inserted, and tighten the bolts until they are snug.

11 Insert the key and check the lock cylinder for proper operation.

12 Tighten the bolts until their heads break off.

13 Refit the steering column as described in Chapter 10, then refit the ignition switch as described previously in this Section.

Steering column switches

14 Remove the three screws from the steering column lower shroud, unclip the upper shroud from it, then work off the lower shroud (refer to Chapter 11, Section 27, if necessary).

15 Remove the driver's airbag as described in Section 21.

16 Remove the steering wheel as described in Chapter 10.

17 Remove the airbag clockspring as described in Section 21.

18 The steering column switches have to be removed as an assembly. First, loosen the switch clamp screw on top. Disconnect both the large wiring plugs from behind the switches, then remove the two screws at the front, and slide the switch assembly off the column **(see illustrations)**.

19 Each switch has two small screws on the front – with these removed, prise the front plate to release the switch pivot peg, and withdraw the switch **(see illustrations)**. Note: *Although each switch can now be removed individually, it is not possible to do this without removing the steering wheel, etc, since the switches hit the facia panel before they are free to be removed.*

20 Refitting is a reversal of removal. Refit the airbag components as described in Section 21, and the steering wheel as described in Chapter 10.

Steering wheel switches

Audio remote control

21 Remove the driver's airbag as described in Section 21.

4.18c Remove the two screws at the front . . .

4.18d . . . then slide the switch assembly off the steering column

22 The switch panel is secured by a total of three screws – two from behind, in line with the wheel's left-hand 'spoke', and one from the front. On our car, however, only one screw was fitted from behind, with the other hole unoccupied. Remove the screws, then withdraw the switch panel and disconnect the wiring plug from it **(see illustrations)**.

4.19a Remove the two small screws on the front of the switch . . .

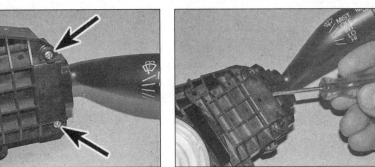

4.19b . . . then prise the front plate to release the switch . . .

4.19c . . . and withdraw it from the assembly

4.22a Remove the steering wheel switch panel screw(s) from behind . . .

4.22b ... and the screw from the front ...

4.22c ... then withdraw the switch panel and disconnect its wiring plug

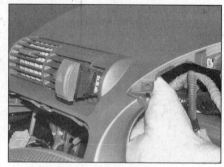

4.27a Working through the instrument panel aperture, push out the switch ...

4.27b ... and disconnect the wiring plug

4.27c The hazard warning light switch bulbs can be unscrewed for renewal

23 The switches themselves are integral with the steering wheel panel, and are not available separately.

24 Refitting is a reversal of removal.

Automatic transmission

25 Refer to Chapter 7B.

Hazard warning light switch

26 Trying to prise this switch out from the front carries a high risk of damaging the switch. Instead, the switch should be pushed out from behind.

27 Remove the instrument panel as described in Section 10. Working through the aperture, release the switch upper and lower clips, then push it out and disconnect the wiring plug. Note that the switch bulbs can be renewed individually (see illustrations).

28 Refitting is a reversal of removal. Refit the instrument panel as described in Section 10.

Heated rear window switch

29 Remove the heater control panel as described in Chapter 3, Section 9.

30 Unclip the switch from the back of the heater control panel. Note that the switch has two bulbs, both of which can be renewed individually (see illustrations).

31 Refitting is a reversal of removal.

Air conditioning switch

32 Remove the heater control panel as described in Chapter 3, Section 9.

33 Unclip the switch from the back of the heater control panel (see illustrations). Note that the switch has two bulbs, both of which can be renewed individually.

34 Refitting is a reversal of removal.

Blower motor switch

35 Remove the heater control panel as described in Chapter 3, Section 9.

36 Carefully prise up the top tab securing

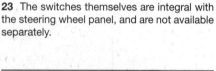

4.30a Use a small screwdriver to release the side clips ...

4.30b ... and withdraw the heated rear window switch from the panel

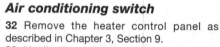

4.30c The switch bulbs can be renewed individually

4.33a Release the switch tabs using a screwdriver ...

4.33b ... and withdraw it from the heater control panel

the switch to the panel, and remove it (see illustrations).

37 Refitting is a reversal of removal.

Electric sunroof switch

38 With care, it may be possible to prise the switch from the headlining, starting at the front edge – however, if this proves difficult, we suggest trying the following. Working as described in Section 6, remove the interior light lens for access to the light unit mounting screws. Remove the screws, take down the light from the headlining, and disconnect its wiring plugs. Working through the hole left by the interior light, push the sunroof switch out from behind.

39 Disconnect the wiring plug, and remove the switch completely.

40 Refitting is a reversal of removal.

Electric window switches

41 Carefully prise off the side cover from the armrest, using a flat-bladed screwdriver to push up and release the three clips along the base of the armrest, at the front (see illustration).

42 Pull the armrest cover away from the door at the front, then work along the armrest, releasing the side clips; finally, pull the cover forwards to release the rear hooked clip (see illustration).

43 Disconnect the wiring plug from the switch panel (see illustration).

44 To remove the switch assembly itself, remove the two or three screws underneath, and take it out of the panel (see illustrations). The armrest can only be removed by taking out the door trim panel as described in Chap-

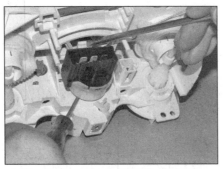

4.36a Use one screwdriver to lift the top tab, and another to prise the switch . . .

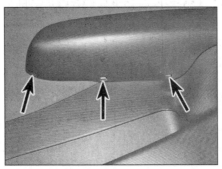

4.41 Press up the three clips along the base of the armrest cover . . .

ter 11 – the armrest is secured by several screws from behind.

45 Refitting is a reversal of removal.

Electric mirror switch

46 Open the driver's door. Taking care not to

4.36b . . . and remove it from the back of the heater control panel

4.42 . . . then pull it away at the front, and unhook it at the rear

mark the trim, prise out the facia end panel alongside the switch (see illustrations).

47 Reach in through the aperture, and push the switch out from behind (see illustration).

48 Disconnect the wiring plug(s) from the back of the switch, and remove it. Note that

4.43 Disconnect the window switch wiring plug

4.44a Remove the screws from below . . .

4.44b . . . and remove the switch assembly (seen with armrest removed)

4.46a Taking care not to mark the trim . . .

4.46b . . . prise out the facia end panel for access to the switch

4.47 Push out the mirror switch from behind

4.48a Disconnect the wiring plug, and remove the switch

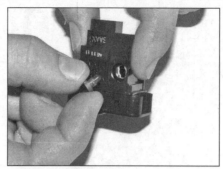

4.48b The mirror switch bulb can be renewed separately

4.55 Disconnect the wiring plug from the switch

the switch bulb can be renewed individually (see illustrations).

49 Refitting is a reversal of removal.

Headlight adjuster switch

50 Open the driver's door. Taking care not to mark the trim, prise out the facia end panel alongside the switch.

51 Reach in through the aperture, squeeze the upper and lower clips, and push the switch out of the facia from behind. To improve access, remove the mirror switch as described previously in this Section.

52 Disconnect the wiring plug(s) from the back of the switch, and remove it. Note that the switch bulb can be renewed individually.

53 Refitting is a reversal of removal.

Handbrake-on warning switch

54 Remove the centre console as described in Chapter 11, Section 28.

55 Disconnect the wiring plug from the switch, then remove the securing screw and withdraw the switch (see illustration).

56 The switch is a simple plunger-type design. If the switch has not been operating properly, it may be possible to restore its proper function by soaking it with lubricant (such as WD-40) and working the plunger several times.

57 Refitting is a reversal of removal.

Fuel cut-off (inertia) switch

58 The inertia switch is located on the left-hand side of the passenger footwell.

59 Remove the passenger's facia closing panel and the passenger footwell kick panel as described in Chapter 11, Section 27.

60 Disconnect the wiring plug from the base of the switch, then remove the two mounting screws and withdraw the switch from the car (see illustration).

61 Refitting is a reversal of removal.

Interior (courtesy) light switch

62 Open the relevant door, then prise back the screw cap from the switch (see illustration).

63 Remove the mounting screw, and withdraw the switch from the door pillar (see illustrations).

64 Disconnect the wiring plug, and remove the switch (see illustration).

> **HAYNES HINT** There is a danger of the wiring plug slipping back inside the door pillar – have a piece of tape ready to stick it to the pillar while the switch is removed.

65 These switches are simple 'plunger' types, and can sometimes suffer from corrosion, which causes them to stick, or have a bad contact. It is worth applying a maintenance spray such as WD-40 to a defective switch, as this may be enough to restore its operation.

66 Refitting is a reversal of removal. Reconnect the switch wiring plug, and test the operation of the interior light before fitting the switch back into position.

Boot light switch

67 The boot light switch is built into the tailgate lock assembly, which is removed as described in Chapter 11.

Brake pedal position (stop-light) switch

68 Refer to Chapter 9.

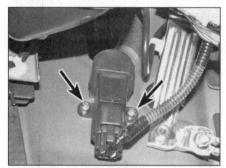

4.60 Disconnect the inertia switch wiring plug, then undo the two screws

4.62 Prise up the screw cap at the top of the switch

4.63a Remove the cross-head screw ...

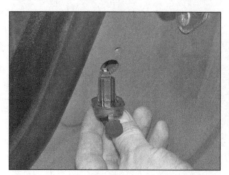

4.63b ... and withdraw the switch from its location

4.64 Disconnect the wiring plug, and remove the switch

5 Bulbs (exterior lights) – renewal

1 Whenever a bulb is renewed, note the following points:

a) *Ensure that the light is switched off, and also switch off the ignition (take out the key). For maximum safety, and particularly when changing the HID headlight bulbs, disconnect the battery negative lead (see Disconnecting the battery).*

b) *Remember that, if the light has just been in use, the bulb may be extremely hot.*

c) *Always check the bulb contacts and holder, ensuring that there is clean metal-to metal contact between the bulb and its live(s) and earth. Clean off any corrosion or dirt before fitting a new bulb.*

d) *Wherever bayonet-type bulbs are fitted, ensure that the live contact(s) bear firmly against the bulb contact.*

e) *Always ensure that the new bulb is of the correct rating, and that it is completely clean before fitting it; this applies particularly to headlight/foglight bulbs (see below).*

Headlight

2 Most models are fitted with conventional twin-filament headlight bulbs. However, high-intensity discharge (HID) bulbs were available as an option – these bulbs operate at a much higher voltage than conventional bulbs, and a different procedure is used to change them. Proceed as described under the appropriate sub-heading below.

3 The bulb is accessed by partially removing the wheel arch plastic liner on the side concerned. Normally, to remove the liner completely would require removing the wheel, but in this case, start the engine and turn the steering so that the roadwheel faces inwards on the side being worked on. Switch off the engine.

4 Use a flat-bladed screwdriver to prise out the two wheel arch liner clips nearest the back of the headlight being worked on (remove more clips than this if it helps). Fold the liner down to access the back of the headlight.

Conventional bulb

5 A conventional bulb can be recognised by the wiring plug and rubber seal fitted to the back of the headlight. Pull the wiring plug straight back off the light **(see illustration)**.

6 Pull off the round rubber cover, noting how it fits over the bulb/wiring plug terminals (the cover may have a pull tab and an arrow marking at the top) **(see illustration)**.

7 Release the bulb's wire retaining clip by pushing the right-hand end forwards and up out of its slot, then pivot the clip to the side. Withdraw the bulb **(see illustrations)**.

5.5 Pull off the headlight bulb wiring plug

8 When handling the new bulb, try and grip it only by the terminals at the rear. Avoid touching the glass with your fingers, as moisture and grease from the skin can cause blackening and rapid failure of this type of bulb. If the glass is accidentally touched, wipe it clean using methylated spirit.

9 Install the new bulb, ensuring that its three locating tabs are correctly seated in the light cut-outs. Secure the bulb in position with the spring clip, the end of which should locate in its slot at the right-hand side.

10 Refit the cover, then reconnect the wiring plug securely to complete.

11 Switch on the headlights, and check the operation on main and dipped beam before clipping the wheel arch liner back in place.

HID bulb

 Warning: HID bulbs operate at 25 000 volts. Make certain that the ignition is switched off (take out the key) before starting work. Do not service the bulbs in wet conditions, or with wet hands.

12 The HID bulb is behind a round plastic cover on the rear of the headlight. To remove the cover, take out the T20 tamper-proof Torx screw at the base of the cover, then turn the cover anti-clockwise to release it.

13 Turn the bulb socket 45° anti-clockwise, and withdraw it from the back of the bulb.

14 Squeeze the ends of the bulb's wire retaining clip together at the top, then swing the clip down to release the bulb.

15 Withdraw the bulb from the back of the headlight.

5.7a Push up the bulb's wire clip on the right-hand side . . .

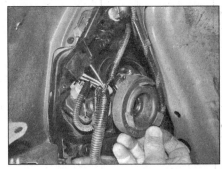

5.6 Take off the rubber cover

16 When handling the new bulb, try and grip it only by the terminals at the rear. Avoid touching the glass with your fingers, as moisture and grease from the skin can cause blackening and rapid failure of this type of bulb.

17 Install the new bulb, ensuring that it is correctly seated. Secure the bulb in position with the spring clip, Hooking both spring ends in place on top of the bulb.

18 Reconnect the bulb socket by offering it in place, then turning it 45° clockwise.

19 Twist on the cover clockwise, and secure with the Torx screw at the base.

20 Switch on the headlights, and check the operation on main and dipped beam before clipping the wheel arch liner back in place.

Front sidelight

21 The bulb is accessed by partially removing the wheel arch plastic liner on the side concerned. Normally, removing this liner completely would require removing the wheel, but in this case, start the engine and turn the steering so that the roadwheel faces inwards on the side being worked on. Switch off the engine.

22 Use a flat-bladed screwdriver to prise out the two wheel arch liner clips nearest the back of the headlight being worked on (remove more clips than this if it helps). Fold the liner down to access the back of the headlight.

23 The sidelight bulbholder is at the very top of the headlight **(see illustration)**.

24 Twist the bulbholder 90° anti-clockwise to

5.7b . . . and withdraw the bulb

5.23 From inside the wheel arch, the sidelight bulb is at the top

5.24 Twist and remove the sidelight bulbholder . . .

5.25 . . . and pull out the wedge-base bulb

release it, and withdraw it from the back of the headlight **(see illustration)**.

25 Pull out the wedge-base bulb, and fit a new one securely in its place **(see illustration)**.

26 Twist the bulbholder back into position, then check the operation of the bulb before clipping the wheel arch liner back in place.

Front direction indicator

27 The direction indicator bulb is on the inner edge of the headlight, and is accessed from the engine compartment.

28 To reach the left-hand bulb, prise out the clip and unhook the plastic access panel from the inner wing at the front corner of the engine compartment **(see illustrations)**.

29 If working on the right-hand bulb, the washer reservoir filler neck must be removed. Use a flat-bladed screwdriver to prise out the clip securing the neck to the front panel, then twist and pull the filler out of the washer

bottle (the filler has an O-ring seal) **(see illustrations)**.

30 Working 'round the corner' through the aperture now available, twist the bulbholder 90° anti-clockwise to release it, and withdraw it from the back of the headlight **(see illustration)**.

31 Pull out the wedge-base bulb, and fit a new one securely in its place **(see illustration)**.

32 Twist the bulbholder back into position, then check the operation of the bulb before refitting the components removed for access.

Front foglight

Early models

33 Unscrew and remove the cross-head screw on the inner side of the light which secures the light unit to the bumper. Pull the surround away at the inside, then unhook the tab at the outer side and withdraw the light. Disconnect the wiring plug from the bulbholder, and remove the light completely.

34 Twist the bulbholder 90° anti-clockwise to release it, and withdraw it from the back of the foglight.

35 The bulb and its holder are one unit – the bulb is not available separately.

36 When handling the new bulb, try and grip it only by the holder part. Avoid touching the glass with your fingers, as moisture and grease from the skin can cause blackening and rapid failure of this type of bulb. If the glass is accidentally touched, wipe it clean using methylated spirit.

37 Fit the new bulb and holder by twisting it clockwise into the back of the light unit.

38 Reconnect the wiring plug, then offer the light back into the bumper, and secure with the screw.

Later models

39 On later models, the foglight bulb is reached through an access panel, from below. The panel fits between the back of the bumper

5.28a For the left-hand indicator, prise out the clip . . .

5.28b . . . and unhook the access panel at the front corner

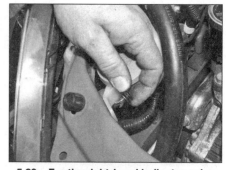

5.29a For the right-hand indicator, prise out the clip . . .

5.29b . . . securing the washer filler neck, then pull it up

5.30 Turn the bulbholder 90° to remove it from the light

5.31 Pull out the wedge-base indicator bulb

and the engine undertray – remove the one or two screws and withdraw the panel.

40 Squeeze down the tab and release the bulbholder wiring plug, pulling it rearwards to remove.

41 Twist the bulbholder 90° anti-clockwise to release it, and withdraw it from the back of the foglight.

42 The bulb and its holder are one unit – the bulb is not available separately.

43 When handling the new bulb, try and grip it only by the holder part. Avoid touching the glass with your fingers, as moisture and grease from the skin can cause blackening and rapid failure of this type of bulb. If the glass is accidentally touched, wipe it clean using methylated spirit.

44 Fit the new bulb and holder by twisting it clockwise into the back of the light unit.

45 Reconnect the wiring plug securely, then refit the access panel.

Wing-mounted side repeater

Method 1

46 Push the light unit rearwards to compress its rear clip, then unhook the front end from the wing and withdraw it **(see illustration)**. Don't use any tools for this, otherwise there is a risk of damaging the paint – if tools must be used, it's worth applying some masking tape around the light first.

Method 2

47 If the light unit is difficult to move, this method is easier, and carries less risk of damaging the wing. Remove the screws/clips

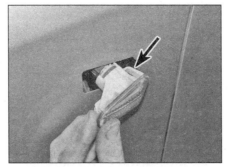

5.46 Removing the wing-mounted side repeater – note the rear clip

securing the lower part of the wheel arch liner, then reach inside and release the light unit from behind **(see illustration)**.

Both methods

48 Twist the bulbholder anti-clockwise to release it, and pull out the wedge-base bulb **(see illustration)**. Make sure that the bulbholder does not disappear back through the hole in the wing – tape it in place temporarily if necessary.

49 Refitting is a reversal of removal. Make sure that the light unit is refitted with the clip facing rearwards, and that it is clipped securely in place.

Mirror-mounted side repeater

50 Where the side repeater lights are built into the mirrors, they are non-renewable LEDs. It appears that the light unit is not available separately, and that if damaged, a new mirror assembly would be needed – check with a Honda dealer.

5.47 Reach inside the wheel arch liner, and unclip the light from behind

Rear lights

51 Open the tailgate and unclip the bulb access panel inside the boot **(see illustrations)**.

52 Remove the relevant bulbholder by turning it a quarter-turn anti-clockwise **(see illustration)**.

53 Any of the wedge-base bulbs can now be removed by pulling them out of the bulbholder **(see illustration)**.

54 Fit the new bulb, then refit the bulbholder securely, and clip the access panel back into place inside the boot.

55 Check the operation of the lights on completion.

Number plate lights

56 Open the tailgate. Press the light unit sideways (Honda say to the right, but on our car, it was to the left) to compress the spring clip, then unhook its edge clip and withdraw the light from the tailgate **(see illustrations)**.

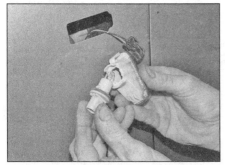

5.48a Twist and remove the bulbholder . . .

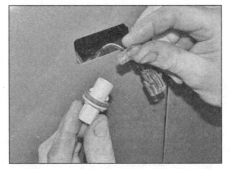

5.48b . . . then pull out the wedge-base bulb

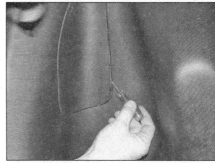

5.51a Using a small screwdriver, unclip . . .

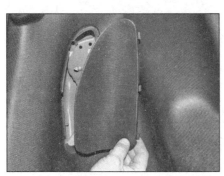

5.51b . . . and remove the rear light bulb access panel

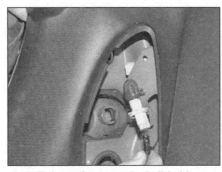

5.52 Twist and remove the bulbholder . . .

5.53 . . . and pull out the bulb

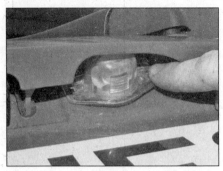

5.56a Press the number plate light to the side . . .

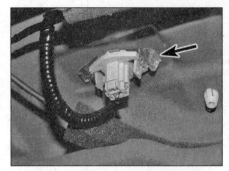

5.56b . . . to compress the spring clip (seen from the inside) . . .

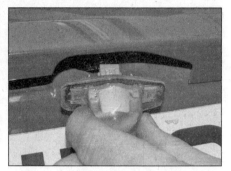

5.56c . . . and withdraw the light from the tailgate

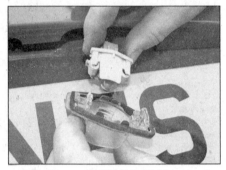

5.57 Squeeze the bulbholder legs, and release it

5.58 Pull out the wedge-base bulb

5.60 Press in the tabs either side, and slide down the light cover

57 Squeeze together the retaining legs and withdraw the bulbholder from the back of the light (see illustration).
58 Pull out the wedge-base bulb, then fit the new one by pushing it firmly into the bulb-holder (see illustration).

59 Clip the bulbholder back into place. Offer the light into the tailgate, right-hand edge first, then clip the light in on its left edge to secure.

High-level stop-light

60 Open the tailgate, and unclip the light unit

cover by pressing the retaining tabs at either end inwards, and withdraw it downwards from the light (see illustration).
61 Remove the bulbholder by turning it a quarter-turn anti-clockwise (see illustration).
62 Pull out the wedge-base bulb, then fit the new one by pushing it firmly into the bulb-holder (see illustration).
63 Twist the bulbholder firmly back into the light, then refit the cover to complete.

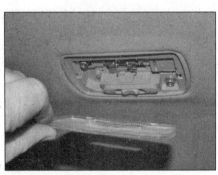

5.61 Twist and remove the bulbholder at the side . . .

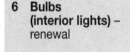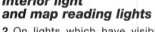

5.62 . . . and pull out the wedge-base bulb

6 Bulbs (interior lights) – renewal

General

1 Refer to Section 5, paragraph 1.

Interior light and map reading lights

2 On lights which have visible switches, carefully prise out the light lens at the front or side (see illustration).
3 On lights which are switched on by pressing the lens, press the outer end of the lens, then prise out the inner end with a small screwdriver and remove the lens (see illustration). If required, the other half of the lens can also be prised out.
4 The bulbs are festoon-type which is held between two spring contacts. Pull out the bulb, and fit a new one, ensuring that it is securely refitted (see illustrations).
5 Clip the light lens (or lenses) back into place to complete.

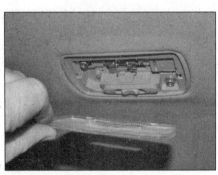

6.2 Typically, the rear interior light lens should be prised out

6.3 The front interior light lenses are removed as shown

6.4a The front interior light on our car had two festoon bulbs . . .

6.4b . . . the rear interior light only has one

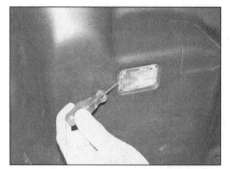

6.6 Prise out the boot light at the rear edge . . .

6.7 . . . and pull out the wedge-base bulb

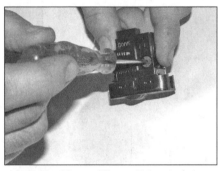

6.12a Many of the switches have bulbholders which can be unscrewed . . .

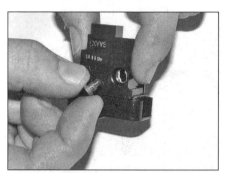

6.12b . . . and removed – note that the bulbs are part of the holder

Luggage compartment light

6 Carefully prise the light unit out from the trim panel, at the rear edge **(see illustration)**. If required, the bulbholder can be disconnected, and the light removed completely.

7 Pull out the wedge-base bulb, then fit the new one by pushing it firmly into the bulbholder **(see illustration)**.

8 Clip the light unit back into the trim panel to complete.

Instrument panel illumination bulbs

9 It appears that all of the instrument panel bulbs are non-renewable LEDs. The instrument panel can be removed as described in Section 10, but any bulb-related problems will have to be referred to a Honda dealer or auto-electrical specialist for repair.

Switch illumination

10 Unusually, some of the switches do have bulbs fitted, which can be renewed individually – note that these bulbs are a special fitment, and may only be available from a Honda dealer.

11 Remove the relevant switch as described in Section 4 for bulb renewal.

12 The bulbholders are typically removed by 'unscrewing' them from the switch, using a small screwdriver in the slot provided **(see illustrations)**. The bulbs and holders will usually be one-piece items.

Heater control unit illumination

13 Remove the heater control unit as described in Chapter 3, Section 9.

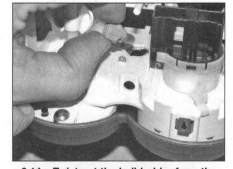

6.14a Twist out the bulbholder from the heater control panel . . .

14 To renew a bulb, twist the relevant bulbholder anti-clockwise and remove it from the rear of the panel. Pull out the wedge-base bulb, and press a new one firmly into place **(see illustrations)**.

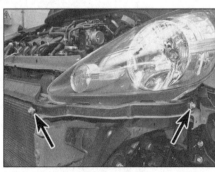

7.2a Remove the headlight's two lower mounting bolts . . .

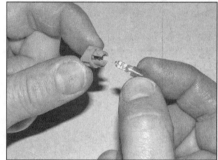

6.14b . . . and pull out the bulb

15 Refit the heater control unit as described in Chapter 3, Section 9.

Automatic transmission selector illumination

16 Refer to Chapter 7B, Section 5.

7 Exterior light units – removal and refitting

Headlight

1 Remove the front bumper as described in Chapter 11 – this is necessary for access to the two lower mounting bolts.

2 Remove the headlight lower mounting bolts first (one each end of the metal bracket), then the two upper bolts **(see illustrations)**.

3 Withdraw the headlight, and disconnect

7.2b ... and the two upper bolts from the wing channel

7.3a Withdraw the headlight ...

7.3b ... then disconnect the headlight adjuster motor ...

7.3c ... and the headlight bulb ...

7.3d ... either disconnect the two bulbholders, or twist them out

the wiring plugs from the headlight bulb and adjuster motor. Either unplug or twist and remove the sidelight and direction indicator bulbholders, and remove the light completely **(see illustrations)**.

4 If a new light is being fitted, unbolt the metal mounting bracket from the base (this is secured by one bolt underneath) and transfer it to the new light.

5 Refitting is a reversal of removal. On completion, check the light operation, and if necessary have the headlight beam alignment checked (see Section 8).

Front direction indicator

6 The front indicator is integral with the headlight.

Front foglight

Early models

7 Unscrew and remove the cross-head screw

on the inner side of the light which secures the light unit to the bumper. Pull the surround away at the inside, then unhook the tab at the outer side and withdraw the light. Disconnect the wiring plug from the bulbholder, and remove the light completely.

8 Refitting is a reversal of removal. If necessary, have the foglight beam alignment checked on completion.

Later models

9 Remove the engine undertray as described in Chapter 11, Section 23.

10 Squeeze down the tab and release the bulbholder wiring plug, pulling it rearwards to remove.

11 Remove the foglight mounting bolts, and withdraw the light from the inside of the bumper.

12 Refitting is a reversal of removal. If necessary, have the foglight beam alignment checked on completion.

Indicator side repeater light

13 Remove the light as described in the bulb renewal procedure in Section 5.

14 Disconnect the wiring plug from the bulbholder, and remove the light completely.

15 Refitting is a reversal of removal.

Rear lights

16 Remove the rear bumper as described in Chapter 11.

17 Remove all the bulbholders from the inside, as described in Section 5. Pull off the bulbholder wiring from the light unit mounting studs.

18 The light unit is secured with three nuts which are removed from the inside. In addition, there is a further bracket underneath, accessible from the outside (which is why the bumper has to be removed). It is simplest to unscrew the two bracket nuts for removal – if a new light is being fitted, remove the centre screw, and transfer the bracket to the new unit **(see illustrations)**.

19 When all the fasteners have been removed, withdraw the light from the car, and recover the foam seal **(see illustration)**. If the seal is in poor condition, a new one should be used when refitting.

20 Refitting is a reversal of removal.

Rear number plate light

21 Remove the light as described in the bulb renewal procedure in Section 5.

22 Disconnect the wiring plug from the bulbholder, and remove the light completely.

23 Refitting is a reversal of removal.

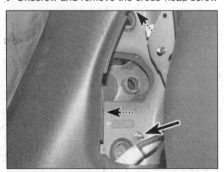

7.18a Remove the three nuts (two hidden) from inside ...

7.18b ... and the two nuts from the mounting bracket underneath

7.19 Withdraw the rear light unit

7.24 Press in the tabs either side, and slide down the light cover

7.25 Disconnect the bulbholder wiring plug

7.26 Unscrew the mounting bolts and remove the light

High-level stop-light

24 Open the tailgate, and unclip the light unit cover by pressing the retaining tabs at either end inwards, and withdraw it downwards from the light (see illustration).
25 Disconnect the wiring plug from the bulbholder at the left-hand side (see illustration).
26 Unscrew and remove the two mounting bolts, and withdraw the light from the tailgate (see illustration).
27 Refitting is a reversal of removal.

8 Headlight beam alignment – general information

All models are equipped with an electrical vertical beam adjuster unit – this can be used to adjust the headlight beam to compensate for the relevant load which the car is carrying. An adjuster wheel is provided on the facia – refer to the car's handbook for further information.

Accurate adjustment of the headlight beam is only possible using optical beam-setting equipment, and this work should therefore be carried out by a Honda dealer or suitably-equipped workshop. Note that the headlight adjuster switch inside the car should be set to its lowest position (0) before any adjustments are made.

For reference, the headlights can be finely adjusted by rotating the adjuster screws fitted to the top of each light unit, using a cross-head screwdriver – the screwdriver tip engages with the toothed adjuster wheel. The screws are accessible through the top of the body front panel. The horizontal adjustment screw is towards the front of the headlight, and the toothed adjuster can be seen easily through the hole in the body front panel. The vertical adjustment screw is further to the rear – a screwdriver with a very long, thin handle will be needed, which should be inserted using the guides moulded into the headlight housing (the adjuster itself is at the base of the headlight).

9 Headlight adjuster components – removal and refitting

Adjuster switch

1 Refer to Section 4.

Adjuster motor

2 Removing the motor is possible without removing the headlight, but refitting it will be much easier if the headlight is removed as described in Section 7.
3 Disconnect the wiring plug from the motor.
4 Remove the cross-head screw, and take off the screwdriver guide bracket (for headlight manual adjustment) (see illustrations).
5 Twist the motor clockwise to free it, then slide it upwards to release the motor's ball fitting from the slot in the headlight (see illustration).

9.4a Remove the cross-head screw . . .

9.5 Slide the motor ball fitting up out of its slot

6 When refitting, remove the headlight bulb and hold the bulb fitting ring against the back of the light with a finger and thumb (see illustration). Slide the ball fitting into the top of the slot and downwards, then twist the motor anti-clockwise to secure it.

10 Instrument panel – removal and refitting

Removal

1 Ensure that the ignition is switched off (take out the key).
2 Remove the three screws from the steering column lower shroud, unclip the upper shroud from it, then work off the lower shroud (refer to Chapter 11, Section 27, if necessary).
3 Adjust the steering column to its lowest

9.4b . . . and take off the screwdriver guide bracket

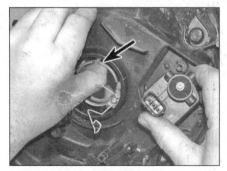

9.6 Hold the bulb fitting ring when refitting the motor

10.4 Unclip and remove the lens surround panel

10.5a Remove the four screws . . .

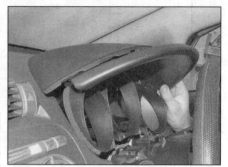

10.5b . . . and take out the inner surround

10.6a Remove the row of five screws . . .

10.6b . . . and take off the visor panel

6 Take off the instrument panel visor next – this has a row of five screws inside (see illustrations).

7 The instrument panel itself has two mounting screws at the base – remove the screws, then disconnect the three wiring plugs (grey, blue and green on our car) along the top of the panel, and lift it out (see illustrations).

Bulb renewal

8 It appears that all of the instrument panel bulbs are non-renewable LEDs. The panel can be removed as described previously in this Section, but any bulb-related problems will have to be referred to a Honda dealer or auto-electrical specialist for repair.

Refitting

9 Refitting is a reversal of removal.

setting, using the lever underneath the steering wheel.

4 To access the instrument panel, the lens surround panel in front must first be unclipped. Pull the bottom edge of the lens surround panel towards the steering wheel to release the clips,

then do the same along the top edge until the lens is free and can be removed (see illustration).

5 The instrument panel inner surround is removed first, and is secured by four screws. Remove the screws and withdraw the surround (see illustrations).

11 Horn(s) – removal and refitting

Removal

1 All models have a horn unit mounted directly below the right-hand headlight (right as seen from the driver's seat).

2 Remove the right-hand front wheel arch liner as described in Chapter 11, Section 23.

3 Unscrew the mounting bolt (see illustrations).

4 Disconnect the wiring plug from the horn, and remove the horn from the front of the car.

Refitting

5 Refitting is a reversal of removal.

10.7a Remove the two screws at the base . . .

10.7b . . . then disconnect the three wiring plugs along the top . . .

10.7c . . . and lift out the instrument panel

11.3a The horn is mounted at the front of the right-hand wheel arch

11.3b Unscrew the horn mounting bolt

Before removing the wiper arm, mark its parked position on the glass using a strip of masking tape.

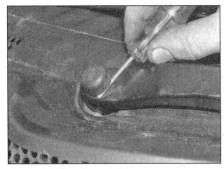

12.2a Prise off the nut cover from the wiper arm . . .

12.2b . . . then unscrew the spindle nut

12.3 Pull off the wiper arm, wiggling it free if necessary

12.4a Lift off the hinged cover . . .

12.4b . . . then unscrew the tailgate wiper arm nut

12 Wiper arms – removal and refitting

Removal

1 Operate the wiper motor, then switch it off so that the wiper arm returns to the park position (see Haynes Hint).

Windscreen wiper arm

2 Prise off the wiper arm spindle nut cover, then slacken and remove the spindle nut (see illustrations).

3 Lift the blade off the glass, and pull the wiper arm off its spindle (see illustration). Note that on some models, the wiper arms may be very tight on the spindle splines – it should be possible to lever the arm off the spindle, using a flat-bladed screwdriver (take care not to damage the scuttle cover panel). In extreme cases, it may even be necessary to use a small puller to free the arm.

Tailgate wiper arm

4 Lift off the hinged cover, then unscrew the spindle nut (see illustrations).

5 Lift the blade off the glass, and pull the wiper arm off its spindle (see illustration). It should be possible to lever the arm off the spindle, using a flat-bladed screwdriver, but in extreme cases, it may even be necessary to use a small puller to free the arm.

Refitting

6 Ensure that the wiper arm and spindle splines are clean and dry, then refit the arm to the spindle. Where applicable, align the wiper blade with the tape fitted on removal.

7 Refit the spindle nut, tightening it securely, and clip the nut cover back into position.

13 Windscreen wiper motor and linkage – removal and refitting

Removal

1 Remove the wiper arms as described in Section 12.

2 Peel off the rubber weatherstrip along the edge of the windscreen scuttle panel (see illustration).

3 Unclip the section of scuttle panel used for access to the brake and clutch fluid reservoirs (see illustration).

12.5 Pull the tailgate wiper arm off the splines

13.2 Peel off the weatherstrip from the front of the scuttle panel

13.3 Unclip the reservoir access panel

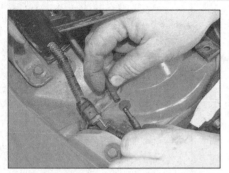

13.4 Disconnect the washer supply hose

13.5a Using pliers from below, release the clips either side . . .

13.5b . . . and one in the centre of the panel

13.6 Pull the panel upwards at the rear edge

4 Disconnect the washer supply hose at the driver's side of the scuttle panel **(see illustration)**.

5 Using pliers from below, release the three clips from the front edge of the windscreen cowl panel **(see illustrations)**.

6 The cowl panel's rear edge is secured under the windscreen by a row of seven clips – starting at one end, pull the panel upwards to release them **(see illustration)**.

7 Unhook the panel rubber ends from the bonnet hinges. The panel can be removed in one piece, or separated at the centre – note how the halves fit together **(see illustration)**.

8 The motor and linkage assembly is secured by three bolts – unscrew and remove them **(see illustrations)**.

9 Disconnect the wiring plug from the wiper motor, and lift out the assembly **(see illustrations)**.

10 Before separating the motor from the linkage, make an alignment mark between the linkage and the cranked arm attached to the motor, to show its parked position (typically, it will be horizontally aligned, along the axis of the motor frame).

11 Remove the spindle nut and washer, and separate the cranked arm from the motor **(see illustration)**. The other end of the cranked arm need not be detached, but for reference, it is on a ball fitting, which can be prised off if required.

12 Remove the two motor mounting screws, and withdraw the motor from the wiper frame.

Refitting

13 Refitting is a reversal of removal, bearing in mind the following points:
  a) Ensure that the motor arm is aligned in the 'parked' position (see paragraph 10) when refitting.
  b) Where they have been disturbed, lightly grease the wiper linkage pivots.
  c) Tighten all nuts and bolts securely.
  d) Ensure that the cowl panel is clipped back into place, and that the rubber trims at each end are tucked back under the wing correctly.
  e) Test the motor's operation before refitting the wiper arms as described in Section 12.

13.7 If required, the panel can be separated at the centre joint

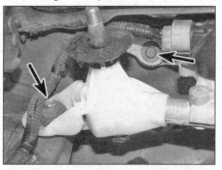

13.8a The motor and linkage assembly has two bolts at the driver's end . . .

13.8b . . . and one more in the centre

13.9a Disconnect the motor wiring plug . . .

13.9b . . . and lift out the motor/linkage assembly

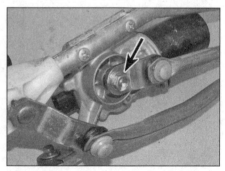

13.11 Wiper motor spindle nut and washer

14 Tailgate wiper motor – removal and refitting

Removal

1 Remove the tailgate wiper arm as described in Section 12.
2 Remove the tailgate main trim panel as described in Chapter 11, Section 27.
3 Disconnect the motor wiring plug (see illustration).
4 Remove the three motor mounting bolts, and withdraw the motor from the tailgate (see illustration).

Refitting

5 Refitting is a reversal of removal. Check the condition of the wiper motor spindle grommet in the tailgate glass, and renew if necessary.

15 Windscreen/tailgate washer system components – removal and refitting

Washer fluid reservoir

Removal

1 First, the washer reservoir filler neck must be removed. Use a flat-bladed screwdriver to prise out the clip securing the neck to the front panel, then twist and pull the filler out of the washer bottle (the filler has an O-ring seal) (see illustrations).
2 Remove the right-hand front wheel arch liner as described in Chapter 11, Section 23.
3 Disconnect the wiring plug and washer tube from each of the two washer pumps – anticipate a small amount of fluid loss when the tubes are disconnected (see illustration). Note the location of each washer tube, as they must be refitted to the correct pump.
4 Alternatively, the two pumps can be prised out of the reservoir, which means they can be left behind on the car – however, the contents of the reservoir will be lost when the pumps are removed. Recover the rubber sealing grommet from each pump, and refit them to the reservoir.
5 Unclip the washer tube from the reservoir guide.
6 Remove the two reservoir mounting bolts, and lower the reservoir into the wheel arch to remove it.

Refitting

7 Refitting is a reversal of removal, noting the following points:
 a) If the pumps were removed, it may be helpful to apply a little washing-up liquid to the rubber sealing grommets to make refitting easier.
 b) Make sure the washer hoses are securely reconnected to their original positions.
 c) Refill the reservoir, then check the operation of the washers before refitting the wheel arch liner.

14.3 Disconnect the wiring plug, then remove the three bolts (arrowed) . . .

14.4 . . . and withdraw the motor from the tailgate

Washer fluid pumps

Removal

8 The pumps are fitted into the washer reservoir. Remove the right-hand front wheel arch liner as described in Chapter 11, Section 23.
9 All models have two pumps – the front one is for the windscreen, with the rear one for the tailgate.
10 Disconnect the wiring plug and washer tube from the pump – anticipate a small amount of fluid loss when the tube is disconnected. If both pumps are being removed, note the location of each washer tube, as they must be refitted to the correct pump.
11 Prise the pump out of the reservoir, and remove it. If the rubber sealing grommet came out with the pump, refit it to the reservoir.

Refitting

12 Refitting is a reversal of removal, noting the following points:
 a) It may be helpful to apply a little washing-up liquid to the rubber sealing grommets to make refitting easier.
 b) Make sure the washer hoses are securely reconnected to their original positions.
 c) Refill the reservoir, then check the operation of the washers before refitting the wheel arch liner.

Windscreen washer jet

Removal

13 Use a small screwdriver to prise the washer jet out of the scuttle panel, then pull off the washer tube and remove it (see illustrations).

15.1a Prise out the filler neck securing clip . . .

15.1b . . . and withdraw the filler neck from the car

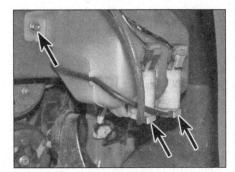

15.3 Fluid reservoir location, showing the two pumps and one of the mounting bolts

15.13a Prise the windscreen washer jet out of the scuttle panel . . .

15.13b . . . and pull off the washer tube

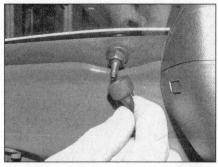

15.15 Pull back the boot and pull off the washer tube

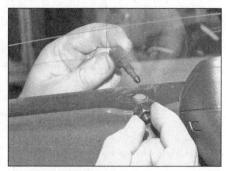

15.16 Unscrew the jet mounting nut, and remove it from the top

16.2 Remove the screws securing the unit to the metal mounting frame

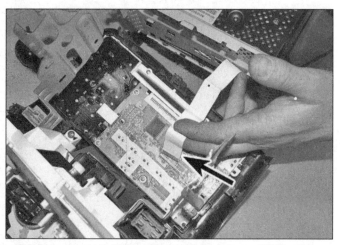

16.3 The rear part of the unit can only be removed if this ribbon cable is detached

Refitting

14 Refitting is a reversal of removal, but make sure that the fluid hose connections are securely remade. It may be helpful to apply a little washing-up liquid to the jet, to make fitting the tube easier.

Tailgate washer jet

Removal

15 At the top of the tailgate, pull back the rubber boot from the base of the jet, then pull off the supply tube **(see illustration)**.
16 Unscrew the jet mounting nut, and withdraw the jet from outside the tailgate **(see illustration)**.

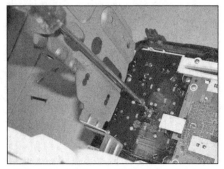

16.5a The front panel bulbholders can be unscrewed . . .

Refitting

17 Refitting is a reversal of removal. Check the condition of the rubber seal at the base of the jet, and tighten the mounting nut securely, to prevent water ingress.

16 Radio unit – removal and refitting

Removal

1 Remove the heater control panel as described in Chapter 3, Section 9.

16.5b . . . and removed if required – the bulbs are fixed

2 In theory, the whole unit can be removed by removing the seven screws securing it to the metal mounting frame on the back of the heater control panel **(see illustration)**.
3 However, when we tried this on our project car, only the back half of the unit came away, attached to a printed circuit board by a ribbon cable **(see illustration)**. Though we did manage to disconnect and reconnect the cable without damage, we would not advise it. It is recommended that the advice of a Honda dealer or car hi-fi specialist is sought before attempting to remove the unit from the panel.
4 With the back half of the unit removed, the front panel can also be unscrewed and removed from the heater control panel, if required.

Illumination bulbs

5 With the radio unit removed (but with the ribbon cable still connected, the illumination bulbholders for the radio front panel are accessible, and can be removed using a screwdriver. As with the switches, however, the bulbs themselves are integral with the holders **(see illustrations)**.

Refitting

6 Refitting is a reversal of removal. Refit the heater control panel as described in Chapter 3, Section 9.

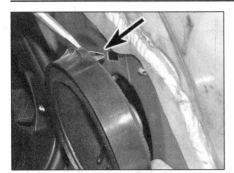

17.2a Release the spring clip at the top . . .

17.2b . . . then unhook the speaker's two lower legs

17.3 Disconnect the speaker wiring plug

17 Speakers –
removed and refitting

Removal

1 Remove the relevant door trim panel as described in Chapter 11, Section 13.
2 The speakers are clipped into the door. Insert a small screwdriver at the top to release the upper clip, then lift the speaker to unhook the two lower legs (see illustrations).
3 Withdraw the speaker from the door, and disconnect the wiring plug (see illustration).

Refitting

4 Refitting is a reversal of removal. Ensure that the speakers are securely clipped or screwed in place.

18 Radio aerial –
removal and refitting

Note: *The aerial mast can be unscrewed from the base, from outside. For good reception (and to discourage theft) always ensure the mast is fully tightened when refitting.*

Removal

1 The aerial base is accessed by removing the front interior light, as follows.
2 Press the outer end of the lens, then prise out the inner end with a small screwdriver and remove the lens (see illustration). The other half of the lens should also be prised out.
3 Remove the two bolts securing the light unit to the headlining, then withdraw it and disconnect its wiring plug (see illustrations).
4 Disconnect the aerial base's earth terminal spade connector, where applicable.
5 Prise off the cap, then unscrew the mounting nut and take off the main aerial lead (see illustration). Withdraw the aerial from the roof. Recover the rubber seal – if this has perished, use a new one when refitting.

Refitting

6 Refitting is a reversal of removal. Ensure that there is a good seal between the aerial

and the roof, to prevent leaks, and good electrical connections on the base of the aerial, or reception will suffer.

19 Immobiliser system and alarm –
general information

Immobiliser system

An engine immobiliser system is fitted as standard to all models, and the system is operated automatically every time the ignition key is inserted/removed.

The immobiliser system ensures that the car can only be started using the original Honda ignition key. The key contains an electronic chip (transponder) which is programmed with a code. When the key is inserted into the

ignition switch, it uses the current present in the reader coil (which is fitted around the switch) to send a signal to the immobiliser electronic control unit (ECU). The ECU checks this code every time the ignition is switched on. If the key code does not match the ECU code, the ECU will disable the fuel pump circuit to prevent the engine being started.

If the ignition key is lost, a new one can be obtained from a Honda dealer. They have access to the correct key code for the immobiliser system of your car, and will be able to supply a new coded key.

If you have any spare keys cut, they will only open the doors, etc, if they are not coded correctly, and will not be capable of starting the engine. For this reason, it may be best to have any spare keys supplied by your Honda dealer, who will also be able to advise you on coding the keys.

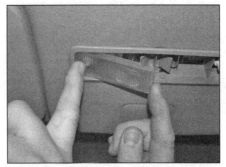

18.2 Press the outer end of the lens, and prise out the inner end to remove

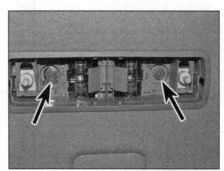

18.3a Remove the two mounting bolts . . .

18.3b . . . and disconnect the light unit wiring plug

18.5 Prise off the cap, and unscrew the aerial mounting nut

Alarm system

Certain models are equipped with an anti-theft alarm system, in addition to the engine immobiliser. Various types of system were offered, depending on specification and market.

The anti-theft alarm system is automatically activated by the central locking system (manually, or via the remote control, where applicable). The alarm system uses the door lock cylinder/lock knob switches, and the tailgate and bonnet lock switches, to detect whether any of them is opened with the alarm set. A security control unit under the facia constantly monitors the switches – if any switch receives an earth signal, the alarm siren will be activated, and the indicators will flash.

This system (sometimes referred to as a 'perimetric' alarm, as it only protects the 'perimeter' of the car) does not prevent a thief from gaining access to the inside of the car by breaking a window – provided the doors, etc, are not opened, the alarm will not go off.

Some models may be fitted with an alarm featuring ultrasonic scanning of the whole inside of the car – with this system, if the ultrasonic beam is broken by any movement inside the car, the alarm will sound. Models with an ultrasonic alarm can be identified by the ultrasonic emitter and receiver grilles in the rear interior light unit.

Any faults with the system will most likely be related to the lock switches or associated wiring, which are covered in the relevant parts of Chapter 11. False alarms may also occur if the doors, bonnet or tailgate are not closing properly for any reason, or if there is a problem with the interior light circuit. On an ultrasonic alarm system, not closing a window or the sunroof properly may also set off the alarm, especially in windy conditions. Any persistent problems not explained by the above should be referred to a Honda dealer for diagnosis – for obvious security reasons, a more detailed description of the system is not included in this manual.

20 Airbag system – general information and precautions

General information

All models are fitted with a driver's airbag mounted in the steering wheel, and a similar airbag for the front seat passenger, mounted in the facia panel. These are designed to prevent serious chest and head injuries during a frontal accident (of sufficient force) within 30° from the left or right of the car centre-line. Some Jazz models also have side airbags, fitted into the front seat side cushions, which are triggered if there is an impact from the side of the car. The control unit for the airbag system is located under the centre of the facia, and performs continual

system diagnostics. Two crash sensors are located at the front of the car, and a side impact sensor is located on the inner sill, in front of each B-pillar.

The airbag system on the Jazz has an adaptive capability – it can adjust the level of protection according to circumstances, and to the number of passengers (or lack of them). If the system's crash sensors detect a less-severe impact, the front airbags may not fire at all. A seat occupancy sensor is fitted to the passenger seat, so the system knows when a front seat passenger is present – when the seat is empty, the passenger front and side airbags are disabled. The occupancy sensor forms part of the seat side cushion, and cannot be renewed separately.

The seat belt tensioners (described in Chapter 11) are also deployed in the event of an accident, and in fact can deploy independently at lower impact levels than the airbags.

The front seat side airbags offer greater passenger protection in a side impact. Although the side airbags are linked to the 'front' airbags, the side airbags will only deploy if the car is struck from the side.

The airbags are inflated by a gas generator, which forces the bag out of the cover in the steering wheel, facia panel, or seat cushion. On the driver's airbag (which turns with the steering wheel) a 'clockspring' rotary connector ensures that a good electrical connection is maintained with the airbag at all times.

⚠ **Warning: When working on the airbag system, always wait at least 3 minutes after disconnecting the battery, as a precaution against accidental deployment of the airbag unit. This period ensures that any stored energy in the back-up capacitor is dissipated. Do not use battery-operated radio key code savers, as these may cause the airbag to be deployed, with the possibility of personal injury.**

Precautions

⚠ **Warning: The following precautions must be observed when working on cars equipped with an airbag system, to prevent the possibility of personal injury.**

General precautions

The following precautions must be observed when carrying out work on a car equipped with an airbag:

a) *Do not disconnect the battery with the engine running.*
b) *Before carrying out any work in the vicinity of the airbag, removal of any of the airbag components, or any welding work on the car, de-activate the system as described in the following sub-Section.*
c) *Do not attempt to test any of the airbag system circuits using test meters or any other test equipment.*
d) *If the airbag warning light comes on,*

or any fault in the system is suspected, consult a Honda dealer without delay. Do not attempt to carry out fault diagnosis, or any dismantling of the components.

When handling an airbag

a) *Transport the airbag by itself, bag upwards.*
b) *Do not put your arms around the airbag.*
c) *Carry the airbag close to the body, bag outwards.*
d) *Do not drop the airbag or expose it to impacts.*
e) *Do not attempt to dismantle the airbag unit.*
f) *Do not connect any form of electrical equipment to any part of the airbag circuit.*

When storing an airbag unit

a) *Store the unit in a cupboard with the airbag upwards.*
b) *Do not expose the airbag to temperatures above 80°C.*
c) *Do not expose the airbag to flames.*
d) *Do not attempt to dispose of the airbag – consult a Honda dealer.*
e) *Never refit an airbag which is known to be faulty or damaged.*

De-activation of airbag system

The system must be de-activated as follows, before carrying out any work on the airbag components or surrounding area.
a) *Remove the ignition key.*
b) *Switch off all electrical equipment.*
c) *Disconnect the battery negative lead (see Disconnecting the battery).*
d) *Insulate the battery negative terminal and the end of the battery negative lead to prevent any possibility of contact.*
e) *Wait for at least 3 minutes before carrying out any further work.*
f) *Ensure that the battery is still disconnected, before reconnecting any airbag wiring.*

21 Airbag system components – removal and refitting

⚠ **Warning: Refer to the precautions given in Section 20 before attempting to carry out work on the airbag components.**

Driver's airbag

Removal

1 De-activate the airbag system as described in Section 20. The airbag unit is an integral part of the steering wheel centre pad.
2 Prise off the rectangular cover at the base/back of the steering wheel **(see illustrations)**.
3 Disconnect the (yellow) airbag wiring plug by sliding back the spring-loaded locking sleeve **(see illustration)**.
4 Unscrew the two airbag mounting Torx bolts, using a T30 Torx bit. The bolts are

21.2a Using a small screwdriver . . .

21.2b . . . prise off the rectangular cover at the base of the wheel

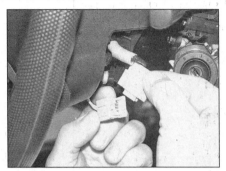

21.3 Slide back the locking sleeve, and disconnect the yellow plug inside

located either side of the wheel, and are deeply recessed – look around the wheel rim to see them **(see illustrations)**. The bolts may be quite tight – ensure that the right size of Torx bit is used.

5 When the bolts are loose, tip the airbag unit backwards out of the steering wheel, then lift it out, feeding the wiring plug through as it is removed. Disconnect the horn wiring plug (spade connector) from the base of the airbag when it is accessible **(see illustrations)**. Move the airbag to a safe place, and always keep the front facing upwards.

6 Discard the airbag mounting bolts – Honda state that new ones should be used when refitting.

Refitting

7 Refitting is a reversal of removal. Feed the wiring back through the wheel, and (with the battery still disconnected) connect the plug

securely. Tighten the new airbag mounting bolts securely, and clip on the wheel's lower cover to complete. Reconnect the battery and check for correct operation of the airbag warning light by switching on the ignition.

Passenger's airbag

Removal

8 De-activate the airbag system as described in Section 20.

9 Remove the glovebox as described in Chapter 11, Section 27.

10 Disconnect the (yellow) airbag wiring plug by sliding back the spring-loaded locking sleeve **(see illustration)**.

11 Remove the three mounting nuts securing the airbag unit to its mounting bracket **(see illustration)**.

12 Protect the top of the facia with strips of masking tape or some cloth. Using a

wide-bladed tool, carefully prise the airbag at the sides to release the retaining tabs, and lift the unit out of the facia.

13 Move the airbag to a safe place, and always keep the front facing upwards.

Refitting

14 Refitting is a reversal of removal. Tighten the mounting nuts securely, and (with the battery still disconected), reconnect the airbag wiring plug. On completion, reconnect the battery and check for correct operation of the airbag warning light by switching on the ignition.

Airbag control unit

Removal

15 When a car is involved in a heavy enough impact to set off the airbags, the event is logged in the airbag control unit. On some cars, even

21.4a The airbag mounting bolt either side of the wheel can be hard to see . . .

21.4b . . . use a Torx bit to unscrew them

21.5a Lift the airbag unit out of the wheel . . .

21.5b . . . and disconnect the horn spade connector at the base

21.10 Disconnect the passenger airbag wiring plug

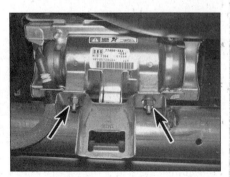

21.11 Two of the three passenger airbag mounting nuts

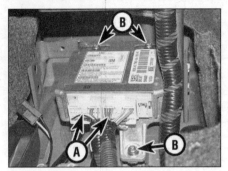

21.18 Airbag control unit wiring plugs (A) and mounting screws (B)

after new airbags are fitted, the 'event code' cannot be cleared from the airbag control unit (so the airbag warning light stays on), and a new control unit has to be fitted. Consult a Honda dealer for advice on this point.

16 Honda state that, before the control unit is removed, as well as disconnecting the battery and waiting three minutes, **all** the airbag and seat belt tensioner wiring plugs must be disconnected. This means disconnecting the driver's and passenger's airbags, the front seat wiring (models with side airbags), and the wiring plugs to the front seat belt inertia reels (refer to Chapter 11 for the last two).

17 Remove the centre console as described in Chapter 11.

18 Fold back the carpet for access to the unit. Disconnect the wiring plugs from the front of the unit, then remove the three Torx screws and withdraw the unit from the floor location **(see illustration)**.

21.24a Disconnect the smaller clockspring connector at the top . . .

21.26 Release the securing tabs, and slide off the clockspring

21.23a Slide the clockspring's yellow connector downwards off its mounting . . .

Refitting

19 Refitting is a reversal of removal, bearing in mind the following points:
a) *The battery must still be disconnected when reconnecting the airbag and seat belt tensioner wiring.*
b) *Make sure that the wiring connectors are securely reconnected.*
c) *Tighten the mounting screws securely.*
d) *On completion, reconnect the battery and check for correct operation of the airbag warning light by switching on the ignition.*

Airbag clockspring (rotary connector)

20 Remove the driver's airbag as described previously in this Section.

21 Remove the steering wheel as described in Chapter 10.

22 Remove the steering column shrouds as described in Chapter 11, Section 27.

21.24b . . . then feed out the wiring from the yellow connector

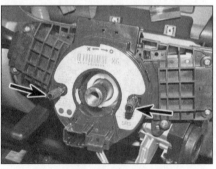

21.28 The clockspring front markings face upwards, and the pins horizontal

21.23b . . . then disconnect it using its spring-loaded sleeve

23 Disconnect the clockspring yellow wiring plug under the column – unclip the plug from the column by sliding it downwards, then slide back its spring-loaded sleeve to disconnect it **(see illustrations)**.

24 Disconnect the clockspring's other wiring plug at the top. Feed out the wiring from the yellow connector, and withdraw it from the top of the clockspring **(see illustrations)**.

25 Before removing the clockspring, note that it has an arrow marking on its front face – this should face upwards. If the same clockspring will be refitted, tape the unit so that it cannot turn once removed.

26 When the wiring has been disconnected, carefully release the upper and lower tabs, and slide the clockspring off the steering column **(see illustration)**.

27 Before fitting the clockspring, it must first be centred. If a new unit is being fitted, note that they are supplied set in the centre position. Similarly, if the old clockspring has not been turned while it was removed, this procedure can be omitted.

28 To centre the unit, gently turn the front face clockwise until it stops. Now turn the front face anti-clockwise by about 2 1/2 turns, and the arrow mark on its face should point straight up – this is the centre position. As a further reference, the two steering wheel locating pins on the front face should be horizontal **(see illustration)**.

29 With the front wheels still pointing straight ahead, offer the clockspring onto the steering column. Note that the direction indicator self-cancelling sleeve's two tabs should be aligned vertically.

30 Feed the clockspring wiring into position, making sure it is routed as before, and connect the wiring plugs. Secure the unit in place by pressing it home so that its upper and lower tabs locate properly.

31 Further refitting is a reversal of removal. On completion, reconnect the battery and check for correct operation of the airbag warning light by switching on the ignition.

Side airbags

32 The side airbags are located internally within the front seat backrest, and no attempt should be made to remove them. Any suspected problems with the side airbag system should be referred to a Honda dealer.

HONDA JAZZ wiring diagrams   **Diagram 1**

Key to symbols

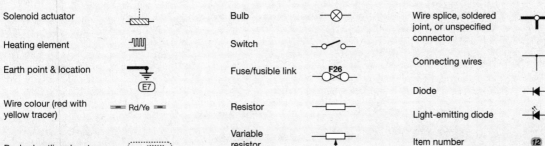

Solenoid actuator	
Heating element	
Earth point & location	(E7)
Wire colour (red with yellow tracer)	Rd/Ye
Dashed outline denotes part of a larger item, containing in this case an electronic or solid state device	
Bulb	
Switch	
Fuse/fusible link	F26
Resistor	
Variable resistor	
Variable resistor	
Wire splice, soldered joint, or unspecified connector	
Connecting wires	
Diode	
Light-emitting diode	
Item number	12
Motor/pump	M

Engine fusebox ④

Fuse	Rating	Circuit protected
F1	80A	Main supply fuse
F2	40A	Main fuse electronic power steering (EPS)
F3	50A	Main fuse ignition
F4	40A	Anti-lock braking system/electronic stability program motor (ABS/ESP)
F5	40A	Heater blower relay
F6	40A	Electric windows
F7	30A	Front foglight/sunroof
F8	15A	Reversing light
F9	10A	Side & tail lights
F10	30A	Engine cooling fan
F11	30A	Air conditioning (A/C) condenser cooling fan
F12	20A	RH headlight
F13	20A	LH headlight
F14	10A	Hazard warning lights
F15	30A	Anti-lock braking system/electronic stability program (ABS/ESP)
F16	10A	Horn, stop lights (without trailer connection)
	15A	Horn, stop lights (with trailer connection)

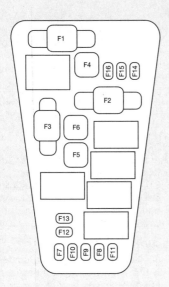

Passenger fusebox ⑥

Fuse	Rating	Circuit protected
F1	10A	Reversing light
F2	15A	Ignition coil 2
F3	7.5A	Instrument cluster, immobiliser, headlight levelling, sunroof, electronic power steering (EPS)
F4	10A	Direction indicators
F5	7.5A	Electronic throttle control system (ETCS)
F6	20A	Front wiper
F7	7.5A	Seat occupancy system (OPDS)
F8	-	Not used
F9	20A	Heated rear window
F10	7.5A	Heater blower, air conditioning
F11	15A	Fuel pump, SRS system
F12	10A	Rear wiper
F13	10A	Safety restraint system (SRS)
F14	15A	IGP
F15	20A	LH rear electric window
F16	20A	RH rear electric window
F17	20A	LH front electric window
F18	10A	Rear foglight
F19	20A	Sunroof, heated mirrors (for some models)
F20	-	Not used
F21	20A	Front fog light (for some models)
F22	-	Not used
F23	-	Not used
F24	15A	Ignition coil 1
F25	7.5A	Anti-lock braking system/electronic stability program (ABS/ESP)
F26	7.5A	Audio system
F27	15A	Accessory socket, cigar lighter
F28	20A	Central locking
F29	20A	RH front electric window

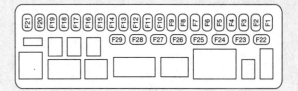

H33694

Wire colours				Key to items		Diagram 2

Wire colours

Bk	Black	Pk	Pink
Ye	Yellow	Vt	Violet
Bu	Blue	Og	Orange
Bn	Brown	Wh	White
Gn	Green	Rd	Red
Gy	Grey	Lgn	Lt. Green

Key to items

1 Battery
2 Alternator
3 Starter motor
4 Engine fusebox
  a = electronic load detection unit
  b = horn relay
  c = engine cooling fan relay
  d = condenser fan relay
  e = compressor clutch relay

5 Ignition switch
6 Passenger fusebox
7 Starter inhibitor relay
8 Transmission switch
9 Power steering control unit
10 Power steering torque sensor
11 Power steering motor
12 Horn switch
13 Horn

14 Steering wheel clock spring
15 Engine cooling fan motor
16 Engine cooling fan switch
17 Condenser cooling fan motor
18 Compressor clutch
19 Thermal protector
20 Condenser (noise filter)
21 Diagnostic connector

H33695

Starting & charging

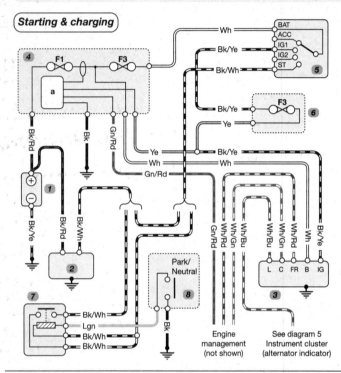

Electronic power steering

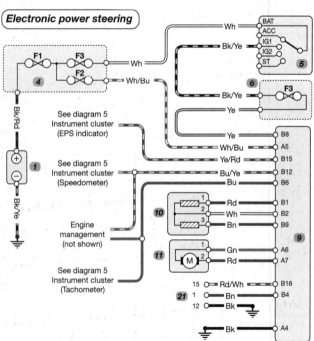

Horn

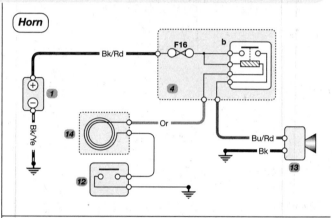

Engine cooling & condenser fans, compressor clutch

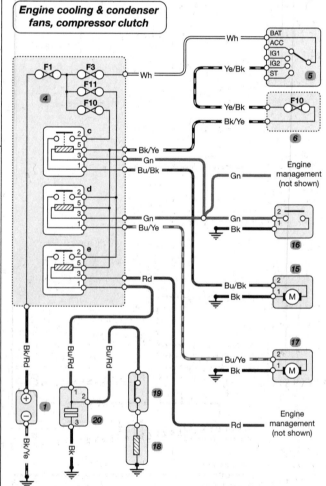

Wire colours

Bk	Black	Pk	Pink
Ye	Yellow	Vt	Violet
Bu	Blue	Og	Orange
Bn	Brown	Wh	White
Gn	Green	Rd	Red
Gy	Grey	Lgn	Lt. Green

Key to items

1 Battery
4 Engine fusebox
   f = headlight relay
5 Ignition switch
6 Passenger fusebox
8 Transmission switch
23 Stop light switch
24 Reversing light switch (M/T)
25 Reversing light relay (A/T)
26 Diode
27 LH stop light

28 RH stop light
29 High level brake light
30 LH reversing light
31 RH reversing light
32 Combination switch
   a = side/headlight
   b = passing
   c = dip switch
   d = foglight switch
   e = direction indicator
33 Tail light relay

34 LH headlight
   a = dip beam
   b = main beam
35 RH headlight
   a = dip beam
   b = main beam
36 LH side light
37 RH side light
38 LH tail light
39 RH tail light
40 Number plate light

41 Rear foglight
42 Hazard warning light switch
43 LH front indicator
44 LH rear indicator
45 LH indicator side repeater
46 RH front indicator
47 RH rear indicator
48 RH indicator side repeater

Diagram 3

H33696

Stop & reversing lights

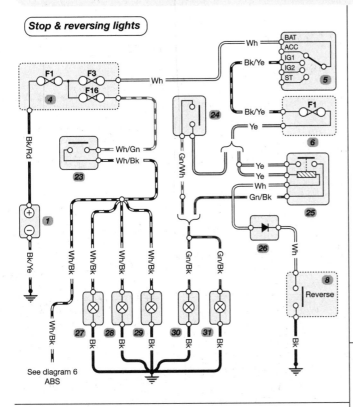

See diagram 6
ABS

Side, head & tail lights

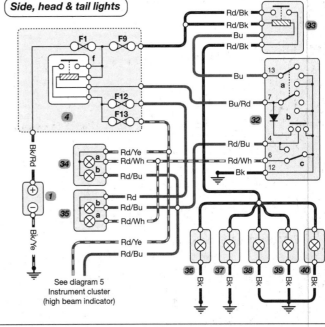

See diagram 5
Instrument cluster
(high beam indicator)

Rear foglights

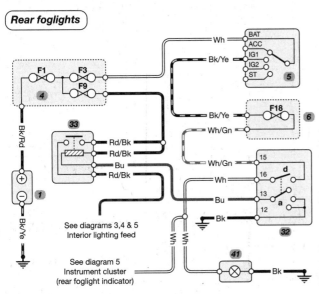

See diagrams 3,4 & 5
Interior lighting feed

See diagram 5
Instrument cluster
(rear foglight indicator)

Direction indicators & hazard warning lights

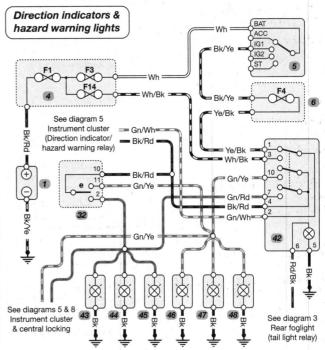

See diagram 5
Instrument cluster
(Direction indicator/
hazard warning relay)

See diagrams 5 & 8
Instrument cluster
& central locking

See diagram 3
Rear foglight
(tail light relay)

Wire colours

Bk	Black	Pk	Pink
Ye	Yellow	Vt	Violet
Bu	Blue	Og	Orange
Bn	Brown	Wh	White
Gn	Green	Rd	Red
Gy	Grey	Lgn	Lt. Green

Key to items

1 Battery
4 Engine fusebox
5 Ignition switch
6 Passenger fusebox
 a = heater blower relay
50 Headlight levelling switch
51 LH headlight levelling motor
52 RH headlight levelling motor
53 Front interior light
54 Rear interior light
55 Tailgate light
56 Tailgate switch
57 Cigar lighter
58 Accessory socket
59 Heated rear window
60 Heated rear window switch
61 Heater panel
62 Heater blower resistors
63 Heater blower motor

Diagram 4

H33697

Headlight levelling

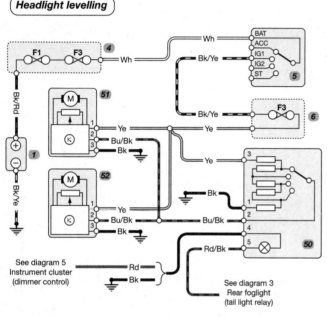

Heater blower

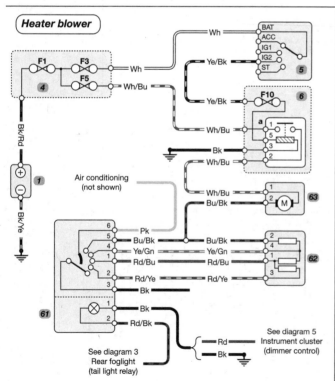

Interior lighting

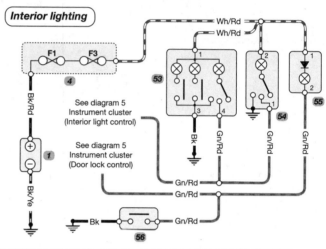

Cigar lighter & accessory socket

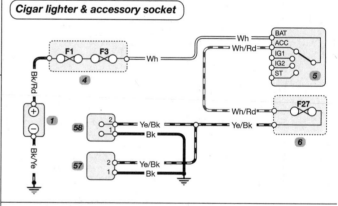

Heated rear window

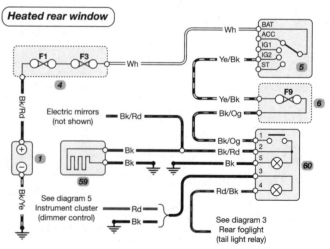

Wire colours

Bk	Black	**Pk**	Pink
Ye	Yellow	**Vt**	Violet
Bu	Blue	**Og**	Orange
Bn	Brown	**Wh**	White
Gn	Green	**Rd**	Red
Gy	Grey	**Lgn**	Lt. Green

Key to items

1 Battery
4 Engine fusebox
5 Ignition switch
6 Passenger fusebox
65 Instrument cluster
66 Vehicle speed sensor
67 Fuel gauge sender unit

68 Low brake fluid switch
69 Handbrake switch
70 Oil pressure switch
71 Driver's door switch
72 Passenger's door switch
73 LH rear door switch
74 RH rear door switch

75 Ignition key switch
76 Driver's seat belt switch
77 Tachometer test connector

Diagram 5

H33698

**Instrument cluster
(warning indicators & gauges)**

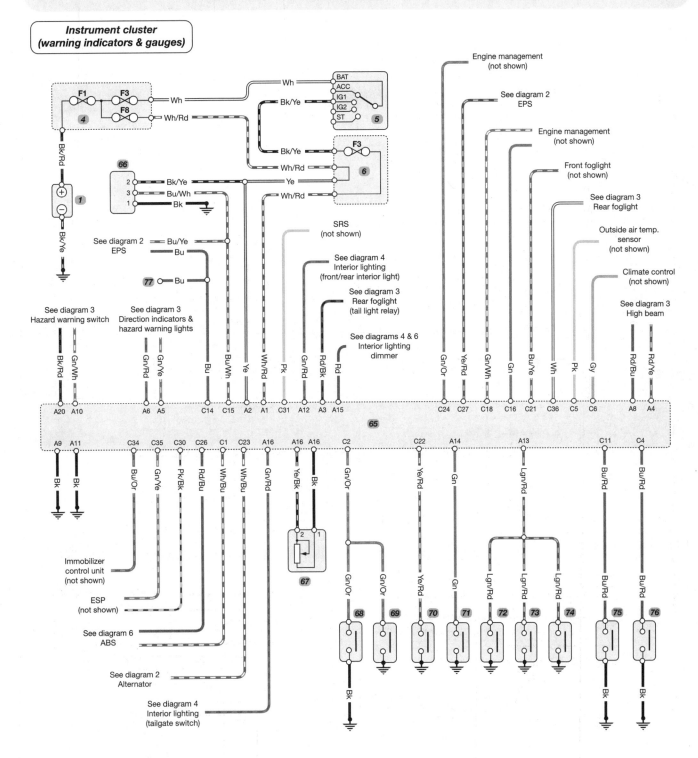

Wire colours

Bk	Black	Pk	Pink
Ye	Yellow	Vt	Violet
Bu	Blue	Og	Orange
Bn	Brown	Wh	White
Gn	Green	Rd	Red
Gy	Grey	Lgn	Lt. Green

Key to items

1 Battery
4 Engine fusebox
5 Ignition switch
6 Passenger fusebox
14 Steering wheel clock spring
21 Diagnostic connector
80 Sunroof open relay
81 Sunroof close relay

82 Sunroof motor
83 Sunroof limit switch
  a = tilt/close
  b = open/close
84 Sunroof switch
  a = tilt
  b = close
  c = open

85 ABS modulator/control unit
86 LH front wheel sensor
87 RH front wheel sensor
88 LH rear wheel sensor
89 RH rear wheel sensor
90 Audio unit
91 Auxiliary input
92 Audio remote controls

Diagram 6

93 LH front door speaker
94 RH front door speaker
95 LH rear door speaker
96 RH rear door speaker

H33699

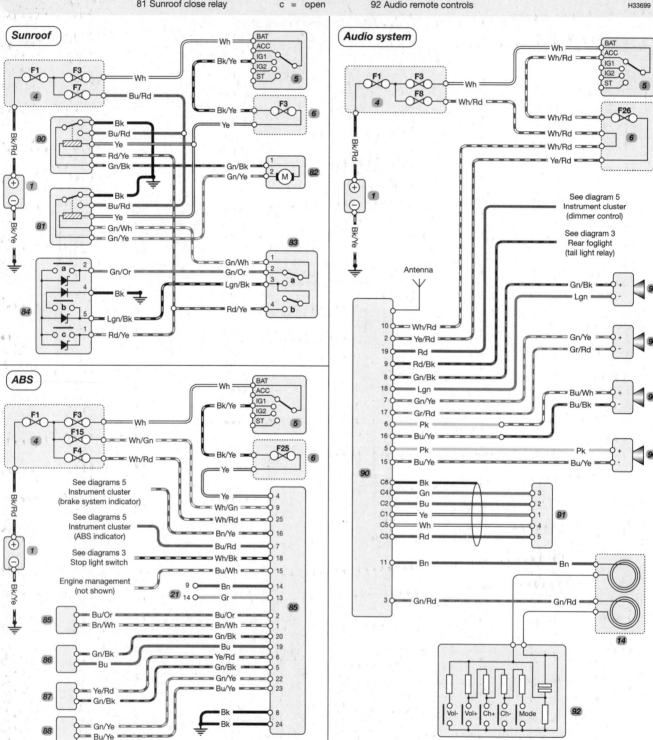

Wire colours

Bk	Black	**Pk**	Pink
Ye	Yellow	**Vt**	Violet
Bu	Blue	**Og**	Orange
Bn	Brown	**Wh**	White
Gn	Green	**Rd**	Red
Gy	Grey	**Lgn**	Lt. Green

Key to items

1 Battery
4 Engine fusebox
5 Ignition switch
6 Passenger fusebox
  b = electric window relay
100 Front washer pump
101 Rear washer pump
102 Front wiper motor
103 Rear wiper motor
104 Wiper switch
  a = washer

104 Wiper switch
  b = front wiper off/int/lo/hi
  c = front wiper off/mist
  d = int. wiper control
  e = rear wiper off/on
105 Driver's window motor
106 Passenger's window motor
107 LH rear window motor
108 RH rear window motor
109 Passenger's window switch
110 LH rear window switch

111 RH rear window switch
112 Electric window master switch
  a = control unit
  b = driver's switch
  c = passenger's switch
  d = LH rear switch
  e = RH rear switch
  f = master switch

Diagram 7

H33700

Wash/wipe

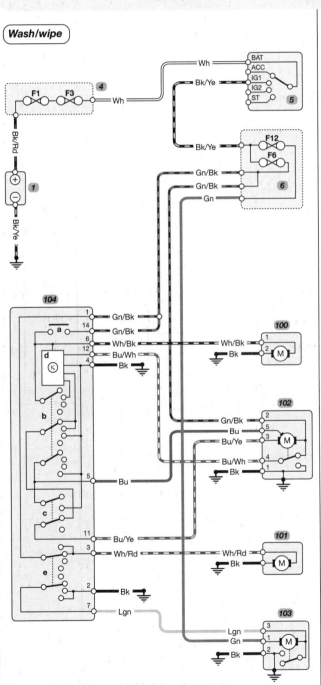

Electric windows

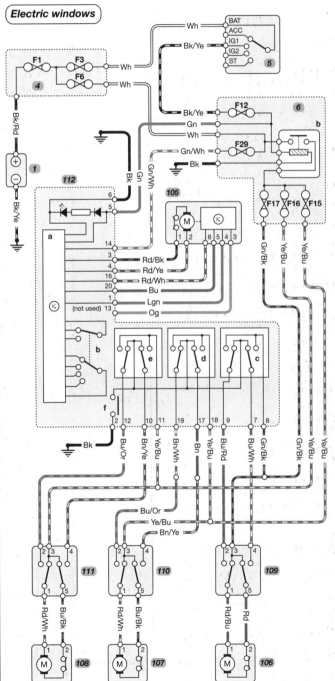

Wire colours

Bk	Black	Pk	Pink
Ye	Yellow	Vt	Violet
Bu	Blue	Og	Orange
Bn	Brown	Wh	White
Gn	Green	Rd	Red
Gy	Grey	Lgn	Lt. Green

Key to items

1 Battery
4 Engine fusebox
5 Ignition switch
6 Passenger fusebox
65 Instrument cluster
112 Electric window master switch
   g = central locking switch
115 LH deadlocking relay
116 RH deadlocking relay
117 Remote receiver unit

118 LH indicator activator relay
119 RH indicator activation relay
120 Central locking lock relay
121 Central locking unlock relay
122 Driver's door lock motor
123 Passenger's door lock motor
124 LH rear door lock motor
125 RH rear door lock motor
126 Tailgate lock motor
127 Driver's door lock switch

128 Passenger's door lock switch
129 LH rear door lock switch
130 RH rear door lock switch
131 Tailgate lock switch
132 Driver's door key switch
133 Passenger's door key switch
134 Tailgate key switch

Diagram 8

H33701

Central locking

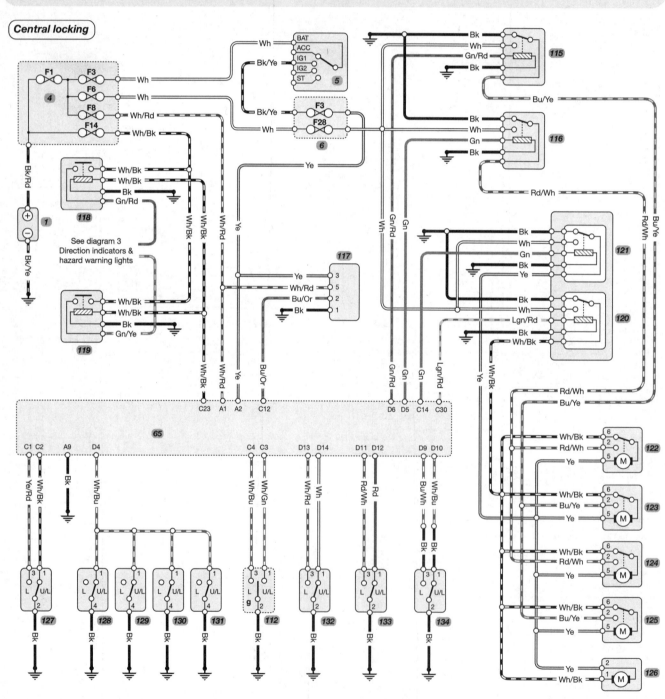

Reference

Dimensions and weights

Note: *All figures are approximate, and vary according to model. Refer to manufacturer's data for exact figures*

Dimensions

Overall length:
Early models.	3830 mm
Later models.	3845 mm
Sport models	3855 mm
Overall width.	1675 mm
Overall height (excluding aerial)	1525 mm

Weights

Kerb weight:

Manual transmission.	977 to 1055 kg	
Automatic transmission	1018 to 1080 kg	
Towing weight:	**Braked**	**Unbraked**
Manual transmission.	1000 kg	450 kg
Automatic transmission	800 kg	450 kg

Conversion factors

Length (distance)

Inches (in)	x 25.4	= Millimetres (mm)	x 0.0394	= Inches (in)
Feet (ft)	x 0.305	= Metres (m)	x 3.281	= Feet (ft)
Miles	x 1.609	= Kilometres (km)	x 0.621	= Miles

Volume (capacity)

Cubic inches (cu in; in³)	x 16.387	= Cubic centimetres (cc; cm³)	x 0.061	= Cubic inches (cu in; in³)
Imperial pints (Imp pt)	x 0.568	= Litres (l)	x 1.76	= Imperial pints (Imp pt)
Imperial quarts (Imp qt)	x 1.137	= Litres (l)	x 0.88	= Imperial quarts (Imp qt)
Imperial quarts (Imp qt)	x 1.201	= US quarts (US qt)	x 0.833	= Imperial quarts (Imp qt)
US quarts (US qt)	x 0.946	= Litres (l)	x 1.057	= US quarts (US qt)
Imperial gallons (Imp gal)	x 4.546	= Litres (l)	x 0.22	= Imperial gallons (Imp gal)
Imperial gallons (Imp gal)	x 1.201	= US gallons (US gal)	x 0.833	= Imperial gallons (Imp gal)
US gallons (US gal)	x 3.785	= Litres (l)	x 0.264	= US gallons (US gal)

Mass (weight)

Ounces (oz)	x 28.35	= Grams (g)	x 0.035	= Ounces (oz)
Pounds (lb)	x 0.454	= Kilograms (kg)	x 2.205	= Pounds (lb)

Force

Ounces-force (ozf; oz)	x 0.278	= Newtons (N)	x 3.6	= Ounces-force (ozf; oz)
Pounds-force (lbf; lb)	x 4.448	= Newtons (N)	x 0.225	= Pounds-force (lbf; lb)
Newtons (N)	x 0.1	= Kilograms-force (kgf; kg)	x 9.81	= Newtons (N)

Pressure

Pounds-force per square inch (psi; lbf/in²; lb/in²)	x 0.070	= Kilograms-force per square centimetre (kgf/cm²; kg/cm²)	x 14.223	= Pounds-force per square inch (psi; lbf/in²; lb/in²)
Pounds-force per square inch (psi; lbf/in²; lb/in²)	x 0.068	= Atmospheres (atm)	x 14.696	= Pounds-force per square inch (psi; lbf/in²; lb/in²)
Pounds-force per square inch (psi; lbf/ln²; lb/ln²)	x 0.069	= Bars	x 14.5	= Pounds-force per square inch (psi; lbf/in²; lb/in²)
Pounds-force per square inch (psi; lbf/in²; lb/in²)	x 6.895	= Kilopascals (kPa)	x 0.145	= Pounds-force per square inch (psi; lbf/in²; lb/in²)
Kilopascals (kPa)	x 0.01	= Kilograms-force per square centimetre (kgf/cm²; kg/cm²)	x 98.1	= Kilopascals (kPa)
Millibar (mbar)	x 100	= Pascals (Pa)	x 0.01	= Millibar (mbar)
Millibar (mbar)	x 0.0145	= Pounds-force per square inch (psi; lbf/in²; lb/in²)	x 68.947	= Millibar (mbar)
Millibar (mbar)	x 0.75	= Millimetres of mercury (mmHg)	x 1.333	= Millibar (mbar)
Millibar (mbar)	x 0.401	= Inches of water (inH₂O)	x 2.491	= Millibar (mbar)
Millimetres of mercury (mmHg)	x 0.535	= Inches of water (inH₂O)	x 1.868	= Millimetres of mercury (mmHg)
Inches of water (inH₂O)	x 0.036	= Pounds-force per square inch (psi; lbf/in²; lb/in²)	x 27.68	= Inches of water (inH₂O)

Torque (moment of force)

Pounds-force inches (lbf in; lb in)	x 1.152	= Kilograms-force centimetre (kgf cm; kg cm)	x 0.868	= Pounds-force inches (lbf in; lb in)
Pounds-force inches (lbf in; lb in)	x 0.113	= Newton metres (Nm)	x 8.85	= Pounds-force Inches (lbf in; lb in)
Pounds-force inches (lbf in; lb in)	x 0.083	= Pounds-force feet (lbf ft; lb ft)	x 12	= Pounds-force inches (lbf in; lb in)
Pounds-force feet (lbf ft; lb ft)	x 0.138	= Kilograms-force metres (kgf m; kg m)	x 7.233	= Pounds-force feet (lbf ft; lb ft)
Pounds-force feet (lbf ft; lb ft)	x 1.356	= Newton metres (Nm)	x 0.738	= Pounds-force feet (lbf ft; lb ft)
Newton metres (Nm)	x 0.102	= Kilograms-force metres (kgf m; kg m)	x 9.804	= Newton metres (Nm)

Power

Horsepower (hp)	x 745.7	= Watts (W)	x 0.0013	= Horsepower (hp)

Velocity (speed)

Miles per hour (miles/hr; mph)	x 1.609	= Kilometres per hour (km/hr; kph)	x 0.621	= Miles per hour (miles/hr; mph)

Fuel consumption*

Miles per gallon, Imperial (mpg)	x 0.354	= Kilometres per litre (km/l)	x 2.825	= Miles per gallon, Imperial (mpg)
Miles per gallon, US (mpg)	x 0.425	= Kilometres per litre (km/l)	x 2.352	= Miles per gallon, US (mpg)

Temperature

Degrees Fahrenheit = (°C x 1.8) + 32   Degrees Celsius (Degrees Centigrade; °C) = (°F - 32) x 0.56

It is common practice to convert from miles per gallon (mpg) to litres/100 kilometres (l/100km), where mpg x l/100 km = 282

Spare parts are available from many sources, including maker's appointed garages, accessory shops, and motor factors. To be sure of obtaining the correct parts, it will sometimes be necessary to quote the vehicle identification number (see *Vehicle identification*). If possible, it can also be useful to take the old parts along for positive identification. Items such as starter motors and alternators may be available under a service exchange scheme – any parts returned should always be clean.

Our advice regarding spare part sources is as follows.

Officially-appointed garages

This is the best source of parts which are peculiar to your car, and which are not otherwise generally available (eg, badges, interior trim, certain body panels, etc). It is also the only place at which you should buy parts if the car is still under warranty.

Accessory shops

These are very good places to buy materials and components needed for the maintenance of your car (oil, air and fuel filters, light bulbs, drivebelts, greases, brake pads, touch-up paint, etc). Components of this nature sold by a reputable shop are of the same standard as those used by the car manufacturer.

Besides components, these shops also sell tools and general accessories, usually have convenient opening hours, charge lower prices, and can often be found close to home. Some accessory shops have parts counters where components needed for almost any repair job can be purchased or ordered.

Motor factors

Good factors will stock all the more important components which wear out comparatively quickly, and can sometimes supply individual components needed for the overhaul of a larger assembly (eg, brake seals and hydraulic parts, bearing shells, pistons, valves). They may also handle work such as cylinder block reboring, crankshaft regrinding, etc.

Tyre and exhaust specialists

These outlets may be independent, or members of a local or national chain. They frequently offer competitive prices when compared with a main dealer or local garage, but it will pay to obtain several quotes before making a decision. When researching prices, also ask what 'extras' may be added – for instance fitting a new valve and balancing the wheel are both commonly charged on top of the price of a new tyre.

Other sources

Beware of parts or materials obtained from market stalls, car boot sales or similar outlets. Such items are not invariably sub-standard, but there is little chance of compensation if they do prove unsatisfactory. In the case of safety-critical components such as brake pads, there is the risk not only of financial loss, but also of an accident causing injury or death.

Second-hand components or assemblies obtained from a car breaker can be a good buy in some circumstances, but his sort of purchase is best made by the experienced DIY mechanic.

Modifications are a continuing and unpublicised process in vehicle manufacture, quite apart from major model changes. Spare parts manuals and lists are compiled upon a numerical basis, the individual vehicle identification numbers being essential to correct identification of the component concerned.

When ordering spare parts, always give as much information as possible. Quote the car model, year of manufacture, body and engine numbers as appropriate.

The *vehicle identification number plate* is located under the bonnet, on the front panel next to the bonnet lock **(see illustration)**. In addition to many other details, it carries the Vehicle Identification Number (VIN), maximum vehicle weight information, and codes for interior trim and body colours.

The *Vehicle Identification Number* (VIN) is given on the vehicle identification plate. It is also stamped into the bulkhead at the rear of the engine compartment, and appears on a tag on the left-hand side of the facia, so that it can be seen through the bottom left-hand corner of the windscreen **(see illustrations)**.

The *engine number* is stamped on the transmission end of the block, on a square area below the clutch bleed screw **(see illustration)**.

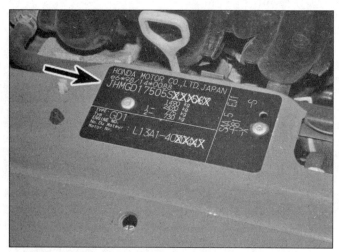

The VIN plate is on the front panel, next to the bonnet lock

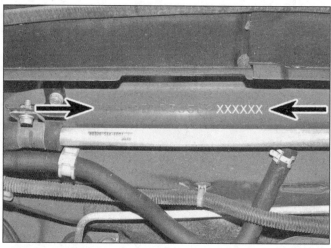

The VIN is stamped into the bulkhead at the back of the engine bay

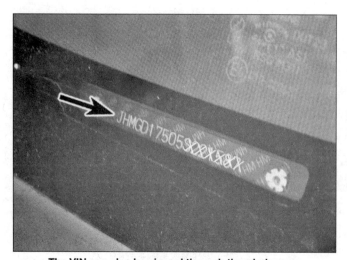

The VIN can also be viewed through the windscreen

The engine number appears on this square area

Whenever servicing, repair or overhaul work is carried out on the car or its components, observe the following procedures and instructions. This will assist in carrying out the operation efficiently and to a professional standard of workmanship.

Joint mating faces and gaskets

When separating components at their mating faces, never insert screwdrivers or similar implements into the joint between the faces in order to prise them apart. This can cause severe damage which results in oil leaks, coolant leaks, etc upon reassembly. Separation is usually achieved by tapping along the joint with a soft-faced hammer in order to break the seal. However, note that this method may not be suitable where dowels are used for component location.

Where a gasket is used between the mating faces of two components, a new one must be fitted on reassembly; fit it dry unless otherwise stated in the repair procedure. Make sure that the mating faces are clean and dry, with all traces of old gasket removed. When cleaning a joint face, use a tool which is unlikely to score or damage the face, and remove any burrs or nicks with an oilstone or fine file.

Make sure that tapped holes are cleaned with a pipe cleaner, and keep them free of jointing compound, if this is being used, unless specifically instructed otherwise.

Ensure that all orifices, channels or pipes are clear, and blow through them, preferably using compressed air.

Oil seals

Oil seals can be removed by levering them out with a wide flat-bladed screwdriver or similar implement. Alternatively, a number of self-tapping screws may be screwed into the seal, and these used as a purchase for pliers or some similar device in order to pull the seal free.

Whenever an oil seal is removed from its working location, either individually or as part of an assembly, it should be renewed.

The very fine sealing lip of the seal is easily damaged, and will not seal if the surface it contacts is not completely clean and free from scratches, nicks or grooves. If the original sealing surface of the component cannot be restored, and the manufacturer has not made provision for slight relocation of the seal relative to the sealing surface, the component should be renewed.

Protect the lips of the seal from any surface which may damage them in the course of fitting. Use tape or a conical sleeve where possible. Lubricate the seal lips with oil before fitting and, on dual-lipped seals, fill the space between the lips with grease.

Unless otherwise stated, oil seals must be fitted with their sealing lips toward the lubricant to be sealed.

Use a tubular drift or block of wood of the appropriate size to install the seal and, if the seal housing is shouldered, drive the seal down to the shoulder. If the seal housing is unshouldered, the seal should be fitted with its face flush with the housing top face (unless otherwise instructed).

Screw threads and fastenings

Seized nuts, bolts and screws are quite a common occurrence where corrosion has set in, and the use of penetrating oil or releasing fluid will often overcome this problem if the offending item is soaked for a while before attempting to release it. The use of an impact driver may also provide a means of releasing such stubborn fastening devices, when used in conjunction with the appropriate screwdriver bit or socket. If none of these methods works, it may be necessary to resort to the careful application of heat, or the use of a hacksaw or nut splitter device.

Studs are usually removed by locking two nuts together on the threaded part, and then using a spanner on the lower nut to unscrew the stud. Studs or bolts which have broken off below the surface of the component in which they are mounted can sometimes be removed using a stud extractor. Always ensure that a blind tapped hole is completely free from oil, grease, water or other fluid before installing the bolt or stud. Failure to do this could cause the housing to crack due to the hydraulic action of the bolt or stud as it is screwed in.

When tightening a castellated nut to accept a split pin, tighten the nut to the specified torque, where applicable, and then tighten further to the next split pin hole. Never slacken the nut to align the split pin hole, unless stated in the repair procedure.

When checking or retightening a nut or bolt to a specified torque setting, slacken the nut or bolt by a quarter of a turn, and then retighten to the specified setting. However, this should not be attempted where angular tightening has been used.

For some screw fastenings, notably cylinder head bolts or nuts, torque wrench settings are no longer specified for the latter stages of tightening, "angle-tightening" being called up instead. Typically, a fairly low torque wrench setting will be applied to the bolts/nuts in the correct sequence, followed by one or more stages of tightening through specified angles.

Locknuts, locktabs and washers

Any fastening which will rotate against a component or housing during tightening should always have a washer between it and the relevant component or housing.

Spring or split washers should always be renewed when they are used to lock a critical component such as a big-end bearing retaining bolt or nut. Locktabs which are folded over to retain a nut or bolt should always be renewed.

Self-locking nuts can be re-used in non-critical areas, providing resistance can be felt when the locking portion passes over the bolt or stud thread. However, it should be noted that self-locking stiffnuts tend to lose their effectiveness after long periods of use, and should then be renewed as a matter of course.

Split pins must always be replaced with new ones of the correct size for the hole.

When thread-locking compound is found on the threads of a fastener which is to be re-used, it should be cleaned off with a wire brush and solvent, and fresh compound applied on reassembly.

Special tools

Some repair procedures in this manual entail the use of special tools such as a press, two or three-legged pullers, spring compressors, etc. Wherever possible, suitable readily-available alternatives to the manufacturer's special tools are described, and are shown in use. In some instances, where no alternative is possible, it has been necessary to resort to the use of a manufacturer's tool, and this has been done for reasons of safety as well as the efficient completion of the repair operation. Unless you are highly-skilled and have a thorough understanding of the procedures described, never attempt to bypass the use of any special tool when the procedure described specifies its use. Not only is there a very great risk of personal injury, but expensive damage could be caused to the components involved.

Environmental considerations

When disposing of used engine oil, brake fluid, antifreeze, etc, give due consideration to any detrimental environmental effects. Do not, for instance, pour any of the above liquids down drains into the general sewage system, or onto the ground to soak away. Many local council refuse tips provide a facility for waste oil disposal, as do some garages. If none of these facilities are available, consult your local Environmental Health Department, or the National Rivers Authority, for further advice.

With the universal tightening-up of legislation regarding the emission of environmentally-harmful substances from motor vehicles, most vehicles have tamperproof devices fitted to the main adjustment points of the fuel system. These devices are primarily designed to prevent unqualified persons from adjusting the fuel/air mixture, with the chance of a consequent increase in toxic emissions. If such devices are found during servicing or overhaul, they should, wherever possible, be renewed or refitted in accordance with the manufacturer's requirements or current legislation.

OIL CARE
OIL BANK LINE
0800 66 33 66
www.oilbankline.org.uk

Note: It is antisocial and illegal to dump oil down the drain. To find the location of your local oil recycling bank, call this number free.

The jack supplied with the car's tool kit should only be used for changing the roadwheels – see *Wheel changing* at the front of this book. When carrying out any other kind of work, raise the car using a hydraulic (or 'trolley') jack, and always supplement the jack with axle stands positioned under the jacking/support points. If the roadwheels do not have to be removed, consider using wheel ramps – if wished, these can be placed under the wheels once the car has been raised using a hydraulic jack, and then lowered onto the ramps so that it is resting on its wheels.

Only ever jack the car up on a solid, level surface. If there is even a slight slope, take great care that the car cannot move as the wheels are lifted off the ground. Jacking up on an uneven or gravelled surface is not recommended, as the weight of the car will not be evenly distributed, and the jack may slip as the car is raised.

As far as possible, do not leave the car unattended once it has been raised, particularly if children are playing nearby.

Before jacking up the front of the car, ensure that the handbrake is firmly applied – it is also advisable to chock behind the rear wheels. Place the jack head under the front jacking points on the door sill (these are elongated tabs on the base of the sill, intended for use with the slotted-head vehicle jack). If the

vehicle jack is not being used, place a block of wood (with a slot cut in, ideally) between the jack head and the sill to prevent damage. Honda also suggest using the front centre-pad on the radiator crossmember (just behind the front bumper) as a support point. Alternatively, if care is taken, most places on the front subframe make an acceptable support point. Always place a flat piece of wood on the jack head, to spread the load and prevent underbody damage **(see illustrations)**.

To raise the rear of the car, chock the front wheels and engage a gear (or select P). Use the two rear jacking points on the door sill, with a slotted block of wood to prevent damage. Rear support points are less easy to find – the rear axle must not be used, and there are brake and fuel pipes to avoid also.

There is a support point inboard of the sill jacking points which can be used, but care should be taken, as the 'target area' is quite small. Honda provide a support point in the centre of the car, just inside the bottom edge of the rear bumper – any jack used here must be substantial, as the weight of the whole rear end is being lifted (there is also a danger of the car tipping sideways). Also, the bottom surface of this central jacking point is not flat – the rear towing eye is incorporated into it – so care must be taken when positioning the jack head. The only alternative is to jack up on the rear sill points, and place axle stands as close to these points as possible. If no work is being carried out on the rear suspension, the car could be jacked up under the rear spring plates, but a substantial jack should be used, as this is not the most stable solution **(see illustrations)**.

To raise the side of the car, prepare the car as described for front AND rear lifting. Place the jack head under the appropriate points.

Do not jack the car under any other part of the sill, sump, floor pan, or directly under any of the steering or suspension components.

Never work under, around, or near a raised car, unless it is adequately supported on stands. Do not rely on a jack alone, as even a hydraulic jack could fail under load.

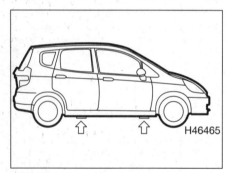

The sill jacking points are elongated tabs

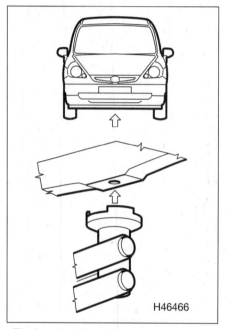

The front jacking point is just behind the front bumper

Jacking the front of the car using the sill jacking point and the front subframe

At the rear, use the sill jacking point, and either . . .

. . . the rear jacking point suggested by Honda . . .

. . . or jack under the rear spring plates

Several systems fitted to the car require battery power to be available at all times, either to ensure their continued operation (such as the clock), or to maintain electronic memory settings which would otherwise be erased. Whenever the battery is to be disconnected, first note the following points, to ensure there are no unforeseen consequences:

a) *First, on any car with central door locking, it is a wise precaution to remove the key from the ignition, and to keep it with you, so that it does not get locked in if the central locking engages when the battery is reconnected.*

b) *During normal operation, the car's engine control module (ECM) learns and stores idling and other engine operating values in its memory. Whenever the battery is disconnected, this information is lost, and has to be relearned. The ECM does this by itself, but until then, there may be surging, hesitation, erratic idle and a generally inferior level of performance. To allow the ECM to relearn these values, start the engine and run it at a fast idle (Honda recommend 3000 rpm) until it reaches its normal operating temperature, then let it idle (with all loads switched off) for at least five minutes, and longer than this if the radiator fan comes on during this time. Next, drive the car as far as necessary – approximately 5 miles of varied driving conditions is usually sufficient – to complete the relearning process.*

c) *If the battery is disconnected while the alarm system is armed or activated, the alarm will remain in the same state when the battery is reconnected. The same applies to the engine immobiliser system. In some cases, the alarm may sound on reconnecting the battery – have the remote control ready to disarm the system.*

d) *If work is being carried out on the car's airbag or seat belt tensioner systems, the battery should be reconnected last – ie, after all the airbag and belt tensioner wiring has been reconnected.*

e) *Where electric windows with 'one-touch' or 'auto' operation are fitted, this function may not work correctly until each window has been reset. This is done by fully opening the window, keeping the button pressed for a few seconds after opening so the system can 'learn' the fully-open position. Close the window, again keeping the button pressed for a second or two.*

f) *Sometimes, the electric power steering will not function properly after the battery is disconnected, or if the battery voltage drops too low. The system will log a fault code, and until the codes are cleared, the steering will not work. Refer to Chapter 10, Section 19, for more information.*

⚠ **Warning: Do not use battery-operated radio key code savers, as these may cause the airbag to be deployed, with the possibility of personal injury.**

Introduction

A selection of good tools is a fundamental requirement for anyone contemplating the maintenance and repair of a motor vehicle. For the owner who does not possess any, their purchase will prove a considerable expense, offsetting some of the savings made by doing-it-yourself. However, provided that the tools purchased meet the relevant national safety standards and are of good quality, they will last for many years and prove an extremely worthwhile investment.

To help the average owner to decide which tools are needed to carry out the various tasks detailed in this manual, we have compiled three lists of tools under the following headings: *Maintenance and minor repair, Repair and overhaul*, and *Special*. Newcomers to practical mechanics should start off with the *Maintenance and minor repair* tool kit, and confine themselves to the simpler jobs around the vehicle. Then, as confidence and experience grow, more difficult tasks can be undertaken, with extra tools being purchased as, and when, they are needed. In this way, a *Maintenance and minor repair* tool kit can be built up into a *Repair and overhaul* tool kit over a considerable period of time, without any major cash outlays. The experienced do-it-yourselfer will have a tool kit good enough for most repair and overhaul procedures, and will add tools from the *Special* category when it is felt that the expense is justified by the amount of use to which these tools will be put.

Maintenance and minor repair tool kit

The tools given in this list should be considered as a minimum requirement if routine maintenance, servicing and minor repair operations are to be undertaken. We recommend the purchase of combination spanners (ring one end, open-ended the other); although more expensive than open-ended ones, they do give the advantages of both types of spanner.

☐ *Combination spanners:*
  Metric - 8 to 19 mm inclusive
☐ *Adjustable spanner - 35 mm jaw (approx.)*
☐ *Spark plug spanner (with rubber insert) - petrol models*
☐ *Spark plug gap adjustment tool - petrol models*
☐ *Set of feeler gauges*
☐ *Brake bleed nipple spanner*
☐ *Screwdrivers:*
  Flat blade - 100 mm long x 6 mm dia
  Cross blade - 100 mm long x 6 mm dia
  Torx - various sizes (not all vehicles)
☐ *Combination pliers*
☐ *Hacksaw (junior)*
☐ *Tyre pump*
☐ *Tyre pressure gauge*
☐ *Oil can*
☐ *Oil filter removal tool*
☐ *Fine emery cloth*
☐ *Wire brush (small)*
☐ *Funnel (medium size)*
☐ *Sump drain plug key (not all vehicles)*

Repair and overhaul tool kit

These tools are virtually essential for anyone undertaking any major repairs to a motor vehicle, and are additional to those given in the *Maintenance and minor repair* list. Included in this list is a comprehensive set of sockets. Although these are expensive, they will be found invaluable as they are so versatile - particularly if various drives are included in the set. We recommend the half-inch square-drive type, as this can be used with most proprietary torque wrenches.

The tools in this list will sometimes need to be supplemented by tools from the *Special* list:

☐ *Sockets (or box spanners) to cover range in previous list (including Torx sockets)*
☐ *Reversible ratchet drive (for use with sockets)*
☐ *Extension piece, 250 mm (for use with sockets)*
☐ *Universal joint (for use with sockets)*
☐ *Flexible handle or sliding T "breaker bar" (for use with sockets)*
☐ *Torque wrench (for use with sockets)*
☐ *Self-locking grips*
☐ *Ball pein hammer*
☐ *Soft-faced mallet (plastic or rubber)*
☐ *Screwdrivers:*
  Flat blade - long & sturdy, short (chubby), and narrow (electrician's) types
  Cross blade – long & sturdy, and short (chubby) types
☐ *Pliers:*
  Long-nosed
  Side cutters (electrician's)
  Circlip (internal and external)
☐ *Cold chisel - 25 mm*
☐ *Scriber*
☐ *Scraper*
☐ *Centre-punch*
☐ *Pin punch*
☐ *Hacksaw*
☐ *Brake hose clamp*
☐ *Brake/clutch bleeding kit*
☐ *Selection of twist drills*
☐ *Steel rule/straight-edge*
☐ *Allen keys (inc. splined/Torx type)*
☐ *Selection of files*
☐ *Wire brush*
☐ *Axle stands*
☐ *Jack (strong trolley or hydraulic type)*
☐ *Light with extension lead*
☐ *Universal electrical multi-meter*

Sockets and reversible ratchet drive

Brake bleeding kit

Torx key, socket and bit

Hose clamp

Angular-tightening gauge

Special tools

The tools in this list are those which are not used regularly, are expensive to buy, or which need to be used in accordance with their manufacturers' instructions. Unless relatively difficult mechanical jobs are undertaken frequently, it will not be economic to buy many of these tools. Where this is the case, you could consider clubbing together with friends (or joining a motorists' club) to make a joint purchase, or borrowing the tools against a deposit from a local garage or tool hire specialist. It is worth noting that many of the larger DIY superstores now carry a large range of special tools for hire at modest rates.

The following list contains only those tools and instruments freely available to the public, and not those special tools produced by the vehicle manufacturer specifically for its dealer network. You will find occasional references to these manufacturers' special tools in the text of this manual. Generally, an alternative method of doing the job without the vehicle manufacturers' special tool is given. However, sometimes there is no alternative to using them. Where this is the case and the relevant tool cannot be bought or borrowed, you will have to entrust the work to a dealer.

- ☐ Angular-tightening gauge
- ☐ Valve spring compressor
- ☐ Valve grinding tool
- ☐ Piston ring compressor
- ☐ Piston ring removal/installation tool
- ☐ Cylinder bore hone
- ☐ Balljoint separator
- ☐ Coil spring compressors (where applicable)
- ☐ Two/three-legged hub and bearing puller
- ☐ Impact screwdriver
- ☐ Micrometer and/or vernier calipers
- ☐ Dial gauge
- ☐ Stroboscopic timing light
- ☐ Dwell angle meter/tachometer
- ☐ Fault code reader
- ☐ Cylinder compression gauge
- ☐ Hand-operated vacuum pump and gauge
- ☐ Clutch plate alignment set
- ☐ Brake shoe steady spring cup removal tool
- ☐ Bush and bearing removal/installation set
- ☐ Stud extractors
- ☐ Tap and die set
- ☐ Lifting tackle
- ☐ Trolley jack

Buying tools

Reputable motor accessory shops and superstores often offer excellent quality tools at discount prices, so it pays to shop around.

Remember, you don't have to buy the most expensive items on the shelf, but it is always advisable to steer clear of the very cheap tools. Beware of 'bargains' offered on market stalls or at car boot sales. There are plenty of good tools around at reasonable prices, but always aim to purchase items which meet the relevant national safety standards. If in doubt, ask the proprietor or manager of the shop for advice before making a purchase.

Care and maintenance of tools

Having purchased a reasonable tool kit, it is necessary to keep the tools in a clean and serviceable condition. After use, always wipe off any dirt, grease and metal particles using a clean, dry cloth, before putting the tools away. Never leave them lying around after they have been used. A simple tool rack on the garage or workshop wall for items such as screwdrivers and pliers is a good idea. Store all normal spanners and sockets in a metal box. Any measuring instruments, gauges, meters, etc, must be carefully stored where they cannot be damaged or become rusty.

Take a little care when tools are used. Hammer heads inevitably become marked, and screwdrivers lose the keen edge on their blades from time to time. A little timely attention with emery cloth or a file will soon restore items like this to a good finish.

Working facilities

Not to be forgotten when discussing tools is the workshop itself. If anything more than routine maintenance is to be carried out, a suitable working area becomes essential.

It is appreciated that many an owner-mechanic is forced by circumstances to remove an engine or similar item without the benefit of a garage or workshop. Having done this, any repairs should always be done under the cover of a roof.

Wherever possible, any dismantling should be done on a clean, flat workbench or table at a suitable working height.

Any workbench needs a vice; one with a jaw opening of 100 mm is suitable for most jobs. As mentioned previously, some clean dry storage space is also required for tools, as well as for any lubricants, cleaning fluids, touch-up paints etc, which become necessary.

Another item which may be required, and which has a much more general usage, is an electric drill with a chuck capacity of at least 8 mm. This, together with a good range of twist drills, is virtually essential for fitting accessories.

Last, but not least, always keep a supply of old newspapers and clean, lint-free rags available, and try to keep any working area as clean as possible.

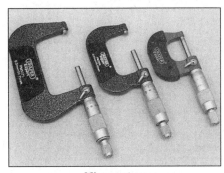

Micrometers

Dial test indicator ("dial gauge")

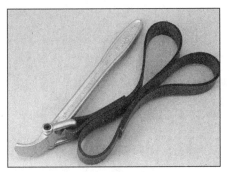

Strap wrench

Compression tester

Fault code reader

This is a guide to getting your vehicle through the MOT test. Obviously it will not be possible to examine the vehicle to the same standard as the professional MOT tester. However, working through the following checks will enable you to identify any problem areas before submitting the vehicle for the test.

It has only been possible to summarise the test requirements here, based on the regulations in force at the time of printing. Test standards are becoming increasingly stringent, although there are some exemptions for older vehicles.

An assistant will be needed to help carry out some of these checks.

The checks have been sub-divided into four categories, as follows:

1 Checks carried out **FROM THE DRIVER'S SEAT**

2 Checks carried out **WITH THE VEHICLE ON THE GROUND**

3 Checks carried out **WITH THE VEHICLE RAISED AND THE WHEELS FREE TO TURN**

4 Checks carried out on **YOUR VEHICLE'S EXHAUST EMISSION SYSTEM**

---

1 Checks carried out **FROM THE DRIVER'S SEAT**

Handbrake

☐ Test the operation of the handbrake. Excessive travel (too many clicks) indicates incorrect brake or cable adjustment.
☐ Check that the handbrake cannot be released by tapping the lever sideways. Check the security of the lever mountings.

Footbrake

☐ Depress the brake pedal and check that it does not creep down to the floor, indicating a master cylinder fault. Release the pedal, wait a few seconds, then depress it again. If the pedal travels nearly to the floor before firm resistance is felt, brake adjustment or repair is necessary. If the pedal feels spongy, there is air in the hydraulic system which must be removed by bleeding.

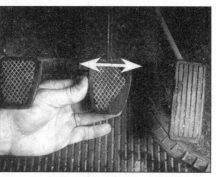

☐ Check that the brake pedal is secure and in good condition. Check also for signs of fluid leaks on the pedal, floor or carpets, which would indicate failed seals in the brake master cylinder.
☐ Check the servo unit (when applicable) by operating the brake pedal several times, then keeping the pedal depressed and starting the engine. As the engine starts, the pedal will move down slightly. If not, the vacuum hose or the servo itself may be faulty.

Steering wheel and column

☐ Examine the steering wheel for fractures or looseness of the hub, spokes or rim.
☐ Move the steering wheel from side to side and then up and down. Check that the steering wheel is not loose on the column, indicating wear or a loose retaining nut. Continue moving the steering wheel as before, but also turn it slightly from left to right.
☐ Check that the steering wheel is not loose on the column, and that there is no abnormal

movement of the steering wheel, indicating wear in the column support bearings or couplings.

Windscreen, mirrors and sunvisor

☐ The windscreen must be free of cracks or other significant damage within the driver's field of view. (Small stone chips are acceptable.) Rear view mirrors must be secure, intact, and capable of being adjusted.

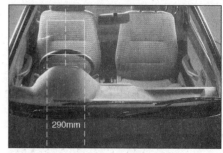

☐ The driver's sunvisor must be capable of being stored in the "up" position.

Seat belts and seats

Note: *The following checks are applicable to all seat belts, front and rear.*

☐ Examine the webbing of all the belts (including rear belts if fitted) for cuts, serious fraying or deterioration. Fasten and unfasten each belt to check the buckles. If applicable, check the retracting mechanism. Check the security of all seat belt mountings accessible from inside the vehicle.

☐ Seat belts with pre-tensioners, once activated, have a "flag" or similar showing on the seat belt stalk. This, in itself, is not a reason for test failure.

☐ The front seats themselves must be securely attached and the backrests must lock in the upright position.

Doors

☐ Both front doors must be able to be opened and closed from outside and inside, and must latch securely when closed.

2 Checks carried out WITH THE VEHICLE ON THE GROUND

Vehicle identification

☐ Number plates must be in good condition, secure and legible, with letters and numbers correctly spaced – spacing at (A) should be at least twice that at (B).

☐ The VIN plate and/or homologation plate must be legible.

Electrical equipment

☐ Switch on the ignition and check the operation of the horn.

☐ Check the windscreen washers and wipers, examining the wiper blades; renew damaged or perished blades. Also check the operation of the stop-lights.

☐ Check the operation of the sidelights and number plate lights. The lenses and reflectors must be secure, clean and undamaged.

☐ Check the operation and alignment of the headlights. The headlight reflectors must not be tarnished and the lenses must be undamaged.

☐ Switch on the ignition and check the operation of the direction indicators (including the instrument panel tell-tale) and the hazard warning lights. Operation of the sidelights and stop-lights must not affect the indicators - if it does, the cause is usually a bad earth at the rear light cluster.

☐ Check the operation of the rear foglight(s), including the warning light on the instrument panel or in the switch.

☐ The ABS warning light must illuminate in accordance with the manufacturers' design. For most vehicles, the ABS warning light should illuminate when the ignition is switched on, and (if the system is operating properly) extinguish after a few seconds. Refer to the owner's handbook.

Footbrake

☐ Examine the master cylinder, brake pipes and servo unit for leaks, loose mountings, corrosion or other damage.

☐ The fluid reservoir must be secure and the fluid level must be between the upper (**A**) and lower (**B**) markings.

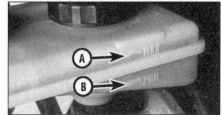

☐ Inspect both front brake flexible hoses for cracks or deterioration of the rubber. Turn the steering from lock to lock, and ensure that the hoses do not contact the wheel, tyre, or any part of the steering or suspension mechanism. With the brake pedal firmly depressed, check the hoses for bulges or leaks under pressure.

Steering and suspension

☐ Have your assistant turn the steering wheel from side to side slightly, up to the point where the steering gear just begins to transmit this movement to the roadwheels. Check for excessive free play between the steering wheel and the steering gear, indicating wear or insecurity of the steering column joints, the column-to-steering gear coupling, or the steering gear itself.

☐ Have your assistant turn the steering wheel more vigorously in each direction, so that the roadwheels just begin to turn. As this is done, examine all the steering joints, linkages, fittings and attachments. Renew any component that shows signs of wear or damage. On vehicles with power steering, check the security and condition of the steering pump, drivebelt and hoses.

☐ Check that the vehicle is standing level, and at approximately the correct ride height.

Shock absorbers

☐ Depress each corner of the vehicle in turn, then release it. The vehicle should rise and then settle in its normal position. If the vehicle continues to rise and fall, the shock absorber is defective. A shock absorber which has seized will also cause the vehicle to fail.

Exhaust system

☐ Start the engine. With your assistant holding a rag over the tailpipe, check the entire system for leaks. Repair or renew leaking sections.

3 Checks carried out **WITH THE VEHICLE RAISED AND THE WHEELS FREE TO TURN**

Jack up the front and rear of the vehicle, and securely support it on axle stands. Position the stands clear of the suspension assemblies. Ensure that the wheels are clear of the ground and that the steering can be turned from lock to lock.

Steering mechanism

☐ Have your assistant turn the steering from lock to lock. Check that the steering turns smoothly, and that no part of the steering mechanism, including a wheel or tyre, fouls any brake hose or pipe or any part of the body structure.

☐ Examine the steering rack rubber gaiters for damage or insecurity of the retaining clips. If power steering is fitted, check for signs of damage or leakage of the fluid hoses, pipes or connections. Also check for excessive stiffness or binding of the steering, a missing split pin or locking device, or severe corrosion of the body structure within 30 cm of any steering component attachment point.

Front and rear suspension and wheel bearings

☐ Starting at the front right-hand side, grasp the roadwheel at the 3 o'clock and 9 o'clock positions and rock gently but firmly. Check for free play or insecurity at the wheel bearings, suspension balljoints, or suspension mountings, pivots and attachments.

☐ Now grasp the wheel at the 12 o'clock and 6 o'clock positions and repeat the previous inspection. Spin the wheel, and check for roughness or tightness of the front wheel bearing.

☐ If excess free play is suspected at a component pivot point, this can be confirmed by using a large screwdriver or similar tool and levering between the mounting and the component attachment. This will confirm whether the wear is in the pivot bush, its retaining bolt, or in the mounting itself (the bolt holes can often become elongated).

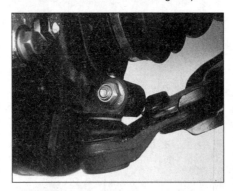

☐ Carry out all the above checks at the other front wheel, and then at both rear wheels.

Springs and shock absorbers

☐ Examine the suspension struts (when applicable) for serious fluid leakage, corrosion, or damage to the casing. Also check the security of the mounting points.

☐ If coil springs are fitted, check that the spring ends locate in their seats, and that the spring is not corroded, cracked or broken.

☐ If leaf springs are fitted, check that all leaves are intact, that the axle is securely attached to each spring, and that there is no deterioration of the spring eye mountings, bushes, and shackles.

☐ The same general checks apply to vehicles fitted with other suspension types, such as torsion bars, hydraulic displacer units, etc. Ensure that all mountings and attachments are secure, that there are no signs of excessive wear, corrosion or damage, and (on hydraulic types) that there are no fluid leaks or damaged pipes.

☐ Inspect the shock absorbers for signs of serious fluid leakage. Check for wear of the mounting bushes or attachments, or damage to the body of the unit.

Driveshafts (fwd vehicles only)

☐ Rotate each front wheel in turn and inspect the constant velocity joint gaiters for splits or damage. Also check that each driveshaft is straight and undamaged.

Braking system

☐ If possible without dismantling, check brake pad wear and disc condition. Ensure that the friction lining material has not worn excessively, (A) and that the discs are not fractured, pitted, scored or badly worn (B).

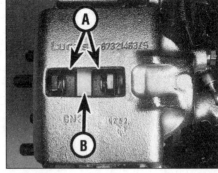

☐ Examine all the rigid brake pipes underneath the vehicle, and the flexible hose(s) at the rear. Look for corrosion, chafing or insecurity of the pipes, and for signs of bulging under pressure, chafing, splits or deterioration of the flexible hoses.

☐ Look for signs of fluid leaks at the brake calipers or on the brake backplates. Repair or renew leaking components.

☐ Slowly spin each wheel, while your assistant depresses and releases the footbrake. Ensure that each brake is operating and does not bind when the pedal is released.

□ Examine the handbrake mechanism, checking for frayed or broken cables, excessive corrosion, or wear or insecurity of the linkage. Check that the mechanism works on each relevant wheel, and releases fully, without binding.

□ It is not possible to test brake efficiency without special equipment, but a road test can be carried out later to check that the vehicle pulls up in a straight line.

Fuel and exhaust systems

□ Inspect the fuel tank (including the filler cap), fuel pipes, hoses and unions. All components must be secure and free from leaks.

□ Examine the exhaust system over its entire length, checking for any damaged, broken or missing mountings, security of the retaining clamps and rust or corrosion.

Wheels and tyres

□ Examine the sidewalls and tread area of each tyre in turn. Check for cuts, tears, lumps, bulges, separation of the tread, and exposure of the ply or cord due to wear or damage. Check that the tyre bead is correctly seated on the wheel rim, that the valve is sound and properly seated, and that the wheel is not distorted or damaged.

□ Check that the tyres are of the correct size for the vehicle, that they are of the same size

and type on each axle, and that the pressures are correct.

□ Check the tyre tread depth. The legal minimum at the time of writing is 1.6 mm over at least three-quarters of the tread width. Abnormal tread wear may indicate incorrect front wheel alignment.

Body corrosion

□ Check the condition of the entire vehicle structure for signs of corrosion in load-bearing areas. (These include chassis box sections, side sills, cross-members, pillars, and all suspension, steering, braking system and seat belt mountings and anchorages.) Any corrosion which has seriously reduced the thickness of a load-bearing area is likely to cause the vehicle to fail. In this case professional repairs are likely to be needed.

□ Damage or corrosion which causes sharp or otherwise dangerous edges to be exposed will also cause the vehicle to fail.

4 Checks carried out on **YOUR VEHICLE'S EXHAUST EMISSION SYSTEM**

Petrol models

□ The engine should be warmed up, and running well (ignition system in good order, air filter element clean, etc).

□ Before testing, run the engine at around 2500 rpm for 20 seconds. Let the engine drop to idle, and watch for smoke from the exhaust. If the idle speed is too high, or if dense blue or black smoke emerges for more than 5 seconds, the vehicle will fail. Typically, blue smoke signifies oil burning (engine wear); black smoke means unburnt fuel (dirty air cleaner element, or other fuel system fault).

□ An exhaust gas analyser for measuring carbon monoxide (CO) and hydrocarbons (HC) is now needed. If one cannot be hired or borrowed, have a local garage perform the check.

CO emissions (mixture)

□ The MOT tester has access to the CO limits for all vehicles. The CO level is measured at idle speed, and at 'fast idle' (2500 to 3000 rpm). The following limits are given as a general guide:
At idle speed – Less than 0.5% CO
At 'fast idle' – Less than 0.3% CO
Lambda reading – 0.97 to 1.03

□ If the CO level is too high, this may point to poor maintenance, a fuel injection system problem, faulty lambda (oxygen) sensor or catalytic converter. Try an injector cleaning treatment, and check the vehicle's ECU for fault codes.

HC emissions

□ The MOT tester has access to HC limits for all vehicles. The HC level is measured at 'fast idle' (2500 to 3000 rpm). The following limits are given as a general guide:
At 'fast idle' – Less then 200 ppm

□ Excessive HC emissions are typically caused by oil being burnt (worn engine), or by a blocked crankcase ventilation system ('breather'). If the engine oil is old and thin, an oil change may help. If the engine is running badly, check the vehicle's ECU for fault codes.

Diesel models

□ The only emission test for diesel engines is measuring exhaust smoke density, using a calibrated smoke meter. The test involves accelerating the engine at least 3 times to its maximum unloaded speed.

Note: *On engines with a timing belt, it is VITAL that the belt is in good condition before the test is carried out.*

□ With the engine warmed up, it is first purged by running at around 2500 rpm for 20 seconds. A governor check is then carried out, by slowly accelerating the engine to its maximum speed. After this, the smoke meter is connected, and the engine is accelerated quickly to maximum speed three times. If the smoke density is less than the limits given below, the vehicle will pass:
Non-turbo vehicles: 2.5m-1
Turbocharged vehicles: 3.0m-1

□ If excess smoke is produced, try fitting a new air cleaner element, or using an injector cleaning treatment. If the engine is running badly, where applicable, check the vehicle's ECU for fault codes. Also check the vehicle's EGR system, where applicable. At high mileages, the injectors may require professional attention.

Engine

- ☐ Engine fails to rotate when attempting to start
- ☐ Engine rotates, but will not start
- ☐ Engine difficult to start when cold
- ☐ Engine difficult to start when hot
- ☐ Starter motor noisy or excessively-rough in engagement
- ☐ Engine starts, but stops immediately
- ☐ Engine idles erratically
- ☐ Engine misfires at idle speed
- ☐ Engine misfires throughout the driving speed range
- ☐ Engine hesitates on acceleration
- ☐ Engine stalls
- ☐ Engine lacks power
- ☐ Engine backfires
- ☐ Oil pressure warning light illuminated with engine running
- ☐ Engine runs-on after switching off
- ☐ Engine noises

Cooling system

- ☐ Overheating
- ☐ Overcooling
- ☐ External coolant leakage
- ☐ Internal coolant leakage
- ☐ Corrosion

Fuel and exhaust systems

- ☐ Excessive fuel consumption
- ☐ Fuel leakage and/or fuel odour
- ☐ Excessive noise or fumes from exhaust system

Clutch

- ☐ Pedal travels to floor – no pressure or very little resistance
- ☐ Clutch fails to disengage (unable to select gears)
- ☐ Clutch slips (engine speed increases, with no increase in vehicle speed)
- ☐ Judder as clutch is engaged
- ☐ Noise when depressing or releasing clutch pedal

Manual transmission

- ☐ Noisy in neutral with engine running
- ☐ Noisy in one particular gear
- ☐ Difficulty engaging gears
- ☐ Jumps out of gear
- ☐ Vibration
- ☐ Lubricant leaks

Automatic transmission

- ☐ Fluid leakage
- ☐ Transmission fluid brown, or has burned smell
- ☐ General gear selection problems
- ☐ Transmission will not downshift (kickdown) with accelerator pedal fully depressed
- ☐ Engine will not start in any gear, or starts in gears other than Park or Neutral
- ☐ Transmission slips, shifts roughly, is noisy, or has no drive in forward or reverse gears

Driveshafts

- ☐ Vibration when accelerating or decelerating
- ☐ Clicking or knocking noise on turns (at slow speed on full-lock)

Braking system

- ☐ Car pulls to one side under braking
- ☐ Noise (grinding or high-pitched squeal) when brakes applied
- ☐ Excessive brake pedal travel
- ☐ Brake pedal feels spongy when depressed
- ☐ Excessive brake pedal effort required to stop car
- ☐ Judder felt through brake pedal or steering wheel when braking
- ☐ Brakes binding
- ☐ Rear wheels locking under normal braking
- ☐ ABS warning light stays on

Suspension and steering

- ☐ Car pulls to one side
- ☐ Wheel wobble and vibration
- ☐ Excessive pitching and/or rolling around corners, or during braking
- ☐ Wandering or general instability
- ☐ Excessively-stiff steering
- ☐ Excessive play in steering
- ☐ Lack of power assistance
- ☐ Tyre wear excessive

Electrical system

- ☐ Battery will not hold a charge for more than a few days
- ☐ Ignition/no-charge warning light remains illuminated with engine running
- ☐ Ignition/no-charge warning light fails to come on
- ☐ Lights inoperative
- ☐ Instrument readings inaccurate or erratic
- ☐ Horn inoperative, or unsatisfactory in operation
- ☐ Windscreen wipers inoperative, or unsatisfactory in operation
- ☐ Windscreen washers inoperative, or unsatisfactory in operation
- ☐ Electric windows inoperative, or unsatisfactory in operation
- ☐ Central locking system inoperative, or unsatisfactory in operation

Introduction

The car owner who does his or her own maintenance according to the recommended service schedules should not have to use this section of the manual very often. Modern component reliability is such that, provided those items subject to wear or deterioration are inspected or renewed at the specified intervals, sudden failure is comparatively rare. Faults do not usually just happen as a result of sudden failure, but develop over a period of time. Major mechanical failures in particular are usually preceded by characteristic symptoms over hundreds or even thousands of miles. Those components which do occasionally fail without warning are often small and easily carried in the car.

With any fault-finding, the first step is to decide where to begin investigations. Sometimes this is obvious, but on other occasions, a little detective work will be necessary. The owner who makes half a dozen haphazard adjustments or replacements may be successful in curing a fault (or its symptoms), but will be none the wiser if the fault recurs, and ultimately may have spent more time and money than was necessary. A calm and logical approach will be found to be more satisfactory in the long run. Always take into account any warning signs or abnormalities that may have been noticed in the period preceding the fault – power loss, high or low gauge readings, unusual smells, etc – and remember that failure of components such as fuses or spark plugs may only be pointers to some underlying fault.

The pages which follow provide an easy-reference guide to the more common problems which may occur during the operation of the car. These problems and their possible causes are grouped under headings denoting various components or systems, such as Engine, Cooling system, etc. The general Chapter which deals with the problem is also shown in brackets; refer to the relevant part of that Chapter for system-specific information. Whatever the fault, certain basic principles apply. These are as follows:

Verify the fault. This is simply a matter of being sure that you know what the symptoms are before starting work. This is particularly important if you are investigating a fault for someone else, who may not have described it very accurately.

Don't overlook the obvious. For example, if the car won't start, is there fuel in the tank? (Don't take anyone else's word on this particular point, and don't trust the fuel gauge either!) If an electrical fault is indicated, look for loose or broken wires before digging out the test gear.

Cure the disease, not the symptom. Substituting a flat battery with a fully-charged one will get you off the hard shoulder, but if the underlying cause is not attended to, the new battery will go the same way. Similarly, changing oil-fouled spark plugs for a new set will get you moving again, but remember that the reason for the fouling (if it wasn't simply an incorrect grade of plug) will have to be established and corrected.

Don't take anything for granted. Particularly, don't forget that a 'new' component may itself be defective (especially if it's been rattling around in the boot for months), and don't leave components out of a fault diagnosis sequence just because they are new or recently-fitted. When you do finally diagnose a difficult fault, you'll probably realise that all the evidence was there from the start.

Consider what work, if any, has recently been carried out. Many faults arise through careless or hurried work. For instance, if any work has been performed under the bonnet, could some of the wiring have been dislodged or incorrectly routed, or a hose trapped? Have all the fasteners been properly tightened? Were new, genuine parts and new gaskets used? There is often a certain amount of detective work to be done in this case, as an apparently-unrelated task can have far-reaching consequences.

Engine

Engine fails to rotate when attempting to start

☐ Battery discharged or faulty (Chapter 5A)
☐ Battery terminal connections loose or corroded (see *Weekly checks*)
☐ Broken, loose or disconnected wiring in the starting circuit (Chapter 5A)
☐ Engine or transmission earth strap broken or disconnected
☐ Defective starter solenoid or ignition switch (Chapter 5A or 12)
☐ Defective starter motor (Chapter 5A)
☐ Starter pinion or flywheel ring gear teeth loose or broken (Chapter 2 or 5A)
☐ Engine suffering 'hydraulic lock' (e.g. from water ingested after driving through a flood, or from a serious internal coolant leak) – consult a Honda dealer for advice
☐ Automatic transmission not in position P or N (Chapter 7B)

Engine rotates, but will not start

☐ Fuel shut-off (inertia) switch energised – after impact or shock (Chapter 4A)
☐ Fuel tank empty
☐ Battery discharged (engine rotates slowly) (Chapter 5A)
☐ Battery terminal connections loose or corroded (see *Weekly checks*)
☐ Ignition components damp or damaged (Chapter 1 or 5B)
☐ Immobiliser fault, or 'uncoded' ignition key being used (Chapter 12 or Roadside repairs)
☐ Crankshaft sensor fault (Chapter 4A)
☐ Broken, loose or disconnected wiring in the ignition circuit (Chapter 1 or 5B)
☐ Worn, faulty or incorrectly-gapped spark plugs (Chapter 1)
☐ Fuel injection system fault (Chapter 4A)
☐ Major mechanical failure (e.g. timing chain failure) (Chapter 2A or 2B)

Engine difficult to start when cold

☐ Battery discharged (Chapter 5A)
☐ Battery terminal connections loose or corroded (see *Weekly checks*)
☐ Worn, faulty or incorrectly-gapped spark plugs (Chapter 1)
☐ Other ignition system fault (Chapter 1 or 5B)
☐ Fuel injection system fault (Chapter 4A)
☐ Wrong grade of engine oil used (*Weekly checks*, Chapter 1)
☐ Low cylinder compressions (Chapter 2A)

Engine difficult to start when hot

☐ Air filter element dirty or clogged (Chapter 1)
☐ Fuel injection system fault (Chapter 4A)
☐ Low cylinder compressions (Chapter 2A)

Starter motor noisy or excessively-rough in engagement

☐ Starter pinion or flywheel ring gear teeth loose or broken (Chapter 2 or 5A)
☐ Starter motor mounting bolts loose or missing (Chapter 5A)
☐ Starter motor internal components worn or damaged (Chapter 5A)

Engine starts, but stops immediately

☐ Low fuel pressure – or low fuel level in tank (Chapter 4A)
☐ Loose or faulty electrical connections in the ignition circuit (Chapter 1 or 5B)
☐ Vacuum leak at the throttle body or inlet manifold (Chapter 4A)
☐ Blocked injectors/fuel injection system fault (Chapter 4A)
☐ EGR valve or control solenoid (Chapter 4B)

Engine idles erratically

☐ Air filter element clogged (Chapter 1)
☐ Vacuum leak at the throttle body, inlet manifold or associated hoses (Chapter 4A)
☐ Worn, faulty or incorrectly-gapped spark plugs (Chapter 1)
☐ Valve clearances incorrect (Chapter 2A)
☐ Uneven or low cylinder compressions (Chapter 2A)
☐ Camshaft lobes worn (Chapter 2A)
☐ Blocked injectors/fuel injection system fault (Chapter 4A)

Engine misfires at idle speed

☐ Worn, faulty or incorrectly-gapped spark plugs (Chapter 1)
☐ Faulty ignition coil(s) (Chapter 5B)
☐ Vacuum leak at the throttle body, inlet manifold or associated hoses (Chapter 4A)
☐ Blocked injectors/fuel injection system fault (Chapter 4A)
☐ Uneven or low cylinder compressions (Chapter 2A)
☐ Disconnected, leaking, or perished crankcase ventilation hoses (Chapter 4B)

Engine (continued)

Engine misfires throughout the driving speed range

- [ ] Fuel pump faulty, or delivery pressure low (Chapter 4A)
- [ ] Fuel tank vent blocked, or fuel pipes restricted (Chapter 4A)
- [ ] Vacuum leak at the throttle body, inlet manifold or associated hoses (Chapter 4A)
- [ ] Worn, faulty or incorrectly-gapped spark plugs (Chapter 1)
- [ ] Faulty ignition coil(s) (Chapter 5B)
- [ ] Uneven or low cylinder compressions (Chapter 2A)
- [ ] Blocked injector/fuel injection system fault (Chapter 4A)
- [ ] EGR valve or control solenoid (Chapter 4B)
- [ ] Blocked catalytic converter (Chapter 4A)
- [ ] High engine operating temperature (Chapter 3)

Engine hesitates on acceleration

- [ ] Worn, faulty or incorrectly-gapped spark plugs (Chapter 1)
- [ ] Vacuum leak at the throttle body, inlet manifold or associated hoses (Chapter 4A)
- [ ] Blocked injectors/fuel injection system fault (Chapter 4A)
- [ ] EGR valve or control solenoid (Chapter 4B)

Engine stalls

- [ ] Vacuum leak at the throttle body, inlet manifold or associated hoses (Chapter 4A)
- [ ] Fuel pump faulty, or delivery pressure low (Chapter 4A)
- [ ] Fuel filter choked (Chapter 1)
- [ ] Fuel tank vent blocked, or fuel pipes restricted (Chapter 4A)
- [ ] Blocked injectors/fuel injection system fault (Chapter 4A)

Engine lacks power

- [ ] Air filter element blocked (Chapter 1)
- [ ] Fuel pipes blocked or restricted (Chapter 4A)
- [ ] Valve clearances incorrect (Chapter 2A)
- [ ] Worn, faulty or incorrectly-gapped spark plugs (Chapter 1)
- [ ] High engine operating temperature (Chapter 3)
- [ ] Accelerator cable problem, or accelerator position sensor faulty (Chapter 4A)
- [ ] Vacuum leak at the throttle body, inlet manifold or associated hoses (Chapter 4A)
- [ ] Blocked injectors/fuel injection system fault (Chapter 4A)
- [ ] Fuel pump faulty, or delivery pressure low (Chapter 4A)
- [ ] EGR valve or control solenoid (Chapter 4B)
- [ ] Uneven or low cylinder compressions (Chapter 2A)
- [ ] Blocked catalytic converter (Chapter 4A)
- [ ] Brakes binding (Chapter 1 or 9)
- [ ] Clutch slipping (Chapter 6)

Engine backfires

- [ ] Vacuum leak at the throttle body, inlet manifold or associated hoses (Chapter 4A)
- [ ] Blocked injectors/fuel injection system fault (Chapter 4A)
- [ ] Blocked catalytic converter (Chapter 4A)
- [ ] Faulty ignition coil(s) (Chapter 5B)

Oil pressure warning light illuminated with engine running

- [ ] Low oil level, or incorrect oil grade (see *Weekly checks*)
- [ ] Faulty oil pressure sensor, or wiring damaged (Chapter 5A)
- [ ] Worn engine bearings and/or oil pump (Chapter 2A or 2B)
- [ ] High engine operating temperature (Chapter 3)
- [ ] Oil pump pressure relief valve defective (Chapter 2A)
- [ ] Oil pump pick-up strainer clogged (Chapter 2A)

Engine runs-on after switching off

- [ ] Excessive carbon build-up in engine (Chapter 2A or 2B)
- [ ] High engine operating temperature (Chapter 3)
- [ ] Fuel injection system fault (Chapter 4A)

Engine noises

Pre-ignition (pinking) or knocking during acceleration or under load

- [ ] Ignition timing incorrect/ignition system fault (Chapter 1 or 5B)
- [ ] Incorrect grade of spark plug (Chapter 1)
- [ ] Incorrect grade of fuel (Chapter 4A)
- [ ] Knock sensor faulty (Chapter 5B)
- [ ] Vacuum leak at the throttle body, inlet manifold or associated hoses (Chapter 4A)
- [ ] Excessive carbon build-up in engine (Chapter 2A or 2B)
- [ ] Blocked injector/fuel injection system fault (Chapter 4A)

Whistling or wheezing noises

- [ ] Leaking inlet manifold or throttle body gasket (Chapter 4A)
- [ ] Leaking exhaust manifold gasket or pipe-to-manifold joint (Chapter 4A)
- [ ] Leaking vacuum hose (Chapter 4, 5 or 9)
- [ ] Blowing cylinder head gasket (Chapter 2A)
- [ ] Partially blocked or leaking crankcase ventilation system (Chapter 4B)

Tapping or rattling noises

- [ ] Valve clearances incorrect (Chapter 2A)
- [ ] Worn valve gear or camshaft (Chapter 2A)
- [ ] Ancillary component fault (water pump, alternator, etc) (Chapter 3, 5A, etc)

Knocking or thumping noises

- [ ] Worn big-end bearings (regular heavy knocking, perhaps less under load) (Chapter 2B)
- [ ] Worn main bearings (rumbling and knocking, perhaps worsening under load) (Chapter 2B)
- [ ] Piston slap – most noticeable when cold, caused by piston/bore wear (Chapter 2B)
- [ ] Ancillary component fault (water pump, alternator, etc) (Chapter 3, 5A, etc)
- [ ] Engine mountings worn or defective (Chapter 2A)
- [ ] Suspension or steering components worn (Chapter 10)

Cooling system

Overheating

- ☐ Insufficient coolant in system (see *Weekly checks*)
- ☐ Thermostat faulty (Chapter 3)
- ☐ Radiator core blocked, or grille restricted (Chapter 3)
- ☐ Cooling fan/switch faulty (Chapter 3)
- ☐ Inaccurate coolant temperature sensor (Chapter 3, 4A)
- ☐ Airlock in cooling system – typically after coolant refilling, or due to a leak (Chapter 1)
- ☐ Expansion tank pressure cap faulty (Chapter 3)
- ☐ Engine management system fault (Chapter 4A)

Overcooling

- ☐ Thermostat faulty (Chapter 3)
- ☐ Inaccurate cylinder head temperature sender (Chapter 3, 4A)
- ☐ Cooling fan/switch faulty (Chapter 3)
- ☐ Engine management system fault (Chapter 4A)

External coolant leakage

- ☐ Deteriorated or damaged hoses or hose clips (Chapter 1)
- ☐ Radiator core or heater matrix leaking (Chapter 3)
- ☐ Expansion tank pressure cap faulty (Chapter 1)
- ☐ Water pump internal seal leaking (Chapter 3)
- ☐ Water pump gasket leaking (Chapter 3)
- ☐ Boiling due to overheating (Chapter 3)
- ☐ Cylinder block core plug leaking (Chapter 2B)

Internal coolant leakage

- ☐ Leaking cylinder head gasket (Chapter 2A)
- ☐ Cracked cylinder head or cylinder block (Chapter 2A or 2B)

Corrosion

- ☐ Infrequent draining and flushing (Chapter 1)
- ☐ Incorrect coolant mixture or inappropriate coolant type (see *Weekly checks*)

Fuel and exhaust systems

Excessive fuel consumption

- ☐ Air filter element dirty or clogged (Chapter 1)
- ☐ Fuel injection system fault (Chapter 4A)
- ☐ Engine management system fault (Chapter 4A)
- ☐ Crankcase ventilation system blocked (Chapter 4B)
- ☐ Tyres under-inflated (see *Weekly checks*)
- ☐ Brakes binding (Chapter 1 or 9)
- ☐ Fuel leak, causing apparent high consumption (Chapter 1 or 4A)

Fuel leakage and/or fuel odour

- ☐ Damaged or corroded fuel tank, pipes or connections (Chapter 4A)
- ☐ Evaporative emissions system fault (Chapter 4B)

Excessive noise or fumes from exhaust system

- ☐ Leaking exhaust system or manifold joints (Chapter 1 or 4A)
- ☐ Leaking, corroded or damaged silencers or pipe (Chapter 1 or 4A)
- ☐ Broken mountings causing body or suspension contact (Chapter 1)

Clutch

Pedal travels to floor – no pressure or very little resistance

- ☐ Air in hydraulic system/faulty master or slave cylinder (Chapter 6)
- ☐ Faulty hydraulic release system (Chapter 6)
- ☐ Clutch pedal return spring detached or broken (Chapter 6)
- ☐ Broken clutch release bearing or fork (Chapter 6)
- ☐ Broken diaphragm spring in clutch pressure plate (Chapter 6)

Clutch fails to disengage (unable to select gears)

- ☐ Air in hydraulic system/faulty master or slave cylinder (Chapter 6)
- ☐ Faulty hydraulic release system (Chapter 6)
- ☐ Clutch disc sticking on transmission input shaft splines (Chapter 6)
- ☐ Clutch disc sticking to flywheel or pressure plate (Chapter 6)
- ☐ Faulty pressure plate assembly (Chapter 6)
- ☐ Clutch release mechanism worn or incorrectly assembled (Chapter 6)

Clutch slips (engine speed increases, with no increase in vehicle speed)

- ☐ Faulty hydraulic release system (Chapter 6)
- ☐ Clutch disc linings excessively worn (Chapter 6)
- ☐ Clutch disc linings contaminated with oil or grease (Chapter 6)
- ☐ Faulty pressure plate or weak diaphragm spring (Chapter 6)

Judder as clutch is engaged

- ☐ Clutch disc linings contaminated with oil or grease (Chapter 6)
- ☐ Clutch disc linings excessively worn (Chapter 6)
- ☐ Faulty or distorted pressure plate or diaphragm spring (Chapter 6).
- ☐ Worn or loose engine or transmission mountings (Chapter 2A)
- ☐ Clutch disc hub or transmission input shaft splines worn (Chapter 6)

Noise when depressing or releasing clutch pedal

- ☐ Worn clutch release bearing (Chapter 6)
- ☐ Worn or dry clutch pedal bushes (Chapter 6)
- ☐ Worn or dry clutch master cylinder piston (Chapter 6)
- ☐ Faulty pressure plate assembly (Chapter 6)
- ☐ Pressure plate diaphragm spring broken (Chapter 6)
- ☐ Broken clutch disc cushioning springs (Chapter 6)

Manual transmission

Noisy in neutral with engine running

- [ ] Lack of oil (Chapter 1)
- [ ] Input shaft bearings worn (noise apparent with clutch pedal released, but not when depressed) (Chapter 7A)*
- [ ] Clutch release bearing worn (noise apparent with clutch pedal depressed, possibly less when released) (Chapter 6)

Noisy in one particular gear

- [ ] Worn, damaged or chipped gear teeth (Chapter 7A)*

Difficulty engaging gears

- [ ] Clutch fault (Chapter 6)
- [ ] Worn, damaged, or poorly-adjusted gearchange cables (Chapter 7A)
- [ ] Lack of lubricant (Chapter 1)
- [ ] Worn synchroniser units (Chapter 7A)*

Jumps out of gear

- [ ] Worn, damaged, or poorly-adjusted gearchange cables (Chapter 7A)
- [ ] Worn synchroniser units (Chapter 7A)*
- [ ] Worn selector forks (Chapter 7A)*

Vibration

- [ ] Lack of lubricant (Chapter 1)
- [ ] Worn bearings (Chapter 7A)*

Lubricant leaks

- [ ] Leaking driveshaft or selector shaft oil seal (Chapter 7A)
- [ ] Leaking housing joint (Chapter 7A)*
- [ ] Leaking input shaft oil seal (Chapter 7A)*

Although the corrective action necessary to remedy the symptoms described is beyond the scope of the home mechanic, the above information should be helpful in isolating the cause of the condition, so that the owner can communicate clearly with a professional mechanic.

Automatic transmission

Note: *Due to the complexity of the automatic transmission, it is difficult for the home mechanic to properly diagnose and service this unit. For problems other than the following, the car should be taken to a dealer service department or automatic transmission specialist. Do not be too hasty in removing the transmission if a fault is suspected, as most of the testing is carried out with the unit still fitted. Remember that, besides the sensors specific to the transmission, many of the engine management system sensors described in Chapter 4A are essential to the correct operation of the transmission.*

Fluid leakage

- [ ] Automatic transmission fluid is usually dark red in colour. Fluid leaks should not be confused with engine oil, which can easily be blown onto the transmission by airflow.
- [ ] To determine the source of a leak, first remove all built-up dirt and grime from the transmission housing and surrounding areas using a degreasing agent, or by steam-cleaning. Drive the car at low speed, so airflow will not blow the leak far from its source. Raise and support the car, and determine where the leak is coming from. The following are common areas of leakage:
  a) *Fluid pan.*
  b) *Dipstick tube (Chapter 1).*
  c) *Transmission-to-fluid cooler unions (Chapter 7B).*
  d) *Radiator fluid cooler unions (Chapter 3).*
  e) *Driveshaft seals.*

Transmission fluid brown, or has burned smell

- [ ] Transmission fluid level low (Chapter 1)

General gear selection problems

- [ ] Chapter 7B deals with checking the selector cable on automatic transmissions. The following are common problems which may be caused by a faulty selector cable or range switch:
  a) *Engine starting in gears other than Park or Neutral.*

  b) *Indicator panel indicating a gear other than the one actually being used.*
  c) *Car moves when in Park or Neutral.*
  d) *Poor gear shift quality or erratic gear changes.*

Transmission will not downshift (kickdown) with accelerator pedal fully depressed

- [ ] Low transmission fluid level (Chapter 1)
- [ ] Accelerator cable problem, or accelerator position sensor faulty (Chapter 4A)
- [ ] Engine management system fault (Chapter 4A)
- [ ] Faulty transmission sensor or wiring (Chapter 7B)
- [ ] Incorrect selector cable adjustment (Chapter 7B)

Engine will not start in any gear, or starts in gears other than Park or Neutral

- [ ] Faulty transmission range switch (Chapter 7B)
- [ ] Faulty transmission sensor or wiring (Chapter 7B)
- [ ] Engine management system fault (Chapter 4A)
- [ ] Incorrect selector cable adjustment (Chapter 7B)

Transmission slips, shifts roughly, is noisy, or has no drive in forward or reverse gears

- [ ] Transmission fluid level low (Chapter 1)
- [ ] Faulty transmission sensor or wiring (Chapter 7B)
- [ ] Engine management system fault (Chapter 4A)

Note: *There are many probable causes for the above problems, but diagnosing and correcting them is considered beyond the scope of this manual. Having checked the fluid level and all the wiring as far as possible, a dealer or transmission specialist should be consulted if the problem persists.*

Driveshafts

Vibration when accelerating or decelerating

☐ Worn inner constant velocity joint (Chapter 8)
☐ Bent or distorted driveshaft (Chapter 8)

Clicking or knocking noise on turns (at slow speed on full-lock)

☐ Worn outer constant velocity joint (Chapter 8)
☐ Lack of constant velocity joint lubricant, possibly due to damaged gaiter (Chapter 8)

Braking system

Note: *Before assuming that a brake problem exists, make sure that the tyres are in good condition and correctly inflated, that the front wheel alignment is correct, and that the car is not loaded with weight in an unequal manner. Apart from checking the condition of all pipe and hose connections, any faults occurring on the anti-lock braking system should be referred to a Honda dealer for diagnosis.*

Car pulls to one side under braking

☐ Worn, defective, damaged or contaminated brake pads/shoes on one side (Chapter 1 or 9)
☐ Seized or partially-seized brake caliper piston or rear wheel cylinder (Chapter 1 or 9)
☐ A mixture of brake pad/shoe materials fitted between sides (Chapter 1 or 9)
☐ Brake caliper mounting bolts loose (Chapter 9)
☐ One rear wheel cylinder leaking – drum brake models (Chapter 9)
☐ Worn or damaged steering or suspension components (Chapter 1 or 10)

Noise (grinding or high-pitched squeal) when brakes applied

☐ Brake pad/shoe material worn down to metal backing (Chapter 1 or 9)
☐ Excessive corrosion of brake disc/drum (may be apparent after the car has been standing for some time (Chapter 1 or 9)
☐ Foreign object (stone chipping, etc) trapped between brake disc and shield (Chapter 1 or 9)

Excessive brake pedal travel

☐ Faulty master cylinder (Chapter 9)
☐ Air in hydraulic system (Chapter 1 or 9)
☐ Faulty vacuum servo unit (Chapter 9)
☐ Rear wheel cylinder leaking – drum brake models (Chapter 9)

Brake pedal feels spongy when depressed

☐ Air in hydraulic system (Chapter 1 or 9)
☐ Rear wheel cylinder leaking – drum brake models (Chapter 9)
☐ Deteriorated flexible rubber brake hoses (Chapter 1 or 9)
☐ Master cylinder mounting nuts loose (Chapter 9)
☐ Faulty master cylinder (Chapter 9)

Excessive brake pedal effort required to stop car

☐ Faulty vacuum servo unit (Chapter 9)
☐ Faulty vacuum pump (Chapter 9)
☐ Disconnected, damaged or insecure brake servo vacuum hose (Chapter 9)
☐ Primary or secondary hydraulic circuit failure (Chapter 9)
☐ Seized brake caliper piston or rear wheel cylinder (Chapter 9)
☐ Brake pads or shoes incorrectly fitted (Chapter 9)
☐ Incorrect grade of brake pads/shoes fitted (Chapter 9)
☐ Brake pads or shoes contaminated (Chapter 1 or 9)

Judder felt through brake pedal or steering wheel when braking

Note: *Under heavy braking on models equipped with ABS, vibration may be felt through the brake pedal. This is a normal feature of ABS operation, and does not constitute a fault.*

☐ Excessive run-out or distortion of front discs (Chapter 1 or 9)
☐ Front brake pads worn (Chapter 1 or 9)
☐ Front brake caliper mounting bolts loose (Chapter 9)
☐ Wear in suspension or steering components or mountings (Chapter 1 or 10)
☐ Front wheels out of balance (see *Weekly checks*)

Brakes binding

☐ Seized brake caliper piston or rear wheel cylinder (Chapter 9)
☐ Incorrectly-adjusted handbrake mechanism (Chapter 9)
☐ Faulty master cylinder (Chapter 9)

Rear wheels locking under normal braking

☐ Rear brake pads/shoes contaminated or damaged (Chapter 1 or 9)
☐ Rear brake discs warped (Chapter 1 or 9)
☐ Seized rear brake caliper piston or rear wheel cylinder (Chapter 9)
☐ ABS fault (Chapter 9)

ABS warning light stays on

☐ Wheel sensor wiring plug corroded, or wiring damaged (Chapter 9)
☐ Other wiring fault – check ABS hydraulic unit in engine compartment (Chapter 9)
☐ ABS fuse blown (Chapter 12)
☐ Low brake fluid level, possibly due to a leak, or system needs bleeding (Chapter 1 or 9)

Suspension and steering

Note: *Before diagnosing suspension or steering faults, be sure that the trouble is not due to incorrect tyre pressures, mixtures of tyre types, or binding brakes.*

Car pulls to one side

- ☐ Defective tyre (see *Weekly checks*)
- ☐ Excessive wear in suspension or steering components (Chapter 1 or 10)
- ☐ Incorrect front wheel alignment (Chapter 10)
- ☐ Accident damage to steering or suspension components (Chapter 1)

Wheel wobble and vibration

- ☐ Front wheels out of balance (vibration felt mainly through the steering wheel) (see *Weekly checks*)
- ☐ Rear wheels out of balance (vibration felt throughout the car) (see *Weekly checks*)
- ☐ Roadwheels damaged or distorted (see *Weekly checks*)
- ☐ Faulty or damaged tyre (see *Weekly checks*)
- ☐ Worn steering or suspension joints, bushes or components (Chapter 1 or 10)
- ☐ Wheel nuts loose (Chapter 1)

Excessive pitching and/or rolling around corners, or during braking

- ☐ Defective shock absorbers (Chapter 1 or 10)
- ☐ Broken or weak spring and/or suspension component (Chapter 1 or 10)
- ☐ Worn or damaged anti-roll bar or mountings (Chapter 1 or 10)

Wandering or general instability

- ☐ Incorrect front wheel alignment (Chapter 10)
- ☐ Worn steering or suspension joints, bushes or components (Chapter 1 or 10)
- ☐ Roadwheels out of balance (see *Weekly checks*)
- ☐ Faulty or damaged tyre (see *Weekly checks*)
- ☐ Wheel nuts loose (Chapter 1)
- ☐ Defective shock absorbers (Chapter 1 or 10)

Excessively-stiff steering

- ☐ Seized steering linkage balljoint or suspension balljoint (Chapter 1 or 10)
- ☐ Incorrect front wheel alignment (Chapter 10)
- ☐ Faulty steering motor or torque sensor (Chapter 10)
- ☐ Faulty steering rack or column (Chapter 10)

Excessive play in steering

- ☐ Worn steering column/intermediate shaft joints (Chapter 10)
- ☐ Worn track rod balljoints (Chapter 1 or 10)
- ☐ Worn steering rack (Chapter 10)
- ☐ Worn steering or suspension joints, bushes or components (Chapter 1 or 10)

Lack of power assistance

- ☐ Faulty steering motor or torque sensor (Chapter 10)
- ☐ Faulty steering rack (Chapter 10)

Tyre wear excessive

Tyres worn on inside or outside edges

- ☐ Tyres under-inflated (wear on both edges) (see *Weekly checks*)
- ☐ Incorrect camber or castor angles (wear on one edge only) (Chapter 10)
- ☐ Worn steering or suspension joints, bushes or components (Chapter 1 or 10)
- ☐ Excessively-hard cornering or braking
- ☐ Accident damage

Tyre treads exhibit feathered edges

- ☐ Incorrect toe setting (tracking) (Chapter 10)

Tyres worn in centre of tread

- ☐ Tyres over-inflated (see *Weekly checks*)

Tyres worn on inside and outside edges

- ☐ Tyres under-inflated (see *Weekly checks*)

Tyres worn unevenly

- ☐ Tyres/wheels out of balance (see *Weekly checks*)
- ☐ Excessive wheel or tyre run-out (buckled wheel rim, faulty tyre)
- ☐ Worn shock absorbers (Chapter 1 or 10)
- ☐ Faulty tyre (see *Weekly checks*)

Electrical system

Note: *For problems associated with the starting system, refer to the faults listed under* **Engine** *earlier in this Section.*

Battery will not hold a charge for more than a few days

- ☐ Battery defective internally – one or more cells failing (Chapter 5A)
- ☐ Battery terminal connections loose or corroded (see *Weekly checks*)
- ☐ Auxiliary drivebelt worn or slipping (Chapter 1)
- ☐ Alternator not charging at correct output (Chapter 5A)
- ☐ Alternator or voltage regulator faulty (Chapter 5A)
- ☐ Short-circuit causing continual battery drain (Chapter 5A or 12)

Ignition/no-charge warning light remains illuminated with engine running

- ☐ Auxiliary drivebelt broken, worn, or slipping (Chapter 1)
- ☐ Internal fault in alternator or voltage regulator (Chapter 5A)
- ☐ Broken, disconnected, or loose wiring in charging circuit (Chapter 5A or 12)

Ignition/no-charge warning light fails to come on

- ☐ Warning light bulb blown (Chapter 12)
- ☐ Broken, disconnected, or loose wiring in warning light circuit (Chapter 5A or 12)
- ☐ Alternator faulty (Chapter 5A)

Lights inoperative

- ☐ Bulb blown (Chapter 12)
- ☐ Corrosion of bulb or bulbholder contacts (Chapter 12)
- ☐ Blown fuse (Chapter 12)
- ☐ Faulty relay (Chapter 12)
- ☐ Broken, loose, or disconnected wiring (Chapter 12)
- ☐ Faulty switch (Chapter 12)

Instrument readings inaccurate or erratic

Instrument readings increase with engine speed

- ☐ Faulty instrument panel voltage regulator (Chapter 12)

Fuel or temperature gauges give no reading

- ☐ Faulty gauge sender unit (Chapter 3, 4A)
- ☐ Wiring open-circuit (Chapter 12)
- ☐ Faulty gauge (Chapter 12)

Fuel or temperature gauges give continuous maximum reading

- ☐ Faulty gauge sender unit (Chapter 3, 4A)
- ☐ Wiring short-circuit (Chapter 12)
- ☐ Faulty gauge (Chapter 12)

Horn inoperative, or unsatisfactory in operation

Horn operates all the time

- ☐ Horn push either earthed or stuck down (Chapter 12)
- ☐ Horn cable-to-horn push earthed (Chapter 12)

Horn fails to operate

- ☐ Blown fuse (Chapter 12)
- ☐ Cable or connections loose, broken or disconnected (Chapter 12)
- ☐ Faulty horn (Chapter 12)

Horn emits intermittent or unsatisfactory sound

- ☐ Cable connections loose (Chapter 12)
- ☐ Horn mountings loose (Chapter 12)
- ☐ Faulty horn (Chapter 12)

Windscreen wipers inoperative, or unsatisfactory in operation

Wipers fail to operate, or operate very slowly

- ☐ Wiper blades stuck to screen, or linkage seized or binding (Chapter 12)
- ☐ Blown fuse (Chapter 12)
- ☐ Battery discharged (Chapter 5A)
- ☐ Wiring/plugs loose, broken or disconnected (Chapter 12)
- ☐ Faulty relay (Chapter 12)
- ☐ Faulty wiper motor (Chapter 12)

Wiper blades sweep over too large or too small an area of the glass

- ☐ Wiper blades incorrectly fitted, or wrong size used (see *Weekly checks*)
- ☐ Wiper arms incorrectly positioned on spindles (Chapter 12)
- ☐ Excessive wear of wiper linkage (Chapter 12)
- ☐ Wiper motor or linkage mountings loose or insecure (Chapter 12)

Wiper blades fail to clean the glass effectively

- ☐ Wiper blade rubbers dirty, worn or perished (see *Weekly checks*)
- ☐ Wiper blades incorrectly fitted, or wrong size used (see *Weekly checks*)
- ☐ Wiper arm tension springs broken, or arm pivots seized (Chapter 12)
- ☐ Insufficient windscreen washer additive to adequately remove road film (see *Weekly checks*)

Electrical system (continued)

Windscreen washers inoperative, or unsatisfactory in operation

One or more washer jets inoperative

- [ ] Blocked (or frozen) washer jet, or washer pump (Chapter 12)
- [ ] Disconnected, kinked or restricted fluid hose (Chapter 12)
- [ ] Insufficient fluid in washer reservoir (see *Weekly checks*)

Washer pump fails to operate

- [ ] Broken or disconnected wiring or connections (Chapter 12)
- [ ] Blown fuse (Chapter 12)
- [ ] Faulty washer switch (Chapter 12)
- [ ] Faulty washer pump (Chapter 12)

Washer pump runs for some time before fluid is emitted from jets

- [ ] Faulty one-way valve in fluid supply hose (Chapter 12)
- [ ] Fluid supply hose leaking (check under or inside car), or partially blocked (Chapter 12)

Electric windows inoperative, or unsatisfactory in operation

Window glass will only move in one direction

- [ ] Faulty switch (Chapter 12)

Window glass slow to move

- [ ] Battery discharged (Chapter 5A)
- [ ] Regulator seized or damaged, or in need of lubrication (Chapter 11)
- [ ] Door internal components or trim fouling regulator (Chapter 11)
- [ ] Faulty motor (Chapter 11)

Window glass fails to move

- [ ] Blown fuse (Chapter 12)
- [ ] Faulty relay (Chapter 12)
- [ ] Broken or disconnected wiring or connections (Chapter 12)
- [ ] Faulty motor (Chapter 11)

One-touch 'auto' feature not working

- [ ] Switch needs resetting after battery disconnection (see *Disconnecting the battery*)

Central locking system inoperative, or unsatisfactory in operation

Complete system failure

- [ ] Remote handset battery discharged, where applicable
- [ ] Blown fuse (Chapter 12)
- [ ] Faulty relay (Chapter 12)
- [ ] Broken or disconnected wiring or connections (Chapter 12)
- [ ] Faulty motor (Chapter 11)

Latch locks but will not unlock, or unlocks but will not lock

- [ ] Remote handset battery discharged, where applicable
- [ ] Faulty master switch (Chapter 12)
- [ ] Broken or disconnected latch operating rods or levers (Chapter 11)
- [ ] Faulty relay (Chapter 12)
- [ ] Faulty motor (Chapter 11)

One solenoid/motor fails to operate

- [ ] Broken or disconnected wiring or connections (Chapter 12)
- [ ] Faulty door lock (Chapter 11)
- [ ] Broken, binding or disconnected latch operating rods or levers (Chapter 11)

A

ABS (Anti-lock brake system) A system, usually electronically controlled, that senses incipient wheel lockup during braking and relieves hydraulic pressure at wheels that are about to skid.

Air bag An inflatable bag hidden in the steering wheel (driver's side) or the dash or glovebox (passenger side). In a head-on collision, the bags inflate, preventing the driver and front passenger from being thrown forward into the steering wheel or windscreen.

Air cleaner A metal or plastic housing, containing a filter element, which removes dust and dirt from the air being drawn into the engine.

Air filter element The actual filter in an air cleaner system, usually manufactured from pleated paper and requiring renewal at regular intervals.

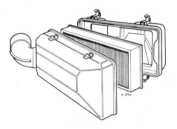

Air filter

Allen key A hexagonal wrench which fits into a recessed hexagonal hole.

Alligator clip A long-nosed spring-loaded metal clip with meshing teeth. Used to make temporary electrical connections.

Alternator A component in the electrical system which converts mechanical energy from a drivebelt into electrical energy to charge the battery and to operate the starting system, ignition system and electrical accessories.

Alternator (exploded view)

Ampere (amp) A unit of measurement for the flow of electric current. One amp is the amount of current produced by one volt acting through a resistance of one ohm.

Anaerobic sealer A substance used to prevent bolts and screws from loosening. Anaerobic means that it does not require oxygen for activation. The Loctite brand is widely used.

Antifreeze A substance (usually ethylene glycol) mixed with water, and added to a vehicle's cooling system, to prevent freezing of the coolant in winter. Antifreeze also contains chemicals to inhibit corrosion and the formation of rust and other deposits that would tend to clog the radiator and coolant passages and reduce cooling efficiency.

Anti-seize compound A coating that reduces the risk of seizing on fasteners that are subjected to high temperatures, such as exhaust manifold bolts and nuts.

Anti-seize compound

Asbestos A natural fibrous mineral with great heat resistance, commonly used in the composition of brake friction materials. Asbestos is a health hazard and the dust created by brake systems should never be inhaled or ingested.

Axle A shaft on which a wheel revolves, or which revolves with a wheel. Also, a solid beam that connects the two wheels at one end of the vehicle. An axle which also transmits power to the wheels is known as a live axle.

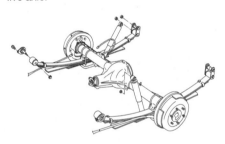

Axle assembly

Axleshaft A single rotating shaft, on either side of the differential, which delivers power from the final drive assembly to the drive wheels. Also called a driveshaft or a halfshaft.

B

Ball bearing An anti-friction bearing consisting of a hardened inner and outer race with hardened steel balls between two races.

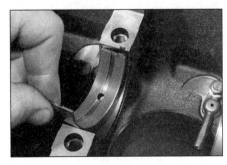

Bearing

Bearing The curved surface on a shaft or in a bore, or the part assembled into either, that permits relative motion between them with minimum wear and friction.

Big-end bearing The bearing in the end of the connecting rod that's attached to the crankshaft.

Bleed nipple A valve on a brake wheel cylinder, caliper or other hydraulic component that is opened to purge the hydraulic system of air. Also called a bleed screw.

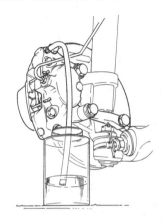

Brake bleeding

Brake bleeding Procedure for removing air from lines of a hydraulic brake system.

Brake disc The component of a disc brake that rotates with the wheels.

Brake drum The component of a drum brake that rotates with the wheels.

Brake linings The friction material which contacts the brake disc or drum to retard the vehicle's speed. The linings are bonded or riveted to the brake pads or shoes.

Brake pads The replaceable friction pads that pinch the brake disc when the brakes are applied. Brake pads consist of a friction material bonded or riveted to a rigid backing plate.

Brake shoe The crescent-shaped carrier to which the brake linings are mounted and which forces the lining against the rotating drum during braking.

Braking systems For more information on braking systems, consult the *Haynes Automotive Brake Manual*.

Breaker bar A long socket wrench handle providing greater leverage.

Bulkhead The insulated partition between the engine and the passenger compartment.

C

Caliper The non-rotating part of a disc-brake assembly that straddles the disc and carries the brake pads. The caliper also contains the hydraulic components that cause the pads to pinch the disc when the brakes are applied. A caliper is also a measuring tool that can be set to measure inside or outside dimensions of an object.

Camshaft A rotating shaft on which a series of cam lobes operate the valve mechanisms. The camshaft may be driven by gears, by sprockets and chain or by sprockets and a belt.

Canister A container in an evaporative emission control system; contains activated charcoal granules to trap vapours from the fuel system.

Canister

Carburettor A device which mixes fuel with air in the proper proportions to provide a desired power output from a spark ignition internal combustion engine.

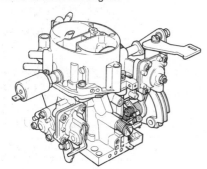

Carburettor

Castellated Resembling the parapets along the top of a castle wall. For example, a castellated balljoint stud nut.

Castellated nut

Castor In wheel alignment, the backward or forward tilt of the steering axis. Castor is positive when the steering axis is inclined rearward at the top.

Catalytic converter A silencer-like device in the exhaust system which converts certain pollutants in the exhaust gases into less harmful substances.

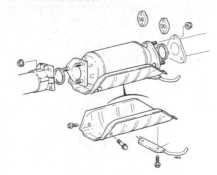

Catalytic converter

Circlip A ring-shaped clip used to prevent endwise movement of cylindrical parts and shafts. An internal circlip is installed in a groove in a housing; an external circlip fits into a groove on the outside of a cylindrical piece such as a shaft.

Clearance The amount of space between two parts. For example, between a piston and a cylinder, between a bearing and a journal, etc.

Coil spring A spiral of elastic steel found in various sizes throughout a vehicle, for example as a springing medium in the suspension and in the valve train.

Compression Reduction in volume, and increase in pressure and temperature, of a gas, caused by squeezing it into a smaller space.

Compression ratio The relationship between cylinder volume when the piston is at top dead centre and cylinder volume when the piston is at bottom dead centre.

Constant velocity (CV) joint A type of universal joint that cancels out vibrations caused by driving power being transmitted through an angle.

Core plug A disc or cup-shaped metal device inserted in a hole in a casting through which core was removed when the casting was formed. Also known as a freeze plug or expansion plug.

Crankcase The lower part of the engine block in which the crankshaft rotates.

Crankshaft The main rotating member, or shaft, running the length of the crankcase, with offset "throws" to which the connecting rods are attached.

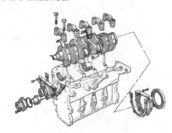

Crankshaft assembly

Crocodile clip See Alligator clip

D

Diagnostic code Code numbers obtained by accessing the diagnostic mode of an engine management computer. This code can be used to determine the area in the system where a malfunction may be located.

Disc brake A brake design incorporating a rotating disc onto which brake pads are squeezed. The resulting friction converts the energy of a moving vehicle into heat.

Double-overhead cam (DOHC) An engine that uses two overhead camshafts, usually one for the intake valves and one for the exhaust valves.

Drivebelt(s) The belt(s) used to drive accessories such as the alternator, water pump, power steering pump, air conditioning compressor, etc. off the crankshaft pulley.

Accessory drivebelts

Driveshaft Any shaft used to transmit motion. Commonly used when referring to the axleshafts on a front wheel drive vehicle.

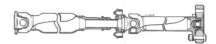

Driveshaft

Drum brake A type of brake using a drum-shaped metal cylinder attached to the inner surface of the wheel. When the brake pedal is pressed, curved brake shoes with friction linings press against the inside of the drum to slow or stop the vehicle.

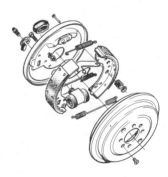

Drum brake assembly

E

EGR valve A valve used to introduce exhaust gases into the intake air stream.

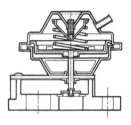

EGR valve

Electronic control unit (ECU) A computer which controls (for instance) ignition and fuel injection systems, or an anti-lock braking system. For more information refer to the *Haynes Automotive Electrical and Electronic Systems Manual*.

Electronic Fuel Injection (EFI) A computer controlled fuel system that distributes fuel through an injector located in each intake port of the engine.

Emergency brake A braking system, independent of the main hydraulic system, that can be used to slow or stop the vehicle if the primary brakes fail, or to hold the vehicle stationary even though the brake pedal isn't depressed. It usually consists of a hand lever that actuates either front or rear brakes mechanically through a series of cables and linkages. Also known as a handbrake or parking brake.

Endfloat The amount of lengthwise movement between two parts. As applied to a crankshaft, the distance that the crankshaft can move forward and back in the cylinder block.

Engine management system (EMS) A computer controlled system which manages the fuel injection and the ignition systems in an integrated fashion.

Exhaust manifold A part with several passages through which exhaust gases leave the engine combustion chambers and enter the exhaust pipe.

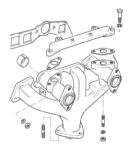

Exhaust manifold

F

Fan clutch A viscous (fluid) drive coupling device which permits variable engine fan speeds in relation to engine speeds.

Feeler blade A thin strip or blade of hardened steel, ground to an exact thickness, used to check or measure clearances between parts.

Feeler blade

Firing order The order in which the engine cylinders fire, or deliver their power strokes, beginning with the number one cylinder.

Flywheel A heavy spinning wheel in which energy is absorbed and stored by means of momentum. On cars, the flywheel is attached to the crankshaft to smooth out firing impulses.

Free play The amount of travel before any action takes place. The "looseness" in a linkage, or an assembly of parts, between the initial application of force and actual movement. For example, the distance the brake pedal moves before the pistons in the master cylinder are actuated.

Fuse An electrical device which protects a circuit against accidental overload. The typical fuse contains a soft piece of metal which is calibrated to melt at a predetermined current flow (expressed as amps) and break the circuit.

Fusible link A circuit protection device consisting of a conductor surrounded by heat-resistant insulation. The conductor is smaller than the wire it protects, so it acts as the weakest link in the circuit. Unlike a blown fuse, a failed fusible link must frequently be cut from the wire for replacement.

G

Gap The distance the spark must travel in jumping from the centre electrode to the side

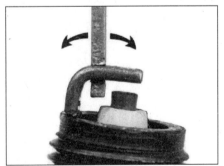

Adjusting spark plug gap

electrode in a spark plug. Also refers to the spacing between the points in a contact breaker assembly in a conventional points-type ignition, or to the distance between the reluctor or rotor and the pickup coil in an electronic ignition.

Gasket Any thin, soft material - usually cork, cardboard, asbestos or soft metal - installed between two metal surfaces to ensure a good seal. For instance, the cylinder head gasket seals the joint between the block and the cylinder head.

Gasket

Gauge An instrument panel display used to monitor engine conditions. A gauge with a movable pointer on a dial or a fixed scale is an analogue gauge. A gauge with a numerical readout is called a digital gauge.

H

Halfshaft A rotating shaft that transmits power from the final drive unit to a drive wheel, usually when referring to a live rear axle.

Harmonic balancer A device designed to reduce torsion or twisting vibration in the crankshaft. May be incorporated in the crankshaft pulley. Also known as a vibration damper.

Hone An abrasive tool for correcting small irregularities or differences in diameter in an engine cylinder, brake cylinder, etc.

Hydraulic tappet A tappet that utilises hydraulic pressure from the engine's lubrication system to maintain zero clearance (constant contact with both camshaft and valve stem). Automatically adjusts to variation in valve stem length. Hydraulic tappets also reduce valve noise.

I

Ignition timing The moment at which the spark plug fires, usually expressed in the number of crankshaft degrees before the piston reaches the top of its stroke.

Inlet manifold A tube or housing with passages through which flows the air-fuel mixture (carburettor vehicles and vehicles with throttle body injection) or air only (port fuel-injected vehicles) to the port openings in the cylinder head.

J

Jump start Starting the engine of a vehicle with a discharged or weak battery by attaching jump leads from the weak battery to a charged or helper battery.

L

Load Sensing Proportioning Valve (LSPV) A brake hydraulic system control valve that works like a proportioning valve, but also takes into consideration the amount of weight carried by the rear axle.

Locknut A nut used to lock an adjustment nut, or other threaded component, in place. For example, a locknut is employed to keep the adjusting nut on the rocker arm in position.

Lockwasher A form of washer designed to prevent an attaching nut from working loose.

M

MacPherson strut A type of front suspension system devised by Earle MacPherson at Ford of England. In its original form, a simple lateral link with the anti-roll bar creates the lower control arm. A long strut - an integral coil spring and shock absorber - is mounted between the body and the steering knuckle. Many modern so-called MacPherson strut systems use a conventional lower A-arm and don't rely on the anti-roll bar for location.

Multimeter An electrical test instrument with the capability to measure voltage, current and resistance.

N

NOx Oxides of Nitrogen. A common toxic pollutant emitted by petrol and diesel engines at higher temperatures.

O

Ohm The unit of electrical resistance. One volt applied to a resistance of one ohm will produce a current of one amp.

Ohmmeter An instrument for measuring electrical resistance.

O-ring A type of sealing ring made of a special rubber-like material; in use, the O-ring is compressed into a groove to provide the sealing action.

O-ring

Overhead cam (ohc) engine An engine with the camshaft(s) located on top of the cylinder head(s).

Overhead valve (ohv) engine An engine with the valves located in the cylinder head, but with the camshaft located in the engine block.

Oxygen sensor A device installed in the engine exhaust manifold, which senses the oxygen content in the exhaust and converts this information into an electric current. Also called a Lambda sensor.

P

Phillips screw A type of screw head having a cross instead of a slot for a corresponding type of screwdriver.

Plastigage A thin strip of plastic thread, available in different sizes, used for measuring clearances. For example, a strip of Plastigage is laid across a bearing journal. The parts are assembled and dismantled; the width of the crushed strip indicates the clearance between journal and bearing.

Plastigage

Propeller shaft The long hollow tube with universal joints at both ends that carries power from the transmission to the differential on front-engined rear wheel drive vehicles.

Proportioning valve A hydraulic control valve which limits the amount of pressure to the rear brakes during panic stops to prevent wheel lock-up.

R

Rack-and-pinion steering A steering system with a pinion gear on the end of the steering shaft that mates with a rack (think of a geared wheel opened up and laid flat). When the steering wheel is turned, the pinion turns, moving the rack to the left or right. This movement is transmitted through the track rods to the steering arms at the wheels.

Radiator A liquid-to-air heat transfer device designed to reduce the temperature of the coolant in an internal combustion engine cooling system.

Refrigerant Any substance used as a heat transfer agent in an air-conditioning system. R-12 has been the principle refrigerant for many years; recently, however, manufacturers have begun using R-134a, a non-CFC substance that is considered less harmful to the ozone in the upper atmosphere.

Rocker arm A lever arm that rocks on a shaft or pivots on a stud. In an overhead valve engine, the rocker arm converts the upward movement of the pushrod into a downward movement to open a valve.

Rotor In a distributor, the rotating device inside the cap that connects the centre electrode and the outer terminals as it turns, distributing the high voltage from the coil secondary winding to the proper spark plug. Also, that part of an alternator which rotates inside the stator. Also, the rotating assembly of a turbocharger, including the compressor wheel, shaft and turbine wheel.

Runout The amount of wobble (in-and-out movement) of a gear or wheel as it's rotated. The amount a shaft rotates "out-of-true." The out-of-round condition of a rotating part.

S

Sealant A liquid or paste used to prevent leakage at a joint. Sometimes used in conjunction with a gasket.

Sealed beam lamp An older headlight design which integrates the reflector, lens and filaments into a hermetically-sealed one-piece unit. When a filament burns out or the lens cracks, the entire unit is simply replaced.

Serpentine drivebelt A single, long, wide accessory drivebelt that's used on some newer vehicles to drive all the accessories, instead of a series of smaller, shorter belts. Serpentine drivebelts are usually tensioned by an automatic tensioner.

Serpentine drivebelt

Shim Thin spacer, commonly used to adjust the clearance or relative positions between two parts. For example, shims inserted into or under bucket tappets control valve clearances. Clearance is adjusted by changing the thickness of the shim.

Slide hammer A special puller that screws into or hooks onto a component such as a shaft or bearing; a heavy sliding handle on the shaft bottoms against the end of the shaft to knock the component free.

Sprocket A tooth or projection on the periphery of a wheel, shaped to engage with a chain or drivebelt. Commonly used to refer to the sprocket wheel itself.

Starter inhibitor switch On vehicles with an automatic transmission, a switch that prevents starting if the vehicle is not in Neutral or Park.

Strut See MacPherson strut.

T

Tappet A cylindrical component which transmits motion from the cam to the valve stem, either directly or via a pushrod and rocker arm. Also called a cam follower.

Thermostat A heat-controlled valve that regulates the flow of coolant between the cylinder block and the radiator, so maintaining optimum engine operating temperature. A thermostat is also used in some air cleaners in which the temperature is regulated.

Thrust bearing The bearing in the clutch assembly that is moved in to the release levers by clutch pedal action to disengage the clutch. Also referred to as a release bearing.

Timing belt A toothed belt which drives the camshaft. Serious engine damage may result if it breaks in service.

Timing chain A chain which drives the camshaft.

Toe-in The amount the front wheels are closer together at the front than at the rear. On rear wheel drive vehicles, a slight amount of toe-in is usually specified to keep the front wheels running parallel on the road by offsetting other forces that tend to spread the wheels apart.

Toe-out The amount the front wheels are closer together at the rear than at the front. On front wheel drive vehicles, a slight amount of toe-out is usually specified.

Tools For full information on choosing and using tools, refer to the *Haynes Automotive Tools Manual*.

Tracer A stripe of a second colour applied to a wire insulator to distinguish that wire from another one with the same colour insulator.

Tune-up A process of accurate and careful adjustments and parts replacement to obtain the best possible engine performance.

Turbocharger A centrifugal device, driven by exhaust gases, that pressurises the intake air. Normally used to increase the power output from a given engine displacement, but can also be used primarily to reduce exhaust emissions (as on VW's "Umwelt" Diesel engine).

U

Universal joint or U-joint A double-pivoted connection for transmitting power from a driving to a driven shaft through an angle. A U-joint consists of two Y-shaped yokes and a cross-shaped member called the spider.

V

Valve A device through which the flow of liquid, gas, vacuum, or loose material in bulk may be started, stopped, or regulated by a movable part that opens, shuts, or partially obstructs one or more ports or passageways. A valve is also the movable part of such a device.

Valve clearance The clearance between the valve tip (the end of the valve stem) and the rocker arm or tappet. The valve clearance is measured when the valve is closed.

Vernier caliper A precision measuring instrument that measures inside and outside dimensions. Not quite as accurate as a micrometer, but more convenient.

Viscosity The thickness of a liquid or its resistance to flow.

Volt A unit for expressing electrical "pressure" in a circuit. One volt that will produce a current of one ampere through a resistance of one ohm.

W

Welding Various processes used to join metal items by heating the areas to be joined to a molten state and fusing them together. For more information refer to the *Haynes Automotive Welding Manual*.

Wiring diagram A drawing portraying the components and wires in a vehicle's electrical system, using standardised symbols. For more information refer to the *Haynes Automotive Electrical and Electronic Systems Manual*.

Note: *References throughout this index are in the form* "**Chapter number**" • "**Page number**". *So, for example, 2B•15 refers to page 15 of Chapter 2B.*

Note: *References throughout this index are in the form* **"Chapter number"** • **"Page number"**. *So, for example, 2B•15 refers to page 15 of Chapter 2B.*

Index REF•31

Note: References throughout this index are in the form **"Chapter number"** • **"Page number"**. *So, for example, 2B•15 refers to page 15 of Chapter 2B.*

Haynes Manuals – The Complete UK Car List

Title	Book No.
ALFA ROMEO Alfasud/Sprint (74 - 88) up to F *	0292
Alfa Romeo Alfetta (73 - 87) up to E *	0531
AUDI 80, 90 & Coupe Petrol (79 - Nov 88) up to F	0605
Audi 80, 90 & Coupe Petrol (Oct 86 - 90) D to H	1491
Audi 100 & 200 Petrol (Oct 82 - 90) up to H	0907
Audi 100 & A6 Petrol & Diesel (May 91 - May 97) H to P	3504
Audi A3 Petrol & Diesel (96 - May 03) P to 03	4253
Audi A4 Petrol & Diesel (95 - 00) M to X	3575
Audi A4 Petrol & Diesel (01 - 04) X to 54	4609
AUSTIN A35 & A40 (56 - 67) up to F *	0118
Austin/MG/Rover Maestro 1.3 & 1.6 Petrol (83 - 95) up to M	0922
Austin/MG Metro (80 - May 90) up to G	0718
Austin/Rover Montego 1.3 & 1.6 Petrol (84 - 94) A to L	1066
Austin/MG/Rover Montego 2.0 Petrol (84 - 95) A to M	1067
Mini (59 - 69) up to H *	0527
Mini (69 - 01) up to X	0646
Austin/Rover 2.0 litre Diesel Engine (86 - 93) C to L	1857
Austin Healey 100/6 & 3000 (56 - 68) up to G *	0049
BEDFORD CF Petrol (69 - 87) up to E	0163
Bedford/Vauxhall Rascal & Suzuki Supercarry (86 - Oct 94) C to M	3015
BMW 316, 320 & 320i (4-cyl) (75 - Feb 83) up to Y *	0276
BMW 320, 320i, 323i & 325i (6-cyl) (Oct 77 - Sept 87) up to E	0815
BMW 3- & 5-Series Petrol (81 - 91) up to J	1948
BMW 3-Series Petrol (Apr 91 - 99) H to V	3210
BMW 3-Series Petrol (Sept 98 - 03) S to 53	4067
BMW 520i & 525e (Oct 81 - June 88) up to E	1560
BMW 525, 528 & 528i (73 - Sept 81) up to X *	0632
BMW 5-Series 6-cyl Petrol (April 96 - Aug 03) N to 03	4151
BMW 1500, 1502, 1600, 1602, 2000 & 2002 (59 - 77) up to S *	0240
CHRYSLER PT Cruiser Petrol (00 - 03) W to 53	4058
CITROËN 2CV, Ami & Dyane (67 - 90) up to H	0196
Citroën AX Petrol & Diesel (87 - 97) D to P	3014
Citroën Berlingo & Peugeot Partner Petrol & Diesel (96 - 05) P to 55	4281
Citroën BX Petrol (83 - 94) A to L	0908
Citroën C15 Van Petrol & Diesel (89 - Oct 98) F to S	3509
Citroën C3 Petrol & Diesel (02 - 05) 51 to 05	4197
Citroën CX Petrol (75 - 88) up to F	0528
Citroën Saxo Petrol & Diesel (96 - 04) N to 54	3506
Citroën Visa Petrol (79 - 88) up to F	0620
Citroën Xantia Petrol & Diesel (93 - 01) K to Y	3082
Citroën XM Petrol & Diesel (89 - 00) G to X	3451
Citroën Xsara Petrol & Diesel (97 - Sept 00) R to W	3751
Citroën Xsara Picasso Petrol & Diesel (00 - 02) W to 52	3944
Citroën ZX Diesel (91 - 98) J to S	1922
Citroën ZX Petrol (91 - 98) H to S	1881
Citroën 1.7 & 1.9 litre Diesel Engine (84 - 96) A to N	1379
FIAT 126 (73 - 87) up to E *	0305
Fiat 500 (57 - 73) up to M *	0090
Fiat Bravo & Brava Petrol (95 - 00) N to W	3572
Fiat Cinquecento (93 - 98) K to R	3501
Fiat Panda (81 - 95) up to M	0793
Fiat Punto Petrol & Diesel (94 - Oct 99) L to V	3251
Fiat Punto Petrol (Oct 99 - July 03) V to 03	4066
Fiat Regata Petrol (84 - 88) A to F	1167
Fiat Tipo Petrol (88 - 91) E to J	1625
Fiat Uno Petrol (83 - 95) up to M	0923
Fiat X1/9 (74 - 89) up to G *	0273
FORD Anglia (59 - 68) up to G *	0001
Ford Capri II (& III) 1.6 & 2.0 (74 - 87) up to E *	0283
Ford Capri II (& III) 2.8 & 3.0 V6 (74 - 87) up to E	1309

Title	Book No.
Ford Cortina Mk I & Corsair 1500 ('62 - '66) up to D*	0214
Ford Cortina Mk III 1300 & 1600 (70 - 76) up to P *	0070
Ford Escort Mk I 1100 & 1300 (68 - 74) up to N *	0171
Ford Escort Mk I Mexico, RS 1600 & RS 2000 (70 - 74) up to N *	0139
Ford Escort Mk II Mexico, RS 1800 & RS 2000 (75 - 80) up to W *	0735
Ford Escort (75 - Aug 80) up to V *	0280
Ford Escort Petrol (Sept 80 - Sept 90) up to H	0686
Ford Escort & Orion Petrol (Sept 90 - 00) H to X	1737
Ford Escort & Orion Diesel (Sept 90 - 00) H to X	4081
Ford Fiesta (76 - Aug 83) up to Y	0334
Ford Fiesta Petrol (Aug 83 - Feb 89) A to F	1030
Ford Fiesta Petrol (Feb 89 - Oct 95) F to N	1595
Ford Fiesta Petrol & Diesel (Oct 95 - Mar 02) N to 02	3397
Ford Fiesta Petrol & Diesel (Apr 02 - 05) 02 to 54	4170
Ford Focus Petrol & Diesel (98 - 01) S to Y	3759
Ford Focus Petrol & Diesel (Oct 01 - 05) 51 to 05	4167
Ford Galaxy Petrol & Diesel (95 - Aug 00) M to W	3984
Ford Granada Petrol (Sept 77 - Feb 85) up to B *	0481
Ford Granada & Scorpio Petrol (Mar 85 - 94) B to M	1245
Ford Ka (96 - 02) P to 52	3570
Ford Mondeo Petrol (93 - Sept 00) K to X	1923
Ford Mondeo Petrol & Diesel (Oct 00 - Jul 03) X to 03	3990
Ford Mondeo Petrol & Diesel (July 03 - 07) 03 to 56	4619
Ford Mondeo Diesel (93 - 96) L to N	3465
Ford Orion Petrol (83 - Sept 90) up to H	1009
Ford Sierra 4-cyl Petrol (82 - 93) up to K	0903
Ford Sierra V6 Petrol (82 - 91) up to J	0904
Ford Transit Petrol (Mk 2) (78 - Jan 86) up to C	0719
Ford Transit Petrol (Mk 3) (Feb 86 - 89) C to G	1468
Ford Transit Diesel (Feb 86 - 99) C to T	3019
Ford 1.6 & 1.8 litre Diesel Engine (84 - 96) A to N	1172
Ford 2.1, 2.3 & 2.5 litre Diesel Engine (77 - 90) up to H	1606
FREIGHT ROVER Sherpa Petrol (74 - 87) up to E	0463
HILLMAN Avenger (70 - 82) up to Y	0037
Hillman Imp (63 - 76) up to R *	0022
HONDA Civic (Feb 84 - Oct 87) A to E	1226
Honda Civic (Nov 91 - 96) J to N	3199
Honda Civic Petrol (Mar 95 - 00) M to X	4050
Honda Civic Petrol & Diesel (01 - 05) X to 55	4611
Honda Jazz (01 - Feb 08) 51 - 57	4735
HYUNDAI Pony (85 - 94) C to M	3398
JAGUAR E Type (61 - 72) up to L *	0140
Jaguar MkI & II, 240 & 340 (55 - 69) up to H *	0098
Jaguar XJ6, XJ & Sovereign; Daimler Sovereign (68 - Oct 86) up to D	0242
Jaguar XJ6 & Sovereign (Oct 86 - Sept 94) D to M	3261
Jaguar XJ12, XJS & Sovereign; Daimler Double Six (72 - 88) up to F	0478
JEEP Cherokee Petrol (93 - 96) K to N	1943
LADA 1200, 1300, 1500 & 1600 (74 - 91) up to J	0413
Lada Samara (87 - 91) D to J	1610
LAND ROVER 90, 110 & Defender Diesel (83 - 07) up to 56	3017
Land Rover Discovery Petrol & Diesel (89 - 98) G to S	3016
Land Rover Discovery Diesel (Nov 98 - Jul 04) S to 04	4606
Land Rover Freelander Petrol & Diesel (97 - Sept 03) R to 53	3929
Land Rover Freelander Petrol & Diesel (Oct 03 - Oct 06) 53 to 56	4623
Land Rover Series IIA & III Diesel (58 - 85) up to C	0529
Land Rover Series II, IIA & III 4-cyl Petrol (58 - 85) up to C	0314

Title	Book No.
MAZDA 323 (Mar 81 - Oct 89) up to G	1608
Mazda 323 (Oct 89 - 98) G to R	3455
Mazda 626 (May 83 - Sept 87) up to E	0929
Mazda B1600, B1800 & B2000 Pick-up Petrol (72 - 88) up to F	0267
Mazda RX-7 (79 - 85) up to C *	0460
MERCEDES-BENZ 190, 190E & 190D Petrol & Diesel (83 - 93) A to L	3450
Mercedes-Benz 200D, 240D, 240TD, 300D & 300TD 123 Series Diesel (Oct 76 - 85)	1114
Mercedes-Benz 250 & 280 (68 - 72) up to L *	0346
Mercedes-Benz 250 & 280 123 Series Petrol (Oct 76 - 84) up to B *	0677
Mercedes-Benz 124 Series Petrol & Diesel (85 - Aug 93) C to K	3253
Mercedes-Benz C-Class Petrol & Diesel (93 - Aug 00) L to W	3511
MGA (55 - 62) *	0475
MGB (62 - 80) up to W	0111
MG Midget & Austin-Healey Sprite (58 - 80) up to W *	0265
MINI Petrol (July 01 - 05) Y to 05	4273
MITSUBISHI Shogun & L200 Pick-Ups Petrol (83 - 94) up to M	1944
MORRIS Ital 1.3 (80 - 84) up to B	0705
Morris Minor 1000 (56 - 71) up to K	0024
NISSAN Almera Petrol (95 - Feb 00) N to V	4053
Nissan Almera & Tino Petrol (Feb 00 - 07) V to 56	4612
Nissan Bluebird (May 84 - Mar 86) A to C	1223
Nissan Bluebird Petrol (Mar 86 - 90) C to H	1473
Nissan Cherry (Sept 82 - 86) up to D	1031
Nissan Micra (83 - Jan 93) up to K	0931
Nissan Micra (93 - 02) K to 52	3254
Nissan Primera Petrol (90 - Aug 99) H to T	1851
Nissan Stanza (82 - 86) up to D	0824
Nissan Sunny Petrol (May 82 - Oct 86) up to D	0895
Nissan Sunny Petrol (Oct 86 - Mar 91) D to H	1378
Nissan Sunny Petrol (Apr 91 - 95) H to N	3219
OPEL Ascona & Manta (B Series) (Sept 75 - 88) up to F *	0316
Opel Ascona Petrol (81 - 88)	3215
Opel Astra Petrol (Oct 91 - Feb 98)	3156
Opel Corsa Petrol (83 - Mar 93)	3160
Opel Corsa Petrol (Mar 93 - 97)	3159
Opel Kadett Petrol (Nov 79 - Oct 84) up to B	0634
Opel Kadett Petrol (Oct 84 - Oct 91)	3196
Opel Omega & Senator Petrol (Nov 86 - 94)	3157
Opel Rekord Petrol (Feb 78 - Oct 86) up to D	0543
Opel Vectra Petrol (Oct 88 - Oct 95)	3158
PEUGEOT 106 Petrol & Diesel (91 - 04) J to 53	1882
Peugeot 205 Petrol (83 - 97) A to P	0932
Peugeot 206 Petrol & Diesel (98 - 01) S to X	3757
Peugeot 206 Petrol & Diesel (02 - 06) 51 to 06	4613
Peugeot 306 Petrol & Diesel (93 - 02) K to 02	3073
Peugeot 307 Petrol & Diesel (01 - 04) Y to 54	4147
Peugeot 309 Petrol (86 - 93) C to K	1266
Peugeot 405 Petrol (88 - 97) E to P	1559
Peugeot 405 Diesel (88 - 97) E to P	3198
Peugeot 406 Petrol & Diesel (96 - Mar 99) N to T	3394
Peugeot 406 Petrol & Diesel (Mar 99 - 02) T to 52	3982
Peugeot 505 Petrol (79 - 89) up to G	0762
Peugeot 1.7/1.8 & 1.9 litre Diesel Engine (82 - 96) up to N	0950
Peugeot 2.0, 2.1, 2.3 & 2.5 litre Diesel Engines (74 - 90) up to H	1607
PORSCHE 911 (65 - 85) up to C	0264

* Classic reprint

Title	Book No.
Porsche 924 & 924 Turbo (76 - 85) up to C	0397
PROTON (89 - 97) F to P	3255
RANGE ROVER V8 Petrol (70 - Oct 92) up to K	0606
RELIANT Robin & Kitten (73 - 83) up to A *	0436
RENAULT 4 (61 - 86) up to D *	0072
Renault 5 Petrol (Feb 85 - 96) B to N	1219
Renault 9 & 11 Petrol (82 - 89) up to F	0822
Renault 18 Petrol (79 - 86) up to D	0598
Renault 19 Petrol (89 - 96) F to N	1646
Renault 19 Diesel (89 - 96) F to N	1946
Renault 21 Petrol (86 - 94) C to M	1397
Renault 25 Petrol & Diesel (84 - 92) B to K	1228
Renault Clio Petrol (91 - May 98) H to R	1853
Renault Clio Diesel (91 - June 96) H to N	3031
Renault Clio Petrol & Diesel (May 98 - May 01) R to Y	3906
Renault Clio Petrol & Diesel (June '01 - '05) Y to 55	4168
Renault Espace Petrol & Diesel (85 - 96) C to N	3197
Renault Laguna Petrol & Diesel (94 - 00) L to W	3252
Renault Laguna Petrol & Diesel (Feb 01 - Feb 05) X to 54	4283
Renault Mégane & Scénic Petrol & Diesel (96 - 99) N to T	3395
Renault Mégane & Scénic Petrol & Diesel (Apr 99 - 02) T to 52	3916
Renault Megane Petrol & Diesel (Oct 02 - 05) 52 to 55	4284
Renault Scenic Petrol & Diesel (Sept 03 - 06) 53 to 06	4297
ROVER 213 & 216 (84 - 89) A to G	1116
Rover 214 & 414 Petrol (89 - 96) G to N	1689
Rover 216 & 416 Petrol (89 - 96) G to N	1830
Rover 211, 214, 216, 218 & 220 Petrol & Diesel (Dec 95 - 99) N to V	3399
Rover 25 & MG ZR Petrol & Diesel (Oct 99 - 04) V to 54	4145
Rover 414, 416 & 420 Petrol & Diesel (May 95 - 98) M to R	3453
Rover 45 / MG ZS Petrol & Diesel (99 - 05) V to 55	4384
Rover 618, 620 & 623 Petrol (93 - 97) K to P	3257
Rover 75 / MG ZT Petrol & Diesel (99 - 06) S to 06	4292
Rover 820, 825 & 827 Petrol (86 - 95) D to N	1380
Rover 3500 (76 - 87) up to E *	0365
Rover Metro, 111 & 114 Petrol (May 90 - 98) G to S	1711
SAAB 95 & 96 (66 - 76) up to R *	0198
Saab 90, 99 & 900 (79 - Oct 93) up to L	0765
Saab 900 (Oct 93 - 98) L to R	3512
Saab 9000 (4-cyl) (85 - 98) C to S	1686
Saab 9-3 Petrol & Diesel (98 - Aug 02) R to 02	4614
Saab 9-5 4-cyl Petrol (97 - 04) R to 54	4156
SEAT Ibiza & Cordoba Petrol & Diesel (Oct 93 - Oct 99) L to V	3571
Seat Ibiza & Malaga Petrol (85 - 92) B to K	1609
SKODA Estelle (77 - 89) up to G	0604
Skoda Fabia Petrol & Diesel (00 - 06) W to 06	4376
Skoda Favorit (89 - 96) F to N	1801
Skoda Felicia Petrol & Diesel (95 - 01) M to X	3505
Skoda Octavia Petrol & Diesel (98 - Apr 04) R to 04	4285
SUBARU 1600 & 1800 (Nov 79 - 90) up to H *	0995
SUNBEAM Alpine, Rapier & H120 (67 - 74) up to N *	0051
SUZUKI SJ Series, Samurai & Vitara (4-cyl) Petrol (82 - 97) up to P	1942
Suzuki Supercarry & Bedford/Vauxhall Rascal (86 - Oct 94) C to M	3015
TALBOT Alpine, Solara, Minx & Rapier (75 - 86) up to D	0337

Title	Book No.
Talbot Horizon Petrol (78 - 86) up to D	0473
Talbot Samba (82 - 86) up to D	0823
TOYOTA Avensis Petrol (98 - Jan 03) R to 52	4264
Toyota Carina E Petrol (May 92 - 97) J to P	3256
Toyota Corolla (80 - 85) up to C	0683
Toyota Corolla (Sept 83 - Sept 87) A to E	1024
Toyota Corolla (Sept 87 - Aug 92) E to K	1683
Toyota Corolla Petrol (Aug 92 - 97) K to P	3259
Toyota Corolla Petrol (July 97 - Feb 02) P to 51	4286
Toyota Hi-Ace & Hi-Lux Petrol (69 - Oct 83) up to A	0304
Toyota Yaris Petrol (99 - 05) T to 05	4265
TRIUMPH GT6 & Vitesse (62 - 74) up to N *	0112
Triumph Herald (59 - 71) up to K *	0010
Triumph Spitfire (62 - 81) up to X *	0113
Triumph Stag (70 - 78) up to T *	0441
Triumph TR2, TR3, TR3A, TR4 & TR4A (52 - 67) up to F *	0028
Triumph TR5 & 6 (67 - 75) up to P *	0031
Triumph TR7 (75 - 82) up to Y *	0322
VAUXHALL Astra Petrol (80 - Oct 84) up to B	0635
Vauxhall Astra & Belmont Petrol (Oct 84 - Oct 91) B to J	1136
Vauxhall Astra Petrol (Oct 91 - Feb 98) J to R	1832
Vauxhall/Opel Astra & Zafira Petrol (Feb 98 - Apr 04) R to 04	3758
Vauxhall/Opel Astra & Zafira Diesel (Feb 98 - Apr 04) R to 04	3797
Vauxhall/Opel Astra Petrol (04 - 07) 04 - 07	4732
Vauxhall/Opel Astra Diesel (04 - 07) 04 - 07	4733
Vauxhall/Opel Calibra (90 - 98) G to S	3502
Vauxhall Carlton Petrol (Oct 78 - Oct 86) up to D	0480
Vauxhall Carlton & Senator Petrol (Nov 86 - 94) D to L	1469
Vauxhall Cavalier Petrol (81 - Oct 88) up to F	0812
Vauxhall Cavalier Petrol (Oct 88 - 95) F to N	1570
Vauxhall Chevette (75 - 84) up to B	0285
Vauxhall/Opel Corsa Diesel (Mar 93 - Oct 00) K to X	4087
Vauxhall Corsa Petrol (Mar 93 - 97) K to R	1985
Vauxhall/Opel Corsa Petrol (Apr 97 - Oct 00) P to X	3921
Vauxhall/Opel Corsa Petrol & Diesel (Oct 00 - Sept 03) X to 53	4079
Vauxhall/Opel Corsa Petrol & Diesel (Oct 03 - Aug 06) 53 to 06	4617
Vauxhall/Opel Frontera Petrol & Diesel (91 - Sept 98) J to S	3454
Vauxhall Nova Petrol (83 - 93) up to K	0909
Vauxhall/Opel Omega Petrol (94 - 99) L to T	3510
Vauxhall/Opel Vectra Petrol & Diesel (95 - Feb 99) N to S	3396
Vauxhall/Opel Vectra Petrol & Diesel (Mar 99 - May 02) T to 02	3930
Vauxhall/Opel Vectra Petrol & Diesel (June 02 - Sept 05) 02 to 55	4618
Vauxhall/Opel 1.5, 1.6 & 1.7 litre Diesel Engine (82 - 96) up to N	1222
VW 411 & 412 (68 - 75) up to P *	0091
VW Beetle 1200 (54 - 77) up to S	0036
VW Beetle 1300 & 1500 (65 - 75) up to P	0039
VW 1302 & 1302S (70 - 72) up to L *	0110
VW Beetle 1303, 1303S & GT (72 - 75) up to P	0159
VW Beetle Petrol & Diesel (Apr 99 - 01) T to 51	3798
VW Golf & Jetta Mk 1 Petrol 1.1 & 1.3 (74 - 84) up to A	0716
VW Golf, Jetta & Scirocco Mk 1 Petrol 1.5, 1.6 & 1.8 (74 - 84) up to A	0726

Title	Book No.
VW Golf & Jetta Mk 1 Diesel (78 - 84) up to A	0451
VW Golf & Jetta Mk 2 Petrol (Mar 84 - Feb 92) A to J	1081
VW Golf & Vento Petrol & Diesel (Feb 92 - Mar 98) J to R	3097
VW Golf & Bora Petrol & Diesel (April 98 - 00) R to X	3727
VW Golf & Bora 4-cyl Petrol & Diesel (01 - 03) X to 53	4169
VW Golf & Jetta Petrol & Diesel (04 - 07) 53 to 07	4610
VW LT Petrol Vans & Light Trucks (76 - 87) up to E	0637
VW Passat & Santana Petrol (Sept 81 - May 88) up to E	0814
VW Passat 4-cyl Petrol & Diesel (May 88 - 96) E to P	3498
VW Passat 4-cyl Petrol & Diesel (Dec 96 - Nov 00) P to X	3917
VW Passat Petrol & Diesel (Dec 00 - May 05) X to 05	4279
VW Polo & Derby (76 - Jan 82) up to X	0335
VW Polo (82 - Oct 90) up to H	0813
VW Polo Petrol (Nov 90 - Aug 94) H to L	3245
VW Polo Hatchback Petrol & Diesel (94 - 99) M to S	3500
VW Polo Hatchback Petrol (00 - Jan 02) V to 51	4150
VW Polo Petrol & Diesel (02 - May 05) 51 to 05	4608
VW Scirocco (82 - 90) up to H *	1224
VW Transporter 1600 (68 - 79) up to V	0082
VW Transporter 1700, 1800 & 2000 (72 - 79) up to V *	0226
VW Transporter (air-cooled) Petrol (79 - 82) up to Y *	0638
VW Transporter (water-cooled) Petrol (82 - 90) up to H	3452
VW Type 3 (63 - 73) up to M *	0084
VOLVO 120 & 130 Series (& P1800) (61 - 73) up to M *	0203
Volvo 142, 144 & 145 (66 - 74) up to N *	0129
Volvo 240 Series Petrol (74 - 93) up to K	0270
Volvo 262, 264 & 260/265 (75 - 85) up to C *	0400
Volvo 340, 343, 345 & 360 (76 - 91) up to J	0715
Volvo 440, 460 & 480 Petrol (87 - 97) D to P	1691
Volvo 740 & 760 Petrol (82 - 91) up to J	1258
Volvo 850 Petrol (92 - 96) J to P	3260
Volvo 940 petrol (90 - 98) H to R	3249
Volvo S40 & V40 Petrol (96 - Mar 04) N to 04	3569
Volvo S40 & V50 Petrol & Diesel (Mar 04 - Jun 07) 04 to 07	4731
Volvo S70, V70 & C70 Petrol (96 - 99) P to V	3573
Volvo V70 / S80 Petrol & Diesel (98 - 05) S to 55	4263

AUTOMOTIVE TECHBOOKS

Title	Book No.
Automotive Electrical and Electronic Systems Manual	3049
Automotive Gearbox Overhaul Manual	3473
Automotive Service Summaries Manual	3475
Automotive Timing Belts Manual – Austin/Rover	3549
Automotive Timing Belts Manual – Ford	3474
Automotive Timing Belts Manual – Peugeot/Citroën	3568
Automotive Timing Belts Manual – Vauxhall/Opel	3577

DIY MANUAL SERIES

Title	Book No.
The Haynes Air Conditioning Manual	4192
The Haynes Car Electrical Systems Manual	4251
The Haynes Manual on Bodywork	4198
The Haynes Manual on Brakes	4178
The Haynes Manual on Carburettors	4177
The Haynes Manual on Diesel Engines	4174
The Haynes Manual on Engine Management	4199
The Haynes Manual on Fault Codes	4175
The Haynes Manual on Practical Electrical Systems	4267
The Haynes Manual on Small Engines	4250
The Haynes Manual on Welding	4176

* Classic reprint

CL23.12/07

Preserving Our Motoring Heritage

< *The Model J Duesenberg Derham Tourster. Only eight of these magnificent cars were ever built – this is the only example to be found outside the United States of America*

Almost every car you've ever loved, loathed or desired is gathered under one roof at the Haynes Motor Museum. Over 300 immaculately presented cars and motorbikes represent every aspect of our motoring heritage, from elegant reminders of bygone days, such as the superb Model J Duesenberg to curiosities like the bug-eyed BMW Isetta. There are also many old friends and flames. Perhaps you remember the 1959 Ford Popular that you did your courting in? The magnificent 'Red Collection' is a spectacle of classic sports cars including AC, Alfa Romeo, Austin Healey, Ferrari, Lamborghini, Maserati, MG, Riley, Porsche and Triumph.

A Perfect Day Out

Each and every vehicle at the Haynes Motor Museum has played its part in the history and culture of Motoring. Today, they make a wonderful spectacle and a great day out for all the family. Bring the kids, bring Mum and Dad, but above all bring your camera to capture those golden memories for ever. You will also find an impressive array of motoring memorabilia, a comfortable 70 seat video cinema and one of the most extensive transport book shops in Britain. The Pit Stop Cafe serves everything from a cup of tea to wholesome, home-made meals or, if you prefer, you can enjoy the large picnic area nestled in the beautiful rural surroundings of Somerset.

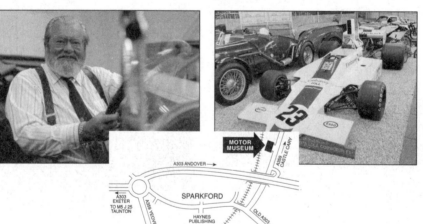

> *John Haynes O.B.E., Founder and Chairman of the museum at the wheel of a Haynes Light 12.*

< *Graham Hill's Lola Cosworth Formula 1 car next to a 1934 Riley Sports.*

The Museum is situated on the A359 Yeovil to Frome road at Sparkford, just off the A303 in Somerset. It is about 40 miles south of Bristol, and 25 minutes drive from the M5 intersection at Taunton.

Open 9.30am - 5.30pm (10.00am - 4.00pm Winter) 7 days a week, *except Christmas Day, Boxing Day and New Years Day*
Special rates available for schools, coach parties and outings Charitable Trust No. 292048